Southern Living
2013 Annual Recipes

Oxmoor House®

Best Recipes of 2013

clockwise from top left:
- Roasted Cherry Hand Pies (page 25)
- Lemon Bar Cheesecake (page 48)
- Gumbo Gravy over Stone-ground Grits (page 26)
- Lemon Tiramisù (page 49)

Maple-Pecan Sticky Buns (page 33)

Asparagus, Orange, and
Lentil Salad (page 63)

Chocolate Zucchini
Cakes (page 91)

clockwise from top left:

- Grilled Salmon Kabobs (page 119)
- Cheese Grits with Poached Eggs (page 82)
- Tomato, Cheddar, and Bacon Pie (page 118)
- Jasmine-Buttermilk Panna Cotta with Berry Sauce (page 65)

clockwise from top left:
- Cheese Straw Tomato Tartlets (page 118)
- Whiskey Pie with Tipsy Berries (page 129)
- Caramelized Sweet Onion Tarte Tatin (page 102)
- Bread-and-Butter Pickled Onions (page 103)

Clockwise from top: Shout Hallelujah Potato Salad (page 143),
Sweet Tea-Brined Fried Chicken
(page 142), Skillet Green Beans
(page 144), Field Pea Relish
(page 144), and Candied Jalapeños
(page 144)

Cucumber Gin & Tonic and
Tomato-Tequila Fizz (page 159)

Blueberry-Cheesecake Ice-Cream
Pie, Strawberry-Pretzel Ice-Cream
Pie, and Key Lime Ice-Cream Pie
(page 196)

Key Lime Icebox Cake, page 213

clockwise from top left:
- Maque Choux Soup (page 203)
- Melon and Crispy Prosciutto Salad (page 201)
- Chicken-Vegetable Kabobs with White BBQ Sauce (page 201)
- Pasta with Burst Tomatoes and Mascarpone (page 200)

clockwise from top left:

• Caramel Apple Blondie Pie (page 230)
• Waldorf Cobb Salad (page 234)
• Grill-Roasted Chicken (page 234)
• Caramel Apple Fantans (page 233)

Molasses-Brined Roasted Chicken (page 252),
Root Vegetable Mash (page 253), and
Sautéed Mushrooms (page 254)

Lemon, Orzo, and
Meatball Soup
(page 243)

Our Year at
Southern Living®

Dear Friends,

Welcome to *Southern Living 2013 Annual Recipes*, the 35th volume of our handy-reference collection. I'm writing you during our busiest time of year here in the South's Most Trusted Kitchen, where our talented team of cooks and editors is putting the finishing touches on the special December double issue. As we cap off another year at *Southern Living* with a Christmas extravaganza of towering white cakes, savory roasts and sides, and festive menus, I'm reminded of how much work goes into guaranteeing the quality of every single recipe.

Here in the South, food is the daily gift we give our friends and families. There's a rhythm to the way we cook depending on the calendar. Each season marks the arrival of fresh ingredients, each month brings forth its own rituals, and each week its own Sunday supper. Want traditional and indulgent recipes for any occasion? You've come to the right place.

Here in the South, food is the daily gift we give our friends and families.

You'll also find fresh solutions, a.k.a our "Quick-Fix Suppers" column, to solve weeknight dinner dilemmas because, let's be honest, we're all busier than we want to be. You may also notice a subtle shift towards healthier dishes and ones that celebrate the bold, new flavors of the new Southern pantry. From entertaining ideas in our "Hospitality" column to a celebration of iconic seasonal ingredients like Vidalia onions in "What to Cook Now," this volume documents how the South cooks and eats now.

So what does all that really mean? This book contains the rock-solid recipes we've always been known for but also an added emphasis on storytelling and how-to advice, including our "Test Kitchen Intervention" column. Some highlights from 2013: A swoon-worthy Lemon Bar Cheesecake; a strategic No-Cook recipe package that beats the summer swelter; a story about cherished spiral-bound Community Cookbooks that touched a chord with our readers; a Two-Step Fresh Peach Pound Cake so good that it caused a run on peach schnapps at local liquor stores by even the most God-fearing of folks; a Tex-Mex Chicken Chili with Lime that you'll want to make for years to come; and the ultimate Thanksgiving cookbook.

Look for more weekly digests from the Test Kitchen on southernliving.com, where you'll find hundreds of new videos that teach you how to make everything from Sweet Tea-Brined Fried Chicken to Salted Caramel-Chocolate Pecan Pie. Tumblr (southernliving. tumblr.com) and Instagram (instagram.com/southernliving), we've got that covered, too. As always, we want to hear from you. To send us a family recipe, ask our team any cooking-related questions, or simply to let us know what feeds your soul, call us at 205-445-6351 or email us at sl_foodedit@timeinc.com. I welcome your questions and story ideas, too; e-mail me at hunter_lewis@timeinc.com.

As we approach our 50th anniversary, we're honored and grateful for your loyalty and readership. The Southern table stands for hospitality above all else, and we look forward to serving up a gracious plenty in 2014.

Cheers,

Hunter

Hunter Lewis
Executive Editor

Contents

Favorite Columns

Each month, we focus on topics that are important to our readers—from delicious menus to healthy options to handy tips for almost anything.

What to Cook Now

• Our healthy spin on these Southern dishes doesn't sacrifice their hearty flavor or satiety at all. Still just as tasty and filling, these lightened-up recipes won't wreck your New Year's resolution for healthy eating. (page 24)

• Serve one of these 4 slow-cooked dishes to family or friends—you'll take the praise and leave all the work to your slow cooker. (page 38)

• Celebrate Easter with our elegant brunch menu. With recipes for soup, salad, biscuits, ham, quiche, and dessert, this spread is fitting for a special family feast. (page 62)

• If you think eggs are only for mornings, think again! Our recipes will have you making "egg-ceptions" for eating this protein-packed food all day long. (page 80)

• Give boring onions a makeover! These 7 recipes spotlight a veggie that's normally on the sidelines, highlighting its flavor, which peaks in the spring. (page 100)

• Tomayto-tomahto no more! These mouthwatering tomato pies will spice up the way you think about this humble summer gem. (page 116)

Full of seasonal veggies and spices, these recipes for soup, salad, pizza, pasta, and kabobs are easy to make and deliver farm-fresh flavor. (page 200)

• Make these brunch recipes the night before and you'll wake up to a fresh and filling morning meal. (page 216)

• Bored with your biscuit? Here is a bounty of other bread options just waiting to be devoured. (page 238)

Quick-Fix Suppers

• For breakfast, lunch, and dinner, the skillet is the kitchen-wonder that does it all. Try these one-pan recipes for easy and delicious food any time of day. (page 29)

• Perk up traditional pasta with these 4 recipes that are as quick as they are tasty. (page 42)

• Colorful and fresh, vegetables are the perfect way to welcome springtime to your table. These 5 recipes chock-full of veggies will liven up your dinners all week long. (page 66)

• It's double-duty time—for your grill, that is! Each of these 4 grill-made meals produces enough leftovers so you can make a separate meal later in the week. (page 86)

• Save time and diversify your menu by mixing and matching any of these soups, salads, and sandwiches that each take less than an hour to make and can be eaten as tasty leftovers for the rest of the week! (page 106)

• Dinners are never easier than when you start with BBQ from your favorite local joint. These recipes will show you how. By adding some fresh veggies and only a few other ingredients, you can whip up a meaty feast in less than an hour. (page 124)

• Cutlets are a great "go-to" for a delicious and simple meal. Here are 7 ways to dress up a thin slice of poultry, pork, and fish, turning them into scrumptious dishes for family and friends. (page 204)

• Conquer your kitchen with these tips for smart and speedy cooking from a Test Kitchen pro and mom-on-the-go. With recipes for fish, steak, chicken, and pork, planning and cooking dinner will be a cinch. (page 220)

• Peppery meatloaf, meaty green beans, chunky soup, and meat-packed sloppy joe dogs—this is the new way to eat ground meats. These recipes show you how to reinvent this weeknight staple and create mouthwatering meals in less than an hour. (page 243)

• These quick recipes are perfect for busy weeknights around the holidays. (page 258)

Save Room

• When our decadent breakfast breads like Maple-Pecan Sticky Buns and Blueberry Coffee Cake are all under 300 calories, there's no reason not to indulge! (page 33)

• More chocolate, less fat? Yes, please! Our Test Kitchen has taken this Dark Chocolate Chunk Cookie where no cookie has gone before. (page 47)

• Whether you're sunburned from too much time at the pool or you're burned out from too much time at the office, our Piña Colada Icebox Pie is the ultimate sweet summer soother. This tropical treat is just as easy and refreshing as its name suggests. (page 77)

• If you ask us, tiny detailed fondant petals covering sweet bites of pound cake are the magical makings of a fairytale treat. One taste of our special Pound Cake Cupcakes and you'll be walking on clouds. (page 89)

• To truly capture summertime spirit in a dessert, two things are certain: It's got to have fresh berries, and it's got to be easy. We've combined these two necessities to create the quintessential summertime dessert—Very Berry Summer Pudding. (page 109)

• A cut above traditional cobbler, these Blackberry-Peach Cobbler Bars are an easily transportable treat for all your summer outings from picnics to neighborhood cookouts to road trips. (page 131)

• Layers of tart Key lime custard stacked upon layers of graham crackers all topped with whipped cream make this Key Lime Icebox Cake a tower of sugary bliss. And because no baking is required, each of the treat's nine layers of deliciousness is also a layer of sweet simplicity for the one who prepares it. (page 213)

• The only thing better than warm apple pie to share is warm apple pie not to share! Our Fried Apple Pie pouches are individual, handheld bundles of gooey goodness that are easy to grab and even easier to eat. (page 224)

• Creamy, decadent, and rich, this Cinderella Cheesecake really did make our dreams come true. (page 247)

Community Cookbook

• Serve these snacks during the big game, and no matter what the scoreboard says, you'll secure a big win. (page 36)

• The spin our readers put on traditional green beans, slaw, and peas and onions won over our Test Kitchen; we're confident that these zesty recipes will supplement your main dishes perfectly. (page 52)

• These appetizers, with their fresh veggies and creamy dips, have spring written all over them. Serve these nibbles at your next garden party and be the talk of the town. (page 76)

• Spring is the time for celebrating new life with family and friends. Whether you're attending a church gathering, baby shower, bridal tea, or graduation ceremony, with one of these recipes on hand, you'll never again have to wonder what food to prepare. (page 98)

• For Mother's Day, serve Mom these granola pancakes for a relaxing and satisfying breakfast in bed, or whip up a refreshing brunch for her using these quinoa salad and couscous recipes. (page 114)

• Packed with pesto, peach, avocado, and pimiento cheese, these salads go beyond garden variety. There's more than one way to eat your greens, and with these rave-worthy recipes you can explore new ways to give classics an update. (page 130)

• Fire up your grill and prepare a Fourth of July feast with spicy salmon, glazed shrimp, and savory chicken to dazzle neighbors, friends, and family. (page 198)

• Before summer is over, squeeze the last bit of fresh seasonal fruit into your desserts. These recipes for a plum tart, berry-laden bars, and peach sorbet will keep summer lingering in your mouth and memory long after the days turn short. (page 214)

• These crispies, cookies, and cheese tots from our readers are must-try treats that are packed with more flavor than their miniature size would suggest. (page 236)

• Adding candy to your baked goodies is a surefire way to load as much gooey chocolate as possible into every bite. Whether you're candy-crazed or simply wondering what to do with all those leftover Halloween treats, these are don't-miss recipes. (page 256)

• Make your Thanksgiving even more memorable with these delicious appetizers. (page 286)

• From a warm and cozy hot chocolate to festive cocktails, discover some beverages that will get your holidays off to a great start. (page 324)

January

Lighten Up Southern Classics

▶ Start the New Year fresh with five hearty Southern dishes built with smart techniques and healthy, vibrant ingredients

Fried Pork Chops with Caramelized Onion Gravy

Fried Pork Chops with Caramelized Onion Gravy

MAKES 6 SERVINGS
HANDS-ON 30 MIN.
TOTAL 1 HOUR, 45 MIN., INCLUDING GRAVY AND SLAW

Try this versatile technique with chicken, beef, or veal cutlets.

- 2 cups panko (Japanese breadcrumbs)
- 1/4 cup finely chopped fresh flat-leaf parsley
- 2 tsp. chopped fresh rosemary
- 1 1/2 tsp. table salt, divided
- 1 1/2 tsp. freshly ground pepper, divided
- 6 (1/2-inch-thick) boneless pork loin chops
- 1/2 cup all-purpose flour
- 4 large egg whites, lightly beaten
- 6 Tbsp. canola oil
  Caramelized Onion Gravy
  Apple-Cabbage Slaw

1. Combine first 3 ingredients, 1/2 tsp. salt, and 1/2 tsp. pepper in a shallow dish. Place each pork chop between 2 sheets of plastic wrap, and flatten to 1/8-inch thickness, using a rolling pin or flat side of a meat mallet.

2. Sprinkle pork with remaining 1 tsp. each salt and pepper. Place flour in a shallow dish; place egg whites in another shallow dish. Dredge pork in flour, dip in egg whites, and dredge in breadcrumb mixture, pressing to adhere; place on a wire rack.

3. Cook half of pork in 1 1/2 Tbsp. hot oil in a large nonstick skillet over medium heat 3 to 4 minutes or until golden. Dab top of pork with 1 1/2 Tbsp. oil using a pastry brush; turn pork over. Cook 3 minutes or until done. Keep warm on a clean wire rack in a jelly-roll pan in a 200° oven. Repeat with remaining pork and 3 Tbsp. oil. Serve with Caramelized Onion Gravy and Apple-Cabbage Slaw.

> **LIGHTEN UP!**
> Pound chops into thin cutlets to create more surface area, then **PAN-FRY THEM**, rather than deep-fry, to crispy perfection.

CARAMELIZED ONION GRAVY

MAKES ABOUT 2 CUPS
HANDS-ON 20 MIN.
TOTAL 1 HOUR, 15 MIN., INCLUDING FLOUR

- 1/2 cup diced sweet onion
- 2 tsp. olive oil
- 1/4 cup Browned Flour (see box above)
- 1 1/2 cups 1% low-fat milk
- 1 Tbsp. jarred chicken soup base
- 1/2 tsp. freshly ground pepper

1. Sauté onion in hot oil in a 3-qt. saucepan over medium heat 6 to 8 minutes or until golden brown.

2. Place Browned Flour in a bowl; gradually whisk in milk until smooth. Add milk mixture to onion, and cook over medium heat, whisking constantly, 3 to 5 minutes or until thickened and bubbly. Whisk in soup base and pepper until blended.

Note: We tested with Superior Touch Better Than Bouillon Chicken Base.

APPLE-CABBAGE SLAW Toss

together **3 cups finely shredded green cabbage; 1 cup finely shredded red cabbage; 1 medium-size Granny Smith apple,** cut into thin strips; **3/4 cup loosely packed fresh flat-leaf parsley leaves;** and **2 Tbsp. Fresh Lemon Vinaigrette. MAKES** 6 to 8 servings

FRESH LEMON VINAIGRETTE Whisk

together **3 Tbsp. fresh lemon juice; 1 tsp. Dijon mustard; 1 tsp. sugar; 1 large garlic clove,** pressed; **1/4 tsp. table salt;** and **1/4 tsp. freshly ground black pepper.** Add **7 Tbsp. olive oil** in a slow, steady stream, whisking constantly, until blended. Serve immediately, or store in refrigerator up to 1 week. Bring to room temperature, and whisk until blended before serving. **MAKES** about 1/2 cup

Roasted Cherry Hand Pies

MAKES 1 DOZEN
HANDS-ON 1 HOUR
TOTAL 4 HOURS, 55 MIN.

Chill the dough to help it hold its shape as it bakes. (Pictured on page 3)

- 1/2 cup butter
- 4 Tbsp. almond paste
- 2 1/2 cups all-purpose flour
- 3/4 tsp. table salt
- 1/4 cup ice-cold vodka
- 4 to 5 Tbsp. ice-cold water
- 1 (12-oz.) package frozen sweet cherries
- 6 Tbsp. Demerara sugar, divided
- 1/2 cup dried cherries
- 1/3 cup seedless raspberry preserves
- 1 Tbsp. butter
- 1 tsp. vanilla bean paste
  Parchment paper
- 1 large egg

1. Cut 1/2 cup butter into small cubes; chill butter and almond paste 15 minutes. Stir together flour and salt. Cut butter and almond paste into flour mixture with a pastry blender until it resembles small peas. Gradually stir in vodka and 1/4 cup ice-cold water with a fork, stirring just until dough begins to form a ball and leaves sides of bowl, adding up to 1 Tbsp. more water if necessary. Place dough on plastic wrap; shape into a flat disk.

2. Divide dough into 12 portions. Shape each into a ball. Flatten each into a 3-inch circle on a lightly floured surface; roll into a 5-inch circle. Stack circles between layers of plastic wrap or wax paper. Cover stack with plastic wrap; chill 2 to 24 hours.

3. Preheat oven to 425°. Spread frozen cherries in a lightly greased 13- x 9-inch baking dish; sprinkle with 4 Tbsp. Demerara sugar. Bake 25 minutes or until juice begins to thicken, stirring every 10 minutes. Remove from oven; immediately scrape cherries and juice into a bowl, using a rubber spatula. Stir in dried cherries and next 3 ingredients; cover with plastic wrap. Cool completely (45 minutes).

4. Working with 1 circle at a time, spoon 1 heaping Tbsp. cherry mixture into center of each dough circle; fold dough over filling. Press edges together with a fork to seal. Place on a parchment paper-lined baking sheet.

5. Whisk together egg and 1 Tbsp. water. Brush pies with egg mixture. Cut 1 to 2 slits in top of each pie; sprinkle with remaining Demerara sugar.

6. Bake at 425° for 15 to 20 minutes or until golden. Remove from pan to a wire rack, and cool 15 minutes.

LIGHTEN UP!

No need to fry these pies! Vodka enhances the crusts' flakiness, so you can use **LESS BUTTER.**

Gumbo Gravy over Stone-ground Grits

MAKES 6 SERVINGS
HANDS-ON 15 MIN.
TOTAL 4 HOURS, 5 MIN., INCLUDING BROWNED FLOUR AND GRITS

With a light gravy, you can indulge in andouille sausage. (Pictured on page 3)

- 1 lb. large raw shrimp, peeled and deveined
- 1 1/2 tsp. Cajun seasoning
- 6 oz. andouille sausage, diced
  Vegetable cooking spray
- 2 tsp. vegetable oil
- 1 cup diced sweet onion
- 1/2 cup diced green bell pepper
- 2 garlic cloves, minced
- 3 Tbsp. Browned Flour (see page 25)
- 1 cup reduced-sodium fat-free chicken broth
- 1 cup sliced fresh okra
- 2 large plum tomatoes, peeled, seeded, and diced
  Slow-Cooker Stone-ground Grits

1. Toss shrimp in Cajun seasoning in a medium bowl.

2. Cook sausage in a large skillet coated with cooking spray over medium heat 5 minutes or until lightly browned. Add oil, onion, and next 2 ingredients; sauté 3 minutes or until tender. Sprinkle Browned Flour over sausage mixture; stir until blended. Stir in chicken broth, and increase heat to medium-high. Bring to a boil, stirring often, and boil, stirring occasionally, 3 minutes or until thickened. Add shrimp, okra, and tomatoes. Cook 5 minutes or just until shrimp turn pink. Serve over grits.

SLOW-COOKER STONE-GROUND GRITS Stir together 1 1/2 **cups uncooked stone-ground yellow grits** and 4 1/2 **cups water** in a 3-qt. slow cooker. Let stand 2 minutes, allowing grits to settle to bottom; tilt slow cooker slightly, and skim off solids using a fine wire-mesh strainer. Cover and cook on HIGH 2 1/2 to 3 hours or until grits are creamy and tender, stirring every 45 minutes. Season with **table salt** and **freshly ground black pepper** to taste. **MAKES** 6 servings

---

LIGHTEN UP!

Browned Flour (page 25) makes a **LOW-FAT GRAVY**, while the slow cooker creates the creamiest grits without cheese or butter.

Vegetarian Enchilada Pies

Vegetarian Enchilada Pies

MAKES 4 SERVINGS
HANDS-ON 30 MIN.
TOTAL 1 HOUR, 25 MIN., INCLUDING SAUCE

Find dried hibiscus flowers (Flor de Jamaica) at Hispanic markets and amazon.com. You can omit them if desired.

- 1 (2-oz.) package dried hibiscus flowers, picked through
- 1 cup thinly sliced sweet onion
- 1 1/2 cups chopped bell pepper
- 1 1/2 cups chopped zucchini
- 1/4 cup olive oil
- 1 (15-oz.) can black beans, drained, rinsed, and mashed
- 1 Tbsp. sugar
- 1 tsp. kosher salt
- 1 tsp. dried oregano
- 1/4 tsp. dried thyme
- 1 cup vegetable broth
- 12 (6-inch) fajita-size corn tortillas*
- 1 1/4 cups (5 oz.) shredded Monterey Jack cheese
  Enchilada Sauce
- 1/2 cup crumbled queso fresco (fresh Mexican cheese)
  Toppings: sour cream, chopped red onion, fresh cilantro leaves

1. Preheat oven to 350°. Bring flowers and 2 cups water to a simmer in a small saucepan over medium heat. Remove from heat; cover and let stand 5 to 8 minutes or until flowers are plump. Drain flowers, and coarsely chop.

2. Sauté flowers, onion, and next 2 ingredients in hot oil in a large skillet over medium heat 10 minutes or until vegetables are tender. Stir in beans and next 4 ingredients, and cook, stirring often, 2 minutes.

3. Pour broth into a shallow dish. Dip 4 tortillas, 1 at a time, in broth, and place 1 inch apart on a foil-lined 15- x 10-inch jelly-roll pan. Divide half of hibiscus mixture among tortillas; top each with about 2 Tbsp. Monterey Jack cheese and 1/4 cup warm Enchilada Sauce. Repeat layers once; top each stack with a tortilla. Spoon 1/4 cup Enchilada Sauce over each stack.

4. Bake at 350° for 20 minutes or until bubbly. Sprinkle with queso fresco and remaining Monterey Jack cheese. Serve with Enchilada Sauce and toppings.

*20 (4-inch) corn tortillas may be substituted. Add 2 more layers, and divide filling accordingly.

LIGHTEN UP!

Dried hibiscus flowers and black beans give these **VEGETARIAN** enchiladas their meaty texture.

ENCHILADA SAUCE

MAKES ABOUT 5 CUPS
HANDS-ON 30 MIN.
TOTAL 30 MIN.

- ¼ cup all-purpose flour
- ¼ cup chili powder
- 6 Tbsp. vegetable oil
- 1 cup minced onion
- 4 garlic cloves, minced
- 2 (8-oz.) cans tomato sauce
- 2 tsp. ground cumin
- 1¼ tsp. table salt
- 1 tsp. dried oregano
- ¼ tsp. ground red pepper

Cook first 2 ingredients in hot oil in a large saucepan over medium heat, stirring often, 2 minutes. Stir in onion; cook, stirring often, 3 minutes or until tender. Add garlic; cook, stirring often, 1 minute. Stir in remaining ingredients and 3 cups water. Cook, stirring often, 15 minutes or until thickened.

Chicken and Sweet Potato Dumplings

MAKES 8 SERVINGS
HANDS-ON 1 HOUR
TOTAL 5 HOURS, 50 MIN., INCLUDING DUMPLINGS

Start with a whole chicken to create a flavorful, refined broth.

- 1 (3¾-lb.) whole chicken
- 2 celery ribs, chopped
- 2 carrots, chopped
- 1 medium onion, quartered
- 4 garlic cloves, crushed
- 3 fresh thyme sprigs
- 1½ tsp. kosher salt
- ½ tsp. black pepper
- ½ medium onion, thinly sliced
- 2 carrots, sliced
- 1 celery rib, thinly sliced
  Sweet Potato Dumplings
  Shaved Parmesan cheese
  Flat-leaf parsley leaves

1. Bring chicken, next 7 ingredients, and water to cover to a boil in a Dutch oven over medium heat. Cover, reduce heat to medium-low, and simmer 1 hour.

2. Remove chicken, reserving broth in Dutch oven. Cool chicken 30 minutes.

3. Meanwhile, cook reserved broth in Dutch oven over low heat 30 minutes.

4. Skin, bone, and shred chicken, reserving bones. Place bones in broth. Cover and chill shredded chicken until ready to use.

Chicken and
Sweet Potato
Dumplings

5. Continue cooking broth, uncovered, over low heat 1 hour or until reduced by one-third. Pour broth through a wire-mesh strainer into a bowl; discard solids. Wipe Dutch oven clean; pour broth back into Dutch oven.

6. Skim fat from broth. Add thinly sliced onion and next 2 ingredients to broth; cook over medium-high heat, stirring occasionally, 20 minutes or until carrots are crisp-tender. Add shredded chicken; return to a simmer.

7. Add Sweet Potato Dumplings to soup. Garnish with Parmesan and parsley; serve immediately.

SWEET POTATO DUMPLINGS

MAKES 4 DOZEN
HANDS-ON 45 MIN.
TOTAL 2 HOURS, 5 MIN.

- 2 medium-size baking potatoes (about ¾ lb.)
- 1 large sweet potato (about ½ lb.)
- ¼ cup freshly grated Parmesan cheese
- 1 large egg
- ½ tsp. chopped fresh rosemary
- ¼ tsp. kosher salt
- ¼ tsp. freshly ground pepper
- ½ cup all-purpose flour

1. Preheat oven to 400°. Prick all potatoes with a fork, and bake on a jelly-roll pan 1 hour.

2. Cool potatoes 20 minutes. Peel and mash until smooth. Add cheese and next 4 ingredients, and stir until smooth. Fold in flour just until blended.

3. Divide dough into 4 equal portions; dust with flour. Roll each into a ¾-inch-diameter rope on a well-floured surface. Cut into 1-inch pieces; place dumplings on a lightly floured baking sheet.

4. Cook dumplings, 10 to 12 at a time, in 3 qt. boiling water over medium-high heat, 3 minutes. Remove with a slotted spoon.

LIGHTEN UP!

Sweet potato creates pillowy, gnocchi-like dumplings and adds **VITAMIN C, BETA CAROTENE, CALCIUM, AND POTASSIUM.**

Build a Better Pantry

*Think the Southern larder is only butter, bacon, and bourbon? Think again.
Here are seven Southern superfoods we cook with all winter long*

❶ BUTTERMILK

Cultured buttermilk is one of the oldest Southern probiotic foods. Drink it until the cows come home because it aids in digestion, is super-rich in calcium, and is good for your complexion. We stirred some into the Cornbread Croutons on page 31.

❷ DARK LEAFY GREENS

Grace your table with a daily dose of these powerhouses. Filled with antioxidants, leafy greens such as collards, kale, and turnip greens can lower cholesterol. See page 32 for our go-to weeknight sauté.

❸ BEANS & PEAS

Canned, frozen, or dried, beans and peas give you long-lasting energy and loads of fiber. Plus, they're a cheap protein. Make a big batch on Sundays for the week or our Hoppin' John Soup on page 31.

EDITOR'S TIP!
Retain nutrients by cooking greens just until they're a vibrant green.

❹ CHICORY COFFEE

Reason #27 why we love New Orleans: dark NOLA-style grounds. The natural plant chemicals in chicory (a ground root added to coffee for body and to mellow bitterness) help protect against cardiovascular disease and relieve pain.

❺ PECANS

These crunchy snacks, salad toppings, and dredges are good for your heart. Their omega-3 fatty acids and vitamin E can help lower bad cholesterol levels and prevent blood clots. Try our lightened pecan sticky buns on page 33.

❻ SWEET POTATOES

With flesh ranging from vibrant orange to deep purple, these fiber-rich gems are loaded with antioxidants that hold up to heat—steaming, boiling, and roasting. See how we turned them into Southern-style dumplings on page 27.

❼ STONE-GROUND GRITS

Not to be confused with instant or the quick-cooking kind, stone-ground grits are whole grains. Benefits include prevention of stroke, diabetes, heart disease, and cancer. Check out page 26 for our creamy slow-cooker recipe.

Stick to a One-Pan Plan

▶ Use the most versatile pan in the kitchen to conjure some weeknight magic, from sizzling stir-frys and perfect pizzas to the crispiest chicken thighs ever

Beef-and-Brussels Sprouts Stir-fry

MAKES 4 SERVINGS

A ripping-hot skillet works as well us a wok to sear food fast. Just be sure to use one that can take the heat, preferably cast-iron or a large, heavy-bottomed stainless. Feel free to substitute any cruciferous vegetable cut into even pieces in place of Brussels sprouts, from broccoli and cauliflower to cabbage and bok choy.

- ½ lb. flank steak
- ¼ tsp. table salt
- ⅛ tsp. freshly ground black pepper
- 2 Tbsp. peanut oil, divided
- ½ cup beef broth or water
- 1 Tbsp. light brown sugar
- 2 Tbsp. soy sauce
- 2 tsp. fresh lime juice
- ½ tsp. cornstarch
- 12 oz. fresh Brussels sprouts, trimmed and halved
- 1 red jalapeño or red serrano pepper, sliced
- 1 Tbsp. grated fresh ginger
- 2 garlic cloves, thinly sliced
- ¼ cup chopped fresh mint
  Hot cooked rice

1. Cut steak diagonally across the grain into thin strips. Sprinkle with salt and pepper.

2. Stir-fry steak, in 2 batches, in 1 Tbsp. hot oil in a large cast-iron or stainless-steel skillet over high heat 2 to 3 minutes or until meat is no longer pink. Transfer to a plate, and wipe skillet clean.

3. Whisk together beef broth and next 4 ingredients in a small bowl until smooth.

4. Stir-fry Brussels sprouts in remaining 1 Tbsp. hot oil over high heat 2 minutes or until lightly browned. Add jalapeño pepper, ginger, and garlic, and stir-fry 1 minute. Pour soy sauce mixture over Brussels sprouts, and bring mixture to a boil. Cook, stirring often, 3 to 4 minutes or until sprouts are tender. Stir in mint and steak. Serve over rice.

Crispy Chicken Thighs with Pasta and Pesto

MAKES 6 SERVINGS

This stove-top-to-oven method yields crisp, durk-golden skin and juicy, tender meat.

- 3½ to 4 lb. skin-on, bone-in chicken thighs (about 7 thighs)
- 2 tsp. kosher salt
- 1 tsp. freshly ground black pepper
- ½ tsp. paprika
- 2 tsp. vegetable oil
- 8 oz. cellentani pasta
- 1 cup chicken broth
  Arugula Pesto

1. Preheat oven to 400°. Sprinkle chicken with salt, pepper, and paprika.

2. Heat oil in a 12-inch cast-iron skillet over high heat until oil just begins to smoke.

3. Place chicken in skillet, skin sides down; reduce heat to medium-high, and cook 15 minutes. Transfer chicken to a plate; discard drippings.

4. Prepare pasta according to package directions. Toss with chicken broth and 3 Tbsp. Arugula Pesto. Add pasta mixture to skillet. Place chicken, skin sides up, on pasta.

5. Bake at 400° for 25 to 30 minutes. Dollop with additional Arugula Pesto.

ARUGULA PESTO Process **2 cups firmly packed arugula, ½ cup firmly packed fresh flat-leaf parsley, ½ cup olive oil, 2 garlic cloves, ¼ cup grated Parmesan cheese, 2 Tbsp. water, 1 tsp. fresh lemon juice, ½ tsp. table salt,** and **¼ tsp. black pepper** in a food processor until smooth. Refrigerate up to 1 week. **MAKES** 1 cup

---

THE THIGH'S THE LIMIT ON FLAVORS
Master the method and you'll have the key to dozens of meals

OLIVES & CAPERBERRIES
Omit pasta, broth, and pesto. Prepare as directed through Step 3. Cut **1 lemon** into ¼-inch-thick rounds. Stir together **1 cup pitted large Spanish olives, 1 cup large caperberries with stems, ¼ cup coarsely chopped almonds,** and **¼ cup dry white wine** in skillet; add lemon slices. Place chicken, skin sides up, in skillet. Bake as directed. Sprinkle with **parsley**.

POBLANOS & ONIONS
Omit pasta, chicken broth, and pesto. Prepare recipe as directed through Step 3. Place **3 large poblano peppers,** seeded and chopped, and **½ large white onion,** chopped, in skillet. Place chicken, skin sides up, in skillet. Bake as directed. Remove from oven, and top with **¼ cup chopped fresh cilantro** and **¼ cup crumbled queso blanco.**

POTATOES & ROSEMARY
Omit pasta, chicken broth, and pesto. Prepare recipe as directed through Step 3. Place **2 lb. small fingerling potatoes,** cut into ½-inch-thick pieces, in a single layer in skillet, and sprinkle with **1 Tbsp. chopped fresh rosemary** and **¼ tsp. table salt.** Place chicken, skin sides up, in skillet, and sprinkle with **¼ tsp. chopped fresh rosemary.** Bake as directed.

Red Pepper, Potato, and Ricotta Frittata

MAKES 6 SERVINGS

Easier than an omelet, this hearty Italian egg dish makes enough to feed a family—all in a single skillet. Use any combination of fillings you'd include in a traditional omelet.

- 1 jarred roasted red bell pepper
- 12 large eggs
- 1/2 cup freshly grated Parmesan cheese
- 3 garlic cloves, minced
- 2 Tbsp. chopped fresh flat-leaf parsley
- 2 Tbsp. chopped fresh chives
- 3/4 tsp. table salt
- 1/4 tsp. black pepper
- 16 frozen rosemary-and-garlic potato wedges, thawed
- 6 Tbsp. ricotta cheese

1. Preheat oven to 350°. Tear roasted red bell pepper into bite-size pieces to equal 1/3 cup.

2. Whisk together eggs, Parmesan cheese, garlic, parsley, chives, salt, pepper, and 1/4 cup water in a large bowl until frothy.

3. Pour half of egg mixture into a lightly greased 10-inch ovenproof nonstick skillet. Place potatoes in a single layer over egg mixture. Pour remaining egg mixture over potatoes. Dot ricotta by tablespoonfuls over egg mixture, and top with red pepper pieces.

4. Bake at 350° for 35 to 40 minutes or until puffy and set. Serve immediately.

Note: We tested with Alexia All Natural Oven Fries with Olive Oil, Rosemary & Garlic.

Whole Wheat Pesto Pizza

MAKES 2 SERVINGS

Double the recipe (making two pizzas) to feed four to six people. Make the Arugula Pesto while the dough stands.

- 1/2 lb. purchased whole wheat pizza dough
- 2 tsp. vegetable oil
- 1 tsp. plain yellow cornmeal
- 2 Tbsp. Arugula Pesto (see page 29) Desired toppings (see below)
- 1/4 cup grated Parmesan cheese
- 1 Tbsp. olive oil

1. Preheat oven to 450°. Let dough stand at room temperature 20 minutes. Coat a 12-inch cast-iron skillet with vegetable oil, and sprinkle with cornmeal.

2. Stretch or roll dough out, and arrange in skillet, gently stretching edges to cover bottom and sides of skillet. Cook over medium heat 2 minutes. Remove from heat, and spread with Arugula Pesto. Add desired toppings; sprinkle with cheese. Brush edges of dough with olive oil.

3. Bake at 450° for 18 minutes or until browned.

TRY THESE TOPPINGS

- Cooked ground turkey sausage, sliced red onion, and sliced sweet mini bell peppers
- Roasted butternut squash, sliced shallots, sun-dried tomatoes, and fresh sage
- Mozzarella cheese slices, plum tomato slices, and basil
- Thinly sliced potatoes, mushrooms, and fontina cheese

Give Comfort in a Jar

▶ Bestow good luck with a New Year's Day soup of good-for-you peas and collards shot through with smoky flavor

Hoppin' John Soup

MAKES 11 CUPS
HANDS-ON 30 MIN.
TOTAL 2 HOURS, 5 MIN., NOT INCLUDING CROUTONS

- 1/2 (16-oz.) package dried black-eyed peas, rinsed and sorted
- 2 lb. smoked turkey wings
- 1/3 cup finely chopped country ham
- 1/4 tsp. dried crushed red pepper
- 2 garlic cloves, minced
- 1 jalapeño pepper, seeded and minced
- 2 carrots, cut into 1-inch pieces
- 1 celery rib, diced
- 1 large sweet onion, diced
- 1 bay leaf
- 2 Tbsp. canola oil
- 1/2 (16-oz.) package fresh collard greens, trimmed and finely chopped
- 1 Tbsp. hot sauce
- 1 Tbsp. apple cider vinegar
  Hot cooked brown rice
  Cornbread Croutons
  Flat-leaf parsley leaves

1. Bring peas, turkey wings, and 6 cups water to a boil in a large Dutch oven. Cover, reduce heat to medium, and simmer 45 minutes or until peas are tender, skimming any foam from surface. Drain peas, reserving 1 1/4 cups liquid. Remove turkey meat from bones. Chop meat.

2. Sauté ham and next 7 ingredients in hot oil in Dutch oven over medium-high heat 10 minutes or until vegetables are tender. Add peas, reserved 1 1/4 cups liquid, turkey meat, collards, hot sauce, and 6 cups water. Bring to a boil; reduce heat to medium, and simmer, stirring occasionally, 30 minutes. Stir in vinegar. Season with salt and pepper. Discard bay leaf. Serve over rice with Cornbread Croutons and parsley.

CORNBREAD CROUTONS

Stir 1/2 **cup chopped fresh cilantro** and **2 jalapeño peppers,** seeded and chopped, into your **favorite cornbread batter.** Bake; cool 10 minutes. Cut into 1-inch cubes. Bake at 375° in a lightly greased jelly-roll pan until edges are golden, stirring halfway through. **MAKES** 6 dozen using a 9-inch pan. (Yield depends on pan size.)

DOWNLOAD OUR LABELS!
Get our gift tags: *southernliving .com/food-gift*

"What's your go-to meal when you get home from work?"

—Allison Creech
Raleigh, North Carolina

▶ **Katie Button** of Asheville's happening tapas bar Cúrate serves up the answer

EVERYDAY TECHNIQUE

Master these eggs and you have a fast and easy protein for topping greens, beans, toast, or pasta.

THE RECIPE

Sautéed Greens with Olive Oil-Fried Eggs

MAKES 2 SERVINGS
HANDS-ON 20 MIN.
TOTAL 30 MIN., NOT INCLUDING EGGS

Serve with crusty bread.

- 2 **cups butternut squash cubes (1 small squash)**
- 4 **Tbsp. olive oil, divided**
- 1 **tsp. kosher salt, divided**
- 1 **medium-size onion, halved and thinly sliced**
- 2 **(5-oz.) packages mixed baby braising greens**
- ¼ **cup blanched hazelnuts, toasted and chopped**
- 2 **Tbsp. dry sherry**
- ¼ **cup crumbled goat cheese**
- 2 **Olive Oil-Fried Eggs**

1. Preheat oven to 450°. Toss squash with 2 Tbsp. olive oil, and spread in a single layer on a baking sheet; sprinkle with ½ tsp. salt. Bake 20 minutes or until squash is soft and golden brown, stirring occasionally.

2. Meanwhile, sauté onion in remaining 2 Tbsp. hot oil in a large skillet over medium heat 10 minutes or until onion is tender. Add greens, next 2 ingredients, and squash, tossing to coat. Sprinkle with remaining ½ tsp. salt. Cook, stirring often, 2 minutes or just until greens begin to wilt. Sprinkle with goat cheese, and top with Olive Oil-Fried Eggs.

Note: We tested with Organic Girl I Heart Baby Kale for mixed baby greens.

OLIVE OIL-FRIED EGGS

The key here is to fry the eggs fast (listen for the sizzle) and baste the yolks with the hot oil until they're opaque.

Pour **light olive oil** to depth of ⅓ inch into a small nonstick skillet (about 1 cup oil for a 6-inch skillet). Heat oil over medium-high heat just until it begins to smoke. Reduce heat to medium. Break **1 egg** into a ramekin or small bowl. Holding dish as close to surface as possible, carefully slip egg into oil. (Oil may splatter.) Spoon oil over egg for about 30 seconds or until white is cooked and crispy on edges. Remove egg from oil using a slotted spoon, dabbing with paper towels to absorb oil; transfer egg to a plate. Sprinkle with **kosher salt** to taste. Repeat with desired number of eggs.
HANDS-ON 5 min., **TOTAL** 5 min.

PULL UP A CHAIR WITH KATIE

LIVES IN
Asheville, NC

LATEST ACHIEVEMENT
A Robb Report nomination for Top New Artist of the Next Generation

FIRST FOOD JOB
Helping my mother set up catering jobs when I was little

PERFECT DINNER GUEST
My husband, Felix, who shares my passion for food

MOST MEMORABLE SOUTHERN MEAL
At the beach in SC: pulled pork with tangy mustard sauce, local peaches, and boiled peanuts

FAVORITE PANTRY STAPLE
Olive oil from a friend's farm in Spain

GO-TO COCKTAIL
Negroni

FAVORITE SOUTHERN INDULGENCE
Homemade pimiento cheese

Indulge Without Guilt

▶ Challenge the Test Kitchen to lighten popular breakfast breads and they'll rise to the occasion. Behold: pure decadence for less than 300 calories.

Maple-Pecan Sticky Buns

MAKES 16 ROLLS
HANDS-ON 20 MIN.
TOTAL 1 HOUR, 30 MIN., INCLUDING SYRUP AND GLAZE

To make ahead, assemble unbaked rolls in pans, cover with plastic wrap, and chill overnight. Let stand 1 1/2 to 2 hours to rise; bake as directed. (Pictured on page 4)

   Sticky Bun Syrup
1 (16-oz.) package hot roll mix
3 Tbsp. butter, melted
1/2 cup firmly packed dark brown sugar
1 tsp. ground cinnamon
   Maple Glaze
1/2 cup chopped toasted pecans

1. Lightly grease 2 (8-inch) round or square cake pans or skillets. Spoon Sticky Bun Syrup into pans.

2. Prepare hot roll dough as directed on back of package; let dough stand 5 minutes.

3. Roll dough into an 18- x 10-inch rectangle. Spread with melted butter. Stir together brown sugar and cinnamon; sprinkle over butter.

4. Roll dough up tightly, starting at 1 long end; cut into 16 slices using a serrated knife. Place 1 slice in center of each prepared pan. Place 7 slices around center roll in each pan.

5. Cover pans loosely with plastic wrap; let rise in a warm place (85°), free from drafts, 30 to 45 minutes or until doubled in bulk.

6. Preheat oven to 350°. Uncover rolls, and bake 15 to 20 minutes or until golden brown and done. Cool in pans on a wire rack 5 minutes. Prepare Maple Glaze, and brush over rolls. Top with toasted pecans.

STICKY BUN SYRUP Whisk together 2/3 cup powdered sugar, 1/4 cup melted butter, 2 Tbsp. maple syrup, and 1 egg white until smooth.

MAPLE GLAZE Melt **3 Tbsp. butter** in a small, heavy saucepan over medium heat. Whisk in 1/4 **cup firmly packed dark brown sugar, 2 Tbsp. maple syrup**, and **a pinch of table salt** until blended. Whisk in **3 Tbsp. milk;** bring mixture to a boil, whisking constantly. Reduce heat to medium-low; simmer, whisking constantly, 3 to 4 minutes or until glaze is golden brown and glossy. Use immediately.

TRY THIS TWIST

APPLE-CINNAMON STICKY ROLLS

Peel and chop **2 Granny Smith apples** (about 3 cups chopped). Place apples in a small microwave-safe bowl, and pour **1 cup apple juice** over apples. Cover tightly with heavy-duty plastic wrap; fold back a small corner to allow steam to escape. Microwave at HIGH 5 minutes or until tender. Drain and cool 15 minutes. Prepare recipe as directed, sprinkling apples over brown sugar mixture before rolling up.

Gluten-Free Banana Bread

MAKES 1 (9- X 5-INCH) LOAF
HANDS-ON 15 MIN.
TOTAL 2 HOURS, 35 MIN.

This recipe was inspired by one from musings-ofahousewife.com. For best results, use a light-colored pan. Or, turn your dark pan into a shiny one by wrapping the outside of it with heavy-duty aluminum foil.

- 1 cup boiling water
- 1/2 cup chopped dates
- 4 large eggs
- 2 cups mashed, very ripe bananas (about 4)
- 3/4 cup granulated sugar
- 1/2 cup unsweetened applesauce
- 1 tsp. vanilla extract
- 1 1/2 cups brown rice flour
- 1/2 cup sorghum flour
- 1 tsp. baking soda
- 1/2 tsp. table salt
- 1/4 tsp. ground nutmeg
- 1/3 cup butter, melted
- 1/2 cup chopped walnuts

1. Preheat oven to 350°. Pour 1 cup boiling water over dates in a small bowl. Let stand 10 minutes. Drain and pat dry.

2. Lightly beat eggs with a whisk in a large bowl. Whisk in bananas and next 3 ingredients until blended.

3. Stir together brown rice flour and next 4 ingredients in a small bowl. Gently stir flour mixture into egg mixture, stirring just until blended. Gently stir in melted butter, walnuts, and dates. Spoon mixture into a lightly greased 9- x 5-inch loaf pan.

4. Bake at 350° for 1 hour to 1 hour and 10 minutes or until a wooden pick inserted in center comes out clean. Cool in pan on a wire rack 10 minutes. Remove from pan to wire rack, and cool completely (about 1 hour).

> **LIGHTEN UP!**
> Brown rice flour and sorghum flour (in the organic section of supermarkets) make a bread so tender, you won't believe it's **GLUTEN-FREE**.

Blueberry Coffee Cake

MAKES 10 SERVINGS
HANDS-ON 20 MIN.
TOTAL 1 HOUR

Combine the dry ingredients the night before for a quick morning start. Serve this cake warm or at room temperature. (Pictured on page 161)

- 1 large egg
- 1/2 cup fat-free milk
- 1/2 cup plain fat-free yogurt
- 3 Tbsp. vegetable oil
- 2 cups all-purpose flour
- 1/2 cup granulated sugar
- 4 tsp. baking powder
- 1/2 tsp. table salt
- 1 1/2 cups frozen blueberries
- 1 Tbsp. all-purpose flour
- 2 Tbsp. turbinado sugar
- 2 Tbsp. sliced almonds
- 1/4 tsp. ground cinnamon

1. Preheat oven to 400°. Whisk together first 4 ingredients in a large bowl.

2. Sift together flour and next 3 ingredients in another bowl. Stir flour mixture into egg mixture just until dry ingredients are moistened.

3. Toss 1 1/4 cups blueberries in 1 Tbsp. flour; fold into batter. Pour into a lightly greased 9-inch springform pan. Sprinkle with remaining 1/4 cup blueberries.

4. Stir together 2 Tbsp. turbinado sugar, sliced almonds, and cinnamon; sprinkle over batter.

5. Bake at 400° for 25 to 30 minutes or until a wooden pick inserted in center comes out clean. Cool in pan on a wire rack 15 minutes; remove sides of pan.

> **LIGHTEN UP!**
> Skim milk and nonfat yogurt make this cake moist and easy on the waistline—**ONLY 219 CALORIES** a slice. Antioxidant-rich blueberries are a bonus.

Gluten-Free
Banana Bread

Gingerbread Muffins with Spiced Nut Streusel

Orange-Honey Buns

MAKES 16 ROLLS
HANDS-ON 20 MIN.
TOTAL 1 HOUR, 35 MIN., INCLUDING SYRUP AND GLAZE

Your microwave and oven (turned off) are perfect draft-free places to let dough rise. You won't believe these delicious breakfast bites are only 213 calories with just 5 grams of fat!

1   cup boiling water
1/2   cup sweetened dried cranberries
      Honey Syrup
1   (16-oz.) package hot roll mix
3/4   cup orange marmalade
      Orange-Honey Glaze

1. Pour 1 cup boiling water over cranberries; let stand 10 minutes. Drain and pat dry.

2. Lightly grease 2 (8-inch) round cake pans. Spoon Honey Syrup into each pan.

3. Prepare hot roll dough as directed on back of package; let dough stand 5 minutes.

4. Roll dough into an 18- x 10-inch rectangle. Spread dough with orange marmalade; sprinkle with prepared cranberries.

5. Roll dough up tightly, starting at 1 long end; cut into 16 slices using a serrated knife. Place 1 slice in center of each prepared pan. Place 7 slices around center roll in each pan.

6. Cover pans loosely with plastic wrap; let rise in a warm place (85°), free from drafts, 30 to 45 minutes or until doubled in bulk.

7. Preheat oven to 350°. Uncover rolls; bake 15 to 20 minutes or until golden brown and done. Cool rolls in pans on a wire rack 5 minutes. Brush rolls with Orange-Honey Glaze.

HONEY SYRUP Whisk together 2/3 cup powdered sugar, 1/4 cup melted butter, 2 Tbsp. honey, and 1 large egg white until smooth.

ORANGE-HONEY GLAZE Whisk together 2/3 cup powdered sugar, 1/2 Tbsp. melted butter, 1/2 tsp. orange zest, 1 Tbsp. fresh orange juice, and 1 tsp. fresh lemon juice in a bowl until blended.

Gingerbread Muffins with Spiced Nut Streusel

MAKES 1 DOZEN
HANDS-ON 15 MIN.
TOTAL 55 MIN., INCLUDING STREUSEL

Bake these easy, melt-in-your-mouth muffins ahead of time, let them cool, and freeze up to one month. Reheat muffins in the oven or microwave for a fast breakfast snack to go.

      Spiced Nut Streusel
2 1/2 cups all-purpose flour
1/3   cup chopped crystallized ginger
3/4   tsp. baking soda
1/2   tsp. table salt
1/2   tsp. ground cinnamon
1/8   tsp. ground cloves
1/4   cup butter, softened
1/4   cup granulated sugar
1/4   cup firmly packed dark brown sugar
1/2   cup unsweetened applesauce
2   large eggs
1   cup hot brewed coffee
1/3   cup unsulphured molasses
12   paper baking cups
      Vegetable cooking spray

1. Preheat oven to 350°. Prepare Spiced Nut Streusel. Process flour and next 5 ingredients in a food processor until ginger is finely ground (about 1 minute).

2. Beat butter at medium speed with a heavy-duty electric stand mixer until creamy. Gradually add sugars, beating until light and fluffy. Beat in applesauce until blended. Add eggs, 1 at a time, beating just until blended after each addition.

3. Combine hot brewed coffee and molasses in a 2-cup glass measuring cup. Add flour mixture to butter mixture alternately with coffee mixture, beginning and ending with flour mixture. Beat at low speed just until blended after each addition.

4. Place 12 paper baking cups in a 12-cup muffin pan, and coat cups with cooking spray. Spoon batter into cups, filling almost full. Sprinkle with Spiced Nut Streusel.

5. Bake at 350° for 18 to 20 minutes or until a wooden pick inserted in center comes out clean. Remove from pan to a wire rack, and cool 10 minutes. Serve warm.

SPICED NUT STREUSEL Stir together 1/4 cup firmly packed dark brown sugar, 1 Tbsp. all-purpose flour, 3/4 tsp. ground cinnamon, and 1/8 tsp. ground cloves in a small bowl; stir in 1/2 cup chopped lightly toasted pecans and 1 Tbsp. melted butter until mixture is crumbly. **MAKES** about 3/4 cup. **HANDS-ON** 5 min., **TOTAL** 5 min.

LIGHTEN UP!

We cut over **HALF OF THE SUGAR AND BUTTER**, brightening up the ginger flavor. Applesauce and coffee add extra moisture minus extra calories.

Bowl-Game Bites

▶ A taste of who and what got the highest raves in the *Southern Living* Test Kitchen.

From the Kitchen of
JULIE HUTSON
CALLAHAN, FLORIDA

"This is surprisingly yummy to have such simple ingredients."

SLOW-COOKER BEEF NACHOS

Season **1 (3-lb.) boneless beef rump roast** with **table salt** and **black pepper**. Brown all sides of roast in **1 Tbsp. hot oil** in a large skillet over high heat. Place in a 6-qt. slow cooker. Add **1 (12-oz.) jar mild banana pepper rings**, **1 (15-oz.) can beef broth**, and **3 garlic cloves**, minced. Cover and cook on LOW 8 hours or until meat shreds easily. Transfer to a cutting board, reserving liquid in slow cooker. Shred roast; return to slow cooker. Keep warm on LOW. Preheat oven to 350°. Place **tortilla chips** on a baking sheet; top with shredded beef, **1 (15-oz.) can black beans**, rinsed; chopped **tomatoes**, finely chopped **onion**, and shredded **Monterey Jack cheese**. Bake 10 minutes. Serve with **cilantro, avocado**, and **sour cream**. MAKES 6 servings

RECIPE Winner SWAP

You can also serve Julie Hutson's Slow-Cooker Beef in slider buns with your favorite sandwich toppings.

From the Kitchen of
URSULA GATTI RAFER
DELRAY BEACH, FLORIDA

"Freeze them for the perfect make-ahead party snack."

CRISPY PORK WONTONS

Stir together **2 cups finely chopped pulled barbecued pork** (without sauce); **1 carrot**, shredded; **2 green onions**, finely chopped; **1 garlic clove**, minced; **3 Tbsp. hoisin sauce**; **2 Tbsp. chicken broth**; and **2 tsp. grated fresh ginger**. Spoon about 1 Tbsp. pork mixture in center of each of **36 wonton wrappers**. Moisten wonton edges with water; bring 1 corner across mixture to form a triangle. Press edges to seal. Cover and steam wontons, in batches, in a lightly greased steamer basket over boiling water 4 minutes or until softened and moist. Stir together 1/4 **cup vegetable oil** and **2 tsp. sesame oil**. Cook wontons, in batches, in hot oil mixture in a large skillet over medium heat 30 seconds to 1 minute on each side or until golden and crispy. Serve with **bottled peanut sauce**, if desired. MAKES 3 dozen

From the Kitchen of
STEPHANIE PARKER
BIRMINGHAM, ALABAMA

"Use any pizza toppings you like. These travel well too."

PEPPERONI-SAUSAGE PIZZA PUFFS

Preheat oven to 375°. Whisk together 3/4 **cup all-purpose flour**, 3/4 **tsp. baking powder**, and 1/2 **tsp. garlic powder** in a large bowl. Whisk in 3/4 **cup milk** and **1 lightly beaten egg**. Stir in **1 cup (4 oz.) shredded mozzarella cheese**, 4 oz. **cooked and crumbled reduced-fat ground pork sausage**, and 1/2 **cup miniature turkey pepperoni**. Let batter stand 10 minutes, and stir until blended. Coat cups of a 24-cup miniature muffin pan well with **vegetable cooking spray**. Spoon batter into muffin cups. Bake 15 to 18 minutes or until puffed and golden. Serve with **warm jarred pizza sauce**. MAKES 2 dozen

February

Feast on Slow-Cooked Comfort

▶ Entertain this: four surprising dinner-party-worthy dishes—from beautifully browned rosemary chicken to a fork-tender pork roast with apples and pancetta—that simmer effortlessly in the slow cooker. And our Chile Verde? Definitely the cream of the crock.

Rosemary-Garlic
Chicken Quarters

Rosemary-Garlic Chicken Quarters

MAKES 6 TO 8 SERVINGS
HANDS-ON 25 MIN.
TOTAL 4 HOURS, 25 MIN.

The key to this dish is to brown the chicken before it goes into the slow cooker. (See "The Art of Browning," opposite page.) (Pictured on page 162)

- 3 carrots or celery ribs
- 5 lb. chicken leg quarters
- 2 Tbsp. chopped fresh rosemary
- 2 tsp. pimentón (sweet smoked Spanish paprika)
- 2 1/2 tsp. kosher salt, divided
- 1 1/4 tsp. freshly ground black pepper, divided
- 12 garlic cloves, sliced
- 3 Tbsp. olive oil
- 1/2 cup chicken broth
- 2 lb. fingerling Yukon gold potatoes, halved
- 1 tsp. olive oil
  Garnish: fresh rosemary

1. Place carrots in a single layer in a 5-qt. slow cooker.

2. Remove skin from chicken, and trim fat. Stir together rosemary, pimentón, 1 1/2 tsp. salt, and 1 tsp. pepper. Rub mixture over chicken.

3. Sauté garlic in 3 Tbsp. hot oil in a large skillet over medium heat 2 minutes or until golden brown. Transfer to a bowl using a slotted spoon; reserve oil in skillet. Cook half of chicken in reserved oil in skillet 3 to 4 minutes on each side or until deep golden brown. Transfer to slow cooker, reserving drippings in skillet. Repeat with remaining chicken.

4. Add broth and garlic to reserved drippings in skillet, and cook 1 minute, stirring to loosen particles from bottom of skillet; pour over chicken in slow cooker. Cover and cook on HIGH 2 hours.

5. Toss potatoes with 1 tsp. oil and remaining 1 tsp. salt and 1/4 tsp. pepper; add to slow cooker. Cover and cook 2 more hours.

6. Transfer chicken and potatoes to a serving platter, and pour juices from slow cooker through a fine wire-mesh strainer into a bowl; skim fat from juices. Serve immediately with chicken and potatoes.

THE ART OF BROWNING

Browning meats and poultry before simmering in the slow cooker yields major depth of flavor plus a picture-perfect presentation, so don't be tempted to skip it. First, pat the meat dry with paper towels before seasoning. Set a heavy stainless steel or well-seasoned cast-iron skillet (not nonstick) over medium to medium-high heat for 2 to 3 minutes or until hot enough for the oil to shimmer—the meat should hiss and sizzle as soon as it hits the pan. Be sure not to crowd the pan; doing so drops the temp, causing the meat to steam rather than form a crisp crust. Don't turn the meat until the bottom is well browned.

Pork with Apples, Bacon, and Sauerkraut

MAKES 6 TO 8 SERVINGS
HANDS-ON 50 MIN.
TOTAL 3 HOURS, 50 MIN.

Find pancetta—unsmoked Italian bacon cured with salt and spices—in the deli section. (Pictured on page 162)

- 1 (3-lb.) boneless pork loin
- ½ tsp. kosher salt
- ½ tsp. freshly ground black pepper
- 6 oz. thinly sliced pancetta or bacon Kitchen string
- 2 Tbsp. olive oil
- 2 small onions, quartered (root end intact)
- 1 (12-oz.) package frozen pearl onions (about 2 cups)
- 2 garlic cloves, thinly sliced
- 3 fresh thyme sprigs
- 2 bay leaves
- 1 (12-oz.) bottle stout or porter beer
- 2 Tbsp. Dijon mustard
- 3 firm apples (such as Gala), divided
- 2 cups jarred sauerkraut, rinsed
- 2 cups finely shredded green cabbage
- 1 Tbsp. chopped fresh flat-leaf parsley
- 1 tsp. fresh lemon juice
- ½ cup apricot preserves
- ¼ cup chicken broth

Pork with Apples, Bacon, and Sauerkraut

1. Trim fat and silver skin from pork. Sprinkle pork with kosher salt and pepper. Wrap top and sides of pork with pancetta. Tie with kitchen string, securing at 1-inch intervals.

2. Cook pork in hot oil in a large skillet over medium heat, turning occasionally, 15 minutes or until deep golden brown. Remove from skillet, reserving drippings in skillet.

3. Place quartered onion and next 4 ingredients in a 6-qt. slow cooker; top with pork.

4. Add beer to reserved drippings in skillet, and cook over medium heat 8 minutes or until liquid is reduced by half, stirring to loosen brown bits from bottom of skillet. Stir in mustard, and pour over pork. Cover and cook on HIGH 2 hours.

5. Peel 2 apples, and cut into large wedges. Add apple wedges, sauerkraut, and cabbage to slow cooker; cover and cook 1 to 2 more hours or until a meat thermometer inserted into thickest portion of pork registers 150° and apples are tender.

6. Cut remaining unpeeled apple into thin strips, and toss with parsley and lemon juice. Season with salt and pepper to taste.

7. Combine preserves and broth in a small saucepan, and cook over medium heat, stirring often, 4 to 5 minutes or until melted and smooth.

8. Brush pork with apricot mixture. Cut pork into slices, and serve with onion mixture, apple-parsley mixture, and additional Dijon mustard.

Green Tomato Chile Verde

MAKES 8 SERVINGS
HANDS-ON 30 MIN.
TOTAL 6 HOURS, 45 MIN., INCLUDING SALSA

We like the tang and body that green tomatoes give this comforting stew. (Pictured on page 162)

- 6 medium-size green tomatoes, divided
- 4 poblano peppers, seeded and divided
- 1 1/2 cups chopped fresh cilantro
- 5 garlic cloves
- 1/2 cup chopped sweet onion
- 1/2 cup hot water
- 1 (5-lb.) boneless pork shoulder roast (Boston butt)
- 2 tsp. ground cumin
- 1 tsp. table salt
- 1 tsp. pepper
- 1/4 cup all-purpose flour
- 1/4 cup olive oil
  Corn tortillas, warmed
  Green Tomato Salsa

1. Chop 3 tomatoes and 1 poblano pepper, and place in a large bowl. Stir in cilantro and next 3 ingredients. Process mixture, in 2 batches, in a blender or food processor until smooth.

2. Coarsely chop remaining tomatoes and peppers, and place in a 6-qt. slow cooker.

3. Trim and discard fat from pork. Cut pork into 2-inch cubes. Combine pork and next 3 ingredients in a large bowl, and toss to coat. Sprinkle with flour, and toss to coat.

4. Cook pork, in batches, in hot oil in a large skillet over medium-high heat, turning occasionally, 10 to 12 minutes or until golden brown. Place pork over tomato mixture in slow cooker. Pour pureed tomato mixture over pork.

5. Cover and cook on LOW 6 to 7 hours or until pork is tender. Season with salt and pepper. Serve chile verde with tortillas and Green Tomato Salsa.

GREEN TOMATO SALSA

MAKES 2 CUPS
HANDS-ON 15 MIN.
TOTAL 15 MIN.

Combine 2 **medium-size green tomatoes,** finely chopped; 1/2 **small onion,** finely chopped; 1 **jalapeño pepper,** seeded and minced; 1/2 cup chopped **fresh cilantro;** 1 Tbsp. **fresh lime juice;** and 1/2 tsp. **table salt** in a bowl. Cover and chill until ready to serve.

Wine-Braised Oxtails

Wine-Braised Oxtails

MAKES ABOUT 6 SERVINGS
HANDS-ON 30 MIN.
TOTAL 6 HOURS, 30 MIN.

(Pictured on page 162)

- 2 carrots, chopped
- 2 medium onions, chopped
- 2 celery ribs, chopped
- 6 garlic cloves, sliced
- 6 fresh flat-leaf parsley sprigs
- 2 bay leaves
- 2 (3-inch) fresh rosemary sprigs
- 5 lb. oxtails
- 2 tsp. kosher salt
- 1 tsp. freshly ground pepper
- 1/4 cup all-purpose flour
- 2 Tbsp. olive oil
- 2 cups dry red wine
- 1 (6-oz.) can tomato paste
- 1 (8-oz.) package fresh mushrooms, quartered
  Hot cooked rice

1. Place first 7 ingredients in a 6-qt. slow cooker.

2. Toss oxtails with salt and pepper. Sprinkle with flour; toss to coat. Cook oxtails, in 2 batches, in hot oil in a large skillet over medium heat 3 to 4 minutes on each side or until well browned. Transfer oxtails to slow cooker, reserving drippings in skillet.

3. Add wine to reserved drippings in skillet; cook 1 minute, stirring to loosen brown bits from bottom of skillet. Whisk in tomato paste; cook, stirring often, 2 minutes. Pour over oxtails.

4. Cover and cook on LOW 5 to 6 hours. Add mushrooms; cook 1 more hour.

5. Remove oxtails and vegetables using a slotted spoon. Discard bay leaves and herbs. Skim fat from juices in slow cooker; season with salt and pepper. Serve immediately over oxtails, vegetables, and hot cooked rice.

> ### SL TEST KITCHEN TIP
>
> Make an easy beef stew by using 1 (5-lb.) boneless chuck roast for oxtails. Trim the fat, and cut into 2-inch pieces.

Master the Art of Making Roux

Use our technique to boost the flavor, color, and aroma of stews, gumbos, and sauces

ROUX IS A RITUAL, a foundation of flavor, and a commitment. To make it, you simply combine fat and flour in a heavy skillet or pot and cook it, stirring *constantly*, to coax out flavor, using the color—blonde to dark brown—as your guidepost. Chefs such as Leah Chase (see page 54) know the only critical key to making roux is following one simple commandment: Thou shalt pay attention. No texting and stirring. From there, it's easy.

STEP 1: Pick your fat. Butter or animal fat adds flavor, but use canola oil for darker Creole and Cajun roux. Its higher smoke point is more forgiving.

STEP 2: Choose your heat. Experts can use a higher flame. Beginners should heat fat in a pan over medium; the roux will take longer but not burn as easily. Add roughly a 1:1 ratio of flour to fat.

STEP 3: ID the roux you want at right. Keep stirring until you match it.

GET IT!

THE CAJUN ROUX SPOON

A whisk works, but this cherrywood spatula is the best tool for making roux. Its flat edge scrapes evenly along the bottom and into the corners of a pan, preventing stubborn bits of flour from scorching (*accentrics.net*).

❶ BLONDE ROUX
Flour is cooked but still light. Stir into sauces such as velouté to add richness and body.

❷ LIGHT BROWN ROUX
Marry this versatile thickener with pan juices from a roast to make gravy.

❸ MEDIUM-BROWN ROUX
Begins losing thickening power but adds toasty flavor. Takes 15 minutes on medium heat.

❹ DARK BROWN ROUX
Takes 20 minutes when cooked fast, up to 1 hour cooked slowly. Gives étouffées and gumbos deep, smoky flavor.

❺ BLESS YOUR HEART
You've gone too far. Cook the roux too long or fast and it will taste burned.

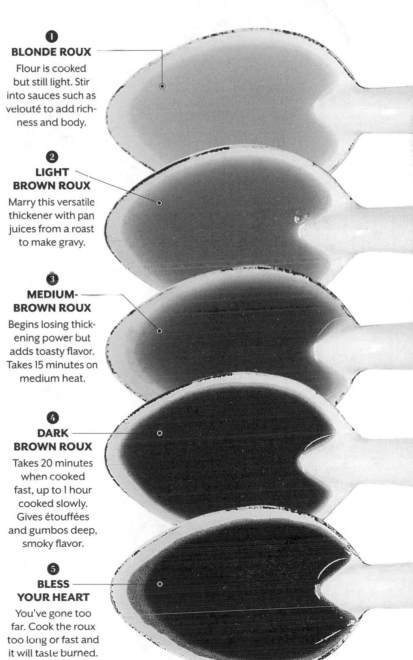

Reinvent Pasta Night

► Liven up this weeknight supper standby with fast, fresh ingredients and our secret to perfect pan sauces––hot pasta water

Fast-and-Fresh
Sausage Ragu

Fast-and-Fresh Sausage Ragu

40 MIN

MAKES 6 TO 8 SERVINGS

Use your favorite breakfast or Italian sausage. For a finer texture, break up the sausage as it cooks using a potato masher. (Pictured on page 168)

1 (16-oz.) package rigatoni pasta
1 (1-lb.) package ground pork sausage with sage
1 medium onion, diced
1 medium zucchini, diced
2 medium carrots, diced
3 garlic cloves, pressed
¼ tsp. dried crushed red pepper
1 (6-oz.) can tomato paste
1 cup dry red wine
1 (28-oz.) can diced tomatoes with basil, garlic, and oregano
Freshly grated Parmesan cheese

1. Cook pasta according to package directions; drain, reserving ½ cup hot pasta water.

2. Meanwhile, cook sausage in a large, 2-inch-deep skillet over medium-high heat, stirring often, 5 minutes or until sausage crumbles and is no longer pink. Add onion, zucchini, and carrots; cook, stirring often, 8 to 10 minutes or until tender. Add garlic and red pepper, and cook, stirring often, 1 to 2 minutes or until garlic is tender. Add tomato paste, and cook, stirring constantly, 1 to 2 minutes. Add wine and reserved pasta water; cook 2 minutes, stirring to loosen bits from bottom of skillet.

3. Add tomatoes, and bring to a boil. Reduce heat to medium, and simmer, stirring occasionally, 10 minutes. Add salt and pepper to taste. Spoon sausage mixture over pasta; sprinkle with cheese.

Quick Chicken Noodle Bowls

MAKES 6 SERVINGS

Fresh lime juice adds extra bright flavor. Bringing the broth back to a boil before serving ensures the snap peas cook to a crisp-tender texture. (Pictured on page 168)

- 6 cups chicken broth
- 4 skinned and boned chicken thighs (about 1 lb.)
- 1/3 cup sliced fresh ginger
- 2 garlic cloves, sliced
- 1/8 tsp. Chinese five spice
- 1 (9.5-oz.) package soba noodles or 8 oz. angel hair pasta
- 1 Tbsp. soy sauce
- 2 to 3 Tbsp. fresh lime juice
  Toppings: thinly sliced sugar snap peas, fresh cilantro and mint leaves, thinly sliced green onions, thinly sliced red chile peppers

1. Bring first 5 ingredients to a boil in a 3-qt. saucepan over medium heat. Cover, reduce heat to low, and simmer 6 to 8 minutes or until chicken is done. Remove chicken, garlic, and ginger with a slotted spoon, reserving broth in saucepan. Discard garlic and ginger. Let chicken cool slightly (10 to 15 minutes); shred chicken.

2. Return broth to a boil over medium heat. Add noodles and soy sauce; cook, stirring to separate noodles, 4 to 5 minutes or until just softened. Remove noodles from broth using tongs, and divide among 6 bowls. Place chicken and desired toppings on noodles. Return broth to a boil over medium heat; remove from heat, and stir in lime juice. Divide broth among bowls.

Burst Tomato and Herb Spaghetti

MAKES 4 SERVINGS

Cover the skillet to prevent splatters as the tomatoes burst.

- 2 medium zucchini, chopped
- 2 Tbsp. olive oil, divided
- 3 garlic cloves, sliced
- 1/4 tsp. dried crushed red pepper
- 1 tsp. kosher salt, divided
- 3 pt. grape tomatoes
- 1/2 tsp. black pepper
- 1 (8-oz.) package spaghetti
- 1 cup coarsely chopped fresh basil
- 1/4 cup coarsely chopped fresh flat-leaf parsley
  Shaved Parmesan cheese

1. Sauté zucchini in 1 Tbsp. hot oil in a large skillet over medium-high heat 5 minutes or until zucchini begins to brown. Add garlic, red pepper, and 1/4 tsp. kosher salt; cook, stirring often, 4 to 5 minutes or until garlic begins to brown. Remove from skillet.

2. Add tomatoes, black pepper, and remaining 1 Tbsp. oil and 3/4 tsp. kosher salt to skillet; cook, stirring occasionally, 2 minutes. Cover, reduce heat to medium, and cook, stirring occasionally, 10 minutes or until tomatoes begin to burst.

3. Cook pasta according to package directions; drain, reserving 1/4 cup hot pasta water. Add pasta, hot pasta water, and zucchini mixture to skillet along with basil and parsley; toss. Top with cheese.

Lemony Broccoli Rabe Pasta

MAKES 4 TO 6 SERVINGS

- 2 tsp. kosher salt
- 1 lb. broccoli rabe, trimmed and cut into 3-inch pieces
- 1 (16- to 17-oz.) package filei, penne, or fusilli
- 3 Tbsp. butter
- 1 Tbsp. olive oil
- 2 garlic cloves, chopped
- 3/4 tsp. dried crushed red pepper
- 2 tsp. lemon zest
- 1/4 cup freshly grated Parmesan cheese
- 1 Tbsp. lemon juice
  Black pepper
- 1 (4-oz.) package goat cheese, crumbled

1. Bring 4 qt. water to a boil in a large Dutch oven. Add 2 tsp. kosher salt, return to a boil, and stir in broccoli rabe. Cook 1 minute or until crisp-tender; drain. Plunge into ice water to stop cooking process; drain.

2. Cook pasta in Dutch oven according to package directions; drain, reserving 1/2 cup hot pasta water.

3. Melt butter with oil in Dutch oven over medium heat; add garlic, and sauté 1 to 2 minutes or until tender. Add red pepper and lemon zest; cook, stirring constantly, 1 minute. Stir in broccoli rabe; cook, stirring constantly, 1 minute. Stir in hot cooked pasta, reserved pasta water, Parmesan, and lemon juice; cook 1 to 2 minutes. Season with kosher salt and black pepper to taste. Top with cheese.

THE POWER OF PASTA WATER

Before you drain off your perfectly cooked pasta (al dente, of course!), scoop out at least 1 cup of that rich, starchy pasta water to make an easy pan sauce. We used 1/4 to 1/2 cup in most of the dishes here, but for most recipes save a little extra in case you want a looser sauce. The cloudy broth marries with butter or oil for silky, creamy results. And because you've cooked your pasta with a proper amount of salt (about 1 Tbsp. kosher salt per quart of water), the leftover liquid delivers flavor too. Use it whenever you feel saucy.

Host an Oscar-Worthy Party

▶ In the role of playing gracious host, Atlanta native Alex Hitz, auther of *My Beverly Hills Kitchen*, is a mega-star. Use his do-ahead menu and tips for your own award-winning performance.

The Menu

appetizer

GOUGÈRES

main

FRIED CHICKEN WINGS

side

BROCCOLI SLAW

dessert

BEST-EVER BROWNIES

Gougères

MAKES 7 TO 8 DOZEN
HANDS-ON 35 MIN.
TOTAL 1 HOUR, 15 MIN.

Use your favorite mix of soft and hard cheeses in these savory one-bite pastry puffs.

- ½ cup milk
- ½ cup butter
- ¾ tsp. table salt
- 1 cup all-purpose flour
- 6 large eggs
- 1½ cups (6 oz.) shredded Gruyère cheese
- 2 Tbsp. grated Parmesan cheese
- 1½ tsp. Dijon mustard
- ⅛ tsp. ground red pepper
  Parchment paper

1. Preheat oven to 425°. Bring first 3 ingredients and ½ cup water to a rolling boil in a 3-qt. saucepan over medium heat; cook, stirring constantly, 1 minute. Add flour all at once, and beat vigorously with a wooden spoon 1 minute or until smooth and pulls away from sides of pan, forming a ball of dough. Remove from heat, and let stand 5 minutes.

2. Transfer dough to bowl of a heavy-duty electric stand mixer. Add eggs, 1 at a time, beating at medium speed until well blended after each addition. (If dough separates, don't worry—it will come back together.) Add Gruyère cheese and next 3 ingredients; beat at high speed 3 minutes or until dough is smooth and glossy. Drop by rounded teaspoonfuls 2 inches apart onto 2 parchment paper-lined baking sheets.

3. Reduce oven temperature to 375°, and bake gougères 10 to 12 minutes, placing 1 baking sheet on middle oven rack and other on lower oven rack. Switch baking sheets, and bake 4 to 6 more minutes or until golden brown. Cool on baking sheets 5 minutes. Repeat procedure with remaining dough.

MAKE-AHEAD TIP

You can make gougères ahead and freeze up to 3 months. To reheat: Place frozen gougères on baking sheets, cover lightly with foil, and bake at 350° for 10 to 15 minutes or until warm.

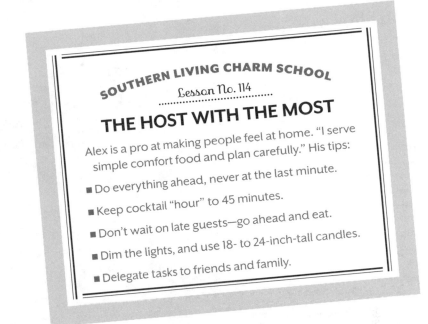

SOUTHERN LIVING CHARM SCHOOL

Lesson No. 114

THE HOST WITH THE MOST

Alex is a pro at making people feel at home. "I serve simple comfort food and plan carefully." His tips:

- Do everything ahead, never at the last minute.
- Keep cocktail "hour" to 45 minutes.
- Don't wait on late guests—go ahead and eat.
- Dim the lights, and use 18- to 24-inch-tall candles.
- Delegate tasks to friends and family.

Fried Chicken Wings

MAKES 6 SERVINGS
HANDS-ON 1 HOUR, 30 MIN.
TOTAL 2 HOURS, 5 MIN.

Alex soaks chicken twice in the egg-milk mixture and double-dredges in the highly seasoned flour for a superior crust.

- 4 lb. chicken wings (about 14 wings)
- ½ cup minced onion
- ¼ cup minced garlic
- ¾ tsp. table salt
- ¼ tsp. black pepper
- 2 large eggs
- 1½ cups milk
- 3 qt. vegetable oil
- 2 cups all-purpose flour
- 3 Tbsp. black pepper
- 1 Tbsp. table salt
- 1 Tbsp. dried oregano
- 1 Tbsp. paprika
- 1½ tsp. chili powder

1. Pat chicken dry. Place chicken and next 4 ingredients in a large bowl; toss to combine. Whisk together eggs and milk; pour over chicken. Let stand 20 minutes.

2. Pour oil into a 7½-qt. Dutch oven; heat to 325°.

3. Whisk together flour and next 5 ingredients in a large bowl.

4. Remove chicken from egg mixture, reserving egg mixture. Drain chicken well.

5. Dredge half of chicken in flour mixture, shaking off excess. Dip chicken in egg mixture, and dredge in flour mixture again.

6. Fry chicken 7 to 9 minutes or until browned. Drain on a wire rack over paper towels. Place on a wire rack in a jelly-roll pan, and keep warm in a 200° oven. (Do not cover.)

7. Return oil to 325°; repeat Steps 5 and 6 with remaining chicken, flour mixture, and egg mixture.

MAKE-AHEAD TIP

Fry chicken up to 1 hour ahead, and keep warm in a 200° oven. Or, make it the day before and chill. Serve it cold, at room temperature, or warm. To reheat: Bake on a wire rack in a jelly-roll pan at 300° for 45 minutes.

Broccoli Slaw

MAKES 6 TO 8 SERVINGS
HANDS-ON 20 MIN.
TOTAL 8 HOURS, 35 MIN., INCLUDING DRESSING

Cooking broccoli in boiling water to a bright green takes only a couple of minutes. Be sure to shock it immediately in ice water to keep the color vibrant.

- 1 lb. fresh broccoli
- 2 tsp. table salt
- 2 cups chopped green cabbage
- 2 cups finely shredded red cabbage
- 3/4 cup diced yellow bell pepper
- 1/2 cup chopped fresh dill
- 1/4 cup minced shallots
- 3/4 tsp. table salt
- 3/4 tsp. black pepper
  Mayo-Sour Cream Dressing

1. Trim 1/2 inch from bottom of broccoli stem. Cut broccoli lengthwise into 4 pieces.

2. Bring salt and 2 qt. water to a boil in a Dutch oven over high heat. Add broccoli; cook 2 minutes or just until broccoli turns bright green. (Do not overcook.) Drain broccoli, and plunge into ice water to stop the cooking process. Let stand 1 to 2 minutes. Drain broccoli, and pat dry between paper towels. Chop broccoli florets and stems.

3. Combine broccoli, green cabbage, and next 6 ingredients in a large bowl. Add 1 cup Mayo-Sour Cream Dressing, and toss to coat. Cover and chill 8 to 24 hours. Add additional dressing, if desired.

MAYO-SOUR CREAM DRESSING

Stir together 3/4 cup **mayonnaise**, 1/2 cup **sour cream**, 1 1/2 Tbsp. **Dijon mustard**, 3/4 tsp. **salt**, 3/4 tsp. **lemon juice**, and 1/4 tsp. **pepper**.

MAKE-AHEAD TIP

Make this easy and delicious winter salad 8 to 24 hours ahead to allow the flavors to meld.

Glam-up Best-Ever Brownies with edible gold leaf ($26; *surlatable.com*).

Best-Ever Brownies

MAKES ABOUT 2 1/2 DOZEN
HANDS-ON 20 MIN.
TOTAL 3 HOURS, 40 MIN.

These are super fudgy. For a more cake-like brownie, bake 5 to 7 minutes longer. (Pictured on page 166)

- 1 (8-oz.) package unsweetened chocolate baking squares, chopped
- 1 1/2 cups butter, cut up
- 4 cups sugar
- 2 cups all-purpose flour
- 6 large eggs
- 1 Tbsp. plus 1/8 tsp. table salt
- 1 Tbsp. vanilla extract
  Edible gold leaf (optional)

1. Preheat oven to 350°. Line a 13- x 9-inch pan with aluminum foil, allowing 2 inches to extend over sides; lightly grease foil.

2. Bring 1 inch of water to a simmer in bottom of a double boiler. Place chocolate and butter in top of double boiler. Cook, stirring occasionally, 5 to 6 minutes or until melted. Cool 10 minutes; transfer to a large bowl. Stir in sugar until blended. Stir in flour and next 3 ingredients just until blended. Pour batter into pan.

3. Bake at 350° for 32 to 35 minutes or until set. Cool in pan 30 minutes. Freeze 2 hours; cut into squares or triangles. Press tops with gold leaf, if desired.

MAKE-AHEAD TIP

Freeze up to 2 months. If using gold leaf, add it just before serving.

Cure your Cravings

▶ How do you sneak gooey melted goodness into every oat-filled bite without the extra fat? Replace half the butter with an extra bar of chocolate.

Dark Chocolate Chunk Cookies

MAKES ABOUT 2 DOZEN
HANDS-ON 15 MIN.
TOTAL 9 HOURS, 50 MIN.

For an even chewier texture, substitute ½ cup hazelnut or almond flour for ½ cup all-purpose flour.

- ¾ **cup uncooked regular oats**
- ¼ **cup butter, softened**
- ¾ **cup firmly packed light brown sugar**
- ½ **cup granulated sugar**
- 2 **large eggs**
- 1 **tsp. vanilla extract**
- 1¾ **cups all-purpose flour**
- ½ **tsp. baking soda**
- ½ **tsp. table salt**
- ¼ **tsp. baking powder**
- 3 **(4-oz.) bittersweet chocolate baking bars, coarsely chopped and divided**
- **Parchment paper**

1. Preheat oven to 400°. Bake oats in a 9-inch pie plate 10 to 12 minutes or until toasted and fragrant, stirring halfway through. Cool completely on a wire rack (about 30 minutes). Process oats in a blender or food processor 1 minute or until finely ground.

2. Beat butter and sugars at medium speed with a heavy-duty electric stand mixer until fluffy. Add eggs and vanilla, beating just until blended.

3. Stir together flour, next 3 ingredients, and ground oats in a small bowl; gradually add to butter mixture, beating just until blended after each addition. Fold in 2¼ cups chopped chocolate (about 2 bars) just until combined. Cover dough, and chill 8 to 12 hours.

4. Preheat oven to 350°. Drop dough by heaping tablespoonfuls onto parchment paper-lined baking sheets (about 6 per sheet).

5. Bake at 350° for 10 to 12 minutes or until golden brown; press remaining chocolate into cookies. Remove from baking sheets to wire racks, cool completely (about 15 minutes).

> **SL TEST KITCHEN TIP**
>
> Pressing some of the chocolate into the hot cookies gives a chunkier look.

Overheard outside the Editor's office:

"Chocolaty, yummy, AND half the fat—my kind of cookie!"

Dreamy Lemon Desserts

▶ Start with one foolproof lemon curd as the building block of nine spoon-licking desserts. From brilliantly simple soufflés to an over-the-top cheesecake wrapped in a buttery shortbread crust, we've got you covered. Now that's sweet!

Lemon Bar Cheesecake

Lemon Bar Cheesecake

MAKES 10 TO 12 SERVINGS
HANDS-ON 40 MIN.
TOTAL 22 HOURS, 45 MIN., INCLUDING CURD AND CANDIED LEMON

Using a dark springform pan ensures a golden brown crust without having to bake before adding the filling. (Pictured on page 3)

- 2 **cups all-purpose flour**
- ½ **cup powdered sugar**
- ¼ **tsp. table salt**
- ½ **cup cold butter, cubed**
- 2 **large egg yolks**
- 1 **to 2 Tbsp. ice-cold water**
- 4 **(8-oz.) packages cream cheese, softened**
- 1 **cup granulated sugar**
- 4 **large eggs**
- 2 **tsp. vanilla extract**
- 2 **cups Quick & Easy Lemon Curd, divided (see opposite page)**
  Candied Lemon Slices (optional)

1. Pulse first 3 ingredients in a food processor 3 or 4 times or just until blended. Add butter, and pulse 5 or 6 times or until crumbly. Whisk together egg yolks and 1 Tbsp. ice-cold water in a small bowl; add to butter mixture, and process until dough forms a ball and pulls away from sides of bowl, adding up to 1 Tbsp. remaining ice-cold water, 1 tsp. at a time, if necessary. Shape dough into a disk; wrap in plastic wrap. Chill 4 to 24 hours.

2. Roll dough into a 14-inch circle on a lightly floured surface. Fit dough into a lightly greased 9-inch dark springform pan, gently pressing on bottom and up sides of pan; trim and discard excess dough. Chill 30 minutes.

3. Meanwhile, preheat oven to 325°. Beat cream cheese at medium speed with an electric mixer 3 minutes or until smooth. Gradually add granulated sugar, beating until blended. Add eggs, 1 at a time, beating just until yellow disappears after each addition. Beat in vanilla.

4. Pour two-thirds of cheesecake batter (about 4 cups) into prepared crust; dollop 1 cup lemon curd over batter in pan, and gently swirl with a knife. Spoon remaining batter into pan.

5. Bake at 325° for 1 hour to 1 hour and 10 minutes or just until center is set. Turn oven off. Let cheesecake stand in oven, with door closed, 15 minutes. Remove cheesecake from oven, and gently run a knife around outer edge of cheesecake to loosen from sides of pan. (Do not remove sides of pan.) Cool completely in pan on a wire rack (about 1 hour). Cover and chill 8 to 24 hours.

6. Remove sides of pan, and transfer cheesecake to a serving platter. Spoon remaining 1 cup lemon curd over cheese-cake, and, if desired, top with Candied Lemon Slices.

CANDIED LEMON SLICES

Cut 2 small **lemons** into ⅛-inch-thick rounds; discard seeds. Stir together 1 cup **sugar,** 2 Tbsp. **fresh lemon juice,** and ¾ cup **water** in a large skillet over medium heat until sugar is dissolved. Add lemon slices, and simmer gently, keeping slices in a single layer and turning occasionally, 14 to 16 minutes or until slightly translucent and rinds are softened. Remove from heat. Place slices in a single layer in a **wax paper**-lined jelly-roll pan, using tongs. Cool completely (about 1 hour). Cover and chill 2 hours to 2 days. Reserve syrup for another use.

IMAGINE THE
**delicious
possibilities** OF
LEMON BARS AND
CHEESECAKE
TOGETHER IN ONE
INDULGENT DESSERT.

LEMON TIRAMISÙ

MAKES 24 SHOOTERS
HANDS-ON 30 MIN.
TOTAL 6 HOURS, 50 MIN., INCLUDING CURD

Be sure to use soft ladyfingers, found in the bakery or produce section. (Pictured on page 3)

1	(8-oz.) container mascarpone cheese
½	cup sugar
2	tsp. vanilla extract
1	cup whipping cream
2	(3-oz.) packages ladyfingers
24	(1 ½-oz.) shot glasses
1 ½	cups Quick & Easy Lemon Curd (see recipe below)
24	fresh raspberries
24	small fresh mint sprigs

1. Stir together first 3 ingredients just until blended.

2. Beat whipping cream at medium speed with an electric mixer until soft peaks form; fold into cheese mixture. Spoon mixture into a zip-top plastic freezer bag. (Do not seal.) Snip 1 corner of bag to make a ½-inch hole.

3. Cut ladyfingers in half crosswise. Press 1 ladyfinger half into bottom of each shot glass. Spoon 1 ½ tsp. lemon curd into each glass. Pipe a small amount of mascarpone mixture into each glass. Repeat layers once with remaining ladyfingers, lemon curd, and mascarpone mixture. Top each with 1 raspberry and 1 mint sprig. Cover and chill 2 hours.

START WITH

quick & easy
lemon curd

We changed the mixing method of our favorite lemon curd, then cooked it in the microwave. The results? Buttery rich and smooth as silk, every time.

STEP ONE

Grate zest from 6 lemons to equal 2 Tbsp. Cut lemons in half; squeeze juice into a measuring cup to equal 1 cup.

STEP TWO

Beat ½ cup butter, softened, and 2 cups sugar at medium speed with an electric mixer until blended. Add 4 eggs, 1 at a time, beating just until blended after each addition. Gradually add lemon juice to butter mixture, beating at low speed just until blended after each addition; stir in zest. (Mixture will look curdled.) Transfer to a 3-qt. microwave-safe bowl.

STEP THREE

Microwave at HIGH 5 minutes, stirring at 1-minute intervals. Microwave, stirring at 30-second intervals, 1 to 2 more minutes or until mixture thickens, coats the back of a spoon, and starts to mound slightly when stirred.

STEP FOUR

Place heavy-duty plastic wrap directly on warm curd (to prevent a film from forming), and chill 4 hours or until firm. Store in an airtight container in refrigerator up to 2 weeks. **MAKES** 2 cups

STOVE-TOP METHOD

Prepare as directed through Step 2, transferring mixture to a heavy 4-qt. saucepan. Cook over medium-low heat, whisking constantly, 14 to 16 minutes. Proceed as directed in Step 4.

Lemon-Yogurt
Crumb Cake

Lemon-Yogurt Crumb Cake

MAKES 8 TO 10 SERVINGS
HANDS-ON 30 MIN.
TOTAL 5 HOURS, 35 MIN., INCLUDING CURD

We love the swirls of lemon curd in this cake, but it's also delicious without it. (Pictured on page 167)

CRUMB TOPPING

1 ½   cups all-purpose flour
⅔   cup granulated sugar
1   Tbsp. lemon zest
1   Tbsp. orange zest
⅛   tsp. table salt
½   cup cold butter, cut into pieces

CAKE BATTER

½   cup butter, softened
1 ½   cups granulated sugar, divided
3   large eggs, separated
1 ½   cups all-purpose flour
⅛   tsp. baking soda
½   cup plain Greek yogurt
1   Tbsp. lemon zest
¾   cup Quick & Easy Lemon Curd (see recipe, page 49)
¼   cup powdered sugar

1. Prepare Crumb Topping: Preheat oven to 350°. Combine first 5 ingredients; cut cold butter into flour mixture with a pastry blender or fork until crumbly. Cover and chill until ready to use.

2. Prepare Cake Batter: Beat softened butter at medium speed with a heavy-duty electric stand mixer until creamy. Add 1 ¼ cups granulated sugar, beating 3 minutes or until fluffy. Add egg yolks, 1 at a time, beating just until yellow disappears.

3. Stir together flour and baking soda; add to butter mixture alternately with yogurt, beginning and ending with flour mixture. Stir in lemon zest.

4. Beat egg whites at high speed until foamy; gradually add remaining ¼ cup granulated sugar, 1 Tbsp. at a time, beating until stiff peaks form. Fold into batter. Pour batter into a greased and floured 9-inch square (2-inch-deep) pan. Dollop with lemon curd; gently swirl with a knife. Sprinkle Crumb Topping over batter.

5. Bake at 350° for 45 to 50 minutes or until a wooden pick inserted in center comes out clean. Remove from oven; dust with powdered sugar. Serve warm, or cool on a wire rack 1 hour.

LEMON CURD ADDS *a twist of sunny citrus flavor* TO OUR FAVORITE CRUMB-TOPPED COFFEE CAKE.

YES, THESE *feather-light soufflés*
DO LOOK TOO GOOD TO EAT. BUT DON'T
LET THAT STOP YOU.

Lemon Soufflés

MAKES 5 (4-OZ.) SERVINGS
HANDS-ON 15 MIN.
TOTAL 4 HOURS, 50 MIN., INCLUDING CURD

Prep the lemon curd up to two weeks ahead and you can serve these in just 30 minutes.

- 2 Tbsp. granulated sugar
- 2 cups Quick & Easy Lemon Curd, divided (see page 49)
- 2 Tbsp. all-purpose flour
- 1/8 tsp. table salt
- 4 large egg whites, at room temperature
- 1/8 tsp. cream of tartar
- 2 Tbsp. powdered sugar

1. Preheat oven to 400°. Lightly coat 5 lightly greased 4-oz. ramekins with granulated sugar, shaking out excess. Place on a jelly-roll pan.

2. Whisk together 1 cup lemon curd and next 2 ingredients in a large bowl.

3. Beat egg whites with cream of tartar at medium speed with an electric mixer 1 to 2 minutes or until soft peaks form. Gently fold one-fourth of egg white mixture into curd mixture using a rubber spatula; fold in remaining egg whites just until blended. Pour gently into ramekins, filling to top. Run tip of thumb around edges of ramekins, wiping clean.

4. Bake at 400° for 10 minutes; reduce heat to 350°, and bake 4 minutes or until soufflés rise and are set. (Center should be slightly loose when shaken.) Dust with powdered sugar. Serve immediately with remaining lemon curd.

5 MORE USES FOR
lemon curd

CAKE DRIZZLE

Top warm gingerbread or toasted pound cake with scoops of dulce de leche ice cream and lemon curd.

CLOUD CAKE

Bake your favorite white cake batter in a 13- x 9-inch pan. Cool in pan on a wire rack 20 minutes. Pierce top of cake every 1 1/2 inches, using the handle of a wooden spoon. Spread 2 cups lemon curd over cake. Cool completely; cover and chill 4 hours. Frost top of cake with sweetened whipped cream.

MAGIC FILLING

Fill layer cakes, cupcakes, or miniature tart shells with lemon curd.

LEMON ETON MESS

Layer lemon curd, coarsely crushed meringue cookies, fresh berries, and sweetened whipped cream in vintage parfait glasses.

BETTER THAN BUTTER

Spread lemon curd on hot biscuits, fresh blueberry muffins, or a basketful of icebox rolls.

Lemon Soufflés

Colorful Winter Sides

▶ A taste of who and what got the highest raves in the *Southern Living* Test Kitchen.

From the Kitchen of
MARI LAPPIN
CARMEL, IN

"When I serve this irresistible dish, I never have to talk my family into eating their veggies."

CARAMELIZED SPICY GREEN BEANS
(Pictured on page 163)

Cook **1 lb. fresh haricots verts** (thin green beans) in boiling salted water to cover 1 minute; drain. Plunge green beans into ice water to stop the cooking process; drain well, pressing between paper towels. Stir together **2 Tbsp. light brown sugar, 1 Tbsp. soy sauce,** and **1/2 tsp. dried crushed red pepper.** Sauté **1 medium-size red bell pepper, sliced; 1/2 medium-size sweet onion, sliced;** and green beans in **1 tsp. hot peanut oil** in a large skillet over high heat 3 to 5 minutes or until beans look blistered. Sprinkle with **3/4 tsp. seasoned salt.** Remove from heat; add soy sauce mixture to green bean mixture, and stir to coat. **MAKES** 4 servings

RECIPE
Winner
SWAP

Salty-sweet flavors, some caramelization, and a bit of spice give these green beans a little pep in their step.

From the Kitchen of
NEALEY DOZIER
DIXIECAVIAR.COM

"By no means is this a 'mayonnaisey' salad— the small amount of mayo just softens the flavor a bit."

CARROT-APPLE-GINGER SLAW

Cut **4 large peeled carrots** (assorted colors such as purple, yellow, and orange) lengthwise into very thin, ribbon-like strips using a vegetable peeler. Cut **2 Granny Smith apples** into 1/8-inch matchsticks, and toss with **1 Tbsp. fresh lemon juice.** Stir together carrots and apples in a large bowl. Whisk together 1/4 **cup apple cider vinegar, 3 Tbsp. mayonnaise, 2 tsp. sugar, 2 tsp. minced fresh ginger,** and 1/4 **tsp. kosher salt.** Pour over carrot mixture, and toss to coat. Cover and chill 1 hour. Fold in **2 Tbsp. chopped fresh flat-leaf parsley** just before serving. **MAKES** 6 to 8 servings

From the Kitchen of
SHEILA SPECTOR
DINNERATSHEILAS.COM

"Frozen peas and onions brighten up a winter day. When spring comes, use fresh."

JAZZED-UP PEAS AND PEARL ONIONS

Melt **1 Tbsp. butter** with **1 Tbsp. extra virgin olive oil** in a large skillet over medium-high heat. Add **1 (14.4-oz.) package frozen pearl onions,** thawed, and **1 tsp. sugar;** sauté 5 to 7 minutes or until onions are caramel colored. Add **2 (14.4-oz.) packages frozen peas,** thawed, and **2 Tbsp. fresh lemon juice;** cook, stirring constantly, 2 to 3 minutes or until thoroughly heated. Remove from heat; stir in 1/4 **cup coarsely chopped fresh flat-leaf parsley, 2 Tbsp. butter,** and 1 1/2 **Tbsp. coarsely chopped fresh dill.** Add **kosher salt** and **freshly ground black pepper** to taste. **MAKES** 8 servings

The South's Most Storied Recipes

THIRTEEN YEARS AGO, AN IMPASSIONED GROUP OF CHEFS, WRITERS, AND FARMERS GATHERED IN ALABAMA.

They came together and vowed to protect the food culture of the South. But what exactly *is* Southern food? And how do you preserve it? Today, the Southern Foodways Alliance continues to grapple with these questions. This is their story.

Nowhere in America can you find more distinct and diverse regional food than the South—from the Lowcountry to Appalachia to the bayous of Cajun country. And only in the South is there an equally distinct and diverse group of food professionals and food enthusiasts who are dedicated to preserving our region's unique culinary traditions. This group, the Southern Foodways Alliance (SFA), is unabashedly committed to celebrating the Southern gastronomic landscape. And it's about time you get to know them.

Founded in Birmingham, Alabama, the SFA has been "putting up" our most prized stories and recipes in the form of oral histories, community cookbooks, and documentary films since 1999, preserving them for generations to come. Today, the 1,200-member-strong organization, helmed by

director John T. Edge and based at the University of Mississippi, sits at the intersection of tradition and advancement.

In *Pride & Joy*, a new feature-length SFA documentary on PBS, viewers will glimpse a snapshot of the people, rituals, and recipes that the organization sets out to document and protect. "Everything we do is about telling some story of the South, a story that advances our understanding of this complicated, beautiful place," says John T. In honor of that film—and because it's time to tell *their* story—we're introducing you to nine influential members, from a young Korean-American chef to a South Carolina peach farmer in her late seventies. Naturally, all of their stories can be told through food. (The recipes begin on the next page.)

> *"IN THE SOUTH, WHITES, BLACKS, EVERYBODY, WE EAT THE SAME THINGS," LEAH SAYS. "WE MAY COOK A LITTLE DIFFERENT, BUT WE EAT THE SAME THINGS."*

LEAH CHASE

Chef/owner, Dooky Chase's Restaurant

LOCATION
New Orleans

RECIPE
Gumbo Z'Herbes

The story of 90-year-old Leah Chase reads like a social history of New Orleans. Creole-born across Lake Pontchartrain, she started waitressing in 1941—part of the first group of female servers in the French Quarter—when the men were off at war. In '46, she began working at her in-laws' restaurant, Dooky Chase's, where jazz greats such as Ray Charles, Duke Ellington, and Sarah Vaughan would congregate. "There was no place else for them to eat when they came to town," Leah says. Then in the 1960s, with desegregation, Leah began "learning what they were doing on the other side," in places like Commander's Palace, where her clientele now had the opportunity to dine. For her, the strength of the SFA is its ability to transcend borders and bring people together over food. Every year on the Thursday before Easter, she cooks up to 100 gallons of her Gumbo Z'Herbes at right, made with nine different types of greens. All of New Orleans, from Catholics to Jews, whites to blacks, flocks to her gumbo pot en masse. "The best way to know people is through food," she says. "Get them to talk about food. Talk over food. It might be about food, but you're also talking about issues."

Gumbo Z'Herbes

MAKES 10 TO 12 SERVINGS
HANDS-ON 55 MIN.
TOTAL 2 HOURS, 50 MIN.

Use any greens, as long as you use 3 1/4 lb. total, but "you will acquire a new friend for every kind of green in the pot—and we hope one of them's rich," says Leah Chase.

- 5 cups chopped mustard greens
- 5 cups chopped collard greens
- 5 cups chopped turnip greens
- 3 cups chopped beet tops (5 oz.)
- 2 cups chopped cabbage
- 2 cups chopped romaine lettuce
- 2 cups chopped watercress
- 1 1/2 cups coarsely chopped spinach
- 1 cup chopped carrot tops (1 1/2 oz.)
- 2 garlic cloves, chopped
- 1 medium onion, chopped
- 1/2 lb. smoked sausage, diced
- 1/2 lb. smoked ham, diced
- 1/2 lb. uncooked beef brisket, diced
- 1/2 lb. dry Spanish chorizo or andouille sausage, diced
- 3 Tbsp. vegetable oil
- 1/4 cup all-purpose flour
- 2 tsp. table salt
- 1/2 tsp. fresh thyme leaves
- 1/2 tsp. ground red pepper
- 1/2 tsp. filé powder
  Hot cooked rice

1. Combine first 11 ingredients and water to cover in a 15-qt. stockpot; cover. Bring to a boil over high heat (about 20 minutes). Uncover; boil, stirring occasionally, 30 minutes. Drain, reserving cooking liquid. Coarsely chop greens.

2. Combine smoked sausage and next 2 ingredients in pot with 2 cups reserved cooking liquid. Bring to a boil. Boil, stirring once, 15 minutes.

3. Meanwhile, cook chorizo in hot oil in a medium skillet over medium-low heat, stirring occasionally, 10 minutes or until browned. Remove with a slotted spoon; drain on paper towels, reserving 3 Tbsp. drippings in skillet.

4. Make a roux: Stir flour into reserved drippings with a wooden spoon, and cook over medium heat, stirring constantly, until flour is medium brown (about 15 minutes; see page 41 as a guide). Add flour mixture to mixture in stockpot; stir well. Add chopped greens mixture and 5 cups reserved cooking liquid. Reduce heat to medium-low; simmer, stirring occasionally, 20 minutes. Stir in salt, thyme, red pepper, and chorizo. Cook, stirring occasionally, 40 minutes. Stir in filé powder; stir vigorously. Serve over hot cooked rice.

JIM GOSSEN

Founder, Louisiana Foods

LOCATION
Grand Isle, LA

RECIPE
Broiled Oysters on the Half Shell

Jim Gossen is an oyster man. He knows the name of every veteran shucker at oyster bars from Casamento's in New Orleans to Swan Oyster Depot in San Francisco and the province and flavor of the oysters each serves. So why do Gulf oysters, his favorite, cost less? And why are they always sold so generically as "Gulf oysters?" It's not quality, Jim says, "it's marketing."

A few years ago, he challenged a gathering of Gulf oystermen. "I brought some oysters [from Canada], and I picked out the prettiest ones," says Jim, an SFA member and founder of Houston-based Louisiana Foods, a seafood wholesaler. "I told all these oystermen, 'These must be three times better than the ones y'all grow because they cost three times more than yours.' " The men shucked and slurped. Then they grumbled. They knew what Jim knew: Their plump bivalves were just as good as the New Brunswick Beau Soleils before them. So Jim helped start a new company, Caminada Bay Oyster Farm, to celebrate the distinctive flavor and brininess of Gulf oyster appellations like Barataria Bay and Creole Bay near his Louisiana home. Houston chef Bryan Caswell of Reef was one of his first customers. "We've got to keep preaching the Gulf," Jim says. "They got such a bad knock because of that damn oil spill. The Gulf has as good a product, or better in some respects, than any part of the world."

At home, Jim and his wife, Diane, make a mean version of broiled oysters served under a crunchy cloak of breadcrumbs. You'll become a believer once the butter and oyster liquor commingle. No marketing or preaching necessary.

Broiled Oysters on the Half Shell

Broiled Oysters on the Half Shell

MAKES 4 TO 6 SERVINGS
HANDS-ON 30 MIN.
TOTAL 35 MIN.

*For an even easier version of **Jim Gossen's** oysters, omit the shells, double the recipe, and broil the oysters in a baking dish. (Pictured on page 164)*

- 2 **dozen medium-size fresh oysters in the shell**
- 2 **Tbsp. butter, divided**
- 2 **Tbsp. olive oil, divided**
- 1 1/2 **cups day-old French-bread breadcrumbs**
- 3/4 **cup minced green onions**
- 1/4 **cup freshly grated Parmigiano-Reggiano cheese**
- 4 **garlic cloves, pressed**
- 4 **Tbsp. minced fresh flat-leaf parsley**
- 2 **tsp. minced fresh thyme**
- 2 **tsp. minced fresh oregano**
- 1/2 **tsp. kosher salt**
- 1/2 **tsp. ground black pepper**
  Pinch of ground red pepper
  Rock salt

1. Shuck oysters, reserving bottom shells and 1 Tbsp. oyster liquor (oyster liquid in shell); discard top shells. Gently loosen oyster from shell, using an oyster knife.

2. Preheat broiler with oven rack 6 inches from heat. Melt 1 Tbsp. butter with 1 Tbsp. olive oil in a large skillet over low heat; stir in breadcrumbs and next 9 ingredients. Remove from heat.

3. Microwave remaining 1 Tbsp. butter and 1 Tbsp. olive oil in a small microwave-safe bowl at HIGH 20 seconds or until butter melts. Stir in reserved oyster liquor.

4. Spread rock salt in a 1/4-inch layer in a 18- x 13-inch shallow pan. Place oysters, in shells, on rock salt. Spoon breadcrumb mixture over oysters; drizzle with butter mixture. Broil 5 to 6 minutes or until top is crisp and browned.

BROILED OYSTERS Omit rock salt. Prepare recipe as directed, doubling ingredient amounts. Shuck oysters, discarding shells, and place oysters in a single layer in a 13- x 9-inch pan. (Pre-shucked oysters work well for this. Reserve 2 Tbsp. oyster liquor.) Top with breadcrumb mixture; broil. **MAKES** 8 to 10 servings

EDWARD LEE

Chef/owner, 610 Magnolia

LOCATION
Louisville, KY

RECIPE
Collard Greens & Kimchi

Edward Lee tasted collards for the first time when he moved from Brooklyn, New York, to Louisville to cook with a fellow chef 10 years ago. "A woman told me, 'This is, historically, poor blacks' food.' I saw it as a cook's way to show love and add nutrition in this one overlooked vegetable." The dish instantly reminded the Korean-American chef of kimchi, which is "[fermented] cabbage, salt, and chili pepper, and it only costs a few pennies. It was the one thing my parents could rely on that was cheap and plentiful." Edward celebrates the two humble ingredients, using sautéed country ham and onions to create a robust harmony of sweet, salty, sour, bitter, and umami flavors. Being a stranger years ago freed the chef to embrace Southern ingredients on his own terms. It also forced him to look inward. "When you're one of 10 Koreans in the state of Kentucky, you ask, 'Who am I?' It's been an incredible journey. Ten years ago, I would never have called the South embracing or accepting. [But] I've never been more at home than in this unique place."

Collards & Kimchi

MAKES 6 TO 8 SERVINGS
HANDS-ON 50 MIN.
TOTAL 50 MIN.

Edward Lee's dish works well with King's Mild Kimchi Korean Marinated Cabbage. (Pictured on page 164)

- 1 Tbsp. butter
- 1 1/2 tsp. lard or bacon drippings
- 1 cup chopped onion
- 1 cup large-diced country ham
- 1 1/2 lb. fresh collard greens, trimmed and coarsely chopped
- 2 1/2 cups reduced-sodium chicken broth
- 2 tsp. soy sauce
- 1 1/2 Tbsp. apple cider vinegar
- 1 (14-oz.) jar mild kimchi, drained and chopped

1. Melt butter with lard in a Dutch oven over medium-high heat until butter begins to foam. Add onion; sauté 3 to 5 minutes or until onion just begins to brown. Add ham, and sauté 3 minutes.

2. Stir in collards and next 2 ingredients. Cover and cook over medium heat, stirring occasionally, to desired degree of doneness (about 10 to 30 minutes, depending on your color and tenderness preference. Collards should be a vibrant green and tender but still have a little chew to them at 10 minutes).

3. Add vinegar, and cook, stirring constantly, 1 minute. Transfer mixture to a large bowl, and toss with kimchi. Serve immediately.

JOHN EGERTON

Historian, writer, and author of *Southern Food*

LOCATION
Nashville

RECIPE
Buttermilk Biscuits

Southerners have historically shown a distinct preference for hot breads: biscuits and cornbread right out of the oven, steaming hoecakes. "We're hotter natured down here—it's born into our culture," says John Egerton, one of the original SFA founders. But it's the biscuit that's been idealized. According to John, the biscuit was even symbolic of your station in life: " 'I feel sorry for that guy—he eats cornbread for breakfast. He can't afford the flour and milk to make a decent biscuit.' "

Then there's the finesse and craft of building the biscuit. "People like to talk about who has the touch, who makes a biscuit better than anybody else," he says. "You never get to the bottom of who does it best, but you never get tired of arguing about it." For John, a good biscuit is made of soft winter-wheat flour such as White Lily, lard or butter, whole-milk buttermilk, salt, and a little baking powder. "I like them crusty on the outside, soft and feathery on the inside," he says. "When you open them, they should be hot enough to fog your glasses. A little butter, some home-made jam. That's the apotheosis of a good biscuit."

Buttermilk Biscuits

MAKES 1 DOZEN
HANDS-ON 15 MIN.
TOTAL 40 MIN.

*Use a 2-inch cutter to make **John Egerton's** biscuits smaller, if desired. Bake in batches.*

- 4 cups all-purpose soft-wheat flour, such as White Lily
- 2 Tbsp. baking powder
- 1 tsp. table salt
- 1 tsp. baking soda
- 1/2 cup cold butter, cubed
- 2 cups buttermilk
  Melted butter

1. Preheat oven to 450°. Sift together first 4 ingredients in a large bowl. Cut butter into flour mixture with a pastry blender until mixture resembles small peas. Stir in buttermilk with a fork until dough forms a ball.

2. Turn dough out onto a well-floured sheet of wax paper. Sprinkle dough with flour, and flatten into a disk. Cover and chill 15 minutes.

3. Remove wax paper, and turn dough out onto a well-floured surface; sprinkle with flour. Pat dough to 1/2-inch thickness. Cut with a 3-inch cutter, reshaping scraps once. Place biscuits 1 inch apart on an ungreased baking sheet.

4. Bake at 450° for 10 to 12 minutes or until golden brown. Brush immediately with melted butter.

John Egerton's Buttermilk Biscuits

DORI SANDERS

Peach Farmer

LOCATION
Filbert, SC

RECIPE
Peach Dumplings

Raised on a peach farm as one of 10 children, Dori Sanders knows food from the ground up. Her father, son of sharecroppers and a rural elementary school principal, saved enough money in 1915 to buy the South Carolina farm that Dori, the 2011 recipient of SFA's Craig Claiborne Lifetime Achievement Award, continues to work. Her family always kept half-gallon Mason jars of canned peaches, preserved when they still clasped summer's warmth. Her mother and older sisters would wrap scraps of biscuit dough around the peaches to make dumplings (at right). "One of my favorite memories is of them scraping up those pieces of dough, assembling them like a jigsaw puzzle." Times were hard. Everything was utilized. "It tasted so good because it was precious," she says. Then she adds emphatically, "We. Lived. Off. The. Farm."

Peach Dumplings

MAKES 10 SERVINGS
HANDS-ON 30 MIN.
TOTAL 1 HOUR, 40 MIN.

*You can substitute canned or fresh biscuits for the piecrust in **Dori Sanders'** dumplings.*

- 1 (14.1-oz.) package refrigerated piecrusts
- 1 (20-oz.) package frozen sliced peaches, thawed and divided or 4 ripe peaches, peeled and sliced
- 1/2 cup sugar
- 1/4 cup butter, melted
- 1/8 tsp. ground cinnamon

1. Preheat oven to 350°. Unroll piecrusts on a lightly floured surface, and roll each into a 10-inch circle. Cut 5 (4-inch) circles from each crust. Roll each circle into an approximately 5 1/2-inch circle.

2. Coarsely chop 2 cups peach slices. Divide chopped peaches among dough, placing in center of each circle (about 1/4 cup per circle). Pull dough edges over peaches, and gather in center, pinching to seal and form a bundle. Place in a lightly greased 11- x 7-inch baking dish. Arrange remaining peaches around bundles.

3. Stir together sugar, next 2 ingredients, and 1/2 cup water until blended. Pour over bundles and peaches.

4. Bake at 350° for 1 hour or until golden brown. Cool 10 minutes.

BILL SMITH

Chef, Crook's Corner, and author of *Seasoned in the South*

LOCATION
Chapel Hill, NC

RECIPE
Pozole

This soup is an amalgamation of styles and cultures that have collided in my kitchen over the years," says Bill Smith. His Mexican-born line cooks taught him how to make it by simmering a whole chicken, then picking the meat clean and stirring it into a heady broth invigorated with fresh and dried chiles, tomatillos, tomatoes, and herbs. Chewy hominy (dried corn kernels that are soaked in lye, boiled, and washed) is the soup's cross-cultural common denominator. "Since hominy is commonly eaten all over the South, it was excuse enough to introduce this onto our menu."

The kitchen lessons work both ways. His Latino "tribe," as he calls it, is family. Bill is the godfather of some of their children, he travels to their homes in Mexico, and he's writing a book about the immigrant experience. "My cooks started out as dishwashers. The economy of North Carolina's Piedmont region really took off, and you could not steal [a cook] away from another kitchen. Then you realize these guys are right beside you, and they've been watching you all along."

Pozole

MAKES 6 TO 8 SERVINGS
HANDS-ON 1 HOUR
TOTAL 4 HOURS, 5 MIN.

(Pictured on page 168)

- 6 qt. water
- 1 (3-lb.) whole chicken
- 1 lb. tomatillos, husks removed
- 2 jalapeño peppers, stemmed
- 1 medium-size yellow onion, chopped
- 6 garlic cloves
- 1 (28-oz.) can crushed tomatoes
- 1 (29-oz.) can Mexican-style or other canned hominy, drained
- 2 Tbsp. dried Mexican oregano
- 4 dried bay leaves
- 2 dried cascabel chiles, stemmed
- 1/2 cup hot water
- 2 tsp. table salt
  Lime wedges
  Garnishes: fresh cilantro, sliced radishes, shredded cabbage

1. Bring 6 qt. of water to a boil over high heat in an 8-qt. stockpot. Remove neck and giblets from chicken. Add chicken, neck, and giblets to boiling water. Return to a boil, and cook 15 minutes. Cover, remove from heat, and let stand 20 minutes. Transfer chicken to a plate, reserving broth in stockpot; discard neck and giblets. Cover and chill chicken until cool enough to handle (about 30 minutes).

2. Meanwhile, combine tomatillos, next 3 ingredients, and 2 1/2 cups reserved broth in a medium saucepan. Bring to rolling boil over medium-high heat, and cook, stirring occasionally, 20 minutes or until garlic is very soft.

3. Skin, bone, and shred chicken, reserving bones, skin, and any juices. Cover and chill chicken until ready to use. Return skin, bones, and juices to broth in stockpot. Bring to a rolling boil over medium-high heat; cook 30 to 45 minutes or until the bones begin to separate. Pour mixture through a fine wire-mesh strainer into a large bowl, discarding solids. Return to pot. Skim fat from broth. Bring broth to a simmer over medium-high heat.

4. Process tomatillo mixture in a blender or food processor until smooth. Stir into broth. Add crushed tomatoes and next 3 ingredients, stirring until blended; bring to a boil. Reduce heat to medium-low; cover and simmer, stirring occasionally, 1 hour.

5. Meanwhile, soak chiles in 1/2 cup hot water in a small bowl for 30 minutes. Drain, reserving soaking liquid. Process chiles and 2 to 3 Tbsp. soaking liquid in a blender or food processor until smooth.

6. Stir 2 tsp. salt and pepper to taste into broth. Pour chile mixture through a fine wire-mesh strainer into broth, discarding solids. Stir in shredded chicken, and simmer 15 minutes. Serve with lime wedges.

Bill Smith's
Pozole

MARCIE COHEN FERRIS

Professor of American Studies, UNC-CH

LOCATION
Chapel Hill, NC

RECIPE
Blackberry Jam Cake

Huddy Cohen, Marcie Cohen Ferris' Jewish mother, is a cake person. A cherished family recipe for blackberry jam cake represents Marcie's Connecticut-born, matzoh-reared mom's assimilation into Southern culture. So how did a confection that originated in Appalachia cement its spot in the repertoire of a Jewish housewife in Blytheville, Arkansas? It all started with a holiday, naturally. Huddy's friend Julia Harrelson baked the cake every Christmas, and its texture and heft appealed to the Cohen family. "Our family is of Eastern European descent," says Marcie, who still bakes the cake in her mother's avocado-green Bundt pan. "We like cakes that are heavy and moist. An angel cake is lovely, but anything that has lots of layers or chiffon, we're not those people."

Blackberry Jam Cake

MAKES 12 SERVINGS
HANDS-ON 30 MIN.
TOTAL 3 HOURS, 45 MIN.

*We based this recipe on one from **Marcie Cohen Ferris'** Matzoh Ball Gumbo: Culinary Tales of the Jewish South.*

- 1 cup buttermilk
- 1 tsp. baking soda
- 1 cup butter, softened
- 2 cups granulated sugar
- 4 large eggs, at room temperature
- 1 tsp. vanilla extract
- 3 cups all-purpose flour
- 1 1/2 tsp. ground cinnamon
- 1 tsp. ground allspice
- 3/4 tsp. ground cloves
- 1/2 tsp. table salt
- 1 (18-oz.) jar seedless blackberry jam
- 1 cup finely chopped toasted pecans
- Powdered sugar (optional)

1. Preheat oven to 350°. Stir together buttermilk and baking soda.

2. Beat butter at medium speed with an electric mixer until creamy. Gradually add granulated sugar, beating until light and fluffy and stopping to scrape bowl as needed. Add eggs, 1 at a time, beating just until blended after each addition. Beat in vanilla.

3. Stir together flour and next 4 ingredients in a large bowl; gradually add to butter mixture alternately with buttermilk mixture, beginning and ending with flour mixture. Beat at low speed just until blended after each addition, stopping to scrape bowl as needed. Add preserves, and beat at low speed just until blended. Stir in pecans. Spoon batter into a greased and floured 10-inch tube pan.

4. Bake at 350° for 1 hour and 5 minutes to 1 hour and 10 minutes or until a long wooden pick inserted in center comes out clean. Cool in pan on a wire rack 10 minutes; remove from pan to wire rack, and cool completely (about 2 hours). Dust cake with powdered sugar just before serving, if desired.

Blackberry Jam Cake

FRANK & PARDIS STITT

Chef/owners, Highlands Bar and Grill

LOCATION
Birmingham

RECIPE
Rabbit Pilau (pronounced PER-loo)

Frank and Pardis Stitt celebrated the fledgling SFA at Highlands on July 22, 1999. The meal almost didn't happen. "I'm kind of anti organization," says Frank. "But we recognized that SFA was an academic and intellectual way of considering what we do: loving our Southern culture, our heritage, our foods." One of the dishes that night was red wine-braised rabbit and pilau, aka pirlau, a Lowcountry rice stew (at right). This marriage of regional ingredients and ideas with French and Italian technique, or "New Southern Cooking," as Frank calls it, has inspired two generations of chefs. Frank and Pardis' restaurants remain vital to our culture, their staff has remained loyal, and the couple's drive is sustained. "I was young and went to the Sistine Chapel and saw Michelangelo's work," Frank recalls. "I was so moved because I knew I would never produce anything of significance relative to that, artistically. [But] we do have the ability to create things with every restaurant experience, to bring some beauty into a person's life."

Rabbit Pilau

MAKES 6 TO 8 SERVINGS
HANDS-ON 1 HOUR
TOTAL 4 HOURS, 5 MIN.

Want to use chicken instead of rabbit in Frank Stitt's braise? Substitute 3 lb. chicken parts and increase salt to 1 ½ tsp.

RABBIT

- 1 Tbsp. dried porcini mushrooms
- 2 ½ cups reduced-sodium chicken broth, divided
- 1 (2 ½-lb.) rabbit, cut into 6 pieces
- 1 tsp. kosher salt
- ½ tsp. freshly ground black pepper
- 2 Tbsp. olive oil
- 2 carrots, diced
- 2 garlic cloves, minced
- 2 cups dry red wine
- ½ cup port
- 1 medium leek
- 6 fresh flat-leaf parsley sprigs
- 4 fresh thyme sprigs
- 2 dried bay leaves
  Kitchen string

PILAU

- 4 Tbsp. unsalted butter, divided
- 3 carrots, diced
- 2 medium onions, chopped
- 1 dried bay leaf
- 2 cups uncooked basmati rice, rinsed
- 3 cups reduced-sodium chicken broth

1. Prepare Rabbit: Preheat oven to 300°. Bring dried mushrooms and ½ cup chicken broth to a boil in a small saucepan over medium heat. Remove from heat, and let stand 30 minutes.

2. Meanwhile, sprinkle rabbit with kosher salt and freshly ground pepper. Cook rabbit, in 2 batches, in hot oil in a heavy ovenproof skillet or enameled cast-iron Dutch oven over medium heat 8 to 10 minutes on each side or until deep golden brown. Transfer to a wire rack in a jelly-roll pan, reserving drippings in skillet.

3. Add carrots and garlic to reserved drippings in skillet, and sauté 4 minutes or until carrots are softened. Stir in wine, port, mushroom mixture, and remaining 2 cups broth; bring to a simmer, stirring occasionally. Skim off foam and fat.

4. Remove and discard root end of leek; remove dark green top of leek. Tie together green leek top, parsley sprigs, and next 2 ingredients with kitchen string. Add herb bundle and rabbit to skillet; bring to a simmer, and cover.

5. Braise at 300° for 15 minutes. Transfer rabbit loin pieces to wire rack in jelly-roll pan. Braise remaining rabbit 30 more minutes. Transfer remaining rabbit to wire rack; cool 15 minutes.

6. Meanwhile, bring liquid in skillet to a simmer over medium heat, and cook 15 minutes or until liquid is reduced by half. Skim off foam and fat. Pour through a fine wire-mesh strainer into a small saucepan; discard solids. Cover and keep warm over low heat.

7. Remove rabbit from bones; shred with 2 forks. Discard bones.

8. Prepare Pilau: Cut reserved leek in half lengthwise; rinse thoroughly under cold running water to remove grit and sand. Cut leek into ½-inch-thick slices.

9. Melt 2 Tbsp. butter in a Dutch oven over medium-high heat. Add carrots, next 2 ingredients, and leek; sauté 2 minutes or until onions and leek just begin to soften. Add rice, and cook, stirring constantly, 1 minute. Add broth, and bring to a boil. Cover, reduce heat to low, and cook 15 minutes or until rice is tender and broth has been absorbed. Discard bay leaf.

10. Stir rabbit into rice; transfer to a platter. Whisk remaining 2 Tbsp. butter into warm braising liquid. Spoon liquid over pilau before serving.

March

Set the Table for Easter Brunch

▶ Celebrate the first sweet days of spring with our sunny brunch menu. A glorious glazed ham and stack of mile-high cornmeal biscuits anchor the menu, while new favorites like an asparagus, lentil, and orange salad keep the meal enticingly fresh and seasonal. Garnish with soft spring colors, seasonal blooms, and balmy breezes.

Watercress-Buttermilk Soup

MAKES 8 TO 10 SERVINGS
HANDS-ON 20 MIN.
TOTAL 3 HOURS, 40 MIN.

Look for watercress with small, bright green leaves and thin stems to make this peppery cold soup. (Pictured on page 164)

- 1 medium leek
- 2 Tbsp. butter
- 1 garlic clove, minced
- 6 cups organic chicken or vegetable broth
- 1 large russet potato (about 1 lb.), peeled and cut into 1-inch cubes
- 1 (5-oz.) package fresh baby spinach
- 2 (4-oz.) packages watercress (about 16 loosely packed cups)
- 1 tsp. kosher salt
- 1/2 tsp. finely ground black pepper
  Pinch of ground red pepper
- 2 cups whole buttermilk
- 1 tsp. fresh lemon juice
  Garnishes: buttermilk, watercress sprigs, chopped fresh chives

1. Remove and discard root end and dark green top of leek. Cut in half lengthwise, and rinse under cold running water to remove grit and sand. Thinly slice leek.

2. Melt butter in a Dutch oven over medium heat; add leek, and sauté 8 to 10 minutes or until tender. Add garlic, and sauté 1 minute.

3. Add broth and potato; cover and cook, stirring occasionally, 20 minutes or until potato is tender. Remove from heat, and add spinach and next 4 ingredients, stirring until spinach is wilted.

4. Puree soup with a blender until smooth; pour into a large bowl. Whisk in buttermilk and lemon juice; add salt and pepper to taste. Serve chilled or at room temperature.

Asparagus, Orange, and Lentil Salad

MAKES 8 CUPS
HANDS-ON 30 MIN.
TOTAL 45 MIN., INCLUDING VINAIGRETTE

Pink lentils add pretty color and texture to this salad. Cook them al dente (like pasta) so they remain firm when tossed with the dressing. (Pictured on page 5)

- 1 medium-size fennel bulb
- 2 large oranges, peeled and sliced
- ¼ tsp. freshly ground black pepper
- 1½ tsp. kosher salt, divided
- 2 lb. fresh asparagus
- 1½ cups dried pink lentils, rinsed
  Champagne-Shallot Vinaigrette
- 2 cups coarsely chopped assorted lettuces
- ½ cup loosely packed fresh flat-leaf parsley leaves

1. Rinse fennel thoroughly. Trim and discard root end of bulb. Trim stalks from bulb, and chop fronds to equal ¼ cup; reserve stalks and remaining fronds for another use. Thinly slice bulb, and toss with oranges, pepper, and ½ tsp. salt. Cover and let stand until ready to use.

2. Meanwhile, cut asparagus tips into 1½-inch pieces, discarding tough ends. Cut stalks diagonally into thin slices.

3. Bring 3 cups water and ½ tsp. salt to a boil in a large saucepan over medium-high heat. Add asparagus, and cook 1 to 2 minutes or until crisp-tender; drain. Plunge into ice water to stop the cooking process; drain. Pat dry with paper towels.

4. Bring 3 cups water and remaining ½ tsp. salt to a boil in saucepan over medium heat. Add lentils; return to a boil. Reduce heat to low, and cook, stirring often, 8 to 10 minutes or until crisp-tender. Drain well, and rinse with cold water. Toss lentils with ¼ cup Champagne-Shallot Vinaigrette.

5. Combine lettuces, parsley, asparagus, fennel mixture, and fennel fronds in a large bowl; toss with remaining vinaigrette. Spoon lentils onto a serving platter; top with asparagus mixture.

Asparagus, Orange, and Lentil Salad

CHAMPAGNE-SHALLOT VINAIGRETTE

MAKES ½ CUP
HANDS-ON 5 MIN.
TOTAL 5 MIN.

Whisk together 3 Tbsp. **Champagne vinegar**, 1 Tbsp. finely chopped **shallots**, 2 tsp. **honey**, 2 tsp. **Dijon mustard**, ½ tsp. **kosher salt**, and ¼ tsp. **freshly ground black pepper** in a small bowl. Gradually whisk in ¼ cup **extra virgin olive oil** until blended.

COMPOSE WITH CARE

To accentuate the textures in Asparagus, Orange, and Lentil Salad, layer oranges and fennel on a platter, then top with asparagus and lentils.

Scalloped Potato and Herb Tart

MAKES 6 TO 8 SERVINGS
HANDS-ON 30 MIN.
TOTAL 4 HOURS, INCLUDING PASTRY

Thinly sliced russet potatoes absorb the richly flavored custard as it bakes and give this quiche its layered texture. (Pictured on page 165)

 Buttery Flaky Pastry (see recipe at right)
1 medium-size baking potato (about 12 oz.), peeled and cut into 1/16-inch-thick slices
1 1/2 tsp. table salt, divided
6 green onions, cut into 1-inch pieces (about 1 cup)
1/2 cup coarsely chopped fresh flat-leaf parsley
1/4 cup coarsely chopped fresh chives
1/2 to 1 Tbsp. coarsely chopped fresh dill
1 cup half-and-half
2 large eggs
1 large egg yolk
1 tsp. fresh thyme leaves
1/2 tsp. freshly ground black pepper
1 cup (4 oz.) shredded Gruyère cheese
1/4 cup (1 oz.) freshly shredded Parmesan cheese

1. Prepare Buttery Flaky Pastry.

2. Preheat oven to 350°. Bring potatoes, 1 tsp. salt, and water to cover to a boil in a large skillet over medium-high heat; cook 5 to 7 minutes or until tender. Drain potatoes, and pat dry with paper towels. Cool 10 minutes.

3. Cook onions in boiling salted water to cover in a small saucepan 2 to 3 minutes or until tender. Drain well, and press between paper towels.

4. Stir together parsley and next 2 ingredients in a small bowl.

5. Whisk together half-and-half, next 4 ingredients, half of parsley mixture, and remaining 1/2 tsp. salt.

6. Spread half of potatoes in bottom of pastry crust. Top with half of Gruyère cheese, half of cooked onions, and half of egg mixture; repeat layers once. Sprinkle with Parmesan cheese.

7. Bake at 350° on an aluminum foil-lined baking sheet 40 to 45 minutes or until center is set. Let stand 10 minutes. Sprinkle with remaining parsley mixture. Serve warm or at room temperature.

BUTTERY FLAKY PASTRY

MAKES 1 (9-INCH) PASTRY SHELL
HANDS-ON 15 MIN.
TOTAL 2 HOURS, 20 MIN.

2 1/2 cups all-purpose flour
1/2 tsp. table salt
1/2 cup cold butter, cut into small cubes
1/4 to 1/2 cup ice-cold water
 Parchment paper

1. Pulse flour and salt in a food processor 3 or 4 times or until combined. Add butter, and pulse 5 or 6 times or until mixture resembles coarse meal. With processor running, gradually add 1/4 cup ice-cold water, and process just until dough forms a ball and pulls away from sides of bowl, adding up to 1/4 cup more ice-cold water if needed.

2. Gently form dough into a flat disk; wrap in plastic wrap, and chill 1 hour to 2 days.

3. Preheat oven to 400°. Roll dough into a 12-inch circle (about 1/8 inch thick) on a lightly floured surface. Fit into a lightly greased 9-inch round tart pan with removable bottom, pressing dough on bottom and up sides into fluted edges.

4. Line dough with parchment paper, and fill with pie weights or dried beans.

5. Bake at 400° for 20 minutes. Remove weights and parchment paper, and bake 15 to 20 more minutes or until bottom is golden. Transfer to a wire rack. Cool completely (about 30 minutes).

Cornmeal-Chive Biscuits

MAKES ABOUT 2 DOZEN
HANDS-ON 20 MIN.
TOTAL 45 MIN.

Press straight down with a biscuit cutter or glass for higher rising biscuits. If you twist the cutter, you'll seal the edges of the dough and the biscuits won't bake as tall.

2 cups self-rising soft-wheat flour
1/2 cup self-rising yellow cornmeal mix
1/2 cup cold butter
1/3 cup chopped fresh chives
1 1/4 cups whole buttermilk
 Parchment paper
2 Tbsp. melted butter

1. Preheat oven to 425°. Combine flour and cornmeal in a large bowl. Cut butter into 1/2-inch-thick slices. Sprinkle butter over flour mixture, and toss. Cut butter into flour mixture with a pastry blender until crumbly. Cover and chill 10 minutes. Stir in chives. Add buttermilk, stirring just until dry ingredients are moistened.

2. Turn dough out onto a floured surface, and knead 3 or 4 times, gradually adding additional self-rising flour as needed. With floured hands, pat dough into a 3/4-inch-thick rectangle (about 9 x 5 inches); dust top with flour. Fold dough over itself in 3 sections, starting with short end (as if folding a letter-size piece of paper). Repeat 2 more times, beginning with patting dough into a rectangle.

3. Pat dough to 1/2-inch thickness. Cut with a 2-inch round cutter, and place, side by side, on a parchment paper-lined or lightly greased jelly-roll pan. (Dough rounds should touch.)

4. Bake at 425° for 13 to 15 minutes or until lightly browned. Remove from oven; brush with 2 Tbsp. melted butter.

Note: We tested with White Lily soft-wheat self-rising flour.

Pepper Jelly and Ginger Glazed Ham

MAKES 12 SERVINGS
HANDS-ON 15 MIN.
TOTAL 5 HOURS

You can use any supermarket bone-in or semi-boneless smoked ham for this recipe, but choose one brined in natural juices. Or order from one of our favorite small Southern producers. (For a list, visit southernliving.com/ham.)

- 1 (9-lb.) smoked, fully cooked bone-in half ham
- 1 Tbsp. olive oil
- 1 tsp. freshly ground black pepper
- 2 cups Riesling or other white wine
- 2 Tbsp. peppercorns
- 1 Tbsp. whole cloves
- 1 Tbsp. fennel seeds
- 2 bay leaves
- 6 cups ginger ale
- 1/2 cup red pepper jelly
- 1 Tbsp. whole grain Dijon mustard Cornmeal-Chive Biscuits (see recipe at left)

1. Preheat oven to 350°. Make shallow cuts in fat of ham 1 inch apart in a diamond pattern. Rub olive oil and ground pepper over ham. Place ham on a rack in a 14- x 11-inch roasting pan. Pour wine into bottom of pan; stir in peppercorns and next 3 ingredients. Add 4 cups water. Cover pan loosely with aluminum foil.

2. Bake, covered, at 350° on lower oven rack 2 hours.

3. Meanwhile, bring ginger ale to a boil in a deep-sided 12-inch skillet over medium-high heat, and boil 25 to 30 minutes or until reduced to 3/4 cup. Remove from heat, and stir in pepper jelly until smooth.

4. Uncover ham, and bake 2 1/2 more hours or until a meat thermometer registers 160° and ham is caramelized, basting every 30 minutes with ginger ale mixture. (Shield ham with foil to prevent excessive browning.) Remove from oven; transfer to a serving platter, reserving 2 cups pan drippings. Let stand 20 minutes before carving.

5. Pour reserved drippings through a fine wire-mesh strainer into a medium saucepan; skim fat. Bring drippings to a boil over high heat, and boil 12 to 15 minutes or until liquid is reduced to 3/4 cup. Remove from heat; stir in mustard. Serve with ham and Cornmeal-Chive Biscuits.

Note: To prepare a 12- to 14-lb. fully cooked bone-in ham, increase red pepper jelly to 1 cup, olive oil to 2 Tbsp., mustard to 1 1/2 Tbsp., and ground pepper to 2 tsp. Prepare recipe as directed, cooking ginger ale mixture 20 to 25 minutes or until reduced to 1 1/2 cups in Step 3, reserving 3 cups drippings in Step 4, and cooking reserved drippings until reduced to 1 1/2 cups in Step 5. **MAKES** 18 to 24 servings. **HANDS-ON** 15 min.; **TOTAL** 4 hours, 55 min.

Jasmine-Buttermilk Panna Cotta with Berry Sauce

MAKES 8 SERVINGS
HANDS-ON 15 MIN.
TOTAL 1 HOUR, 10 MIN., INCLUDING SAUCE (PLUS 1 DAY FOR CHILLING)

The key to making these easy desserts is to soften the unflavored gelatin in cold water before dissolving in a hot liquid. (Pictured on page 7)

- 1 tsp. unflavored gelatin
- 1 Tbsp. cold water
- 2 cups heavy cream
- 1/2 cup sugar
- 1 (3-inch) orange peel strip, white part removed
- 3 regular-size jasmine tea bags
- 1 vanilla bean
- 2 cups whole buttermilk
- 1/8 tsp. table salt Berry Sauce

1. Sprinkle gelatin over cold water; let stand 10 minutes.

2. Meanwhile, combine cream and next 3 ingredients in a medium saucepan over medium heat. Split vanilla bean; scrape seeds into cream mixture, and place bean in mixture.

3. Cook over medium heat, stirring constantly, 5 minutes or just until mixture begins to boil. Remove from heat; immediately stir in gelatin mixture until smooth. Let stand 5 minutes.

4. Discard tea bags and vanilla bean. Stir in buttermilk and salt. Strain into a heat-proof glass measuring cup. Divide among 8 (6-oz.) glasses. Cover and chill 24 hours. Serve with Berry Sauce.

BERRY SAUCE

MAKES 2 CUPS
HANDS-ON 10 MIN.
TOTAL 40 MIN.

- 6 oz. fresh raspberries
- 3/4 cup coarsely chopped fresh strawberries
- 2 Tbsp. sugar
- 1 1/2 tsp. fresh lemon juice
- 1/4 tsp. vanilla bean paste

Coarsely mash 3/4 cup raspberries and next 4 ingredients in a bowl; let stand 30 minutes. Stir in remaining raspberries just before serving.

Jasmine-Buttermilk Panna Cotta with Berry Sauce

Brighten Up Your Plate

▶ Spring vegetables are here! So hit the market and use the season's bounty to cook five colorful weeknight meals short on prep time and full of garden-fresh flavor

Spring Salmon and Vegetable Salad

MAKES 4 TO 6 SERVINGS

Line your pan with foil for easy cleanup. The dressing will keep in the fridge up to one week.

- ½ **lb. fresh asparagus**
- 1 **cup sugar snap peas**
- 1¼ **lb. skinless salmon fillets, cut into 2-inch chunks**
- ½ **tsp. table salt**
- ¼ **tsp. black pepper**
- 6 **cups chopped romaine lettuce hearts**
- ½ **cup uncooked shelled fresh or frozen edamame, thawed**
- ¼ **cup sliced radishes**
  Creamy Herb Dressing

1. Preheat broiler with oven rack 6 inches from heat. Snap off tough ends of asparagus. Cut asparagus into 1-inch-long pieces, and cook with sugar snap peas in boiling salted water 2 to 3 minutes or until crisp-tender; drain. Plunge into ice water; drain.

2. Sprinkle salmon with salt and pepper; broil on a lightly greased rack in a broiler pan 3 to 4 minutes or to desired degree of doneness.

3. Arrange lettuce, edamame, radishes, asparagus mixture, and salmon on a serving plate. Drizzle with dressing.

CREAMY HERB DRESSING Whisk together ½ cup **buttermilk**, ¼ cup **mayonnaise**, 3 Tbsp. chopped **fresh herbs** (such as mint, dill, and chives), 1 Tbsp. **fresh lemon juice**, and **table salt and black pepper**. Chill 30 minutes.

Spring Salmon and Vegetable Salad

Seared Steak with Potato-Artichoke Hash

MAKES 4 TO 6 SERVINGS

For easier grill management and faster cooking, cut larger steaks into two pieces. (Pictured on page 170)

- 2 tsp. light brown sugar
- 1 1/2 tsp. kosher salt
- 1 tsp. ground black pepper
- 1/4 tsp. ground red pepper
- 1 (1 1/2- to 1 3/4-lb.) flank, skirt, or tri-tip steak
- 4 Tbsp. olive oil, divided
- 1 (22-oz.) package frozen potato wedges, thawed
- 3 Tbsp. butter
- 1 medium-size sweet onion, chopped
- 1 (9-oz.) package frozen artichoke hearts, thawed
- 3 garlic cloves, minced
- 3 Tbsp. coarsely chopped fresh flat-leaf parsley
- 3 Tbsp. drained capers
- 1 Tbsp. fresh lemon juice

1. Stir together brown sugar and next 3 ingredients. Rub steak with sugar mixture, and let stand 5 minutes.

2. Heat 1 Tbsp. olive oil in a cast iron grill pan over high heat. Add steak; cook, turning once, until seared, 12 to 16 minutes for medium-rare. Remove from skillet; cover loosely with aluminum foil. (Alternatively, cook steak on gas or charcoal grill.)

3. Meanwhile, cook potatoes in remaining 3 Tbsp. hot oil in a large skillet over medium-high heat, stirring occasionally, 10 to 12 minutes or until golden. Remove from skillet.

4. Melt 2 Tbsp. butter in skillet. Add onion, and cook, stirring often, 5 to 7 minutes or until tender. Add artichokes and garlic; cook, stirring often, 5 minutes. Stir in parsley, next 2 ingredients, potatoes, and remaining 1 Tbsp. butter; cook, stirring often, 2 to 3 minutes.

5. Cut steak diagonally across the grain into thin slices, and serve with potato mixture. Add salt and pepper to taste.

Note: We tested with Alexia All Natural Oven Reds with Olive Oil, Parmesan & Roasted Garlic potatoes.

Lemon Pork Chops with Quinoa Salad

MAKES 6 SERVINGS

Best way to cook quinoa? Simmer, drain, and let it stand, covered, to steam; then fluff.

- 6 (1/2-inch-thick) bone-in center-cut pork rib chops (about 4 lb.)
- 2 Tbsp. lemon-herb seasoning
- 1 3/4 tsp. kosher salt, divided
- 6 Tbsp. olive oil, divided
- 1 1/2 cups uncooked quinoa
- 1 (8-oz.) package fresh sugar snap peas
- 1 garlic clove, sliced
  Lemon-Garlic Vinaigrette (see recipe at right)
- 1/3 cup loosely packed fresh flat-leaf parsley leaves
- 1/4 cup chopped dry-roasted almonds

1. Rub pork chops with herb seasoning and 1 tsp. kosher salt. Sear half of pork in 2 1/2 Tbsp. hot olive oil in a large skillet over medium-high heat 4 to 5 minutes on each side or until browned and cooked through. Keep pork warm on a wire rack in a 200° oven. Repeat procedure with 2 1/2 Tbsp. olive oil and remaining pork. Wipe skillet clean.

2. Bring quinoa, 1/2 tsp. kosher salt, and 4 cups water to a boil in large saucepan over high heat. Cover, reduce heat to medium-low, and simmer 8 to 10 minutes or until tender; drain. Return to saucepan; cover. Let stand 10 minutes.

3. Cut sugar snap peas in half crosswise. Heat remaining 1 Tbsp. olive oil in skillet over medium-high heat; cook peas in hot oil 1 minute or until bright green and tender. Sprinkle with remaining 1/4 tsp. salt. Add garlic; sauté 1 minute. Remove from heat.

4. Fluff quinoa with a fork. Add quinoa and Lemon-Garlic Vinaigrette to sugar snap pea mixture, and toss to coat. Stir in parsley and almonds. Serve with pork.

LEMON-GARLIC VINAIGRETTE

Whisk together 2 Tbsp. **lemon juice**; 1 Tbsp. **olive oil**; 2 **garlic cloves**, minced; 1/4 tsp. **kosher salt**; and 1/4 tsp. **black pepper**.

Lemon Pork Chops with Quinoa Salad

Roasted Carrots
with Avocado and
Feta Vinaigrette

Grilled Chicken and New Potatoes

(35 MIN)

MAKES 4 SERVINGS

Use a foil packet as a fuss-free cooking vessel for the leeks and potatoes (or any vegetable).

- 1 medium leek
- 1 ½ lb. small new potatoes, halved
- 2 Tbsp. crushed red pepper-and-garlic seasoning (such as McCormick), divided
- 4 Tbsp. olive oil, divided
- 1 ½ tsp. table salt, divided
- 1 ½ lb. chicken breast tenders
- 2 Tbsp. fresh lemon juice, divided
- 2 bunches green onions

1. Preheat grill to 350° to 400° (medium-high) heat. Remove and discard root end and dark green top of leek. Cut in half lengthwise, and rinse thoroughly under cold running water to remove grit and sand. Cut into thin slices.

2. Toss together leek, potatoes, 1 Tbsp. garlic seasoning, 3 Tbsp. olive oil, and 1 tsp. salt.

3. Divide leek mixture among 2 large pieces of heavy-duty aluminum foil. Bring foil sides up over mixture; double fold top and sides to seal, making packets.

4. Grill foil packets, covered with grill lid, 12 minutes.

5. Meanwhile, toss together chicken, 1 Tbsp. lemon juice, and remaining 1 Tbsp. garlic seasoning, 1 Tbsp. olive oil, and ½ tsp. salt.

6. Shake foil packets, using tongs, and return to grill. At the same time, grill chicken, covered with grill lid, 5 minutes; turn chicken. Place green onions on grill, and grill chicken, onions, and foil packets 4 to 5 minutes or until chicken is done.

7. Open foil packets carefully, using tongs. Arrange grilled vegetables, chicken, and green onions on a serving plate. Drizzle with remaining 1 Tbsp. lemon juice.

Roasted Carrots with Avocado and Feta Vinaigrette

(30 MIN)

MAKES 4 SERVINGS

In this salad, char, spice, and creaminess meld. The key to roasting veggies is to use similarly sized pieces. Spread them evenly on a baking sheet, and roast in a very hot oven until just tender. (Pictured on page 171)

- 2 lb. small carrots in assorted colors
- 1 Tbsp. sorghum syrup or honey
- 4 Tbsp. extra virgin olive oil, divided
- 1 tsp. kosher salt
- 1 tsp. ground cumin
- ½ tsp. freshly ground black pepper
- ¼ tsp. dried crushed red pepper
- 1 shallot, minced
- 2 Tbsp. red wine vinegar
- 2 oz. feta, blue, or goat cheese, crumbled
- 1 medium-size ripe avocado, sliced
- 2 Tbsp. fresh cilantro leaves
- 1 Tbsp. roasted, salted, and shelled pepitas (pumpkin seeds)

1. Preheat oven to 500°. Toss carrots with sorghum and 2 Tbsp. olive oil. Sprinkle with kosher salt and next 3 ingredients; toss to coat. Place carrots in a lightly greased jelly-roll pan. Bake 15 to 20 minutes or until tender, stirring halfway through.

2. Stir together shallot and vinegar. Add salt and pepper to taste. Stir in remaining 2 Tbsp. olive oil; stir in feta.

3. Arrange carrots and avocado on a serving platter. Drizzle with vinaigrette. Sprinkle with cilantro and pepitas.

Fry Without Fear

In The Way to Fry, *his new cookbook out this month,*
Southern Living *Test Kitchen pro* **Norman King** *demystifies this regional art*

▶ **AS A CURIOUS COOK**, I rely on science as much as Southern wisdom. Take shallow frying, a technique we've improved in five easy steps. The only equipment you need is a wire rack, tongs, and a heavy skillet, which promotes even browning and a crispy crust as heat radiates up from the bottom of the pan. Think of the recipe for **Country Fried Steak** (below) as a versatile road map for all sorts of thin cuts, from pork chops and green tomatoes to catfish fillets and chicken cutlets.

❶ THE SEASONING

Stir together 1 1/2 cups **self-rising white cornmeal mix,** 1 1/2 Tbsp. chopped **fresh oregano,** and 3/4 tsp. **black pepper** in a shallow dish. Sprinkle both sides of 4 to 6 **cubed steaks** (about 1 1/2 lb.) with 1 tsp. **kosher salt** and 1/4 tsp. **black pepper.** "Season the dredging mixture *and* steaks so there's flavor in every bite," Norman says.

❷ THE "3 D'S"

Set up a dredging station: Arrange 2 shallow dishes next to the cornmeal mixture. Place 1 1/2 cups each **all-purpose flour** and **low-fat buttermilk** (or whole milk) in separate dishes. "Then dredge-dip-dredge." Dredge steaks in flour; shake off excess. Dip in buttermilk. Dredge in cornmeal mixture, pressing to adhere.

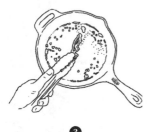

❸ THE TEMP

"Proper oil temperature is key to frying right. Try my method." Place 1 **bacon slice** in a 12-inch cast-iron skillet. Add 2 cups **vegetable oil;** cook over medium heat. When the bacon is crisp (about 5 minutes), the oil is at 350°— and flavored. Transfer bacon to paper towels, reserving oil in skillet.

❹ THE FRY

Nestle steaks in skillet, 2 at a time, and fry until golden brown and crisp (3 to 4 minutes per side). "The steaks aren't submerged in oil, so I carefully spoon hot oil over the tops with a metal spoon during the first minute of frying. This promotes even browning on top while the steaks get crispy underneath."

❺ THE DRAIN

Transfer steaks to a wire rack set over paper towels. Keep warm on wire rack in a jelly-roll pan in a 200° oven. "This prevents them from getting soggy while you finish frying the remaining steaks." Crumble bacon, and reserve for gravy. For our favorite gravy recipes, go to *southernliving.com/gravy.*

Party Like the Lee Bros.

▶ Who better to share a charming Charleston menu than Southern food experts **Matt Lee** and **Ted Lee.** Do try this casual fare from their new cookbook on your own porch, deck, or patio.

The Menu

THE HUGO

SAVORY BENNE
WAFERS

ROMAINE WITH
TOASTED PECANS
AND PICKLED
STRAWBERRIES

RICE AND HAM
CROQUETTES WITH
TOMATO SAUCE

SMOKED EGG SALAD
TOASTS

PICKLED SHRIMP
WITH FENNEL

GRAPEFRUIT CHESS
TART

▶ **THERE'S AN EASE** to assembling parties in Charleston that comes from the city's compact, walkable design and its social traditions," say authors and food personalities Matt Lee and Ted Lee. As the brothers spent formative years here, that social spirit rubbed off, shaping their culinary careers. In their third cookbook, *The Lee Bros. Charleston Kitchen,* they bring this great city, its people, and its recipes to life.

Romaine with Toasted Pecans and Pickled Strawberries

MAKES 10 TO 12 SERVINGS
HANDS-ON 20 MIN.
TOTAL 1 HOUR, 20 MIN.

Use this recipe as a template for every season, substituting seasonal fruit such as plums, figs, or grapes for the berries. If your strawberries are large, cut them into eighths. (Pictured on page 169)

- 1/2 cup white wine vinegar
- 1/2 tsp. kosher salt
- 2 tsp. honey
- 1 (16-oz.) container fresh strawberries, quartered
- Freshly ground black pepper
- 1 Tbsp. white wine vinegar
- 2 tsp. Dijon mustard
- 6 Tbsp. light olive oil
- 3 romaine lettuce hearts
- 1 cup pecan halves, toasted
- 1 (4-oz.) blue cheese wedge, crumbled* (optional)

1. Combine first 2 ingredients and 1 1/2 cups water in a large bowl; whisk in honey until salt is dissolved and honey is blended. Add strawberries; cover and let stand 1 hour.

2. Pour strawberry mixture through a wire mesh strainer into a medium bowl; reserve 2 Tbsp. liquid. Transfer strawberries to a bowl. Season with kosher salt and freshly ground pepper to taste.

3. Whisk together 1 Tbsp. vinegar, Dijon mustard, and reserved 2 Tbsp. strawberry liquid in a bowl. Add oil in a slow, steady stream, whisking constantly until smooth.

4. Cut lettuce hearts in half crosswise, keeping top 6 inches of each and reserving ends for another use. Place lettuce tops on a serving platter. Top with strawberries, pecans, and, if desired, cheese; drizzle with vinegar mixture.

*1 (4-oz.) goat cheese log, crumbled, may be substituted.

SOUTHERN LIVING CHARM SCHOOL
Lesson No. 115

HOW TO PARTY ON THE PORCH

- Go minimal with a bar, a food table, and precious few chairs. The porch railing should be sturdy!

- The mix is key: Invite people of all ages and recruit guests to help pour drinks and pass trays.

- Set up box fans in windows or on side tables and offer unscented bug spray during warmer months.

- The host sets the stage but shouldn't hog it. While well planned, a party should remain flexible enough to head off in a slightly different direction.

PORCH FARE
Strawberries and blue cheese add sweet and tangy notes to a simple romaine salad.

Rice and Ham Croquettes
with Tomato Sauce

Rice and Ham Croquettes with Tomato Sauce

MAKES 10 SERVINGS
HANDS-ON 1 HOUR
TOTAL 2 HOURS, 20 MIN., INCLUDING SAUCE

These ham-studded rice fritters are the Lowcountry version of Italian arancini.

- 3 cups cooked long-grain rice
- 1 1/2 cups finely diced country ham or prosciutto (about 6 oz.)
- 1/2 cup finely chopped green onions, white and light green parts only
- 1 (3-oz.) package cream cheese, softened to room temperature
- 2 large eggs
- 2 Tbsp. milk
- 1 1/4 cups panko (Japanese breadcrumbs)
  Vegetable oil
  Tomato Sauce, warm

1. Preheat oven to 225°. Stir together first 4 ingredients in a large bowl until blended; season with salt and pepper to taste. Lightly beat 1 egg, and gently stir into rice mixture until blended. Stir together milk and remaining egg in a small bowl until blended; place breadcrumbs in a shallow bowl.

2. Form rice mixture into 1-inch balls, using wet hands. Dip balls in egg mixture, and roll in breadcrumbs, shaking off excess.

3. Pour oil to depth of 1 1/2 inches into a Dutch oven; heat over medium-high heat to 340°. Fry croquettes, in batches, 4 to 5 minutes or until golden brown. Transfer to an oven-safe platter lined with paper towels, and keep warm in a 225° oven. Serve croquettes with warm Tomato Sauce.

TOMATO SAUCE

MAKES 3 CUPS
HANDS-ON 15 MIN.
TOTAL 1 HOUR, 20 MIN.

- 1 cup diced sweet onion
- 4 garlic cloves, thinly sliced
- 1/2 tsp. kosher salt
- 1/4 tsp. freshly ground black pepper
- 1/4 cup olive oil
- 1 (28-oz.) can crushed tomatoes
- 1/4 tsp. dried crushed red pepper

Sauté first 4 ingredients in hot oil in a large saucepan over medium heat 6 minutes or until fragrant and onion is tender. (Do not brown.) Add tomatoes and red pepper; cover and bring to a simmer. Reduce heat to low, and cook, partially covered and stirring occasionally, 1 hour or until thickened.

SERVE WITH STYLE

The Lees mix vintage and silver dishes for their casual, eclectic table.

Grapefruit Chess Tart

MAKES 12 SERVINGS
HANDS-ON 30 MIN.
TOTAL 2 HOURS, 40 MIN.

We adapted this recipe to work in a 12- x 8-inch rectangular or 9-inch round tart pan with a removable bottom as well as a 9-inch pie plate. Serve with whipped cream for an extra touch of sweetness. (Pictured on page 169)

- 1 (14.1-oz.) package refrigerated piecrusts
- 2 red or pink grapefruit
- 3/4 tsp. kosher salt
- 3 large egg whites
- 2 large egg yolks
- 1/2 cup whipping cream, at room temperature
- 4 Tbsp. butter, melted
- 1 cup sugar
- 3 Tbsp. all-purpose flour
- 2 Tbsp. plain white cornmeal
  Garnish: fresh mint sprigs

1. Preheat oven to 425°. Unroll piecrusts, and stack on a lightly floured surface. Roll piecrusts into a 14- x 10-inch oval. Fit piecrust into a lightly greased 12- x 8-inch rectangular tart pan with removable bottom; press into fluted edges. Trim off excess crust. Line piecrust with aluminum foil or parchment paper, and fill with pie weights or dried beans. Place pan on a baking sheet.

2. Bake at 425° for 10 minutes. Remove weights and foil, and bake 7 to 8 more minutes or until browned. Cool completely on baking sheet on a wire rack (about 15 minutes). Reduce oven temperature to 300°.

3. Meanwhile, grate zest from grapefruit to equal 1 tsp. Peel grapefruit; section over a bowl to catch juice, reserving 1/3 cup juice and segments separately. Reserve any remaining juice for another use. Whisk zest and salt into 1/3 cup juice.

4. Whisk together egg whites and yolks in a large bowl until creamy and light in color; whisk in cream and butter.

5. Stir together sugar, flour, and cornmeal in a medium bowl. Gradually whisk sugar mixture into egg mixture, one-third at a time, until blended. Whisk in grapefruit juice mixture. Spoon filling into cooled tart shell.

6. Bake at 300° for 20 minutes; remove from oven, and arrange grapefruit sections on tart. Bake 30 to 35 more minutes or until fruit is browned and filling is set. Cool tart on a wire rack 1 hour before serving.

Smoked Egg Salad Toasts

MAKES 8 APPETIZER SERVINGS
HANDS-ON 40 MIN.
TOTAL 50 MIN.

Liven up egg salad with the distinctive Low-country flavor of smoke. (Think hardwood-roasted oysters and pulled pork barbecue.) Serve these also as an open-face sandwich. (Pictured on page 169)

- 8 large eggs
- 1 Tbsp. applewood indoor barbecue chips for stove-top smokers
  Vegetable cooking spray
- 3 Tbsp. mayonnaise
- 2 Tbsp. buttermilk
- 2 tsp. hot sauce
- 1/4 tsp. kosher salt
- 8 (4-inch-square) whole wheat bread slices, crusts removed
- 2 oz. baby arugula or baby lettuces

1. Bring 4 qt. water to a boil in a Dutch oven over high heat. Reduce heat to low. When water is just simmering, gently lower eggs into water using a skimmer or ladle. Simmer 14 minutes. Drain immediately, and return eggs to pan. Fill pan with cold water and ice. Let stand until cool enough to handle (about 10 minutes).

2. Meanwhile, place wood chips in center of a broiler pan. Wrap broiler rack with heavy-duty aluminum foil, and lightly coat top with cooking spray. Place rack in broiler pan.

3. Remove eggs from ice water. Tap each egg firmly on the counter until cracks form all over the shell. Peel under cold running water. Cut eggs in half lengthwise, and carefully remove yolks. Place yolks in a medium bowl. Place egg whites on rack of broiler pan.

4. Partially cover broiler pan tightly with heavy-duty foil, folding back 1 corner to create a 1/2-inch opening. Place over medium-high heat on stove-top. When you see the first wisp of smoke, cover tightly with foil. Smoke 6 minutes. Remove from heat; let stand 2 minutes. Remove whites from pan; coarsely chop.

5. Press yolks through a fine wire-mesh strainer into a bowl. Stir in mayonnaise and next 3 ingredients until mixture is smooth and resembles cake batter. Fold in egg whites.

6. Toast bread; cut in half diagonally. Top with egg salad and top with arugula.

Note: We tested with Hellmann's Mayonnaise and Whole Foods Market Prairie bread. Purchase indoor smoking chips at *kitchenemporium.com*.

Pickled Shrimp with Fennel

MAKES 8 SERVINGS
HANDS-ON 40 MIN.
TOTAL 2 HOURS

Marinated, plump shrimp and crunchy sliced fennel make great passed hors d'oeuvres with toothpicks and an even better no-fuss cold salad. (Pictured on page 174)

- 1 small fennel bulb
- 1 Tbsp. kosher salt
- 2 lb. large raw shrimp, peeled and deveined
- 1 cup fresh lemon juice
- 1/2 cup white wine vinegar
- 1 small serrano or bird pepper, seeded and thinly sliced
- 1 1/2 tsp. kosher salt
- 1 tsp. sugar
- 1 cup thinly sliced white onion

1. Slice fennel bulb thinly, reserving fronds. Chop fronds to equal 1 Tbsp. Fill a large bowl halfway with ice and water.

2. Bring 1 Tbsp. kosher salt and 2 qt. water to a boil in a Dutch oven over high heat. Remove from heat; add shrimp, and let stand, stirring once, 1 minute or just until shrimp turn pink.

3. Transfer shrimp to ice water, using a slotted spoon. Reserve 2 cups hot cooking liquid in a medium bowl. Let shrimp stand 10 minutes, stirring once. Transfer shrimp to a paper towel-lined plate, reserving ice water in bowl.

4. Whisk lemon juice and next 4 ingredients into reserved hot cooking liquid until salt and sugar dissolve. Place bowl in reserved ice water, and whisk lemon juice mixture until cooled to room temperature (about 10 minutes).

5. Remove lemon juice mixture from ice water; discard ice water, reserving chilled bowl for shrimp. Stir together onion, fennel slices, chopped fennel fronds, and shrimp in chilled bowl. Pour cooled lemon juice mixture over shrimp mixture. Cover and chill 1 hour to 2 days. Serve with a slotted spoon.

BACK-UP DUTY Serve cold dishes, such as Pickled Shrimp with Fennel, in small bowls. Have more in the fridge at the ready.

The Hugo

Savory Benne Wafers

MAKES ABOUT 6 DOZEN

HANDS-ON 30 MIN.

TOTAL 2 HOURS, 35 MIN.

The Lees turned the sweet benne wafer, a Lowcountry staple, into a crisp, one-bite cocktail snack. Benne, aka sesame seeds, can be found in bulk at health food stores.

- 1/4 **cup plus 2 tsp. benne (sesame) seeds**
- 2 **cups all-purpose flour**
- 1 1/2 **tsp. kosher salt**
- 1/4 **tsp. ground red pepper**
- 3/4 **cup cold unsalted butter, cut into small pieces**
- 1/4 **cup ice-cold water**
  Parchment paper

1. Preheat oven to 325°. Cook sesame seeds in a heavy skillet over medium heat, stirring often, 6 to 7 minutes or until browned and fragrant. (Seeds will be the color of pecans.) Transfer to a plate. Cool completely (about 20 minutes).

2. Process flour, next 2 ingredients, and 1 Tbsp. seeds in a food processor 30 seconds or until seeds are finely ground. (Seeds should be the same consistency as flour.) Add butter, and pulse 5 or 6 times or until mixture resembles small peas and is crumbly. Add half of ice-cold water, 1 Tbsp. at a time, and pulse 2 or 3 times or just until combined. Add 1 Tbsp. sesame seeds and remaining water; process 10 to 15 seconds or until dough forms a ball and pulls away from sides of bowl.

3. Place dough on a lightly floured surface. Shape into a 1 1/2-inch-thick flat disk; cut into 4 wedges.

4. Dust top of 1 dough wedge with flour; roll dough to 1/16-inch thickness on a lightly floured surface. Sprinkle with 2 tsp. sesame seeds; roll gently to press seeds into dough. Cut dough with a 2-inch round cutter. Place wafers 1/2 inch apart on parchment paper-lined baking sheets. Repeat procedure with remaining dough wedges and sesame seeds.

5. Bake at 325° for 23 to 25 minutes or until lightly browned. Cool completely on baking sheets on wire racks (about 20 minutes). Store in an airtight container up to 3 days.

The Hugo

MAKES 8 SERVINGS

HANDS-ON 10 MIN.

TOTAL 10 MIN.

Make this rum-and-ginger drink ahead, if you like. Follow directions through Step 1; cover and chill up to 24 hours. Proceed with Step 2 when you're ready to serve.

- 2 **cups dark rum**
- 1 **cup fresh lime juice (about 8 limes)**
- 1/2 **cup store-bought ginger juice**
- 5 **Tbsp. plus 1 tsp. sugar**
- 8 **dashes of bitters (optional)**
- 1 **(1-liter) bottle club soda, chilled**
  Garnish: lime slices

1. Combine first 4 ingredients and, if desired, bitters in a pitcher; stir until sugar dissolves.

2. Pour mixture into 8 (10-oz.) rocks glasses filled with ice; top with club soda.

Obey the Laws of Buffet Feng Shui

▶ Southerners are known for having charisma and poise no matter the circumstances. In today's on-the-go culture, mastering that art has never been more important. Form and function unite in a masterfully arranged buffet.

Vary the Height
Stack books under table linens to help elevate certain dishes (less messy ones, without sauces) and to add a little design panache.

Identify Dishes
Include place cards stating the name of each item and any good-to-know information for guests (contains peanuts, for example).

Save Utensils for Last
Place napkins and silverware at the end of the buffet line. Guests won't have to fuss with them while piling up their plates.

Have a Clear Beginning
For a visual cue on where to form the line, start with a tall stack of plates. Pull table out from the wall so traffic flows down both sides.

Give Some Support
Place empty saucers throughout the buffet so guests have a spot to rest those sticky serving spoons.

Position Strategically
Place food you have limited supply of at the end of the line. Guests will be less tempted to take a giant scoop if their plate is nearly full.

EVERY SOUTHERNER SHOULD HAVE...
A SIGNATURE COCKTAIL

Because pineapple has been a symbol of hospitality since the days of the early American colonies, we stirred up a twist for each season, including this springy punch.

PINEAPPLE-RUM-TEA PUNCH Process 4 cups cubed **fresh pineapple**, ½ cup **sugar**, and ½ cup **fresh lime juice** in a blender or food processor 30 seconds or until smooth, stopping to scrape down sides as needed. Pour through a fine wire-mesh strainer into a large pitcher, pressing to release juices. Discard solids. Bring 2 cups **water** to a boil in a medium saucepan over medium-high heat. Remove from heat, and add 4 regular-size **green tea bags** (such as Tazo All Natural Zen Green Tea).

Cover and steep 7 minutes. Discard tea bags. Stir tea into pineapple mixture; cover and chill 4 to 6 hours. Gently stir 1 (20-oz.) bottle chilled **lemon-lime soft drink** and 1 cup **light rum** into pineapple mixture just before serving. Place 2 cups **pineapple sherbet** in a punch bowl or individual glasses. Pour pineapple mixture over sherbet. Serve immediately. **MAKES** about 7 ½ cups. **HANDS-ON** 15 min.; **TOTAL** 4 hours, 30 min.

Spring Appetizers

▶ A taste of who and what got the highest raves in the *Southern Living* Test Kitchen.

From the Kitchen of
SUSAN WEBER
DUNWOODY, GEORGIA

"This easy appetizer dip is delicious in a grilled lamb pita. You can also use it as a spread for burgers or a crudité platter."

GREEN PEA HUMMUS

Cook 1 cup **fresh or frozen, thawed sweet peas** in boiling salted water to cover 1 to 3 minutes or just until crisp-tender; drain. Plunge sweet peas into ice water to stop the cooking process; drain. Pulse blanched sweet peas, 1/4 cup **olive oil**, 2 Tbsp. **chopped fresh mint**, 1 **garlic clove**, and 1/4 tsp. **table salt** in a food processor 4 or 5 times or until smooth. Store in an airtight container in refrigerator up to 3 days. Serve with **assorted vegetables** (such as baby bell peppers, radish halves, sugar snap peas, and endive leaves) and **toasted bread slices**. MAKES about 3/4 cup

RECIPE
Winner
SWAP

Green Pea Hummus makes a pretty platter for baby showers, Easter brunch, or any spring gathering.

From the Kitchen of
ALI EBRIGHT
KANSAS CITY, MO

"In place of phyllo shells, you also can bake wonton wrappers in lightly greased mini muffin cups at 350° for 5 minutes. Be sure to press the wonton edges flat against the sides before baking so they are open for filling when they crisp up."

SPINACH-ARTICHOKE CUPS

Preheat oven to 350°. Drain 1/2 (10-oz.) package **frozen chopped spinach,** thawed, pressing between paper towels. Stir together drained spinach; 1 (14-oz.) can **artichoke hearts,** drained and chopped; 1/2 cup **sour cream;** 1/2 (8-oz.) package **cream cheese,** softened; 1/2 cup (2 oz.) shredded **mozzarella cheese;** 1/4 cup **freshly grated Parmesan cheese;** and a dash of **freshly ground black pepper.** Place 45 **frozen mini-phyllo pastry shells** on a baking sheet. Spoon spinach mixture into shells (about 2 tsp. per cup), pressing into bottom of each cup. Bake 25 minutes or until golden and bubbly. Serve immediately. MAKES 15 appetizer servings

From the Kitchen of
ASHLEY VAN BEEK
BIRMINGHAM, AL

"Make two recipes for a larger crowd. Bake one for the start of your party and the second later so it's hot and fresh."

HOT CHICKEN DIP

Preheat oven to 350°. Place 2 (8-oz.) packages **cream cheese,** softened, and 1 (10 3/4-oz.) can **cream of chicken soup** in a large bowl; beat at medium speed with an electric mixer until smooth and fluffy. Stir in 1 (12.5-oz.) can **premium chunk white chicken breast in water,** drained and flaked; 1/3 cup coarsely chopped jarred **pickled sliced jalapeño peppers;** and 1 Tbsp. **pickled jalapeño pepper juice** from jar. Spoon into a lightly greased 8-inch baking dish. Bake 25 to 30 minutes or until top is browned and bubbly. Serve with **corn chip scoops** or **tortilla chips.** MAKES 10 servings

Make an Easy Icebox Pie

▶ Forget the rolling pin and tricked-out lattice topping—just pat the crust in the pan, add a little tropical flair (we're talking a delicious pineapple-coconut filling here), then bake and chill

Piña Colada Icebox Pie

MAKES 8 SERVINGS
HANDS-ON 25 MIN.
TOTAL 6 HOURS, 20 MIN.

Press the crumb mixture all the way up the sides of the pie plate before baking; otherwise, you'll end up with a thick, uneven crust that's too shallow to hold the filling. (Pictured on page 173)

- 2 **cups pecan shortbread cookie crumbs (about 16 cookies)**
- 1 **cup sweetened flaked coconut**
- 1/4 **cup butter, melted**
- 1/3 **cup sugar**
- 2 **Tbsp. cornstarch**
- 1 **(8-oz.) can crushed pineapple in juice**
- 1 **(8-oz.) package cream cheese, softened**
- 1 1/2 **cups cream of coconut, divided**
- 2 **large eggs**
- 1 **cup whipping cream**
  Garnishes: lightly toasted shaved coconut, pineapple wedges, fresh pineapple mint sprigs

1. Preheat oven to 350°. Stir together first 3 ingredients; firmly press on bottom and up sides of a lightly greased 9-inch pie plate. Bake 10 to 12 minutes or until lightly browned. Transfer to a wire rack; cool completely (about 30 minutes).

2. Stir together sugar and cornstarch in a small heavy saucepan; stir in pineapple. While stirring constantly, bring to a boil over medium-high heat; cook (keep stirring!) 1 minute or until thickened. Remove from heat, and cool completely (about 20 minutes).

3. Beat cream cheese at medium speed with a heavy-duty electric stand mixer, using whisk attachment, until smooth. Gradually add 1 cup cream of coconut, beating at low speed just until blended. (Chill remaining 1/2 cup cream of coconut until ready to use.) Add eggs, 1 at a time, beating just until blended after each addition.

TEST KITCHEN TIP!
Pineapple mint adds texture with its variegated leaves, but any mint will do.

4. Spread cooled pineapple mixture over bottom of piecrust; spoon cream cheese mixture over pineapple mixture.

5. Bake at 350° for 38 to 42 minutes or until set. Cool completely on a wire rack (about 1 hour). Cover and chill 4 hours.

6. Beat whipping cream at high speed until foamy. Gradually add remaining 1/2 cup cream of coconut, beating until soft peaks form; spread over pie.

Note: We tested with Keebler Sandies Pecan Shortbread and Coco López Cream of Coconut.

TOASTED COCONUT

Simply bake shaved coconut in a single layer in a shallow pan at 325° for 7 to 9 minutes or until lightly browned, stirring occasionally.

"How do you cook the perfect rack of lamb?"

—Anna Skubel
Alexandria, Virginia

▶ Chef **Wesley True** of Montgomery, Alabama's True shares his Easter secrets

BARE BONES

Most racks are sold "frenched," meaning the meat and fat have been removed from the upper bones.

TRIMMING THE FAT

You can trim the thick layer of fat on the outside of the rack to ¼ inch for quicker cooking. Or don't. "Fat adds wonderful flavor," Wesley says.

Rack of Lamb with Carrot Salad

MAKES 4 SERVINGS
HANDS-ON 25 MIN.
TOTAL 1 HOUR, 15 MIN., INCLUDING VINAIGRETTE

- 1 (1½-lb.) **frenched rack of lamb** (8 ribs)
- 2 tsp. **olive oil**
- 1 tsp. **table salt**
- ¼ tsp. **black pepper**
- 2 Tbsp. **vegetable oil**
- 1 **carrot**
- 2 bunches **frisée, torn**
- ¼ cup loosely packed fresh **mint leaves, torn**
  Orange-Pecan Vinaigrette

1. Preheat oven to 300°. Rub lamb with 2 tsp. olive oil; sprinkle with salt and pepper (**A**). Let stand 10 minutes.

2. Cook lamb in 2 Tbsp. hot oil in a large skillet over high heat 8 to 10 minutes or until browned, turning twice (**B**). Place lamb on a lightly greased wire rack in a roasting pan. Bake at 300° for 20 minutes or until a meat thermometer inserted into thickest portion registers 140° to 145° (medium-rare) or to desired degree of doneness (**C**). Remove lamb from pan; cover with aluminum foil, and let stand 10 minutes.

3. Meanwhile, cut carrot lengthwise into very thin, ribbon-like strips using a vegetable peeler. Toss frisée, mint, and carrot strips with desired amount of Orange-Pecan Vinaigrette.

4. Slice lamb into chops. Serve with salad and remaining Orange-Pecan Vinaigrette.

ORANGE-PECAN VINAIGRETTE

MAKES ABOUT 1 CUP
HANDS-ON 10 MIN.
TOTAL 10 MIN.

Whisk together ¼ cup **sherry vinegar,** 3 Tbsp. chopped toasted **pecans,** 2 Tbsp. **orange marmalade,** ½ tsp. **table salt,** and ¼ tsp. **black pepper** until blended. Add ¾ cup **extra virgin olive oil** in a slow, steady stream, whisking until smooth.

TRUE'S 3 TRUTHS TO COOKING LAMB

"Rack of lamb is actually pretty simple if you remember three main points," below.

A "Home cooks often want to marinate lamb, but I've never seen that in a restaurant. **Seasoning only with table salt and black pepper** lets the flavor of the lamb come through."

B "You want the skillet smoking hot. Put the lamb, fat side down, in the skillet and leave it alone for a minute until it's brown. Then flip it and let it brown; then flip it again. This crisps up the fat and gives a nice brown exterior while preventing the edges from overcooking in the oven."

C "Baking lamb at 300° keeps the meat from tightening up so that it comes out very tender. Putting the lamb on a wire rack allows the hot air to circulate around the lamb."

April

Break Out of Your Shell

▶ Protein-rich eggs kick off the day in the best way, but here they take on a whole new after-sundown vibe as pub-style appetizers and hearty meatless mains—seriously savory recipes you'll crave for dinner, lunch, and yes, breakfast.

Bistro Salad with Bacon, Eggs, and Mushrooms

Bistro Salad with Bacon, Eggs, and Mushrooms

MAKES 6 SERVINGS
HANDS-ON 25 MIN.
TOTAL 25 MIN.

Creamy eggs, the star of this entrée, play well off the bitter greens and earthy 'shrooms.

- 6 cups loosely packed torn curly endive
- 3 cups loosely packed arugula
- 1/2 cup loosely packed fresh flat-leaf parsley leaves
- 2 Tbsp. chopped fresh chives
- 6 oz. slab bacon slices, thinly sliced crosswise
- 1 shallot, minced
- 1/4 cup Champagne vinegar
- 2 tsp. Dijon mustard
- 2/3 cup plus 2 Tbsp. extra virgin olive oil
  Kosher salt and freshly ground pepper to taste
- 3/4 cup halved baby portobello mushrooms
- 6 medium-cooked large eggs, halved
- 12 artisan bread slices, toasted

1. Combine first 4 ingredients in a large bowl; cover with a damp paper towel, and chill.

2. Cook bacon in a medium skillet over medium heat 5 minutes or until crisp. Remove with a slotted spoon, and drain on paper towels, reserving 2 Tbsp. drippings.

3. Sauté shallot in 1 Tbsp. reserved hot drippings over medium heat 1 to 2 minutes or until lightly browned. Remove from heat, and stir in vinegar and mustard. Add oil in a slow, steady stream, whisking constantly until smooth. Add salt and pepper to taste. Transfer to a small bowl. Wipe skillet clean.

4. Cook mushrooms in skillet in remaining 1 Tbsp. reserved hot drippings over medium-high heat, stirring occasionally, 5 to 7 minutes or until tender. Sprinkle with a pinch of kosher salt.

5. Toss endive mixture with 1/4 cup vinaigrette, and divide among 6 salad plates. Top with eggs, mushrooms, bacon, and bread slices. Serve with remaining vinaigrette.

Scrambled Egg and Crêpe Casserole

Scrambled Egg and
Crêpe Casserole

Scrambled Egg and Crêpe Casserole

MAKES ABOUT 1 DOZEN
HANDS-ON 30 MIN.
TOTAL 2 HOURS, 30 MIN.,
INCLUDING SAUCE AND CRÊPES

This is a twist on classic Gentlemen's Casserole. Also wrap the crêpes around smoked salmon or veggies for summer rolls.

- 3 **Tbsp. butter, divided**
- 1 **cup finely chopped baked ham**
- 1/2 **cup thinly sliced green onions**
- 14 **large eggs, beaten**
- 1/2 **tsp. table salt**
- 1/2 **tsp. freshly ground black pepper**
  Cheese Sauce
  Fresh Herb Crêpes

1. Preheat oven to 350°. Melt 1 Tbsp. butter in a large nonstick skillet over medium-high heat; add ham, and sauté 3 to 4 minutes or until golden brown. Remove from skillet, and wipe skillet clean.

2. Melt remaining 2 Tbsp. butter in skillet over medium-low heat. Add green onions; sauté 1 minute. Add eggs, salt, and pepper, and cook, without stirring, 1 to 2 minutes or until eggs begin to set on bottom. Gently draw cooked edges away from sides and across bottom of skillet to form large curds, using a spatula. Repeat procedure, cooking until eggs are thickened but still moist (about 6 to 7 minutes). Remove from heat, and gently fold in ham and 2 cups Cheese Sauce.

3. Spoon about 1/3 cup egg mixture down the center of each crêpe; roll up. Place in a lightly greased 13- x- 9-inch baking dish (or divide among smaller dishes). Spoon remaining Cheese Sauce over crêpes. Bake at 350° for 15 to 20 minutes or until sauce is bubbly.

CHEESE SAUCE

MAKES ABOUT 4 CUPS
HANDS-ON 15 MIN.
TOTAL 15 MIN.

Melt 1/3 cup **butter** in a heavy saucepan over medium-low heat; whisk in 1/3 cup **all-purpose flour** until smooth. Cook, whisking constantly, 2 minutes. Gradually whisk in 3 cups **milk**; cook over medium heat, whisking constantly, 5 minutes or until thickened. Remove from heat, and whisk in 2 cups (8 oz.) freshly shredded **sharp white Cheddar cheese** and 3/4 tsp. **table salt** until smooth.

FRESH HERB CRÊPES

MAKES ABOUT 1 DOZEN
HANDS-ON 20 MIN.
TOTAL 1 HOUR, 20 MIN.

- 1 **cup all-purpose flour**
- 1 **cup milk**
- 3 **large eggs**
- 1/2 **tsp. table salt**
- 1/2 **cup chopped fresh herbs (such as parsley, chives, basil, and tarragon)**
  Vegetable cooking spray

1. Whisk together first 4 ingredients until blended. Cover and chill 1 hour. Stir in herbs.

2. Coat bottom of a 6-inch crêpe pan or heavy skillet with cooking spray; place over medium heat until hot.

3. Pour a scant 1/4 cup batter into pan; quickly tilt pan in all directions so batter evenly covers bottom of pan. Cook 1 minute or until crêpe can be shaken loose from pan. (Do not turn crêpe.) Place crêpe on a dish towel to cool. Repeat procedure with remaining batter, coating pan with cooking spray between batches.

Note: To make ahead, stack cooled crêpes between sheets of wax paper, and place in a zip-top plastic freezer bag. Store in refrigerator up to 2 days.

DUAL ROLES
Eggs are the main ingredient in both the crêpes and filling. Folding cheese sauce into the scrambled eggs keeps them moist when baked.

Dirty Rice Scotch Eggs

MAKES 6 SERVINGS
HANDS-ON 40 MIN.
TOTAL 1 HOUR, 10 MIN.

When deep-frying, choose an oil with a high smoke point, such as canola or peanut oil.

- 1 cup finely chopped spicy smoked sausage
- 1/4 cup finely chopped sweet onion
- 1/4 cup finely chopped celery
- 1/4 cup finely chopped bell pepper
- 2 1/2 cups cooked jasmine rice
- 1 Tbsp. Worcestershire sauce
- 1 tsp. Cajun seasoning
- 1/4 tsp. dry mustard
- 2 large eggs
- 1/4 cup fine, dry breadcrumbs
- 6 hard-cooked eggs
  Vegetable oil

1. Sauté sausage in a large skillet over medium heat 3 to 4 minutes or until crisp. Add onion and next 2 ingredients; sauté 3 to 4 minutes or until vegetables are tender. Remove from heat, and stir in rice and next 3 ingredients. Cool 30 minutes. Stir in 2 large eggs and breadcrumbs.

2. Gently press rice mixture evenly around hard-cooked eggs to cover, using wet hands.

3. Pour oil to depth of 2 inches into a Dutch oven; heat over medium heat to 360°. Fry eggs, in 3 batches, 3 minutes or until golden brown, turning often. Drain on a wire rack over paper towels.

Cheese Grits with Poached Eggs

MAKES 6 SERVINGS
HANDS-ON 40 MIN.
TOTAL 1 HOUR

Grits and eggs are a great canvas for any flavor variation, such as this Tex-Mex take. (Pictured on page 7)

- 2 cups milk
- 1 1/2 tsp. table salt
- 1 cup stone-ground grits
- 1 1/2 cups (6 oz.) freshly shredded pepper Jack cheese
- 2 Tbsp. butter
- 1/2 tsp. white vinegar
- 6 large eggs
  Pico de Gallo
  Tortilla strips

1. Bring milk, salt, and 4 cups water to a boil in a medium saucepan over medium-high heat. Gradually whisk in grits; return to a boil. Reduce heat to medium-low, and simmer, stirring occasionally, 20 to 25 minutes or until thickened. Remove from heat, and stir in cheese and butter. Cover and keep warm.

2. Pour water to depth of 2 inches into a large saucepan. Bring to a boil; reduce heat, and maintain at a light simmer. Add vinegar. Break eggs, and slip into water, 1 at a time, as close as possible to surface of water. Simmer 3 to 5 minutes or to desired degree of doneness. Remove with a slotted spoon. Trim edges, if desired. Spoon grits into 6 bowls; top with Pico de Gallo, eggs, and tortilla strips.

PICO DE GALLO

MAKES 1 1/2 CUPS
HANDS-ON 10 MIN.
TOTAL 10 MIN.

Stir together 1 medium **tomato,** chopped; 2 **jalapeño peppers,** seeded and chopped; 1 small **onion,** chopped; 1/2 cup coarsely chopped **fresh cilantro;** 1/4 cup **fresh 'Florida Super Sweet' corn kernels;** 1 **garlic clove,** pressed; 2 Tbsp. **fresh lime juice;** and 1 tsp. **table salt** in a bowl. Stir in 2 coarsely chopped **avocados** just before serving.

Asparagus Mimosa

MAKES 4 SERVINGS
HANDS-ON 10 MIN.
TOTAL 10 MIN.

(Pictured on page 173)

Trim 1 lb. **fresh asparagus;** cook in boiling salted water to cover 1 to 2 minutes or until crisp-tender. Drain. Plunge into ice water; drain. Toss with 1 tsp. **cider vinegar,** 1 tsp. **extra virgin olive oil,** 1/8 tsp. **kosher salt,** and 1/8 tsp. **freshly ground black pepper.** Place on a serving platter; top with 1 grated **hard-cooked egg,** 2 Tbsp. sautéed finely diced **spicy smoked sausage,** and 1 tsp. chopped **fresh chives.** Serve with **hot sauce.**

CHEEP CHIC: MARBLED EGGS

Pickled beets give Chinese tea eggs a colorful flavor makeover.

MARBLED EGGS

MAKES 6 EGGS
HANDS-ON 10 MIN.
TOTAL 2 HOURS, 50 MIN.

To get a finely etched marbled look, peel eggs after 2 hours. For more pronounced pick-led-beet flavor and uniform color, chill eggs for the full 24 hours.

Bring 3 medium-size fresh **beets,** peeled and thinly sliced; 2 1/2 cups **water;** 1 cup **apple cider vinegar;** 1/3 cup **sugar;** 1/4 cup **table salt;** 1/4 cup thinly sliced **red onion;** and 1 tsp. **dried crushed red pepper** to a boil in a medium saucepan over medium-high heat. Reduce heat to medium-low; simmer 15 to 20 minutes or until onion is tender. Remove from heat. Crack 6 large **hard-cooked eggs** all over using back of a wooden spoon. Submerge eggs in beet mixture, and let stand 15 minutes. Cover and chill 2 to 24 hours.

How to use them: Take your favorite deviled egg recipe up a notch. Add a festive note to salad niçoise. Halve and top with sour cream and caviar or smoked trout roe. Or, serve picnic-style with sea salt, pepper, and a six pack of cold beer.

Southern-Style Smørrebrød

Sparked by the leisurely pleasures of the cocktail-and-canapé Mad Men era, smørrebrød (Danish open-faced sandwiches) are the latest craze in stress-free entertaining. With a little clever prep, you can set out an impressive DIY spread in under an hour. Now we'll toast to that. Skål, y'all! (Pictured on page 172)

START HEARTY

Opt for a rustic pumpernickel, rye, or sourdough—the bread lays the foundation and needs to be sturdy enough to support high-rise toppings. Trim the crusts and go bite-size, or indulge in full-on knife-and-fork dinner fare. Brush bread slices with melted butter or olive oil, and bake at 400° for 8 to 10 minutes or until crisp.

ADD A CREAMY NOTE

Set out a few versatile spreads that guests can mix and match with different toppings; The New Egg Salad and Sour Cream-Herb Sauce are two of our favorites. Other great options include garlic-and-herb cheeses, flavored butters, rémoulade, and country-style mustards.

THE NEW EGG SALAD

MAKES 4 CUPS
HANDS-ON 15 MIN.
TOTAL 3 HOURS, 20 MIN.

Bring ½ cup **vegetable broth** to a boil over medium-high heat. Stir in ¼ cup **julienne-cut sun-dried tomatoes**; cover, remove from heat, and let stand 5 minutes. Drain tomatoes, pat dry with paper towels, and chop. Grate 12 **hard-cooked eggs** using large holes of a box grater; place in a large bowl. Stir in tomatoes, ¼ cup finely chopped **celery**, and 2 Tbsp. finely chopped **sweet onion**. Stir together ½ cup **Greek yogurt**, 3 Tbsp. **mayonnaise**, 1 Tbsp. **chopped fresh flat-leaf parsley**, 1 Tbsp. **prepared horseradish**, 1 tsp. **hot sauce**, 1 tsp. **Worcestershire sauce**, ¾ tsp. **celery salt**, and ¼ tsp. **black pepper** in a bowl until blended. Fold into egg mixture. Chill up to 3 days.

SOUR CREAM-HERB SAUCE

MAKES ¾ CUP
HANDS-ON 5 MIN.
TOTAL 2 HOURS, 5 MIN.

Stir together ½ cup **sour cream**, 2 Tbsp. **mayonnaise**, 1 Tbsp. chopped **capers**, 1 tsp. chopped **fresh dill**, 1 tsp. **fresh lemon juice**, and a pinch of **ground red pepper** until blended. Chill up to 3 days.

GET CREATIVE

Toppings can be minimal or lavish—anything goes as long as it looks great and the flavors play well together: thinly sliced meats and cheeses, bacon, pickled shrimp, smoked trout, hard-cooked eggs, crabmeat. Also consider condiments such as bacon marmalade and tomato chutney.

FINISH FRESH

Think color and crunch. Pickled squash and onions, julienned peppers, thinly sliced cucumbers and radishes, peppery watercress, fresh herbs, sprouts and microgreens, grape tomatoes, and slivers of fresh seasonal fruit.

OUR FAVE COMBOS

PAIR WITH SOUR CREAM-HERB SAUCE AND SLICED HARD-COOKED EGGS.

1. Salami, pickled okra, and olive salad
2. Smoked trout, green apple, and dill
3. Shrimp, cornichons, and radicchio
4. Shrimp, cucumber, and chervil or parsley

PAIR WITH EGG SALAD

5. Tomato, feta, and sprouts
6. Tomato, bacon, and watercress

Crack the Egg Code

Welcome to Eggs 101. Your curriculum today: the SL way to cook in the shell and peel

▶ **LIKE STEAK, EGGS HAVE** different degrees of doneness. It's all about the timing. We cooked dozens of them in search of the most consistently tender whites and evenly cooked yolks for our egg story (page 80). Here's what we found: Place six eggs in a single layer in a 4-qt. stainless steel saucepan; add 5½ cups water (or just enough to cover the eggs), and bring to a simmer. Start your timer, maintain water at a bare simmer, and cook to preferred doneness, using the times below as your guide. Drain the eggs, and soak them under a steady stream of tap water until cool to the touch (about 1 minute). Then get cracking.

❶ SOFT-COOKED
5 MINUTES
White is just set, and yolk is creamy. Serve on its own, over pasta, or on toast.

❷ MEDIUM-COOKED
8 MINUTES
Yolk is almost opaque and just firm. Great for composed salads.

❸ HARD-COOKED
10 MINUTES
The all-purpose egg. Yolk is bright yellow and just cooked all the way through.

❹ BLESS YOUR HEART!
You have ring-around-the-yolk because you boiled them for too long. Don't toss them; they're still edible. Many cultures prize long-cooked eggs.

TIP

We buy large Grade A eggs in the *SL* Test Kitchen. To test their freshness beyond the stamp on the carton, place an egg in a glass of water. If it sinks, it's fresh; if it remains suspended, it's okay; if the egg floats, it has lost density—discard it.

EASY PEELING

Myths abound. Here's the truth, no yoke.

MYTH #1 Add cooking oil to the water so the shells slide right off. Wrong.

MYTH #2 Cooking fresh eggs with baking soda makes them easier to peel. Jury's still out.

MYTH #3 Adding vinegar makes peeling a breeze. Wrong, though if cracked, it keeps eggs from splitting while boiling.

MYTH #4 Chilling eggs before peeling eases the process. Wrong.

THE *SL* VERDICT There's more than one way to crack and peel an egg, but we prefer gently tapping all sides of the egg on a flat surface and peeling it under running water so the shell comes off quickly and easily.

Capture Spring in a Bottle

▶ This season's best-dressed salads start with a trio of versatile vinaigrettes that serve double duty as sauces and marinades

Ginger-Basil Vinaigrette

Use this as a sauce for fish or shrimp, crisp lettuces, avocado, or rice. Process 1/2 cup loosely packed **fresh basil leaves**, chopped; 2 Tbsp. **fresh lemon juice**; 2 tsp. minced **fresh ginger**; 1 **garlic clove**, minced; 1 tsp. **honey**; and 1/2 tsp. **kosher salt** in a food processor until smooth. With processor running, pour 2/3 cup **grapeseed oil** through food chute in a slow, steady stream, processing until smooth. **MAKES** about 3/4 cup

Red Pepper Jelly Vinaigrette

Pair this sweet, piquant vinaigrette with fresh greens and tangy goat cheese. It also works as a marinade for chicken or pork. Whisk together 6 Tbsp. red wine vinegar; 1/3 cup olive oil; 3 Tbsp. red pepper jelly; 1 shallot, minced (about 2 Tbsp.); 1 Tbsp. coarse-grained mustard; 1/4 tsp. kosher salt; and 1/4 tsp. black pepper in a small bowl. **MAKES** about 1 cup

Peach-Poppy Seed Vinaigrette

Pair with any lettuce, or drizzle over grilled pork. Process 3/4 cup frozen sliced peaches or mango, thawed; 3 Tbsp. peach preserves; 2 Tbsp. plus 2 tsp. apple cider vinegar; 1/2 tsp. Dijon mustard; and 1/2 tsp. kosher salt in a food processor until smooth. With processor running, pour 1/2 cup canola oil through food chute in a slow stream. Process until smooth; stir in 1 1/2 tsp. poppy seeds. **MAKES** 1 1/4 cups

Grill Once, Eat Twice

▶ Make your grill work overtime to give you eight simple, fresh, and quick weeknight options

Pork Tenderloins with Balsamic Strawberries

Pork Tenderloins with Balsamic Strawberries

45 MIN

MAKES 4 SERVINGS

- 1 (3-lb.) package pork tenderloins
- ½ tsp. freshly ground black pepper
- 2 tsp. kosher salt, divided
- 10 bacon slices
- 2 (8-oz.) packages haricots verts (thin green beans)
- 2 Tbsp. olive oil, divided
- 4 garlic cloves, divided
- ½ cup balsamic vinegar
- ⅓ cup strawberry preserves
- ½ cup quartered fresh strawberries

1. Preheat grill to 400° to 500° (high) heat. Sprinkle pork with pepper and 1 tsp. salt; wrap 5 bacon slices around each tenderloin, and secure with wooden picks.

2. Place green beans, 1 Tbsp. olive oil, 2 garlic cloves, and remaining 1 tsp. salt in center of a 24- x 18-inch piece of heavy-duty aluminum foil; toss to coat. Bring up sides of foil over beans; double fold top and side edges to seal, making a packet.

3. Turn off one side of grill. Arrange pork and foil packet over unlit side, and grill, covered with grill lid, 25 to 30 minutes.

4. Mince remaining 2 garlic cloves; sauté in remaining 1 Tbsp. hot olive oil in a skillet over medium-high heat 2 to 3 minutes or until golden. Add vinegar; bring to a boil over medium-high heat. Boil 5 minutes. Remove from heat, and stir in preserves. Reserve half of mixture for basting. Stir fresh strawberries into remaining mixture.

5. Remove foil packet from grill; transfer pork to lit side. Baste pork with reserved strawberry mixture. Grill 5 more minutes over lit side, turning once. Remove pork from grill; reserve 1 tenderloin for Pork Pesto Panini. Slice remaining tenderloin, and serve with strawberry mixture and green beans.

LEFTOVER DINNER

PORK PESTO PANINI Cut reserved pork from Pork Tenderloins with Balsamic Strawberries into 18 thin slices. Drain 1 (7-oz.) jar **roasted red bell peppers**; cut peppers into 6 pieces. Spread 2 tsp. **pesto** on each of 6 **artisan bread** slices. Top each with 3 pork slices, 1 red pepper piece, 1 (1-oz.) **Havarti cheese** slice, and 1 bread slice. Cook in a preheated panini press 2 to 3 minutes or until golden. **MAKES** 6 servings

Grilled Lime Shrimp and Vegetable Rice

40 MIN

MAKES 4 SERVINGS

- 1 (13.66-oz.) can coconut milk
- 2 garlic cloves, minced
- 1 tsp. table salt
- 3 Tbsp. red pepper jelly
- 2 Tbsp. olive oil
- 1 tsp. Asian hot chili sauce (such as Sriracha)
- 1 tsp. lime zest
- 6 Tbsp. fresh lime juice, divided
- 2 lb. peeled, large raw shrimp
- 1¼ cups uncooked jasmine rice
- 2 ears fresh corn
- 5 assorted mini bell peppers
- 1 sweet onion, cut into ½-inch slices
- 2 tsp. olive oil
- ½ cup chopped fresh herbs (such as flat-leaf parsley, mint, basil, and cilantro)

1. Preheat grill to 350° to 400° (medium-high) heat. Bring first 3 ingredients and ⅔ cup water to a boil in a medium saucepan over high heat.

2. While coconut milk mixture comes to a boil, whisk together red pepper jelly, next 3 ingredients, and ¼ cup fresh lime juice in a small bowl. Reserve 2 Tbsp. lime mixture. Combine remaining lime mixture and shrimp. Let stand 20 minutes.

3. Meanwhile, stir rice into boiling coconut milk mixture. Cover, reduce heat to low, and simmer 20 minutes or until liquid is absorbed. Remove from heat, and keep covered.

4. While shrimp marinates and rice simmers, brush corn, peppers, and onion with 2 tsp. olive oil, and grill, covered with grill lid, 8 minutes or until slightly charred, turning halfway through. Remove and discard seeds from peppers; chop peppers. Cut kernels from corn cobs. Discard cobs. Chop onion. Combine peppers, corn, and onion in a bowl.

5. Remove shrimp from marinade, discarding marinade. Grill shrimp, covered with grill lid, 3 minutes on each side or just until shrimp turn pink. Remove shrimp from grill; sprinkle with 1 Tbsp. lime juice, and toss with reserved 2 Tbsp. lime mixture. Reserve half of shrimp for Lime Shrimp Rolls. Stir remaining 1 Tbsp. lime juice into rice. Stir rice mixture and herbs into grilled vegetables. Serve remaining shrimp over rice-and-vegetable mixture.

Grilled Lime Shrimp and Vegetable Rice

LEFTOVER DINNER

LIME SHRIMP ROLLS Preheat oven to 375°. Coarsely chop **reserved shrimp** from Grilled Lime Shrimp and Vegetable Rice. Stir together ½ cup chopped **celery,** ⅓ cup **mayonnaise,** ½ tsp. **lime zest,** 1 Tbsp. **fresh lime juice,** ½ tsp. chopped **fresh tarragon,** and shrimp in a bowl. Stir together 2 Tbsp. **melted butter** and 1 **garlic clove,** pressed; spread on cut sides of 4 **hot dog buns.** Bake 7 to 8 minutes or until toasted. Place 1 **lettuce leaf** in each roll; top with shrimp mixture. Serve with **lime wedges.** **MAKES** 4 servings

Grilled Steak Salad with Walnut Dressing

MAKES 4 SERVINGS

Add a side of fresh blueberries, strawberries, or mango.

- 1 small red onion, thinly sliced
- 1/2 cup olive oil
- 1 cup coarsely chopped walnuts
- 1 garlic clove, thinly sliced
- 2 lb. flat-iron, hanger, or tri-tip steak
- 2 Tbsp. olive oil
- 1 Tbsp. Chicago steak seasoning
- 1 tsp. kosher salt, divided
- 2 large red onions, cut into 1/2-inch-thick slices
- 1/3 cup white wine vinegar
- 1 Tbsp. dark brown sugar
- 1 Tbsp. whole grain Dijon mustard
- 1/4 tsp. black pepper
- 1 romaine lettuce heart, torn
- 2 oz. crumbled blue cheese

1. Preheat grill to 350° to 400° (medium-high) heat. Sauté 1 thinly sliced small onion in 1/2 cup hot olive oil in a large skillet over medium-high heat 3 to 4 minutes or until golden and tender. Add walnuts and garlic; cook, stirring occasionally, 3 to 4 minutes or until walnuts just begin to turn golden brown. Remove from heat, and cool 5 minutes.

2. Rub steak with 1 Tbsp. olive oil, steak seasoning, and 1/2 tsp. salt. Toss 1/2-inch onion slices with remaining 1 Tbsp. olive oil.

3. Grill steak, covered with grill lid, 5 to 7 minutes on each side or to desired degree of doneness. At the same time, grill thick onion slices, covered with grill lid, 4 to 5 minutes on each side or until golden brown. Remove steak and onions from grill, and let stand 5 minutes. Thinly slice steak. Reserve half of steak and onions for Steak Wraps.

4. Whisk together vinegar, brown sugar, and mustard in a medium bowl. Gradually whisk in walnut mixture. Add 1/4 tsp. pepper and remaining 1/2 tsp. salt. Reserve 1/2 cup vinaigrette for Steak Wraps.

5. Toss lettuce and grilled onions with 1/4 cup vinaigrette in a large bowl; arrange on a serving platter. Top with grilled steak. Sprinkle with crumbled blue cheese. Serve with remaining 1/4 cup vinaigrette.

⌐ **LEFTOVER DINNER** ⌐

STEAK WRAPS Coarsely chop **reserved onions** from Grilled Steak Salad with Walnut Dressing. Stir together 4 oz. softened **cream cheese** and reserved 1/2 cup **vinaigrette** until smooth. Spread on 1 side of 4 (9-inch) **plain wraps**. Top each with 10 **baby spinach leaves**. Divide reserved steak and onions among wraps; sprinkle with 2 oz. crumbled **blue cheese**. Roll up. **MAKES** 4 wraps

Grilled Spicy Cilantro Chicken

MAKES 4 TO 6 SERVINGS

- 2/3 cup olive oil
- 2 Tbsp. fresh lemon juice
- 4 medium-size jalapeño peppers, seeded
- 2 bunches fresh cilantro (about 3 cups loosely packed leaves)
- 2 bunches fresh mint (about 1 cup loosely packed leaves)
- 4 garlic cloves
- 1 tsp. table salt
- 1 tsp. ground ginger
- 12 small skinned and boned chicken thighs
- 8 plum tomatoes, halved
   Freshly ground black pepper
   Assorted chopped fresh herbs
   Naan bread

1. Preheat grill to 350° to 400° (medium-high) heat. Process first 4 ingredients and 1/4 cup water in a blender until smooth. Add mint and next 3 ingredients, and process until smooth, stopping to scrape down sides as needed.

2. Rub 1/2 cup cilantro mixture over chicken; cover and chill 10 minutes. Reserve 1/2 cup cilantro mixture for Grilled Chicken Naan Pizza and 1/2 cup to serve with chicken.

3. Grill chicken, covered with grill lid, 5 to 6 minutes on each side or until done. Remove from grill, and let stand 5 minutes.

4. Meanwhile, grill tomato halves 3 to 5 minutes or just until they begin to blister. Sprinkle with salt and pepper, drizzle with desired amount of olive oil, and top with chopped fresh herbs. Grill naan 1 to 2 minutes on each side or just until puffy and soft.

5. Reserve 6 chicken thighs and 4 tomato halves for Grilled Chicken Naan Pizza. Serve remaining chicken and tomatoes with grilled naan bread and reserved 1/2 cup cilantro mixture.

⌐ **LEFTOVER DINNER** ⌐

GRILLED CHICKEN NAAN PIZZA Preheat oven to 450°. Thinly slice 6 **Grilled Spicy Cilantro Chicken thighs.** Place 2 **naan breads** on a parchment paper-lined baking sheet; spread each with 1 Tbsp. reserved **cilantro mixture;** layer each with 1/2 cup sliced chicken, 4 reserved **plum tomato halves,** and 4 fresh **mozzarella cheese** slices. Bake 7 to 8 minutes or until cheese melts. Top with **arugula.** Serve with remaining cilantro mixture. **MAKES** 4 servings

Grilled Steak Salad with Walnut Dressing

Stir Up a Little Cupcake Magic

▶ A Thumbelina version of the tube-pan classic, these Pound Cake Cupcakes are pretty enough for a fairy-tale princess—and only a muffin tin away.

Pound Cake Cupcakes

MAKES 30 CUPCAKES
HANDS-ON 30 MIN.
TOTAL 1 HOUR, 55 MIN., NOT INCLUDING BLOSSOMS

(Pictured on page 175)

1	cup butter, softened
2½	cups sugar
6	large eggs
3	cups all-purpose flour
1	tsp. baking powder
1	(8-oz.) container mascarpone cheese, softened
3	tsp. vanilla extract, divided
30	paper baking cups
9	(2-oz.) vanilla candy coating squares, coarsely chopped
½	cup whipping cream
2	Tbsp. butter, softened
	Sky blue food coloring paste
	Hydrangea Blossoms

1. Preheat oven to 350°. Beat 1 cup butter at medium speed with an electric mixer until fluffy; gradually add sugar, beating well. Add eggs, 1 at a time, beating just until blended after each addition.

2. Stir together flour and baking powder. Add flour mixture to butter mixture alternately with mascarpone cheese, beginning and ending with flour mixture. Beat at low speed just until blended after each addition. Stir in 2 tsp. vanilla. Place 30 paper baking cups in 3 (12-cup) standard-size muffin pans; spoon batter into cups using a 4 Tbsp. (¼-cup) cookie scoop.

3. Bake at 350° for 20 to 23 minutes or until a wooden pick inserted in centers comes out clean. Remove from pans to wire racks, and cool completely.

4. Microwave vanilla candy coating and whipping cream in a 1-qt. microwave-safe bowl at MEDIUM (50% power) 1½ minutes. Stir mixture, and microwave 1 more minute or until candy coating is almost melted, gently stirring at 30-second intervals. Whisk until melted and smooth. (Do not overheat or overwhisk.) Whisk in 2 Tbsp. softened butter and remaining 1 tsp. vanilla. Tint with desired amount of food coloring paste.

5. Working quickly, dip tops of cupcakes in candy mixture. Place right-side-up on a wire rack. (If mixture begins to harden, microwave 10 to 15 seconds, and stir until smooth.) Top with blossoms.

EDITOR'S TIP

Make blossoms weeks ahead and store at room temp in airtight container away from sunlight.

HYDRANGEA BLOSSOMS

Ready-to-use fondant is just as easy to cut and shape as Play-Doh. A hydrangea gumpaste cutter set (*petalcrafts.com*) adds realistic details. Find fondant and color dust at craft stores or *wilton.com*.

1

Dust work surface with cornstarch. Thinly roll fondant; stamp with petal veiner included in kit.

2

Cut blossoms with petal cutter. Press petal edges between fingertips; shape and let harden on candy gummy rings until firm enough to lift.

3

Accent petals with dark blue color dust. Mold anthers; let harden, and brush with yellow dust. Dot petal centers with corn syrup; add anthers.

Cakes in Bloom

▶ In honor of the spring party season, five of our all-time favorite cakes take delicious flights of fancy. The original Hummingbird Cake (our most requested recipe ever!) celebrates its 35th anniversary with swirls of browned butter frosting. Gilding the lily? Mmm...maybe. But seriously, can there be too much of a good thing when it comes to a freshly baked cake?

35th Anniversary
Hummingbird Cake

35th Anniversary Hummingbird Cake

MAKES 12 SERVINGS
HANDS-ON 30 MIN.
TOTAL 8 HOURS, 40 MIN., INCLUDING FILLING AND FROSTING

Over-ripe bananas (yellow peels splotched with brown flecks) are best for baking. You won't get the same depth of flavor or moistness without them.

- 3 cups all-purpose flour
- 2 cups sugar
- 1 tsp. baking soda
- 1 tsp. table salt
- 1 tsp. ground cinnamon
- 2 cups diced ripe bananas (about 3 medium)
- 3 large eggs, beaten
- 1 cup chopped toasted pecans
- 1 cup vegetable oil
- 1 (8-oz.) can crushed pineapple, undrained
- 2 tsp. vanilla extract
  Cream Cheese Custard Filling
  Browned Butter Frosting

1. Preheat oven to 350°. Stir together first 5 ingredients in a large bowl; stir in bananas and next 5 ingredients, stirring just until dry ingredients are moistened. Pour batter into 4 greased and floured 9-inch square or round cake pans.

2. Bake at 350° for 20 to 25 minutes or until a wooden pick inserted in center comes out clean. Cool in pans on wire racks 10 minutes; remove from pans to wire racks, and cool completely (about 1 hour).

3. Spread Cream Cheese Custard Filling between layers. Spread Browned Butter Frosting on top and sides of cake. Chill 1 hour before serving. Store in refrigerator.

35TH ANNIVERSARY HUMMINGBIRD CAKE

We updated the original with a banana pudding-inspired custard filling and browned butter frosting. As for the cake layers? They're original. We recognize perfection when we taste it.

CREAM CHEESE CUSTARD FILLING

MAKES ABOUT 2 ²/₃ CUPS
HANDS-ON 20 MIN.
TOTAL 7 HOURS, 20 MIN.

- ³/₄ cup sugar
- ¹/₃ cup all-purpose flour
- 3 large eggs
- 1¹/₂ cups milk
- 1 (8-oz.) package cream cheese, cubed and softened
- 1 Tbsp. vanilla extract

Whisk together first 2 ingredients in a heavy saucepan; whisk in eggs and milk until smooth. Cook over medium heat, whisking constantly, 8 to 10 minutes or until mixture reaches a chilled pudding-like thickness. Bring to a boil, whisking constantly; boil, whisking constantly, 1 minute. Remove from heat, and whisk in cream cheese and vanilla until cheese melts. Cool to room temperature (about 1 hour). Place plastic wrap directly on mixture (to prevent a film from forming), and chill 6 to 24 hours.

BROWNED BUTTER FROSTING

MAKES ABOUT 3 CUPS
HANDS-ON 20 MIN.
TOTAL 1 HOUR, 20 MIN.

- 1 cup butter
- 1 (16-oz.) package powdered sugar
- ¹/₄ cup milk
- 1 tsp. vanilla extract

1. Cook butter in a small heavy saucepan over medium heat, stirring constantly, 8 to 10 minutes or until butter begins to turn golden brown. Remove pan immediately from heat, and pour butter into a small bowl. Cover and chill 1 hour or until butter is cool and begins to solidify.

2. Beat butter at medium speed with an electric mixer until fluffy; gradually add sugar alternately with milk, beginning and ending with sugar. Beat at low speed until well blended after each addition. Stir in vanilla.

GET THE LOOK: Double the frosting recipe. Fit a pastry bag with a basket-weave tip; fill with frosting. Pipe basket-weave pattern around sides of cake, refilling bag as needed. Use a star tip to pipe ruffle around top of cake.

Chocolate Zucchini Cakes

MAKES 6 (5- X 3-INCH) CAKES
HANDS-ON 30 MIN.
TOTAL 2 HOURS, 45 MIN., INCLUDING FROSTING

Adding freshly grated zucchini to the batter yields luxuriously dense, moist results. The frosting sets up quickly, so prepare it after cooling the cakes. (Pictured on page 6)

- 2 cups sugar
- ¹/₂ cup butter, softened
- ¹/₂ cup canola oil
- 3 large eggs
- 2¹/₃ cups all-purpose flour
- ²/₃ cup unsweetened cocoa
- 1 tsp. baking soda
- 1 tsp. table salt
- ¹/₂ tsp. ground cinnamon
- ²/₃ cup whole buttermilk
- 2 cups grated unpeeled zucchini (about 2 medium)
- 1 (4-oz.) semisweet chocolate baking bar, finely chopped
- 2 tsp. vanilla extract
- 6 (5- x 3-inch) disposable aluminum foil loaf pans, lightly greased
  Chocolate Fudge Frosting

1. Preheat oven to 350°. Beat first 3 ingredients at medium speed with a heavy-duty electric stand mixer until light and fluffy. Add eggs, 1 at a time, beating just until blended after each addition. Sift together flour and next 4 ingredients; add to butter mixture alternately with buttermilk, beginning and ending with flour mixture. Beat at low speed just until blended after each addition. Stir zucchini and next 2 ingredients into batter until blended. Spoon batter into lightly greased loaf pans, filling two-thirds full.

2. Bake at 350° for 30 to 35 minutes or until a wooden pick inserted in center comes out clean. Cool completely in pans on wire racks (about 1 hour).

3. Prepare Chocolate Fudge Frosting. Spoon hot frosting over cooled cakes (about ¹/₄ cup each); cool completely (about 30 minutes).

Chocolate Zucchini Cakes

CHOCOLATE FUDGE FROSTING

MAKES ABOUT 2 CUPS
HANDS-ON 15 MIN.
TOTAL 15 MIN.

- ¹/₃ cup butter
- ¹/₃ cup unsweetened cocoa
- ¹/₃ cup milk
- ¹/₄ cup sour cream
- 2 tsp. vanilla extract
- 3 cups powdered sugar

Cook first 3 ingredients in a large saucepan over medium heat, stirring constantly, 3 to 4 minutes or until butter melts. Remove from heat; whisk in sour cream and vanilla until blended. Gradually add powdered sugar, beating at medium speed with an electric mixer until mixture is smooth. Use immediately.

CHOCOLATE ZUCCHINI CAKES

Spiked with a triple hit of chocolate (we're talking rich sour cream-fudge frosting here), these are definitely not your garden-variety zucchini cakes.

Green Tea-
Honeysuckle
Cake

Green Tea-Honeysuckle Cake

MAKES 12 SERVINGS

HANDS-ON 30 MIN.

TOTAL 3 HOURS, 15 MIN., INCLUDING GLAZE

Matcha, *a Japanese green tea powder, adds vivid green color and a delicate flavor. Look for it in Asian grocery stores and gourmet markets, or order online. Store tightly covered in the fridge. (It oxidizes quickly.) If you can't find* matcha, *pulverize regular green tea in a spice grinder. (Pictured on page 173)*

1	**cup butter, softened**
1/2	**cup shortening**
2 1/2	**cups sugar**
1/4	**cup honey**
6	**large eggs**
3	**cups all-purpose flour**
1	**tsp. baking powder**
1/2	**tsp. table salt**
3/4	**cup milk**
2	**tsp. matcha (green tea powder)**
	Honeysuckle Glaze

1. Preheat oven to 325°. Beat butter and shortening at medium speed with a heavy-duty electric stand mixer until creamy. Gradually add sugar, beating until light and fluffy. Add honey, beating until blended. Add eggs, 1 at a time, beating just until blended after each addition.

2. Stir together flour and next 2 ingredients. Add to butter mixture alternately with milk, beginning and ending with flour mixture. Beat at low speed just until blended after each addition. Transfer 2 1/2 cups batter to a 2-qt. bowl, and stir in matcha until blended.

3. Drop 2 scoops of plain batter into a greased and floured 10-inch (16-cup) Bundt pan, using a small cookie scoop (about 1 1/2 inches); top with 1 scoop of matcha batter. Repeat procedure around entire pan, covering bottom completely. Continue layering batters in pan as directed until all batter is used.

4. Bake at 325° for 1 hour and 5 minutes to 1 hour and 15 minutes or until a long wooden pick inserted in center comes out clean.

5. During last 10 minutes of baking, prepare Honeysuckle Glaze. Remove cake from oven, and gradually spoon 1 cup hot Honeysuckle Glaze over cake in pan, allowing glaze to soak into cake after each addition. Reserve remaining glaze. Cool cake completely in pan on a wire rack (about 1 hour and 30 minutes).

6. Remove cake from pan; spoon reserved glaze over cake.

GREEN TEA-HONEYSUCKLE CAKE

Spring-green ribbons of matcha-flavored batter and a homemade honeysuckle glaze elevate a basic vanilla butter cake to gourmet status. Bonus: It tumbles from the pan perfectly fluted and party ready.

HONEYSUCKLE GLAZE

MAKES ABOUT 1 2/3 CUPS
HANDS-ON 10 MIN.
TOTAL 10 MIN.

- 3/4 cup sugar
- 1/2 cup butter
- 1/3 cup honey
- 1/3 cup orange liqueur

Bring all ingredients and 3 Tbsp. water to a boil in a 1-qt. saucepan over medium heat, stirring often; reduce heat to medium-low, and boil, stirring constantly, 3 minutes.

Note: We tested with Grand Marnier orange liqueur.

Strawberries and Cream Cake

MAKES 12 SERVINGS
HANDS-ON 30 MIN.
TOTAL 72 HOURS, 10 MIN., INCLUDING FILLING AND FROSTING

We used 6 (8-inch) disposable aluminum foil cake pans, so we could fill all the pans at once. This way, if you bake the layers in batches, the second batch is ready to go in the oven as soon as the first is done.

- 2 cups sifted cake flour
- 2 1/2 tsp. baking powder
- 1/3 tsp. table salt
- 1 1/4 cups sugar, divided
- 1/2 cup canola oil
- 1/4 cup fresh lemon juice
- 4 large egg yolks
- 8 large egg whites
- 1 tsp. cream of tartar
  Strawberry Jam Filling
  Strawberry Frosting

1. Preheat oven to 350°. Stir together first 3 ingredients and 1 cup sugar in a large bowl. Make a well in center of mixture; add oil, next 2 ingredients, and 1/4 cup water. Beat at medium-high speed with an electric mixer 3 to 4 minutes or until smooth.

2. Beat egg whites and cream of tartar at medium-high speed until soft peaks form. Gradually add remaining 1/4 cup sugar, 1 Tbsp. at a time, beating until stiff peaks form. Gently stir one-fourth of egg white mixture into flour mixture; gently fold in remaining egg white mixture. Spoon batter into 6 greased and floured 8-inch round cake pans.

3. Bake at 350° for 12 to 15 minutes or until a wooden pick inserted in center comes out clean. Cool in pans on wire racks 10 minutes; remove from pans to wire racks, and cool completely (about 1 hour).

4. Spread filling between cake layers, leaving a 1/4-inch border around edges (about 2/3 cup between each layer). Cover cake with plastic wrap, and chill 8 to 24 hours. Spread Strawberry Frosting on top and sides of cake. Chill 2 hours before serving.

STRAWBERRY JAM FILLING

MAKES ABOUT 4 CUPS
HANDS-ON 20 MIN.
TOTAL 9 HOURS, 50 MIN.

Serve any extra filling along with the cake, or refrigerate up to 1 week and enjoy home-made jam for breakfast!

- 4 cups mashed fresh strawberries
- 2 1/2 cups sugar
- 1 (3-oz.) package strawberry-flavored gelatin

1. Stir together strawberries and sugar in a large saucepan; let stand 30 minutes.

2. Bring strawberry mixture to a boil over medium heat; boil 5 minutes. Remove from heat, and stir in gelatin until dissolved; cool completely (about 1 hour). Cover and chill 8 hours.

STRAWBERRY FROSTING

MAKES ABOUT 3 1/2 CUPS
HANDS-ON 10 MIN.
TOTAL 30 MIN.

For maximum volume and a silky smooth texture, make sure the whipping cream and sour cream are ice cold when blended.

- 1 Tbsp. strawberry-flavored gelatin
- 2 Tbsp. boiling water
- 1 cup whipping cream
- 1/4 cup sugar
- 1 (8-oz.) container sour cream

1. Stir together first 2 ingredients in a small bowl; cool completely (about 20 minutes).

2. Beat whipping cream and gelatin mixture at high speed with an electric mixer until foamy; gradually add sugar, beating until soft peaks form. Stir in sour cream, 1/4 cup at a time, stirring just until blended after each addition.

STRAWBERRIES AND CREAM CAKE

Imagine a multi-layered fusion of fresh strawberry pie and feather-light sponge cake. Unlike the original strawberry cake-mix classic, this one's made from scratch.

Sweet Talk

BAKING A BEAUTIFUL CAKE IS, WELL, EASY AS PIE. HERE ARE A FEW TIPS AND TRICKS TO ENSURE YOUR LAYERS STACK UP TO PERFECTION.

MEASURE ACCURATELY. Extra sugar or leavening will cause a cake to fall; too much flour makes it dry.

GREASE PANS with solid vegetable shortening. Margarines with a high liquid-to-fat ratio and butter (which is about 20 percent water) can cause layers to stick to the pan.

BAKE AND FREEZE completely cool cake layers in zip-top plastic freezer bags up to 1 month before assembling and frosting, if desired.

MAKE AND CHILL pastry cream or fruit fillings up to 1 day ahead. For a firmly set filling, don't tempt fate and trim the required chill time.

PIPE A RING of frosting just inside the top edge of each cake layer to hold the filling and prevent bulging. Add filling, and spread to edge of ring.

WRAP CAKES in plastic wrap after filling, and chill 8 to 24 hours to allow the layers to settle before spreading the frosting.

Boiling Point

▶ Roll up your sleeves and crank the music for the South's ultimate springtime feast. Chef Tim Byres celebrates crawfish season with a Texas twist.

In the South,

it's not unusual for a party to begin with a very large pot and a wood fire. We're funny that way. Southerners own the art of outdoor cooking, and you'd be hard-pressed to find a livelier example than a crawfish boil. (FYI, if you prefer to use large, sweet Gulf shrimp instead, no one will complain.) We love a rowdy boil because it's as much an occasion as a meal. The fragrant pot and tumble of ingredients beckon us outside around a table, elbow-to-elbow with friends and fingers dusted with red spice. It's a juicy, loud, messy, and delicious seasonal pleasure—mudbugs are at their best right now. Tim Byres, one of the smartest young chefs around, gets it. His restaurants, SMOKE and Chicken Scratch (part of a large alfresco space with live music, room for kids to play, and a garden), are devoted to cooking over fire, from-scratch food, and community. We love the funky, rustic edge he's brought to shiny Dallas. And we love his Texas-spin on the boil even more.

The Crawfish Boil

MAKES 10 TO 12 SERVINGS
HANDS-ON 20 MIN.
TOTAL 2 HOURS, 35 MIN.,
INCLUDING SAUCE AND SPICE MIX

Chef Tim Byres' boil works great with shrimp too. It's a one-pot meal in itself with spiced potatoes, sausage, and fresh corn, but no one will complain if you also serve a bowl of bracing slaw, bean salad, pitchers of margaritas, and a mile-high Tequila-Key Lime Meringue Pie (recipes, pages 96-97). Cook the crawfish on the stovetop in two batches for ease. Or, if you have a 10-gal. pot and propane cooker (or wood fire), boil the crawfish outside all in one go. To do so, simply double the first five ingredients and water.

- 3 celery ribs, cut into 2-inch pieces
- 1/2 lemon, cut into 1/8-inch-thick slices
- 1/2 yellow onion, coarsely chopped
- 1 1/2 cups Crawfish Spice Mix
  Tejano Red Sauce, divided
- 5 1/2 lb. red new potatoes (about 30)
- 6 (1/4-lb.) andouille sausage links
- 6 ears fresh corn, cut in half
- 20 lb. live fresh crawfish, purged (see Crawfish Connection, below, right)*

1. Pour 3 1/4 gal. water into a 7 1/2-gal. heavy stockpot; add celery, lemon, onion, spice mix, and 1 1/2 cups red sauce. Bring to a boil; add potatoes. Boil 20 minutes or until potatoes can be pierced easily with a knife. Transfer potatoes to a large, clean cooler to keep warm. Add sausage to pot; boil 5 minutes. Add corn; boil 5 minutes. Transfer sausage and corn to cooler.

2. Add half of crawfish to stockpot; boil 8 to 10 minutes or until crawfish tails curl. Transfer crawfish to a large bowl; toss with desired amount of Tejano Red Sauce. Transfer to cooler. Repeat boiling procedure with remaining crawfish. Serve with corn, sausage, and potatoes.

***6 to** 8 lb. unpeeled, large raw shrimp may be substituted. Boil 3 minutes or just until shrimp turn pink.

HANDS-ON: SHED THE SHELL

1. Twist and snap head away from tail.

2. Peel away shell from widest part of tail.

3. Hold tip of tail; gently pull out tender meat.

CRAWFISH SPICE MIX

MAKES ABOUT 3 CUPS
HANDS-ON 10 MIN.
TOTAL 10 MIN.

Dill, marjoram, and coriander add an aromatic twist to the traditional Cajun seasoning. Use this mix for any kind of seafood boil.

- 3/4 cup mustard seeds
- 3/4 cup coriander seeds
- 1/2 cup kosher salt
- 1/4 cup celery seeds
- 1/4 cup dried marjoram
- 1/4 cup dill seeds
- 2 Tbsp. sugar
- 1 Tbsp. whole allspice
- 1 Tbsp. ground red pepper
- 1 tsp. whole cloves
- 20 bay leaves, crushed

Stir together all ingredients, and store in an airtight container up to 2 months.

TEJANO RED SAUCE

MAKES 5 CUPS
HANDS-ON 20 MIN.
TOTAL 1 HOUR, 5 MIN.

This versatile sauce takes its acidity from tomatillos, not vinegar, and its earthy spice from guajillo chiles, which can be found in many supermarkets and Latin groceries. Toast the chiles first to coax out their flavor. Use the sauce to spice up the crawfish boil, or drizzle it on tacos, grilled chicken, or eggs.

- 2 lb. tomatillos, husks removed
- 4 oz. dried guajillo chiles
- 16 garlic cloves
- 4 tsp. olive oil
- 2 1/2 tsp. salt

1. Preheat oven to 500°. Cut tomatillos in half or quarters, depending on size.

2. Spread chiles in a single layer on a baking sheet; toast 1 to 2 minutes or until chiles puff and become fragrant. (Chiles burn quickly, so keep a watchful eye.) Cut chiles open with kitchen shears; remove seeds. Cut off stems.

3. Sauté garlic in hot oil in a large saucepan over medium-high heat 2 minutes or until garlic begins to brown. Add tomatillos, salt, and 1 qt. water. Bring to a boil, and cook, stirring often, 4 minutes. Add chiles, and cook, stirring occasionally, 5 to 10 minutes or until tomatillos are soft and peppers have rehydrated. Cool 10 minutes.

4. Purée mixture, in batches, in a blender or food processor. Pour through a fine wiremesh strainer into a container, discarding solids. Cool completely. Refrigerate in an airtight container up to 4 days.

CRAWFISH CONNECTION: ORDER, CLEAN, BOIL

Order direct from *lacrawfish.com* or *cajungrocer.com*, and figure on 2 lb. live crawfish per person. To purge crawfish of mud and debris, place them in a 48-qt. cooler with a pourable spout. Add cold water and 2 cups salt. Gently stir crawfish; let stand 3 minutes. Open spout, tilt cooler, and rinse crawfish with a steady stream of cold water until water runs clear.

Woodshed
Margarita

Woodshed Margarita

MAKES 5 1/2 CUPS
HANDS-ON 10 MIN.
TOTAL 50 MIN., NOT INCLUDING TEQUILA

- 1 cup sugar
- 2 1/2 cups Cedar-Infused Tequila or any white, silver, or gold tequila
- 1 1/4 cups fresh lime juice
- 1/2 cup orange liqueur (such as Cointreau)
  Limes, thinly sliced

1. Bring sugar and 1 cup water to a boil over medium-high heat; boil, stirring occasionally, 5 minutes or until sugar dissolves. Remove from heat; cool to room temperature (about 30 minutes). Refrigerate in an airtight container up to 1 week.

2. Stir together sugar mixture, tequila, lime juice, and orange liqueur in a pitcher. Serve over ice with lime slices.

CEDAR-INFUSED TEQUILA Place 6 **cedar grilling papers**, broken into pieces, in a 1-qt. jar. Pour in 1 (750-milliliter) bottle **white or gold tequila**. Cover and let stand at room temperature 2 to 4 days. (The longer it sits, the more intense the cedar flavor.) Pour tequila through a fine wire-mesh strainer lined with a **coffee filter or cheesecloth** into a clean 1-qt. jar. Refrigerate, covered, up to 3 months. **MAKES** about 3 cups

Blue Cheese Coleslaw

MAKES 9 CUPS
HANDS-ON 35 MIN.
TOTAL 35 MIN.

Stir in the red cabbage just before serving so the slaw doesn't turn pink.

- 3/4 cup sour cream
- 2 Tbsp. white vinegar
- 1 Tbsp. green hot sauce
- 1 tsp. kosher salt
- 1/2 tsp. celery seeds
- 3/4 cup crumbled blue cheese
- 1/2 large head green cabbage, shredded
- 1 medium carrot, shredded
- 4 thinly sliced green onions
- 1 1/2 cups shredded red cabbage

Whisk together first 5 ingredients and 1/2 cup blue cheese in a very large bowl. Add green cabbage, carrot, and half of green onions; toss to coat. Just before serving, transfer to a serving bowl, and stir in red cabbage. Sprinkle with remaining blue cheese and green onions.

Bean-Jicama Salad

MAKES 10 TO 12 SERVINGS
HANDS-ON 30 MIN.
TOTAL 13 HOURS, 35 MIN.

The key to cooking tender beans with the skins intact? A long soak and gentle simmer.

- 2 lb. dried pinto beans
- 2 dried ancho chile peppers
- 1 bunch fresh oregano
  Kitchen string
- 2 Tbsp. ground cumin
- 1 1/2 qt. hot water
- 1 large yellow onion, diced
- 3 to 5 large jalapeño peppers, seeded and diced (about 3/4 cup)
- 1/2 cup minced garlic (15 to 20 cloves)
- 3 Tbsp. olive oil
- 8 green onions, sliced
- 3/4 cup sherry vinegar
- 1/4 cup extra virgin olive oil
- 2 Tbsp. plus 1 tsp. kosher salt, divided
- 1 medium jicama (about 1 lb.), peeled and cut into thin strips
- 1/2 cup chopped fresh cilantro
- 1/3 cup fresh lime juice

1. Rinse and sort beans according to package directions. Place in a large Dutch oven; add water to 3 inches above beans. Cover and let soak 8 hours. Drain.

2. Preheat oven to 500°. Spread chiles in a single layer on a baking sheet; toast 1 to 2 minutes or until chiles puff and become fragrant. Cut chiles open with kitchen shears; remove seeds. Cut off stems.

3. Tie oregano bunch with kitchen string. Return beans to Dutch oven; add oregano, chiles, cumin, and 1 1/2 qt. hot water. Bring to a boil over high heat. Cover, reduce heat to low, and simmer, stirring occasionally, 2 to 2 1/2 hours or until beans are tender, adding more water as needed.

4. Remove oregano and chiles from bean mixture; discard. Spoon beans in a single layer on a baking sheet; cool completely (about 40 minutes). Cover and chill 3 hours.

5. Sauté onion, jalapeños, and garlic in 3 Tbsp. hot oil in a large skillet over medium-high heat 8 to 10 minutes or until onion is tender and slightly charred.

6. Toss together beans, sautéed vegetables, green onions, vinegar, 1/4 cup oil, and 2 Tbsp. kosher salt in a large bowl.

7. Toss together jicama, cilantro, lime juice, and remaining 1 tsp. salt. Serve over bean salad.

Tequila-Key Lime Meringue Pie

MAKES 10 TO 12 SERVINGS
HANDS-ON 30 MIN.
TOTAL 4 HOURS, 10 MIN.

1 1/2 cups graham cracker crumbs
6 Tbsp. melted butter
1/3 cup sugar
1 tsp. ground cinnamon
1/4 tsp. kosher salt
8 large egg yolks
2 (14-oz.) cans sweetened condensed milk
3/4 cup Key lime juice
2 Tbsp. lime zest
1 Tbsp. tequila
3 Tbsp. cold water
1 1/2 Tbsp. cornstarch
2/3 cup boiling water
4 large egg whites
1 1/2 tsp. cream of tartar
1 cup sugar
1 1/2 tsp. vanilla extract
1/8 tsp. kosher salt

1. Preheat oven to 350°. Stir together first 5 ingredients; firmly press mixture on bottom and up sides of a lightly greased 9 1/2-inch deep-dish pie plate. Bake 15 minutes or until crust is lightly browned. Transfer to a wire rack, and cool completely (about 30 minutes).

2. Whisk together egg yolks and next 4 ingredients in a large bowl; pour mixture into cooled crust. Bake at 350° for 25 minutes or until set. Cool completely on a wire rack (about 1 hour).

3. Preheat oven to 375°. Whisk 3 Tbsp. cold water into cornstarch in a 1-qt. saucepan; whisk in 2/3 cup boiling water. Cook over medium heat, whisking constantly, 1 minute or until a thick gel forms. Remove from heat; cool completely (about 30 minutes).

4. Beat 4 egg whites and cream of tartar at medium-high speed with a heavy-duty electric stand mixer, using whisk attachment, until foamy. Gradually add 1 cup sugar; beat until glossy, stiff peaks form. Beat in vanilla and salt. Slowly beat in cornstarch mixture. Beat 3 minutes.

5. Spread meringue over cooled pie, and bake at 375° for 15 minutes or until meringue is golden brown. Transfer to wire rack, and cool completely (about 45 minutes). Serve at room temperature, or cover and chill 8 to 24 hours.

Tequila-Key Lime
Meringue Pie

All recipes adapted from *Smoke: New Firewood Cooking*© by Tim Byres. Published by Rizzoli.

Spring Shower Recipes

▶ A taste of who and what got the highest raves in the *Southern Living* Test Kitchen.

RECIPE *Winner* **SWAP**

Serve this versatile pasta as a pretty side at a spring luncheon or as a quick main course on busy weeknights.

From the Kitchen of
MARIAN COOPER CAIRNS
BIRMINGHAM, AL

"Add cooked shrimp for a heartier main, or white beans for a vegetarian option."

ZUCCHINI-MINT PASTA

Melt 2 Tbsp. **butter** with 2 Tbsp. **olive oil** in a large nonstick skillet over medium-high heat; add 2 **shallots**, diced, and sauté 2 minutes. Add 1 1/2 lb. small **zucchini**, sliced; sauté 5 minutes or until zucchini is tender. Stir in 1 minced **garlic clove**, and cook 1 minute. Remove from heat; stir in 2 Tbsp. **fresh lemon juice**, 2 tsp. **lemon zest**, 1 tsp. **kosher salt**, and 1/2 tsp. **freshly ground black pepper**. Toss in 1 (9-oz.) package **refrigerated fettuccine pasta**, cooked, or 1 (8.8-oz.) package **pappardelle pasta**, cooked; 1/2 cup thinly sliced **fresh mint**; 1/2 cup chopped **toasted walnuts**; and 1/4 cup **freshly grated Parmesan cheese**. Sprinkle with 4 oz. **crumbled feta cheese** just before serving. **MAKES** 4 to 6 main-dish or 6 to 8 side-dish servings

---

From the Kitchen of
VICKIE MOSES PERKINS
DERIDDER, LA

"Serve with a slotted spoon."

CREAMY, SPICY CUCUMBERS

Peel, seed, and slice 4 large **cucumbers**. Stir together 1 cup **mayonnaise**, 1/4 cup **white vinegar**, 1/4 cup **evaporated milk**, 3 Tbsp. **sugar**, 1 tsp. **dried parsley flakes**, 2 tsp. **hot sauce**, 1/2 tsp. **table salt**, 1/2 tsp. **garlic powder**, and 1/2 tsp. **pepper**. Toss in cucumbers and 1 bunch **green onions**, sliced. Chill 8 to 24 hours. **MAKES** 6 cups

---

From the Kitchen of
BRYAN WELLS
CHARLOTTE, NC

"Add club soda if you wish."

STRAWBERRY-LIME GREEN TEA COOLER

Pour 3 cups **boiling water** over 2 regular-size **green tea bags**; cover and steep 5 minutes. Discard tea bags. Stir in 1 cup **cold water**. Cool 30 minutes. Process 1 (16-oz.) container **fresh strawberries, hulled**; 1 (12-oz.) can **frozen limeade concentrate**, thawed; and 1/4 cup **honey** in a blender until smooth. Pour into a pitcher. Stir in tea; serve on ice. **MAKES** 8 cups

---

From the Kitchen of
CRYSTAL KINNARD
MABLETON, GA

"Blanch peas in boiling salted water until crisp-tender. Then plunge into ice water."

THREE-PEA SALAD

Whisk together 2 Tbsp. **fresh lemon juice**; 1 tsp. **Dijon mustard**; 2 **garlic cloves**, pressed; 1/2 tsp. **table salt**; 1/2 tsp. **sugar**; and 1/2 tsp. **freshly ground black pepper**. Whisk in 1/4 cup **olive oil** until smooth. Add 2 cups each blanched **fresh sweet peas**, trimmed **snow peas**, and trimmed **sugar snap peas**. Add 1 1/2 cups thinly sliced **radishes**. Toss gently to coat. **MAKES** 8 servings

May

Sweet on Vidalias

▶ Nothing says spring quite like a Georgia Vidalia. Hand-planted in the rich, loamy soil of rain-washed fields, these are the stuff only Southern dreams (and crispy cornmeal-crusted onion rings) are made of. The season is fleeting, so savor the bounty now.

Sweet Onion Stack

Sweet Onion Stacks

MAKES 4 SERVINGS
HANDS-ON 1 HOUR, 15 MIN.
TOTAL 1 HOUR, 30 MIN.

Salty strips of bacon and a tart Champagne vinaigrette play against the layered richness of sweet char-grilled onions and creamy goat cheese. Feel free to mix and match the stacks. (Pictured on page 178)

1/2	cup butter
6	fresh thyme sprigs
1/3	cup bourbon
4	(8-oz.) sweet onions
1/4	cup Champagne vinegar
1	tsp. grated sweet onion
1/2	tsp. kosher salt
1/2	tsp. chopped fresh thyme
1/2	tsp. freshly ground black pepper
1/2	tsp. Dijon mustard
1/3	cup olive oil
12	to 16 tomato slices
1/2	(4-oz.) package goat cheese, softened
16	fresh basil leaves
4	thick bacon slices, cooked and halved
4	cups firmly packed mixed salad greens with fresh herbs

1. Preheat grill to 300° to 350° (medium) heat. Cook first 3 ingredients in a 2-qt. heavy saucepan over medium heat, stirring constantly, 2 minutes.

2. Cut each onion crosswise into 3 slices. Grill onion slices, covered with grill lid, 32 minutes, turning every 4 minutes and basting with bourbon mixture with each turn during last half of grill time. Remove from grill, wrap in aluminum foil, and let stand 10 minutes.

3. Meanwhile, whisk together vinegar and next 5 ingredients. Add oil in a slow, steady stream, whisking constantly until smooth. Whisk before serving.

4. Sprinkle tomato slices with salt and pepper to taste. Place 1 tomato slice (or stack 2) on each of 4 plates. Top each with 1 onion slice, and spread with 1 1/2 tsp. goat cheese. Top each stack with 2 basil leaves and 1 bacon piece. Repeat layers once. Top with remaining onions. Spoon 1 Tbsp. vinaigrette over each stack.

5. Toss greens with 3 Tbsp. vinaigrette, and serve immediately with Sweet Onion Stacks and remaining vinaigrette.

Grilled Sweet Onion-and-Mango Chutney

MAKES 6 TO 8 SERVINGS
HANDS-ON 40 MIN.
TOTAL 50 MIN.

This is our new go-to topping for anything grilled, from turkey burgers to pork tenderloin. Try swapping the mango for sliced peaches, plums, or nectarines.

- 2 large sweet onions, cut into 1/2-inch slices
- 2 mangoes, peeled and cut into 1/2-inch slices
- 2 Tbsp. olive oil
- 1/2 cup white wine vinegar
- 1/3 cup firmly packed light brown sugar
- 2 Tbsp. minced fresh ginger
- 1 tsp. lime zest
- 1/2 tsp. table salt
- 1 jalapeño pepper, seeded and minced
- 1/3 cup chopped fresh cilantro
- 2 Tbsp. fresh lime juice

1. Preheat grill to 300° to 350° (medium) heat. Brush both sides of onion and mangoes with olive oil. Grill onions, covered with grill lid, 5 to 6 minutes on each side until softened and grill marks appear. At same time, grill mangoes 2 to 3 minutes on each side or until softened and grill marks appear. Remove from grill; cover and let stand 15 minutes.

2. Meanwhile, bring vinegar and next 4 ingredients to a boil in a small saucepan over medium-high heat. Reduce heat to low, and simmer 5 minutes. Add jalapeño, and simmer 5 minutes. Remove from heat; transfer to a bowl.

3. Chop onion and mangoes, and stir into vinegar mixture. Stir in cilantro and lime juice. Serve chutney warm or at room temperature.

Caramelized Onion and Swiss Popovers

MAKES 8 SERVINGS
HANDS-ON 10 MIN.
TOTAL 1 HOUR, 35 MIN., INCLUDING ONIONS

A hot pan and oven temp get popovers off to a high-rising start; lowering the temp midway through baking helps prevent an out-of-the-oven collapse.

- 1 cup all-purpose flour
- 1 cup 2% reduced-fat milk, at room temperature
- 3 large eggs, at room temperature
- 2 Tbsp. butter, melted
- 3/4 tsp. table salt
- 1/4 cup (1 oz.) freshly shredded Swiss cheese
- 1/4 cup Caramelized Sweet Onions, chopped (recipe at right)
- 1 Tbsp. chopped fresh chives
- 4 tsp. canola oil

1. Preheat oven to 425°. Heat a 12-cup muffin pan in oven 10 minutes.

2. Meanwhile, process first 5 ingredients in a blender or food processor 20 to 30 seconds or until smooth. Stir in cheese and next 2 ingredients.

3. Remove pan from oven; pour 1/2 tsp. oil into each of 8 muffin cups, filling center 6 cups and middle cup on each end. Heat in oven 5 minutes. Remove from oven. Divide batter among oiled muffin cups; return to oven immediately.

4. Bake 15 to 20 minutes or until puffed and lightly browned around edges. Reduce oven temperature to 350°; bake 10 minutes or until tops are golden brown.

5. Transfer to a wire rack; cool 3 to 4 minutes before serving.

CARAMELIZED SWEET ONIONS

MAKES ABOUT 3 CUPS
HANDS-ON 45 MIN.
TOTAL 45 MIN.

The trick: Cook the onions slowly, allowing the natural sugars to caramelize. Make several batches, and store in freezer.

- 12 cups sliced sweet onions (about 2 1/2 lb.)
- 1 tsp. table salt

Heat a large nonstick skillet over medium heat. Add sweet onions, and cook, stirring often, 30 minutes or until onions are caramel colored, sprinkling with salt halfway through.

Note: Store in refrigerator in an airtight container or zip-top plastic freezer bag up to 1 week, or freeze up to 2 months.

Caramelized Sweet Onion Tarte Tatin

MAKES 6 SERVINGS
HANDS-ON 25 MIN.
TOTAL 55 MIN.

For maximum flavor, use a high-quality brand of frozen puff pastry dough that tastes of butter and gives rise to crisp, flaky layers. (See "Note" below.) (Pictured on page 8)

- 3 Tbsp. butter
- 1 Tbsp. sugar
- 8 small sweet onions (about 1 1/2 lb.), halved crosswise
- 1 tsp. kosher salt
- 2 Tbsp. balsamic vinegar
- 1 frozen puff pastry sheet, thawed
  Garnishes: fresh thyme sprigs, freshly ground black pepper

1. Preheat oven to 375°. Melt butter in a 12-inch ovenproof skillet over medium-low heat; swirl to coat bottom. Sprinkle with sugar.

2. Place 12 to 14 onion halves in skillet, cut sides down, with sides touching. Cut remaining onion halves into quarters, and place, cut sides down, in gaps between onions in skillet.

3. Cover and cook onions 10 minutes, adding salt and 1 Tbsp. water halfway through. Add vinegar; cover and cook 3 to 5 minutes or until onions are caramelized. Remove from heat.

4. Roll pastry sheet into a 12-inch square on a lightly floured surface; cut into a 12-inch round. Place pastry round over onions in skillet.

5. Bake at 375° for 30 minutes or until golden. Remove from oven, and immediately invert onto a serving plate.

Note: We tested with Dufour Pastry Kitchens Classic Puff Pastry.

Crispy Fried Sweet Onion Rings

MAKES 6 SERVINGS
HANDS-ON 40 MIN.
TOTAL 2 HOURS, 40 MIN.

Store any leftover dredging mixture (from Step 3) in an airtight container in refrigerator up to 2 weeks. Make sure your oil is hot enough, and that it comes back up to temp, before adding the second batch of onions.

- 2 large sweet onions, cut into 3/8-inch-thick slices
- 3 cups buttermilk
  Vegetable oil
- 2 cups all-purpose flour
- 1 cup plain yellow cornmeal
- 2 tsp. table salt
- 1/2 tsp. ground red pepper

1. Separate onion slices into rings, and place in a 9-inch square baking dish. Pour buttermilk over onion rings. Cover and chill 2 to 24 hours.

2. Pour oil to depth of 2 inches into a Dutch oven; heat to 360°.

3. Stir together flour and next 3 ingredients in a shallow dish. Dredge onion rings in flour mixture, and place on a baking sheet. Discard buttermilk.

4. Fry onion rings, in batches, 2 minutes or until golden brown, turning once. Drain on paper towels.

5. Serve onion rings immediately, or keep warm in a 200° oven until ready to serve.

Caramelized Onion-Herb Butter

MAKES ABOUT 1 1/4 CUPS
HANDS-ON 10 MIN.
TOTAL 10 MIN., NOT INCLUDING ONIONS

Stir together 1 cup **butter**, softened; 1/4 cup minced **Caramelized Sweet Onions** (see page 101); 1 Tbsp. chopped **fresh chives**; 1 Tbsp. chopped **fresh flat-leaf parsley**; 1 **garlic clove**, minced; 1 tsp. **lemon zest**; and 1/8 tsp. each **kosher salt** and **freshly ground black pepper**.

Caramelized Sweet
Onion Tarte Tatin

Bread-and-Butter
Pickled Onions

MAKES 3 PT.
HANDS-ON 20 MIN.
TOTAL 10 HOURS, 10 MIN.

Dialing back the sugar in the versatile brine lets the natural sweetness of the onions and vegetables shine in these quick and easy refrigerator pickles.

- 1 lb. sweet onions, halved and cut into ¼-inch-thick slices
- 1 lb. Kirby cucumbers, cut into ¼-inch-thick slices
- 2 garlic cloves, thinly sliced
- 1 fresh red chile pepper, halved, seeded, and thinly sliced
- 2 Tbsp. kosher salt
- 2 cups apple cider vinegar
- 1½ cups sugar
- 1 tsp. mustard seeds
- ½ tsp. ground turmeric

1. Toss together first 5 ingredients in a large bowl. Cover and let stand 1 hour. Transfer to a colander; drain 20 minutes. Pack into 3 (1-pt.) jars, filling to ½ inch from top.

2. Bring vinegar and next 3 ingredients to a boil in a small saucepan over medium-high heat; boil, stirring constantly, 1 minute or until sugar dissolves. Let stand 5 minutes.

3. Pour vinegar mixture over onion mixture in jars, filling to ½ inch from top. Cool completely (about 20 minutes). Cover with lids, and chill 8 hours before serving. Store in refrigerator up to 2 weeks.

BREAD-AND-BUTTER PICKLED ONIONS WITH GREEN TOMATOES Prepare recipe as directed, substituting green tomatoes, cut into ½-inch pieces, for cucumbers.

BREAD-AND-BUTTER PICKLED ONIONS WITH RADISHES Prepare recipe as directed, substituting radishes, cut into ¼-inch slices, for cucumbers; white vinegar for cider vinegar; and celery seeds for turmeric. Add 2 fresh tarragon sprigs to each jar just before covering.

BREAD-AND-BUTTER PICKLED ONIONS WITH CARROTS Prepare recipe as directed, substituting carrots, cut into ¼-inch-thick slices, for cucumbers; a serrano pepper for red chile pepper; and cumin seeds for mustard seeds.

Bread-and-Butter
Pickled Onions

SWITCHING SIDES

CREAMY ONION PUREE

Move over potatoes. This is a mash made in heaven.

Onion Puree

MAKES 4 SERVINGS

A quick spin in the processor transforms long-simmered onions into a silken puree.

Tie 4 **fresh thyme sprigs** with kitchen string. Melt 3 Tbsp. **butter** in a large skillet over medium-high heat; add 1 Tbsp. **olive oil**; 6 large **sweet onions**, thinly sliced; and thyme sprigs, stirring to coat. Sprinkle with 1½ tsp. **kosher salt,** and reduce heat to medium-low. Cover and cook, stirring occasionally, 1 hour or until onions are tender. Discard thyme sprigs. Drain onions, using a fine wire-mesh strainer and reserving liquid for another use. Process onions in a food processor 30 to 60 seconds or until smooth. Serve immediately.

Preserve the Season's Harvest

Four quick ways to freeze the fresh-picked flavor of summer berries

THERE'S NOTHING quite as soul-crushing as eating an out-of-season berry. That's why we capture the cobbler-sweet taste of the locally grown jewels by freezing them at their peak. Berries frozen with sugar better retain their color and texture, while those frozen without are perfect for adding to quick breads or cakes. Just before freezing, gently wash berries in cool water, and pat them dry with paper towels. Remove and discard stems, leaves, and any under-ripe or damaged fruit. Pick one of the methods below, or mix and match. No matter how you freeze 'em, we guarantee you'll never be tempted to buy bland again.

❶ SLICED, CRUSHED, OR PUREED BERRIES

Add ¹/₃ to ³/₄ cup sugar per quart of berries; gently stir until sugar dissolves. Spoon into plastic freezer jars, leaving ¹/₂-inch headspace. Wipe jar rims clean; secure lids. Freeze up to 12 months.

BEST USES: Top off short-cakes, stir into yogurt, layer in an ice-cream parfait.

❷ DRY SUGAR PACK

Pat 1 quart of berries just until damp. Gently toss with ¹/₂ to ³/₄ cup sugar. Place in a single layer on a jelly-roll pan; freeze until firm. Pack into plastic freezer containers; cover and seal. Freeze up to 12 months.

BEST USES: Add frozen berries to cobblers or pies, stir into pancake batter.

❸ QUICK FREEZE

Place berries in a single layer on a jelly-roll pan; freeze until firm. Pack into zip-top plastic freezer bags, leaving 1-inch headspace. Squeeze out excess air; seal and freeze up to 8 months.

BEST USES: Add frozen berries to muffin, cake, or quick bread batter; spoon over oatmeal or cereal.

❹ SYRUP PACK

Stir together 1 quart cold water and 2 ¹/₂ cups sugar until sugar dissolves. Pack berries in widemouth canning jars; cover with syrup, leaving ¹/₂-inch headspace. Wipe jar rims clean; secure lids. Freeze up to 12 months.

BEST USES: Thaw in fridge; drain, reserving syrup, and use like fresh berries.

Make Your Own Extract

▶ Easy homemade vanilla extract is the gift that keeps on giving. Choose bourbon or vodka as your base, then let the vanilla bean do the work. The longer it steeps, the better the flavor

TAKE IT
Look for those gift-worthy corked Boston jars ($2.09) at *specialtybottle.com*

Bottomless Vanilla Extract

MAKES 3 (½-PT.) JARS
HANDS-ON 15 MIN.
TOTAL 45 MIN., PLUS AT LEAST 1 WEEK FOR STANDING

Homemade extract is something every baker should have. It's more flavorful and generally less expensive than store-bought versions. Cooking speeds up the infusion, but you can omit the process by letting the mixture stand an extra week. Then use it in frostings and baked goods.

- 3 **vanilla beans**
- 3 **cups bourbon or vodka**

1. Split 1 vanilla bean, and scrape seeds into a clean ½-pt. jar. If desired, cut bean in half crosswise. Place in jar. Repeat procedure with remaining beans and 2 (½-pt.) jars.

2. Cook bourbon in a large saucepan over medium heat 5 minutes. (Do not cook longer than 5 minutes or it can overheat and ignite.) Pour 1 cup bourbon into each jar. Cool mixture to room temperature (about 30 minutes).

3. Cover jars tightly, and let stand at room temperature 1 to 2 weeks before using, shaking jars once a day. (For a cleaner look, pour liquid through a fine wire-mesh strainer into clean bottles with tight-fitting lids; discard solids.) Store in a cool, dark place up to 1 year.

Note: When cooking alcohol, be sure to use a large saucepan to contain vapors. Do not heat longer than 5 minutes—the vapors can ignite. The vodka version has the purest vanilla flavor. Though both extracts turn a rich brown after 1 week, the bourbon version is slightly darker.

DOWNLOAD OUR LABELS!
Get our gift tags: southernliving.com/food-gift

homemade

·BOURBON·
VANILLA EXTRACT

Create a Fresh Combo

▶ Mix and match any of these soups, salads, and sandwiches for a hearty (not heavy!) meal. Save the leftovers—tonight's supper is tomorrow's bagged lunch

Yellow Squash and Curry Stew with Basil & Parsley

Carrot, Apple, and Ginger Soup with Chives

Vegetable Soup with Basil Pesto

3 EASY SOUPS

 45 MIN | ## Yellow Squash and Curry Stew

MAKES 4 SERVINGS

Have a windfall of yellow squash? This makes good use of summer's bounty. Roasting the squash in the oven concentrates flavor; curry powder gives it a sweet and fragrant kick. (Pictured on page 177)

- 2 lb. yellow squash, coarsely chopped
- 1 medium-size sweet onion, coarsely chopped
- 1 pt. grape tomatoes
- 3 garlic cloves, thinly sliced
- 2 Tbsp. olive oil
- 2 tsp. curry powder
- 1/4 tsp. dried crushed red pepper
- 1 1/2 tsp. kosher salt, divided
- 3 cups organic vegetable or chicken broth, divided
- 2 Tbsp. butter
- 1 Tbsp. fresh lime juice
- 1/2 cup torn fresh basil
- 1/4 cup loosely packed fresh flat-leaf parsley leaves

1. Preheat oven to 450°. Toss together first 7 ingredients and 1 tsp. salt. Arrange in a single layer in a 15- x 10-inch jelly-roll pan.

2. Bake at 450° for 30 to 35 minutes or until vegetables are tender and lightly browned, stirring halfway through. Remove from oven; process 2 cups squash mixture and 1 cup broth in a blender or food processor until smooth. Divide remaining squash mixture among 4 shallow soup bowls.

3. Stir together vegetable puree and remaining 2 cups broth in a 3-qt. saucepan; bring to a boil over medium heat, stirring occasionally. Remove from heat; whisk in butter, lime juice, and remaining 1/2 tsp. salt.

4. Spoon broth mixture over squash mixture in bowls. Sprinkle with fresh herbs, and serve immediately.

Carrot, Apple, and Ginger Soup

MAKES 8 SERVINGS

To save time peeling and chopping, a 1-lb. package of baby carrots may be substituted. (Pictured on page 177)

- 2   shallots, chopped
- 2   Tbsp. olive oil
- 1   lb. carrots, chopped
- 1   Gala apple, peeled and chopped
- 2 to 3 tsp. minced fresh ginger
- 6   cups organic vegetable broth
- 1   tsp. orange zest
- 1   tsp. kosher salt
- 2   tsp. fresh lime juice
- ¹/₂   tsp. freshly ground black pepper
  Garnishes: chopped fresh chives, freshly ground black pepper

1. Sauté shallots in hot oil in a large Dutch oven over medium heat 2 to 3 minutes or until tender. Stir in carrots and apple; cook, stirring often, 2 to 4 minutes or until apple is tender. Add ginger, and cook, stirring constantly, 1 minute. Stir in broth and zest; bring to a boil over medium-high heat. Cover, reduce heat to medium-low, and simmer, stirring occasionally, 30 minutes or until carrots are tender. Stir in salt, lime juice, and pepper.

2. Remove from heat. Process mixture with a handheld blender until smooth.

OUR FAVORITE COMBOS

Try a few of our favorite supper pairings, or customize your own weeknight combos.

1. Carrot, Apple, and Ginger Soup; Asian Chicken Salad Wraps; Chopped Salad

2. Vegetable Soup with Basil Pesto, Biscuit BLTs, Spinach and Avocado Salad

3. Yellow Squash and Curry Stew, Avocado and Sprout Sandwiches, Fruit Salad

4. Carrot, Apple, and Ginger Soup; Chopped Salad; Grilled Cheese & Apple Sandwiches

---

Vegetable Soup with Basil Pesto

MAKES ABOUT 10 CUPS

Our chunky take on pistou is chock-full of veggies, beans, and pasta. Serve it with lemon wedges. (Pictured on page 177)

- 2   medium carrots, chopped
- 2   celery ribs, chopped
- 1   large sweet onion, chopped
- 4   garlic cloves, minced
- 1   tsp. minced fresh thyme
- 1   Tbsp. olive oil
- 2   (32-oz.) containers organic vegetable broth
- 2   plum tomatoes, seeded and chopped
- 1   medium zucchini, chopped
- 1¹/₄   tsp. kosher salt
- ¹/₂   tsp. freshly ground black pepper
- 1   (15-oz.) can cannellini beans, drained and rinsed
- ¹/₂   cup uncooked mini farfalle (bow-tie) pasta
  Basil Pesto

1. Sauté carrots and next 4 ingredients in hot oil in a Dutch oven over medium-high heat 8 to 10 minutes or until vegetables are tender. Stir in broth, tomatoes, zucchini, kosher salt, and freshly ground black pepper; bring to a boil. Reduce heat to medium-low, and simmer, stirring occasionally, 10 minutes.

2. Stir in beans and pasta, and cook, stirring occasionally, 10 to 12 minutes or until pasta is tender. Top each serving with 1 to 2 tsp. Basil Pesto.

BASIL PESTO

MAKES ABOUT ¹/₂ CUP

If you're short on time, reach for a good-quality refrigerated pesto at the supermarket to substitute for this homemade blend. You can also use this pesto to dress up canned soups, spread on pizza, or brush on grilled vegetables.

- 2   cups firmly packed fresh basil leaves
- ¹/₂   cup grated Parmesan cheese
- 3   Tbsp. extra virgin olive oil
- 1   garlic clove, chopped
- ¹/₂   tsp. kosher salt

Process all ingredients in a food processor until finely ground. Refrigerate in an airtight container up to 1 week.

---

1 DRESSING, 3 SALADS

LEMON-BASIL VINAIGRETTE

MAKES ABOUT ¹/₂ CUP

Toss any of these salads or your favorite mixed greens with this go-to vinaigrette.

Whisk together ¹/₄ cup **olive oil**; ¹/₄ cup **fresh lemon juice**; 1 Tbsp. chopped **fresh basil**; 1 Tbsp. **white balsamic vinegar**; 1 **garlic clove**, minced; 1 tsp. **sugar**; ¹/₂ tsp. **table salt**; and ¹/₄ tsp. **freshly ground black pepper** in a small bowl until blended. Refrigerate up to 2 days.

SPINACH AND AVOCADO SALAD

Combine **fresh baby spinach**; **English cucumber**, cut into ribbons; ripe **avocado**, coarsely chopped; **kiwifruit**, peeled and sliced into ¹/₄-inch pieces; and toasted sliced **almonds**. Serve with Lemon-Basil Vinaigrette.

FRUIT SALAD

Combine chopped **fresh nectarines**, **mango**, **cantaloupe**, **honeydew melon**, and **mint** with sliced **strawberries** and thinly sliced **jicama** in a large bowl. Serve with Lemon-Basil Vinaigrette. (Omit garlic from vinaigrette.)

CHOPPED SALAD

Combine chopped **fresh Bibb lettuce**, **Gala apples**, **English cucumber**, **sugar snap peas**, **yellow bell pepper**, **red onion**, **celery**, **flat-leaf parsley**, and **broccoli** with thinly sliced **radishes** in a large bowl. Serve with Lemon-Basil Vinaigrette.

4 HEARTY SANDWICHES

❶ Biscuit BLTs

MAKES 8 SERVINGS
HANDS-ON 10 MIN.
TOTAL 10 MIN.

Feel free to substitute fresh basil for Bibb lettuce if you wish.

- ½ cup mayonnaise
- 2 Tbsp. Basil Pesto (see page 107)
- 8 frozen biscuits, baked
- 8 thick bacon slices, cooked and halved
- 8 Bibb lettuce leaves
- 8 plum tomato slices

Stir together mayonnaise and pesto. Spread on cut sides of biscuits. Layer biscuit bottoms with bacon, lettuce, and tomatoes; top with biscuit tops.

❷ Avocado and Sprout Sandwiches

MAKES 4 SERVINGS
HANDS-ON 15 MIN.
TOTAL 15 MIN.

Customize to suit your taste.

- 3 Tbsp. red pepper jelly
- 8 sourdough bread slices
- 8 (1-oz.) provolone cheese slices
- 1 large avocado, cut into 12 slices
- ½ cup bean sprouts
- 3 Tbsp. toasted pumpkin seeds
  Kosher salt and freshly ground black pepper
- 4 Tbsp. ⅓-less-fat cream cheese, softened

Spread pepper jelly on 1 side of 4 bread slices; layer each with cheese, avocado, and sprouts. Sprinkle with pumpkin seeds and salt and pepper to taste. Spread cream cheese on 1 side of remaining bread slices; place on sandwiches, cheese sides down.

❸ Grilled Cheese & Apple Sandwiches

MAKES 4 SERVINGS
HANDS-ON 30 MIN.
TOTAL 30 MIN.

No panini press? Cook sandwiches in a skillet 4 minutes on each side with a pan on top.

- 8 tsp. honey mustard
- 8 hearty whole grain bread slices
- 8 sharp Cheddar cheese slices
- 1 large Granny Smith apple, thinly sliced
  Vegetable cooking spray

Spread about 1 tsp. mustard on 1 side of each bread slice. Place 1 cheese slice on each of 4 bread slices; top with apples. Top with remaining cheese and bread, mustard sides down. Coat both sides of sandwiches with cooking spray. Cook sandwiches in a preheated panini press 8 to 10 minutes or until golden brown.

❹ Asian Chicken Salad Wraps

MAKES 8 SERVINGS
HANDS-ON 15 MIN.
TOTAL 15 MIN.

Use your favorite flavored wraps from the bread or deli section.

- 1 lb. deli chicken salad
- ½ cup thinly sliced fresh snow peas
- ½ cup crunchy rice noodles (such as La Choy)
- 1 Tbsp. grated fresh ginger
- 4 sun-dried tomato sandwich wraps
- 4 Tbsp. chopped fresh cilantro

Stir together first 4 ingredients. Spread each wrap with ½ cup chicken salad mixture; sprinkle each with 1 Tbsp. cilantro. Roll up tightly, and cut in half.

Make-Ahead Berry Pudding

▶ Take the heat off summer entertaining with this fresh and easy tiramisù twist—no baking required. Just tuck layers of ladyfingers and saucy, sweet berries into a dish. Then sit back and chill.

EDITOR'S TIP
Weighing down the pudding compresses the ladyfingers and berries into sliceable, cakelike layers.

Very Berry Summer Pudding

MAKES 6 TO 8 SERVINGS
HANDS-ON 25 MIN.
TOTAL 13 HOURS, 15 MIN.

Serve this juicy showstopper with sweetened whipped cream, or dollop on extra tiramisù flavor by folding together equal parts sweetened whipped cream and mascarpone cheese. (Pictured on page 176)

- 2 cups sliced fresh strawberries
- 2 cups fresh cherries, pitted and halved
- 2 cups fresh raspberries
- 2 cups fresh blackberries
- 1 cup fresh blueberries
- 1/2 cup sugar
- 1/4 cup orange liqueur
- 3 (3-oz.) packages soft ladyfingers
  Garnishes: fresh berries, fresh mint sprigs

1. Stir together first 6 ingredients in a large, heavy stainless steel saucepan; let stand 30 minutes, stirring occasionally. Add 1/2 cup water, and cook over medium-low heat, stirring occasionally, 8 to 10 minutes or just until berries begin to break down and release their juices. Remove from heat, and stir in orange liqueur; cool 20 minutes.

2. Line a 2-qt. soufflé dish with plastic wrap. Spoon 1 cup berry mixture into prepared dish, spreading to cover bottom. Arrange ladyfingers in a single layer on berry mixture, pressing together and trimming as needed to fit snugly and cover berry mixture. Repeat layers twice, dividing remaining berry mixture evenly between layers.

3. Cover loosely with plastic wrap, and place a small plate (approximately the same diameter as the inside of the dish) directly on top. Place 2 or 3 heavy cans on plate, and chill 12 hours. Unmold pudding onto a serving plate.

"How do you grill the perfect piece of fish?"

—Margie Haber
Chapel Hill, NC

▶ Chef Jeremiah Bacon of Charleston's The Macintosh shares his secrets

Grilled Triggerfish with Potato Salad

MAKES 4 SERVINGS
HANDS-ON 10 MIN.
TOTAL 10 MIN.

Freshness counts with a recipe this elemental. Jeremiah opts for meaty, just-caught trigger-fish, but any firm-fleshed fillets will work—just adjust the cooking time depending on the thickness.

> Vegetable cooking spray
> 4 (6-oz.) triggerfish, amberjack, cobia, mahi-mahi, swordfish, mackerel, or salmon fillets
> 2 Tbsp. extra virgin olive oil
> 1/2 tsp. table salt
> 1/4 tsp. freshly ground black pepper
> 4 lemon wedges or 1 tsp. lemon zest (optional)

(A) Coat cold cooking grate of grill with cooking spray, and place on grill. Preheat grill to 400° (medium-high) heat. **(B)** Brush both sides of fish with olive oil; sprinkle with salt and pepper. Place fish on cooking grate, and grill, covered with grill lid, 4 minutes or until grill marks appear and fish no longer sticks to grate. **(C)** Using a metal spatula, carefully turn fish over, and grill, without grill lid, 2 minutes or just until fish flakes with a fork **(D).** Serve with lemon wedges or sprinkle with zest, if desired.

SIMPLE POTATO SALAD

MAKES 4 TO 6 SERVINGS
HANDS-ON 15 MIN.
TOTAL 45 MIN.

> 2 lb. small fingerling potatoes, halved or quartered
> 2 tsp. kosher salt, divided
> 1/2 cup mayonnaise
> 1 Tbsp. red wine vinegar
> 1 Tbsp. whole grain mustard
> 2 tsp. chopped fresh flat-leaf parsley
> 1 tsp. freshly ground black pepper
> 1 garlic clove, minced
> 1/8 tsp. ground red pepper

1. Bring potatoes, 1 tsp. salt, and water to cover to a boil in a Dutch oven over medium-high heat. Reduce heat to medium-low, and cook, covered, 10 to 12 minutes or until potatoes are tender; drain. Place in a bowl; cool 15 minutes.

2. Meanwhile, stir together mayonnaise, next 6 ingredients, and remaining 1 tsp. salt in a small bowl.

3. Pour desired amount of dressing over potatoes; toss to coat. (Reserve any remaining dressing for another use.) Serve at room temperature.

JEREMIAH'S GUIDE TO GRILLING FISH

Master the method with his four simple tips.

A "A clean, hot grill is important because it creates a nonstick surface for the fish." Heat your gas grill, or build a charcoal fire. Use a grill brush to clean off any gunk.

B "Season the fish with salt and pepper just before grilling. Lemon is fine at the end, but don't overdo it. You want the flavor of the fish to speak for itself."

C A thin metal spatula is best for turning fish. "If the fish sticks, it's not ready. Grill it 1 to 2 minutes more."

D "You know when the fish is done when the color is an even light brown and the flesh just begins to flake. If the fillet is thick, like grouper, use a cake tester. It will slide through the flesh without resistance when the fish is done."

The Thrill of the 'Chase

▶ Trot out your wide-brimmed hat and best picnic fare for an afternoon social at the Steeplechase, Nashville's most time-honored rite of spring.

IT'S 8:30 a.m., 12 miles south of downtown Nashville, where the concrete loop gives way to rolling pastures. A young blonde plates three dozen country ham biscuits. Her friends, prim in seersucker dresses and high-to-the-heavens hats, put the finishing touches on a peony arrangement while their beaus raise cups filled with Tennessee whiskey. The group is getting a four-hour head start on the Iroquois Steeplechase, a 72-year-old annual rite as sacred to Middle Tennessee as tailgating is to SEC football.

To the uninitiated, a horse race by any other name is just Derby. But Steeplechase isn't that. Started in 1941 by a group of businessmen and avid foxhunters looking to make Middle Tennessee's pasture races more official, Steeplechase is composed of seven races for horses ages three and older. The animals are trained to clear hurdles, as opposed to their lean Derby counterparts who speed down flat courses. In the world of steeplechase racing, Nashville races have the most cachet and fattest purses of the spring season.

For the 25,000 devotees who parade down the turf at Percy Warner Park in May, Steeplechase is like Mardi Gras, a once-a-year chance for unapologetic revelry—with a little more style. In the early afternoon, Thoroughbreds stride down the stretch, clearing 4-foot fences with the agility of Olympic athletes. But the main event is almost an afterthought, a theatrical backdrop for a boisterous party. Polished families line up sedan-to-sedan long before the first horses leave the paddock. Gentlemen's bets are placed among friends, often with rounds of drinks on the line instead of money.

Continued on next page

But the people who trace their roots to Tennessee's horse culture—the ones whose box seats have been passed down through generations—are there for the steeds. Just ask Margaret Menefee Gillum, whose brother was a rider in 1949 and who has missed only two races since the Steeplechase began—both times her husband was on active military duty. "A lot of people just go for the party now," she says. "But horse people still run the races."

For box-seat holders and those with high-dollar Hunt Club tickets, rainy afternoons and empty cups are no issue. Both splurges guarantee live music and coveted seating. Hunt Club tickets offer all you can eat and drink, while box-seat holders have access to the lavish Paddock Club and Iroquois Society tents. No matter where you sit, it's tradition to take a turn in the infield: the raucous, often muddy, space within the track loop where the twenty- and thirtysomething crowds swill Coors Light and jockey for the best party. "The infield is like Talladega in an upscale way," says Amy Cochran, who has adopted Steeplechase as a spring ritual since moving to Nashville six years ago. "You're expected to wear your Sunday best, but you also know you're going to get messy."

As the day goes on, Tory Burch wedges are swapped for Hunter Wellies, which hold up better in the muck. And after the fifth race, hat-adorned ladies make their way to the bell tower, where prizes are awarded for the best toppers. The fickle spring sky turns to rain, and the women wince ever so slightly as they wait for the winners to be announced. They know that to embrace Steeplechase you can't be a fair-weather fan. And so the show goes on, one mud-stained, seersucker-clad moment after another. It's tradition, after all.

The Winning Spread

▶ Skip the bucket of fried chicken (been there, done that) and mint juleps (this isn't the Derby, after all) and follow our Steeplechase menu for a make-ahead tailgate that will impress even the most discerning of guests.

Beef Tenderloin Crostini

MAKES 3 DOZEN
HANDS-ON 45 MIN.
TOTAL 1 HOUR, 35 MIN.

(Pictured on page 176)

Cilantro Sauce

- 2 tsp. cumin seeds
- 1 1/2 cups firmly packed fresh cilantro leaves
- 1/3 cup olive oil
- 1 garlic clove
- 2 Tbsp. fresh lime juice
- 1/2 tsp. kosher salt

Mango-Red Onion Relish

- 1/2 cup diced red onion
- 1 tsp. olive oil
- 1 large mango, diced
- 1/4 cup diced red bell pepper
- 1 jalapeño pepper, seeded and minced
- 1 Tbsp. Champagne vinegar

Beef Tenderloin

- 1 lb. beef tenderloin fillets
- 1 Tbsp. olive oil
- 1 tsp. kosher salt
- 1/2 tsp. freshly ground black pepper
- 1/8 tsp. garlic powder

Remaining Ingredient

Herbed Cornbread Crostini

1. Prepare Cilantro Sauce: Place a small skillet over medium-high heat until hot; add cumin seeds, and cook, stirring constantly, 1 to 2 minutes or until toasted. Cool 10 minutes. Process cilantro, next 4 ingredients, 2 Tbsp. water, and toasted cumin seeds in a blender until smooth, stopping to scrape down sides as needed. Cover and chill until ready to serve.

2. Prepare Relish: Sauté onion in 1 tsp. hot olive oil in a small skillet over medium-high heat 6 to 8 minutes or until onion is tender. Transfer to a medium bowl, and stir in mango, next 3 ingredients, and salt and pepper to taste.

3. Prepare Beef Tenderloin: Rub steaks with 1 Tbsp. olive oil. Sprinkle with 1 tsp. salt and next 2 ingredients. Place a grill pan over medium-high heat until hot; cook steaks 8 minutes on each side or to desired degree of doneness. Let stand 5 minutes. Thinly slice steak.

4. Assemble: Top flat sides of Herbed Cornbread Crostini with relish and steak; drizzle with Cilantro Sauce.

HERBED CORNBREAD CROSTINI

MAKES 3 DOZEN

Freeze crostini 1 month ahead.

Preheat oven to 450°. Stir together 2 cups **self-rising white cornmeal mix** and 2 Tbsp. **sugar** in a large bowl; make a well in center of mixture. Whisk together 2 large **eggs**; 1/2 cup **sour cream**; 1/2 cup **buttermilk**; and 1/2 cup **butter**, melted, in a medium bowl. Add to cornmeal mixture, stirring just until dry ingredients are moistened. Fold in 2 Tbsp. each chopped **fresh chives** and **parsley**. Spoon batter into 3 lightly greased 12-cup muffin pans (about 1 Tbsp. per cup), spreading batter to cover bottoms of cups. Bake 8 minutes or until set. Immediately remove from pans to wire racks. Serve warm.

Corn-Avocado
Salad

Corn-Avocado Salad

MAKES 12 SERVINGS
HANDS-ON 20 MIN.
TOTAL 1 HOUR

Chill salad up to 24 hours ahead before adding the avocado. (Pictured on page 176)

- 2 cups fresh corn kernels (about 4 ears)
- 1 Tbsp. olive oil
- 3 lb. assorted small heirloom cherry or pear tomatoes, halved
- 1 English cucumber, sliced into half moons
- 1 cup thinly sliced radishes
- 1/3 cup Champagne vinegar
- 1/4 cup extra virgin olive oil
- 1 large shallot, finely chopped
- 2 tsp. country-style Dijon mustard
- 1 tsp. kosher salt
- 1/2 tsp. freshly ground black pepper
- 2 avocados, chopped
- 1 (1-oz.) package fresh basil leaves, torn

1. Preheat oven to 450°. Toss corn with 1 Tbsp. olive oil, and spread in a single layer in a jelly-roll pan. Bake 7 to 8 minutes or until golden brown. Cool 10 minutes. Combine corn, tomatoes, and next 2 ingredients.

2. Whisk together vinegar and next 5 ingredients in a large bowl; add tomato mixture, and toss to coat. Gently stir in avocado. Let stand 20 minutes, stirring occasionally. Top with basil just before serving.

Next-Day Pickled Shrimp

MAKES 12 TO 15 APPETIZER SERVINGS
HANDS-ON 20 MIN.
TOTAL 8 HOURS, 20 MIN.

(Pictured on page 176)

- 3 lb. peeled, jumbo cooked shrimp with tails
- 1 small red onion, sliced
- 1 medium-size yellow bell pepper, sliced
- 4 fresh bay leaves
- 1 cup canola oil
- 1 cup white balsamic vinegar
- 3 Tbsp. sugar
- 1 Tbsp. lemon zest
- 3 Tbsp. fresh lemon juice
- 1 Tbsp. Dijon mustard
- 1 Tbsp. hot sauce
- 1 tsp. kosher salt
- 2 garlic cloves, pressed
- 1 tsp. dried crushed red pepper

Layer first 4 ingredients in an airtight container. Whisk together oil and next 9 ingredients; pour over shrimp mixture. Cover and chill 8 to 24 hours, stirring occasionally. Serve with a slotted spoon.

Moonshine-Cherry Blush

MAKES 10 1/2 CUPS
HANDS-ON 10 MIN.
TOTAL 10 MIN., NOT INCLUDING MOONSHINE

(Pictured on page 176)

- 1/3 cup sugar
- 1/4 cup loosely packed fresh mint leaves
- 1/4 cup loosely packed fresh basil leaves
- 1 cup Basil-Lemon Moonshine
- 1 cup grenadine
- 1/3 cup fresh lemon juice
- 8 cups sparkling water
  Garnishes: lemon slices, fresh basil leaves, maraschino cherries

Process first 3 ingredients in a blender about 20 seconds or until herbs are minced. Stir together moonshine, next 2 ingredients, and sugar mixture in a pitcher until sugar dissolves. Gently stir in sparkling water. Serve immediately over ice.

BASIL-LEMON MOONSHINE

MAKES 1 QT.
HANDS-ON 15 MIN.
TOTAL 25 MIN., PLUS 1 DAY FOR CHILLING

Basil-Lemon Moonshine is great by itself on the rocks.

Cook 1/4 cup **sugar** and 3 Tbsp. **water** in a saucepan over medium heat, stirring often, 5 minutes or until sugar dissolves. Cool 10 minutes. Stir in 3 cups shredded fresh **basil**, 1 (750-milliliter) bottle **moonshine** (such as Ole Smoky Original Tennessee Moonshine), and 2 (2- x 1-inch) **lemon peel strips.** Pour into a large glass jar. Seal with lid, and chill 24 hours to 2 weeks. Strain into a bowl; discard solids. Return to jar. Add 6 fresh **basil leaves** and 2 (2- x 1-inch) **lemon peel strips.** Refrigerate up to 2 months.

Berry Pies

MAKES 10 PIES
HANDS-ON 30 MIN.
TOTAL 1 HOUR, 5 MIN.

- 2 (6-oz.) packages fresh raspberries
- 1 cup chopped fresh strawberries
- 1/2 cup sugar
- 2 Tbsp. cornstarch
- 1/2 tsp. almond extract
- 2 (14.1-oz.) packages refrigerated piecrusts, divided
- 2 Tbsp. butter, cubed
- 1 large egg yolk
- 1 Tbsp. sugar

1. Preheat oven to 425°. Gently toss together first 5 ingredients.

2. Unroll 2 piecrusts on a lightly floured surface. Cut crusts into 10 rounds using a 4-inch round cutter. Fit into 10 lightly greased 3-inch fluted tart pans; press into edges. Spoon berry mixture into pans; dot with butter.

3. Unroll remaining 2 piecrusts on lightly floured surface. Cut into 10 (4-inch) rounds. Cut 3 (1-inch) stars from top of each round. Place rounds over filling in each tart pan; press into fluted edges to seal. Top each tart with 3 stars, leaving cutouts open for steam to escape. Freeze pies on an aluminum foil-lined 15- x 10-inch jelly-roll pan 10 minutes.

4. Meanwhile, whisk together egg yolk and 1 Tbsp. water. Brush tops of pies with egg mixture; sprinkle with 1 Tbsp. sugar.

5. Bake pies on jelly-roll pan at 425° for 24 to 26 minutes or until bubbly and golden brown.

Treats for Mom

▶ A taste of who and what got the highest raves in the *Southern Living* Test Kitchen

RECIPES FROM
THE SOUTH'S
Tastiest
BLOGS
★

From the Kitchen of
LINDSAY LANDIS
LOVEANDOLIVEOIL.COM
NASHVILLE, TN

"Any grain or mix of grains, such as quinoa or barley, will do. Peaches add a sweet finish."

ROASTED VEGETABLE COUSCOUS

Preheat oven to 400°. Peel 3 medium-size **fresh beets** and 2 **carrots.** Cut beets and carrots into 1-inch pieces, discarding beet stems. Toss with 1 Tbsp. **olive oil,** 1 tsp. **kosher salt,** and ¼ tsp. **black pepper.** Place in a single layer in center of a large piece of heavy-duty aluminum foil. Bring up foil sides over vegetables; double fold top and sides to seal, making a packet. Place on a baking sheet; bake 25 to 30 minutes or until tender. Cook 1½ cups uncooked **Israeli (pearl) couscous** according to package directions; toss with 1 Tbsp. each olive oil and **balsamic vinegar,** 2 tsp. chopped **fresh thyme,** ½ tsp. **kosher salt,** and ¼ tsp. **black pepper.** Top with roasted vegetables, ¾ cup diced **fresh peaches or mango,** ½ cup crumbled **feta cheese,** and **fresh thyme sprigs. MAKES** 4 to 6 servings

From the Kitchen of
CELESTE WARD
SUGARANDSPICEBYCELESTE.COM
BIRMINGHAM, AL

"Crispy prosciutto complements the sweet strawberries."

STRAWBERRY-PECAN QUINOA SALAD

Bring 4 cups **water** and 1 cup uncooked **quinoa** to a boil. Cover, reduce heat to medium-low, and simmer 8 to 10 minutes or until tender; drain. Return to saucepan; cover and let stand 10 minutes. Stir together ⅓ cup diced **red onion,** 1 Tbsp. chopped **fresh flat-leaf parsley,** 3 Tbsp. **grapeseed oil,** 1 Tbsp. **apple cider vinegar,** 1 tsp. **lemon zest,** 1 Tbsp. **fresh lemon juice,** ¼ tsp. **kosher salt,** and ¼ tsp. **freshly ground black pepper.** Sauté 1 (4-oz.) package **prosciutto,** torn into strips, in 1 Tbsp. hot **olive oil** in a large nonstick skillet over medium heat 3 to 4 minutes or until slightly crisp; drain well. Toss together onion mixture, prosciutto, quinoa, 1 cup **toasted pecan halves,** 1 cup quartered fresh **strawberries,** 1 cup crumbled **feta cheese,** and ½ cup loosely packed **arugula. MAKES** 4 servings

From the Kitchen of
KATHY "MAMA" COFFEY
MAMAS-SOUTHERN-COOKING.COM
STOCKBRIDGE, GA

"You don't have to sacrifice flavor for a healthy breakfast."

GRANOLA PANCAKES

Bring 1 cup **water** and 2 Tbsp. **butter** to a boil over medium-high heat in a saucepan. Remove from heat. Stir in ⅓ cup uncooked **multigrain hot cereal** (such as Bob's Red Mill). Let stand 10 minutes. Stir in 1¼ cups **milk;** 1 cup **granola** (such as Special K Low Fat Granola); 1 **large egg,** lightly beaten; and 2 Tbsp. **honey** until blended. Stir together 1 cup **all-purpose flour,** ½ cup **whole wheat flour,** 2 tsp. **baking powder,** and ¼ tsp. **salt.** Gradually stir milk mixture into flour mixture just until moistened. Pour about ¼ cup batter for each pancake onto a hot buttered griddle or nonstick skillet. Cook 3 minutes or until tops are covered with bubbles and edges look cooked. Turn and cook 2 minutes or until done. Keep warm in a 200° oven up to 30 minutes. **MAKES** 1 dozen

June

Tomato Pies

▶ Introducing four juicy new twists on the summer classic, from a heroic Cheddar, bacon, and herb number to party-perfect Cheese Straw Tomato Tartlets. Now that's ripe!

TEST KITCHEN TIP
Mix, match, and marinate tomatoes of different sizes and colors to create a tart topping.

Tomato-Goat Cheese Tart with Lemon-Basil Vinaigrette

Tomato-Goat Cheese Tart with Lemon-Basil Vinaigrette

MAKES 6 SERVINGS
HANDS-ON 30 MIN.
TOTAL 3 HOURS, 45 MIN., INCLUDING VINAIGRETTE

Cookbook author Sheri Castle shared her recipe, a family favorite, with us. Be sure to drain the ricotta before mixing with the goat cheese. Spread it gently into the delicate crust so it won't pull away from the pan. (Pictured on page 179)

Cheesecloth or coffee filter
¾ cup whole-milk ricotta cheese
Vegetable cooking spray
1 ¾ cups finely crushed buttery round crackers (about 42 crackers)
6 Tbsp. freshly grated Parmesan cheese
6 Tbsp. butter, melted
1 tsp. freshly ground black pepper, divided
¾ lb. assorted small tomatoes, halved
1 tsp. kosher salt, divided
6 oz. goat cheese, softened
6 green onions, sliced (about ½ cup)
2 tsp. fresh thyme leaves
2 tsp. lemon zest
Lemon-Basil Vinaigrette

1. Line a fine wire-mesh strainer with 3 layers of cheesecloth or 1 coffee filter. Place strainer over a bowl. Spoon ricotta into strainer. Let stand at room temperature 2 hours; discard any accumulated liquid.

2. Preheat oven to 350°. Coat a 12- x 4-inch tart pan with cooking spray. Stir together crushed crackers, next 2 ingredients, and ½ tsp. pepper; press firmly on bottom and up sides of pan. Place on a baking sheet.

3. Bake at 350° for 12 to 15 minutes or until golden brown. Cool on a wire rack 35 minutes.

4. Meanwhile, toss tomatoes with ½ tsp. kosher salt and remaining ½ tsp. pepper in a bowl. Let stand 30 minutes.

5. Stir together goat cheese, next 3 ingredients, strained ricotta, and remaining ½ tsp. salt in a bowl until smooth. Spoon gently into prepared crust, and spread to edges.

6. Bake at 350° for 20 to 25 minutes or until lightly browned.

7. Spoon tomatoes over warm tart, using a slotted spoon. Serve immediately with Lemon-Basil Vinaigrette.

LEMON-BASIL VINAIGRETTE

Process 1 cup firmly packed **fresh basil leaves**; ¼ cup **extra virgin olive oil**; 1 Tbsp. **Champagne vinegar or white wine vinegar**; 2 tsp. **lemon zest**; 1 Tbsp. **fresh lemon juice**; 1 tsp. **honey**; and 1 **garlic clove**, minced, in a blender or food processor 3 to 4 seconds or until smooth. **MAKES** ½ cup. **HANDS-ON** 5 min., **TOTAL** 5 min.

COMPANY'S COMIN'

Tomato-Goat Cheese Tart

Bake this showstopper in a 12- x 4-inch or 9-inch round tart pan, and serve immediately for the crispiest crust.

Savory Tomato Cobbler

Savory Tomato Cobbler

MAKES 6 TO 8 SERVINGS
HANDS-ON 45 MIN.
TOTAL 1 HOUR, 55 MIN.

Stone-ground cornmeal adds texture to the biscuit-like crust, but you can use plain cornmeal or your favorite biscuit recipe. (Pictured on page 179)

- 1 medium-size sweet onion, chopped
- 1 Tbsp. olive oil
- 1 large tomato, chopped
- 3 garlic cloves, minced
- 3 lb. assorted small tomatoes, divided
- 1 Tbsp. Champagne vinegar or white wine vinegar
- 1 Tbsp. cornstarch
- 1 tsp. kosher salt
- 1 tsp. freshly ground black pepper
- 1 tsp. fresh thyme leaves
- 1½ cups self-rising soft-wheat flour (such as White Lily)
- ½ cup stone-ground yellow cornmeal
- ½ tsp. baking powder
- ½ cup cold butter, cut into ¼-inch-thick pieces
- ¾ cup (6 oz.) freshly shredded Jarlsberg cheese
- ¼ cup chopped fresh basil
- 2 Tbsp. chopped fresh chives
- 1¼ cups buttermilk

1. Preheat oven to 375°. Sauté onion in hot oil in a large skillet over medium-high heat 5 to 6 minutes or until tender. Add chopped tomato, garlic, and 1½ cups small tomatoes, and sauté 10 minutes or until tomatoes are softened. Remove from heat, and stir in vinegar and next 4 ingredients.

2. Place remaining small tomatoes in a 13- x 9-inch baking dish. Spoon onion mixture over tomatoes, and gently toss to coat. Bake at 375° for 10 minutes.

3. Meanwhile, stir together flour and next 2 ingredients in a large bowl. Cut butter into flour with a pastry blender until mixture resembles small peas; cover and chill 10 minutes. Stir cheese and next 2 ingredients into cold flour mixture. Add buttermilk, stirring just until dry ingredients are moistened. Dollop mixture by ½ cupfuls onto tomato mixture. (Do not spread.)

4. Bake at 375° for 30 to 35 minutes or until golden brown. Cool on a wire rack 30 minutes before serving.

WEEKNIGHT WARRIOR

Savory Tomato Cobbler

Serve this casserole with a green salad for supper or with eggs for a scrumptious breakfast.

Cheese Straw Tomato Tartlets

MAKES ABOUT 2 DOZEN
HANDS-ON 30 MIN.
TOTAL 3 HOURS, 25 MIN.

This short-crust (non-rising) cheese dough forms a delicate shell for these juicy little wonders. (Pictured on page 8)

CRUST

- 2 1/2 cups all-purpose flour
- 1/2 tsp. kosher salt
- 1/4 to 1/2 tsp. dried crushed red pepper
- 3/4 cup cold butter, cut into pieces
- 1 1/2 cups (6 oz.) shredded extra-sharp white Cheddar cheese
- 1/2 to 3/4 cup ice-cold water

FILLING

- 2 pt. red and yellow cherry or grape tomatoes, cut in half lengthwise
- 3 garlic cloves, finely chopped
- 2 Tbsp. chopped fresh basil
- 1 Tbsp. chopped fresh oregano
- 1 Tbsp. chopped fresh flat-leaf parsley
- 2 Tbsp. red wine vinegar
- 2 Tbsp. extra virgin olive oil
- 1 tsp. kosher salt
- 1/4 tsp. freshly ground black pepper
  Crumbled feta or shaved Parmesan cheese

1. Prepare Crust: Pulse first 3 ingredients in a food processor 3 or 4 times or until combined. Add butter, and pulse 5 or 6 times or until crumbly. Stir in cheese. With processor running, gradually add 1/2 cup ice-cold water, and process until dough forms a ball and pulls away from sides of bowl, adding more water, 1 Tbsp. at a time, if necessary.

2. Divide dough in half; place each half on a large piece of plastic wrap. Shape each into a flat disk. Wrap in plastic wrap, and chill 2 to 24 hours.

3. Prepare Filling: Toss together tomatoes and next 8 ingredients; let stand 1 to 1 1/2 hours.

4. Preheat oven to 400°. Roll 1 dough disk to 1/4-inch thickness on a lightly floured surface. Cut into 12 rounds using a 2 1/2-inch round cutter, rerolling dough as needed; press into cups of a lightly greased 12-cup miniature muffin pan. (Dough will come slightly up sides.) Repeat procedure with remaining dough disk and another muffin pan. Divide tomato mixture among cups.

5. Bake at 400° for 40 to 45 minutes or until golden. Remove from pans. Cool completely on a wire rack (about 15 minutes). Sprinkle with cheese.

Cheese Straw Tomato Tartlets

Tomato, Cheddar, and Bacon Pie

MAKES 6 TO 8 SERVINGS
HANDS-ON 45 MIN.
TOTAL 3 HOURS

We raised the ante on classic tomato pie with a sour cream crust studded with bacon, layers of colorful tomatoes, and plenty of cheese and herbs to tie it all together. For best results, seed the tomatoes and drain the slices before baking. (Pictured on page 7)

CRUST

- 2 1/4 cups self-rising soft-wheat flour (such as White Lily)
- 1 cup cold butter, cut up
- 8 cooked bacon slices, chopped
- 3/4 cup sour cream

FILLING

- 2 3/4 lb. assorted large tomatoes, divided
- 2 tsp. kosher salt, divided
- 1 1/2 cups (6 oz.) freshly shredded extra-sharp Cheddar cheese
- 1/2 cup freshly shredded Parmigiano-Reggiano cheese
- 1/2 cup mayonnaise
- 1 large egg, lightly beaten
- 2 Tbsp. fresh dill sprigs
- 1 Tbsp. chopped fresh chives
- 1 Tbsp. chopped fresh flat-leaf parsley
- 1 Tbsp. apple cider vinegar
- 1 green onion, thinly sliced
- 2 tsp. sugar
- 1/4 tsp. freshly ground black pepper
- 1 1/2 Tbsp. plain yellow cornmeal

1. Prepare Crust: Place flour in bowl of a heavy-duty electric stand mixer; cut in cold butter with a pastry blender or fork until mixture resembles small peas. Chill 10 minutes.

2. Add bacon to flour mixture; beat at low speed just until combined. Gradually add sour cream, 1/4 cup at a time, beating just until blended after each addition.

3. Spoon mixture onto a heavily floured surface; sprinkle lightly with flour, and knead 3 or 4 times, adding more flour as needed. Roll to a 13-inch round. Gently place dough in a 9-inch fluted tart pan with 2-inch sides and a removable bottom. Press dough into pan; trim off excess dough along edges. Chill 30 minutes.

4. Meanwhile, prepare Filling: Cut 2 lb. tomatoes into 1/4-inch-thick slices, and remove seeds. Place tomatoes in a single layer on paper towels; sprinkle with 1 tsp. salt. Let stand 30 minutes.

5. Preheat oven to 425°. Stir together Cheddar cheese, next 10 ingredients, and remaining 1 tsp. salt in a large bowl until combined.

6. Pat tomato slices dry with a paper towel. Sprinkle cornmeal over bottom of crust. Lightly spread 1/2 cup cheese mixture onto crust; layer with half of tomato slices in slightly overlapping rows. Spread with 1/2 cup cheese mixture. Repeat layers, using remaining tomato slices and cheese mixture. Cut remaining 3/4 lb. tomatoes into 1/4-inch-thick slices, and arrange on top of pie.

7. Bake at 425° for 40 to 45 minutes, shielding edges with foil during last 20 minutes to prevent excessive browning. Let stand 1 to 2 hours before serving.

Build a Better Kabob

▶ Stepping up your skewer game is as simple as layering bright and bold flavors with unexpected ingredients. Here, five surprising new combos, guaranteed to ignite your imagination. En garde!

Grilled Salmon Kabobs

Grilled Salmon Kabobs

MAKES 6 SERVINGS
HANDS-ON 30 MIN.
TOTAL 3 HOURS, 30 MIN.

Spice-crusted salmon teams up with the smoky crunch of grilled cucumbers. (If you think cukes are best saved for gazpacho and tea sandwiches, you're in for a delicious surprise.) A creamy yogurt raita, spiked with fresh dill and tangy bits of pickled okra, cools it all down. (Pictured on page 7)

3	tsp. ground coriander
2	tsp. ground cumin
1	tsp. table salt
1/2	tsp. ground red pepper
1	(2 1/4-lb.) whole skinless salmon fillet, cut into 1-inch cubes
1	cup plain yogurt
1/3	cup finely chopped pickled okra
1	Tbsp. olive oil
2	tsp. chopped fresh dill
1 1/2	tsp. fresh lemon juice
6	(12-inch) wooden or metal skewers
3	Kirby cucumbers
12	grape tomatoes
	Garnish: chopped fresh dill

1. Stir together first 4 ingredients in a bowl; transfer to a large zip-top plastic freezer bag. Add salmon, seal bag, and turn gently to coat. Chill 3 hours, turning occasionally.

2. Meanwhile, stir together yogurt and next 4 ingredients; cover and chill until ready to serve. Soak wooden skewers in water 30 minutes. (Omit if using metal skewers.)

3. Preheat grill to 350° to 400° (medium-high) heat. Scrape outside of cucumbers lengthwise using tines of a fork, scoring skin all the way around; cut into half moons.

4. Remove salmon from marinade, discarding marinade. Thread salmon, cucumbers, and tomatoes alternately onto skewers, leaving a 1/8-inch space between pieces.

5. Grill, covered with grill lid, 5 to 6 minutes on each side or to desired degree of doneness. Serve with yogurt mixture.

Steak and Fingerling Potato Kabobs

MAKES 6 SERVINGS
HANDS-ON 45 MIN.
TOTAL 4 HOURS, 20 MIN., INCLUDING VINAIGRETTE

Low in starch with a creamy texture and paper-thin skin, fingerlings hold their shape when grilled. Parboiling jump-starts the cooking process, so they take on a crispy finish just about the time the steak is done.

- 14 (8-inch) wooden or metal skewers, divided
- 16 small fingerling potatoes, halved
- 2 lb. boneless rib-eye, tri-tip, or flank steaks, trimmed and cut into 1 1/2-inch pieces
  Béarnaise Vinaigrette, divided
- 1/4 cup butter, melted
- 1 cup firmly packed baby arugula
- 1 cup loosely packed fresh flat-leaf parsley leaves
- 1/2 cup torn fresh basil
- 1/4 cup chopped fresh chives
- 1/4 cup loosely packed fresh mint leaves, torn
- 3 Tbsp. drained capers

1. Soak 8 wooden skewers in water 30 minutes. (Omit if using metal skewers.)

2. Meanwhile, bring potatoes and water to cover to a boil in a Dutch oven over medium-high heat; cook 10 minutes or just until crisp-tender. Drain.

3. Combine steak and 1/2 cup vinaigrette in a large zip-top plastic freezer bag. Thread 8 potato halves onto 1 double set of skewers (2 skewers side-by-side), leaving a 1/8-inch space between pieces; repeat with 3 double sets of skewers and remaining potatoes. Cut 4 to 8 crosswise slits 1/4 inch deep on top of each potato. Combine potatoes and 1/2 cup vinaigrette in another large zip-top plastic freezer bag. Seal bags, and chill 3 hours, turning occasionally.

4. Meanwhile, soak remaining 6 wooden skewers in water 30 minutes. (Omit if using metal skewers.)

5. Preheat grill to 350° to 400° (medium-high) heat. Remove steak and potatoes from marinades, discarding marinades. Thread steak onto 6 skewers, leaving a 1/8-inch space between pieces. Sprinkle with desired amount of salt and pepper.

6. Grill potatoes and steak at the same time, covered with grill lid, 6 to 7 minutes on each side or until steak reaches desired degree of doneness and potatoes are golden brown, basting potatoes and steak with melted butter with each turn.

7. Toss together arugula, next 5 ingredients, and 2 Tbsp. vinaigrette. Serve kabobs with arugula salad and remaining vinaigrette.

EDITOR'S TIP

To ensure quick, even cooking, keep steak pieces uniform in size and don't tightly pack the skewers.

BÉARNAISE VINAIGRETTE

MAKES ABOUT 2 CUPS
HANDS-ON 5 MIN.
TOTAL 5 MIN.

A light, fresh take on the French classic, this versatile sauce delivers the tarragon-rich spark of the original without the dairy.

Whisk together 3/4 cup **white wine vinegar;** 1/4 cup chopped **fresh tarragon;** 1/4 cup **fresh lemon juice;** 3 **shallots,** minced; 2 **garlic cloves,** minced; 1 Tbsp. **Dijon mustard;** 2 tsp. **sugar;** 1 1/2 tsp. **table salt;** and 1 tsp. **freshly ground black pepper** in a bowl until blended. Add 1/2 cup **canola oil** and 1/2 cup **olive oil,** 1 at a time in a slow, steady stream, whisking constantly until mixture is smooth.

Grilled Balsamic-Molasses Bacon

MAKES 6 TO 8 SERVINGS
HANDS-ON 30 MIN.
TOTAL 1 HOUR

Tie fresh rosemary sprigs to the handle of a wooden spoon with garden sisal or kitchen string, and use as an aromatic basting brush for the bacon. (Pictured on page 179)

- 14 (8-inch) wooden skewers
- 6 Tbsp. molasses
- 3 Tbsp. balsamic vinegar
- 1/4 tsp. ground red pepper
- 14 thick applewood-smoked bacon slices
- 3 fresh rosemary sprigs
  Freshly ground black pepper

1. Soak wooden skewers in water 30 minutes. Preheat grill to 250° to 300° (low) heat.

2. Stir together molasses and next 2 ingredients. Thread 1 bacon slice onto each skewer.

3. Grill bacon, covered with grill lid, 15 to 18 minutes or until bacon begins to brown, turning every 6 minutes. Baste with half of molasses mixture, using rosemary sprigs as a brush; grill, covered with grill lid, 5 minutes. Turn bacon, and baste with remaining molasses mixture, using rosemary sprigs. Grill, covered with grill lid, 5 minutes or until browned and crisp. Remove from grill. Sprinkle with freshly ground pepper to taste. Serve bacon immediately.

EDITOR'S TIP

A high-voltage mix of balsamic vinegar, red pepper, and molasses caramelizes into a finger-licking glaze.

Buttermilk-and-Honey Chicken Kabobs

MAKES 6 TO 8 SERVINGS
HANDS-ON 30 MIN.
TOTAL 3 HOURS, 30 MIN., NOT INCLUDING SAUCES

A buttermilk marinade ensures tender meat and juicy flavor. The kabobs are delicious on their own, but even better with Toasted Pecan Pesto or Romesco Sauce (recipes at right).

- ¼ cup hot sauce
- ¼ cup tomato paste
- 3 Tbsp. honey
- 1 cup buttermilk
- ½ small sweet onion, grated
- 6 garlic cloves, minced
- 1 Tbsp. cracked black pepper
- 2¼ tsp. salt, divided
- 3 lb. skinned and boned chicken thighs, trimmed and cut into 2-inch chunks
- 10 (6-inch) wooden or metal skewers
  Vegetable cooking spray
  Grilled lemon halves
  Toasted Pecan Pesto or Romesco Sauce

1. Whisk together first 3 ingredients in a large bowl until smooth; whisk in buttermilk, next 3 ingredients, and 2 tsp. salt until blended.

2. Place buttermilk mixture and chicken in a large zip-top plastic freezer bag; seal and chill 3 hours.

3. Meanwhile, soak wooden skewers in water 30 minutes. (Omit if using metal skewers.)

4. Coat cold cooking grate of grill with cooking spray, and place on grill. Preheat grill to 350° to 400° (medium-high) heat. Remove chicken from marinade, discarding marinade. Thread chicken onto skewers, leaving a ⅛-inch space between pieces; sprinkle with remaining ¼ tsp. salt.

5. Grill kabobs, covered with grill lid, 6 to 8 minutes on each side or until chicken is done. Serve with lemon halves and Toasted Pecan Pesto or Romesco Sauce.

TOASTED PECAN PESTO

MAKES 1 ¼ CUPS
HANDS-ON 15 MIN.
TOTAL 1 HOUR, 15 MIN.

To preserve the vibrant green color, pour a thin layer of olive oil directly over the top of the pesto before covering and storing it in the refrigerator.

- 2½ cups loosely packed fresh basil leaves
- ⅔ cup olive oil
- ½ cup chopped toasted pecans
- ½ cup loosely packed fresh mint leaves
- 2 garlic cloves, sliced
- 1 Tbsp. fresh lemon juice
- ¾ tsp. salt
- ¼ tsp. dried crushed red pepper

Process all ingredients in a food processor until smooth, stopping to scrape down sides as needed. Cover and chill 1 to 8 hours before serving.

ROMESCO SAUCE

MAKES 1 CUP
HANDS-ON 15 MIN.
TOTAL 15 MIN.

Toasted pecans add a Southern twist to this rustic puree of roasted peppers, garlic, and olive oil. We love it on anything grilled. Or try it tossed with hot cooked pasta or spread on a crusty baguette.

- 1 (12-oz.) jar roasted red bell peppers, drained
- ⅓ cup chopped toasted pecans
- 2 garlic cloves, sliced
- 2 Tbsp. olive oil
- 1 Tbsp. red wine vinegar
- ½ tsp. sugar
- ¼ tsp. salt
- ⅛ tsp. ground red pepper

Process all ingredients in a food processor until smooth.

Buttermilk-and-Honey Chicken Kabobs

Shrimp, Watermelon, and Halloumi Kabobs

Shrimp, Watermelon, and Halloumi Kabobs

MAKES 6 SERVINGS
HANDS-ON 40 MIN.
TOTAL 1 HOUR, 15 MIN., INCLUDING VINAIGRETTE

Addictively briny, halloumi cheese is a favorite for grilling. (Pictured on page 179)

- 36 unpeeled, jumbo raw shrimp (about 2 lb.)
- 12 (12-inch) wooden or metal skewers
   Cilantro-Lime Marinade
- 12 oz. halloumi cheese, cut into 1 1/2-inch cubes*
- 24 (2-inch) watermelon cubes
- 3 Tbsp. fresh cilantro leaves, torn
- 3 Tbsp. fresh mint leaves, torn

1. Peel shrimp, leaving tails on; devein, if desired.

2. Soak wooden skewers in water 30 minutes. (Omit if using metal skewers.)

3. Meanwhile, combine shrimp and 1/2 cup Cilantro-Lime Marinade in a large zip-top plastic freezer bag. Combine cheese and 1/3 cup Cilantro-Lime Marinade in another large zip-top plastic freezer bag. Seal bags, turning to coat; chill 30 minutes, turning occasionally.

4. Preheat grill to 350° to 400° (medium-high) heat. Remove shrimp and cheese from marinades, discarding marinades. Thread shrimp, watermelon, and cheese alternately onto skewers, leaving a 1/8-inch space between pieces.

5. Grill kabobs, covered with grill lid, 4 to 5 minutes on each side or just until shrimp turn pink. Sprinkle with cilantro and mint. Serve with remaining Cilantro-Lime Marinade.

*Firm feta cheese may be substituted.

CILANTRO-LIME MARINADE

MAKES 2 CUPS
HANDS-ON 5 MIN.
TOTAL 5 MIN.

This quick-to-fix vinaigrette doubles as a marinade and dipping sauce. Adjust the amount of sugar according to taste.

Whisk together 1 cup **red wine vinegar;** 1/3 cup chopped **fresh cilantro;** 2 Tbsp. seeded and minced **jalapeño pepper;** 1 Tbsp. **sugar;** 2 Tbsp. **lime zest;** 1/4 cup **fresh lime juice;** 2 Tbsp. **Dijon mustard;** 2 **garlic cloves,** pressed; and 1 tsp. **kosher salt** until blended. Add 1 cup **canola oil** in a slow, steady stream, whisking constantly until smooth.

Grill Veggies Like a Pro

Achieving perfectly charred and crisp-tender results is all in the timing

▶ **GRILL** vegetables the *SL* way and they'll give your rib-eyes a run for their money. Here's how: Start with a clean grill heated to 400°. Cut vegetables into large, even pieces to maximize surface area, lightly brush with olive oil, and season with salt and pepper. Grill with the lid closed. Resist the urge to fiddle with the veggies as they sear, and use the times below as your guide to flip.

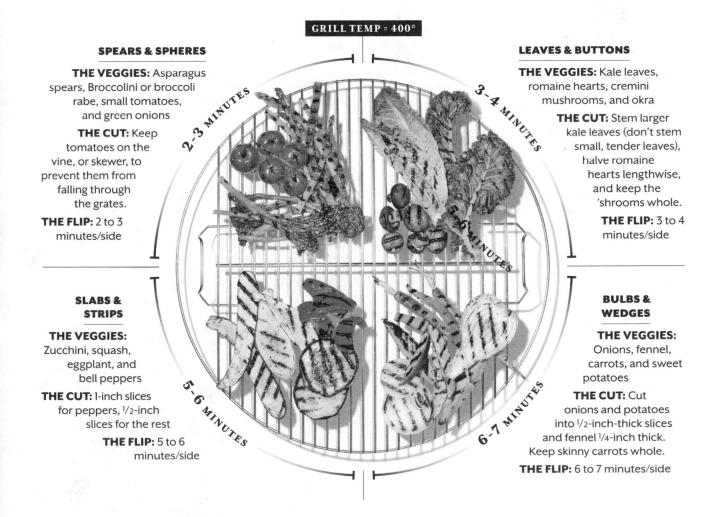

GRILL TEMP = 400°

SPEARS & SPHERES

THE VEGGIES: Asparagus spears, Broccolini or broccoli rabe, small tomatoes, and green onions

THE CUT: Keep tomatoes on the vine, or skewer, to prevent them from falling through the grates.

THE FLIP: 2 to 3 minutes/side

2–3 MINUTES

LEAVES & BUTTONS

THE VEGGIES: Kale leaves, romaine hearts, cremini mushrooms, and okra

THE CUT: Stem larger kale leaves (don't stem small, tender leaves), halve romaine hearts lengthwise, and keep the 'shrooms whole.

THE FLIP: 3 to 4 minutes/side

3–4 MINUTES

5–6 MINUTES

SLABS & STRIPS

THE VEGGIES: Zucchini, squash, eggplant, and bell peppers

THE CUT: 1-inch slices for peppers, 1/2-inch slices for the rest

THE FLIP: 5 to 6 minutes/side

5–6 MINUTES

BULBS & WEDGES

THE VEGGIES: Onions, fennel, carrots, and sweet potatoes

THE CUT: Cut onions and potatoes into 1/2-inch-thick slices and fennel 1/4-inch thick. Keep skinny carrots whole.

THE FLIP: 6 to 7 minutes/side

6–7 MINUTES

Pick up a Pound of 'Cue

▶ Keep your cool with summer-fresh meals guaranteed to make weeknight cooking a breeze. The secret? Start with pulled pork or chicken from your favorite barbecue joint

Summer Brunswick Stew

MAKES 10 SERVINGS

A light, summery broth lets the flavors of fresh-picked corn and lady peas shine. Stir in whatever barbecue sauce you have on hand—some are bolder or sweeter than others, so start with the minimum amount and adjust according to taste.

- 1 large sweet onion, diced
- 2 Tbsp. olive oil
- 2 garlic cloves, minced
- 6 cups chicken broth
- 2 cups fresh lady peas or butter peas
- 1 lb. pulled barbecued pork (without sauce)
- 1 lb. Yukon gold potatoes, peeled and diced (about 2 cups)
- 2 cups fresh corn kernels (about 4 ears)
- 1 to 1 1/2 cups barbecue sauce
- 2 cups peeled and diced tomatoes

Sauté onion in hot oil in a Dutch oven over medium heat 5 minutes or until tender; add garlic, and sauté 1 minute. Add broth and peas; bring to a boil, stirring often. Cover, reduce heat to medium-low, and simmer, stirring occasionally, 15 minutes or until peas are tender. Stir in pork and next 3 ingredients; cover and simmer, stirring occasionally, 15 minutes or until potatoes are tender. Add tomatoes, and season with salt and pepper to taste.

Note: We tested with Kraft Original Barbecue Sauce.

Farmers' Market Pasta Salad

MAKES 8 TO 10 SERVINGS

Cook the pasta al dente (1 or 2 minutes shorter than package directions specify) so it holds its shape when tossed with the vegetables and vinaigrette. Ripe for riffs, the salad is also delicious with cheese-filled tortellini.

- 2 cups halved baby heirloom tomatoes
- 2 small zucchini, thinly sliced into half moons
- 1 small red bell pepper, cut into thin strips
- 1 cup fresh corn kernels
- 1 cup diced firm, ripe fresh peaches (about 2 medium)
- 1/2 cup thinly sliced green onions Parmesan Vinaigrette
- 1 (8-oz.) package penne pasta*
- 2 cups shredded smoked chicken (about 10 oz.)
- 1/3 cup torn fresh basil
- 1/3 cup torn fresh cilantro

1. Toss together first 7 ingredients in a large bowl, and let stand 10 minutes.

2. Meanwhile, prepare pasta according to package directions. Add hot cooked pasta and chicken to tomato mixture; toss gently to coat. Season with salt and pepper to taste. Transfer to a serving platter, and top with basil and cilantro.

*1 (20-oz.) package refrigerated cheese-filled tortellini may be substituted.

PARMESAN VINAIGRETTE

MAKES ABOUT 1 CUP

Process 1/2 cup freshly grated **Parmesan cheese**, 1/2 cup **olive oil**, 2 tsp. **lemon zest**, 3 Tbsp. fresh **lemon juice**, 1 Tbsp. balsamic **vinegar**, 2 **garlic cloves**, 2 tsp. **freshly ground black pepper**, and 1/2 tsp. **table salt** in a blender or food processor until smooth. Add 1/4 cup each chopped fresh **basil** and **cilantro**; pulse 5 or 6 times or just until blended.

Farmers' Market Pasta Salad

Korean Cabbage Wraps with Sweet-and-Sour Cucumber Salad

MAKES 18 WRAPS

A robust cousin of Sriracha, gochujang is a spicy-sweet fermented chili paste used in Korean dishes. Here it adds depth of flavor to a Korean-style barbecue sauce. Find it in the Asian section of supermarkets or at Walmart.

Sweet-and-Sour Cucumber Salad
- ½ cup reduced-sodium soy sauce
- ¼ cup rice wine vinegar
- 2 Tbsp. light brown sugar
- 2 Tbsp. dark sesame oil
- 2 Tbsp. *gochujang* (Korean chili paste)*
- 1 Tbsp. grated fresh ginger
- 1 garlic clove, pressed
- 1 lb. pulled barbecued pork (without sauce)
- 18 savoy or napa cabbage leaves
  Chopped oil-roasted cocktail peanuts

1. Prepare Sweet-and-Sour Cucumber Salad.

2. While salad chills, process soy sauce and next 6 ingredients in a blender or food processor until smooth.

3. Spoon about ¼ cup pork into each cabbage leaf; drizzle with soy sauce mixture. Spoon Sweet-and-Sour Cucumber Salad over pork, using a slotted spoon. Top with desired amount of peanuts.

*2 tsp. Asian hot chili sauce (such as Sriracha) may be substituted.

Note: We tested with Annie Chun's Go-Chu-Jang Korean Sweet & Spicy sauce, available online at *anniechun.com*.

SWEET-AND-SOUR CUCUMBER SALAD

MAKES 8 TO 10 SERVINGS

Whisk together 3 Tbsp. **rice wine vinegar**, 2 Tbsp. **sugar**, 1 tsp. **Dijon mustard**, and ¼ tsp. each **table salt** and **freshly ground black pepper** in a bowl. Add 3 Tbsp. **canola oil** in a slow, steady stream, whisking constantly until well blended. Add 1 **English cucumber**, seeded and thinly sliced into half-moons; 2 **shallots**, minced; and 2 Tbsp. chopped **fresh cilantro**. Toss to coat. Cover and chill 15 minutes.

Pulled Pork Griddle Cakes

MAKES 16 GRIDDLE CAKES

Fresh Cherry Salsa, spiked with pepper jelly, puts these pork-rich griddle cakes over the top. Self-rising cornmeal mix, which includes both leavening and salt, adds just the right amount of lift and tenderness. Hungry for more? Serve with extra 'cue.

- 1½ cups self-rising white cornmeal mix
- ½ cup all-purpose flour
- 1 Tbsp. sugar
- 1⅔ cups buttermilk
- 3 Tbsp. butter, melted
- 2 large eggs, lightly beaten
- 2 cups chopped pulled barbecued pork (without sauce)
  Fresh Cherry Salsa

1. Whisk together cornmeal mix and next 5 ingredients just until moistened; stir in pulled pork.

2. Pour about ¼ cup batter for each griddle cake onto a hot, lightly greased griddle or large nonstick skillet. Cook 3 to 4 minutes or until tops are covered with bubbles and edges look dry and cooked; turn and cook other side 2 to 3 minutes or until done. Serve immediately with salsa.

FRESH CHERRY SALSA

MAKES 2 ½ CUPS

Whisk together ½ cup **red pepper jelly**, 1 Tbsp. **lime zest**, ¼ cup **fresh lime juice**, and ¼ tsp. **dried crushed red pepper** in a small bowl. Stir in 2 cups pitted, coarsely chopped **fresh cherries**; ¾ cup diced **fresh nectarines**; and ⅓ cup each chopped **fresh cilantro** and **chives**.

Korean Cabbage Wraps with Sweet-and-Sour Cucumber Salad

Host a Backyard Bash

▶ North Carolina native and Grill Girl Elizabeth Karmel shares a make-ahead menu that proves firing up the grill is the easiest way to pull off an elegant summer gathering

The Menu

starters

FROZEN PEACH
OLD FASHIONEDS

BUTTERMILK-RICOTTA
CHEESE DIP

main course

GRILLED SUMMER
VEGETABLE PLATTER
WITH VEGGIE
VINAIGRETTE

SMOKED BEEF
TENDERLOIN WITH
CHIMICHURRI SAUCE

CHARRED CORN
WITH GARLIC-HERB
BUTTER

dessert

WHISKEY PIE WITH
TIPSY BERRIES AND
VANILLA ICE CREAM

PREP-AHEAD PLAN

"Even the most accomplished cooks plan ahead," says seasoned hostess Elizabeth Karmel. "That is the key to throwing a party that the host enjoys as much as the guests."

1 WEEK

☐ **STIR UP Garlic-Herb Butter:** Chill up to 1 week, or freeze up to 3 months.

☐ **MIX Hill Country Rub:** Store in an airtight container up to 3 months.

☐ **BLEND Chimichurri Sauce:** Chill up to 1 week.

2 DAYS

☐ **PREPARE Buttermilk-Ricotta Cheese Dip:** After straining, chill up to 2 days.

☐ **BLEND Veggie Vinaigrette:** Chill up to 2 days (if serving with the vegetable platter).

1 DAY

☐ **BAKE Whiskey Pie:** Chill up to 24 hours.

☐ **SLICE Grilled Summer Vegetables:** Prep and chill in zip-top plastic bags up to 24 hours.

☐ **SMOKE Beef Tenderloin:** Prepare through Step 5, and chill up to 24 hours.

DAY OF

☐ **4 HOURS** Make Tipsy Berries

☐ **1 HOUR** Preheat grill. Grill veggies.

☐ **30 MINUTES** Grill corn. Crank up the grill temp, and sear the beef (Step 6 of recipe). Then slice, serve, and take a bow.

**Frozen Peach
Old Fashioneds**

Buttermilk-Ricotta Cheese Dip

MAKES 1 1/2 CUPS
HANDS-ON 40 MIN.
TOTAL 13 HOURS, 10 MIN.

If you've never tried homemade ricotta, then you're in for a tasty surprise. This will change the way you think about the store-bought kind. Be sure to stir only when indicated in the recipe.

>   3 cups whole milk (preferably organic)
> 1 1/2 cups whole buttermilk (preferably organic)
>   1 cup heavy cream (preferably organic)
> 1/4 tsp. kosher salt
>   Cheesecloth
>   Extra virgin olive oil
>   Sea salt and dried crushed red pepper
>   Assorted crackers

1. Bring first 4 ingredients to a simmer, without stirring, in a heavy nonaluminum Dutch oven (about 9 1/2 inches in diameter) over medium heat; cook, without stirring, 20 to 25 minutes or just until bubbles appear and temperature reaches 175° to 180°. (Do not boil.)

2. Stir gently, and return to a simmer. Cook, without stirring, 5 to 6 minutes or until temperature reaches 190°. (Do not boil or stir. Mixture will look curdled.) Remove from heat, and let stand 30 minutes.

3. Line a fine wire-mesh strainer with 3 layers of cheesecloth, and place over a bowl. Spoon mixture into strainer. Cover with cheesecloth; chill 12 to 24 hours. Remove cheese, discarding strained liquid.

4. Spoon cheese into a serving bowl; drizzle with olive oil, and sprinkle with salt and crushed red pepper. Serve with crackers. Refrigerate dip in an airtight container up to 2 days.

PRETTY GARNISH
Top Buttermilk-Ricotta Cheese Dip with lemon rind strips and a mix of parsley, basil, mint, and dill.

Frozen Peach
Old Fashioneds

MAKES 8 SERVINGS
HANDS-ON 10 MIN.
TOTAL 10 MIN.

Served ice cold, these refreshing cocktails keep your guests cool.

>   2 cups frozen peach slices, slightly thawed
>   1 cup bourbon
>   1 cup peach nectar
>   1 cup peach sorbet, softened
> 1/2 to 1 tsp. orange bitters
>   Pinch of kosher salt
>   1 to 3 Tbsp. superfine sugar
>   Garnishes: fresh mint sprigs, peach slices

Pulse first 4 ingredients in a blender 4 or 5 times or until combined. Add bitters and salt, and process 30 to 45 seconds or until smooth. Stir in sugar. Serve immediately.

Note: We tested with Angostura Orange Bitters.

Grilled Summer Vegetable Platter

MAKES 8 TO 10 SERVINGS
HANDS-ON 45 MIN.
TOTAL 1 HOUR, 15 MIN.

Start with this mix of vegetables, or simply use what you have on hand. See our complete veggie grilling guide on page 123.

- 3 (12-inch) wooden or metal skewers
- 1 pt. cherry tomatoes
- 1 lb. fresh asparagus
- 4 small zucchini or yellow squash (about 1 lb.), cut lengthwise into ½-inch slices
- 2 small sweet potatoes (about ½ lb.), peeled and cut into ½-inch wedges
- 5 sweet mini bell peppers, halved
- 1 (8-oz.) container fresh mushrooms
- 1 medium eggplant (about 1 lb.), cut into ½-inch slices
- 2 small bunches green onions
  Olive oil
  Salt and black pepper
  Veggie Vinaigrette

1. Soak wooden skewers in water 30 minutes. (Omit if using metal skewers.)

2. Preheat grill to 350° to 400° (medium-high) heat. Thread tomatoes 1 inch apart onto skewers. Snap off and discard tough ends of asparagus.

3. Brush zucchini, next 5 ingredients, tomatoes, and asparagus with olive oil; sprinkle with desired amount of salt and black pepper.

4. Grill sweet potatoes, covered with grill lid, 6 minutes on each side or until tender. At the same time, grill zucchini, peppers, mushrooms, and eggplant 4 to 6 minutes on each side or until crisp-tender. Grill green onions, asparagus, and tomatoes 2 to 3 minutes on each side or until tender and grill marks appear. Remove from grill, and brush with vinaigrette. Arrange on a serving platter. Serve with remaining vinaigrette.

VEGGIE VINAIGRETTE Process ¾ cup **extra virgin olive oil**; 9 **jarred anchovy fillets**, drained; 6 **garlic cloves**, chopped; 3 Tbsp. **red wine vinegar**; 2 Tbsp. **drained capers**; and a pinch of **ground black pepper** in a food processor until smooth. **MAKES** about 1 cup

---

TEST KITCHEN TIP
....
Instead of skewers, you can use tomatoes still on the vine for easy grilling.

Grilled Summer Vegetable Platter

Smoked Beef Tenderloin

MAKES 8 TO 10 SERVINGS
HANDS-ON 35 MIN.
TOTAL 15 HOURS, 20 MIN., INCLUDING RUB, CREAM, AND SAUCE

Instead of tenderloin, you can try the other cuts listed below as easy, budget-friendlier substitutions.

- 1 (5-lb.) beef tenderloin, trimmed
  Wood chips
- 2 Tbsp. olive oil
- 2 Tbsp. Hill Country Rub
  Vegetable cooking spray
  Chimichurri Sauce (recipe, opposite page)

1. Cover tenderloin, and let stand at room temperature 1 hour.

2. Meanwhile, soak wood chips in water 30 minutes. Prepare smoker according to manufacturer's directions, bringing internal temperature to 300°; maintain temperature for 15 to 20 minutes.

3. Pat tenderloin dry; brush with olive oil, and sprinkle with Hill Country Rub.

4. Drain wood chips, and place on coals. Place tenderloin on cooking grate; cover with smoker lid.

5. Smoke tenderloin, maintaining temperature inside smoker at 300°, for 45 minutes or until a meat thermometer inserted in thickest portion registers 130°. Let stand at room temperature 30 minutes; cover and chill 12 to 24 hours.

6. Coat cold cooking grate of grill with cooking spray, and place on grill. Preheat grill to 400° to 450° (high) heat. Place chilled tenderloin on cooking grate, and grill 2 minutes on each side. Let stand 5 minutes before slicing. Serve with Chimichurri Sauce.

BUDGET-FRIENDLY STEAKS

Feel free to substitute one of these for the tenderloin. Reduce the rub to 1¼ tsp., decrease smoker temp to 250°, and follow smoking times below.
Tri-tip steak: 1½ lb. for 20 min.
Flank steak: 1 lb. for 15 min.

HILL COUNTRY RUB Stir together 1½ cups **kosher salt**, ¼ cup **coarsely ground black pepper**, and 2 Tbsp. **ground red pepper**. Store in an airtight container up to 3 months. **MAKES** 1¾ cups

CHIMICHURRI SAUCE Process 4 cups firmly packed fresh **flat-leaf parsley leaves**, ³/₄ cup **olive oil**, 4 **garlic cloves**, 3 Tbsp. each **fresh lemon juice** and **sherry vinegar** or **red wine vinegar**, 2 Tbsp. minced **shallot**, 1 tsp. **kosher salt**, ½ tsp. **freshly ground black pepper**, and ½ tsp. **dried crushed red pepper** in a food processor until finely chopped. **MAKES** about 1 ½ cups

Charred Corn with Garlic-Herb Butter

MAKES 8 SERVINGS
HANDS-ON 35 MIN.
TOTAL 35 MIN.

Use the husks as handles by pulling them back and tying the ends with kitchen string. Soak in cold water at least 10 minutes before grilling to prevent burning.

    8   ears fresh corn, husks removed
        Extra virgin olive oil
        Garlic-Herb Butter
        Sea salt and freshly ground
        black pepper

Preheat grill to 350° to 400° (medium-high) heat. Brush corn with olive oil. Grill corn, covered with grill lid, 20 minutes or until charred, turning every 4 to 5 minutes. (Some kernels will begin to char and pop.) Remove from grill; brush corn with Garlic-Herb Butter. Sprinkle with salt and pepper to taste. Serve immediately with remaining butter.

GARLIC-HERB BUTTER Stir together 1 (5.2-oz.) container **buttery garlic-and-herb spreadable cheese** (such as Boursin), softened; ½ cup **butter**, softened; 2 tsp. minced **curly leaf parsley**; and **sea salt** and **freshly ground black pepper** to taste. **MAKES** about 1 ½ cups

Whiskey Pie with Tipsy Berries

Whiskey Pie with Tipsy Berries

MAKES 8 SERVINGS
HANDS-ON 15 MIN.
TOTAL 3 HOURS, 25 MIN.

Offer with a scoop of vanilla ice cream, and you can simply top with a mix of your favorite fresh summer fruit. (Pictured on page 8)

    1²/₃   cups finely crushed graham cracker
           crumbs*
      3   Tbsp. sugar
     ¼   cup butter, melted
      2   Tbsp. all-purpose flour
      1   cup sugar
      3   large eggs, beaten
      1   cup buttermilk
     ½   cup butter, melted
      2   Tbsp. bourbon
      1   tsp. vanilla extract
     ⅛   tsp. sea salt
           Pinch of freshly grated nutmeg
           Tipsy Berries

1. Preheat oven to 350°. Stir together first 3 ingredients; firmly press on bottom and up sides of a 9-inch pie plate. Bake 10 to 12 minutes or until fragrant. Cool completely on a wire rack (about 30 minutes). Reduce oven temperature to 325°.

2. Whisk together flour and 1 cup sugar. Whisk in eggs until sugar is dissolved. Whisk in buttermilk and next 5 ingredients until smooth. Pour into crust.

3. Bake at 325° for 45 to 50 minutes or until puffy and golden. Cool completely on a wire rack (about 1 hour). Chill until ready to serve. Serve with Tipsy Berries.

*Chocolate graham crackers may be substituted.

TIPSY BERRIES Stir together 1 (16-oz.) container **fresh strawberries**, sliced; 1 cup **fresh blueberries**; ½ cup fresh **raspberries**; ¼ cup **shaved fresh coconut**; 2 Tbsp. **bourbon**; and 2 tsp. **sugar**. Let stand 30 minutes. Serve with a slotted spoon. **MAKES** about 2 ½ cups

Fresh Summer Salads

▶ A taste of who and what got the most raves in the *Southern Living* Test Kitchen.

RECIPES FROM
THE
SOUTH'S
Tastiest
BLOGS
★

From the Kitchen of
PAULA JONES
BELLALIMENTO.COM
YOUNGSVILLE, NC

"Being originally from Georgia, I love a good peach!"

GRILLED PEACH-AND-AVOCADO SALAD

Preheat grill to 350° to 400° (medium-high) heat. Process 1 large **peach,** peeled and chopped; 6 Tbsp. **canola oil;** 2 Tbsp. **Champagne vinegar or white wine vinegar;** and 1/2 tsp. **honey** in a blender until smooth. Add 1/4 tsp. **kosher salt** and 1/8 tsp. **freshly ground black pepper.** Gently toss 3 large **peaches,** peeled and halved, and 2 **firm avocados,** peeled and quartered, in 1 Tbsp. canola oil and salt and pepper to taste. Grill, covered with grill lid, 2 minutes on each side or until charred. Slice and serve over 6 cups loosely packed **arugula.** Top with peach vinaigrette and 1/2 cup freshly grated **Manchego or Parmesan. MAKES** 6 servings

From the Kitchen of
GEORGIA JOHNSON
THECOMFORTOFCOOKING.COM
AUSTIN, TX

"This is my go-to summer dish, full of vibrant Mediterranean flavors. Fresh pesto is best."

PESTO CAPRESE POTATO SALAD

Bring 2 lb. **baby yellow potatoes,** halved, and water to cover to a boil in a large Dutch oven over medium-high heat; cook 8 to 10 minutes or until tender. Drain; rinse under cold running water. Gently toss together potatoes; 1/2 to 3/4 cup **Easy Pesto;** 6 oz. **grape or cherry tomato halves;** 6 oz. **fresh mozzarella cheese,** cut into bite-size pieces; 1/2 tsp. **kosher salt;** and 1/2 tsp. **freshly ground black pepper.** Refrigerate in an airtight container up to 1 week. **MAKES** 6 servings

EASY PESTO Pulse 2 cups firmly packed **fresh basil leaves,** 2 **garlic cloves,** and 1/4 cup **pine nuts** in a food processor until coarsely chopped. Add 2/3 cup **extra virgin olive oil;** process until smooth. Stir in 1/2 cup **freshly grated Parmesan cheese,** 3/4 tsp. **kosher salt,** and 1/4 tsp. **freshly ground black pepper. MAKES** 1 1/4 cups

From the Kitchen of
MICHAL THORNTON
THEHUMIDITY.BLOGSPOT.COM
GULFPORT, MS

"Creamy pimiento cheese is a delicious Southern twist on the typical blue cheese dressing."

WEDGE SALAD WITH PIMIENTO CHEESE DRESSING

Sauté 4 oz. **mild andouille sausage,** diced, in a small nonstick skillet over medium heat 5 minutes or until crispy. Drain on paper towels, and cool. Drain 1 (4-oz.) jar **diced pimiento;** reserve 1 Tbsp. pimiento. Process 1 cup (4 oz.) shredded **sharp Cheddar cheese,** 1 cup **mayonnaise,** 1/2 cup **buttermilk,** 1 tsp. **hot sauce,** 1/4 tsp. **kosher salt,** 1/4 tsp. **freshly ground black pepper,** and remaining pimiento in a food processor or blender 20 to 30 seconds or until smooth. Add reserved 1 Tbsp. pimiento, and pulse 2 times or just until blended. (Mixture should be slightly chunky.) Place 4 **iceberg lettuce wedges,** cut sides up, on plates, and drizzle with pimiento cheese dressing. Top each wedge with diced sausage and 1/4 cup **cherry tomatoes,** halved. **MAKES** 4 servings

Raise the Bar on Summer Cobbler

▶ Looking for a picnic-perfect treat that's a cut above the classic fruit-filled cobbler? Consider it found.

EDITOR'S TIP
Toffee-glazed pecan pieces add a streusel-like crunch to the tops of these fruity bars.

Blackberry-Peach Cobbler Bars

MAKES 10 TO 12 SERVINGS
HANDS-ON 20 MIN.
TOTAL 2 HOURS, 20 MIN.

- 1 cup butter, softened
- 1 cup firmly packed light brown sugar
- 1 1/2 cups granulated sugar, divided
- 4 large eggs
- 1 Tbsp. vanilla extract
- 1 tsp. baking powder
- 3/4 tsp. table salt
- 3 1/4 cups all-purpose flour, divided
- 3 (6-oz.) packages fresh blackberries (about 4 cups)
- 4 cups peeled and sliced fresh firm, ripe peaches
- 3 Tbsp. bourbon
- 1 cup roasted glazed pecan pieces

1. Preheat oven to 350°. Beat first 2 ingredients and 1 cup granulated sugar at medium speed with an electric mixer until creamy. Add eggs, 1 at a time, beating just until blended after each addition. Stir in vanilla.

2. Stir together baking powder, salt, and 3 cups flour; gradually add to butter mixture, beating just until blended. Spread three-fourths of batter in a greased and floured 13- x 9-inch pan; sprinkle with blackberries.

3. Stir together remaining 1/2 cup granulated sugar and 1/4 cup flour in a medium bowl; add peaches and bourbon, stirring to coat. Spoon mixture over blackberries.

4. Stir pecans into remaining batter; dollop over peach mixture.

5. Bake at 350° for 1 hour or until golden and bubbly. Cool completely on a wire rack (about 1 hour). Cut into bars.

Note: We tested with Diamond of California Glazed Pecans.

Southern Living®

2 ★ 0 ★ 1 ★ 3

'CUE

AWARDS

IN THE SOUTH, BARBECUE IS MEAT, SMOKE, SAUCE, SIDES, RAMSHACKLE JOINTS, COMMUNITY, AND A WHOLE LOT OF OPINIONS ABOUT WHO DOES IT BEST. IN OUR SECOND ANNUAL 'CUE AWARDS, WE DIVE DEEP INTO THE RITUALS AND FLAVORS OF THIS BELOVED SOUTHERN TRADITION

2013 'CUE AWARDS READERS' CHOICE

BEST RIB-STICKIN' JOINTS

SL readers sure love some 'cue, so we asked you who reigns for ribs. Here, your votes for the best spots across the region to hunker down with a slab

1 **FIERY RON'S HOME TEAM BBQ**
Charleston, SC

Aaron Siegel breaks all the old-school BBQ rules at his two juke joint-inspired hangouts. He's open seven days a week, serves cold beer *and* cocktails, and sports live tuneage. But when it comes to ribs, he's a purist: red oak, a simple dry rub, no basting, no sauce. Simply put, it works. *hometeambbq.com*

2 **SOUTHERN SOUL BARBEQUE**
St. Simons Island, GA

Under the portico of an old (and rebuilt) gas station, massive wooden farm tables fan out to seat the 'cue-loving faithful 60 at a time. Folks pack in for the salt- and sugar-cured ribs, smoked rotisserie-style and glazed with pan drippings, and righteous hoppin' John. *southernsoulbbq.com*

3 **SAM'S BBQ1**
Marietta, GA

Sam Huff joined the ranks of boss hog through 14 years as a weekend warrior on the competition circuit. Now his lightly lacquered baby backs, tender with a little give, pretty much own Atlanta. *bbq1.net*

4 **BIG BOB GIBSON BAR-B-Q**
Decatur, AL

If these St. Louis-cut spareribs are the perfect marriage of meat, spice, and hickory smoke (and they are), then we're glad to join the honeymoon. *bigbobgibson.com*

5 **CORKY'S RIBS & BBQ**
Memphis, TN

Unlike most temples of 'cue, where menus proffer a simple range of ribs, pulled pork, chicken, and maybe brisket, this East Memphis landmark dishes up everything from barbecue nachos and tamales to sides of spaghetti. But if you're making a pilgrimage here, you really need to decide only one thing: wet or dry? *corkysbbq.com*

RUNNERS-UP

6. **Jim 'N Nick's Bar-B-Q** Locations around the South; *jimnnicks.com*

7. **Charles Vergos' Rendezvous** Memphis, TN; *hogsfly.com*

8. **Dreamland BBQ** Locations in AL and GA; *dreamlandbbq.com*

9. **Central BBQ** Memphis, TN; *cbqmemphis.com*

10. **The Salt Lick** Driftwood, TX; *saltlickbbq.com*

11. **Hubba Hubba Smokehouse** Flat Rock, NC; *hubbahubba smokehouse.com*

12. **Stubb's Bar-B-Q** Austin, TX; *stubbsaustin.com*

13. **Archibald's Drive In** Northport, AL; *205/345-6861*

14. **The Shed Barbecue & Blues Joint** Locations in MS and AL; *theshedbbq.com*

15. **The Bar-B-Q Shop** Memphis, TN; *901/272-1277*

THE NEW 'CUE CLASSICS

BARBECUE TITANS tend to earn their creds over decades. Occasionally, remarkable upstarts come along that open to instant acclaim, cementing their place as community institutions. At **Franklin Barbecue** (*franklinbarbecue.com*) in Austin, Aaron and Stacy Franklin serve brisket and sausage out of an East Austin building where the queues are as legendary as the 'cue. Franklin's success is debunking the notion that transcendent barbecue is the province solely of small towns. So is **Saw's BBQ** (*sawsbbq.com*) in Birmingham, where locals have embraced Mike Wilson's four-year-old dive as if it has been around for decades. You'll need both hands for his hickory-scented ribs, as thick as double-cut pork chops, with a gorgeous char. At Atlanta's **Heirloom Market BBQ** (*heirloommarketbbq.com*), Cody Taylor (from Tennessee and Texas) and Jiyeon Lee (a former Korean pop star) reflect the city's international vibe with their Korean Spicy Pork Sandwich—smoked shoulder bathed in *gochujang* (sweet chile paste) atop a potato bun with kimchi coleslaw. Unorthodox, yes. But giddy, multigenerational crowds fill the joint's eight-person communal table, eager for an ambrosial taste of barbecue's evolution in the ever-diversifying South.

2·0·1·3
'CUE
AWARDS
BLUE-RIBBON
RECIPE

THE ULTIMATE SMOKY, SWEET
RIBS

We challenged our Test Kitchen to a ribs smackdown. Taste how Memphis native **Pam Lolley** smoked the competition

MAKES 4 TO 6 SERVINGS
HANDS-ON TIME 45 MIN.
TOTAL TIME 15 HOURS, 10 MIN., INCLUDING RUB, BRAISING LIQUID, AND SAUCE

2 (2 1/2- to 3-lb.) slabs St. Louis-style pork ribs
   Smoky Dry Rub
1 cup applewood smoking chips
   Rib Braising Liquid
   Sweet-and-Spicy Barbecue Sauce

1. Rinse slabs, and pat dry. Remove thin membrane from back of each slab by slicing into it and pulling it off. (This will make ribs more tender.) Rub both sides of slabs with Smoky Dry Rub (about 3 to 4 Tbsp. per slab), pressing gently to adhere. Wrap each slab in plastic wrap, and chill 8 to 12 hours. Soak wood chips in water 30 minutes.

2. Prepare smoker according to manufacturer's directions, bringing internal temperature to 225° to 250°; maintain temperature 15 to 20 minutes.

3. Drain wood chips, and place on coals. Place slabs, meat sides up, on cooking grate; cover with smoker lid.

4. Smoke slabs, maintaining temperature inside smoker between 225° and 250°, for 3 1/2 hours.

5. Remove slabs from smoker. Place each slab, meat side down, on a large piece of heavy-duty aluminum foil. (Foil should be large enough to completely wrap slab.) Bring up edges of foil to contain liquid. Pour half of Rib Braising Liquid over each slab. Tightly wrap each slab in foil. Return slabs, meat sides down, to smoker. Cook, covered with lid, 1 to 1 1/2 hours, checking for tenderness after 1 hour.

6. Remove slabs; unwrap and discard foil. Generously brush both sides of slabs with Sweet-and-Spicy Barbecue Sauce.

7. Return slabs to smoker, and smoke 20 minutes or until caramelized.

SMOKY DRY RUB Stir together 1/4 cup firmly packed **dark brown sugar**, 2 Tbsp. **smoked paprika**, 1 Tbsp. **kosher salt**, 2 tsp. **garlic salt**, 2 tsp. **chili powder**, 2 tsp. **ground black pepper**, 1 tsp. **onion salt**, 1 tsp. **celery salt**, 1 tsp. **ground red pepper**, and 1 tsp. **ground cumin**. Store in an airtight container at room temperature up to 1 month. **MAKES** 1/2 cup

RIB BRAISING LIQUID Stir together 1 cup **apple juice**, 1 Tbsp. **Smoky Dry Rub**, 2 tsp. **balsamic vinegar**, and 1 minced **garlic clove**. Chill in an airtight container up to 1 week. **MAKES** 1 cup

SWEET-AND-SPICY BARBECUE SAUCE Sauté 1/2 cup chopped **sweet onion**, 2 minced **garlic cloves**, and 1 seeded and minced **jalapeño pepper** in 1 Tbsp. hot **olive oil** in a large saucepan over medium-high heat 4 to 5 minutes or until tender. Stir in 1 (32-oz.) bottle **ketchup** (such as Heinz), 1 cup firmly packed **dark brown sugar**, 1 cup **apple cider vinegar**, 1/2 cup **apple juice**, 1/2 cup **honey**, 1 Tbsp. **Worcestershire sauce**, 1 tsp. **kosher salt**, 1 tsp. **freshly ground black pepper**, 1 tsp. **celery seeds**, and 1/2 tsp. **dried crushed red pepper**. Bring to a boil, stirring occasionally. Reduce heat to low; simmer, stirring occasionally, 30 minutes. Use immediately, or refrigerate in an airtight container up to 1 month. **MAKES** 5 cups

TWO MORE METHODS

CHARCOAL

Pile hot coals on one side of grill, leaving other side empty. Let grill heat up, covered with grill lid, 10 minutes or until inside temperature reaches 225° to 250°. (Don't have a built-in gauge? Insert a thermometer in top air vent of grill. Stay between 225° and 250°, adjusting vent as needed.)
Prepare recipe as directed in Step 1. Omit Steps 2 through 4.
Place soaked and drained chips directly on hot coals.
Grill slabs, meat sides up, on unlit side of grill, covered with grill lid, 3 1/2 hours, keeping inside grill temp between 225° and 250°. Proceed with Steps 5 and 6.
Return slabs to unlit side of grill, meat sides up; grill, covered with grill lid, 20 minutes or until caramelized.

GAS

Light one side of gas grill, heating to 250° (low) heat, leaving other side unlit. Keep inside grill temp between 225° and 250°.
Prepare recipe as directed in Step 1. Omit Steps 2 through 4.
Place soaked and drained chips in center of a 12-inch square of heavy-duty aluminum foil, and wrap tightly to form a packet. Pierce several holes in top of packet; place directly on lit side of grill.
Grill slabs, meat sides up, on unlit side of grill, covered with grill lid, 3 1/2 hours, keeping inside grill temp between 225° and 250°. Proceed with Steps 5 and 6.
Return slabs to unlit side of grill, meat sides up; grill, covered with grill lid, 20 minutes or until caramelized.

STATE CHAMPION
SLAW

The state of your 'cue dictates the cut of your cabbage.
A region-by-region guide

BARBECUE SLAW does more than decorate your plate. By soaking its seasoned dressing into the meat, slaw adds moisture as well as complementary flavors, playing against the smokiness and fattiness of the different regional styles. Tart, sweet, creamy, crunchy, here's how the layers stack up.

CENTRAL TEXAS SLAW

Whisk together 1/4 cup **white vinegar,** 1/4 cup **extra virgin olive oil,** 2 Tbsp. **sugar,** 3 to 4 Tbsp. **fresh lime juice,** 1 1/2 tsp. **kosher salt,** 1/2 tsp. **ground coriander,** 1/4 tsp. **ground cumin,** 1/4 tsp. **ground red pepper,** and 1/4 tsp. **freshly ground black pepper** in a large bowl. Add 2 cups thinly sliced **red cabbage;** 2 cups thinly sliced **white cabbage;** 1/2 cup shredded **carrot;** 1 medium **jalapeño pepper** (with seeds), thinly sliced; 1/2 **red bell pepper,** thinly sliced; and 1/2 **yellow bell pepper,** thinly sliced. Toss to coat. Chill 1 hour before serving, tossing occasionally. Stir in 1/2 cup chopped **fresh cilantro** just before serving. **MAKES** about 4 cups.
HANDS-ON 15 min.; **TOTAL** 1 hour, 15 min.

MEMPHIS SLAW

Whisk together 1 Tbsp. **light brown sugar,** 2 tsp. **kosher salt,** 1 tsp. **paprika,** 1/2 tsp. **dry mustard,** 1/2 tsp. **dried oregano,** 1/2 tsp. **freshly ground black pepper,** 1/4 tsp. **granulated garlic,** 1/4 tsp. **ground coriander,** and 1/4 tsp. **onion powder** in a bowl. Whisk in 1/2 cup **mayonnaise** and 1/4 cup **apple cider vinegar** until sugar dissolves. Cut 1/2 head **cabbage** (about 1 lb.) into thick slices; cut slices crosswise. Fold cabbage, 1 cup diced **green bell pepper,** and 1 cup diced **red onion** into mayonnaise mixture until coated. Let stand 1 hour before serving, tossing occasionally. **MAKES** 8 cups. **HANDS-ON** 15 min.; **TOTAL** 1 hour, 15 min.

EASTERN NORTH CAROLINA SLAW

Whisk together 1/2 cup **white vinegar,** 1/4 cup **sugar,** 1 tsp. **kosher salt,** and 1/4 tsp. **freshly ground black pepper.** Add 1/2 head **green cabbage** (about 1 lb.), grated, and 1/2 cup chopped **celery;** toss to coat. Let stand 1 hour before serving, tossing occasionally. Serve with **hot sauce.**
MAKES 4 cups. **HANDS-ON TIME** 15 min.; **TOTAL TIME** 1 hour, 15 min.

WESTERN NORTH CAROLINA SLAW

Whisk together 1/3 cup **ketchup,** 1/3 cup **apple cider vinegar,** 2 Tbsp. **sugar,** 1/2 tsp. **kosher salt,** 1/2 tsp. **freshly ground black pepper,** and 1/4 tsp. **hot sauce** in a bowl. Add 1/2 head **cabbage** (about 1 lb.), grated, and 1/4 large **sweet onion,** grated; toss to coat. Let stand 1 hour before serving, tossing occasionally. **MAKES** about 4 cups.
HANDS-ON TIME 15 min.; **TOTAL TIME** 1 hour, 15 min.

SOUTH CAROLINA SLAW

Place 1/2 head thinly sliced **cabbage** (about 1 lb.) and 1 cup grated **carrot** in a bowl. Whisk together 1/2 cup **apple cider vinegar,** 1/4 cup **sugar,** 1/4 cup **vegetable oil,** 2 Tbsp. **Dijon mustard,** 2 tsp. **dry mustard,** 1 tsp. **celery seeds,** 1 tsp. **kosher salt,** and 1/2 tsp. **freshly ground black pepper** in a saucepan until sugar dissolves; bring to a boil over medium-high heat. Pour over cabbage mixture; toss to coat. Serve immediately.
MAKES 6 cups. **HANDS-ON TIME** 15 min., **TOTAL TIME** 15 min.

OBEY YOUR STATE SLAWS

THE REGION	THE MEAT	THE KEY INGREDIENT	THE CHOP
SOUTH CAROLINA	Whole hog or pork shoulder	Mustard	Shredded or thinly sliced
CENTRAL TEXAS	Beef brisket and shoulder clod sliced across grain	Jalapeño and cilantro	Shredded or thinly sliced
MEMPHIS, TENNESSEE	Pulled pork or ribs (dry and wet)	Dry rub spices	Chopped or coarsely chopped
EASTERN NORTH CAROLINA	Chopped whole hog	Extra-tart vinegar	Finely chopped
WESTERN NORTH CAROLINA	Chopped or pulled pork shoulder	Ketchup	Finely chopped

2·0·1·3
'CUE
AWARDS
EDITOR'S
PICK

THE PERFECT
PIT STOP

The ritual of barbecue starts with the woodpile and ends with the best sandwich ever. Yes, ever. Executive Editor **Hunter Lewis** revisits his hometown joint

ALLEN & SON BAR-B-QUE *(919/942-7576)* sits at the nexus of Old 86 and Millhouse Road on the outskirts of Chapel Hill, North Carolina. A few miles off I-40, it's the first place I go whenever I fly home via RDU. I ate my first real chopped pork sandwich here. Recently my daughter did too. In high school, my buddies and I burned a path down the back roads, skipping class for a taste of pitmaster Keith Allen's handiwork. The teachers always smelled the telltale wood smoke on us. Turns out this sandwich is worth more than a week of detention.

START

THE WOODPILE
Owner **Keith Allen** hauls hickory to the restaurant and splits the wood with a steel wedge and a maul. Some mistake the no-nonsense Keith for a lumberjack or retired tight end. He is a pitmaster.

THE COUNTER
Step up to the window, and place your to-go order or pay your bill. The house sauce is for sale in Mason jars. A board advertises the specials: peach cobbler, chocolate chess pie, cherry pie.

7

THE AMBIENCE
Tackle shop meets BBQ joint. Smoke-stained painted cinder block walls, framed accolades from the press, taxidermy galore, and oilcloth-lined tables: The place just feels, and smells, right.

You can't manufacture authenticity. Allen & Son in Chapel Hill, NC, is the mecca for pork shoulders smoked, chopped, and seasoned in the Eastern North Carolina way.

THE PITS Keith transports the hickory by wheelbarrow to feed the fire in a huge brick fireplace, where it burns down to nuggets of coals. He shovels the coals into the two pits that sit on each side of the fireplace.

3

THE MEAT Whole pork shoulders, chicken halves, and ribs sizzle on the grates, dripping fat onto the coals. The smoke infuses the meat, and the gentle heat slowly breaks down and tenderizes it.

THE SEASONING Keith douses the 'cue with a fatty Eastern NC-style, red pepper-spiced vinegar sauce. This marriage of vinegar sauce with Western NC pork shoulder cookery befits a Piedmont town in the middle of the state.

5

THE CHOP In the kitchen, Keith uses two machete-like blades that he calls "lamb breakers" to aggressively and rhythmically break down steaming hunks of pork shoulder into piles of chopped barbecue.

4

THE CROWD The veteran staff shepherds platters and never-ending pitchers of perfectly sweetened tea to the tables full of country and city folks, white collar and blue collar, Duke and Carolina fans.

THE SANDWICH The smoky 'cue is zippy and rich. Ask for the tart, minced slaw on top. The squishy bun can't hold all the business together and practically melts away as the sandwich sits idle during gulps of tea. Heaven.

9

FINISH

THE SWEETEST
SMOKE

When a beloved Tennessee joint burned to the ground, a community rallied to rebuild. As it turns out, the *real* barbecue experience is only partly about the meat

IT WAS A PERFECT SATURDAY for a barbecue sandwich in Humboldt, Tennessee, late July 2012: clear blue skies and pleasantly humid temps. But Rein Fertel stood waist-deep in all that remained of the pit at Sam's Bar-B-Q. Like a barbecue archeologist, he set to pickax-hacking through layers of mortar, cemented hardwood ash, and hog fat, attempting to find the foundational brick masonry layer buried beneath the detritus collected from 25 years of smoking pork shoulders.

Just weeks before, Sam's pit room caught fire and, because swine grease explodes like napalm, incinerated the restaurant down to its cinder block walls. Over two days, he joined a couple dozen volunteers from the Southern Foodways Alliance, the Fatback Collective, and Jim 'N Nick's Bar-B-Q to help rebuild this tiny smoke shack in western Tennessee. Barbecue devotees came from across town and as far away as South Carolina, all endeavoring to resurrect a bit of barbecue history.

For the past five years, he has worked as a barbecue documentarian, a culinary-centric oral historian tracking down the stories behind the food. He spins odometers in search of chopped pork sandwiches and butcher paper satchels of brisket. But that weekend in Humboldt, he came closer than he ever has to the heart of barbecue. What is it about this American culinary art form—a transcendent merger of salt and sweet, smoke and spice with flesh—that

could make him travel 500 miles, labor in 90-something-degree heat, and not even get a taste of meat or sauce?

For Rein, it starts with the story. Samuel Donald opened his barbecue joint in 1988 after retiring from a lifetime of factory work and cattle farming. He smoked his shoulders all day and night over hickory and oak coals. His vinegar-and-spice sauce was known throughout West Tennessee. (A customer once offered $200 for a gallon.) But according to his daughter Seresa Ivory, who, with her husband, Jon, has owned the joint since Sam's passing in 2011, Sam's favorite part of the job was the sweat-soaked hours spent working alongside his hand-built barbecue pit, where friends and customers would join him for storytelling and fellowship around the fire.

As Rein excavated the remnants of Sam's pit, he could not help but flash back to the past years he has spent unearthing barbecue's history. When he started documenting 'cue culture, he accepted anyone and everyone's definition of barbecue. Third-generation pitmasters in the Carolinas insisted that barbecue is whole hog smoked over hickory for 12-plus hours. Texans said barbecue is beef. More heterodox barbecuers cooked everything, every way. Mutton and beef; poultry and pork; on the backyard grill or in the smokehouse; chopped, pulled, shredded, or sliced. As long as fire met meat, he agreed, it was all barbecue.

But as he dug deeper into barbecue's past, he wanted more. His definition felt incomplete.

Rein climbed out of Sam's pit and handed the pickax to fellow volunteer Rodney Scott, who serves up peerless whole hog at Scott's Bar-B-Que in Hemingway, South Carolina. A month earlier, Rodney had shared with him his philosophy: sauce, smoke, and even meat don't matter. For Rodney, barbecue is a reunion, a party, an opportunity "for everybody to come and join in and enjoy each other's company." Whether you form a team on the competition circuit, gather for family cookouts, or share a slab of ribs with a neighbor, barbecue is rarely, if ever, a solitary activity.

Rodney's comment exemplified what Rein witnessed at Sam's: a group of folks getting together in the name of barbecue. Many of them, including Rein, had never tasted a Sam's pulled pork sandwich, yet they craved being a part of its revival. All that weekend they talked barbecue, shared stories about barbecue, and made plans to visit each other and eat barbecue.

In November, Rein drove back out to Humboldt to visit the newly reopened Sam's Bar-B-Q. First thing, he made a pilgrimage out to the smokehouse to see the pit that Sam built, and they rebuilt. He stood marveling at the beauty of the restoration, and pondered just how much barbecue he would eat that day.

July

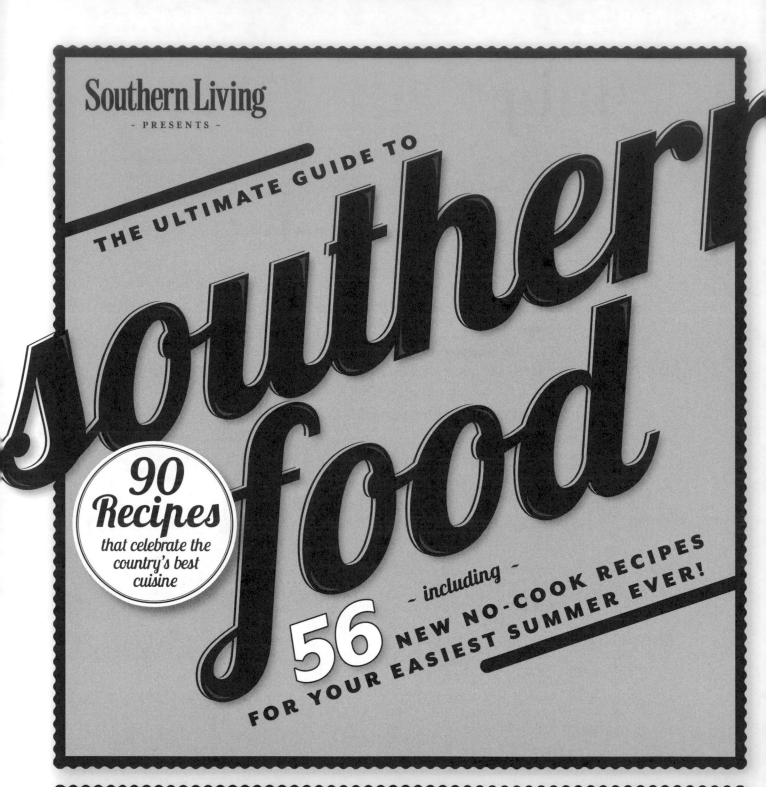

Southern Living
~ PRESENTS ~

THE ULTIMATE GUIDE TO

southern food

90 Recipes that celebrate the country's best cuisine

56 ~ including ~ **NEW NO-COOK RECIPES FOR YOUR EASIEST SUMMER EVER!**

~ A SPECIAL SECTION FEATURING ~

the soul:
Celebrate the tradition of food and fellowship at Dinner on the Grounds
opposite page

the community:
Taste your way through some of our favorite community cookbooks
page 146

the bounty:
Learn smart and tasty new ways to cook your farm-stand finds
page 150

plus!
Beat the heat with a season of no-cook solutions
page 155

Spread the Gospel

▶ Dinner on the Grounds—a soulful Southern tradition of gracious plenty—celebrates two things we do best: feast and fellowship. With these new classic recipes, get ready to pass the plate.

A SUNDAY MEMORY
By Scott Peacock

mong the most vivid images of my childhood is a plain country church, starkly set against open fields in the shimmering heat of an Alabama summer. It is my grandmother's church, my father's mother, Grandmaw Peacock. Less than 8 miles from where my family lives in the small town of Hartford, it is a place we visit only once or twice a year. Primitive and unair-conditioned, it brings me endless fidgeting discomfort. Remarkably, this church, like others around the South, is also the setting for what stands as one of the most memorable and voluptuous food experiences of my life: Dinner on the Grounds.

It is Homecoming Sunday, a reunion of sorts, the day set aside each year when church members who have moved away return. More than just a house of worship, the church is a gathering place and social center for the community, and the occasion is as much an affirmation of fellowship as it is religious observance. Many travel great distances to attend; some, like my father, come from just a few miles down the road. The centerpiece of this all-day celebration is a lavish outdoor, covered-dish feast prepared by the women of the church. It is a generous affair.

Chairs arranged under a makeshift arbor of cut tree limbs and branches are reserved for the eldest of the congregation, who, following the blessing, are given first choice in the serving line. Others eat standing, seated on the ground, or perched on truck tailgates. The women, in homemade dresses and aprons, stand duty, replenishing bowls and platters as needed, waving dish towels and advertising fans to shoo away the flies.

A long running table improvised from old doors and sawhorses is draped and filled to the edges with all the favorites: platters and platters of fried chicken, each from a different stove and skillet; corn pudding, fragrant with nutmeg, butter, and vanilla; butter beans, both speckled and plain; the full gamut of field peas; corn pones and yeast rolls; fried okra that is crisp and greaseless; whole baked ham, sweet-glazed and sticky; myriad incarnations of deviled eggs and potato salad; and sweet iced tea by the barrel.

In a separate area, ice-cream churns are cranked by hand and desserts are laid out in glorious excess. Cakes—there are all kinds, including the thin 20-layered variety particular to this corner of Alabama. And chocolate; fresh coconut; lemon cheese; pound cake, of course; and, because it is so temperamental to make, the most prized of all, caramel. Deep pans of fruit cobbler, wild blackberry and peach, lie lathed with strips of rich pastry. And pies reside in full double rows: pecan, buttermilk, muscadine, sweet potato, and my very favorite of all, egg custard.

This food, made by the same hands that grew it, exemplifies country cooking, simple and pure, rendered with uncommon knowledge and finesse. As the lines pass along the table, people cannily and discreetly seek out the dishes made by the finest cooks. But everything is good. And somehow, simply through taste, something of the land, the community, and each individual cook is conveyed and understood.

Sweet Tea-Brined Fried Chicken

MAKES 6 TO 8 SERVINGS

A marriage of Southern favorites: Our salty-sweet brine of brown sugar and freshly brewed tea infuses this picnic-perfect chicken with juicy flavor before frying. Bonus: The tannins in tea act as a natural tenderizer.

- 2 family-size tea bags
- ½ cup firmly packed light brown sugar
- ¼ cup kosher salt
- 1 small sweet onion, thinly sliced
- 1 lemon, thinly sliced
- 4 garlic cloves, halved
- 1 Tbsp. cracked black pepper
- 2 cups ice cubes
- 1 (3 ½-lb.) cut-up whole chicken
- 2 cups self-rising flour
- 1 cup self-rising white cornmeal mix
- 2 Tbsp. freshly ground black pepper
- 2 tsp. table salt
- 1 tsp. ground red pepper
  Vegetable oil

1. Bring 4 cups water to a boil in a 3-qt. heavy saucepan; add tea bags. Remove from heat; cover and steep 10 minutes.

2. Discard tea bags. Stir in brown sugar and next 5 ingredients, stirring until sugar dissolves. Cool completely (about 45 minutes); stir in ice. (Mixture should be cold before adding to chicken.)

3. Cut chicken breasts in half crosswise. Place tea mixture and all chicken pieces in a large zip-top plastic freezer bag; seal. Place bag in a shallow baking dish, and chill 24 hours.

4. Remove chicken from marinade, discarding marinade. Drain chicken well.

5. Whisk together flour and next 4 ingredients in a medium bowl. Spoon 1 cup flour mixture into a brown paper bag or large zip-top plastic freezer bag. Place one piece of chicken in bag; seal and shake to coat. Remove chicken, and transfer to a wire rack. Repeat procedure with remaining chicken, adding more flour mixture to bag as needed. Let chicken stand 30 minutes to form a crust.

6. Pour oil to depth of 1 ½ inches into a cast-iron Dutch oven; heat over medium heat to 325°. Fry chicken, in batches, 15 to 22 minutes or until browned and done, turning occasionally. Drain on a wire rack over paper towels.

Note: If using a 12-inch-wide (2 ¼-inch-deep) cast-iron skillet, pour oil to depth of 1 inch.

Tomato-and-Fruit Salad

Tomato-and-Fruit Salad

MAKES 8 TO 10 SERVINGS

This colorful dish captures the best flavors of summer on one cool platter. A fresh basil dressing spiked with orange marmalade merges the sweet with the savory.

- 2 lb. watermelon, sliced
- 2 lb. honeydew melon, sliced
- 1 fresh peach, sliced
- 2 nectarines, sliced
- 2 red plums, cut into wedges
- 1 green tomato, sliced
- 1 lb. assorted heirloom tomatoes, sliced or cubed
- 1 (12-oz.) package baby heirloom tomatoes, halved
- 6 to 8 fresh basil leaves, torn
  Basil-Orange Vinaigrette

Arrange first 9 ingredients on a serving platter. Serve with Basil-Orange Vinaigrette.

BASIL-ORANGE VINAIGRETTE

MAKES 1 ⅓ CUPS

Pulse ½ cup **sweet orange marmalade** (such as Smucker's); ⅓ cup **red wine vinegar**; 6 fresh **basil leaves**, torn; 1 Tbsp. grated **fresh ginger**; 1 **garlic clove**, sliced; ½ tsp. **kosher salt**; and ½ tsp. **freshly ground black pepper** in a blender or food processor until blended. With blender running, pour ½ cup **canola oil** through food chute in a slow, steady stream, processing until smooth.

Zucchini, Squash, and Corn Casserole

Zucchini, Squash, and Corn Casserole

MAKES 8 TO 10 SERVINGS

To make breadcrumbs, pulse torn slices of day-old sandwich bread in the food processor. (Pictured on page 180)

1 1/2 lb. yellow squash, cut into 1/4-inch-thick slices

1 1/2 lb. zucchini, cut into 1/4-inch-thick slices

1/4 cup butter, divided

2 cups diced sweet onion

2 garlic cloves, minced

3 cups fresh corn kernels

1 1/2 cups (6 oz.) freshly shredded white Cheddar cheese

1/2 cup sour cream

1/2 cup mayonnaise

2 large eggs, lightly beaten

2 tsp. freshly ground black pepper

1 tsp. table salt

1 1/2 cups soft, fresh breadcrumbs, divided

1 cup freshly grated Asiago cheese, divided

1. Preheat oven to 350°. Bring first 2 ingredients and water to cover to a boil in a Dutch oven over medium-high heat, and boil 5 minutes or until crisp-tender. Drain; gently press between paper towels.

2. Melt 2 Tbsp. butter in a skillet over medium-high heat; add onion, and sauté 10 minutes or until tender. Add garlic, and sauté 2 minutes.

3. Stir together squash, onion mixture, corn, next 6 ingredients, and 1/2 cup each breadcrumbs and Asiago cheese just until blended. Spoon mixture into a lightly greased 13- x 9-inch baking dish.

4. Melt remaining 2 Tbsp. butter. Stir in remaining 1 cup breadcrumbs and 1/2 cup Asiago cheese. Sprinkle over casserole.

5. Bake at 350° for 45 to 50 minutes or until golden brown and set. Let stand 15 minutes before serving.

Shout Hallelujah Potato Salad

MAKES 12 SERVINGS

Bragging rights for this flavor-packed, perfectly balanced favorite (from The Southern Foodways Alliance Community Cookbook) *go to Blair Hobbs of Oxford, Mississippi.*

5 lb. Yukon gold potatoes

4 large hard-cooked eggs, peeled

1 Tbsp. table salt

1 cup plus 2 Tbsp. mayonnaise

1 cup sweet salad cube pickles, drained

1/2 cup chopped red onion

1/2 cup chopped green bell pepper

1/2 cup chopped celery

1/4 cup chopped fresh flat-leaf parsley

1/4 cup yellow mustard

1 (4-oz.) jar diced pimiento, drained

2 Tbsp. seasoned rice wine vinegar

2 Tbsp. fresh lemon juice

1 Tbsp. extra virgin olive oil

1 to 2 jalapeño peppers, seeded and minced

1 to 2 tsp. celery salt

4 drops of hot sauce

1/2 tsp. smoked paprika

1. Cook potatoes in boiling water to cover 20 minutes or until tender; drain and cool 15 minutes. Peel potatoes, and place in a large bowl. Add eggs, and chop mixture into bite-size pieces. Sprinkle with salt; toss to coat.

2. Stir together mayonnaise and next 13 ingredients; gently stir into potato mixture. Sprinkle with paprika; add black pepper to taste. Serve immediately, or cover and chill up to 2 days.

Skillet Green Beans

MAKES 8 TO 10 SERVINGS

Pencil-thin green beans laced with crispy bits of pan-fried bacon and Candied Jalapeños turn up the heat on tradition.

- 2 lb. haricots verts (thin green beans), trimmed
- 4 thick hickory-smoked bacon slices, cut crosswise into 1/4-inch-thick pieces
- 6 large shallots, quartered
- 1 Tbsp. olive oil
- 1/4 cup syrup from Candied Jalapeños
- 2 Tbsp. red wine vinegar
  - Kosher salt
  - Freshly ground black pepper
  - Candied Jalapeños
  - Field Pea Relish

1. Cook green beans in boiling salted water to cover 3 to 4 minutes or until crisp-tender; drain. Plunge beans into ice water to stop the cooking process; drain.

2. Cook bacon in a large skillet over medium heat 5 to 6 minutes or until crisp. Remove with a slotted spoon, and drain on paper towels, reserving 2 Tbsp. drippings in skillet.

3. Sauté shallots in hot olive oil and reserved hot drippings over medium heat 8 to 10 minutes or until golden brown and tender. Stir in jalapeño syrup and vinegar. Increase heat to medium-high; add green beans. Sauté 5 minutes or until hot. Add salt and pepper to taste. Toss with bacon. Serve with jalapeños and relish.

CANDIED JALAPEÑOS

MAKES 1 1/3 CUPS

This is our new go-to summer condiment. Chill at least 48 hours ahead so the jalapeños have time to take on a fiery-sweet crunch.

Drain 1 (12-oz.) jar **pickled jalapeño pepper slices**, discarding liquid and reserving jar and lid. Toss together jalapeño slices; **4 red chile peppers**, sliced; 3/4 cup **sugar**; and 1 tsp. loosely packed **lime zest**. Let stand 5 minutes, stirring occasionally. Spoon into reserved jar, scraping any remaining sugar mixture from bowl into jar. Cover with lid, and chill 48 hours to 1 week, shaking jar several times a day to dissolve any sugar that settles.

FIELD PEA RELISH

MAKES ABOUT 4 CUPS

Perfect for anything fried, grilled, or fresh from the garden—it's just that good and easy, no special jars or canning required.

Whisk together 1/4 cup **canola oil**; 1/4 cup **fresh lime juice**; 3 Tbsp. chopped **fresh cilantro**; 3 Tbsp. minced **Candied Jalapeños**; 1 **garlic clove**, pressed; and 1/4 tsp. **table salt** in a large bowl. Add 3 cups **assorted cooked fresh field peas**, 1/2 cup diced **red onion**, and 1/2 cup diced **red bell pepper**, tossing to coat. Cover and chill 12 hours, stirring occasionally.

Two-Step Fresh Peach Pound Cake

MAKES 10 TO 12 SERVINGS

Turn out a high-rise cake with a moist, tender crumb by layering the ingredients in the bowl in the order specified. Don't have a stand mixer with a 4-qt. bowl and paddle attachment? Prep the batter in the traditional way.

- 4 cups all-purpose flour
- 3 cups sugar
- 2 cups butter, softened
- 1/2 cup milk
- 1/2 cup peach schnapps
- 6 large eggs
- 2 tsp. vanilla extract
- 2 1/2 cups diced fresh peaches

1. Preheat oven to 325°. Place flour, sugar, butter, milk, peach schnapps, eggs, and vanilla (in that order) in 4-qt. bowl of a heavy-duty electric stand mixer. Beat at low speed 1 minute, stopping to scrape down sides. Beat at medium speed 2 minutes. Stir in peaches. Pour into a greased and floured 10-inch (16-cup) tube pan.

2. Bake at 325° for 1 hour and 30 minutes to 1 hour and 35 minutes or until a wooden pick inserted in center comes out clean. Cool in pan on a wire rack 20 minutes. Remove from pan to wire rack; cool completely (about 1 hour).

Butterscotch Banana Pudding Pie

MAKES 8 TO 10 SERVINGS

Stop the meringue from shrinking by spreading just over the inside edge of the crust, covering the hot filling.

- 74 vanilla wafers (1 [11-oz.] package), divided
- 1/2 cup finely chopped toasted pecans
- 1/2 cup butter, melted
- 2 (1.4-oz.) chocolate-covered toffee candy bars, finely chopped
- 2 large ripe bananas, sliced
  - Butterscotch Filling
- 4 large egg whites
- 1/2 cup sugar

1. Preheat oven to 350°. Pulse 44 wafers in a food processor 8 to 10 times or until coarsely crushed. (Yield should be about 2 cups.) Stir together crushed wafers, pecans, and butter until blended. Firmly press on bottom, up sides, and onto lip of a lightly greased 9-inch pie plate.

2. Bake at 350° for 10 to 12 minutes or until lightly browned. Transfer to a wire rack; sprinkle candy bars over crust. Cool completely (about 30 minutes).

3. Arrange bananas over candy bars. Prepare filling, and spread half of hot filling over bananas; top with 20 vanilla wafers in a single layer. Spread remaining hot filling over wafers. (Filling will be about 1/4 inch higher than crust.)

4. Beat egg whites at high speed with an electric mixer until foamy. Gradually add sugar, 1 Tbsp. at a time, beating until stiff peaks form and sugar dissolves. Spread meringue over hot filling, sealing edges. Insert remaining 10 vanilla wafers halfway into meringue around outer edge of pie.

5. Bake at 350° for 10 to 12 minutes or until golden brown. Remove from oven to a wire rack. Cool completely (about 1 hour). Chill 4 to 6 hours or until firm.

BUTTERSCOTCH FILLING

MAKES ABOUT 2 1/2 CUPS

Whisk together 3/4 cup **firmly packed light brown sugar**, 1/3 cup **all-purpose flour**, and 1/8 tsp. **table salt** in a heavy saucepan; whisk in 6 large **egg yolks** and 2 cups **milk** until well blended. Cook over medium-low heat, whisking constantly, 10 to 12 minutes or until a chilled pudding-like thickness. (Mixture will just begin to bubble and will be thick enough to hold soft peaks when whisk is lifted.) Remove from heat; stir in 2 tsp. **vanilla extract**. Use immediately.

Patchwork Cobbler

MAKES 10 TO 12 SERVINGS

Topped with squares of sugar-crusted pastry, this cobbler shows off summer fruits in a rich, just-sweet-enough filling.

CRUST

- 2 cups all-purpose flour
- 3 Tbsp. granulated sugar
- 1/4 tsp. table salt
- 1 cup cold butter, cut into pieces
- 1 large egg yolk
- 3 Tbsp. ice-cold milk

FILLING

- 8 cups peeled and sliced firm, ripe peaches (about 7 large or 3 lb.)
- 6 cups sliced red plums (about 9 medium or 2 lb.)
- 2 cups fresh blueberries
- 2 tsp. vanilla extract
- 1 3/4 cups granulated sugar
- 1/2 cup all-purpose flour
- 1/4 cup butter, melted
- 1 large egg
  Sanding sugar or sparkling sugar

1. Prepare Crust: Stir together first 3 ingredients in a large bowl. Cut 1 cup butter into flour mixture with a pastry blender until mixture resembles coarse meal. Whisk together egg yolk and milk; stir into flour mixture just until dough starts to form a ball. Shape dough into a flat disk using lightly floured hands. Wrap disk in plastic wrap, and chill 1 to 24 hours.

2. Prepare Filling: Preheat oven to 425°. Place peaches and next 3 ingredients in a large bowl. Stir together 1 3/4 cups sugar and 1/2 cup flour; sprinkle over peach mixture, and gently stir. Spoon into a lightly greased 13- x 9-inch or shallow 3-qt. baking dish. Drizzle with melted butter.

3. Place dough disk on a lightly floured surface; sprinkle with flour. Place a piece of plastic wrap over dough disk. (This makes the dough easier to roll.) Roll dough to 1/8-inch to 1/4-inch thickness; cut into 2-inch squares. Arrange squares in a patchwork pattern over peach mixture, leaving openings for steam to escape.

4. Whisk together egg and 2 Tbsp. water; brush dough with egg mixture. Sprinkle with sanding sugar or sparkling sugar.

5. Bake on lowest oven rack at 425° for 40 to 55 minutes or until crust is deep golden and peach mixture is bubbly, shielding edges with foil during last 5 to 10 minutes to prevent excessive browning. Transfer to a wire rack; cool 1 hour.

Patchwork Cobbler

Spiral Bound South

▶ Long before Pinterest, there was the community cookbook, an authentic collection of shared recipes that told the story of a people and a place. We cooked from dozens of our dog-eared favorites to unearth 18 vintage recipes for today's home cook.

FOREWORD BY
Kelly Alexander

Central heating, French rubber goods, and cookbooks are three amazing proofs of man's ingenuity in transforming necessity into art, and of these, cookbooks are perhaps most lastingly delightful," wrote the great food authority— and, yes, cookbook author—M.F.K. Fisher. Anyone who's been immersed in a cookbook knows she's right, because a good one rewards us with much more than recipes. It provides us glimpses into the way people live and eat, giving us ideas for meals to share with our own families. The cookbooks that do this best aren't slick, art-directed tomes written by celebrities or restaurant chefs: Community cookbooks are the ones that capture our hearts.

These are the softcover, spiral-bound productions made and sold as fund-raisers by bands of ladies' auxiliaries, church sisterhoods, Hadassah chapters, parent-teacher associations, and other such groups. The books' defining characteristic is that they are composed of recipes created by local home cooks, people who could be your own next-door neighbors. They are often charmingly illustrated fonts of nostalgia, places we can turn to recall our grandmothers' signature specialties.

Historians write that the first of these cookbooks was published in 1864 by a band of women hoping to help pay for the medical care of Union soldiers in the Civil War. It is no surprise that the South, with our sacred food traditions, took to the concept. No doubt the single most renowned example is *Charleston Receipts,* first published in 1950 by the storied port city's Junior League. In it we find a wide-sweeping look at the dishes that made up the Lowcountry canon, including red rice and Awendaw (see page 149)—dishes associated with Charleston, South Carolina, to this day.

Short by nature, these books exist to showcase one small community, not to provide an exhaustive, encyclopedic perspective. Aficionados snap them up off used-book store shelves and garage sale tables. They visit the handful of shops around the country that are dedicated to selling these historic markers of how we eat, including Kitchen Witch Cookbooks in New Orleans and Heirloom Book Company in Charleston. They peruse the special collections at universities around the country, including Virginia Tech, Alabama, and Harvard.

Nowadays, chefs love snapping up these volumes as much as home cooks do. Most aren't looking for precise formulas for re-creating, say, Awendaw; they're looking to determine the essence of our food traditions. Sean Brock, the venerated chef at McCrady's in Charleston, says, "When you hold a vintage cookbook, you are holding people's history."

And despite the great range of communities, certain archetypal recipes appear over and over again from one book to the next: divinity, congealed salads of all colors and flavors; bowls of icy, boozy punches; chicken salads of every persuasion (see opposite page and page 148).

It's these quirks, the commonalities and the uniquities, that give these local cookbooks significance beyond their nostalgic value. They live on in our kitchens and in our hearts because, when it comes to Southern food, they show where we've been and where we just might go.

Chicken Salad with Wild Rice

Chicken Salad with Wild Rice

MAKES 4 TO 6 SERVINGS

A brightly flavored vinaigrette puts a fresh spin on traditional mayo-based chicken salads. From Meet Me at the Garden Gate *by the Junior League of Spartanburg.*

- ½ **cup uncooked wild rice**
- 2 **cups chopped cooked chicken tenders**
- ½ **cup thinly sliced green onions**
- ½ **cup chopped celery**
- ½ **cup chopped toasted, blanched almonds**
  Tarragon Vinaigrette
- 1 **cup loosely packed watercress leaves**

Rinse rice in a fine wire-mesh strainer. Bring 1 ½ cups salted water to a boil over medium-high heat in a small saucepan. Stir in rice, and return to a boil. Reduce heat to low; cover and simmer, stirring occasionally, 40 to 50 minutes or until tender. Drain rice, and rinse under cold water; drain. Stir together chicken, next 3 ingredients, and rice in a large bowl until combined. Drizzle desired amount of Tarragon Vinaigrette over salad; toss to coat. Chill 1 hour. Toss with watercress and desired amount of remaining vinaigrette before serving.

TARRAGON VINAIGRETTE

MAKES ABOUT ¾ CUP

Gradually add ½ cup **olive oil** to ¼ cup **white wine vinegar** in a small bowl, whisking constantly until smooth. Whisk in 1 Tbsp. chopped **fresh tarragon**, 1 tsp. **kosher salt**, and ½ tsp. **freshly ground black pepper**.

Fresh Rosemary Muffins

MAKES 1 DOZEN

Spiral-bounds offer a cornucopia of delights for the linen-lined bread basket. Redolent of rosemary, these savory, crowd-pleasing muffins boast a goat cheese filling. From Stop and Smell the Rosemary *by the Junior League of Houston.*

- ¾ **cup milk**
- ¼ **cup golden raisins**
- ¼ **cup raisins**
- ¼ **cup currants**
- 1 **Tbsp. chopped fresh rosemary**
- ¼ **cup unsalted butter**
- 1 ½ **cups all-purpose flour**
- ½ **cup sugar**
- 2 **tsp. baking powder**
- ¼ **tsp. table salt**
- 1 **large egg, lightly beaten**
- 4 **oz. goat cheese**

Preheat oven to 350°. Cook first 5 ingredients in a heavy saucepan over medium heat, stirring often, 2 minutes or just until it begins to steam; remove from heat. Add butter; stir until butter melts. Cool completely. Combine flour and next 3 ingredients in a large bowl; make a well in center of mixture. Stir together egg and milk mixture until well blended; add to flour mixture, stirring just until moistened. Spoon one-third of batter into 1 lightly greased 12-cup muffin pan; add 2 tsp. goat cheese to each muffin cup. Spoon remaining batter over goat cheese, filling each cup two-thirds full. Bake at 350° for 20 to 24 minutes or until golden brown. Cool in pan on a wire rack 3 minutes. Remove from pan.

Coconut Custard Pie

MAKES 8 SERVINGS

The recipes in this ethereal collection are indeed divine, and the coconut custard is, dare we say, the best we've ever tasted. From The Church Ladies' Divine Desserts *by Brenda Rhodes Miller.*

Preheat oven to 350°. Stir together 1 ½ cups **graham cracker crumbs,** ⅓ cup melted **butter,** and ¼ cup **sugar;** press on bottom and up sides of a lightly greased 9-inch pie plate. Bake 12 minutes. Cool completely on a wire rack. Increase oven temp to 425°. Whisk together 3 large **eggs,** well beaten; 2 cups **whipping cream;** ¾ cup **sweetened flaked coconut;** ½ cup **sugar;** and 1 tsp. **vanilla extract;** pour into crust. Bake at 425° for 15 minutes. Reduce oven temp to 325°. Shield edges with foil; bake 20 minutes or until set. Cool completely.

Dueling Jezebels

MAKES 4 CUPS

Southerners are, by nature, opinionated about their food, which is why you'll find so many variations of popular recipes like Jezebel Sauce in community cookbooks. The origins of this pineapple-and-horseradish-spiked party favorite are linked to the Gulf Coast, and its name to Queen Jezebel, the biblical bad girl who inspired the eponymous 1938 film starring Bette Davis as a bold and saucy Southern belle. From Savory & Sage *by the Tallahassee Garden Club.*

Whisk together 1 (18-oz.) jar **apple jelly**, 1 (18-oz.) jar **pineapple preserves**, 1 (5.25-oz.) jar **prepared horseradish**, 1/3 cup **dry mustard**, and 1 Tbsp. **cracked black pepper** in a large bowl. Serve with a cheese log or ham.

Blue & White's Chicken Salad

MAKES 4 TO 6 SERVINGS

Clever cookbook committees could often woo coveted recipes from local cafes and restaurants. Birmingham's Blue & White Cafe closed years ago, but its chicken salad still receives rave reviews whenever it's served. Honeycup Uniquely Sharp Mustard is essential to the unique flavor, so no subs, please! From The Collection, an Anniversary Cookbook *by Mountain Brook Baptist Church.*

- 1 3/4 lb. cooked chicken breast tenders, chilled and chopped (about 4 cups)
- 3 to 4 celery ribs, diced (including some leaves)
- 1 cup toasted walnuts, coarsely chopped
- 1 cup mayonnaise (such as Hellmann's)
- 1/2 cup honey mustard (such as Honeycup Uniquely Sharp Mustard)
- 1 tsp. freshly ground black pepper

Stir together all ingredients in a large bowl until blended. Serve immediately.

Chicken Salad Exotique

MAKES 4 TO 6 SERVINGS

During the halcyon days of department store tearooms, the basic makings of this staple took an adventurous turn. The change was duly noted in community cookbooks. Here, we re-create four cosmopolitan favorites to pair with our Summer Sangria Salad.

- 1/2 cup mayonnaise
- 1/2 cup sour cream
- 2 Tbsp. minced shallots
- 1 Tbsp. chopped fresh tarragon
- 4 cups diced cooked chicken
- 2 cups halved seedless red grapes
- 1 cup diced celery
- 1 cup slivered almonds, toasted

Whisk together first 4 ingredients in a large bowl; stir in chicken and next 2 ingredients. Add salt and pepper to taste. Chill 3 hours. Stir in almonds just before serving.

CURRIED CHICKEN SALAD Omit shallots, tarragon, grapes, and almonds. Whisk 1/4 cup finely chopped **green onions**, 1 Tbsp. grated **fresh ginger,** and 2 tsp. **curry powder** into mayonnaise mixture. Stir 3/4 cup each **golden raisins** and diced **yellow bell pepper** into chicken mixture. Stir in 3/4 cup toasted **sweetened flaked coconut** and top with 1/2 cup chopped **lightly salted roasted peanuts** just before serving.

POPPY SEED CHICKEN SALAD Omit tarragon and grapes. Whisk 2 Tbsp. chopped **fresh basil**, 1 Tbsp. **orange zest**, 3 Tbsp. **honey**, and 1 tsp. **poppy seeds** into mayonnaise mixture. Stir 1 cup **sweetened dried cranberries** into chicken mixture. Stir in 1 cup chopped toasted **pecans** just before serving.

MANGO CHICKEN SALAD Omit shallots, tarragon, grapes, and almonds. Whisk 1/4 cup diced **red onion**; 2 **jalapeño peppers,** seeded and minced; 3 Tbsp. chopped **fresh cilantro;** and 1 Tbsp. **lime zest** into mayonnaise mixture. Stir 1 1/2 cups diced **fresh mango** into chicken mixture just before serving.

Summer Sangria Salad

MAKES 6 TO 8 SERVINGS

Once upon a time, smart suburban hostesses considered a shimmering, fruit-filled gelatin ring perfect make-ahead party fare. Rediscover the glories with this modern interpretation.

- 2 cups peeled and diced fresh peaches
- 1 cup diced fresh strawberries
- 2 Tbsp. sugar
- 2 tsp. lime zest
- 2 Tbsp. fresh lime juice
- 1 1/2 cups dry white wine
- 1 (3-oz.) package strawberry-flavored gelatin
- 1 (3-oz.) package lemon-flavored gelatin
- 2 cups chilled lemon-lime soft drink
- 1 cup fresh raspberries

Stir together first 5 ingredients in a medium bowl.

Bring wine to a boil in a small saucepan over medium-high heat. Stir together boiling wine and both packages of gelatin in a large glass bowl; stir 2 minutes or until gelatin dissolves, using a rubber spatula and scraping down sides of bowl as needed. Stir in soft drink.

Fill a large bowl with ice. Place bowl containing gelatin mixture in ice, and let stand 10 minutes or until consistency of un-beaten egg whites, stirring frequently. Stir in peach mixture and raspberries. Spoon mixture into a 6-cup ring mold; cover and chill 8 hours or until firm. Unmold onto a cake stand or serving platter.

Big Easy Barbecue Shrimp

MAKES 6 SERVINGS

Created in 1954 at Pascal's Manale Italian restaurant in New Orleans, Barbecue Shrimp soon became a spiral-bound classic. The seasonings may vary, but it's always served with a crusty loaf of French bread for soaking up the buttery sauce. This recipe, from Elizabeth Ross of Dallas, first ran to rave reviews in our September 2006 issue.

- 3 lb. unpeeled, large raw shrimp
- ¾ cup butter
- ¼ cup Worcestershire sauce
- ¼ cup ketchup
- 3 bay leaves
- 2 lemons, sliced
- 2 Tbsp. Old Bay seasoning
- 1 Tbsp. Italian seasoning
- 2 Tbsp. Asian chili-garlic sauce
- 2 tsp. hot sauce
- 1 (16-oz.) French bread baguette, sliced

Preheat oven to 325°. Place shrimp in a shallow aluminum foil-lined broiler pan. Stir together butter and next 8 ingredients in a saucepan over low heat until butter melts; pour over shrimp. Bake 25 minutes, stirring and turning shrimp after 10 minutes. Serve with French bread.

Old Kentucky Bourbon Marinade

MAKES ABOUT 2 CUPS

This is the little black dress of marinades—sophisticated yet simple. It works with beef, pork, or chicken, and will see you through endless seasons of backyard grilling and entertaining. From Splendor in the Bluegrass *by the Junior League of Louisville.*

- ¾ cup soy sauce
- ½ cup bourbon
- ¼ cup canola or corn oil
- ¼ cup Worcestershire sauce
- 3 Tbsp. coarsely ground black pepper
- 2 Tbsp. light brown sugar
- 1 Tbsp. spicy brown mustard
- 4 garlic cloves, minced
- 1 tsp. ground white pepper
- ½ tsp. ground ginger

Whisk together all ingredients and ¼ cup water in a bowl.

Note: We tested with Old Forester Kentucky Straight Bourbon Whisky.

Mrs. Ralph Izard's Awendaw

MAKES 6 TO 8 SERVINGS

In honor of all those company-perfect casseroles found in community cookbooks, we were tempted to include a recipe for chicken tetrazzini, rumored (somewhat falsely) to have been created in Charleston for the great soprano Luisa Tetrazzini. We opted instead for Mrs. Izard's Awendaw, a creamy, richly flavored fusion of grits and spoonbread with a soufflé-like texture. It's astoundingly good, any time of day, with everything from panfried breakfast sausage to molasses grilled pork tenderloin. So good and versatile, in fact, that our Test Kitchen developed three irresistible twists. From Charleston Receipts.

- 1½ tsp. table salt, divided
- 1½ cups uncooked regular grits
- 1½ Tbsp. butter
- 3 large eggs, lightly beaten
- 1½ cups milk
- ¾ cup plain white cornmeal

Preheat oven to 375°. Bring 1 tsp. salt and 6 cups water to a boil in a large saucepan over medium-high heat. Gradually whisk in grits, and return to a boil. Reduce heat to medium-low, and cook, whisking often, 15 minutes or until thickened.

Remove grits from heat, and whisk in butter. Whisk about one-fourth of hot grits mixture into eggs; whisk egg mixture into remaining hot grits mixture. Gradually whisk in milk. Whisk in cornmeal and remaining ½ tsp. salt. Pour grits mixture into a lightly greased 2½-qt. baking dish.

Bake at 375° for 1 hour to 1 hour and 10 minutes or until golden brown and set.

CHEESE AWENDAW Prepare recipe as directed, stirring in 2 cups (8 oz.) shredded **smoked Gouda cheese** and ½ tsp. **ground red pepper** after cornmeal.

GARLIC-AND-HERB AWENDAW Prepare recipe as directed, stirring in 1 cup freshly grated **Parmesan cheese;** ¼ cup each finely chopped **fresh flat-leaf parsley, basil,** and **chives;** 2 Tbsp. chopped **fresh tarragon;** 3 **garlic cloves,** pressed; and 1 tsp. **freshly ground black pepper** after cornmeal.

FRESH CORN AWENDAW Cut kernels from fresh ears of **corn** to equal 2 cups, and place in a bowl. Using the dull side of a knife blade, scrape milk and remaining pulp from cobs into bowl. Prepare recipe as directed, increasing salt to 1 tsp. in Step 2 and stirring in corn kernels after cornmeal.

Nancy Reagan's Vienna Chocolate Bars

MAKES 3 DOZEN

The occasional celebrity recipe added a certain cachet to community cookbooks. After visiting the Neshoba County Fair (billed as Mississippi's Giant Houseparty) during Ronald Reagan's 1980 bid for the presidency, Nancy shared this supreme creation. The buttery layers of shortbread and fruit topped with crisp meringue definitely get our vote. From Giant Houseparty Cookbook *by The Philadelphia-Neshoba County Chamber of Commerce.*

- 1 cup butter, softened
- 1½ cups granulated sugar, divided
- 2 large egg yolks
- 2½ cups all-purpose flour
- 1 (10-oz.) jar seedless raspberry preserves
- 1 cup semisweet chocolate morsels
- 4 large egg whites, at room temperature
- ¼ tsp. table salt
- 2 cups finely chopped pecans, lightly toasted

Preheat oven to 350°. Line a 15- x 10-inch jelly-roll pan with aluminum foil; lightly grease foil. Beat butter and ½ cup sugar at medium speed with a heavy-duty electric stand mixer until well blended. Add egg yolks, and beat until combined. Gradually add flour, beating at low speed 1 to 2 minutes or just until combined. Press mixture onto bottom of prepared pan.

Bake at 350° for 15 to 20 minutes or until golden brown. Remove from oven, and spread preserves over crust. Sprinkle with chocolate morsels.

Beat egg whites and salt at high speed, using whisk attachment, until foamy. Gradually add remaining 1 cup sugar, 1 Tbsp. at a time, beating until glossy and stiff peaks form. Fold in pecans. Gently spread egg white mixture over chocolate mixture.

Bake at 350° for 30 to 35 minutes or until meringue is browned and crispy. Cool completely on a wire rack (1 hour). Cut into bars.

Note: We tested with Dickinson's Pure Seedless Cascade Mountain Red Raspberry Preserves.

Cook the Bounty

▶ 4 chefs + 4 ingredients = 16 fresh, easy, and fast recipe solutions for gardeners, farm shares, and the farmers' market set.

*w*e wait all year for the moment when gardens groan under the weight of fat, juicy tomatoes, okra pods hang heavy on the vine, and bushelfuls of basil shoot skyward. "For anyone who cooks, this is the time of year when you start getting excited," says Vishwesh Bhatt, chef of Snackbar in Oxford, Mississippi. "The bounty opens up the horizons of what you can do." Let's be honest, though. This sheer abundance also leads even the best of us down a cart path full of culinary ruts. There's only so much pesto one can process before summer's blessings begin to feel more like a curse. Enter Vishwesh and three of his peers. We tapped each to tackle an everyday vegetable or herb and share their creative solutions. No fussy ingredients. No "cheffy" techniques. Just 16 new and smart ways to cook during the most bountiful season of the year.

cucumber

THE CHEF: **Vivian Howard**

ON CUCUMBER: *"I'm always looking for texture on the plate. Cucumbers offer great texture and crunch."*

BUY IT: *"Look for smooth, firm, medium-size cucumbers. Bigger ones are more watery and have more seeds."*

STORE IT: *Room temp, like tomatoes. If you must, store no more than 3 days in a zip-top bag in the fridge crisper.*

RESTAURANT:
Chef & Farmer
Kinston, NC

Cucumber-Ginger Limeade

MAKES 4 SERVINGS

Try this cooler with gin, vodka, rum, or tequila.

Process 1 1/2 cups peeled, seeded, and coarsely chopped **cucumbers** and 1 1/2 cups **water** in a blender or food processor 15 to 20 seconds or until smooth. Transfer to a pitcher, and stir in **Ginger-Lime Syrup** and 1 cup **fresh lime juice.** Serve over **ice.** Garnish with cucumber slices.

GINGER-LIME SYRUP

MAKES 1 1/3 CUPS

Process 1 1/2 cups **sugar**, 1 cup peeled and coarsely chopped **ginger**, and 1 1/2 Tbsp. **lime zest** (about 3 limes) in a food processor 15 seconds. Transfer to a small saucepan, and stir in 2 cups **water.** Cook over medium heat 10 minutes. Remove from heat, and let stand 10 minutes. Pour through a fine wire-mesh strainer, discarding solids.

Cucumber-Basil Dressing

MAKES ABOUT 8 CUPS

Tomatoes, meet a new best friend.

- 4 cups peeled, seeded, and thinly sliced cucumbers
- 2 tsp. table salt
- 1 1/2 cups Greek yogurt
- 1 1/2 cups mayonnaise (such as Duke's)
- 2 Tbsp. finely grated sweet onion
- 1 Tbsp. finely grated garlic
- 1/2 cup chopped fresh basil
- 1/2 cup whole buttermilk
- 1/4 cup fresh lemon juice
- 1 Tbsp. sugar
- 1/2 tsp. kosher salt
- 1/2 tsp. freshly ground pepper

Toss together first 2 ingredients; drain in a colander 30 minutes. Whisk together yogurt and next 9 ingredients. Stir in cucumbers; let stand 30 minutes. Refrigerate up to 2 days.

Cucumber-and-Charred Red Onion Relish

MAKES 4 TO 6 SERVINGS

Chop the veggies as finely or coarsely as you like; spoon over grilled meat.

- 6 cups peeled, seeded, and chopped cucumbers
- 4 tsp. kosher salt, divided
- 2 medium-size red onions, cut into 1/4-inch slices
- 2 Tbsp. olive oil
- 1 garlic clove, finely grated
- 1/2 cup chopped fresh mint
- 1/2 cup chopped fresh flat-leaf parsley
- 1/3 cup sherry vinegar
- 1/4 cup chopped fresh oregano
- 1 Tbsp. sugar
- 2 1/2 Tbsp. fresh lemon juice
- 1 1/4 tsp. dried crushed red pepper

1. Toss together cucumbers and 3 tsp. salt; drain cucumber mixture in a colander 30 minutes.

2. Meanwhile, preheat grill to 350° to 400° (medium-high) heat. Brush onions with olive oil, and sprinkle with remaining 1 tsp. salt. Grill onions 3 to 4 minutes on each side or until charred and tender. Cool 10 minutes.

3. Stir together cucumbers, onions, garlic, and remaining ingredients. Let stand 30 minutes.

Scallion-and-Benne Cucumber Noodles

Scallion-and-Benne Cucumber Noodles

MAKES 4 TO 6 SERVINGS

Slice the cucumbers just until you reach the seeds, but no farther or the noodles become raggedy. Pair with fish or shrimp.

- 6 large cucumbers
- 4 tsp. kosher salt
- 2/3 cup thinly sliced green onions, green parts only
- 1/2 cup plus 2 Tbsp. rice vinegar
- 2 Tbsp. honey
- 1 tsp. sesame oil
  Toasted sesame seeds

1. Peel cucumbers; cut into thin strips using the julienne blade of a mandoline. (Yield should be about 8 cups.) Toss together cucumbers and salt, and drain in a colander 30 minutes.

2. Toss together green onions, next 3 ingredients, and drained cucumbers. Sprinkle with sesame seeds.

Cucumber Basil Dressing

squash

THE CHEF: **Whitney Otawka**

ON SQUASH: *"Last year, I fell in love with petite varieties. Try all shapes and sizes."*

BUY IT: *"Look for firm flesh, no bruises or softening of the skin, no cuts or scrapes. Too big and the seeds get too intrusive."*

STORE IT: *At room temperature, or in the crisper drawer of the fridge if you must.*

RESTAURANT:
Farm 255
Athens, GA

Chilled Zucchini Soup

MAKES 6 1/2 CUPS

Sauté 1/2 cup diced **sweet onion**, 1/2 cup diced **fennel bulb,** and 3 **garlic cloves,** sliced, in 1 Tbsp. hot **olive oil** in a large Dutch oven over medium-high heat 5 minutes; add 5 cups diced **zucchini** (about 2 1/2 lb.), and sauté 3 minutes. Stir in 2 cups **organic vegetable broth** and 1 cup **water;** bring to a simmer. Cook 15 minutes or until vegetables are tender. Remove from heat. Process with a handheld blender 4 minutes or until smooth. Stir in 1/2 cup **whole buttermilk,** 2 tsp. **kosher salt,** 2 tsp. **Champagne vinegar,** 1 tsp. **lemon zest,** and 1 tsp. **fresh lemon juice.** Let stand at room temperature 15 minutes. Cover and chill 2 hours or up to 2 days.

Grilled Squash and Salsa Verde

MAKES 4 TO 6 SERVINGS

- 4 or 5 assorted medium squash (about 3 1/2 lb.)
- 3 Tbsp. olive oil
- 1/4 tsp. kosher salt
- 1 cup raw, unsalted, shelled pepitas (pumpkin seeds), toasted
  Salsa Verde
- 1/4 cup crumbled goat cheese

1. Preheat grill to 300° to 350° (medium) heat. Cut squash lengthwise into 1/4-inch-thick slices. Toss with olive oil and salt. Grill 10 minutes or until lightly caramelized.

2. Place squash on a serving platter. Top with pepitas, salsa, and goat cheese.

SALSA VERDE Combine 7 **fresh tomatillos,** husks removed; 1/2 small **onion;** 1 tsp. **kosher salt;** and **water** to cover in a deep saucepan. Bring to a boil; boil 3 to 5 minutes or until tender. Drain and cool. Process tomatillo mixture, 2 Tbsp. chopped **fresh cilantro,** 2 Tbsp. **fresh lime juice,** and 1 tsp. **kosher salt** in a blender 10 to 20 seconds or until slightly chunky.

Fried Zucchini Straws

MAKES 6 SERVINGS

- 2 cups all-purpose flour
- 1 tsp. paprika
- 1/2 tsp. garlic powder
- 1 Tbsp. kosher salt, divided
- 4 large eggs, lightly beaten
- 4 cups panko (Japanese breadcrumbs)
- 4 Tbsp. all-purpose flour
- 1/2 tsp. dried oregano
- 1/4 tsp. black pepper
- 2 medium zucchini (about 1 lb.), cut into 1/4-inch-thick strips
  Canola oil
- 1 cup grated Parmesan cheese

1. Combine 2 cups flour, next 2 ingredients, and 1 tsp. salt in a shallow dish. Whisk together eggs and 3 Tbsp. water in another dish.

2. Process breadcrumbs in a food processor 10 to 15 seconds or until finely ground. Combine breadcrumbs, 4 Tbsp. flour, oregano, pepper, and remaining 2 tsp. salt in a third shallow dish.

3. Dredge zucchini, in batches, in flour mixture; dip in egg mixture, and dredge in breadcrumb mixture.

4. Pour oil to depth of 2 inches into a Dutch oven; heat over medium heat to 325°. Fry zucchini, in batches, 1 to 2 minutes or until golden. Drain on a wire rack over paper towels. Sprinkle with Parmesan cheese.

Squash Frittata

MAKES 4 SERVINGS

- 6 large eggs, lightly beaten
- 2 Tbsp. heavy cream
- 1/2 tsp. kosher salt, divided
- 1/4 lb. fingerling potatoes, cut into 1/4-inch-thick slices
- 2 Tbsp. canola oil
- 1 Tbsp. butter
- 4 small zucchini, cut into 1/4-inch-thick slices (about 2 cups)
- 4 Tbsp. freshly grated Parmesan cheese
  Garnishes: chopped fresh chives, flat-leaf parsley, and basil; freshly ground black pepper

1. Preheat oven to 350°. Whisk together eggs, cream, and 1/4 tsp. salt.

2. Cook potatoes in hot oil in a 10-inch ovenproof nonstick skillet over medium-high heat, stirring often, 1 minute. Sprinkle with remaining 1/4 tsp salt. Reduce heat to medium, and cook, stirring often, 3 to 4 minutes or until light golden brown on both sides. Transfer potatoes to a bowl.

3. Return skillet to heat; melt 1 tsp. butter in skillet. Add zucchini; cook, stirring often, 2 to 3 minutes or until crisp-tender. Add remaining 2 tsp. butter to skillet; let melt. Add potatoes, stirring to coat.

4. Pour egg mixture over potatoes. Reduce heat to medium-low; cook 1 minute. Sprinkle with cheese.

5. Bake at 350° for 8 to 9 minutes or until center is set. Remove from oven; invert onto a serving plate.

okra

THE CHEF:
Vishwesh Bhatt

RESTAURANT:
Snackbar; *Oxford, MS*

ON OKRA: *"The ingredients of the South are the ingredients I grew up with in Gujarat, India. It took me a while to process that okra came to the U.S. and India from Africa."*

BUY IT: *"Look for a nice, small pod that's bright green and tender to the touch. The bigger, the tougher."*

STORE IT: *In the fridge in a zip-top plastic bag. Wash just before using.*

Pimiento Cheese-Stuffed Pickled Okra

MAKES 4 CUPS

Stir together 4 cups (1 lb.) shredded **Cheddar cheese;** 1 (7-oz.) jar diced **pimiento;** 1/2 cup **mayonnaise;** 1 Tbsp. minced **bread-and-butter pickles;** 1 Tbsp. **Dijon mustard;** 1 tsp. **kosher salt;** 1 **garlic clove,** minced; 1 tsp. **ground red pepper;** 2 tsp. **fresh lemon juice;** and 2 dashes of **hot sauce.**

TO SERVE: Cut desired amount of **pickled okra pods** in half lengthwise. Gently scoop out seeds. Spoon pimiento cheese into okra halves. Garnish with **smoked paprika.**

Charred Okra

MAKES 6 SERVINGS

    3   limes
    2   lb. medium-size fresh okra
    1   Tbsp. garam masala
    2   Tbsp. olive oil
    2   garlic cloves, minced
 1 1/2 tsp. kosher salt
 1 1/2 tsp. freshly ground black pepper
  1/4   cup chopped fresh cilantro

1. Grate zest from 2 limes to equal 2 1/2 Tbsp.; squeeze juice from same 2 limes to equal 5 Tbsp. Cut remaining lime into 8 wedges.

2. Toss together okra, next 5 ingredients, lime zest, and lime juice in a bowl. Cover and chill 1 hour.

3. Preheat grill to 350° to 400° (medium-high) heat. Remove okra from marinade, discarding marinade. Grill okra, without grill lid, 10 to 15 minutes or just until tender and lightly charred, turning often. Sprinkle with cilantro; serve with lime wedges.

Okra-and-Potato Hash

MAKES 4 TO 6 SERVINGS

While traditional, the spices are not crucial. Salt and pepper will work just fine.

    1   Tbsp. whole brown mustard seeds
  1/3   cup vegetable oil
    1   small sweet onion, minced
    2   garlic cloves, minced
    2   tsp. minced fresh ginger
  1/2   lb. small russet potatoes, diced
  1/2   tsp. ground red pepper
  1/4   tsp. kosher salt
 1 1/2 lb. fresh okra, cut into 1/8-inch-thick slices
    2   tsp. ground cumin
    2   tsp. ground coriander
    1   tsp. ground turmeric
 1 1/2 Tbsp. sesame seeds, toasted

Cook mustard seeds in hot oil in a wok or large heavy skillet over medium-high heat 10 seconds or just until seeds begin to pop. Add onion and next 2 ingredients; sauté 2 minutes or until fragrant. Stir in potatoes, red pepper, and salt; cover, reduce heat to low, and cook, stirring occasionally, 5 minutes. Uncover; stir in okra, next 3 ingredients, and salt to taste. Cook, uncovered, over low heat, stirring occasionally, 8 to 10 minutes or until potatoes and okra are tender. Sprinkle with sesame seeds just before serving.

Spicy Okra Fries

Spicy Okra Fries

MAKES 4 TO 6 SERVINGS

Take fried okra to the next level.

    2   medium tomatoes, seeded
  1/4   cup fresh lime juice
    2   Tbsp. Worcestershire sauce
    1   Tbsp. dark molasses
        Vegetable oil
    2   lb. medium okra, cut lengthwise into thin strips
    2   shallots, minced
  1/2   cup roasted peanuts, coarsely chopped
    1   Tbsp. garam masala
        Ground red pepper
  1/4   cup chopped fresh mint
  1/4   cup chopped fresh cilantro
        Yogurt Sauce

1. Dice tomatoes. Stir together lime juice and next 2 ingredients until blended.

2. Pour oil to depth of 2 inches into a Dutch oven; heat to 375°. Fry okra, in batches, 7 to 10 minutes or until crispy and deep golden brown; drain on paper towels.

3. Toss together shallots, next 2 ingredients, okra, tomatoes, 3 Tbsp. lime juice mixture, and red pepper to taste in a large bowl. Sprinkle with mint and cilantro. Serve with Yogurt Sauce and remaining lime juice mixture.

YOGURT SAUCE

MAKES 1 1/4 CUPS

Whisk together 1 cup **plain Greek yogurt** and 1 tsp. **apple cider vinegar** until blended. Whisk in 2 Tbsp. finely diced **apple,** 2 Tbsp. finely diced **red onion,** 1 Tbsp. chopped **fresh chives,** and 2 Tbsp. fresh **lime juice.**

mint & basil

THE CHEF: **Jason Alley**

ON MINT & BASIL: *"We don't use fancy techniques, so we rely on herbs and citrus to brighten flavors."*

BUY IT: *"Look for vibrant, stiff stems and clean tops. If it looks beautiful, it will probably taste great."*

STORE IT: *Cut at the base. Store in water just like cut flowers. Chill mint. Store basil at room temperature in a zip-top plastic bag.*

RESTAURANT:
Pasture and **Comfort**
Richmond, VA

Mint-Honeydew Ice

Mint-Honeydew Ice

MAKES 2 QT.

This creamier cousin of sorbet makes a perfect palate cleanser. You can also scoop it into a glass or paper cone and top with a glug of rum or bourbon for a play on a frozen mint julep.

- 8 cups cubed honeydew melon
- 1 1/2 cups loosely packed fresh mint leaves
- 1 1/2 cups simple syrup
- 4 1/2 tsp. fresh lemon juice
  Pinch of salt
  Bourbon or rum (optional)

Stir together first 5 ingredients, and process, in 2 batches, in a blender or food processor until smooth. Pour mixture into freezer container of a 1-gal. electric ice-cream maker, and freeze according to manufacturer's instructions. (Instructions and times may vary.) Drizzle with bourbon or rum just before serving, if desired.

Mint-Champagne Shrub

MAKES 8 SERVINGS

Shrub cocktails get their tart pucker from vinegar.

- 1 1/2 cups loosely packed fresh mint leaves
- 1/3 cup superfine sugar
- 1/2 cup elderflower liqueur
- 1/3 cup Champagne vinegar
- 1/4 cup fresh lemon juice
- 3 1/2 Tbsp. fresh lime juice
  Chilled sparkling wine
  Garnish: fresh mint leaves

Muddle first 2 ingredients in a cocktail shaker to release flavors; add elderflower liqueur and next 3 ingredients. Fill shaker with ice; cover with lid, and shake vigorously until thoroughly chilled (about 30 seconds). Strain into 8 (8-oz.) glasses; top with sparkling wine.

Peanut-Basil Relish

MAKES 4 SERVINGS

Try this chunky pesto riff as a sauce on fish or pork, tossed with cellophane or vermicelli noodles, or stirred into chicken noodle soup.

- 3 cups firmly packed fresh basil leaves, coarsely chopped
- 3/4 cup unsalted roasted peanuts, coarsely chopped
- 1 serrano pepper, seeded and minced
- 1 garlic clove, minced
- 1 bunch green onions (green parts only), thinly sliced
- 2 Tbsp. fish sauce or 1 tsp. anchovy paste
- 1/8 tsp. sesame oil
- 3 to 4 Tbsp. olive oil

Stir together first 7 ingredients; slowly stir in olive oil until blended.

Basil-Shallot Green Goddess Dressing

MAKES 8 CUPS

"This is what happens when Green Goddess sleeps with Ranch," Jason says. Use it on any salad, though it's particularly good on tomato salad. "Or use it as a dunking sauce for something fried, like fried green tomatoes."

- 3 cups firmly packed fresh basil leaves
- 1 cup whole buttermilk
- 1/4 cup apple cider vinegar
- 1 shallot, sliced
- 2 cups mayonnaise (such as Duke's)
- 2 cups sour cream

Process first 4 ingredients in a blender or food processor until smooth. Transfer to a large bowl, and whisk in mayonnaise, sour cream, and table salt and black pepper to taste. Serve dressing immediately, or cover and chill up to 3 days.

ULTIMATE
southern
food
ISSUE

the southern living
no-cook
summer guide

OUR COOLEST SUPPERS, laid-back party ideas, and iciest treats start here. Give the oven and stove the summer off by employing fresh farm-stand finds and ingredients from the deli, BBQ joint, and seafood counter

Watermelon "Steak" Salad

MAKES 8 SERVINGS **HANDS-ON** 30 MIN.
TOTAL 35 MIN., INCLUDING VINAIGRETTE

Not your mother's fruit salad. A cold, thick, steak-like slice of ripe watermelon pairs unexpectedly well with salty Cotija cheese and a smoky vinaigrette. Also try it with leftover grilled chicken or beef. (Pictured on page 180)

- 1 medium-size red onion, sliced
- 1 cup seasoned rice wine vinegar
- 1 garlic clove, minced
- 1 Tbsp. sugar
- 1½ tsp. table salt
- 12 cups assorted tender salad greens (such as mâche, watercress, arugula, and Bibb)
- 1 cup crumbled Cotija or feta cheese Smoky Dijon Dressing
- 8 (1¼-inch-thick) chilled seedless watermelon slices, rinds removed
- ¾ cup salted pepitas or sunflower seeds

1. Stir together first 5 ingredients and ¼ cup water in a glass bowl. Cover and chill 2 hours. (Mixture can be made and chilled up to 2 days ahead.) Remove onions from marinade, discarding marinade.

2. Toss together greens, cheese, 1 cup red onions, and desired amount of dressing in a large bowl. Top each watermelon slice with 1½ cups greens mixture. Sprinkle with pepitas. Serve immediately with remaining vinaigrette and onions.

SMOKY DIJON DRESSING Whisk together ⅔ cup **olive oil,** ⅓ cup **red wine vinegar,** 2 Tbsp. **honey,** 2 tsp. **pimentón** (sweet smoked Spanish paprika), and 2 tsp. **coarse-grained Dijon mustard.** Add **kosher salt** and **black pepper** to taste. **MAKES** about 1 cup. **HANDS-ON** 5 min., **TOTAL** 5 min.

Texas Caviar Rice and Beans

MAKES 4 TO 6 SERVINGS **HANDS-ON** 20 MIN.
TOTAL 45 MIN., INCLUDING VINAIGRETTE

Turn a Lone Star State appetizer into a simple weeknight main dish. Customize with any topping, such as guacamole, salsa, or a dollop of sour cream. (Pictured on page 180)

- 1 (15.8-oz.) can black-eyed peas, drained and rinsed
- 1 (15-oz.) can black beans, drained and rinsed
- ⅓ cup finely chopped roasted red bell peppers
- ¼ cup finely chopped poblano pepper Texas Vinaigrette, divided
- 2 (8.8-oz.) pouches fully cooked basmati rice
- 1¼ cups halved grape tomatoes
- 1 cup (4 oz.) shredded pepper Jack cheese
- ¾ cup loosely packed fresh cilantro leaves
- ⅔ cup thinly sliced celery
- ⅓ cup thinly sliced green onions Tortilla chips
- Garnish: sliced pickled jalapeño peppers

1. Stir together first 4 ingredients and ¼ cup Texas Vinaigrette in a microwave-safe glass bowl; let stand 20 minutes, stirring occasionally. Microwave at HIGH 2 minutes or until thoroughly heated, stirring at 30-second intervals.

2. Heat rice according to package directions; fluff with a fork. Divide bean mixture, rice, tomatoes, and next 4 ingredients among 4 to 6 individual plates. Serve with tortilla chips and remaining vinaigrette.

Note: We tested with Tasty Bite Basmati Rice.

TEXAS VINAIGRETTE Whisk together ½ cup **olive oil;** ¼ cup **fresh lime juice;** 2 Tbsp. chopped **fresh cilantro;** 1 Tbsp. **hot sauce;** 1 garlic clove, minced; ½ tsp. **chili powder;** and ½ tsp. **ground cumin.** Add **kosher salt** and **black pepper** to taste. **MAKES** about 1 cup. **HANDS-ON** 5 min., **TOTAL** 5 min.

Texas Caviar Rice and Beans

Barbecue-Peach Summer Rolls

MAKES 12 TO 16 ROLLS **HANDS-ON** 35 MIN.
TOTAL 45 MIN., INCLUDING SAUCE

Look for rice paper rounds in the international aisle of large grocery stores or at Asian markets.

Hot water
12 to 16 (8- to 9-inch) round rice paper sheets
2 small peaches, peeled and thinly sliced
12 to 16 Bibb lettuce leaves
1 English cucumber, cut into thin strips
1 large ripe avocado, thinly sliced
1 lb. shredded barbecued pork (without sauce), warm
1 Granny Smith apple, peeled and cut into thin strips
1 1/2 cups torn fresh mint, cilantro, and basil
Sweet Pepper-Peanut Sauce

1. Pour hot water to depth of 1 inch into a large shallow dish. Dip 1 rice paper sheet in hot water briefly to soften (about 15 to 20 seconds). Pat dry with paper towels.

2. Place softened rice paper on a flat surface. Place 1 or 2 peach slices in center of rice paper; top with 1 lettuce leaf, 2 cucumber strips, 1 avocado slice, about 3 Tbsp. pork, 3 or 4 apple strips, and 1 1/2 to 2 Tbsp. herbs. Fold sides over filling, and roll up, burrito style. Place roll, seam side down, on a serving platter. Cover with damp paper towels to keep from drying out.

3. Repeat procedure with remaining rice paper and filling ingredients. Serve with Sweet Pepper-Peanut Sauce.

SWEET PEPPER-PEANUT SAUCE

Stir together 1 cup **sweet pepper relish** (such as Howard's); 1/2 cup finely chopped **cocktail peanuts**; 3 Tbsp. **fresh lime juice**; 2 Tbsp. **lite soy sauce**; 4 tsp. **toasted sesame oil**; 1 Tbsp. grated **fresh ginger**; 2 finely chopped **green onions**; 2 **garlic cloves**, minced; and 2 tsp. **Asian hot chili sauce** (such as Sriracha). Cover and chill until ready to serve. **MAKES** about 1 1/2 cups. **HANDS-ON** 10 min., **TOTAL** 10 min.

Zucchini-Mushroom "Linguine"

Zucchini-Mushroom "Linguine"

MAKES 4 MAIN-DISH OR 6 TO 8 SIDE-DISH
SERVINGS **HANDS-ON** 20 MIN. **TOTAL** 50 MIN.

Cutting zucchini into thin strips is easy and makes a fresh substitute for pasta. Add thinly sliced ribbons of salami for a meatier meal.

1 (3.5-oz.) package fresh shiitake mushrooms*
1/3 cup extra virgin olive oil
2 Tbsp. fresh lemon juice
1/2 shallot, minced
1/2 tsp. table salt
1/2 tsp. freshly ground pepper
1 1/2 lb. small zucchini
3 Tbsp. thinly sliced chives
3 Tbsp. chopped fresh basil
1/3 cup chopped toasted, salted pecans
Freshly grated pecorino or Parmesan cheese

1. Cut stems from mushrooms and, if desired, reserve for another use. Cut mushroom caps into thin slices. Whisk together olive oil and next 4 ingredients in a large bowl. Stir in mushrooms, and let stand 10 minutes.

2. Meanwhile, cut zucchini lengthwise into 1/8- to 1/4-inch-thick slices. Stack 2 or 3 slices on a cutting board, and cut lengthwise into thin strips (similar to linguine). Repeat with remaining zucchini.

3. Toss zucchini in olive oil mixture. Let stand 20 minutes, stirring occasionally. Fold in chives and basil. Transfer to a serving platter; sprinkle with pecans and cheese. Serve immediately.

*1/2 (8-oz.) package button mushrooms may be substituted.

Keep Your Cool

Barbecue-Peach Summer Rolls: Make a small batch to kick-start the party, then offer a platter of the fresh ingredients with the dipping sauce so guests can build their own. Just dip the rice paper sheets in hot water as directed, and wrap with a damp towel to keep them soft.

Bloody Mary Tomato Salad with Quick Pickled Shrimp

MAKES 6 TO 8 SERVINGS **HANDS-ON** 15 MIN.
TOTAL 2 HOURS, 30 MIN., INCLUDING VINAIGRETTE AND SHRIMP

Mix and match colorful assorted tomatoes, such as 'Beefsteak,' 'Brandywine,' and 'Cherokee Purple.' Their rich, meaty flavor counters the dressing's tang and zip. Don't overlook the tender inside leaves of the celery bunch—they're quite delicious, and they add an herbal note to the dish.

- 3 lb. assorted tomatoes, sliced
- 1/3 cup diagonally sliced celery
  Bloody Mary Vinaigrette
  Quick Pickled Shrimp
- 1/2 cup firmly packed celery leaves
  Garnishes: chilled dilly beans, lemon slices, fresh flat-leaf parsley

Arrange tomatoes and sliced celery on a large chilled platter. Sprinkle with table salt and black pepper to taste. Drizzle with desired amount of Bloody Mary Vinaigrette. Spoon Quick Pickled Shrimp over tomatoes. Top with celery leaves. Serve immediately with remaining vinaigrette.

Bloody Mary Tomato Salad with Quick Pickled Shrimp

BLOODY MARY VINAIGRETTE

Whisk together 1/2 cup **spicy Bloody Mary mix,** 1/4 cup **olive oil,** 2 Tbsp. **fresh lemon juice,** 1 Tbsp. **prepared horseradish,** 1 tsp. **freshly ground black pepper,** 1 tsp. **hot sauce,** 3/4 tsp. **celery salt,** and 1/2 tsp. **Worcestershire sauce.** **MAKES** about 1 cup. **HANDS-ON** 5 min., **TOTAL** 5 min.

Note: We tested with Zing Zang Bloody Mary Mix.

QUICK PICKLED SHRIMP Stir

together 1 **lemon,** thinly sliced; 1/3 cup thinly sliced **red onion;** 1/4 cup **olive oil;** 3 Tbsp. **red wine vinegar;** 2 Tbsp. each chopped **fresh dill** and **flat-leaf parsley;** 1 1/4 tsp. **Creole seasoning;** and 1 **garlic clove,** minced, in a large bowl; transfer to a zip-top plastic freezer bag. Add 1 lb. **peeled, medium-size cooked shrimp,** turning to coat. Seal and chill 2 to 6 hours. Remove shrimp, discarding marinade. Sprinkle shrimp with **table salt** and **freshly ground black pepper** to taste. **MAKES** 6 to 8 servings. **HANDS-ON** 10 min.; **TOTAL** 2 hours, 10 min.

Fresh Fact
~
Perk up precooked shrimp by simply tossing them in very hot water for 30 seconds. Then plunge immediately into ice water to stop the cooking process. Drain well.

Picnic in a Glass

MAKES 6 TO 8 SERVINGS **HANDS-ON** 20 MIN.
TOTAL 3 HOURS, INCLUDING DRESSING

This Southern spin on Middle Eastern fattoush salad can be assembled in the morning before taking off to your picnic, tailgate, or work so the flavors meld and pita chips soften. Serve it directly from the jars. We love widemouthed Weck jars, though any style will do.

- 1 (19-oz.) can chickpeas, drained and rinsed
- 2 Tbsp. chopped fresh flat-leaf parsley
- 2 Tbsp. chopped fresh mint
- 2 Tbsp. fresh lemon juice
- 5 Tbsp. olive oil, divided
- 1 (2 1/2- to 3-lb.) deli-roasted chicken, skinned, boned, and shredded
- 3/4 cup chopped radishes
- 1/4 cup finely chopped red onion
- 1 pt. grape tomatoes, halved
- 1 1/2 cups chopped English cucumbers
  Yogurt Dressing
- 3 cups coarsely crushed pita chips
  Lemon wedges

1. Stir together first 4 ingredients and 2 Tbsp. olive oil; stir in shredded chicken. Add table salt and black pepper to taste; let stand 15 minutes.

2. Meanwhile, stir together radishes, onion, and 1 Tbsp. olive oil. Stir together tomatoes and 1 Tbsp. olive oil. Stir together cucumbers and remaining 1 Tbsp. olive oil. Season each mixture with salt and pepper to taste.

3. Layer chickpea mixture, radish mixture, 3/4 cup Yogurt Dressing, tomato mixture, pita chips, and cucumber mixture in a 4-qt. bowl; top with remaining Yogurt Dressing. Cover and chill 2 to 4 hours. Serve with lemon wedges and additional pita chips.

YOGURT DRESSING Stir together

1 cup **Greek yogurt;** 4 oz. **feta cheese,** finely crumbled; 2 Tbsp. chopped **fresh dill;** 5 Tbsp. **buttermilk;** 2 tsp. **lemon zest;** 2 Tbsp. **fresh lemon juice;** and 1 **garlic clove,** minced. Add **table salt** and **black pepper** to taste. Let stand 15 minutes. **MAKES** about 2 1/2 cups. **HANDS-ON** 10 min., **TOTAL** 25 min.

Note: For a thicker dressing, reduce buttermilk to 4 Tbsp.

TEST KITCHEN  INTERVENTION

A LITTLE PROFESSIONAL HELP FROM OUR KITCHEN TO YOURS

Keep Your Kitchen Cool

*Don't get all hot and bothered. Contributing editor **Marian Cooper Cairns,** who created this issue's no-cook recipes, rolls out her fuss-free blueprint for the smartest ways (not) to cook all summer long.*

▶ **SWELTERING TEMPS** drive even the most experienced cooks out of the kitchen. The solution? Outsmart the thermometer by marrying peak summer produce with savvy supermarket shopping. The best no-cook dishes begin with ultra-fresh vegetables and layer in convenience ingredients like rotisserie chicken. Season with bright flavors like lemon juice or herbs. Then add crunch with nuts, seeds, radishes, or cukes.

FOUR WAYS TO BEAT THE HEAT

❶

PURCHASE PROTEINS

Let the grocery store and barbecue joint do the roasting, smoking, or boiling. Pick up ready-to-serve ribs, pulled pork, rotisserie chicken, steamed shrimp, deli meats, or canned beans to give your meal more no-cook mileage.

❷

USE YOUR CHEF'S KNIFE

Now's the time to sharpen your knife know-how. Use it to cleverly cut fruit and veggies into new shapes, such as thick watermelon steaks or long, thin strands of zucchini or cucumber noodles—a healthy, no-cook pasta alternative.

❸

TAP INTO HOT WATER

No need to boil! Straight from the tap, hot water will transform dried rice noodles and tiny grains like bulgur and couscous into hearty meals in minutes. If your tap water isn't steamy enough, use your microwave.

❹

FREEZE THE ICE-CREAM MAKER

Always store the insert to your ice-cream machine in the freezer to get a head start, and chill your ice-cream mixture in the fridge before freezing so that it will freeze faster and take on a creamier texture.

Summer Tomato Trick

Adding salt to these gems concentrates flavor and softens their texture without cooking.

Toss 1 lb. halved cherry tomatoes with 1 tsp. salt in a colander. Let stand over a bowl 1 hour.

Use the seasoned tomatoes in salads and pastas and the juice in dressings or cocktails.

no-cook party menu

ULTIMATE southern food ISSUE

MAKE IT EASY BREEZY.
Cocktails, charcuterie, and a mix of make-ahead salads amount to the chillest dinner party ever

Fresh Fact

It's not just for looks; garnishing adds fragrance and flavor to any cocktail. **AT LEFT:** sliced cucumbers and a lime wedge. **AT RIGHT:** grape tomato halves with a sprig of mint.

Cucumber Gin & Tonic

(Pitured on page 10)

Cut 3 **Kirby cucumbers** into ½-inch-thick slices and 2 **limes** into 6 wedges; muddle in a bowl to release flavors. Stir in 2 cups **gin** and ½ cup **tonic concentrate** (such as Jack Rudy Cocktail Co. Small Batch Tonic); let stand 30 minutes. Press through a fine wire-mesh strainer into a large container, using back of a spoon. Discard solids. Cover and chill 1 to 2 hours. Cut 1 **Kirby cucumber** and 1 **lime** into ¼-inch-thick slices. Fill a large pitcher with **ice cubes**; add cucumber and lime slices. Stir in gin mixture and 2 cups chilled **club soda**. **MAKES** about 4 cups

Tomato-Tequila Fizz

(Pitured on page 10)

Muddle ¾ cup **grape tomato halves**; ¼ cup loosely packed **mint leaves**; 1 **lime**, cut into wedges; and ¼ tsp. **kosher salt** in a medium bowl to release flavors. Stir in 2 cups **tequila** and ¼ cup **light agave nectar**; let stand 15 minutes. Press mixture through a fine wire-mesh strainer into a large container, using back of a spoon. Discard pulp and seeds. Cover and chill 1 to 2 hours. Fill a large pitcher with **ice cubes**; add ¼ cup **grape tomato halves** and **fresh mint sprigs**. Add chilled tomato mixture and 4 cups chilled **club soda**. Stir gently. **MAKES** about 6 cups

Easy Summer Appetizer Board

MAKES 8 SERVINGS **HANDS-ON** 15 MIN.
TOTAL 4 HOURS, INCLUDING PIMIENTO CHEESE AND PEACHES (RECIPES ON FOLLOWING PAGE)

Start your party the casual, crowd-friendly way, and let guests help themselves to a variety of bites. No Southern appetizer board is complete without spicy-sweet pickled okra. Our new obsession: Wickles Wicked Okra (wicklespickles.com). We also recommend Olli Salumeria salami, slow-cured in Virginia and found in gourmet grocery stores across the South, but you can choose any of your favorite cured meats.

8   oz. thinly sliced salami, prosicutto, or country ham
1   (16-oz.) jar sweet-hot pickled okra, chilled and drained
1½   cups toasted salted pecans
¼   cup whole grain Dijon mustard
      Torn bread or crackers

White Cheddar-Chive Pimiento Cheese

MAKES ABOUT 2 CUPS **HANDS-ON** 15 MIN. **TOTAL** 30 MIN.

Here's the secret to nice pimiento-cheese texture: Grate the cheese by hand, half on the large holes of a box grater and half on the small holes. Choose an aged sharp Cheddar cheese for extra bite. Chopped chives and Dijon mustard add piquant punch in place of grated onion.

- 1 (12-oz.) block aged sharp white Cheddar cheese
- 1/3 cup plus 2 Tbsp. mayonnaise
- 1 (4-oz.) jar diced pimiento, drained and rinsed
- 1/3 cup thinly sliced fresh chives
- 1 Tbsp. Dijon mustard
- 1/2 tsp. Worcestershire sauce
- 1/4 tsp. ground red pepper
- 1/4 tsp. freshly ground black pepper

Grate half of cheese using the large holes of a box grater; grate remaining half of cheese using the small holes of box grater. Stir together mayonnaise and next 6 ingredients. Stir in Cheddar cheese until well blended. Let stand 15 minutes. Serve immediately, or cover and chill up to 3 days.

Riesling Peaches

MAKES 2 CUPS **HANDS-ON** 15 MIN. **TOTAL** 3 HOURS, 15 MIN.

These sweet summer gems pair perfectly with cured meats over torn bread with a little Dijon mustard, and work double-duty as a final flourish spooned over our irresistible homemade Buttermilk Ice Cream (see page 196). Or make a simple peach shortcake by sandwiching the peaches in a warm scone with sweetened whipped cream. Swap in any summer fruit and 1 Tbsp. chopped fresh basil or 1 tsp. chopped fresh rosemary for the thyme, if desired.

- 2 cups peeled and chopped fresh ripe peaches (about 2 large)
- 1/2 cup dry Riesling wine
- 1 to 2 Tbsp. light brown sugar
- 1 Tbsp. apple cider vinegar
- 1 tsp. coarsely chopped fresh thyme
- 1/4 tsp. freshly ground black pepper
  Pinch of kosher salt
  Garnish: fresh thyme sprigs

Stir together first 7 ingredients in a serving bowl. Cover peach mixture, and chill 3 to 24 hours to let flavors marinate, stirring occasionally. Serve with a slotted spoon.

Whipped-Cream Corn Salad

MAKES 2 1/2 CUPS **HANDS-ON** 10 MIN. **TOTAL** 25 MIN.

1. Process 1 cup **fresh corn kernels** in a blender or food processor 30 to 60 seconds or until smooth and creamy. Stir together pureed corn, 1 1/4 cups **fresh corn kernels,** 1/4 tsp. **kosher salt,** and 1/4 tsp. **freshly ground black pepper** in a large bowl.

2. Beat 1/2 cup **heavy cream** at high speed with an electric mixer until stiff peaks form. Fold into corn mixture. Let stand 15 minutes. Stir gently. Serve immediately, or let stand up to 2 hours.

Note: To make ahead, prepare recipe as directed through Step 1. Cover and chill up to 24 hours. Let stand at room temperature 30 minutes, and proceed with recipe.

Sweet-Hot Cukes and Peppers

MAKES 8 SERVINGS **HANDS-ON** 30 MIN. **TOTAL** 3 HOURS, 30 MIN.

Stir together 1 1/2 large **English cucumbers,** thinly sliced (about 1 lb.); 1 (8-oz.) package **sweet mini bell peppers,** thinly sliced; 1/2 medium-size **red onion,** sliced; 1 or 2 **serrano peppers,** seeded and thinly sliced; 2 **garlic cloves,** minced; and 2 tsp. **kosher salt** in a large bowl. Stir together 1/3 cup **Champagne vinegar,** 1/4 cup **sugar,** 1 Tbsp. **toasted sesame seeds,** 1/2 tsp. **mustard seeds,** and 1/4 tsp. **celery seeds** in a small bowl. Let both mixtures stand, stirring occasionally, 1 hour. Drain cucumber mixture. (Do not rinse.) Pour vinegar mixture over cucumber mixture; stir to coat. Chill 2 to 24 hours. Serve with a slotted spoon.

Easy Appetizer Board

ENJOY!

Fresh Fig Salad

Whisk together 1/4 cup **olive oil;** 1 Tbsp. **fig preserves;** 3 Tbsp. **white wine vinegar;** 1 **garlic clove,** minced; and **salt** and **pepper** to taste. Refrigerate in an airtight container up to 1 week. Serve over **arugula, prosciutto slices, fresh fig halves,** and shaved **Manchego cheese.** Sprinkle with toasted chopped **pistachios. MAKES** about 1/2 cup

Blueberry Coffee Cake
(page 34)

clockwise from top left:
• Pork with Apples, Bacon, and Sauerkraut (page 39)
• Wine-Braised Oxtails (page 40)
• Rosemary-Garlic Chicken Quarters (page 38)
• Green Tomato Chile Verde (page 40)

Caramelized Spicy Green
Beans (page 52)

clockwise from top left:
- Broiled Oysters on the Half Shell (page 55)
- Collards & Kimchi (page 56)
- Watercress-Buttermilk Soup (page 62)
- Green Pea Hummus (page 76)

Scalloped Potato and
Herb Tart (page 64)

**Best-Ever
Brownies
(page 46)**

Lemon-Yogurt Crumb
Cake (page 50)

clockwise from top left:

- **Fast-and-Fresh Sausage Ragu** (page 42)
- **Quick Chicken Noodle Bowls** (page 43)
- **Pozole** (page 58)

clockwise from top left:

- Romaine with Toasted Pecans and Pickled Strawberries (page 71)
- Pickled Shrimp with Fennel (page 73)
- Smoked Egg Salad Toasts (page 73)
- Grapefruit Chess Tart (page 72)

Seared Steak with Potato-Artichoke Hash (page 67)

Roasted Carrots with Avocado and Feta Vinaigrette (page 68)

From top, clockwise:
Salami, pickled okra, and olive salad;
Smoked trout, green apple, and dill;
Shrimp, cornichons, and radicchio;
Shrimp, cucumber, and chervil or parsley;
Tomato, feta, and sprouts with egg salad; and Tomato, bacon, and watercress with egg salad (page 83)

clockwise from top left:
- Asparagus Mimosa (page 82)
- Muffuletta Deviled Eggs (page 264)
- Piña Colada Icebox Pie (page 77)
- Green Tea-Honeysuckle Cake (page 92)

Pickled Shrimp with
Fennel (page 73)

**Pound Cake Cupcakes,
page 89**

clockwise from top left:
- Very Berry Summer Pudding (page 109)
- Beef Tenderloin Crostini (page 112)
- Moonshine-Cherry Blush (page 113)
- Corn-Avocado Salad and Next-Day Pickled Shrimp (page 113)

from top:
- Yellow Squash and Curry
  Stew (page 106)
- Carrot, Apple, and Ginger
  Soup (page 107)
- Vegetable Soup with
  Basil Pesto (page 107)

Sweet Onion Stack
(page 100)

clockwise from top left:
- Savory Tomato Cobbler (page 117)
- Tomato-Goat Cheese Tart with Lemon-Basil Vinaigrette (page 116)
- Shrimp, Watermelon, and Halloumi Kabobs (page 122)
- Grilled Balsamic-Molasses Bacon (page 120)

clockwise from top left:
• Zucchini, Squash, and Corn Casserole (page 143)
• Carrot-Avocado Tabbouleh (page 193)
• Watermelon "Steak" Salad (page 155)
• Texas Caviar Rice and Beans (page 155)

Firecracker
Grilled Salmon,
page 198

Plum Shortbread
Tart (page 214)

clockwise from top left:
- Turkey Cutlets with
Tomato Cream Sauce
(page 206)
- Spiced Eggplant Cutlets
(page 208)
- Pork Grillades with
Pepper Jelly-Peach Sauce
(page 207)
- Peanut Chicken Scaloppine
(page 204)

BBQ-Ranch Popcorn
(page 212)

Ginger & Lime Marinated Melon;
Roasted Green Bean, Apple, and
Bacon Sandwich; and Cucumber-
and-Sugar Snap Salad, pages 211–212

clockwise from top left:
- Whiskey Whoopie Pies (page 228)
- Slow-Cooker Beef Sliders with Pickled Peppers (page 226) and Buffalo Chicken Meatball Sliders (page 227)
- Broccoli Salad Dip and Hot Brown Fondue (page 226)

Apple, Lemon, and Gin Shandy and
Homemade Cherry Soda (page 225)

Country Ham and Gouda
Grit Cakes with Tomato
Gravy (page 219)

Rosemary Chicken with Corn
Quinoa (page 222)

Apple Bread Pudding
(page 255)

Chocolate Crinkle Candy Surprise Cookies (page 256)

Sloppy Cola Joe Dogs (page 244)

Carrot-Avocado Tabbouleh

(Pictured on page 180)

MAKES 8 SERVINGS **HANDS-ON** 20 MIN.
TOTAL 3 HOURS, 20 MIN.

Combine 1 cup **bulgur wheat**, 1 cup boiling water, and ¼ tsp. **kosher salt** in a large bowl. Cover and let stand 1 hour or until water is absorbed. Meanwhile, cut 6 oz. **baby rainbow carrots** lengthwise into very thin, ribbon-like strips using a mandoline or Y-shaped vegetable peeler. Toss together bulgur; carrots; 5 large **radishes**, sliced; 5 **green onions**, diagonally sliced; ⅔ cup coarsely chopped **fresh flat-leaf parsley**; ½ cup coarsely chopped **fresh mint**; 1 Tbsp. loosely packed **lemon zest**; 2 Tbsp. **fresh lemon juice**; and 2 Tbsp. **extra virgin olive oil** in a large bowl. Season with ½ tsp. **freshly ground black pepper** and ½ tsp. **kosher salt**. Cover and chill 2 to 4 hours. Fold in 1 small **avocado**, diced, and ¼ cup **roasted salted sunflower kernels**. Add table salt and black pepper to taste.

BLT Salad with Olive Vinaigrette

MAKES 8 SERVINGS **HANDS-ON** 20 MIN.
TOTAL 25 MIN., INCLUDING VINAIGRETTE

Microwave 8 thick **bacon slices** according to package directions until crisp. Break slices into large pieces. Toss 1 pt. **cherry tomatoes**, halved, with ¼ cup **Kalamata Olive Vinaigrette**; add **table salt** and **black pepper** to taste. Arrange leaves from 2 **romaine lettuce hearts** and ⅓ cup loosely packed **fresh basil leaves** on a large platter; cover and chill up to 1 hour. Place 4 **hard-cooked eggs**, peeled and quartered, around lettuce. Spoon tomatoes over lettuce; sprinkle with bacon and 4 oz. **Gorgonzola cheese**, coarsely crumbled. Add table salt and black pepper to taste just before serving. Serve with remaining vinaigrette.

KALAMATA OLIVE VINAIGRETTE

Whisk together ½ cup **extra virgin olive oil**, ⅓ cup finely chopped **kalamata olives**, ¼ cup **red wine vinegar**, 2 Tbsp. each chopped **fresh basil** and **oregano**, 2 minced **garlic cloves**, and ½ tsp. **sugar**. Add **table salt** and **black pepper** to taste. **MAKES** about 1 cup. **HANDS-ON** 5 min., **TOTAL** 5 min.

Carrot-Avocado
Tabbouleh

Snappy Beans and Peas with Pecorino

MAKES 8 SERVINGS **HANDS-ON** 30 MIN.
TOTAL 30 MIN.

Process 1 cup grated **pecorino** or **Parmesan cheese** (about 1 ½ oz.); ½ cup **olive oil**; ¼ cup **fresh lemon juice**; 1 **garlic clove**, minced; 1 tsp. **anchovy paste**; and 1 tsp. **Dijon mustard** in a blender until smooth; add **table salt** and **black pepper** to taste. Place ½ lb. **haricots verts** (thin green beans), trimmed and cut into thirds, and 2 cups **water** in a microwave-safe bowl. Cover tightly with plastic wrap, folding back a small edge to allow steam to escape. Microwave at HIGH 2 to 3 minutes or until crisp-tender; plunge into ice water. Drain; pat dry. Repeat with ½ lb. fresh **yellow wax beans**, trimmed, and ½ lb. **sugar snap peas**, trimmed. Combine beans; sugar snaps; 2 cups thinly sliced **radicchio**; ⅔ cup **roasted walnut halves**; ½ cup **frozen green peas**, thawed; 1 large **shallot**, finely chopped; and ¼ cup thinly sliced **chives**. Chill up to 1 hour. Add desired amount of olive oil mixture to bean mixture; toss to coat. Sprinkle with salt and pepper to taste before serving.

no-cook quick fix

ULTIMATE *southern food* ISSUE

HURRY UP AND RELAX. These almost effortless weeknight meals are as fresh as the farmers' market and faster than lightning (bugs)

Summer Gazpacho with Avocado West Indies Salad

MAKES 4 TO 6 SERVINGS

Serve this immediately on busy weeknights for a fresh and light meal. Or make ahead and chill to let the flavors brighten even more.

- 1 medium-size red heirloom tomato
- 1 cup diced seedless watermelon
- 1 cup diced strawberries
- 1 Kirby cucumber, diced
- 1 cup diced peaches
- 1 jalapeño pepper, seeded and minced
- 1 1/2 cups fresh orange juice
- 1/3 cup finely chopped sweet onion
- 1 1/2 Tbsp. chopped fresh basil
- 1 1/2 Tbsp. chopped fresh mint
- 2 Tbsp. extra virgin olive oil
- 1 Tbsp. red wine vinegar
- 1/2 tsp. kosher salt
  Avocado West Indies Salad
  Whole grain crackers

1. Cut tomato in half; gently squeeze to remove seeds. Discard seeds, and chop tomato. Combine tomato and next 12 ingredients in a large pitcher. Serve immediately, or cover and chill up to 24 hours.

2. Meanwhile, prepare Avocado West Indies Salad. Spoon gazpacho into bowls. Top with Avocado West Indies Salad or serve salad alongside Gazpacho. Serve with crackers.

AVOCADO WEST INDIES SALAD

Gently stir together 1 medium **avocado,** chopped; 8 oz. fresh **jumbo lump crabmeat,** drained; 1/3 cup diced **sweet onion;** 2 Tbsp. chopped **fresh basil;** 3 Tbsp. **apple cider vinegar;** 3 Tbsp. **extra virgin olive oil;** and 1/4 tsp. each **kosher salt** and **freshly ground black pepper.** Serve immediately, or chill up to 2 hours.

Family-style Muffuletta

MAKES 6 SERVINGS

Porchetta, a seasoned boneless pork roast, can be found in the deli case, but you can use any cold cuts here. For a make-ahead twist, wrap the sandwich tightly with plastic wrap, and chill under the weight of a heavy cast-iron skillet up to 8 hours.

- ³/₄ cup chopped assorted olives
- ³/₄ cup coarsely chopped jarred artichoke hearts
- 1 medium carrot, grated
- 2 Tbsp. chopped fresh basil
- 1 Tbsp. chopped fresh oregano
- 3 Tbsp. extra virgin olive oil
- 1 Tbsp. red wine vinegar
- 1 garlic clove, minced
  Kosher salt
  Freshly ground black pepper
- 1 (16-oz.) ciabatta bread loaf
- 3 Tbsp. coarse-grained Dijon mustard
- ¹/₂ lb. thinly sliced deli porchetta
- 1 (4-oz.) package thinly sliced Italian chorizo
- 1 (3-oz.) package thinly sliced prosciutto
- 8 (1-oz.) provolone cheese slices
- ¹/₃ cup sliced red onion
- 2 cups loosely packed arugula

1. Stir together first 8 ingredients. Add salt and pepper to taste. Cut ciabatta loaf in half lengthwise. Scoop out soft bread from both halves, leaving a ¹/₂-inch-thick shell. (Reserve soft center of loaf for another use, if desired.)

2. Spoon olive mixture into bottom half of bread loaf, and spread mustard on top half. Layer meats and cheese slices on top of olive mixture. Top with onions and arugula. Cover with bread top, mustard side down. Cut loaf into wedges or slices.

Note: 1 cup jarred Italian olive salad, drained, may be substituted for olive mixture.

Salmon Tostadas with Zucchini-Radish Slaw

MAKES 4 TO 6 SERVINGS

Stir together ¹/₂ cup **sour cream;** 1 tsp. **lime zest;** 1 **garlic clove,** minced; ¹/₄ tsp. **ground chipotle chile pepper;** 1 Tbsp. **fresh lime juice;** and **salt** and **pepper** to taste. Toss together 2 ¹/₂ cups shredded **savoy cabbage;** 1 cup grated **zucchini;** 5 **radishes,** thinly sliced; ¹/₃ cup loosely packed fresh **cilantro leaves;** 1 **jalapeño pepper,** thinly sliced; 2 Tbsp. **olive oil;** 3 Tbsp. **fresh lime juice;** and salt and pepper to taste. Let stand 15 minutes. Flake 1 to 2 (4-oz.) **hot-smoked salmon fillets** or **smoked trout** into pieces, discarding skin. Spread sour cream mixture over 6 **tostada shells,** and top with salmon and cabbage mixture. Cut 1 **avocado** into 6 wedges. Top tostadas with avocado wedges; serve immediately.

Brisket and Rice Noodles with Pineapple Salsa

MAKES 4 SERVINGS

Pulled pork or cooked shrimp can stand in for the brisket.

- 1 Tbsp. kosher salt
- ¹/₂ (8.8-oz.) package thin rice noodles
- ¹/₂ fresh pineapple, peeled, cored, and finely chopped
- 1¹/₂ small Kirby cucumbers, seeded and sliced
- ¹/₃ cup thinly sliced red onion
- 2 Tbsp. chopped fresh cilantro
- 1¹/₂ Tbsp. seasoned rice wine vinegar
- 3 Tbsp. hoisin sauce
- 2 Tbsp. roasted peanut oil
- 2 Tbsp. fresh lime juice
- 1 Tbsp. fish sauce
- 1 tsp. Asian hot chili sauce (such as Sriracha)
- 4 cups shredded romaine lettuce
- 1 lb. shredded smoked beef brisket, warm
- ¹/₂ cup sliced pickled Peppadew peppers
- ¹/₂ cup assorted torn mint, basil, and cilantro

Salmon Tostadas with Zucchini-Radish Slaw

1. Microwave 8 cups water and 1 Tbsp. kosher salt at HIGH in a large microwave-safe glass bowl 2 minutes. Submerge noodles in water; let stand 20 minutes or until tender. Drain.

2. Meanwhile, toss together pineapple and next 4 ingredients; add table salt and black pepper to taste.

3. Whisk together hoisin sauce, next 4 ingredients, and 2 Tbsp. water. Combine drained noodles and 2 Tbsp. hoisin sauce mixture in a medium bowl, tossing to coat.

4. Divide lettuce among 4 bowls. Top with noodles, pineapple mixture, brisket, and peppers. Drizzle with desired amount of remaining hoisin mixture. Sprinkle with herbs, and serve immediately.

no-cook ice-cream desserts

A NEW FREEZER FAVORITE HAS ARRIVED. One genius (and easy!) master recipe and four over-the-top variations provide an endless summer of sweet and creamy ideas, from towering cookie sandwiches to make-and-take pies

Buttermilk Ice Cream

MAKES ABOUT 1 QT. **HANDS ON** 15 MIN.
TOTAL 3 HOURS

Cream cheese and tangy buttermilk give this master recipe its creamy texture and eliminate the need to cook a traditional custard base. Stir in fresh fruit, chopped candy bars, crushed cookies, or spices. Try it in cookie sandwiches or irresistible pies.

- 1 **(8-oz.) package cream cheese,** softened to room temperature
- 1 1/2 cups **half-and-half**
- 3/4 cup **sugar**
- 1/2 cup **whole buttermilk**
- 1 1/2 tsp. **vanilla bean paste***
- 1/8 tsp. **salt**

1. Process all ingredients in a blender 30 seconds or until very smooth. Cover and chill at least 2 hours or up to 2 days.

2. Pour mixture into freezer container of a 1 1/2-qt. electric ice-cream maker, and freeze according to manufacturer's instructions. (Instructions and times may vary.)

3. Serve immediately, or transfer to an airtight container, and freeze up to 1 week.

*Vanilla extract may be substituted.

Keep Your Cool
–
No ice-cream maker? No problem. Substitute 1 qt. of store-bought ice cream (2 cups for each layer) in any of these pies. Try new flavors, like salted caramel gelato. Frozen yogurt or sherbet works too.

Build Your Own Ice-Cream Pie

These simple pies are fit for any occasion. Try one of our combos on this page, or choose your own adventure by mixing and matching flavors. Simply pick a cookie crust, add a homemade ice cream (on facing page), and top with sweetened whipped cream and summer fruit or sundae toppings. Just be sure to freeze the pie after adding each layer to ensure easy assembly and a layered look. (Pictured on page 11)

Blueberry-Cheesecake Ice-Cream Pie

MAKES 8 TO 10 SERVINGS

THE CRUST: Process 1 (10-oz.) package **shortbread cookies** (such as Lorna Doone) in a food processor until finely ground. Stir together shortbread crumbs and 1/3 cup **butter,** melted. Press mixture on bottom and up sides of a lightly greased 9-inch pie plate. Freeze 30 minutes or until set.

THE FILLING: Spread 1/4 cup **blueberry preserves** (such as Smucker's) on bottom of crust, and freeze 10 minutes. Spread half of **Blueberry-Cheesecake Ice Cream** (opposite page) over preserves, and freeze 15 minutes. Repeat layers once with 1/4 cup preserves and remaining ice cream, freezing as directed above after each layer.

THE TOPPING: Top with **sweetened whipped cream, fresh blueberries** and **blackberries,** and **lemon twists.**

Strawberry-Pretzel Ice-Cream Pie

MAKES 8 TO 10 SERVINGS

THE CRUST: Process 1 (9-oz.) package **chocolate wafer cookies** (such as Famous Chocolate Wafers) in a food processor until finely ground. Stir together cookie crumbs and 1/2 cup **butter,** melted. Press mixture on bottom and up sides of a lightly greased 9-inch pie plate. Freeze 30 minutes or until set.

THE FILLING: Spread half of 1 (11.75-oz.) jar **hot fudge topping** (such as Smucker's) on bottom of crust; freeze 10 minutes. Spread half of **Strawberry-Pretzel Ice Cream** (opposite page; omit basil in ice cream, if desired) over fudge topping; freeze 15 minutes. Spread remaining fudge topping over pie, and sprinkle with 1/2 cup chopped **pretzels;** freeze 10 minutes. Spread with remaining ice cream, and freeze 15 minutes.

THE TOPPING: Top with **sweetened whipped cream, strawberry slices, pretzel sticks,** and **shaved chocolate.**

Key Lime Ice-Cream Pie

MAKES 8 TO 10 SERVINGS

THE CRUST: Process 1 (8.8-oz.) package **crisp, gourmet cookies** (such as Lotus Biscoff) in a food processor until finely ground. Stir together crumbs and 1/3 cup **butter,** melted. Press on bottom and up sides of a lightly greased 9-inch pie plate. Freeze 30 minutes or until set.

THE FILLING: Spread half of 1 (10-oz.) jar **lemon curd** on bottom of crust, and freeze 10 minutes. Spread half of **Avocado-Key Lime Pie Ice Cream** (opposite page) over lemon curd; freeze 15 minutes. Repeat layers with remaining lemon curd and ice cream, freezing as directed above after each layer.

THE TOPPING: Beat 2 cups **whipping cream,** 1/4 cup **powdered sugar,** and 1/8 tsp. **coconut extract** at medium speed with an electric mixer until soft peaks form; spread over top of pie. Top with **macadamia nuts, toasted coconut curls,** and **Key lime slices.**

**AVOCADO-KEY LIME PIE
ICE CREAM:** Prepare recipe as
directed, adding 1 1/2 medium-
size ripe **avocados**, chopped;
1 tsp. **Key lime zest**; and
1/4 cup **fresh Key lime juice**
with cream cheese in Step 1.
Stir 3/4 cup coarsely crumbled
graham crackers into prepared ice cream. Freeze 1 hour
before serving.

THE COOKIE:
White chocolate-macadamia
nut cookies

**LEMON MERINGUE ICE
CREAM:** Prepare recipe as
directed. Whisk together
6 Tbsp. **lemon curd**, 2
Tbsp. **sour cream**, 2 tsp.
lemon zest, and 1 Tbsp.
lemon juice. Swirl lemon
mixture and 6 crushed
meringue cookies into
prepared ice cream. Freeze
1 hour before serving.

THE COOKIE:
Gingersnaps

**BLUEBERRY-
CHEESECAKE ICE
CREAM:** Prepare recipe
as directed, adding 1/4 tsp.
almond extract to cream
cheese mixture in Step 1.
Mash together 1 cup **fresh
blueberries**, 3 Tbsp.
blueberry preserves,
and 2 tsp. **lemon zest.**
Stir mixture into prepared
ice cream. Freeze 1 hour
before serving.

THE COOKIE:
Snickerdoodles

**STRAWBERRY-
PRETZEL ICE CREAM:**
Prepare recipe as directed.
Stir together 1 cup chopped
fresh strawberries,
1/4 cup **strawberry
preserves**, and 2 Tbsp.
chopped **fresh basil.** Stir
strawberry mixture and
3/4 cup crushed **pretzel
sticks** into prepared ice
cream. Freeze 1 hour
before serving.

THE COOKIE:
Sugar cookies

Fresh Takes on Summer Grilling

▶ A taste of who and what online got the most raves in the *Southern Living* Test Kitchen.

RECIPES FROM THE SOUTH'S *Tastiest* BLOGS

From the Kitchen of
AMY CLARKE
FAIRFAX, VA
THE-SAVVY-KITCHEN.COM

"Perfect for family or company, this recipe is rich in flavor but light enough to keep your waistline in check."

FIRECRACKER GRILLED SALMON
(Pictured on page 181)

Place 6 (6-oz.) **salmon fillets** in a large zip-top plastic freezer bag. Whisk together 1/2 cup **vegetable oil,** 1/4 cup reduced-sodium **soy sauce,** 1/4 cup **balsamic vinegar,** 1 Tbsp. **honey,** 2 tsp. finely chopped **garlic,** 2 tsp. **dried crushed red pepper,** 1 1/2 tsp. **ground ginger,** 1 tsp. **sesame oil,** 1/2 tsp. **table salt,** and 1/4 tsp. **onion powder.** Pour over salmon, reserving 1/4 cup mixture. Seal and chill 30 minutes. Preheat grill to 400° (high) heat. Remove salmon from marinade; discard marinade. Grill salmon, without grill lid, 4 to 5 minutes or until fish is cooked through and flakes with a fork, turning occasionally and basting with reserved marinade. Remove and discard skin. **MAKES** 6 servings

From the Kitchen of
DAVID OLSON
GRAND RAPIDS, MI
ABACHELORANDHISGRILL.COM

"My love of the Gulf Coast inspired this spicy-sweet dish."

MANGO-CHILI-GLAZED GRILLED SHRIMP

Preheat grill to 350° to 400° (medium-high) heat. Process 1 large **mango,** peeled and cubed; 1/4 cup loosely packed **fresh mint leaves;** 1 tsp. **lime zest;** 4 Tbsp. **fresh lime juice;** 2 Tbsp. bottled **sweet chili sauce;** 1 Tbsp. grated **fresh ginger;** 2 **garlic cloves,** minced; 1 tsp. **dried crushed red pepper;** 1 tsp. **olive oil;** and 1/2 tsp. each **kosher salt** and **freshly ground black pepper** in a food processor 15 seconds or until combined. Stir together 2 lb. peeled and deveined large, raw **shrimp** and 1/2 cup mango mixture; let stand 5 minutes. Remove shrimp from marinade, discarding marinade. Grill shrimp, covered with grill lid, 2 to 3 minutes on each side or just until shrimp turn pink. Toss shrimp with 4 to 6 Tbsp. mango mixture. Serve with remaining mango mixture. **MAKES** 6 to 8 servings

From the Kitchen of
ROBYN STONE
CARROLLTON, GA
ADDAPINCH.COM

"My family's go-to meal—grilled chicken with caprese salad on the side—inspired this easy dish."

CAPRESE GRILLED CHICKEN

Preheat grill to 350° to 400° (medium-high) heat. Cook 1/2 cup good-quality **balsamic vinegar** in a 2-qt. saucepan over medium-high heat 4 to 5 minutes or until slightly thickened; remove from heat, and whisk in 1 Tbsp. **butter.** Sprinkle desired amounts of **kosher salt** and **freshly ground black pepper** over 6 large **tomato slices** and 6 skinned and boned **chicken breasts.** Grill chicken, covered with grill lid, 6 to 8 minutes on each side or until done. Brush chicken with 2 Tbsp. balsamic mixture; top each with 2 **fresh basil leaves** and 2 **fresh mozzarella cheese slices.** Cover with grill lid, and grill 3 minutes or just until cheese melts. Remove from grill; top each chicken breast with 1 tomato slice; drizzle with remaining balsamic sauce. Top with torn basil. **MAKES** 6 servings

August

Savor the Flavors of Late Summer

▶ Save time and money with these fast and farm-fresh recipes from **Caroline Wright,** author of *Twenty-Dollar, Twenty-Minute Meals*

Pasta with Burst
Tomatoes and
Mascarpone

Pasta with Burst Tomatoes and Mascarpone

MAKES 6 SERVINGS
HANDS-ON 15 MIN.
TOTAL 15 MIN.

Blister and burst tomatoes under the broiler to hide imperfections and concentrate flavor. Use extras to fill omelets or sandwiches. (Pictured on page 13)

- 1 (24-oz.) package frozen cheese-filled ravioli
- 3 pt. assorted grape tomatoes
- 1 large tomato, chopped
- 2 garlic cloves, chopped
- 2 Tbsp. olive oil
- 1/4 cup butter, cubed
- 1 Tbsp. fresh lemon juice
- 3/4 tsp. kosher salt
- 1/4 tsp. freshly ground black pepper
- 1/2 cup torn assorted fresh herbs (such as parsley and basil)
- 1 (8-oz.) container mascarpone cheese

1. Prepare pasta according to package directions.

2. Meanwhile, preheat broiler with oven rack 4 to 5 inches from heat. Stir together tomatoes, garlic, and olive oil in a 15- x 10-inch jelly-roll pan. Broil 5 to 8 minutes or until tomatoes are charred, stirring halfway through.

3. Transfer tomato mixture to a large bowl. Stir in butter, next 3 ingredients, and 1/4 cup fresh herbs. Spoon over hot cooked ravioli; dollop with cheese. Sprinkle with remaining 1/4 cup fresh herbs. Serve immediately.

Note: We tested with Celentano Cheese Ravioli.

Melon and Crispy Prosciutto Salad

MAKES 4 SERVINGS
HANDS-ON 20 MIN.
TOTAL 20 MIN.

Build the base of this sweet, salty, and crunchy salad with any melon. (Pictured on page 13)

- 1 (4-oz.) package prosciutto
- 6 Tbsp. chopped fresh mint
- 4 Tbsp. olive oil
- 3 Tbsp. white wine vinegar
- 3 Tbsp. honey
- 3/4 tsp. kosher salt
- 1/2 tsp. freshly ground pepper
- 10 cups loosely packed baby greens (such as arugula)
- 1/2 honeydew melon, peeled, seeded, and coarsely chopped (about 6 cups)
- 1 (4-oz.) package feta cheese, crumbled
- 1/2 cup pistachios, coarsely chopped

1. Arrange half of prosciutto on a paper towel-lined microwave-safe plate; cover with a paper towel. Microwave at HIGH 2 minutes or until crisp. Repeat procedure with remaining prosciutto. Break prosciutto into large pieces.

2. Whisk together mint and next 5 ingredients.

3. Toss greens and chopped melon with vinaigrette, and top with cooked prosciutto, crumbled feta cheese, and chopped pistachios.

Chicken-Vegetable Kabobs with White BBQ Sauce

Chicken-Vegetable Kabobs with White BBQ Sauce

MAKES 4 SERVINGS
HANDS-ON 25 MIN.
TOTAL 50 MIN., INCLUDING SOAKING SKEWERS

Swap new veggies to transform the meal. Go Mediterranean with cauliflower florets and eggplant. (Pictured on page 13)

- 4 (12-inch) wooden skewers
- 1 Tbsp. coarsely chopped fresh rosemary
- 2 Tbsp. olive oil
- 2 garlic cloves, minced
- 1/2 tsp. kosher salt
- 1/2 tsp. loosely packed orange zest
- 1/2 tsp. ancho chile powder
- 1/2 tsp. freshly ground black pepper
- 6 skinned and boned chicken thighs (about 1 lb.), cut into 1 1/2-inch pieces
- 1 small zucchini, cut into 1 1/2-inch pieces
- 1 small summer squash, cut into 1 1/2-inch pieces
- 1 red bell pepper, cut into 1 1/2-inch pieces
- White BBQ Sauce

1. Soak wooden skewers in water 30 minutes. Preheat grill to 350° to 400° (medium-high) heat. Whisk together rosemary and next 6 ingredients in a bowl. Add chicken and next 3 ingredients; toss to coat. Thread chicken and vegetables alternately onto skewers; discard marinade.

2. Grill kabobs, covered with grill lid, 12 to 14 minutes or until chicken is done, turning occasionally. Let stand 5 minutes; serve with sauce.

WHITE BBQ SAUCE

MAKES ABOUT 1 CUP

Stir together 3/4 cup **mayonnaise**; 2 Tbsp. **white wine vinegar**; 1 **garlic clove**, pressed; 1 1/2 tsp. **coarsely ground black pepper**; 1 1/2 tsp. **spicy brown mustard**; 1 tsp. prepared **horseradish**; 1/2 tsp. **sugar**; and 1/2 tsp. **table salt**. Refrigerate up to 1 week.

Skillet Kale Pizza

MAKES 4 SERVINGS
HANDS-ON 20 MIN.
TOTAL 1 HOUR, 40 MIN.

- 1 lb. bakery pizza dough
  Vegetable cooking spray
- ½ cup sliced red onion
- 1 garlic clove, sliced
- 2 Tbsp. olive oil, divided
- 4 cups firmly packed coarsely chopped kale
- 1 tsp. chopped fresh rosemary
- 1 Tbsp. red wine vinegar
- 2 tsp. plain yellow cornmeal
- ½ cup crumbled blue cheese
- ½ cup (2 oz.) shredded fontina cheese
- ¼ tsp. dried crushed red pepper

1. Place dough in a large bowl coated with cooking spray; lightly coat dough with cooking spray. Cover with a clean cloth, and let rise in a warm place (85°), free from drafts, 1 hour.

2. Roll dough into a 14-inch circle on a lightly floured surface; cover with plastic wrap.

3. Preheat oven to 450°. Cook onion and garlic in 1 Tbsp. hot oil in a 12-inch cast-iron skillet over medium-high heat, stirring often, 2 minutes or until onion is tender. Add kale and rosemary. Cook, stirring constantly, 2 minutes or just until wilted. Stir in vinegar. Add salt to taste. Transfer to a bowl.

4. Wipe skillet clean. Reduce heat to medium. Coat skillet with 2 tsp. oil; sprinkle with cornmeal. Arrange dough in skillet, gently stretching edges to cover bottom and sides of skillet. Cook over medium heat 2 minutes. Remove from heat. Top with kale mixture and cheeses. Brush edges with remaining 1 tsp. oil.

5. Bake at 450° for 12 to 15 minutes or until crust is golden. Sprinkle with red pepper.

Zucchini Fritters with Herb-and-Mozzarella Salad

MAKES 4 SERVINGS
HANDS-ON 25 MIN.
TOTAL 25 MIN.

Squeezing the zucchini in paper towels helps remove excess water for a crisp, latke-like crust.

- ½ cup finely crumbled cornbread
- ¼ cup all-purpose flour
- 2 tsp. loosely packed lemon zest
- 1 tsp. kosher salt
- ¾ tsp. baking powder
- ½ tsp. black pepper
- 1 large egg, lightly beaten
- 3 medium zucchini (about 1½ lb.), coarsely shredded
- ½ cup peanut oil
- 1 Tbsp. olive oil
- 1 Tbsp. drained capers
- 1 Tbsp. fresh lemon juice
- 1 (8-oz.) tub fresh small mozzarella cheese balls, drained
- ½ cup coarsely chopped assorted fresh herbs (such as parsley, basil, and mint)

1. Stir together first 7 ingredients in a medium bowl. Place one-third of zucchini on two layers of paper towels, and squeeze out excess liquid. Repeat with remaining zucchini, discarding paper towels after each use.

2. Heat peanut oil in a large nonstick skillet over medium heat. Stir together zucchini and cornbread mixture.

3. Drop 4 to 5 firmly packed ¼ cupfuls zucchini mixture into hot oil; press lightly to flatten. Cook 3 to 4 minutes on each side or until golden brown. Drain on a wire rack over paper towels. Repeat with remaining zucchini mixture.

4. Stir together olive oil and next 2 ingredients; toss with mozzarella and herbs. Top fritters with herb salad before serving.

Zucchini Fritters with Herb-and-Mozzarella Salad

Maque Choux Soup

MAKES 6 CUPS
HANDS-ON 40 MIN.
TOTAL 40 MIN.

Run a knife along just-cut cobs to catch sweet corn milk in a bowl. It'll add flavor and creamy texture. (Pictured on page 13)

- 3 cups fresh corn kernels (about 6 ears)
- 1 medium-size orange bell pepper, chopped
- ¼ tsp. ground cumin
- ¼ tsp. ground coriander
- 1 (32-oz.) container chicken broth
- ¾ tsp. kosher salt
- ½ tsp. freshly ground black pepper
- ½ cup sour cream
- 3 Tbsp. plain white cornmeal
  Toppings: cooked bacon, fresh flat-leaf parsley leaves, fresh lime juice

1. Stir together first 2 ingredients. Place a large cast-iron skillet over medium-high heat until hot. Add half of corn mixture; cook, stirring constantly, 4 minutes or until vegetables begin to char. Transfer mixture to a 3-qt. saucepan. Add remaining corn mixture to skillet; cook, stirring constantly, 4 minutes or until vegetables begin to char. Stir in cumin and coriander; cook, stirring constantly, 2 to 3 minutes or until fragrant.

2. Add 2 cups broth to corn mixture in saucepan, and process with a handheld blender 1 to 2 minutes or until slightly smooth. Add remaining corn mixture and 2 cups broth to saucepan; bring to a light boil over medium heat. Reduce heat to medium-low, and simmer, stirring often, 5 minutes. Stir in salt and pepper.

3. Whisk together sour cream and cornmeal in a heatproof bowl. Whisk in ½ cup hot soup. Add sour cream mixture to soup. Simmer, stirring occasionally, 5 minutes or until thickened.

Maque Choux Soup

Sizzle Up Supper

▶ Thin cutlets of pork, poultry, fish, and even eggplant are the keys to cooking up an easy meal. Let your nonstick skillet do the work, and you're golden.

Peanut Chicken Scaloppine and Squash Ribbon Salad

COAT IT!

GET THE CRUNCH YOU CRAVE WITH EVERYTHING FROM PEANUTS TO POTATO FLAKES. SEE MORE IDEAS ON PAGE 209.

Peanut Chicken Scaloppine

MAKES 4 SERVINGS

Work in two batches so you don't crowd the cutlets in the pan. (Pictured on page 183)

- 4 (4-oz.) chicken breast cutlets
- 1 1/2 tsp. kosher salt, divided
- 1/2 tsp. freshly ground black pepper, divided
- 1/4 cup all-purpose flour
- 2 large eggs, lightly beaten
- 1 cup panko (Japanese breadcrumbs)
- 1/2 cup salted dry-roasted peanuts, finely chopped
- 4 Tbsp. canola oil
  Squash Ribbon Salad

1. Place each chicken cutlet between 2 sheets of heavy-duty plastic wrap, and flatten to 1/4-inch thickness, using a rolling pin or flat side of a meat mallet. Sprinkle with 1 tsp. salt and 1/4 tsp. pepper.

2. Place flour in a shallow dish. Place eggs in another shallow dish. Stir together panko, peanuts, and remaining 1/2 tsp. salt and 1/4 tsp. pepper in a third shallow dish. Dredge chicken in flour, dip in eggs, and dredge in panko mixture, pressing to adhere.

3. Cook half of chicken in 1 Tbsp. hot canola oil in a large nonstick skillet over medium heat 3 minutes or until golden brown. Turn chicken, add 1 Tbsp. canola oil to skillet, and cook 3 minutes or until done. Place on a wire rack in a jelly-roll pan. Keep warm in a 200° oven. Repeat procedure with remaining chicken and canola oil. Serve with Squash Ribbon Salad.

SQUASH RIBBON SALAD

MAKES 4 SERVINGS

Cut 1 lb. each **zucchini** and **yellow squash** lengthwise into thin, ribbon-like strips using a vegetable peeler. Toss together zucchini, squash, 3 cups loosely packed **arugula**, 1 cup loosely packed **fresh flat-leaf parsley leaves**, 2 Tbsp. **fresh lemon juice**, and 1 1/2 tsp. **extra virgin olive oil**. Add salt and pepper to taste.

Crispy Lemon Catfish

MAKES 4 SERVINGS

Cook times can vary depending on the thickness of the fish.

    Vegetable oil
  1 cup **instant potato flakes**
 1/2 tsp. loosely packed **lemon zest**
  4 **(4-oz.) catfish fillets**
 1/2 tsp. **kosher salt**
 1/2 tsp. **black pepper**
 3/4 cup **milk**
    Marinated Slaw

1. Pour oil to depth of 1 inch into a large deep skillet; heat to 350°. Stir together potato flakes and lemon zest. Sprinkle catfish with salt and pepper. Dip catfish in milk; dredge in potato flake mixture, pressing gently to adhere.

2. Fry catfish, in batches, 3 to 5 minutes on each side or until golden brown and fish just flakes with a fork. Drain on a wire rack over paper towels. Serve with Marinated Slaw.

MARINATED SLAW

MAKES 4 SERVINGS

Combine 1 (16-oz.) package shredded **coleslaw mix**; 1 1/2 cups **fresh corn kernels** (about 3 ears); 2 medium-size **Kirby cucumbers**, sliced into half-moons; 1/2 cup chopped fresh **cilantro**; 1 cup jarred mild **banana pepper rings**, drained; and 2 **garlic cloves**, minced, in a large zip-top plastic freezer bag. Whisk together 1 cup **rice vinegar**, 1 Tbsp. **sugar**, 1 1/2 tsp. **kosher salt**, 1/2 tsp. **ground cumin**, 1/2 tsp. **dried crushed red pepper**, and 1/2 tsp. **black pepper**; add to bag. Seal bag, and turn to coat. Let stand 30 minutes. Drain; transfer to a serving bowl. Stir in 1/2 cup **mayonnaise** to coat.

Peppery Pork Biscuits

MAKES 10 TO 12 SERVINGS

This is better than any drive-through breakfast item. We love the time-saving convenience of frozen biscuits. Save even more time by spreading these with your favorite store-bought jam for a savory-sweet combo.

  1 lb. **pork tenderloin**
 1/2 cup **all-purpose flour**
 1/4 cup **plain white cornmeal**
1 1/2 tsp. **freshly ground black pepper**
  1 tsp. **table salt**, divided
 1/2 cup **milk**
 1/2 cup **vegetable oil**
 10 to 12 **frozen biscuits**, baked
    Fig-Onion Jam

1. Remove silver skin from tenderloin, leaving a thin layer of fat. Cut tenderloin into 1-inch-thick pieces. Place each piece between 2 sheets of heavy-duty plastic wrap, and flatten to 1/8- to 1/4-inch thickness, using a rolling pin or flat side of a meat mallet.

2. Stir together flour, cornmeal, pepper, and 1/2 tsp. salt in a shallow dish. Pour milk into a bowl.

3. Sprinkle both sides of pork with remaining 1/2 tsp. salt. Dredge in flour mixture, shaking off excess. Dip in milk, and dredge in flour mixture again.

4. Fry pork, in 2 batches, in hot oil in a 12-inch cast-iron skillet over medium heat 3 to 4 minutes on each side or until golden brown. Drain on a wire rack over paper towels. Serve on biscuits with jam.

FIG-ONION JAM

MAKES ABOUT 1 CUP

Stir in chopped fresh figs for added flavor and texture.

Sauté 1/3 cup chopped **sweet onion** in 1 tsp. hot **olive oil** in a medium saucepan over medium heat 4 minutes. Add 1 tsp. chopped **fresh rosemary** and 1/4 tsp. **dried crushed red pepper**, and sauté 1 minute. Stir in 1 (11.5-oz.) jar **fig preserves**, 1 tsp. fresh **lemon juice**, and 1/4 tsp. **kosher salt**. Cook, stirring often, 1 minute or until hot. Serve warm.

Peppery Pork Biscuits and Fig-Onion Jam

Turkey Cutlets with Tomato Cream Sauce

Turkey Cutlets with Tomato Cream Sauce

MAKES 4 SERVINGS

Here's our new spaghetti-dinner riff on saltimbocca. Use any noodle you wish, or try with chicken cutlets. (Pictured on page 183)

- 1/2 cup all-purpose flour
- 1 Tbsp. cornstarch
- 1 lb. turkey cutlets
- 1/2 tsp. kosher salt
- 1/4 tsp. freshly ground black pepper
- 1/4 cup olive oil, divided
- 1/4 cup loosely packed fresh sage leaves
- 1/2 large shallot, sliced
- 1/2 cup dry white wine
- 1 cup chicken broth
- 2 medium tomatoes, seeded and diced
- 1/4 cup heavy cream
- 1/4 cup freshly grated Parmesan cheese
- 8 oz. hot cooked thin spaghetti

1. Stir together flour and cornstarch in a shallow dish. Sprinkle turkey with salt and pepper. Dredge turkey in flour mixture, shaking off excess.

2. Cook turkey in 2 Tbsp. hot oil in a large skillet over medium-high heat 2 to 3 minutes on each side or until golden. Drain on paper towels.

3. Heat remaining 2 Tbsp. oil in skillet; add sage. Cook, stirring often, 2 to 3 minutes or until crisp and fragrant. Remove with a slotted spoon; drain on paper towels. Add shallots, and sauté 2 to 3 minutes or until tender. Add wine, and cook 3 to 4 minutes or until mixture is reduced by half, stirring to loosen brown bits from bottom of skillet. Add broth, next 2 ingredients, and turkey. Bring to a boil over medium-high heat; reduce heat to medium-low, and simmer 10 minutes or until mixture is thickened. Sprinkle with Parmesan cheese. Serve over pasta; top with crispy sage leaves.

FLASH IN THE PAN

Our secret to golden goodness? A nonstick skillet. It needs less oil for pan-frying, and cleanup is a breeze. No need for a fancy model. Just use a 12-inch or larger to avoid overcrowding.

Pork Grillades with Pepper Jelly-Peach Sauce

MAKES 4 SERVINGS

Keep the cutlets on a wire rack in the oven to ensure each batch stays warm. Prepare the Summer Corn Grits first, letting it simmer on the stove while you pan-fry the cutlets and make the sauce. (Pictured on page 183)

- 1 lb. (¼-inch-thick) pork loin cutlets
- ½ tsp. kosher salt
- ¼ tsp. freshly ground black pepper
- 1 Tbsp. olive oil
- 2 Tbsp. finely chopped shallots or onion
- 1 to 2 tsp. chopped fresh thyme
- ¼ cup dry white wine
- 3 Tbsp. red pepper jelly
- 1 large peach, peeled and chopped
- 1 medium tomato, diced
- Summer Corn Grits
- Garnish: fresh thyme leaves

1. Sprinkle pork with salt and pepper. Cook, in batches, in hot oil in a large skillet over medium-high heat 3 minutes on each side or until done. Transfer pork to a wire rack in a jelly-roll pan, and keep warm in a 200° oven.

2. Add shallots and thyme to skillet; sauté 1 minute or until tender. Stir in wine and pepper jelly until smooth. Stir in peach and tomato, and cook, stirring often, 2 to 3 minutes or until thoroughly heated. Add salt and pepper to taste. Pour sauce over pork, and serve immediately with grits.

SUMMER CORN GRITS

MAKES 4 TO 6 SERVINGS

Scrape the milky liquid from the corncobs, and add it with the kernels for extra summery flavor.

Sauté 1½ cups **fresh corn kernels** (about 3 ears) and 1 **garlic clove**, minced, in 2 tsp. hot **olive oil** in a medium saucepan over medium-high heat 2 to 3 minutes or until corn is tender. Transfer mixture to a small bowl. Add 4 cups **water** to saucepan, and bring to a boil over medium-high heat. Stir in 1 cup uncooked **stone-ground grits** and 1 tsp. **kosher salt**; return to a boil, stirring occasionally. Cover, reduce heat to low, and cook, stirring occasionally, 30 to 35 minutes or until tender. Stir in corn mixture, and add salt to taste.

Pork Grillades with Pepper Jelly-Peach Sauce

CHOOSE THE BEST CUTLETS

WHETHER POUNDING YOUR OWN OR BUYING PRECUT CONVENIENCE, THINK THIN. THESE ARE THE BEST CUTLETS FOR THE PAN.

POULTRY
Pounded chicken breasts cook up fast. Try tenders and turkey cutlets too. For extra-juicy flavor, pound boneless, skinless chicken thighs.

PORK
Look for packs of sliced loin cutlets, thin boneless pork chops, or bone-in breakfast chops. Or make your own with tenderloin or loin. See how on page 209.

FISH
Thin, meaty fillets (catfish, flounder, and smallish snapper and triggerfish) make easy cutlets, no pounding required. They're ready when you are.

Spiced Eggplant Cutlets

Grilled Chipotle Chicken

DUST IT!

DRIED HERBS, SPICES, AND RUBS ADD PUNCHY, ZINGY FLAVOR—PERFECT FOR GRILLING AND BROILING.

Spiced Eggplant Cutlets

MAKES 4 TO 6 SERVINGS

Eggplant slices tend to shrink significantly as they cook, so start with hearty 1-inch-thick slabs. (Pictured on page 183)

- 2 tsp. paprika
- 2 tsp. chopped fresh thyme
- 1 tsp. ground cumin
- 1 tsp. kosher salt
- 2 small eggplants
- 3/4 cup olive oil
- 2 garlic cloves, minced
  Chickpea-Feta Salad

1. Preheat grill to 350° to 400° (medium-high) heat. Stir together first 4 ingredients in a small bowl. Cut eggplants lengthwise into 1-inch-thick slices. Stir together olive oil and garlic.

2. Sprinkle both sides of eggplant slices with paprika mixture. Brush both sides with olive oil mixture.

3. Grill eggplant, covered with grill lid, 4 to 5 minutes on each side or until slightly charred and tender. Serve immediately with Chickpea-Feta Salad.

CHICKPEA-FETA SALAD

MAKES 4 TO 6 SERVINGS

Stir together 1 (15.5-oz.) can **chickpeas,** drained and rinsed; 2 **red bell peppers,** diced; 1 small **shallot,** minced; 2 Tbsp. **fresh lemon juice;** 2 Tbsp. **olive oil;** and 1/2 tsp. **kosher salt** in a large bowl. Fold 1 cup coarsely chopped **fresh herbs** (such as basil, oregano, and parsley) into chickpea mixture. Top with 1/2 cup crumbled **feta cheese** just before serving.

Grilled Chipotle Chicken

MAKES 4 SERVINGS

Try Mexican oregano for extra zing.

- 2 lb. skinned and boned chicken thighs
- 2 Tbsp. light brown sugar
- 1/2 tsp. dried oregano
- 1/2 tsp. ground chipotle chile pepper
- 1/2 tsp. kosher salt
  Okra and Tomatoes

1. Preheat grill to 350° to 400° (medium-high) heat. Place each chicken thigh between 2 sheets of heavy-duty plastic wrap, and flatten to 1/4-inch thickness, using a rolling pin or flat side of a meat mallet. Combine sugar and next 3 ingredients; rub over chicken.

2. Grill chicken, covered with grill lid, 2 to 3 minutes on each side or until done. Remove from grill, and cover with aluminum foil to keep warm. Serve with Okra and Tomatoes.

OKRA AND TOMATOES

MAKES 4 SERVINGS

Thinly slice 8 oz. fresh **okra** and 1 large **shallot;** sauté in 2 Tbsp. hot **olive oil** in a large skillet over medium-high heat 6 to 8 minutes or until okra is golden brown; transfer to a bowl. Heat 1 Tbsp. olive oil in skillet. Add 1 large **green tomato,** chopped; 1 pt. **grape tomatoes,** halved; and 2 **garlic cloves,** minced. Cook, stirring often, 2 minutes or until softened. Combine tomatoes and okra mixture. Stir in 1/3 cup torn **fresh basil,** 1/4 cup **fresh flat-leaf parsley leaves,** 1/2 tsp. **table salt,** and 1/2 tsp. freshly ground **black pepper.**

Create a Cheaper Cutlet

▶ **CUTLETS WILL MAKE YOU** a smarter, faster weeknight cook because the path from seasoning to browning to plating takes mere minutes. They'll even fatten your wallet too. As we developed the recipes for "Sizzle Up Supper" on page 204, we sliced and pounded our own pork cutlets, saving us a whopping $2 a pound vs. buying presliced and packaged ones. Here's how to outsmart the supermarket meat counter.

① MAKE YOUR OWN PORK CUTLETS

Using a sharp knife, trim any connective tissue or excess fat from a 3- to 4-lb. pork loin. Working from one end of the loin, cut a ½-inch-thick medallion by slicing crosswise. Repeat to make about 20 medallions.

② POUND THEM THIN

Arrange 1 medallion on an 11- x 24-inch sheet of heavy-duty plastic wrap. Fold short ends together to cover pork. Using a meat mallet, pound to ¼- to ⅛-inch thickness. Refrigerate up to 2 days; freeze 2 months. Try also with turkey tenders.

③ THINK BEYOND BREADCRUMBS

Dredge any cutlet in ¼ cup seasoned flour, dip in an egg wash of 2 lightly beaten eggs, and then dredge with any of **our new dreamcoats** (below). To store, freeze the dreamcoats in airtight containers up to 3 months.

A. PORK RINDS & ROSEMARY

Stir together 2 cups crushed fried pork rinds, 2 Tbsp. minced fresh rosemary, ½ tsp. garlic powder, and ¼ tsp. dried crushed red pepper.

B. WASABI PEAS & ALMONDS

Stir together 1½ cups crushed wasabi peas, 1 cup crushed wasabi-and-soy sauce almonds, and ⅛ tsp. each kosher salt and ground red pepper.

C. PITA CHIPS & CHIPOTLE

Stir together 2½ cups crushed pita chips, 2 tsp. orange zest, ½ tsp. kosher salt, and ¼ tsp. each ground chipotle chile pepper and ground cumin.

D. CAJUN POTATO CHIPS

Stir together 2½ cups crushed Cajun-seasoned kettle-cooked potato chips and 1 tsp. Cajun seasoning.

Pack a Perfect Picnic

▶ Paired with a patch of grass and charming take-out containers, this easy and impressive make-ahead menu will enliven any outdoor gathering

The Menu

STARTERS & SIDES
BBQ-RANCH POPCORN

SUMMER RICE SALAD

CUCUMBER-AND-SUGAR
SNAP SALAD

GINGER & LIME
MARINATED MELON

MAIN COURSE
ROASTED GREEN BEAN, APPLE,
AND BACON SANDWICHES

DESSERT
BLACKBERRY-LIMEADE BARS

Summer Rice Salad

MAKES 8 TO 10 SERVINGS
HANDS-ON 30 MIN.
TOTAL 30 MIN.

Ditch a mayonnaise-laden potato salad for this fresh, minty number. Drizzle the versatile dressing over fresh fruit or grilled fish or veggies.

Stir together 1 small **shallot**, minced; 3 Tbsp. **white wine vinegar;** 1 Tbsp. loosely packed **lime zest;** 2 Tbsp. **fresh lime juice;** 1 tsp. **Dijon mustard;** and 1 tsp. **honey** in a large bowl. Whisk in ½ cup **extra virgin olive oil** until blended. Add 4 cups cooked **basmati rice**, chilled; 2 cups thinly sliced **napa cabbage;** 1½ cups thinly sliced **English cucumbers;** 1 cup diced **red bell pepper;** ½ cup thinly sliced **green onions;** ½ cup chopped **fresh mint;** ⅓ cup chopped **fresh chives;** and ⅓ cup chopped **fresh flat-leaf parsley;** toss. Add **salt** to taste. Cover and chill up to 4 hours.

Ginger & Lime Marinated Melon

MAKES 8 SERVINGS
HANDS-ON 15 MIN.
TOTAL 3 HOURS, 15 MIN.

Skewer the melon after marinating for easy-to-eat melon pops.

- 1 (3½-lb.) cantaloupe
- 1 (2-inch) piece fresh ginger, peeled
  Cheesecloth or coffee filter
- 2 Tbsp. Demerara sugar
- 1 tsp. loosely packed lime zest
- 1 Tbsp. fresh lime juice
- ¼ tsp. kosher salt

Peel, seed, and slice cantaloupe into ½-inch-thick wedges. Grate ginger to equal 1 Tbsp., using large holes of a box grater. Place grated ginger in a piece of cheesecloth or a coffee filter. Squeeze juice from grated ginger into a large bowl; discard solids. Add cantaloupe, sugar, and remaining ingredients to bowl; toss to coat. Pack mixture into 2 (1-qt.) wide-mouth canning jars; pour any accumulated juices into jars. Cover with metal lids, and screw on bands. Chill 3 to 8 hours.

Ginger & Lime Marinated Melon; Roasted Green Bean, Apple, and Bacon Sandwiches; and Cucumber-and-Sugar Snap Salad

Cucumber-and-Sugar Snap Salad

MAKES 8 SERVINGS
HANDS-ON 20 MIN.
TOTAL 20 MIN.

No cukes or sugar snaps on hand? Almost any raw veggie will do. Try using bell peppers, jicama, or fresh corn kernels. (Pictured on page 185)

- ¼ cup Greek yogurt
- ¼ cup sour cream
- 1 garlic clove, minced
- 2 Tbsp. chopped fresh mint
- 1 Tbsp. chopped fresh dill
- ½ tsp. kosher salt
- ½ tsp. freshly ground black pepper
- 1 oz. feta cheese, crumbled
- 1 cup fully cooked shelled frozen edamame (green soybeans), thawed
- 1 cup fresh sugar snap peas, cut into ¼-inch pieces
- ½ English cucumber, diced (about 1 cup)
- 2 celery ribs, diced (about 1 cup)
- 6 to 8 radishes, cut into thin strips (about ⅓ cup)
- ¼ cup finely chopped red onion

1. Stir together first 7 ingredients in a small bowl; stir in feta cheese.

2. Toss together edamame and next 5 ingredients in a large bowl. Stir yogurt mixture into vegetable mixture. Serve immediately, or cover and chill up to 4 hours.

Roasted Green Bean, Apple, and Bacon Sandwiches

MAKES 8 SERVINGS
HANDS-ON 20 MIN.
TOTAL 2 HOURS, 40 MIN.

A green bean sandwich? Trust us on this one. We fell for the combo of tender beans, crisp apples, salty Parm, and tangy dressing. Keep it tidy by hollowing out the baguette to create a cradle for the fillings. (Pictured on page 185)

- 1 lb. fresh green beans, trimmed
- 2 tsp. olive oil
- 1/4 tsp. freshly ground black pepper
- 1 tsp. kosher salt, divided
- 6 thick bacon slices
- 1/2 cup torn fresh dill
- 1/2 cup olive oil
- 1 tsp. firmly packed lemon zest
- 2 tsp. Dijon mustard
- 1 small shallot, minced
- 4 Tbsp. fresh lemon juice, divided
- 1 medium-size Red Delicious apple
- 2 (8 1/2-oz.) French bread baguettes, cut in half horizontally
- 4 oz. Parmigiano-Reggiano cheese, thinly sliced
  Wax paper

1. Preheat oven to 425°. Toss green beans with 2 tsp. olive oil, pepper, and 1/4 tsp. salt. Place beans in a single layer in a jelly-roll pan, and bake 10 minutes. Remove from oven, and chill 10 minutes.

2. Arrange bacon in a single layer in jelly-roll pan. Bake at 425° for 12 minutes or until crisp. Drain on paper towels.

3. Whisk together dill, next 4 ingredients, 3 Tbsp. lemon juice, and remaining 3/4 tsp. salt. Let stand 5 minutes.

4. Meanwhile, cut apple into thin slices, and toss with remaining 1 Tbsp. lemon juice.

5. Spoon vinaigrette onto top halves of baguettes. Layer beans, bacon, apple, and cheese on bottom halves. Cover with top halves of baguettes; wrap tightly in wax paper. Chill up to 2 hours. Slice sandwiches before serving.

Crafty moment
Trim and tape chevron sandwich bags into cute cones.

BBQ-Ranch Popcorn

MAKES 8 SERVINGS
HANDS-ON 10 MIN.
TOTAL 10 MIN.

Try other flavors, like chili powder-lime zest and cinnamon-sugar. (Pictured on page 184)

1. Stir together 1 (1-oz.) envelope **Ranch dressing mix,** 2 tsp. **smoked paprika,** and 1 tsp. **light brown sugar** in a small bowl. Prepare 1 (86.8-gram) bag **gourmet microwave popcorn** according to package directions, and pour into a large bowl. Sprinkle immediately with half of Ranch mixture, tossing to coat.

2. Prepare another bag of popcorn according to package directions. Add to bowl with seasoned popcorn, and toss with remaining Ranch mixture. Store popcorn in an airtight container up to 2 days.

Note: We tested with Orville Redenbacher's Gourmet White Corn popcorn.

Whip Up a No-Bake Cake

▶ Layers of tangy-sweet Key lime custard and graham crackers stack up to make one quick and easy layer cake with just enough pucker to take the heat off summer

Key Lime Icebox Cake

MAKES 8 TO 10 SERVINGS

Add the lime juice once you've fully cooked the custard to let the cornstarch thicken the mixture properly. (Pictured on page 12)

- 3/4 cup granulated sugar
- 1/4 cup cornstarch
- 1/8 tsp. kosher salt
- 4 large egg yolks
- 2 cups half-and-half
- 3 Tbsp. butter
- 2 Tbsp. Key lime zest*
- 1/2 cup fresh Key lime juice*
- 45 graham cracker squares
- 1 cup whipping cream
- 1/4 cup powdered sugar

1. Whisk together first 3 ingredients in a heavy saucepan. Whisk together egg yolks and half-and-half in a bowl. Gradually whisk egg mixture into sugar mixture; bring to a boil over medium heat, whisking constantly. Boil, whisking constantly, 1 minute; remove from heat. Whisk in butter and zest until butter melts. Gradually whisk in juice just until blended. Pour into a metal bowl, and place bowl on ice. Let stand, stirring occasionally, 8 to 10 minutes or until custard is cold and slightly thickened.

2. Meanwhile, line bottom and sides of an 8-inch square pan with plastic wrap, allowing 4 inches to extend over sides. Place 9 graham crackers, with sides touching, in a single layer in bottom of pan to form a large square. (Crackers will not completely cover bottom.)

3. Spoon about 3/4 cup cold custard over crackers; spread to edge of crackers. Repeat layers 3 times with crackers and remaining custard, ending with custard; top with remaining 9 crackers. Pull sides of plastic wrap tightly over cake; freeze in pan 8 hours.

4. Lift cake from pan, and place on a platter; discard plastic wrap. Cover loosely; let stand 1 hour.

5. Beat whipping cream at high speed with an electric mixer until foamy; gradually add powdered sugar, beating until soft peaks form. Spread on top of cake.

*Regular (Persian) lime zest and juice may be substituted.

FROZEN ASSETS

Store in freezer up to 1 month: Place frozen wrapped cake in a zip-top freezer bag. Frost and serve.

Fresh Fruit Desserts

▶ A taste of who and what online got the most raves in the *Southern Living* Test Kitchen

RECIPES FROM
THE
SOUTH'S
Tastiest
BLOGS
★

From the Kitchen of
KELLY STERLING

FORT LAUDERDALE, FL
SNAILSVIEW.COM

"I like to use fresh organic fruit for optimal sweetness. You can use plums, peaches, or nectarines."

PLUM SHORTBREAD TART

Preheat oven to 350°. Pulse 3/4 cup **all-purpose flour;** 1/4 cup toasted **slivered almonds,** and a pinch of **sea salt** in a food processor 3 times or until combined. Beat 1/3 cup **powdered sugar** and 1/4 cup **butter,** softened, at medium speed with an electric mixer 5 minutes or until pale and fluffy. Gradually add flour mixture and 1 **large egg yolk,** beating at low speed until a dough forms. Press dough into a lightly greased 13- x 4-inch tart pan with removable bottom. Chill 10 minutes. Bake 14 minutes or until golden. Cool completely. Whisk 6 **large egg yolks** until thick and pale. Whisk together 1/2 cup **sugar,** 6 Tbsp. **all-purpose flour,** and a pinch of **sea salt.** Combine 2 cups **milk** and 1 Tbsp. loosely packed **lemon zest** in a saucepan; cook over medium heat, stirring constantly, 5 minutes or just until it begins to steam. Whisk in sugar mixture, whisking constantly just until bubbles appear. Gradually stir one-fourth of hot milk mixture into yolks; add to remaining hot milk mixture, stirring constantly. Bring mixture to a low boil over medium heat; remove from heat. Stir in 2 Tbsp. each **butter** and **amaretto liqueur.** Transfer to a bowl; place plastic wrap directly onto custard. Cool 1 hour. Spread into crust; top with 4 thinly sliced **plums.** Brush with 1 Tbsp. warm **apricot preserves. MAKES** 8 servings

From the Kitchen of
REBECCA CRUMP

NASHVILLE, TN
EZRAPOUNDCAKE.COM

"For easy peeling, score an 'x' on each peach. Boil in water 1 minute. Cool peaches in ice, and peel."

FRESH PEACH SORBET

Process 2 lb. ripe **peaches,** peeled and chopped, in a food processor until smooth; strain into a bowl. Stir together 1 cup warm **water,** 1/2 cup **sugar,** and 1 Tbsp. **vodka** or **orange liqueur** until sugar dissolves. Stir sugar mixture into peach puree. Chill 2 hours. Pour into container of a 1-qt. ice-cream maker; prepare according to manufacturer's instructions. Freeze in an airtight container. **MAKES** 1 qt.

From the Kitchen of
MEGHAN CASSIDY

CHEVY CHASE, MD
COSMOCOOKIE.BLOGSPOT.COM

"I use Key limes for bright flavor. These bars are best served chilled."

BLACKBERRY-LIMEADE BARS

Preheat oven to 350°. Line bottom and sides of an 8-inch square pan with **parchment paper,** allowing 3 inches to extend over sides. Beat 1/2 cup **butter,** softened, and 1/4 cup **sugar** at medium speed with an electric mixer until smooth. Stir together 1 cup **all-purpose flour** and 1/4 tsp. **table salt;** gradually add to butter mixture, beating at low speed just until blended after each addition. Press dough into bottom of prepared pan. Bake 20 to 25 minutes or until lightly browned. Whisk together 1 1/2 cups **sugar,** 1/2 cup **all-purpose flour,** 1 Tbsp. loosely packed **Key lime zest,** and 1/4 tsp. salt in a large bowl. Whisk in 1 large **egg** and 3 large **egg whites** just until blended. Process 2 cups fresh **blackberries** in a blender until smooth. Pour pureed berries through a fine wire-mesh strainer into sugar mixture, discarding seeds; whisk in 2/3 cup fresh **Key lime juice.** Pour over warm crust; bake 30 to 35 minutes or until center is set. Cool on wire rack 30 minutes. Cover with plastic wrap; chill 2 hours. Lift from pan, using parchment paper as handles. Cut into bars. **MAKES** 16 (2-inch) bars

September

Wake Up Brunch

▶ Mix and match these make-ahead recipes for a fresh twist on our morning favorites

Breakfast Sausage-Egg Pizza

Breakfast Sausage-Egg Pizza

MAKES 4 TO 6 SERVINGS
HANDS-ON 20 MIN.
TOTAL 2 HOURS

Feel free to fry the eggs in a skillet and add to the just-cooked pizza.

- 1 lb. store-bought pizza dough
  Vegetable cooking spray
- ½ medium-size sweet onion, sliced
- 1 red bell pepper, sliced
- ½ (8-oz.) package sliced baby portobello mushrooms
- 2 Tbsp. olive oil, divided
- 1 tsp. plain yellow cornmeal
  Mornay Sauce
- ½ (1-lb.) package ground pork sausage, cooked and crumbled
- 6 large eggs, at room temperature

1. Place dough in a large bowl coated with cooking spray; lightly coat dough with cooking spray. Cover with plastic wrap, and let rise in a warm place (85°), free from drafts, 1 hour or just until doubled in bulk.

2. Preheat oven to 425°. Sauté onion and next 2 ingredients in 1 Tbsp. hot oil in a large skillet 3 to 5 minutes or until onion and bell pepper are crisp-tender.

3. Roll dough to about ¼-inch thickness (about 14 x 10 inches) on a lightly floured surface; cover with plastic wrap. Let stand 5 minutes.

4. Brush a 15- x 10-inch jelly-roll pan with remaining 1 Tbsp. oil; sprinkle with corn-meal. Transfer dough to pan. Spread Mornay Sauce over dough, and sprinkle with sausage and onion mixture. Break eggs over pizza.

5. Bake at 425° for 20 to 25 minutes or until eggs are cooked how you like them and crust is crisp.

MORNAY SAUCE

MAKES 1 ¼ CUPS

Melt 2 Tbsp. **butter** in a heavy saucepan over medium-low heat; whisk in 2 Tbsp. **all-purpose flour** until smooth. Cook, whisking constantly, 2 minutes. Gradually whisk in 1 cup **half-and-half**; increase heat to medium, and cook, whisking constantly, 3 to 5 minutes or until thickened. Remove from heat, and whisk in 1 cup (4 oz.) freshly grated **Parmesan cheese**, ½ tsp. freshly ground **pepper**, and ¼ tsp. **kosher salt**.

Fall Vegetable Hash

MAKES 8 SERVINGS
HANDS-ON 35 MIN.
TOTAL 35 MIN.

Sub any of your favorite root vegetables for the potatoes and turnips.

- 4 thick bacon slices
- 2 Tbsp. olive oil
- 1 medium-size sweet onion, chopped
- 1 medium-size sweet potato (about 10 oz.), peeled and cut into 1/2-inch cubes
- 2 medium turnips (about 12 oz.), peeled and cut into 1/2-inch cubes
- 1 Tbsp. white wine vinegar
- 1 lb. small fresh Brussels sprouts, quartered
- 2 garlic cloves, sliced

1. Cook bacon in a 12-inch cast-iron skillet over medium heat, turning occasionally, 8 to 10 minutes or until crisp. Remove bacon; drain, reserving 2 Tbsp. drippings in skillet. Coarsely chop bacon.

2. Add oil to hot drippings in skillet. Cook onion and sweet potato in hot oil and drippings over medium heat, stirring occasionally, 5 minutes. Add turnips; cook, stirring occasionally, 8 minutes.

3. Combine vinegar and 2 Tbsp. water. Add Brussels sprouts, garlic, and vinegar mixture to skillet. Cover and cook, stirring occasionally, 5 minutes or until vegetables are tender. Stir in bacon; add salt and pepper to taste.

Mixed Greens with French Toast Croutons

MAKES 8 SERVINGS
HANDS-ON 15 MIN.
TOTAL 25 MIN., INCLUDING CROUTONS

A jar of presectioned oranges works in a pinch.

- 1/2 cup extra virgin olive oil
- 1/4 cup white wine vinegar
- 1 tsp. loosely packed orange zest
- 1/4 cup fresh orange juice
- 1 small shallot, minced
- 1 Tbsp. honey
- 1 tsp. fresh thyme leaves
- 3/4 tsp. kosher salt
- 1/4 tsp. dry mustard
- 1 (6-oz.) package spring greens mix
- 1 (6.5-oz.) package sweet butter lettuce
- 2 navel oranges, sectioned
  French Toast Croutons

1. Whisk together olive oil and next 8 ingredients. Arrange salad greens, oranges, and croutons on a platter. Serve with vinaigrette.

French Toast Croutons

MAKES 8 SERVINGS

Preheat oven to 375°. Cut 4 (1-inch) **challah bread slices** into 1/2-inch cubes. Stir together 1 tsp. **sugar** and 1 tsp. **ground cinnamon** in a large bowl. Add bread cubes and 1/2 cup **butter,** melted; toss to coat. Bake in a single layer on a baking sheet 10 minutes or until crisp. Cool completely.

Fall Vegetable Hash

Fruit Salad with Citrus-Basil Syrup

Spinach-and-Herb Pastatta

Poppy Seed-Ginger Muffins

Spinach-and-Herb Pastatta

MAKES 8 SERVINGS
HANDS-ON 40 MIN.
TOTAL 1 HOUR, 45 MIN.

Introducing the pastatta: a comforting, hearty casserole that's a cross between baked pasta and frittata.

- 1 (10-oz.) package frozen chopped spinach, thawed
- 1 (16-oz.) package mezze penne pasta
- 2 1/2 Tbsp. butter
- 3 large shallots, sliced
- 2 Tbsp. all-purpose flour
- 1 1/2 cups half-and-half
- 1/2 cup ricotta cheese
- 1 cup (4 oz.) freshly shredded Asiago cheese, divided
- 10 large eggs, lightly beaten
- 1/3 cup loosely packed fresh flat-leaf parsley leaves, coarsely chopped
- 1 Tbsp. finely chopped chives
- 2 tsp. kosher salt
- 1 tsp. freshly ground pepper
   Garnishes: fresh flat-leaf parsley leaves, shaved Parmesan cheese

1. Preheat oven to 325°. Drain spinach well, pressing between paper towels.

2. Prepare pasta according to package directions.

3. Meanwhile, melt butter in a medium saucepan over medium heat; add shallots, and sauté 5 minutes or until golden brown. Whisk in flour until smooth; cook 1 minute, whisking constantly. Gradually whisk in half-and-half; cook over medium heat, whisking constantly, until thickened and bubbly. Whisk in ricotta and 1/2 cup Asiago cheese until smooth. Remove from heat.

4. Whisk eggs in a bowl until frothy. Fold in shallot mixture, spinach, parsley, and next 3 ingredients. Stir in cooked pasta.

5. Sprinkle 1/4 cup Asiago cheese on inside rim of a lightly greased 9-inch springform pan. Pour pasta mixture into pan.

6. Bake at 325° for 55 minutes to 1 hour and 10 minutes or until set. Let stand 10 minutes. Remove sides of pan. Sprinkle with remaining 1/4 cup Asiago cheese.

Poppy Seed-Ginger Muffins

MAKES 1½ DOZEN
HANDS-ON 15 MIN.
TOTAL 40 MIN.

Add more orange juice to the glaze, about 1 tsp. at a time, to make it as thin or thick as you'd like.

MUFFINS

- ¾ cup butter, softened
- 1⅓ cups granulated sugar
- 2 large eggs, separated
- 3 cups cake flour
- 3½ tsp. baking powder
- ¼ tsp. table salt
- 1¼ cups milk
- 1 Tbsp. loosely packed orange zest
- 2 tsp. grated fresh ginger
- 2 tsp. vanilla extract
- 4 tsp. poppy seeds

GLAZE

- 1½ cups powdered sugar
- 2 Tbsp. fresh orange juice

1. Prepare Muffins: Preheat oven to 350°. Beat butter at medium speed with a heavy-duty electric stand mixer until creamy. Gradually add granulated sugar, beating until light and fluffy. Add egg yolks, 1 at a time, beating just until blended after each addition.

2. Stir together flour and next 2 ingredients. Stir together milk and next 3 ingredients. Add flour mixture to butter mixture alternately with milk mixture, beginning and ending with flour mixture. Beat at low speed just until blended after each addition. Beat egg whites until stiff peaks form; fold into batter. Stir in poppy seeds. Spoon into lightly greased 12-cup muffin pans, filling three-fourths full.

3. Bake at 350° for 18 to 20 minutes or until a wooden pick inserted in center comes out clean. Cool in pans on wire racks 5 minutes; transfer to wire racks.

4. Prepare Glaze: Stir together powdered sugar and orange juice. Drizzle over warm muffins.

Country Ham and Gouda Grit Cakes with Tomato Gravy

MAKES 6 SERVINGS
HANDS-ON 1 HOUR
TOTAL 5 HOURS, 35 MIN.

Make grits and sauce a day ahead. Grit cakes (browned in a skillet) also make a tasty supper side. (Pictured on page 188)

HAM AND GRITS

- ½ cup diced country ham
- 1 cup heavy cream
- ¼ cup butter
- 1 tsp. kosher salt
- 1 cup quick-cooking grits
- 1 garlic clove, minced
- 1½ cups (6 oz.) freshly shredded Gouda cheese, divided

TOMATO GRAVY

- 1 cup finely chopped sweet onion
- 2 garlic cloves, minced
- 1 Tbsp. extra virgin olive oil
- 1 (28-oz.) can Italian-style peeled tomatoes
- 2 Tbsp. chopped fresh basil
- 1½ tsp. sugar
- 1 tsp. kosher salt
- ½ tsp. ground red pepper

POACHED EGGS

- 1½ Tbsp. white vinegar
- 6 large eggs

1. Prepare Ham and Grits: Sauté diced ham in a small skillet over medium heat 3 to 5 minutes or until lightly browned. Drain on paper towels.

2. Bring cream, next 2 ingredients, and 3 cups water to a boil in a medium saucepan over high heat. Gradually whisk in grits; return to a boil. Reduce heat to low; cook, whisking often, 5 minutes or until thickened. Stir in garlic, ham, and 1 cup Gouda cheese; cook, stirring occasionally, 1 to 2 minutes or until cheese melts. Spread in a lightly greased 13- x 9-inch pan; cover and chill 4 hours or until set.

3. Prepare Tomato Gravy: Sauté onion and garlic in hot oil in a 3-qt. saucepan over medium heat 2 to 3 minutes or until tender. Stir in tomatoes and 1 cup water. Bring to a boil, stirring constantly and crushing tomatoes with spoon. Reduce heat to low, and simmer, stirring occasionally, 15 to 20 minutes or until slightly thickened. Stir in basil and next 3 ingredients.

4. Prepare Poached Eggs: Add water to depth of 3 inches in a large saucepan. Bring to a boil; reduce heat, and maintain at a light simmer. Add vinegar. Break eggs, and slip into water, 1 at a time, as close as possible to surface. Simmer 3 to 5 minutes or to desired degree of doneness. Remove with a slotted spoon. Trim edges, if desired.

5. Assemble: Preheat oven to 375°. Invert chilled grits onto a cutting board. Cut into 12 (3-inch) squares; place in a single layer, overlapping slightly, in a 13- x 9-inch baking dish. Spoon gravy over grits. Bake 20 minutes or until thoroughly heated. Top with remaining ½ cup Gouda and poached eggs.

Fruit Salad with Citrus-Basil Syrup

MAKES 6 SERVINGS
HANDS-ON 20 MIN.
TOTAL 45 MIN.

Bring 1 cup **water** and ½ cup **sugar** to a boil over medium heat. Remove from heat, and stir in ¼ cup firmly packed **fresh basil leaves**, 1 Tbsp. firmly packed **orange zest**, and 1 Tbsp. firmly packed **lemon zest**. Let stand 20 minutes. Meanwhile, combine ½ lb. **peaches**, peeled and sliced; ½ lb. **plums**, sliced; and 1 lb. **apricots**, sliced, in a large bowl. Pour sugar mixture through a fine wire-mesh strainer into a bowl; discard solids. Stir ¼ to ½ cup syrup and 2 Tbsp. chopped fresh basil into fruit; reserve remaining syrup for another use.

Cocoa-Coconut Coffee Cooler

MAKES ABOUT 8 CUPS
HANDS-ON 15 MIN.
TOTAL 1 HOUR, 15 MIN.

This is almost a dessert! Stir in 1 cup dark rum or bourbon for an even more festive sipper.

Whisk together 4 cups strong brewed hot **chicory coffee**, ½ cup **sugar**, and ¼ cup **unsweetened cocoa** in a large pitcher until cocoa and sugar dissolve. Whisk in 2 cups **half-and-half**, 1 (13.5-oz.) can **coconut milk**, 2 tsp. **vanilla extract**, and ¼ tsp. **coconut extract** until blended. Chill 1 to 24 hours. Stir just before serving over ice.

Marry Fast with Fresh

▶ Test Kitchen pro and busy mom Vanessa McNeil Rocchio wows with her smart approach to speedy suppers

Parchment-Baked Fish and Tomatoes

Parchment-Baked Fish and Tomatoes

MAKES 4 SERVINGS
HANDS-ON 15 MIN.
TOTAL 30 MIN.

Aluminum foil can be subbed for parchment to make the packets.

- 1 (8-oz.) package haricots verts (thin green beans)
- 1 red bell pepper, thinly sliced
- 1/2 small red onion, thinly sliced
- 2 large tomatoes, chopped
- 2 Tbsp. drained capers
- 1/3 cup green olives, quartered
  Parchment paper
- 4 (4- to 5-oz.) fresh white fish fillets (such as snapper, triggerfish, flounder, or grouper)
- 1 tsp. table salt
- 1/2 tsp. freshly ground black pepper
- 2 Tbsp. olive oil
- 1 lemon, quartered
- 1/4 cup torn fresh basil

1. Preheat oven to 400°. Divide first 6 ingredients among 4 (17-inch) squares of parchment paper. Top each with 1 fish fillet. Sprinkle fish with salt and pepper; drizzle with olive oil. Squeeze juice from lemon over fish; place 1 lemon wedge on each fillet. Bring parchment paper sides up over mixture; double fold top and sides to seal, making packets. Place packets on a baking sheet.

2. Bake at 400° for 15 to 20 minutes or until a thermometer registers 140° to 145° when inserted through paper into fish. Place each packet on a plate, and cut open. Sprinkle fish with basil. Serve immediately.

Steak with Mushroom Gnocchi

MAKES 4 SERVINGS
HANDS-ON 40 MIN.
TOTAL 45 MIN.

- 2 (1-inch-thick) rib-eye steaks (about 2 lb.)
- 1 tsp. kosher salt
- 1 tsp. freshly ground pepper
- ¼ cup butter, softened
- 2 Tbsp. country-style Dijon mustard
- 1 Tbsp. chopped fresh tarragon, parsley, or chives
  Mushroom Gnocchi

1. Preheat grill to 350° to 400° (medium-high) heat. Rub steaks with salt and pepper; let stand 10 minutes.

2. Meanwhile, stir together butter, mustard, and tarragon.

3. Grill steaks, covered with grill lid, 8 to 10 minutes on each side or to desired degree of doneness. Remove from grill, and spread with tarragon butter. Serve with Mushroom Gnocchi.

MUSHROOM GNOCCHI

MAKES 4 SERVINGS

You can also toss this with cooked baby red potato quarters, instead of gnocchi.

Prepare 1 (16-oz.) package **gnocchi** (such as Gia Russa) according to package directions. Melt 2 Tbsp. **butter** in a large skillet over medium-high heat. Add 1 (16-oz.) package fresh **button mushrooms,** quartered, and 1 (4-oz.) package fresh **gourmet mushroom blend;** sauté 3 minutes or until lightly browned and liquid evaporates. Add 3 Tbsp. sliced fresh **shallots** and 4 **garlic cloves,** thinly sliced; sauté 2 minutes or until shallots are tender. Add 2 Tbsp. butter to skillet; cook 2 minutes or until lightly browned. Add gnocchi; gently toss. Stir in ½ cup loosely packed **fresh flat-leaf parsley leaves** and ½ tsp. each **kosher salt** and **pepper.**

Steak with Mushroom Gnocchi

Glazed Pork with Fresh Plums

MAKES 4 SERVINGS
HANDS-ON 20 MIN.
TOTAL 30 MIN.

- 2 (1 ¼-lb.) pork tenderloins
- 1 tsp. salt
- ½ tsp. freshly ground pepper
- 2 Tbsp. olive oil
- ½ large red onion, cut into ¼-inch slices
- 3 medium plums, quartered
- 3 Tbsp. white or regular balsamic vinegar
- 3 Tbsp. plum preserves
- 1 tsp. fresh thyme leaves

1. Preheat oven to 400°. Sprinkle pork with salt and pepper. Cook in hot oil in a large ovenproof skillet over high heat 3 to 4 minutes on each side or until browned. Add onion and plums. Bake 15 minutes or until a meat thermometer inserted into thickest portion registers 145°.

2. Transfer pork, onion, and plums to a serving platter, reserving drippings in skillet. Cover pork loosely with aluminum foil, and let stand 10 minutes.

3. Meanwhile, stir vinegar and preserves into drippings; cook over medium-high heat, stirring constantly, 3 to 5 minutes or until slightly thickened. Remove from heat; stir in thyme. Pour over pork and plum mixture.

ENJOY!

Muscadine Syrup

Bring 2 ½ cups **purple muscadine juice** and 2 Tbsp. **sugar** to a boil in a saucepan over medium-high heat, stirring until sugar dissolves. Reduce heat to medium-low, and simmer 25 minutes or until reduced to 1 cup. Cool completely (about 30 minutes). Store in refrigerator.

MAKES 1 cup
HANDS-ON 10 min.
TOTAL 1 hour, 5 min.

Rosemary Chicken with Corn Quinoa

MAKES 4 SERVINGS
HANDS-ON 40 MIN.
TOTAL 40 MIN.

(Pictured on page 189)

- 4 skinned and boned chicken breasts (2 lb.)
- 1 tsp. kosher salt
- ½ tsp. freshly ground pepper
- ½ tsp. minced fresh rosemary
- 2 Tbsp. olive oil
  Fresh Corn Quinoa

Sprinkle chicken with salt, pepper, and rosemary. Cook in hot oil in a large skillet over medium-high heat 6 minutes on each side or until done. Serve with quinoa.

FRESH CORN QUINOA

MAKES 4 SERVINGS

Bring 1 ¼ cups uncooked **red quinoa,** ½ tsp. **kosher salt,** and 4 cups **water** to a boil. Cover, reduce heat to medium, and simmer 8 to 10 minutes or until tender; drain. Cover and let stand 15 minutes. Meanwhile, sauté 4 **shallots** or 2 **small onions,** quartered, in 1 Tbsp. hot **olive oil** in a large skillet over medium heat 3 minutes or until tender. Add 2 **garlic cloves,** minced; sauté 1 minute. Add 2 cups **fresh corn kernels** and 6 cups shredded **greens** (such as chard); cook 2 minutes or just until wilted. Add quinoa, ½ cup torn **basil,** ¼ cup torn **mint,** and 2 Tbsp. **fresh lemon juice.**

Rosemary Chicken with Corn Quinoa

Caramel Control

Follow our easy guide for spoon-lickin' results

▶ **COOKING SUGAR SYRUP TO MAKE CARAMEL,** the process that creates the decadent sauce's robust, bittersweet flavors and rich aroma, happens quickly, so prep your ingredients in advance and stand ready at the stove. Inspired by a Julia Child recipe, here's our tried-and-true method.

Easy Caramel Sauce

1. Bring 1 cup **sugar,** ⅓ cup **water,** and 2 tsp. **fresh lemon juice** (to prevent crystals from forming) to a boil in a tall, heavy saucepan over medium-high heat; boil 3 minutes or until sugar melts and liquid is clear, swirling pan occasionally. Cover; boil 1 minute.

2. Remove lid. Boil, gently swirling often and checking color and temp every 5 to 10 seconds, about 4 minutes or until a candy thermometer reaches 345° to 350° and mixture is medium to dark amber. (Follow our Spoon Guide below.) Remove from heat.

3. Gradually whisk in 1 cup **heavy cream.** (Mixture will bubble and spatter.) Cook, whisking constantly, over low heat 1 minute or until smooth. Remove from heat; stir in 2 tsp. **vanilla extract** and a pinch of **sea salt.** Transfer to a serving bowl or pitcher. Chill, covered, up to 1 week.

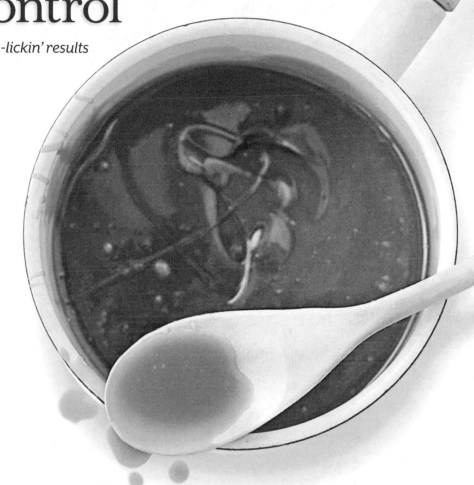

THE SPOON GUIDE No candy thermometer? No problem! Simply cook the sugar syrup until you attain a medium- or dark-amber hue.

Pale Gold
TEMP: 310°-315°
Almost there!
Keep an eye
on that pan.
▼

Medium Amber
TEMP: 345°-348°
Stop here for a mellow
flavor.
▼

Dark Amber
TEMP: 350°-355°
Stop! This base creates
the deepest flavor.
▼

▲ **Light Amber**
TEMP: 330°-335°
You're within
seconds. Keep
swirling.

Fry Up Sweet Comfort

▶ Called "apple jacks" in some parts of the South, these handheld gems boast fabulous flavor

Fried Apple Pies

MAKES 1½ DOZEN
HANDS-ON 30 MIN.
TOTAL 4 HOURS, 18 MIN.

There's enough filling to make a second batch of these delicious pies, or you can freeze it for later. Serve warm or at room temperature.

DOUGH

- 2½ cups self-rising flour
- 2 Tbsp. granulated sugar
- ½ cup shortening
- ¾ cup buttermilk

APPLE FILLING

- 1 (5-oz.) package dried apples
- 2 Tbsp. granulated sugar
- 2 Tbsp. light brown sugar
- 1½ tsp. fresh lemon juice
- ¼ tsp. ground cinnamon
- ⅛ tsp. table salt

CINNAMON SUGAR

- ¼ cup granulated sugar
- 1 Tbsp. ground cinnamon

REMAINING INGREDIENT

Vegetable oil

1. Prepare Dough: Stir together flour and sugar. Cut shortening into flour mixture with a pastry blender or fork until crumbly. Add buttermilk, stirring just until dry ingredients are moistened. Shape dough into a disk; wrap in plastic wrap. Chill 12 to 24 hours.

2. Meanwhile, prepare Filling: Bring apples and water to cover (about 3½ cups) to a boil in a large saucepan over medium-high heat. Reduce heat to low, and simmer, stirring occasionally, 1 hour. Remove from heat; cover and let stand 1 hour.

3. Drain apples; place in a large bowl. Coarsely mash apples with 2 Tbsp. granulated sugar and next 4 ingredients. (A pastry blender does a great job.) Cover and chill 12 to 24 hours.

4. Prepare Cinnamon Sugar: Stir together ¼ cup granulated sugar and 1 Tbsp. cinnamon.

5. Pour oil to depth of 2 inches into a Dutch oven; heat over medium-high heat to 350°. Turn dough out onto a lightly floured surface. Divide into 18 portions; shape into balls. Flatten into 3-inch circles; roll into 5-inch circles. Working with 1 circle at a time, spoon 1 Tbsp. filling into center of each circle; brush edge with water. Fold dough over filling. Press edges with a fork to seal.

6. Fry, in batches, in hot oil 3 to 4 minutes or until golden. Transfer to a paper towel-lined baking sheet. Sprinkle both sides of hot pies with cinnamon sugar.

TEST KITCHEN TIP!
Keep the oil temp at 350° and each batch will boast a golden brown crust.

Tackle Your Tailgate

▶ You'll be the fan favorite with this make-ahead, easy-to-transport game-day menu. Saturdays in the South are as much about food as they are about football. This year, step up your game with a make-ahead menu that will shave time off the clock and, if you're hitting the road, will go from kitchen to cooler with ease. And it doesn't stop there. See page 228 for 15 varsity frosting colors to decorate a sheet cake, we developed to-the-drop formulas for 15 varsity frosting colors to decorate a sheet cake that's sure to score points.

DRINKS

Apple, Lemon, and Gin Shandy

(Pictured on page 187)

Puree 3 large **Granny Smith apples**, peeled and chopped; 1/2 cup **fresh lemon juice**; and 3 Tbsp. **fresh shredded ginger** in a blender. Pour mixture through a fine wire-mesh strainer into a large pitcher, pressing to release juices; discard solids. Stir in 1/2 cup **Simple Syrup** and 2 cups **gin**. Chill 2 hours. Stir in 1 (12-oz.) bottle chilled **Pilsner beer** or **club soda**. Serve over **ice**. Garnish with apple and lemon slices. **MAKES** 8 servings

EXTRA POINT!
(Bow) tie one on! Use this preppy staple to keep track of who's drinking what.

SIMPLE SYRUP

Bring 1 cup **sugar** and 1/2 cup **water** to a boil in a small saucepan over medium-high heat. Reduce heat to low, and cook, stirring often, 3 to 5 minutes or until sugar is dissolved. Let stand 30 minutes or until cool. Refrigerate up to 1 week. **MAKES** 1 1/4 cups

Homemade Cherry Soda

(Pictured on page 187)

Bring 2 (12-oz.) packages **frozen dark, sweet pitted cherries**; 1 1/2 cups **Demerara sugar**; and 1 cup **water** to a boil in a large saucepan over medium-high heat. Reduce heat to low; simmer, stirring occasionally, 15 to 20 minutes or until cherries are tender. Let stand 30 minutes. Press mixture through a fine wire-mesh strainer into a pitcher, using back of a spoon to squeeze out juices; discard pulp. Stir in 1/2 cup **fresh lime juice** and 1/4 cup liquid from **jarred maraschino cherries**. Chill 2 to 24 hours. Stir together 3 Tbsp. cherry mixture and 1 cup **club soda** for each serving. Serve over ice in 16-oz. glasses. **MAKES** 16 servings

DIPS

Broccoli Salad Dip

MAKES 2 ½ CUPS
HANDS-ON 20 MIN.
TOTAL 20 MIN.

Spin the old-school salad into a dip, and pair with everything from crudités to pretzel rods. (Pictured on page 186)

- ½ lb. fresh broccoli
- 6 oz. cream cheese, softened
- ⅔ cup low-fat Greek yogurt
- ¼ cup apple cider vinegar
- 2 tsp. sugar
- ¼ tsp. kosher salt
- 4 thick bacon slices, cooked and chopped
- ½ cup coarsely chopped cashews
- ½ cup (2 oz.) shredded sharp Cheddar cheese
- ⅓ cup minced red onion

1. Remove and discard large leaves and tough ends of stalks from broccoli. Peel and coarsely chop stems; coarsely chop florets.

2. Process cream cheese and next 4 ingredients in a food processor until smooth. Add broccoli; pulse 12 to 15 times or until finely chopped. Fold bacon and remaining ingredients into cream cheese mixture. Serve immediately, or chill up to 3 days.

Broccoli Salad Dip and Hot Brown Fondue

Hot Brown Fondue

MAKES ABOUT 5 CUPS
HANDS-ON 15 MIN.
TOTAL 15 MIN.

(Pictured on page 186)

- 2 Tbsp. butter
- 2 Tbsp. all-purpose flour
- 2 cups milk
- ¾ tsp. paprika
- ¼ tsp. table salt
- 2 cups chopped white American cheese (8 oz.)
- 2 cups (8 oz.) shredded Swiss cheese
- 1 (4-oz.) jar diced pimiento, drained
- 1 lb. deli-roasted turkey, minced
- 6 bacon slices, cooked and crumbled
- 3 green onions, coarsely chopped
  Toast points

1. Melt butter in a medium saucepan over medium heat; whisk in flour until smooth. Cook, whisking constantly, 1 minute. Gradually whisk in milk; bring to a boil, whisking constantly.

2. Reduce heat to low; whisk in paprika and salt. Gradually add cheeses, whisking until smooth after each addition. Remove from heat; whisk in pimiento and next 3 ingredients. Transfer to a fondue pot or slow cooker on WARM. Serve with toast points.

Note: To make ahead, refrigerate fondue in an airtight container up to 3 days. Reheat in a saucepan, slow cooker, or fondue pot.

SLIDERS

Slow-Cooker Beef Sliders with Pickled Peppers

MAKES 16 SERVINGS
HANDS-ON 30 MIN.
TOTAL 7 HOURS, INCLUDING PEPPERS

Rev up your slow cooker the night before, and on game day, tote it to the game, plug it in, and let your crowd build their own sandwiches. (Pictured on page 186)

- 1 (3 ¼- to 3 ¾-lb.) boneless chuck roast, trimmed
- 2 tsp. kosher salt
- 1 ½ tsp. freshly ground black pepper
- 1 Tbsp. vegetable oil
- 1 medium-size sweet onion, coarsely chopped
- 2 carrots, coarsely chopped
- 4 celery ribs, coarsely chopped
- 2 garlic cloves
- 2 cups beef broth
- ½ cup dry red wine
- 4 fresh thyme sprigs
- 2 Tbsp. prepared horseradish
- ¼ cup loosely packed fresh flat-leaf parsley leaves, chopped
- ¼ cup chopped fresh chives
- 16 hearty dinner rolls, split
  Pickled Peppers

1. Rub roast with salt and pepper. Cook in hot oil in a Dutch oven or large cast-iron skillet over medium-high heat 2 to 3 minutes on all sides until browned. Place roast, onion, and next 6 ingredients in a 6-qt. slow cooker.

2. Cover and cook on HIGH 6 to 8 hours or until meat is tender. Remove roast and vegetables; discard vegetables. Shred meat. Pour liquid from slow cooker through a fine wire-mesh strainer into a 4-cup measuring cup, and let stand about 15 minutes. Remove fat from cooking liquid, and discard.

3. Stir together shredded meat, horseradish, next 2 ingredients, and 1 cup reserved cooking liquid; discard remaining liquid. Add salt and pepper to taste. Serve on rolls with Pickled Peppers.

Note: Keep beef mixture warm in slow cooker on WARM up to 2 hours. We tested with Pepperidge Farm Stone Baked French Artisan Rolls.

PICKLED PEPPERS Stir together 2 cups sliced **red** and **yellow sweet mini bell peppers**, 1 cup sliced **pepperoncini salad peppers**, 1 tsp. **pepperoncini juice** from jar, 1/4 cup loosely packed **fresh flat-leaf parsley leaves**, 1/4 cup thinly sliced **fresh chives**, and 1 tsp. **extra virgin olive oil** in a medium bowl. Add **salt** and **pepper** to taste. **MAKES** about 3 cups. **HANDS-ON** 10 min., **TOTAL** 10 min.

Buffalo Chicken Meatball Sliders

MAKES 32 SERVINGS
HANDS-ON 30 MIN.
TOTAL 1 HOUR, 45 MIN.

(Pictured on page 186)

- 1 Tbsp. kosher salt
- 2 tsp. fennel seeds
- 1 tsp. black peppercorns
- 2 lb. ground chicken
- 1/2 cup firmly packed fresh flat-leaf parsley leaves, chopped
- 1/2 cup finely grated Parmesan cheese
- 1/2 small sweet onion, grated
- 2 large eggs, lightly beaten
- 2 garlic cloves, minced
- 1 Tbsp. extra virgin olive oil
- 1 (5-oz.) bottle Buffalo-style hot sauce
- 32 small rolls or buns, split
     Blue Cheese Sauce
     Garnishes: thinly sliced celery, fresh flat-leaf parsley leaves

1. Place first 3 ingredients in a mortar bowl or spice grinder; grind to a fine powder, using a pestle or spice grinder. Place chicken, next 6 ingredients, and crushed spices in a large bowl. Combine mixture with hands until blended and smooth (2 minutes). Cover and chill 1 hour.

2. Preheat oven to 400°. Drop mixture by rounded spoonfuls 1 1/2 inches apart onto a lightly greased aluminum foil-lined jelly-roll pan, using a medium-size cookie scoop (about 1 1/2 inches).

3. Bake at 400° for 10 to 12 minutes or until done. Toss meatballs with hot sauce. Serve on split rolls with Blue Cheese Sauce.

BLUE CHEESE SAUCE Process 1 cup **crumbled blue cheese**; 1/2 cup **heavy cream**; 1/4 cup **sour cream**; 1/2 **shallot**, minced; 1/2 tsp. firmly packed **lemon zest**; and 2 Tbsp. **fresh lemon juice** in a food processor or blender until smooth and creamy. Season with **salt** and **pepper** to taste.

Buffalo Chicken Meatball Sliders and Slow-Cooker Beef Sliders

EXTRA POINT! Pickled Peppers do double-duty as sandwich toppings or a stand-alone snack.

DESSERTS

Whiskey Whoopie Pies

MAKES 12 TO 14 SANDWICH COOKIES
HANDS-ON 45 MIN.
TOTAL 1 HOUR, 40 MIN.

Freeze the assembled whoopie pies in zip-top plastic bags up to 3 weeks before your tailgate. Defrost in the fridge overnight. (Pictured on page 186)

COOKIES

1	cup granulated sugar
1/2	cup butter, softened
1/4	tsp. table salt
1	large egg
1	large egg yolk
1 3/4	cups all-purpose flour
1/2	cup unsweetened cocoa
1	tsp. baking soda
1 1/2	cups buttermilk
	Parchment paper

FILLING

1	(8-oz.) package cream cheese, softened
1/4	cup butter, softened
2	Tbsp. whiskey
3 1/2	cups powdered sugar
3/4	cup toasted chopped pecans

1. Prepare Cookies: Preheat oven to 350°. Beat first 3 ingredients at medium speed with a heavy-duty electric stand mixer until light and fluffy. Add egg and egg yolk; beat just until blended.

2. Sift together flour and next 2 ingredients; add to butter mixture alternately with buttermilk, beginning and ending with flour mixture. Beat at low speed just until blended after each addition. Drop batter by level spoonfuls onto parchment paper-lined baking sheets, using a medium-size cookie scoop (about 1 1/2 inches).

3. Bake at 350° for 10 minutes. Cool on baking sheets 5 minutes; cool on wire racks completely.

4. Prepare Filling: Beat cream cheese and next 2 ingredients at medium speed until smooth. Add powdered sugar, 1/2 cup at a time, beating at low speed just until blended after each addition.

5. Assemble: Turn half of cooled cookies over, flat sides up. Dollop each with about 2 Tbsp. filling, and sprinkle with pecans. Top with remaining cookies; press gently to spread filling to edges. Serve immediately. Or place pies on a parchment paper-lined baking sheet, cover with plastic wrap, and freeze 8 to 24 hours or until firm. Store in freezer up to 3 weeks. Let stand 1 hour before serving.

White Sheet Cake

MAKES 12 TO 15 SERVINGS
HANDS-ON 20 MIN.
TOTAL 2 HOURS, 15 MIN.

1 1/4	cups butter, softened
2 1/4	cups sugar
7	large egg whites, at room temperature
3 1/2	cups cake flour
4	tsp. baking powder
1	Tbsp. vanilla extract
	Vanilla Buttercream Frosting

1. Preheat oven to 325°. Beat butter and sugar at medium speed with a heavy-duty electric stand mixer until fluffy. Gradually add egg whites, one-third at a time, beating well after each addition.

2. Sift together cake flour and baking powder; gradually add to butter mixture alternately with 1 cup water, beginning and ending with flour mixture. Stir in vanilla. Pour batter into a greased and floured 13-x 9-inch pan.

3. Bake at 325° for 45 to 50 minutes or until a wooden pick inserted in center comes out clean. Cool completely in pan on a wire rack (about 1 hour). Remove from pan to a serving platter. Spread top and sides of cake with frosting.

VANILLA BUTTERCREAM FROSTING

MAKES ABOUT 5 CUPS
HANDS-ON 10 MIN.
TOTAL 10 MIN.

Customize the icing with your team colors. Find the recipes at right.

1	cup butter, softened
1/2	cup milk
1	Tbsp. vanilla extract
2	(16-oz.) packages powdered sugar

Beat butter at medium speed with an electric mixer until creamy. Stir together milk and vanilla. Gradually add powdered sugar to butter mixture alternately with milk mixture, beating at low speed just until blended after each addition and scraping down sides of bowl as needed.

TOUCHDOWN! TEAM ICING COLOR FORMULAS

Recipes are for 1 cup Vanilla Buttercream Frosting. One drop is the size of a 4 mm round nail head. Gel paste will thicken after bottles are opened. If your gel paste comes out in drops larger than the 4 mm round nail head, count 1 large drop as 3 drops. We tested with AmeriColor Soft Gel Paste colors (from $1.35/color for a 3/4-oz. bottle). Because our formulas were tested with AmeriColor, we suggest using their products for results equal to our own. For a list of retailers, visit americolorcorp.com.

Georgia: 3/4 tsp. plus 8 drops Red Red; 8 drops Burgundy; 8 drops Maroon

Alabama: 1/4 tsp. Super Red; 8 drops Maroon; 4 drops Regal Purple

Texas A&M: 1/4 tsp. Maroon

Florida State: 1/4 tsp. Maroon; 8 drops Warm Brown; 8 drops Regal Purple

Vanderbilt: 1/8 tsp. plus 4 drops Warm Brown; 8 drops Avocado; 8 drops Lemon Yellow; Wilton Gold Sparkle Gel on top

Louisiana: 1/4 tsp. plus 8 drops Egg Yellow

Tennessee: 1/4 tsp. plus 4 drops Orange

Virginia Tech: 1/8 tsp. plus 2 drops Orange; 5 drops Red Red

Oklahoma State: 1/4 tsp. plus 1/8 tsp.
plus 4 drops Terra-cotta; 1/8 tsp. plus 4 drops Lemon Yellow; 8 drops Warm Brown

Texas: 1/8 tsp. Orange; 2 drops Maroon; 1 drop Lemon Yellow

Appalachian State: 10 drops Electric Yellow; 5 drops Gold; 2 drops Bright White

Marshall: 1/8 tsp. Leaf Green; 5 drops Forest Green; 1 drop Super Black

West Virginia: 1/4 tsp. plus 1/8 tsp. plus 4 drops Navy Blue; 5 drops Super Black

Mississippi: 1/2 tsp. Navy Blue; 1/8 tsp. plus 4 drops Super Black; 8 drops Regal Purple

Clemson: 1/8 tsp. plus 8 drops Regal Purple; 2 drops Super Black

---

LIGHTEN UP MAMA'S...
Seven-Layer Dip

Mama's Way: *Tex-Mex party stalwart* **Our Way:** *Southern-meet-Mediterranean conversation starter*

New Seven-Layer Dip

MAKES 16 SERVINGS
HANDS-ON 20 MIN.
TOTAL 1 HOUR, 20 MIN.

Sub any of your favorite legumes, pickles, veggies, or hummus to make this versatile party dish.

LAYER 1
Process 2 (15.8-oz.) cans **great Northern beans**, drained and rinsed; 2 **garlic cloves**; ¼ cup firmly packed **fresh basil leaves**; 3 Tbsp. **olive oil**; 1 Tbsp. **fresh lemon juice**; and ½ tsp. **kosher salt** in a food processor until smooth, stopping to scrape bowl as needed. Cover and chill until ready to assemble.

LAYERS 2, 3 & 4
Rinse ⅓ cup **minced red onion** in cold water, and pat dry. Cut 1 pt. **grape tomatoes** into halves. Stir together ¼ cup **sliced pickled okra** and ¼ cup **pitted Castelvetrano olives**, sliced.

LAYER 5
Stir together ½ cup **reduced-fat sour cream**, ⅓ cup chopped **fresh flat-leaf parsley**, 3 Tbsp. chopped **fresh mint**, 1 tsp. **lemon zest**, 1 Tbsp. **lemon juice**, and ¾ tsp. **ground cumin** in a medium bowl. Cover and chill until ready to assemble.

LAYER 6
Stir together 1 (15-oz.) can **black-eyed peas**, drained and rinsed; 1 medium-size **red bell pepper**, chopped; 1 **jalapeño pepper**, seeded and minced; 1 Tbsp. **hot sauce**; and ¼ tsp. **freshly ground black pepper.** Cover and chill until ready to assemble.

LAYER 7
½ cup **crumbled feta cheese**

ASSEMBLY
Layer bean mixture; minced onion, tomatoes, pickled okra mixture; sour cream mixture, black-eyed pea mixture, and feta cheese in an 11- x 7-inch baking dish. Cover and chill 1 to 2 hours before serving. Serve with **pita** or **multigrain chips** and **crudités.**
PER SERVING: CALORIES 100; **FAT** 5g (Sat 2g); **PROTEIN** 4g; **CARB** 11g; **CHOL** 8mg; **SODIUM** 243mg; **CALC** 68mg

OLD SCHOOL
Creamy layers of sour cream, guac, refried beans, cheese, and often, a flavor base bolstered by taco seasoning

NEW SCHOOL
Creamy hummus and fresh herbs. Pickled okra and marinated black-eyed peas add piquant punch.

REPORT CARD
Half the calories and nearly half the fat and sodium

Take Your Pick

▶ Sweet or Savory: 7 ways to celebrate the apple, autumn's most versatile fruit

THE SWEET

Caramel Apple Blondie Pie

MAKES 8 TO 10 SERVINGS

HANDS-ON 40 MIN.

TOTAL 4 HOURS, 30 MIN.

Buttery rich layers of tender cake and caramelized apples add up to one sweet combo. The secret to the crisp, flaky crust? Baking in a cast-iron skillet on a lower oven rack. (Pictured on page 14)

- 6 large Granny Smith apples (about 3 lb.)
- 2 Tbsp. all-purpose flour
- 2 cups firmly packed light brown sugar, divided
- 1 cup butter, divided
- 1 1/2 cups all-purpose flour
- 1 1/2 tsp. baking powder
- 1/2 tsp. table salt
- 3 large eggs, lightly beaten
- 3 Tbsp. bourbon
- 3/4 cup coarsely chopped toasted pecans
- 1/2 (14.1-oz.) package refrigerated piecrusts
  Apple Cider Caramel Sauce

1. Peel apples, and cut into 1/4-inch-thick wedges. Toss with 2 Tbsp. flour and 1/2 cup brown sugar in a large bowl. Melt 1/4 cup butter in a large skillet over medium-high heat; add apple mixture, and sauté 15 minutes or until apples are tender and liquid is thickened. Remove from heat; cool completely (about 30 minutes).

2. Meanwhile, preheat oven to 350°. Melt remaining 3/4 cup butter. Stir together 1 1/2 cups flour and next 2 ingredients in a large bowl. Add eggs, bourbon, 3/4 cup melted butter, and remaining 1 1/2 cups brown sugar, stirring until blended. Stir in pecans.

3. Fit piecrust into a 10-inch cast-iron skillet, gently pressing piecrust all the way up the sides of skillet. Spoon two-thirds of apple mixture over bottom of piecrust, spreading and gently pressing apple slices into an even layer using the back of a spoon. Spoon batter over apple mixture; top with remaining apple mixture.

4. Place pie on lower oven rack, and bake at 350° for 1 hour and 10 minutes to 1 hour and 20 minutes or until a wooden pick inserted in center comes out with a few moist crumbs. Remove from oven; cool pie completely on a wire rack.

5. Drizzle cooled pie with ⅓ cup Apple Cider Caramel Sauce. Serve with remaining sauce.

APPLE CIDER CARAMEL SAUCE

MAKES ABOUT 1 ¼ CUPS
HANDS-ON 25 MIN.
TOTAL 1 HOUR, 10 MIN.

For straight-up apple flavor, start with fresh-pressed cider from a farm stand.

- 1 cup apple cider
- 1 cup firmly packed light brown sugar
- ½ cup butter
- ¼ cup whipping cream

Cook cider in a 3-qt. saucepan over medium heat, stirring often, 10 minutes or until reduced to ¼ cup. Stir in remaining ingredients. Bring to a boil over medium-high heat, stirring constantly; boil, stirring constantly, 2 minutes. Remove from heat, and cool completely. Refrigerate up to 1 week. To reheat, microwave at HIGH 10 to 15 seconds or just until warm; stir until smooth.

Apple-Pecan Carrot Cake

MAKES 10 SERVINGS
HANDS-ON 30 MIN.
TOTAL 3 HOURS, 30 MIN., INCLUDING SAUCE AND FROSTING

Top a showstopping crown of Mascarpone Frosting with swirls of Apple Cider Caramel Sauce and a scattering of salty-sweet Spiced Pecans (minus the ground red pepper; page 234). Caramel sauce, rather than frosting, sandwiches together the moist cake layers.

- 2 ⅓ cups finely chopped lightly toasted pecans, divided
- 2 cups all-purpose flour
- 2 tsp. baking soda
- 2 tsp. apple pie spice
- ½ tsp. table salt
- 3 large eggs, lightly beaten
- 2 cups sugar
- ¾ cup vegetable oil
- ¾ cup buttermilk
- 2 tsp. vanilla extract
- 2 cups peeled and grated Granny Smith apples
- 1½ cups grated carrots
- ⅔ cup plus 2 Tbsp. Apple Cider Caramel Sauce (see recipe above)
  Mascarpone Frosting

1. Preheat oven to 350°. Sprinkle 1 ⅓ cups toasted pecans into 2 well-buttered shiny 9-inch round cake pans; shake to coat bottom and sides of pans.

2. Stir together flour and next 3 ingredients.

3. Stir together eggs and next 4 ingredients in a large bowl until blended. Add flour mixture, stirring just until blended. Fold in apples, carrots, and remaining 1 cup pecans. Pour batter into prepared pans.

4. Bake at 350° for 30 to 35 minutes or until a wooden pick inserted in center comes out clean. Cool in pans on wire racks 10 minutes. Remove from pans to wire racks, and cool completely (about 1 hour).

5. Place 1 cake layer, pecan side down, on a serving plate. Spread top of cake layer with ⅔ cup Apple Cider Caramel Sauce;

top with remaining cake layer, pecan side down. Spread Mascarpone Frosting over top of cake. Drizzle 2 Tbsp. Apple Cider Caramel Sauce over frosting, and swirl sauce into frosting. Serve immediately.

MASCARPONE FROSTING

MAKES ABOUT 3 CUPS
HANDS-ON 10 MIN.
TOTAL 10 MIN.

- 1 (8-oz.) container mascarpone cheese
- ¼ cup powdered sugar
- 2 tsp. vanilla extract
- 1 cup whipping cream

Whisk together first 3 ingredients in a large bowl just until blended. Beat whipping cream at medium speed with an electric mixer until stiff peaks form. Gently fold into mascarpone mixture.

FIVE ORCHARD-FRESH FAVORITES

SEPTEMBER BRINGS A BOUNTY OF CRISP FALL APPLES, EACH WITH UNIQUE CHARACTERISTICS — FROM TART 'GRANNY SMITHS' (A NATURAL FOR SAVORY DISHES) TO CANDY-SWEET 'FUJIS' (A 'RED DELICIOUS'-VIRGINIA 'RALL'S JANET' HYBRID). MANY LESSER KNOWN VARIETIES ARRIVE IN PEAK SEASON AND APPEAR ONLY BRIEFLY, SO ENJOY THEM NOW.

No. 1
JONAGOLD

No. 2
GALA

No. 3
GOLDEN DELICIOUS

No. 4
HONEYCRISP

No. 5
McINTOSH

1. Versatile, sweet-tart cross between a 'Jonathan' and 'Golden Delicious,' best enjoyed soon after harvest.
2. Crisp, aromatic and sweet; a favorite for eating out of hand. Try it julienned in our Waldorf Cobb Salad.
3. Mellow and sweet with a medium-firm texture; a versatile old-fashioned favorite that's perfect for baking.
4. Crisp and honey-sweet with a juicy bite; perfect for snacking or baking. Can sub for 'Braeburns' in our Caramel Apple Fantans.
5. Juicy and aromatic with a hint of spice and soft, creamy texture that breaks down easily when cooked. Excellent for applesauce.

illustrations by JOHN BURGOYNE

Caramel Apple Fantans

MAKES 1 DOZEN
HANDS-ON 50 MIN.
TOTAL 2 HOURS, 45 MIN.

Use any firm cooking apple, such as 'Jona-gold' or 'Honeycrisp,' or a combo for extra flavor and texture. (Pictured on page 14)

DOUGH

- 1 (¼-oz.) envelope active dry yeast
- 1 cup warm water (105° to 115°)
- 1 tsp. granulated sugar
- 1 large egg
- ¼ cup granulated sugar
- ¼ cup butter, melted
- 1 tsp. salt
- 1½ to 2 cups bread flour
- 1½ cups whole wheat flour

FILLING

- 9 Tbsp. butter, softened and divided
- 3 cups peeled and diced Braeburn apples (about 3 large)
- ½ cup golden raisins
- ¼ cup firmly packed light brown sugar
- ¾ cup granulated sugar
- 1 Tbsp. ground cinnamon
- ¾ cup chopped toasted pecans

GLAZE

- ⅓ cup butter
- ⅓ cup firmly packed light brown sugar

1. Prepare Dough: Combine first 3 ingredients in bowl of a heavy-duty electric stand mixer; let stand 5 minutes. Stir in egg, next 3 ingredients, and 1½ cups bread flour. Beat at medium speed, using paddle attachment, 1 minute or until smooth. Gradually beat in whole wheat flour and enough remaining bread flour to make a soft dough.

2. Turn dough out onto a well-floured surface, and knead until smooth and elastic (6 to 8 minutes), sprinkling surface with bread flour as needed. Place dough in a lightly greased large bowl, turning to grease top. Cover with plastic wrap, and let rise in a warm place (85°), free from drafts, 45 to 55 minutes or until doubled in bulk.

3. Meanwhile, prepare Filling: Melt 1 Tbsp. butter in a large skillet over medium-high heat. Add apples and next 2 ingredients, and sauté 4 to 5 minutes or until apples are crisp-tender. Cool completely (about 30 minutes).

FANTASTIC FANTANS

MASTER THE ART OF SHAPING DELECTABLE PULL-APART FANTANS IN FOUR SIMPLE STEPS

1 Roll out and top the dough (through Step 4 of recipe). Use the steady pressure of a pizza wheel or chef's knife to cut dough into 5 (12- x 4-inch) strips.

2 Stack strips of dough on top of one another. Don't fret about perfection, but do tuck back in any apple or pecan pieces that tumble from between the layers.

3 Using a knife, cut stacked strips crosswise into 6 rectangles; cut rectangles in half to make 12 (2-inch) squares.

4 Turn stacked squares, cut sides up, and place in lightly greased muffin cups for a final rise before baking.

4. Punch dough down; turn out onto a lightly floured surface. Roll into a 20- x 12-inch rectangle. Spread remaining 8 Tbsp. softened butter over dough. Stir together ¾ cup granulated sugar and cinnamon; sprinkle over butter, and top with pecans and apple mixture.

5. Cut dough into 5 (12- x 4-inch) strips; stack dough strips. (See above.) Replace any apples and pecans that fall out. Cut stack into 6 (4- x 2-inch) rectangles; cut each rectangle in half crosswise to form 12 (2-inch) squares. Place stacked squares, cut sides up, into cups of a lightly greased 12-cup muffin pan. Cover loosely with plastic wrap; let rise in a warm place (85°), free from drafts, 45 minutes to 1 hour or until rolls rise about ¾ inch above rim of pan.

6. Preheat oven to 375°. Bake 18 to 20 minutes or until deep golden brown. Cool in pan on a wire rack 5 minutes. Remove from pan to a wire rack.

7. Prepare Glaze: Bring ⅓ cup butter and ⅓ cup brown sugar to a boil in a 1-qt. heavy saucepan over medium heat, stirring constantly; boil 1 minute, stirring constantly. Remove from heat; drizzle over top of warm rolls.

THE SAVORY

Grill-Roasted Chicken

MAKES 6 SERVINGS
HANDS-ON 45 MIN.
TOTAL 7 HOURS, 30 MIN.

An aromatic rack of early fall apples and vegetables catches all the chicken's flavorful juices. (Pictured on page 14)

- 4 cups apple juice
- 1/2 cup bourbon
- 1/4 cup firmly packed light brown sugar
- 1/4 cup kosher salt
- 1 Tbsp. cracked pepper
- 2 cups ice cubes
- 1 (5-lb.) whole chicken
  Kitchen string
- 2 Tbsp. light brown sugar
- 3 Tbsp. olive oil
- 3 Tbsp. balsamic vinegar
- 5 medium-size assorted apples, quartered
- 1 1/2 lb. shallots, peeled and halved
- 1 lb. small sweet potatoes, quartered
- 2 Tbsp. chopped fresh flat-leaf parsley

1. Bring apple juice to a boil in a heavy 3-qt. saucepan. Remove from heat, and stir in bourbon and next 3 ingredients, stirring until sugar and salt are dissolved. Cool completely (about 20 minutes); stir in ice.

2. Remove neck and giblets from chicken; reserve for another use. Place chicken and apple juice mixture in a 2-gal. zip-top plastic freezer bag; seal. Place bag in a shallow baking dish, and chill 4 hours, turning bag occasionally.

3. Remove chicken from brine, discarding brine; pat chicken dry with paper towels. Tie chicken legs together with kitchen string, and tuck chicken wingtips under.

4. Whisk together 2 Tbsp. brown sugar and next 2 ingredients in a large bowl. Add apples and next 2 ingredients, tossing to coat. Place mixture in a single layer in a lightly greased shallow roasting pan. Sprinkle with desired amount of kosher salt and freshly ground black pepper. Place chicken, breast side up, on top of apple mixture in pan.

5. Light one side of grill, heating to 350° to 400° (medium-high) heat; leave other side unlit. Place pan over unlit side, and grill, covered with grill lid, 45 minutes. Stir apple mixture. Grill, covered with grill lid, 1 hour and 15 minutes to 1 hour and 20 minutes or until a meat thermometer inserted into chicken thigh registers 165° and vegetables are tender. (Shield after 45 minutes to prevent excessive browning.) Remove from grill, cover chicken and vegetables with foil, and let stand 20 minutes. Transfer chicken to a serving platter. Toss apples and vegetables with pan juices to coat; sprinkle with parsley.

Waldorf Cobb Salad

MAKES 8 SERVINGS
HANDS-ON 30 MIN.
TOTAL 2 HOURS, 5 MIN., INCLUDING PECANS AND VINAIGRETTE

This makes a company-perfect sidekick for anything roasted or grilled. The concentrated flavor of an apple cider reduction, plus a shot of sorghum syrup, add rich complexity, not just sweetness, to the vinaigrette. (Pictured on page 14)

- 2 large Gala apples
- 3 Tbsp. fresh lime juice
- 2 medium avocados
- 3 cups shredded romaine lettuce
- 3 cups shredded iceberg lettuce
- 1 cup loosely packed watercress leaves
- 1 pt. grape tomatoes, halved
- 1 cup (4 oz.) shredded white Cheddar cheese
- 4 oz. Gorgonzola cheese, crumbled
- 6 thick bacon slices, cooked and crumbled
  Spiced Pecans
  Cider-Sorghum Vinaigrette (see opposite page)

1. Cut apples into 1/8-inch matchsticks; toss with 2 Tbsp. lime juice. Peel and quarter avocados; toss with remaining 1 Tbsp. lime juice.

2. Toss together romaine lettuce and next 2 ingredients; arrange on a large serving platter. Arrange tomatoes, next 4 ingredients, apples, and avocado over salad greens. Serve with Cider-Sorghum Vinaigrette.

SPICED PECANS

MAKES 1 1/2 CUPS
HANDS-ON 5 MIN.
TOTAL 55 MIN.

Preheat oven to 350°. Pour 1 1/2 cups **apple juice** over 1 1/2 cups **pecan halves** in a small bowl. Let stand 15 minutes; drain. Stir together 3 Tbsp. **sugar,** 1 tsp. **apple pie spice,** 1/8 tsp. **table salt,** and, if desired, 1/8 tsp. **ground red pepper** in a medium bowl; add pecans, tossing to coat. Spread in a single layer in a lightly greased, aluminum foil-lined 15- x 10-inch pan. Bake 15 minutes or until lightly toasted, stirring once. Cool in pan on a wire rack 20 minutes; separate pecans with a fork.

Grill-Roast Chicken

CIDER-SORGHUM VINAIGRETTE

MAKES 2 1/4 CUPS
HANDS-ON 20 MIN.
TOTAL 40 MIN.

- 1 cup apple cider
- 1 (3-inch) cinnamon stick
- 1/2 cup apple cider vinegar
- 1/3 cup sorghum syrup
- 1 shallot, minced
- 2 Tbsp. bourbon
- 1 Tbsp. Dijon mustard
- 1 tsp. table salt
- 1 tsp. freshly ground black pepper
- 1 cup canola oil

1. Cook first 2 ingredients in a 3-qt. saucepan over medium heat, stirring occasionally, 10 minutes or until cider is reduced to 1/4 cup. Remove from heat, and cool completely (about 20 minutes).

2. Transfer cider mixture to a bowl, discarding cinnamon stick. Whisk in vinegar and next 6 ingredients. Add oil in a slow, steady stream, whisking constantly until smooth.

Caramelized Onion-and-Apple Tassies

MAKES 2 DOZEN
HANDS-ON 45 MIN.
TOTAL 2 HOURS, 30 MIN.

Be sure to press the cream cheese pastry dough all the way up the sides of the mini muffin cups so the tart shells will be deep enough to hold a generous amount of filling.

- 1/2 cup butter, softened
- 1/2 (8-oz.) package cream cheese, softened
- 1 cup (4 oz.) shredded Asiago cheese, divided
- 1 1/4 cups all-purpose flour
- 2 Tbsp. butter
- 1 3/4 cups diced sweet onion
- 1 3/4 cups peeled and diced Granny Smith apples (about 2 large)
- 1 Tbsp. light brown sugar
- 1 Tbsp. balsamic vinegar
- 1/2 tsp. freshly ground black pepper
- 1/8 tsp. table salt
- 4 bacon slices, cooked and finely chopped
- 2 tsp. fresh thyme leaves

1. Beat first 2 ingredients and 1/2 cup Asiago cheese at medium speed with an electric mixer until creamy. Gradually add flour, beating at low speed until blended. Shape mixture into 24 balls; place on a baking sheet. Cover and chill 1 hour.

2. Meanwhile, melt 2 Tbsp. butter in a medium skillet over medium heat; add onion, and sauté 5 minutes. Add apple and next 4 ingredients, and cook, stirring occasionally, 10 minutes or until golden brown. Remove from heat, and cool completely.

3. Preheat oven to 350°. Place dough balls into cups of a lightly greased 24-cup miniature muffin pan; press dough into muffin cups, forming a shell. Sprinkle bacon into shells; top with apple mixture, mounding mixture slightly. Sprinkle with remaining 1/2 cup Asiago cheese.

4. Bake at 350° for 20 to 25 minutes or until golden brown. Remove from pan to a wire rack, and sprinkle with thyme.

Cider-Poached Shrimp with Jezebel Apple Salsa

MAKES 6 SERVINGS
HANDS-ON 15 MIN.
TOTAL 1 HOUR, 45 MIN., INCLUDING SALSA

Ready to move beyond the classic shrimp cocktail? We thought so! Hard cider (fermented apple juice) infuses the shrimp with a faint hint of sweetness and subtle fruitiness. Cook shrimp up to 1 day ahead, then stir together a quick and colorful salsa just before serving.

- 2 lb. peeled, large raw shrimp with tails
- 3 1/2 cups hard cider
- 2 tsp. table salt
- 6 cups ice cubes
  Jezebel Apple Salsa

Devein shrimp. Bring cider and salt to a boil in a Dutch oven over medium-high heat. Add shrimp; remove from heat. Cover and let stand 5 minutes or until shrimp turn pink. Stir in ice; let stand 5 minutes. Remove shrimp; chill 1 to 24 hours. Serve with salsa.

JEZEBEL APPLE SALSA

MAKES 3 CUPS
HANDS-ON 15 MIN.
TOTAL 15 MIN.

- 1/4 cup apple jelly
- 1 3/4 tsp. prepared horseradish
- 1 1/2 tsp. lime zest
- 4 1/2 tsp. fresh lime juice
- 1/4 tsp. dry mustard
- 1/8 tsp. dried crushed red pepper
- 2 cups diced Granny Smith apples
- 3/4 cup diced fresh mango
- 1/2 cup diced red bell pepper
- 1/3 cup diced red onion
- 1/3 cup chopped fresh cilantro

Whisk together first 6 ingredients in a medium bowl. Stir in apples and next 4 ingredients.

Bite-Size Treats

▶ A taste of who and what online got the most raves in the *Southern Living* Test Kitchen.

RECIPES FROM
THE
SOUTH'S
Tastiest
BLOGS

From the Kitchen of
ROBIN WILSON

SIMPLYSOUTHERNBAKING.COM
ALTAMONTE SPRINGS, FL

"You can also use yellow and pink food coloring gel to make peach. Practice on a piece of wax paper, adding a little at a time to achieve your perfect shade. I serve these to family and friends, and there's never a square left."

ORANGE DREAMSICLE CRISPY TREATS

Melt ¼ cup **butter** in a large Dutch oven over medium-low heat. Add 1 (10-oz.) package **miniature marshmallows**, stirring until melted. Remove from heat. Stir in 1 ½ tsp. **vanilla extract.** Add ½ cup **orange cake mix** (such as Duncan Hines Orange Supreme), blending well. Stir in 6 cups **crisp rice cereal** and 1 (12-oz.) package **white chocolate morsels** until well coated. Spread mixture into a lightly greased 13- x 9-inch pan. Cool completely (about 30 minutes). Meanwhile, stir together 3 cups **powdered sugar**, 6 Tbsp. **softened butter**, 5 to 6 Tbsp. **orange juice**, ¼ tsp. **vanilla extract,** ¼ tsp. **orange extract,** and desired amount of **peach food coloring gel.** Spread over cereal mixture. Let stand 1 hour before cutting. **MAKES** 32 bars

From the Kitchen of
JESSICA PENDERGRASS

URBANSACREDGARDEN.COM
LOUISVILLE, KY

"These cookies are the perfect remedy for an afternoon slump. For a chewy, moist cookie that isn't overdone, remove them from the oven when edges are just lightly browned."

OATMEAL ENERGY COOKIES

Preheat oven to 350°. Microwave ½ cup **butter** in a microwave-safe bowl at HIGH 30 to 40 seconds or until butter is partially melted. (Butter will have lumps.) Whisk together partially melted butter, ¼ cup plus 3 Tbsp. **honey**, 2 large **eggs**, and 1 tsp. **vanilla extract** in a large bowl. Whisk together 1 ¾ cups **white whole wheat flour**, 1 tsp.

baking powder, and ¼ tsp. **table salt** in a large bowl. Stir in 1 ½ cups uncooked **regular oats**; ½ cup **milk chocolate morsels**; ½ cup **bittersweet chocolate morsels**; ¼ cup **walnuts,** coarsely chopped; ¼ cup **granulated sugar**; ¼ cup firmly packed **dark brown sugar**; ¼ cup **roasted, salted pumpkin seeds**; and ¼ cup **sweetened dried cranberries**. Add flour mixture to butter mixture, stirring just until combined. (Do not overmix.) Shape dough into 2-inch balls, and place dough balls 1 inch apart on **parchment paper**-lined baking sheets. Bake, in batches, 15 minutes or until edges of cookies are lightly browned. Cool cookies on baking sheets 5 minutes; transfer cookies to wire racks, and let cool completely (about 20 minutes). **MAKES** 2 ½ dozen cookies

From the Kitchen of
HEATHER DISARRO

HEATHERSDISH.COM
LITTLE ROCK, AR

"I serve this with a simple mixture of equal parts sour cream, Greek yogurt, and mayonnaise spiced up with curry powder, ground red pepper, salt, and pepper."

SWEET POTATO-GOAT CHEESE TOTS

Grate 2 large **sweet potatoes,** peeled, and 1 medium-size **russet potato,** peeled, into a bowl using small holes of a box grater. Pat potatoes dry with paper towels. Stir together grated potatoes; 1 (4-oz.) **goat cheese log,** softened; 2 Tbsp. **all-purpose flour;** 1 Tbsp. grated **sweet onion;** 1 tsp. **table salt;** and ½ tsp. **black pepper** until well blended. Divide mixture into 4 equal portions; shape each portion into a 12- x 1-inch log. Wrap each portion in plastic wrap, and freeze 30 minutes or until slightly firm. Unwrap dough, and cut each dough log into about 15 (¾-inch-thick) slices. Heat 4 cups **vegetable oil** in a heavy saucepan over medium-low heat to 330°. Fry potato slices, in batches, 3 to 5 minutes or until golden and crisp. Drain on paper towels. Immediately sprinkle potato tots with **fine sea salt. MAKES** about 6 dozen potato tots

October

Go Beyond the Biscuit

▶ Justly famous for our flaky biscuits, it's high time we celebrate other classically Southern—and divinely delicious—breads that fill our region's basket

Potato Loaves
(opposite page)

New Orleans Calas
(page 242)

Sally Lunn
(right)

Any Flavor Buttermilk
Coffee Cake (page 241)

YEAST BREADS

Soft, pillowy, and served hot are the only imperatives of good Southern yeast bread. Although these recipes take a pinch more patience than quick breads, nothing tastes quite as comforting or makes the kitchen smell more inviting.

Sally Lunn

MAKES 8 TO 10 SERVINGS
HANDS-ON 15 MIN.
TOTAL 2 HOURS

- 1 cup warm milk (100° to 110°)
- 1 (¼-oz.) envelope active dry yeast
- 1 tsp. sugar
- 4 cups all-purpose flour
- ¼ to ½ cup sugar
- 1 tsp. table salt
- 3 large eggs, lightly beaten
- ½ cup warm water (100° to 110°)
- ½ tsp. baking soda
- ½ cup butter, melted

1. Stir together first 3 ingredients in a 2-cup glass measuring cup; let stand 5 minutes.

2. Stir together flour and next 2 ingredients in a large bowl. Stir in eggs until well blended. (Dough will look shaggy.) Stir together warm water and baking soda. Stir yeast mixture, soda mixture, and melted butter into flour mixture until well blended.

3. Spoon batter into a well-greased 10-inch (14-cup) tube pan. Cover with plastic wrap, and let rise in a warm place (80° to 85°), 45 minutes to 1 hour or until doubled in bulk.

4. Preheat oven to 400°. Carefully place pan in oven. (Do not agitate dough.) Bake 25 to 30 minutes or until a wooden pick inserted in center comes out clean. Remove from pan to a wire rack, and cool 30 minutes before slicing.

Potato Rolls

MAKES 2 DOZEN
HANDS-ON 1 HOUR, 15 MIN.
TOTAL 5 HOURS, 45 MIN.

- 1 medium-size russet potato (about 8 oz.), peeled and cut into 1-inch pieces
- 2 (1/4-oz.) envelopes active dry yeast
- 1 cup warm water (105° to 115°)
- 1/2 cup sugar
- 2 large eggs
- 1/4 cup vegetable oil
- 1 Tbsp. fresh lemon juice
- 2 tsp. table salt
- 6 1/2 cups all-purpose flour
- 3 Tbsp. melted butter, divided

1. Bring potato and water to cover to a boil in a saucepan over medium heat; boil 10 to 12 minutes or until tender. Drain, reserving 1 cup liquid, and cool potato 15 minutes. Press potato through a potato ricer or food mill, and cool completely (about 30 minutes).

2. Stir together yeast, 1 cup warm water, 2 tsp. sugar, and reserved cooking liquid in bowl of a heavy-duty electric stand mixer; let stand 5 minutes. Stir in eggs, next 3 ingredients, potato, 3 cups flour, and remaining sugar. Beat at medium speed, using paddle attachment, until smooth. Gradually beat in remaining 3 to 3 1/2 cups flour until a soft dough forms.

3. Turn dough out onto a well-floured surface, and knead until smooth and elastic (about 4 to 6 minutes), sprinkling with flour as needed. Place dough in a lightly greased large bowl, turning to grease top. Cover and let rise in a warm place (80° to 85°), about 1 hour or until doubled in bulk.

4. Punch dough down; turn out onto a lightly floured surface, and divide in half.

5. Gently shape each half into 12 (2 1/2-inch) balls, and place in 2 greased 10-inch round cake pans. Brush tops with 2 Tbsp. melted butter. Cover and let rise in a warm place (80° to 85°), 1 hour or until doubled in bulk.

6. Preheat oven to 375°. Bake 25 to 30 minutes or until rolls are deep golden brown. Remove from pans to a wire rack, and brush with remaining melted butter. Cool completely.

POTATO LOAVES Prepare recipe through Step 4. Roll each dough half into an 18- x 9-inch rectangle. Starting at 1 short end, roll up each rectangle, jelly-roll fashion, pressing to seal edges as you roll. Pinch ends of dough, and tuck ends under. Place each roll, seam side down, in a lightly greased 9- x 5-inch loaf pan. Proceed with recipe as directed, baking 30 to 35 minutes or until deep golden brown.

Sorghum-Oat Bread

MAKES 2 LOAVES
HANDS-ON 25 MIN.
TOTAL 4 HOURS, 20 MIN.

Be sure the oat mixture has cooled before mixing with the yeast.

- 2 1/4 cups boiling water
- 1 cup uncooked regular oats
- 1/4 cup butter
- 1/2 cup firmly packed dark brown sugar
- 2 Tbsp. sorghum syrup
- 1 Tbsp. fresh lemon juice
- 1/2 cup warm water (100° to 110°)
- 1 Tbsp. active dry yeast
- 1 tsp. granulated sugar
- 4 cups bread flour
- 1 1/2 cups whole wheat flour
- 1 Tbsp. table salt
- 1 tsp. ground cinnamon
- 2 Tbsp. butter, melted

1. Stir together first 3 ingredients in bowl of a heavy-duty electric stand mixer until butter melts. Stir in brown sugar and next 2 ingredients. Cool until lukewarm (20 to 30 minutes).

2. Meanwhile, stir together 1/2 cup warm water, yeast, and granulated sugar in a 1-cup glass measuring cup; let stand 5 minutes.

3. Stir together bread flour and next 3 ingredients in a medium bowl. Stir yeast mixture into oat mixture. Gradually add flour mixture to oat mixture, beating on low speed until well blended.

4. Sprinkle a flat surface generously with bread flour. Turn dough out, and knead until smooth and elastic (about 6 to 8 minutes), sprinkling surface with bread flour as needed. Place dough in a lightly greased large bowl, turning to grease top. Cover and let rise in a warm place (80° to 85°), about 1 hour or until doubled in bulk.

5. Punch dough down; turn out onto a lightly floured surface. Divide dough in half. Roll each half into an 18- x 9-inch rectangle. Starting at short end, tightly roll up each rectangle, jelly-roll fashion, pressing to seal edges as you roll. Pinch ends of dough to seal, and tuck ends under dough. Place each dough roll, seam side down, in a lightly greased 9- x 5-inch loaf pan. Cover and let rise in a warm place (80° to 85°) 1 hour or until doubled in bulk.

6. Preheat oven to 350°. Bake 30 to 35 minutes or until loaves are golden brown and sound hollow when tapped. Remove from pans to a wire rack, and brush loaves with melted butter. Cool completely (about 1 hour).

FOOL PROOF RISE

Baking in a cold kitchen? Turn your microwave into a proofbox: Heat 2 cups water in a glass measuring cup for 4 minutes. Move water to back of microwave. Set dough, covered in a bowl, in the center. Shut the door (with microwave off); let rise.

CORNBREAD

In the South, there are as many names for cornbread as there are china patterns. No matter what you call it—corn dodgers, johnnycakes, corn pones, scratch backs—cornbread is a simple wonder that will be forever welcome at even the most lavish table.

Skillet Cornbread

MAKES 6 TO 8 SERVINGS
HANDS-ON 20 MIN.
TOTAL 40 MIN.

Quickly incorporate the hot bacon drippings into the batter with a fork. When you pour it back into the hot skillet, listen for the sizzle. That sound means your crust will be dark golden and crisp.

- 2 Tbsp. bacon drippings
- 1 1/2 cups stone-ground white cornmeal
- 1/4 cup all-purpose flour
- 2 tsp. sugar
- 1 tsp. baking powder
- 1 tsp. baking soda
- 3/4 tsp. table salt
- 2 cups buttermilk
- 1 large egg

1. Preheat oven to 450°. Place bacon drippings in a 10-inch cast-iron skillet, and heat in oven 8 to 10 minutes or until drippings begin to gently smoke.

2. Meanwhile, stir together cornmeal and next 5 ingredients in a large bowl. Stir together buttermilk and egg in a medium bowl.

3. During last minute skillet is heating in oven, stir buttermilk mixture into cornmeal mixture until just combined. Pour hot drippings into cornmeal mixture, and quickly stir to incorporate. Pour mixture into hot skillet, and immediately place in oven.

4. Bake at 450° for 18 to 20 minutes or until golden brown and cornbread pulls away from sides of skillet. Remove from skillet, and serve immediately.

GRIDDLE CAKES Place bacon drippings in skillet, and heat over medium-high heat 2 to 3 minutes or until drippings begin to gently smoke. Add 1 cup fresh corn kernels and 1/4 cup finely chopped sweet onion to drippings, and sauté 3 to 4 minutes or until lightly charred. Stir together cornmeal and next 7 ingredients in a large bowl. Stir in corn mixture. Pour about 2 Tbsp. batter for each griddle cake onto a hot buttered griddle or into a large nonstick skillet. Cook 2 to 3 minutes or until tops are covered with bubbles and edges look dry and cooked. Turn and cook 2 to 3 minutes or until golden brown. Place in a single layer on a baking sheet, and keep warm in a 200° oven up to 30 minutes. **MAKES** 2 DOZEN. **HANDS-ON** 30 MIN., **TOTAL** 35 MIN.

GET THAT CRUST CRISP Heat your skillet or pan before pouring in the batter.

THE MEAL TICKET Yellow cornmeal is a hint sweeter than white, with a stronger corn flavor. Regardless, they can be used interchangeably in recipes. Our favorite brands include Hodgson Mill, Dixie Lily, and Quaker.

PICK A SIZE
Make these muffins into loaves!
Spoon batter into 2 greased
8- x 4-inch loaf pans, and
bake 55 minutes.

Pumpkin Streusel Muffins

MAKES 2 DOZEN
HANDS ON 20 MIN.
TOTAL 1 HOUR, 15 MIN., INCLUDING STREUSEL

- ³⁄₄ cup butter, softened
- 1 (8-oz.) package cream cheese, softened
- 1 cup granulated sugar
- 1 cup firmly packed light brown sugar
- 2 large eggs
- 3 cups all-purpose flour
- 1 tsp. pumpkin pie spice
- ¹⁄₂ tsp. baking powder
- ¹⁄₂ tsp. baking soda
- ¹⁄₂ tsp. table salt
- 1¹⁄₂ cups canned pumpkin
- ¹⁄₂ cup toasted chopped pecans
- ¹⁄₂ cup sweetened dried cranberries
- ¹⁄₂ tsp. vanilla extract
  Pumpkin Pie Streusel

1. Preheat oven to 350°. Beat butter and cream cheese at medium speed with a heavy-duty electric stand mixer until creamy. Gradually add sugars, beating until light and fluffy. Add eggs, 1 at a time, beating just until blended after each addition.

2. Stir together flour and next 4 ingredients; gradually add to butter mixture, beating at low speed. Stir in pumpkin and next 3 ingredients.

3. Spoon batter into 2 lightly greased (12-cup) muffin pans, filling two-thirds full. Sprinkle with Pumpkin Pie Streusel.

4. Bake at 350° for 25 minutes or until a wooden pick inserted in center comes out clean. Cool in pans on wire racks 5 minutes; remove from pans to wire racks, and cool 20 minutes.

Note: We tested with Craisins Original Dried Cranberries.

PUMPKIN PIE STREUSEL Stir together ¹⁄₂ cup chopped **pecans**, ¹⁄₂ cup firmly packed **light brown sugar**, 1 Tbsp. **all-purpose flour**, 1 Tbsp. **melted butter**, and ¹⁄₄ tsp. **pumpkin pie spice**.

GO GLUTEN-FREE!
Substitute 1¹⁄₂ cups each sorghum flour and brown rice flour for the all-purpose flour in Pumpkin Streusel Muffins. Both flours are available at *bobsredmill.com* ($3.29 and up).

BREAKFAST BREADS

Muffins, coffee cakes, and hot fried delights are heralds of hospitality. They're the quick breads we bake to wake up houseguests, thank friends, and comfort neighbors.

Any Flavor Buttermilk Coffee Cake

MAKES 8 SERVINGS
HANDS-ON 15 MIN.
TOTAL 1 HOUR, 5 MIN.

Customize your topping with any fruit-nut combo. We like plum preserves, sliced plums, and almonds, or strawberry jam, sliced strawberries, and pecans.

- 2 cups all-purpose flour
- 3 tsp. baking powder
- ¹⁄₂ tsp. baking soda
- ¹⁄₄ tsp. table salt
- 2 large eggs
- 1 cup buttermilk
- ¹⁄₂ cup granulated sugar
- 4 Tbsp. shortening, melted
- ¹⁄₄ cup fruit preserves or jam
- 1 cup diced or sliced fresh fruit
- ¹⁄₄ cup chopped nuts
- 1 tsp. granulated sugar
- 1 cup powdered sugar
- 2¹⁄₂ Tbsp. buttermilk

1. Preheat oven to 350°. Sift together first 4 ingredients. Whisk together eggs and next 3 ingredients in a large bowl. Whisk flour mixture into egg mixture.

2. Pour batter into a lightly greased 9-inch round cake pan. Dollop preserves by teaspoonfuls over batter, and gently swirl with a knife. Top with diced fruit and chopped nuts. Sprinkle with 1 tsp. granulated sugar.

3. Bake at 350° for 38 to 45 minutes or until golden brown. Cool in pan on a wire rack 5 minutes. Remove from pan to wire rack, and cool 5 minutes.

4. Whisk together powdered sugar and 2¹⁄₂ Tbsp. buttermilk. Drizzle over warm coffee cake.

New Orleans Calas

MAKES 2 1/2 DOZEN
HANDS-ON 45 MIN.
TOTAL 10 HOURS, 10 MIN.

The Calas Women, as they were called, ped-dled these hot breakfast fritters—whose name comes from the African word "kárá"—each morning in the French Quarter. The street vendors have vanished, so we honor them here with a classic rice-dough recipe too delicious to ever disappear.

- 1/2 **cup uncooked medium-grain rice**
- 3/4 **tsp. table salt, divided**
- 1/2 **cup warm water (100° to 110°)**
- 1 1/4 **tsp. active dry yeast**
- 1 **tsp. granulated sugar**
- 3 **large eggs, lightly beaten**
- 1 1/4 **cups all-purpose flour**
- 1/4 **cup granulated sugar**
- 1/4 **tsp. ground nutmeg**
  Vegetable oil
  Powdered sugar

1. Bring 6 cups water to a boil in a sauce-pan over medium-high heat. Stir in rice and 1/4 tsp. salt. Reduce heat to medium, and cook, stirring often, 25 to 30 minutes. (Rice will be very soft and thick.) Remove from heat, and drain. Place 1 1/2 cups cooked rice in a bowl, discarding remaining rice. Mash rice with a potato masher 30 seconds. Cool 20 minutes or until lukewarm.

2. Stir together warm water, yeast, and 1 tsp. granulated sugar in a 1-cup glass mea-suring cup; let stand 5 minutes. Stir yeast mixture into rice. Cover with plastic wrap, and let stand in a warm place (80° to 85°), free from drafts, 8 to 12 hours.

3. Stir eggs into rice mixture. Combine flour, next 2 ingredients, and remaining 1/2 tsp. salt. Stir flour mixture into rice mix-ture. Cover with plastic wrap, and let stand in a warm place (80° to 85°), free from drafts, 30 minutes.

4. Meanwhile, pour oil to depth of 3 inches into a deep cast-iron skillet or large Dutch oven; heat to 350°. Drop dough by rounded tablespoonfuls into hot oil, and fry, in batches, 3 minutes or until golden brown. Drain on paper towels. Sprinkle with pow-dered sugar, and serve immediately.

Note: We tested with Water Maid Medium-Grain Enriched Rice.

TEST KITCHEN TIPS

Work ahead: Refrigerate the rice batter overnight (Step 2) to deepen its flavor. Finish the dough and fry the next morning.

Don't jump the gun and fry before your oil reaches 350° or your fritters will be greasy.

This batter is sticky! Coat the measuring spoon with vegetable cooking spray before scooping and the dough will slide gently into the frying oil.

Escape the Daily Grind

▶ Liven up your weeknight cooking routine with five fresh takes on ground meat dinners

Lemon, Orzo, and Meatball Soup

MAKES ABOUT 3 QT.

(Pictured on page 16)

- 1 lb. ground chicken
- 1 large egg, lightly beaten
- 1/4 cup fine, dry breadcrumbs
- 1 tsp. kosher salt
- 4 tsp. loosely packed lemon zest, divided
- 1 tsp. dried crushed rosemary, divided
- 3 Tbsp. olive oil, divided
- 1 medium-size sweet onion, chopped
- 3 carrots, thinly sliced
- 2 garlic cloves, minced
- 2 (32-oz.) containers chicken broth
- 5 to 6 Tbsp. lemon juice
- 3/4 cup orzo pasta
- 1/4 cup freshly grated Parmesan cheese
- 1/2 cup fresh flat-leaf parsley leaves

1. Combine first 4 ingredients, 2 tsp. lemon zest, and 1/2 tsp. rosemary in a medium bowl. Shape into 30 (1-inch) meatballs (about 1 level tablespoonful each).

2. Sauté meatballs, in 2 batches, in 1 Tbsp. hot oil per batch in a Dutch oven over medium heat 3 to 4 minutes or until browned. Remove, using a slotted spoon.

3. Sauté onion and next 2 ingredients in remaining 1 Tbsp. hot oil in Dutch oven over medium-high heat 3 to 5 minutes or until tender. Stir in broth, lemon juice, and remaining 2 tsp. zest and 1/2 tsp. rosemary. Bring to a boil, stirring occasionally. Add orzo. Reduce heat to medium; simmer, stirring occasionally, 7 to 9 minutes or until pasta is almost tender.

4. Stir in meatballs; simmer, stirring occasionally, 5 to 7 minutes or until meatballs are thoroughly cooked. Add salt and pepper to taste. Top with cheese and parsley.

Sloppy Cola Joe
Dogs

Salsa Verde Corn Chip Pie

35 MIN

MAKES 6 SERVINGS

Make this Texas Friday-night-football favorite your Tuesday supper.

- 2 cups frozen whole kernel yellow corn, thawed
- 5 tsp. olive oil, divided
- 1 (9-oz.) package garlic pork sausage links, casings removed
- 1 medium-size sweet onion, chopped
- 2 tsp. chili powder
- 1 tsp. ground cumin
- 1 (16-oz.) bottle salsa verde
- 2 (4.5-oz.) cans chopped green chiles
- 1 (16-oz.) can navy beans, drained and rinsed
- 2 Tbsp. fresh lime juice
- 6 cups original corn chips
- 1 cup (4 oz.) shredded pepper Jack cheese
- Toppings: cilantro, radishes, avocado

1. Sauté corn in 3 tsp. hot olive oil in a large skillet over medium heat 3 to 4 minutes or until corn begins to char. Remove corn from skillet.

2. Sauté sausage in skillet over medium-high heat 6 to 8 minutes or until browned. Remove from skillet, and drain on paper towels.

3. Sauté onion in remaining 2 tsp. hot oil in skillet over medium-high heat 4 to 5 minutes or until tender. Stir in chili powder and cumin; cook, stirring often, 2 to 3 minutes. Stir in salsa, chiles, and sausage. Cook over medium heat, stirring often, 7 to 8 minutes or until slightly thickened. Remove from heat; stir in beans, lime juice, and corn.

4. Divide chips among 6 plates. Spoon sausage mixture over chips; top with half of cheese. Serve with toppings and remaining cheese.

Note: We tested with Herdez Salsa Verde and Fritos Original Corn Chips.

Sloppy Cola Joe Dogs

25 MIN

MAKES 8 SERVINGS

Our Test Kitchen couldn't get enough of these new sloppy joes enlivened with a splash of cola, which gives the ground beef a sweet boost that plays well off the filling's spices. Try these with traditional or split-top hot dog buns or hoagie rolls. Garnish with your favorite coleslaw for crunch and color. (Pictured on page 192)

- 1 medium-size red onion, thinly sliced
- 2 Tbsp. olive oil
- 1 1/2 lb. ground round
- 1 (6-oz.) can tomato paste
- 1 garlic clove, minced
- 1 Tbsp. Worcestershire sauce
- 1 cup spicy, fruity cola soft drink (such as Dr Pepper)
- 1/2 cup jarred sliced pepperoncini salad peppers
- Ground red pepper
- 8 hot dog buns or hoagie rolls
- Store-bought coleslaw

1. Sauté onion in hot oil in a large skillet over medium-high heat 4 to 5 minutes or until onions are caramel colored.

2. Add ground beef to skillet, and cook over medium-high heat, stirring often, 5 to 6 minutes or until meat crumbles and is no longer pink; drain.

3. Return beef mixture to skillet. Stir in tomato paste and next 2 ingredients, and cook, stirring occasionally, 3 to 4 minutes or until mixture thickens and color darkens. Stir in cola and 1/2 cup water, and cook, stirring constantly, 6 to 8 minutes or until bubbly. Remove from heat, and stir in pepperoncini peppers; add salt and red pepper to taste.

4. Serve beef mixture immediately on buns with coleslaw.

Pepper Relish Mini Meatloaves

MAKES 6 TO 8 SERVINGS

Use pepper relish to add sweet-savory punch and a pretty glaze.

- 1/2 cup soft, fresh breadcrumbs
- 1/4 cup spicy-hot vegetable juice
- 1/4 cup buttermilk
- 1 cup minced sweet onion (about 1 medium)
- 1 Tbsp. olive oil
- 1 3/4 lb. ground round
- 1/4 cup finely chopped fresh basil
- 1 large egg, lightly beaten
- 1 Tbsp. Dijon mustard
- 1 tsp. kosher salt
- 1/2 tsp. freshly ground black pepper
- 1 cup hot pepper relish, divided
  Garnish: fresh basil

1. Preheat oven to 450°. Stir together first 3 ingredients; let stand 5 minutes.

2. Meanwhile, sauté onion in hot oil in a medium-size nonstick skillet over medium heat 5 minutes or just until tender.

3. Stir together bread mixture, onion, ground beef, next 5 ingredients, and 2 Tbsp. relish just until blended.

4. Shape into 8 loaves (about 1/2 cup each); place in cups of a lightly greased 8-cup mini loaf pan. (Each cup will be about 3 1/2 x 2 1/2 inches. Or arrange on a lightly greased wire rack in a foil-lined jelly-roll pan.)

5. Bake at 450° for 25 to 30 minutes or until a meat thermometer registers 155°, brushing with 1/3 cup relish during last 10 minutes of baking. Remove from oven; let stand 5 minutes. Serve with remaining relish.

Note: We tested with Howard's Hot Pepper Relish.

 ## Pork-and-Green Bean Stir-fry

MAKES 4 SERVINGS

The key to this dish is developing a nice char on the green beans. To do so, heat the oil in your skillet until it almost smokes before adding the beans. Let them sear, stirring every 20 to 30 seconds, and they'll take on color. Feel free to sub thinly sliced strips of red bell pepper instead of hot chiles.

- 1 1/2 lb. ground pork
- 2 garlic cloves, thinly sliced
- 1/2 tsp. table salt
- 1/4 tsp. ground red pepper
- 1 (8-oz.) package haricots verts (thin green beans)
- 1 Tbsp. peanut oil or vegetable oil
- 3/4 cup triple-ginger or regular teriyaki sauce
- 1/2 tsp. loosely packed lime zest
- 1 Tbsp. fresh lime juice
  Hot cooked rice or thin rice noodles
  Garnishes: thinly sliced red jalapeño pepper, lime halves

1. Brown ground pork and next 3 ingredients in a large stainless steel skillet over medium-high heat, stirring often, 7 to 8 minutes or until meat crumbles and is no longer pink; drain. Wipe skillet clean.

2. Cook green beans in hot oil in skillet over medium-high heat, stirring occasionally, 4 to 5 minutes or until just tender and slightly charred.

3. Stir together teriyaki sauce and next 2 ingredients.

4. Stir pork mixture into green beans. Stir in teriyaki mixture, tossing to coat. Serve immediately over rice or noodles.

Note: We tested with Kikkoman Triple Ginger Takumi Collection Teriyaki Sauce.

TEST KITCHEN

A LITTLE PROFESSIONAL HELP FROM OUR KITCHEN TO YOURS

Conquer the Rise

▶ **DON'T BE INTIMIDATED** by yeast; embrace it. A friendly fungus, yeast is the microscopic magic that leavens bread and gives it its unique texture and flavor. At the grocery store, you'll see instant (or "rapid-rise") and active dry yeast. We recommend active dry—the activation (Step 2, below) means the yeast is alive and ready to go to work. Follow our steps and your bread will rise to the occasion.

1

STORE

Use yeast packets before the expiration date. To store yeast after it has been opened, refrigerate the granules in an airtight container.

2

ACTIVATE

Stir active dry yeast into warm water (100° to 110°). Too cold and the granules will remain dormant; too hot and the yeast will die. Yeast loves sugar, so add a pinch to speed up activation (aka "proofing"). If bubbles appear, you're golden. That's the gas that makes bread rise.

3

MIX

Mix the bubbly brew with flour to make a shaggy dough. Most recipes call for a pinch of salt, not just for flavor but to slow the activation process, keeping the yeast in check so it doesn't activate too fast.

4

KNEAD

Knead the dough to create gluten, which behaves like bubble gum. It traps tiny gas bubbles produced by the yeast and stretches to give bread its springy texture.

5

RISE

Bubbles multiply and grow as the yeast starts fermenting, which gives bread its unique flavor and texture. After this first rise, shape the dough, let it rise briefly again, and bake it!

Bake Up an Enchanting Dessert

▶ A chewy ring of brownie-batter crust folds over creamy and luscious peanut butter cheesecake. Yes, please!

Cinderella Cheesecake

MAKES 10 TO 12 SERVINGS
HANDS-ON 45 MIN.
TOTAL 11 HOURS, 5 MIN., INCLUDING TOPPING

Recipe from Savor the Moment *by the Junior League of Boca Raton.*

BROWNIE CRUST

- 3 (1-oz.) unsweetened chocolate baking squares
- 1/4 cup unsalted butter
- 1/2 cup sifted all-purpose flour
- 1/8 tsp. table salt
- 1/8 tsp. baking powder
- 2 large eggs
- 1 cup firmly packed light brown sugar
- 1 1/2 tsp. vanilla extract
- 1/2 (1-oz.) bittersweet chocolate baking square, finely chopped

CHEESECAKE FILLING AND TOPPING

- 1 1/2 (8-oz.) packages cream cheese, softened
- 1 cup firmly packed light brown sugar
- 3 large eggs
- 1/2 cup sour cream
- 1 1/3 cups creamy peanut butter
   Sour Cream Topping
   Chocolate curls

1. Prepare Brownie Crust: Preheat oven to 350°. Microwave first 2 ingredients in a small microwave-safe bowl at MEDIUM (50% power) 1 1/2 minutes or until melted, stirring at 30-second intervals. Stir together flour, salt, and baking powder in a bowl.

2. Beat 2 eggs and 1 cup brown sugar at medium-high speed with an electric mixer 3 to 4 minutes or until batter forms thin ribbons when beaters are lifted. Add vanilla, bittersweet chocolate, and melted chocolate mixture, and beat just until blended. Stir in flour mixture just until combined.

3. Spread 1 cup brownie mixture on bottom of a greased and floured 9-inch springform pan. Bake at 350° on center oven rack 13 to 15 minutes or until set. Cool on a wire rack 10 minutes; freeze 15 minutes. Remove from freezer; spread remaining brownie batter up sides of pan to 1/4 inch from top, sealing batter to bottom crust.

4. Prepare Filling: Beat cream cheese and 1 cup brown sugar at medium speed with a heavy-duty electric stand mixer until blended. Add 3 eggs, 1 at a time, beating just until yellow disappears after each addition. Beat in sour cream just until blended. Beat in peanut butter until blended.

5. Pour filling into prepared crust. (Mixture will not completely fill crust.) Bake at 350° for 35 minutes or until center is almost set.

6. Remove from oven. Spread Sour Cream Topping over center of cheesecake, leaving a 2-inch border around edge. Bake at 350° for 1 more minute. Remove from oven; gently run a knife around edge of cheesecake to loosen. Cool completely on a wire rack.

7. Cover and chill 8 to 12 hours. Remove sides of pan. Top with chocolate curls.

SOUR CREAM TOPPING Stir together 3/4 cup sour cream and 2 tsp. granulated sugar in a small bowl until smooth.

Note: We tested with Jif peanut butter.

GET THE LOOK!
Fill a decorating bag with 1/2 cup peanut butter, and pipe with a rosette tip.

Wow 'em with Chili

▶ Stew up a quick and casual Halloween get-together with this soul-satisfying one-pot meal of chicken-and-sweet-potato chili with cheese toast

Tex-Mex Chicken Chili with Lime

MAKES 3 QT.
HANDS-ON 30 MIN.
TOTAL 1 HOUR, 5 MIN.

Store-bought rotisserie chicken shortcuts the cook time, while white ale adds spice, body, and flavor.

- 1 Tbsp. butter
- 2 Tbsp. olive oil
- 1 large white onion, diced
- 1 medium-size red onion, diced
- 1 poblano or bell pepper, seeded and diced
- 1 red or green jalapeño pepper, seeded and diced
- 1 large sweet potato, peeled and chopped
- 2 tsp. ground cumin
- 2 tsp. chipotle powder
- 2 tsp. kosher salt
- 3 garlic cloves, minced
- 2 (16-oz.) cans navy beans, drained
- 1 (12-oz.) bottle white ale
- 4 cups shredded deli-roasted chicken
- 4 cups chicken broth
  Toppings: Lime Cream, fresh cilantro, green onions, lime wedges

1. Melt butter with oil in a Dutch oven over medium heat. Add white onion and next 7 ingredients, and sauté 8 minutes or until translucent. Add garlic, and cook 30 seconds.

2. Stir in beans and beer, and cook 5 minutes or until liquid is reduced by half. Add chicken and broth; bring to a boil over high heat. Reduce heat to medium-low, and simmer 30 minutes until thickened. Serve with desired toppings.

Note: We tested with Blue Moon Belgian White Wheat Ale.

LIME CREAM Combine 1 cup sour cream and zest and juice of 1 lime. Season with salt to taste. **MAKES** 1 CUP

GREEN CHILE CHEESE TOAST Stir together 1 cup (4 oz.) each shredded **pepper Jack cheese** and **white Cheddar cheese**, ³/4 cup **mayonnaise**, ¹/2 cup freshly grated **Parmesan cheese**, 1 (4.5-oz.) can diced **green chiles,** and 1 Tbsp. Ranch **dressing mix.** Spread on toasted French bread slices. Broil 5 inches from heat until bubbly.

LIGHTEN UP MAMA'S...
Traditional Lasagna

Mama's Way: *Layered meat-and-cheese casserole* **Our Way:** *Hearty vegetarian rolls with fresh basil*

Tomato-Basil Lasagna Rolls

MAKES 10 SERVINGS
HANDS-ON 35 MIN.
TOTAL 1 HOUR, 35 MIN.

Canned artichokes give the rich filling its meaty heft. Feel free to sub sautéed 'shrooms or spinach.

- 10 uncooked lasagna noodles
- 1 cup finely chopped sweet onion
- 2 tsp. olive oil
- 3 garlic cloves, minced and divided
- 1 (24-oz.) jar tomato-and-basil pasta sauce
- 1½ tsp. sugar
- ¼ tsp. dried crushed red pepper
- 1 cup low-fat ricotta cheese
- 2 oz. ⅓-less-fat cream cheese, softened
- 1 (14-oz.) can baby artichoke hearts, drained and quartered
- 1 large egg white, lightly beaten
- ¼ cup torn fresh basil
- ¼ cup (1 oz.) freshly shredded Parmesan cheese
- Toppings: fresh basil, Parmesan cheese

1. Preheat oven to 350°. Cook pasta according to package directions for al dente. Drain pasta (do not rinse); arrange in a single layer on a piece of lightly greased aluminum foil or wax paper.

2. Sauté onion in hot oil in a 3-qt. saucepan over medium heat 7 to 8 minutes or until caramelized. Add two-thirds of minced garlic, and cook, stirring constantly, 1 minute. Stir in tomato sauce and next 2 ingredients. Bring mixture to a boil, stirring often. Reduce heat to low; simmer, stirring often, 5 minutes. Remove from heat.

3. Stir together ricotta and cream cheese until smooth. Stir in artichoke hearts, next 3 ingredients, and remaining minced garlic. Spread ¼ cup cheese mixture on 1 noodle. Roll up firmly, and place, seam side down, into a lightly greased 11- x 7-inch baking dish. Repeat with remaining noodles and cheese. Spoon tomato sauce over lasagna rolls.

4. Bake, covered, at 350° for 45 to 50 minutes or until thoroughly heated and bubbly. Let stand 5 minutes. Sprinkle with desired toppings.

Note: We tested with Classico Tomato & Basil pasta sauce.

PER SERVING (NOT INCLUDING TOPPINGS):
CALORIES 190; **FAT** 5g (sat 1.5g); **PROTEIN** 9g; **CARB** 28g; **CHOL** 11mg; **SODIUM** 590mg; **CALC** 120mg

OLD SCHOOL
Classic casserole layered with noodles, ground beef, tomato sauce, and cheese...lots of cheese. *Mamma mia!*

NEW SCHOOL
Pretty spiraled-up noodles stuffed with creamy vegetable filling and topped with sweet 'n' spicy tomato sauce.

REPORT CARD
We cut the calories in half and the fat by more than 70% while making the portion sizes more easily defined.

From Plow to Chow

▶ As the air turns crisp, a new season of produce fills the rows at photographer Helen Norman's Star Bright Farm. To celebrate, she gathers family and friends around her Maryland table for a harvest feast.

THE SETTING

There was serendipity involved when photographer Helen Norman went looking for an idyllic stone house to buy in the rolling countryside of Maryland. Her brother, Drew Norman, owned an organic farm near White Hall and was hoping to expand his business with more acreage. So, when the property right next door to Drew, complete with a charming stone house, went on the market, the stars aligned. Over the years, the neighboring farms have hosted countless family dinners. "We've always brought everyone together to enjoy each other, eat good food, and talk about what's growing in the field," says Helen. "We like to say our dining room is wherever we choose to gather." For this dinner, it was Helen's old barn that, thanks to a Belgian block floor and chandelier, feels more suited for a dining table than a tractor. "It's very much a grab-your-chair-and-meet-us-in-the-barn type of dinner," says Helen. But while the gathering is casual, she doesn't hold back on her favorite part: setting the table. Feed sacks topped with an indigo linen runner and a mix of blue-and-white china establish the table's vintage, rustic feel and complement the rich russet hues of the barn, fall leaves, and piles of fresh apples.

4 WAYS TO GET HELEN'S LOOK

1. The Place Setting
Layer various patterns. Helen starts every setting with a matching dinner plate from her late mother's china collection, and then tops each with a different transferware salad plate.

2. The Centerpiece
Raid your china cabinet. Various pewter and silver serving pieces are scattered down the table, some with heaps of apples and others with small arrangements of foliage and hydrangeas.

3. The Place Cards
Look to nature. Helen simply gathers colorful leaves from her yard and writes each guest's name with a gold paint pen.

4. The Decor
Display the bounty. Pots of vintage hydrangeas, herbs, and cabbages pair perfectly with bushel basketfuls of wine-red apples.

THE MENU

Inspired by the bounty of squash, beets, and apples growing on and near Helen and Drew's neighboring farms, friend and collaborator Bill Scepansky, a local chef, created this fall menu. Bill's rustic cooking doesn't require expensive or trendy ingredients—just simple, patient technique, such as brining chicken and roasting its carcass to make a jus, to elevate and showcase the elemental flavors of a dish. "Everything has become so much about fast food," says Helen, who is working with Bill on an upcoming cookbook, *Plow to Chow*. "We try to make our meals much more into a celebration."

Apple-Onion Soup

MAKES 8 CUPS
HANDS-ON 1 HOUR, 10 MIN.
TOTAL 2 HOURS

Slowly caramelizing onions in butter over low heat coaxes out their sweetness and adds deeper flavor to this ever-so-sweet fall soup.

- 2 Tbsp. butter
- 2 medium-size sweet onions, thinly sliced
- 1 garlic clove
- 1 bay leaf
- 2 medium-size Gala or Honeycrisp apples, peeled and cut into 1/4-inch-thick slices
- 6 cups organic chicken broth
- 1/2 cup apple cider
- 1 medium-size russet potato, peeled and cut into 1/4-inch-thick slices
- 1/2 cup heavy cream
- 1 Tbsp. fresh lemon juice
- 1 1/2 to 2 tsp. kosher salt
- 1 tsp. freshly ground black pepper
  Cheese Puff Pastries

1. Melt butter in a large Dutch oven over low heat. Add onions and next 2 ingredients, and cook, stirring often, 30 to 35 minutes or until onions are caramel colored. (Adjust heat to prevent scorching.) Add apples, and cook, stirring often, 5 minutes. Add broth and next 2 ingredients. Increase heat to medium, and bring to a boil, stirring occasionally. Reduce heat to medium-low, and simmer, stirring occasionally, 20 to 25 minutes or until apples and potato are tender. Remove from heat, and let stand 15 minutes. Discard bay leaf.

2. Process mixture with a handheld blender until smooth. Add cream and lemon juice. Return to low heat; simmer, stirring often, 15 minutes. Add salt and pepper. Serve with Cheese Puff Pastries.

Note: We tested with Swanson Certified Organic Chicken Broth.

CHEESE PUFF PASTRIES

MAKES 14 TO 16
HANDS-ON 20 MIN.
TOTAL 1 HOUR, 5 MIN.

Preheat oven to 400°. Let 1 **frozen puff pastry sheet** (from 1 [17.3-oz.] package) stand at room temperature, covered with a cloth towel, 30 minutes or until partially thawed. Unfold pastry sheet on a lightly floured surface. Whisk together 1 large **egg** and 2 tsp. **milk.** Brush pastry sheet with egg mixture, and sprinkle with 1/2 cup freshly grated **Parmesan cheese,** 2 Tbsp. freshly grated **sharp Cheddar cheese,** and 1/2 tsp. thinly sliced **chives.** Cover pastry with plastic wrap, and gently press cheese and chives into pastry to adhere, using a rolling pin. Remove plastic wrap; sprinkle pastry with 1/4 tsp. **kosher salt** and 1/8 tsp. **paprika.** Cut with a 2 1/2-inch round cutter, and place 1 inch apart on a **parchment paper**-lined baking sheet. Bake at 400° for 10 to 15 minutes or until golden brown. Remove from oven to a wire rack, and cool 5 minutes.

Apple-Onion Soup topped with Cheese Puff Pastries

Molasses-Brined Roasted Chicken

MAKES 8 SERVINGS
HANDS-ON 45 MIN.
TOTAL 8 HOURS, 25 MIN., NOT INCLUDING JUS

The brined, roasted chicken is juicy, rich, and great on its own, but the jus, a concentrated homemade stock, is worth the effort. As for the birds, ask your butcher for two chickens, cut into four pieces each, reserving the carcasses to make the jus. Or buy leg quarters or airline breasts (first wing joint attached) and make the jus with the extra wings and backbones. (Pictured on page 15)

- 1/2 **cup kosher salt**
- 1/2 **cup dark molasses**
- 2 **cups ice cubes**
- 1 **sweet onion, thinly sliced**
- 2 **fresh thyme sprigs**
- 2 **garlic cloves, peeled and sliced**
- 1/2 **tsp. black peppercorns**
- 2 **(4- to 5-lb.) whole chickens, cut into 4 pieces each (boneless breasts with first wing joint intact, legs whole with bone in, carcasses reserved)***
- 1/2 **tsp. garlic salt**
- 2 **Tbsp. canola oil**
- 8 **garlic cloves, unpeeled**
- 2 **fresh thyme sprigs**
  Roasted Chicken Jus (optional)

1. Bring 4 cups water to a boil in a large Dutch oven over medium-high heat. Add kosher salt and molasses. Reduce heat to low, and simmer, stirring occasionally, 2 to 3 minutes or until salt and molasses dissolve. Transfer to a very large bowl; add ice and next 4 ingredients. Let stand, stirring occasionally, 30 minutes or until mixture cools to room temperature. Cover and chill 30 minutes to 1 hour or until cold.

2. Submerge chicken in cold brine. Cover and chill 6 to 8 hours.

3. Preheat oven to 400°. Remove chicken from brine; rinse and pat dry. Sprinkle with garlic salt.

4. Heat 1 Tbsp. oil in a 14-inch nonstick or cast-iron skillet over medium-high heat. Add 4 unpeeled garlic cloves, 1 thyme sprig, and half of chicken. Cook 5 minutes or until skin is browned and crisp. (The molasses in the brine will brown the skin quickly.) Turn chicken and garlic, and cook 5 minutes or until browned. Remove chicken, and place on a wire rack in a jelly-roll pan. Wipe skillet clean. Repeat with remaining oil, chicken, garlic, and thyme.

5. Bake chicken, skin side up, at 400° for 10 to 20 minutes or until a meat thermometer inserted into thickest portion registers 165°. (Breasts will cook faster than legs, so check for doneness after 10 minutes.) Cover with foil. Let stand 10 minutes before slicing. Serve with Roasted Chicken Jus, if desired.

*8 chicken leg quarters or 8 chicken breasts, airline cut, may be substituted.

Note: We tested with Diamond Crystal Kosher Salt.

ROASTED CHICKEN JUS

MAKES 4 1/2 CUPS
HANDS-ON 55 MIN.
TOTAL 3 HOURS

Reserved carcasses from Molasses-Brined Roasted Chicken*
1/2 sweet onion, thinly sliced
1 small carrot, sliced
1 celery rib, sliced
1 fresh thyme sprig
1 Tbsp. canola oil
1 cup dry white wine
1 tsp. cornstarch
1 Tbsp. minced fresh flat-leaf parsley
1 tsp. minced fresh chives

1. Preheat oven to 450°. Chop each carcass into 4 pieces; place in a lightly greased jelly-roll pan. Roast, turning occasionally, 35 to 45 minutes or until browned.

2. Cook onion and next 3 ingredients in hot oil in a Dutch oven over medium-high heat, stirring occasionally, 3 to 4 minutes or until tender. (Do not overcook.)

3. Add white wine to onion mixture, increase heat to high, and bring to a boil. Boil, stirring occasionally, 3 to 5 minutes or until wine is reduced by three-fourths. Add carcass pieces and water to cover by 2 inches. Return to a boil over high heat; reduce heat to low, and simmer, stirring occasionally, 1 1/2 hours.

4. Pour sauce through a fine wire-mesh strainer into a small saucepan, discarding solids. Let stand 10 minutes, and skim fat from sauce. Bring sauce to a boil over medium-high heat.

5. Whisk together cornstarch and 1 Tbsp. water. Whisk cornstarch mixture into sauce. Return to a boil over medium-high heat, stirring constantly. Reduce heat to low, and simmer 10 minutes or to desired consistency. Stir in parsley and chives; add salt and pepper to taste.

*2 to 3 lb. chicken backbones or wings may be substituted.

Root Vegetable Mash

Root Vegetable Mash

MAKES 8 TO 10 SERVINGS
HANDS-ON 20 MIN.
TOTAL 1 HOUR, 5 MIN.

Whipped, tender root vegetables and creamy roasted garlic elevate the typical mash. Any root will do. (Pictured on page 15)

1 garlic bulb
1 large rutabaga (about 1 lb.), peeled and cut into 1-inch cubes
1 lb. celery root, peeled and cut into 1-inch cubes
3 large russet potatoes (about 2 1/2 lb.), peeled and quartered
3/4 cup milk
1/4 cup unsalted butter
1 1/2 tsp. freshly ground black pepper
1 tsp. kosher salt
1 Tbsp. thinly sliced fresh chives (optional)

1. Preheat oven to 425°. Cut off pointed end of garlic bulb; place bulb on a piece of aluminum foil. Fold to seal. Bake 30 minutes; cool 10 minutes.

2. Meanwhile, bring rutabaga, celery root, and salted water to cover to a boil in a Dutch oven, and boil 15 minutes or until tender. Drain. Bring potatoes and salted water to cover to a boil in a 4-qt. saucepan, and boil 15 minutes or until tender. Drain. Combine rutabaga mixture and potatoes in Dutch oven.

3. Cook milk in a small saucepan over low heat 3 to 5 minutes or until thoroughly heated.

4. Add butter, next 2 ingredients, and hot milk to rutabaga mixture. Squeeze pulp from 2 roasted garlic cloves into mixture; reserve remaining garlic for another use. Mash vegetable mixture with a potato masher until light and fluffy. (Use a food processor for a silkier texture.) Add chives, if desired. Serve immediately.

Fall Salad with Beets and Apples

MAKES 6 TO 8 SERVINGS
HANDS-ON 35 MIN.
TOTAL 5 HOURS

Perfectly balanced with different flavors, textures, and colors, this salad is a colorful addition to any fall spread.

1 lb. red or yellow beets, peeled and thinly sliced into half moons
1/2 cup white balsamic vinegar
1/2 cup white wine vinegar
5 Tbsp. honey
2 tsp. kosher salt
1/2 medium-size sweet onion, cut into thin strips
1/2 cup extra virgin olive oil
2 Tbsp. white wine vinegar
1 tsp. spicy brown mustard
6 thick applewood-smoked bacon slices, cooked and crumbled
1 Gala apple (about 8 oz.), thinly sliced
3 cups firmly packed baby arugula
3 cups loosely packed frisée, torn
1/2 cup loosely packed fresh flat-leaf parsley leaves
1/4 cup toasted chopped walnuts

1. Microwave beets and water to cover in a microwave-safe bowl at HIGH 8 to 10 minutes or until crisp-tender. Let stand 30 minutes. Drain and rinse beets.

2. Stir together white balsamic vinegar, next 3 ingredients, and 2 Tbsp. water; pour into a large zip-top plastic freezer bag. Add beets and onion. Seal and chill 4 hours.

3. Drain beets and onion, reserving 1/3 cup pickling liquid. Discard remaining liquid. Whisk together olive oil, next 2 ingredients, and reserved 1/3 cup pickling liquid until smooth. Add salt and pepper to taste. Toss together bacon, next 5 ingredients, and desired amount of dressing. Serve with beets, onions, and remaining dressing.

Sautéed Mushrooms

MAKES 8 SERVINGS.
HANDS-ON 35 MIN.
TOTAL 35 MIN.

Any types of mushrooms work well here. Sear them in batches, without crowding, in a hot skillet so that they will take on color without steaming. (Pictured on page 15)

  1 (8-oz.) package stemmed and sliced fresh shiitake mushrooms
  4 1/2 Tbsp. olive oil
  2 large portobello mushrooms (about 8 oz.), stemmed, cleaned, and chopped
  1 (8-oz.) package stemmed and sliced oyster mushrooms*
  2 Tbsp. butter
  3 Tbsp. minced shallots
  2 garlic cloves, chopped
  1/2 tsp. kosher salt
  1/2 tsp. freshly ground black pepper
  3 tsp. sliced fresh chives

1. Cook shiitake mushrooms in a single layer in 1 1/2 Tbsp. hot oil in a 10- to 12-inch nonstick skillet over high heat, stirring often, 4 to 6 minutes or until browned. Transfer to a medium bowl. Repeat procedure two more times with portobello mushrooms, oyster mushrooms, and remaining oil.

2. Melt butter in skillet over medium-high heat; add shallot, and sauté 2 to 3 minutes or until tender. Stir in garlic; cook 1 minute. Add mushrooms, salt, and pepper; toss gently to coat. Remove from heat; stir in chives. Serve warm.

*Crimini or button mushrooms may be substituted.

Candied Roasted Squash

MAKES 8 TO 12 SERVINGS
HANDS-ON 20 MIN.
TOTAL 45 MIN.

A recipe with only three ingredients calls for smart technique and a little bit of finesse. Score the squash flesh to create more surface area for caramelizing.

Preheat oven to 450°. Cut 1 small **kabocha** or **butternut squash** (about 3 to 4 lb.), halved and seeded, into 2-inch wedges; cut each wedge in half crosswise. (If using butternut, cut into smaller pieces.) Score a crisscross pattern 1/4 inch deep into squash flesh, using a sharp knife. Stir together 1/2 cup melted **butter** and 3 Tbsp. **light brown sugar** until sugar dissolves. Brush one-third of butter mixture over all sides of squash. Place squash, flesh sides down, in a lightly greased aluminum foil-lined 15- x 10-inch jelly-roll pan. Bake at 450° for 10 minutes. Turn squash over; spread with half of remaining butter mixture. Bake 12 to 14 minutes or until tender. Remove from oven; increase oven temperature to broil. Brush squash with remaining butter mixture. Broil 2 to 3 minutes or until well caramelized. Sprinkle with **salt** and **pepper** to taste. Serve warm.

Apple Bread Pudding

MAKES 8 TO 10 SERVINGS
HANDS-ON 25 MIN.
TOTAL 2 HOURS, 30 MIN., INCLUDING ANGLAISE AND APPLES

Serve this family-style from a baking dish, or divide with a 3-inch round cutter for an elegant presentation. (Pictured on page 190)

- 2 Tbsp. butter
- 3 large apples, such as Honeycrisp (about 1 1/2 lb.), peeled and cut into 1/4- to 1/2-inch cubes
- 3 cups heavy cream
- 4 large eggs
- 1 large egg yolk
- 1/4 cup granulated sugar
- 1 tsp. ground cinnamon
- 1 (16-oz.) cinnamon-raisin bread loaf, cut into 3/4-inch cubes
- 4 Tbsp. turbinado sugar
  Apple Brandy Crème Anglaise
  Sautéed Apples

1. Preheat oven to 375°. Melt butter in a large nonstick skillet over medium-high heat; add apples, and cook, stirring occasionally, 8 to 10 minutes or until softened and lightly browned.

2. Whisk together cream and next 4 ingredients in a large bowl until smooth. Stir in bread cubes; let mixture stand 5 minutes. Stir in cooked apples.

3. Sprinkle 2 Tbsp. turbinado sugar into a buttered 13- x 9-inch baking dish. Add bread-and-apple mixture to dish, and spread in an even layer. Sprinkle with remaining 2 Tbsp. turbinado sugar.

4. Bake at 375° for 40 to 45 minutes or until light golden and center is set. (Bread pudding will puff to top of dish and pull away slightly from sides as it bakes.) Cool 10 minutes. Serve warm with Apple Brandy Crème Anglaise and Sautéed Apples.

Note: We tested with Panera Bread Cinnamon Raisin Bread. To make ahead, cover and chill baked and cooled bread pudding overnight. Let stand 20 minutes; reheat in a 350° oven 20 minutes.

APPLE BRANDY CRÈME ANGLAISE

MAKES ABOUT 1 1/3 CUPS
HANDS-ON 50 MIN.
TOTAL 1 HOUR, 50 MIN.

Whisk together 1 cup **heavy cream,** 2 large **egg yolks,** and 1/4 cup **sugar** in a 2-qt. saucepan, and cook over medium heat, whisking constantly (so mixture doesn't scorch or scramble), 8 to 10 minutes or until mixture thinly coats back of a wooden spoon. Pour through a fine wire-mesh strainer into a bowl. Stir in 2 Tbsp. **apple brandy** or **bourbon.** Add 1 **cinnamon stick,** if desired. Fill a large bowl with ice. Place bowl containing cream mixture in ice, and let stand, stirring constantly, 30 minutes. Remove cinnamon stick. Cover and chill 1 hour to 3 days.

SAUTÉED APPLES

MAKES ABOUT 2 CUPS
HANDS-ON 15 MIN.
TOTAL 15 MIN.

Melt 2 Tbsp. **butter** in a large skillet over medium heat; add 2 large **Granny Smith apples,** peeled and diced, and sauté 2 minutes. Stir in 3 Tbsp. **sugar** and 2 tsp. **fresh lemon juice.** Cook, stirring often, 6 to 8 minutes or until golden.

Ways to Bake with Candy

▶ A taste of who and what online got the most raves in the *Southern Living* Test Kitchen.

From the Kitchen of
MEGAN PORTA

PIPANDEBBY.COM

"Be careful not to overbake these cookies. Ten minutes is the sweet spot for most ovens."

CHOCOLATE CRINKLE CANDY SURPRISE COOKIES

(Pictured on page 191) Beat 1 1/2 cups granulated **sugar**; 1/2 cup plus 2 Tbsp. **butter,** softened; 2 large **eggs;** and 2 tsp. **vanilla extract** at medium speed with an electric mixer until mixture is blended and smooth. Stir together 2 cups **all-purpose flour,** 1 cup **unsweetened cocoa,** 2 tsp. **baking powder,** and 1 tsp. **table salt.** Gradually add to butter mixture, beating just until blended. Shape dough into a ball, and wrap in plastic wrap. Chill 2 to 4 hours. Preheat oven to 350°. Remove dough from plastic wrap; shape dough into 30 (1-inch) balls (about 1 Tbsp. each), and place 1 inch apart on **parchment paper**-lined baking sheets. Flatten each ball into a 2-inch disk. Place 1 **chocolate-covered caramel candy** (such as Rolo) into center of each disk, and wrap dough around candy to form a ball. Bake 10 minutes or until slightly flattened. Cool on baking sheets 8 minutes. Sprinkle cookies with powdered sugar. Serve cookies immediately. **MAKES** 30 cookies

From the Kitchen of
JENNIFER McHENRY

BAKEORBREAK.COM

"Growing up in Mississippi, baking was a way of life. If someone you love is a fan of chocolate and caramel, these are a quick, easy way to create a little happiness."

CARAMEL-CHOCOLATE CHIP COOKIE BARS

Preheat oven to 350°. Whisk together 1 1/2 cups **all-purpose flour,** 1/2 tsp. **baking powder,** and 1/2 tsp. **table salt.** Beat 1 1/2 cups firmly packed **light brown sugar** and 3/4 cup **butter,** softened, at medium speed with an electric mixer until fluffy. Add 2 **large eggs,** 1 at a time, beating until blended after each addition. Add 1 1/2 tsp. **vanilla**

extract, beating until blended. Gradually add flour mixture, beating at low speed just until blended. Stir in 1/2 cup **milk chocolate morsels** just until combined. Spread batter in a lightly greased 8-inch square pan. Microwave 1/2 cup **caramel bits** (or 12 caramels) and 2 Tbsp. **heavy cream** in a microwave-safe bowl at MEDIUM (50% power) 2 minutes or until melted, stirring at 30-second intervals. Pour caramel mixture over batter, and gently swirl with a knife. Bake 35 to 40 minutes or until a wooden pick inserted in center comes out clean. (Center will rise and fall while baking.) Cool completely in pan on a wire rack (about 1 hour) before cutting. **MAKES** 16 squares

Note: We tested with Kraft Premium Caramel Bits.

From the Kitchen of
SHELLY JARONSKY

COOKIESANDCUPS.COM

"When I spent summers in Florida with my grandma, we would bake almost every day. I love this recipe because it's special enough to serve to guests, but easy enough to make often."

TRIPLE FUDGE BROWNIES

Bake 1 (18.75-oz.) package **brownie mix** in a 9-inch square pan according to package directions. Cool completely. Chop 1 (10-oz.) bag **miniature chocolate-covered whipped nougat bars.** Sprinkle half of chopped bars over cooled brownies. Pour **water** to a depth of 1 inch into bottom of a double boiler over medium heat; bring to a boil. Reduce heat to low, and simmer; place 2 cups **semisweet chocolate morsels** in top of a double boiler over simmering water. Pour 1 (14-oz.) can **sweetened condensed milk** over morsels, and cook, stirring occasionally, 5 to 6 minutes or until chocolate is melted. Spread melted chocolate mixture over brownies. Press remaining chopped candy bars into chocolate. Chill 30 minutes. Cut into bars. **MAKES** 16 squares

Note: We tested with Ghirardelli Chocolate Supreme Brownie Mix and 3 Musketeers candy bars.

November

Beyond the Bird

▶ Weeknights just got easier. Serve supper on the double with hearty, seasonal entrées paired with fresh sides.

Collard Green Carbonara

MAKES 6 TO 8 SERVINGS
HANDS-ON 35 MIN.
TOTAL 35 MIN.

Pasta carbonara is the ultimate quick dinner. It's rich, satisfying, and works during the week but is worthy of weekend company.

- 12 oz. uncooked spaghetti
- 6 thick hickory-smoked bacon slices, chopped
- 1 medium-size red onion, halved and sliced
- 2 garlic cloves, minced
- 4 cups firmly packed chopped fresh collards
- 3 large pasteurized eggs, lightly beaten
- 1 large pasteurized egg yolk, lightly beaten
- 1 tsp. kosher salt
- 1 tsp. ground black pepper
- ½ tsp. dried crushed red pepper
- 3 cups (12 oz.) freshly shredded Parmigiano-Reggiano cheese

1. Cook pasta according to package directions.

2. Meanwhile, cook bacon in a large skillet over medium-high heat 5 to 6 minutes or until crisp; drain on paper towels, reserving drippings in skillet.

3. Sauté onion in hot drippings 4 to 5 minutes or until golden brown and tender. Add garlic; sauté 1 minute. Add collards; sauté 5 minutes. Remove from heat. Add bacon.

4. Whisk together eggs, egg yolk, next 3 ingredients, and 2½ cups cheese in a large bowl. Drain pasta, reserving ½ cup pasta water, and immediately pour hot pasta into egg mixture; toss to coat. (The heat from the pasta will partially cook the eggs.) Add collard mixture; toss to combine. Stir in enough pasta water to reach desired consistency. Sprinkle with remaining ½ cup cheese.

save time! Tender collards are minutes away! Remove the tough center stalks and discard. Stack the leaves and roll them up, like a cigar. Cut crosswise into ⅛-inch-thick strips. The strips will cook in a jiffy.

FRESH CITRUS SALAD Peel 2 small red **grapefruits** and 2 large **navel oranges**; cut into rounds, and arrange on a serving platter. Whisk together ¼ cup **sweet orange marmalade**, 2 Tbsp. **raspberry vinegar**, and 2 tsp. grated **fresh ginger**. Toss marmalade mixture with ½ cup each diced **avocado** and diced **strawberries**; spoon over citrus slices. **MAKES** 6 to 8 servings

Spice-Rubbed Pork With Roasted Butternut Salad

MAKES 6 TO 8 SERVINGS
HANDS-ON 45 MIN.
TOTAL 55 MIN.

- 2 (³/₄-lb.) pork tenderloins
- 3 Tbsp. olive oil, divided
- 1½ Tbsp. pork dry rub (such as McCormick Grill Mates Pork Rub)
- 3 cups coarsely chopped butternut squash
- 6 cups arugula
- 1 small ripe Bartlett pear, thinly sliced
- ½ (4-oz.) package goat cheese, crumbled
- ¼ cup chopped dried cherries
  Toasted Pecan Vinaigrette

1. Preheat grill to 350° to 400° (medium-high) heat. Remove silver skin from tenderloins, leaving a thin layer of fat. Brush with 1 Tbsp. oil, and rub with dry rub.

2. Preheat oven to 400°. Toss squash with remaining 2 Tbsp. oil; place in a single layer in a lightly greased foil-lined 15- x 10-inch jelly-roll pan. Bake 20 minutes or until squash is just tender and begins to brown, stirring once halfway through. Remove from oven, and cool 10 minutes.

3. Meanwhile, grill pork, covered with grill lid, 10 minutes on each side or until a meat thermometer inserted into thickest portion registers 145°. Remove from grill, and let stand 10 minutes. Cut pork diagonally into thin slices.

4. Toss together squash, arugula, and next 3 ingredients on a serving platter; add salt and black pepper to taste. Serve squash salad with Toasted Pecan Vinaigrette and sliced pork.

TOASTED PECAN VINAIGRETTE

Whisk together ¼ cup **balsamic vinegar**, 2 Tbsp. **light brown sugar**, 2 Tbsp. minced **shallots**, 1 Tbsp. **Dijon mustard**, ½ tsp. **table salt**, and ½ tsp. **freshly ground black pepper** until blended. Add ½ cup **canola oil** in a slow, steady stream, whisking until smooth. Whisk in ½ cup finely chopped toasted **pecans**. **MAKES** 1½ cups

Black Bean Cakes With Avocado-Corn Salsa

MAKES 6 SERVINGS
HANDS-ON 15 MIN.
TOTAL 40 MIN.

- ³/₄ cup diced red onion
- 4 Tbsp. canola oil, divided
- 2 garlic cloves, pressed
  Avocado-Corn Salsa
- 1 Tbsp. taco seasoning mix
- 2 (15-oz.) cans black beans, drained and rinsed
- ½ cup panko (Japanese breadcrumbs)
- 1 large egg, lightly beaten
- ⅓ cup chopped fresh cilantro
- 1½ cups (6 oz.) shredded pepper Jack cheese, divided
- 6 tostada shells
- ½ cup (2 oz.) shredded Cheddar cheese

1. Sauté onion in 1 Tbsp. hot oil in a small skillet over medium-high heat 4 minutes or until tender. Stir in garlic. Remove from heat.

2. Prepare Avocado-Corn Salsa; chill until ready to serve.

3. Mash together taco seasoning and 2 cups black beans in a large bowl with a fork. Stir in panko, next 2 ingredients, onion mixture, 1 cup pepper Jack cheese, and remaining black beans until well blended. Shape mixture into 6 (½-inch-thick) patties.

4. Cook patties in remaining 3 Tbsp. hot oil in a large nonstick skillet over medium heat 4 to 5 minutes on each side or until golden brown.

5. Preheat oven to 400°. Place tostadas on a 15- x 10-inch jelly-roll pan; top with Cheddar and remaining pepper Jack cheese. Bake until cheese melts. Top with black bean cakes and salsa.

AVOCADO-CORN SALSA

Whisk together 1 Tbsp. **lime zest,** ¼ cup **fresh lime juice**, 2 Tbsp. **canola oil**; 1 tsp. **Dijon mustard**, and ¼ tsp. **dried crushed red pepper** in a large bowl. Stir in 2 cups **fresh corn kernels**; 1 cup halved **grape tomatoes**; 1 small **avocado**, diced; ⅓ cup diced **red onion**; and 2 Tbsp. each chopped **fresh basil** and **cilantro**. Add **table salt** and **black pepper**. **MAKES** 6 servings

Spice-Rubbed Pork With Roasted Butternut Salad

Coconut Chicken with Pineapple Fried Rice

MAKES 4 SERVINGS
HANDS-ON 15 MIN.
TOTAL 50 MIN.

- 4 (6-oz.) skinned and boned chicken breasts
- 1/4 cup cornstarch
- 1 Tbsp. Caribbean jerk seasoning
- 2 large egg whites
- 1 cup sweetened flaked coconut
- 1 cup panko (Japanese breadcrumbs)
- 3 Tbsp. canola oil
  Pineapple Fried Rice

1. Preheat oven to 325°. Place each chicken breast between 2 sheets of plastic wrap; flatten to 1/2-inch thickness, using a rolling pin or flat side of a meat mallet.

2. Stir together cornstarch and jerk seasoning in a shallow dish. Whisk egg whites just until foamy in another shallow dish. Stir together coconut and breadcrumbs in a third shallow dish.

3. Dredge chicken breasts, 1 at a time, in cornstarch mixture; dip in egg whites, and dredge in coconut, pressing gently to adhere.

4. Cook chicken in hot oil in a large non-stick ovenproof skillet over medium heat 1 to 2 minutes on each side or until golden. Transfer skillet to oven, and bake at 325° for 15 to 20 minutes or until chicken is done. Sprinkle with table salt and black pepper to taste. Serve with fried rice.

PINEAPPLE FRIED RICE Melt 3 Tbsp. **butter** in a large nonstick skillet over medium-high heat; add 1 cup diced **fresh pineapple,** 3/4 cup diced **sweet onion,** and 1 tsp. **Asian chili-garlic sauce,** and sauté 6 to 8 minutes or until onions are lightly caramelized. Add 3 cups cold cooked **basmati rice,** 1/2 cup diced **red bell pepper,** 3 Tbsp. chopped **fresh cilantro,** and 2 tsp. **lime zest;** stir-fry 5 minutes or until thoroughly heated. Remove from heat, and stir in 1/2 cup loosely packed **cilantro leaves.** Add **table salt** to taste. **MAKES** 4 servings

save money

Meat marked "family pack" is the best deal per pound. You'll buy at least 3 pounds, so cook what you need and freeze what's left using our guidelines (page 283).

mix 'n' match

Built for flexibility, these meals pair simple, hearty entrées with fresh, light side dishes. You can mix 'n' match or replace any component with store-bought items like rotisserie chicken or your favorite deli side.

Bulgogi Flank Steak

MAKES 6 SERVINGS
HANDS-ON 35 MIN.
TOTAL 12 HOURS, 45 MIN.

- 1/2 cup soy sauce
- 1/4 cup firmly packed light brown sugar
- 1/4 cup chopped green onions
- 1/4 cup dark sesame oil
- 2 Tbsp. dry sherry
- 2 Tbsp. minced fresh garlic
- 1 Tbsp. grated fresh ginger
- 1 tsp. dried crushed red pepper
- 1 (2-lb.) flank steak

1. Combine first 8 ingredients in a 2-gal. zip-top plastic freezer bag; add steak. Seal bag, and chill 12 hours. Remove steak from marinade, discarding marinade.

2. Preheat grill to 400° to 450° (high) heat. Grill steak, covered with grill lid, 9 minutes on each side or to desired degree of doneness. Let stand 10 minutes. Cut diagonally across the grain into thin slices. Sprinkle with table salt and black pepper to taste.

THAI-STYLE CABBAGE Whisk together 2 Tbsp. **light brown sugar**, 2 tsp. **lime zest**, 2 Tbsp. **fresh lime juice**, 1 1/2 Tbsp. **fish sauce**, and 1 tsp. **Asian chili-garlic sauce** in a large bowl. Stir in 1/2 cup coarsely chopped **roasted peanuts** and 1/4 cup each sliced **green onions** and chopped **fresh cilantro**. Toss peanut sauce with 4 cups firmly packed sliced **napa cabbage** and 1 to 2 thinly sliced **radishes**. Serve immediately. **MAKES** 6 servings

THAI-STYLE NOODLES Prepare Thai-Style Cabbage as directed, omitting radishes and substituting 1 (8-oz.) package wide **lo mein noodles**, prepared according to package directions, for napa cabbage.

Note: We tested with Ka·Me Wide Lo Mein Noodles.

Three-Ingredient Slow-Cooker Barbecue Pork

MAKES 6 TO 8 SERVINGS
HANDS-ON 10 MIN.
TOTAL 8 HOURS, 10 MIN.

Just three ingredients and 10 minutes of prep work make this a quick-fix supper. Start the slow cooker first thing in the morning and dinner will be ready by 5 p.m. Serve over rice, on hamburger buns, or in loaded baked potatoes, with a side of Orange-Walnut Slaw.

- 1 (3- to 4-lb.) boneless pork shoulder roast (Boston butt), trimmed
- 1 (18-oz.) bottle barbecue sauce (such as Cattlemen's Kansas City Classic Barbecue Sauce)
- 1 (12-oz.) can cola soft drink

Place pork in a lightly greased 6-qt. slow cooker; pour barbecue sauce and cola over pork. Cover and cook on LOW 8 to 10 hours or until meat shreds easily with a fork. Transfer pork to a cutting board; shred with 2 forks, removing any large pieces of fat. Skim fat from sauce, and stir pork into sauce.

ORANGE-WALNUT SLAW Whisk together 1 tsp. **orange zest**, 1/4 cup **orange juice**, 3 Tbsp. **sherry vinegar**, 1 Tbsp. minced **shallot**, 1 Tbsp. **honey**, and 1 tsp. **Dijon mustard** in a medium bowl. Stir in 3/4 cup coarsely chopped **roasted walnuts**. Season with **table salt** and **freshly ground black pepper** to taste. Toss walnut dressing with 1 (16-oz.) package **coleslaw mix** and 1 firm **Bartlett pear**, chopped. **MAKES** 6 to 8 servings

Speedy Sandwich Sauces

Turn your ho-hum leftover turkey sandwich into a gourmet lunch with our Food Editors' go-to sandwich condiments. The best part? There's no shopping needed. Each sauce can be made with ingredients found in your refrigerator. To build a spectacular sandwich, slather any of the sauces below on toasted slices of your favorite bread. Then pile on the leftover turkey and top with thinly sliced red onion, crisp lettuce leaves, and a juicy slice of tomato.

*From Deputy Food Director **Whitney Wright**:*

THE CAESAR SPECIAL Stir together 1 cup **mayonnaise**, 3 Tbsp. grated **Parmesan cheese**, 1/2 tsp. **lemon zest**, 2 Tbsp. **fresh lemon juice**, 1/2 tsp. **freshly ground black pepper**, and 1/4 tsp. **table salt** in a small bowl. Refrigerate in an airtight container up to 5 days. **MAKES** 1 cup

*From Test Kitchen Director **Robby Melvin**:*

SOUR CREAM-AND-PICKLED ONION SAUCE Stir together 3/4 cup **mayonnaise**, 1/2 cup chopped **green onions**, 1/3 cup minced **pickled cocktail onions**, 1/4 cup **sour cream**, and 1 Tbsp. **pickled onion juice from jar** in a small bowl. Add **table salt** and **freshly ground black pepper** to taste. Refrigerate sauce in an airtight container up to 5 days. **MAKES** 1 cup

*From Executive Editor **Hunter Lewis**:*

THREE-MILE THOUSAND ISLAND SAUCE Stir together 1 cup **mayonnaise**, 1/4 cup **ketchup**, 1/4 cup minced **pickled jalapeño peppers***, 2 Tbsp. **prepared horseradish**, and 2 to 4 tsp. **Asian hot chili sauce** (such as Sriracha) in a small bowl. Add **table salt** to taste. Refrigerate in an airtight container up to 5 days. **MAKES** 1 cup

*Sweet pickle relish may be substituted.

Southern Living

CORDIALLY INVITES YOU TO

Our Progressive

THANKSGIVING
DINNER

CELEBRATE THE PIES (AND TURKEY, GREEN
BEANS, AND CASSEROLES) THAT BIND WITH
A MISSISSIPPI HOSTESS, ALABAMA CHEESEMAKER,
GEORGIA DESIGNER, TWO TEXAS CHEFS,
AND OUR TEST KITCHEN PROS

20 13

EASY & ELEGANT
HOLIDAY
APPETIZERS
WITH WHITNEY MILLER

MISSISSIPPI'S NEWEST FACE IN FOOD SHARES HER TALENT FOR MINGLING CHERISHED **FAMILY RECIPES** WITH **MODERN HOSPITALITY**

Cornmeal Tarts with Ricotta Pimiento Cheese

MAKES 5 DOZEN
HANDS-ON 30 MIN.
TOTAL 2 HOURS, 35 MIN.

Feel free to make and freeze the muffins ahead. Then thaw, fill, and bake before serving.

Preheat oven to 400°. Stir together 2 cups **self-rising white cornmeal mix**; 2 cups **buttermilk**; 1/2 cup **all-purpose flour**; 2 **large eggs,** lightly beaten; 1/4 cup **butter,** melted; and 2 Tbsp. **sugar** just until moistened. Spoon batter into 2 lightly greased miniature muffin pans, filling two-thirds full. Bake, in batches, 15 minutes or until golden brown. Cool 5 minutes. Scoop about 1 tsp. from top of each muffin; discard or reserve for another use. Spoon about 1 tsp. **Ricotta Pimiento Cheese** into each muffin; place on a baking sheet. Bake at 400° for 3 to 4 minutes or until cheese melts.

RICOTTA PIMIENTO CHEESE Stir together 1 cup (4 oz.) shredded **pepper Jack cheese,** 3/4 cup (3 oz.) shredded **sharp Cheddar cheese,** 1/2 cup **whole-milk ricotta cheese,** 2 Tbsp. **mayonnaise,** 1 Tbsp. drained **diced pimiento,** 1/4 tsp. **ground black pepper,** 1/8 tsp. **table salt,** and 1/8 tsp. **ground red pepper** in a small bowl. Store in refrigerator up to 3 days. **MAKES** about 1 1/2 cups

Zucchini-and-Squash Pickles

MAKES 1 QT.
HANDS-ON 1 HOUR
TOTAL 2 HOURS, 40 MIN.

- 2 medium zucchini (about 12 oz.)
- 2 medium-size yellow squash (about 12 oz.)
- 1 red onion, halved and cut into 1/8-inch-thick slices
  Parchment paper
- 2 1/2 Tbsp. kosher salt
- 1/2 cup apple cider vinegar
- 1/2 cup rice vinegar
- 3/4 cup sugar
- 1 tsp. celery seeds
- 1 tsp. mustard seeds
- 1/4 tsp. dry mustard

1. Cut zucchini and yellow squash lengthwise into 1/8-inch-thick slices, using a mandoline or sharp knife. Spread zucchini, yellow squash, and onion in a single layer on 2 parchment paper-lined baking sheets. Sprinkle with salt. Let stand 1 hour. Transfer to a colander, rinse, and drain. Place in a widemouthed 1-qt. jar, filling to 1/2 inch from top.

2. Bring vinegars to a boil in a medium saucepan over medium heat. Add sugar; cook, stirring constantly, 3 to 5 minutes or until dissolved. Stir in next 3 ingredients. Bring to a boil, immediately remove from heat, and pour over vegetables. Cool 1 hour. Cover and chill 3 days before serving. Refrigerate up to 2 months.

My family's Thanksgiving fare, once a traditional dinner prepared single-handedly by my great-grandmother Mary Strahan, has turned into a collaborative feast that begins the moment everyone arrives home. My contribution is always the relish tray, a platter of finger foods, spreads, fresh rolls, and pickles that stave off anxious appetites and keep everyone out of the kitchen while my mother, grandmother, and aunts finish up dinner.

For me, a great relish tray includes a variety of flavors and textures and has something for everyone, from sweet spreads and tart pickles to savory one-bite appetizers. And, more important, it's the perfect place to showcase beloved family recipes, like my grandmother's lemony pear preserves, alongside new traditions like my turnip green pesto. This year, I'm incorporating a spin on the deviled egg that is a nod to my parents' favorite sandwich, the New Orleans muffuletta, and also making a warm pimiento cheese mini-muffin. And because, as my Nanny Ida says, nothing tastes as wonderful as homemade bread, I'll bake both my rosemary focaccia and Mrs. Monty's famous yeast rolls. (The recipe has been in our family for more than 100 years.) Springy rolls are just the thing for sandwiching ham and stacking with a colorful array of condiments.

However you kick off your Thanksgiving tradition, whether it's with a big relish tray or just a single appetizer, the feast before the feast should be just as memorable as the main event. After all, it's the first taste that reminds everyone they are home and together again.

Muffuletta Deviled Eggs

(Pictured on page 173) Place 12 **large eggs** in a single layer in a stainless steel saucepan. (Do not use nonstick.) Add **water** to depth of 3 inches. Bring to a rolling boil. Cover, remove from heat, and let stand 15 minutes. Tap each egg on the counter until cracks form all over the shell. Peel under cold running water. Slice eggs in half lengthwise; remove yolks. Mash yolks with a fork in a bowl. Stir in 1/4 cup **mayonnaise** until smooth. Fold in 6 Tbsp. **Olive Salad.** Spoon mixture into egg white halves. Heat a small skillet over low heat 1 to 2 minutes or until hot. Add 3 oz. very thinly sliced **salami,** and cook, stirring often, 2 to 3 minutes or until lightly browned and crisp.

Remove from skillet, and drain on paper towels. Top eggs with salami and chopped chives. Serve immediately, or cover and chill up to 24 hours.

OLIVE SALAD Pulse 1 (16-oz.) jar **mixed pickled vegetables,** undrained; 1 (7-oz.) jar **pimiento-stuffed Spanish olives,** drained; 1 (6-oz.) jar **pitted kalamata olives,** drained; 2 Tbsp. **extra virgin olive oil;** 1/2 tsp. drained **capers;** 1/2 tsp. **dried oregano;** 1/2 tsp. **black pepper;** 1 minced **garlic clove;** 1/8 tsp. **paprika;** and 1/8 tsp. **ground red pepper** in a food processor 5 times or until coarsely chopped. Use immediately, or refrigerate up to 1 week. **MAKES** 4 cups

Pear Preserves

Cook 8 **Bartlett pears,** peeled and cut into 1/4-inch-thick slices; 3 cups **sugar;** and 2 thinly sliced **lemons** in a heavy 3-qt. saucepan over medium heat, stirring often, 5 to 7 minutes or until sugar dissolves. Increase heat to medium-high; cook, stirring occasionally, 30 minutes or until mixture is thick and golden and pears are tender. Cool 10 minutes. Spoon into 3 (1-pt.) widemouthed jars. Store in refrigerator up to 3 weeks. **MAKES** 3 pt.

Rosemary Focaccia Bread

MAKES 10 TO 12 SERVINGS
HANDS-ON 30 MIN.
TOTAL 3 HOURS

- 1 (1/4-oz.) envelope active dry yeast
- 1 2/3 cups lukewarm water (100° to 110°)
- 4 1/2 cups bread flour
- 1/4 cup extra virgin olive oil
- 1 Tbsp. table salt
- 2 Tbsp. fresh rosemary leaves, divided
- 3 Tbsp. extra virgin olive oil
- 1 tsp. kosher salt

1. Stir together yeast and warm water in bowl of a heavy-duty electric stand mixer; let stand 5 minutes.

2. Add bread flour, 1/4 cup oil, and 1 Tbsp. table salt to yeast mixture. Beat on low speed, using paddle attachment, 10 seconds or until blended. Increase speed to medium. Beat 45 seconds or until dough is smooth. Add 1 Tbsp. rosemary. Replace paddle attachment with dough hook; increase speed to medium-high, and beat 4 minutes. (Dough will be sticky.)

3. Turn dough onto a floured surface, and knead until smooth and elastic (about 1 minute). Place in a greased bowl, turning to coat. Cover dough with plastic wrap, and let rise in a warm place (80° to 85°), free from drafts, 1 hour or until doubled in bulk.

4. Press dough into a well greased 15- x 10-inch jelly-roll pan, pressing to about 1/4-inch thickness. Cover with a kitchen towel, and let rise in a warm place 1 hour.

5. Preheat oven to 475°. Press handle of a wooden spoon into dough to make indentations at 1-inch intervals; drizzle with 3 Tbsp. oil. Sprinkle with kosher salt and remaining 1 Tbsp. rosemary. Bake 14 to 16 minutes or until top is light brown. Remove from pan to a wire rack, and cool 10 minutes.

Muffuletta Deviled Eggs

Mrs. Monty's Rolls

Turnip Green Pesto

Rosemary Focaccia Bread

Pickled Beets

MAKES 4 PT.
HANDS-ON 50 MIN.
TOTAL 1 HOUR, 45 MIN., PLUS 2 DAYS FOR CHILLING

Remove skins from roasted beets while they're still warm by gently wiping with a paper towel.

4 1/2 lb. medium-size fresh beets
1/2 medium-size red onion, thinly sliced
1 tsp. extra virgin olive oil
1 1/3 cups sugar
1 1/3 cups apple cider vinegar
2 Tbsp. kosher salt
8 whole cloves
4 (3-inch) cinnamon sticks

1. Preheat oven to 400°. Remove tops and ends of beets, and wash. Place beets and onion on a foil-lined baking sheet. Drizzle with oil, and toss to coat. Cover tightly with foil. Bake 40 to 50 minutes or until tender.

2. Transfer beets, onion, and any liquid to a bowl; cool 15 minutes. Peel beets; cut into 1/4-inch-thick slices. Cut slices into 1/4-inch-wide sticks. Layer beets and onion in 4 (1-pt.) widemouthed jars, filling to 1/2 inch from top.

3. Bring sugar, next 2 ingredients, and 1 1/3 cups water to a boil in a medium saucepan, stirring often. Boil 5 minutes or until sugar dissolves. Pour into jars, just covering beet mixture. Discard any remaining vinegar mixture. Add 2 cloves and 1 cinnamon stick to each jar. Cover with lids; screw on bands. Chill 2 days before serving. Store up to 1 month.

Turnip Green Pesto

MAKES ABOUT 2 CUPS
HANDS-ON 15 MIN.
TOTAL 20 MIN.

"My younger cousins enjoy this recipe as much as the adults," Whitney says. "I'm not sure they know they're eating their greens!"

1 (1-lb.) package fresh turnip greens, chopped
2 1/2 Tbsp. chopped toasted walnuts
1 garlic clove
3/4 tsp. kosher salt
1/4 tsp. black pepper
6 Tbsp. extra virgin olive oil
3 Tbsp. fresh lemon juice
1 Tbsp. honey
2 Tbsp. freshly grated Parmesan cheese

1. Bring 4 qt. water to a boil in an 8-qt. stockpot. Add greens; cook 30 seconds. Remove greens, and pat dry with paper towels.

2. Process greens, walnuts, and next 3 ingredients in a food processor 2 to 3 minutes or until a paste forms, stopping to scrape down sides. With processor running, pour oil and lemon juice through food chute in a steady stream, processing until smooth. Add honey and cheese, and pulse 3 or 4 times or until blended. Add kosher salt and black pepper to taste. Serve immediately, or place plastic wrap directly on pesto (to help retain color), and refrigerate up to 1 week. Let stand 10 minutes before serving.

Note: We tested with Glory Turnip Greens.

Mrs. Monty's Rolls

MAKES ABOUT 3 DOZEN
HANDS-ON 40 MIN.
TOTAL 4 HOURS, 10 MIN.

1 (1/4-oz.) envelope active dry yeast
2 cups warm water (100° to 110°)
1/2 cup sugar
3 Tbsp. shortening, softened
1 tsp. table salt
1 large egg, lightly beaten
6 to 6 1/2 cups sifted all-purpose flour
3 Tbsp. butter, softened
2 Tbsp. butter, melted

1. Combine yeast and water in a large bowl; let stand 5 minutes. Stir in sugar and next 3 ingredients. Whisk in 3 cups sifted flour, 1 cup at a time, until combined. Gradually stir in more flour to make a soft dough (about 3 to 3 1/2 cups). Using floured hands, shape dough into a smooth ball. Place dough in a well-greased bowl, turning to grease top. Cover with plastic wrap. Let rise in a warm place 2 hours or until doubled in bulk.

2. Punch dough down. Roll dough out to 1/4-inch thickness on a floured surface. Cut dough into rounds with a 3-inch round cutter, rerolling scraps once. Lightly press each round into a 4-inch oval. Spread 1/4 tsp. softened butter on half of each oval. Fold unbuttered half over to form a half-moon shape; place 2 inches apart on 2 lightly greased baking sheets. Cover and let rise in a warm place 40 minutes or until doubled in bulk.

3. Preheat oven to 375°. Bake, in batches, 14 to 15 minutes or until golden brown. Transfer to a wire rack; brush with melted butter.

GEORGIA
THANKSGIVING

※ WITH JAMES FARMER ※

JOIN ONE OF THE SOUTH'S
MOST DYNAMIC YOUNG DESIGNERS
AT HIS FAMILY TABLE,
WHERE **OLD SOUTH** MIXES WITH **NEW**

Fall is the season I relish most. Its flavors, scents, textures, colors, and temperance meld together into a tableau of delight, and we kick off the season with a celebratory feast that brings our families and friends together. As I look across my Thanksgiving table here in Middle Georgia, I am filled with nostalgia and flooded with memories— Aunt Irene's silver, hydrangeas from Granddaddy's garden, my great-grandmother's turkey plates, the blue-and-white jars Mimi and Granddaddy found on their honeymoon in Japan. These are the objects that weave together our familial tapestry. They also inform my work. Mixing the old with the new, forging ahead with new traditions while honoring the old, that is my go-to style.

This Thanksgiving will be my family's first without Mimi, but her cast-iron skillets, roasting pans, silver, and china are all still with us, and so are her down-home recipes. In her kitchen, we will roast a turkey as she did by seasoning it simply with salt and pepper and serving it with an old-fashioned gravy enriched with both giblets and chopped boiled eggs. We'll also simmer a sweet conserve to spoon over slices of the spiral-cut ham, and we'll bake her rich, buttermilk-laden cornbread dressing. But without Mimi here at the stove to guide me, I can't help but wonder if her recipes, what she always referred to as "suggestive guidelines," will taste the same. "Was Mimi's cup of sugar a cup proper or a scant cup?" I wonder. "Did she use all the celery in the dressing?"

More important than the dressing's flavor and the glint of Mimi's silver and china on the table, what we'll remember most about her is the way she embodied the very essence of a Southern lady with her generosity of spirit. So as we gather around the table for this feast to begin the season, two words fill my family's hearts and minds: thanks and giving. *Thanks*, Mimi, for *giving* us such a legacy to uphold.

James Farmer is an Editor-at-Large at *Southern Living*. His most recent book is *A Time to Cook: Dishes from My Southern Sideboard*.

Salt-and-Pepper Roasted Turkey

MAKES 8 TO 10 SERVINGS
HANDS-ON 20 MIN.
TOTAL 4 HOURS, 25 MIN.

With a turkey this simple and with so few ingredients, focus on the techniques that matter most. First, pat the turkey very dry, which will help it achieve a crispier skin in the oven. Then season liberally with kosher salt. Season the cavity, gently under the skin, and again on the surface of the skin to enhance the flavor from the skin to the bone.

1 (11- to 12-lb.) whole fresh turkey
⅓ cup canola oil, divided
2 Tbsp. kosher salt, divided
1 Tbsp. freshly ground black pepper, divided
  Kitchen string

1. Preheat oven to 325°. Remove giblets and neck from turkey, and if desired, reserve for gravy. Rinse turkey with cold water; pat dry. Drain cavity well; pat dry. Loosen and lift skin from turkey breast without totally detaching skin. Rub 2 Tbsp. oil, 2 tsp. salt, and 1 tsp. pepper under skin and inside cavity.

2. Place turkey, breast side up, on a lightly greased roasting rack in a large roasting pan. Tie ends of legs together with kitchen string; tuck wing tips under. Brush turkey with remaining oil, and sprinkle with remaining salt and pepper.

3. Bake at 325° for 3 hours and 45 minutes to 4 hours or until a meat thermometer inserted into thigh registers 165°. Let stand 20 minutes before carving.

> *" MIXING THE OLD WITH THE NEW, FORGING AHEAD WITH NEW TRADITIONS WHILE HONORING THE OLD, THAT IS MY GO-TO STYLE. "*

Old-Fashioned Giblet-Egg Gravy

MAKES ABOUT 2 1/2 CUPS
HANDS-ON 30 MIN.
TOTAL 30 MIN.

"My family likes our gravy thin and soupy, but you can thicken yours as desired," James says. Feel free to omit the egg or giblets, but do start with homemade chicken or turkey stock or the best broth you can buy.

- 3 Tbsp. butter
- 1 medium-size yellow onion, finely chopped
- 2 garlic cloves, minced
- 3 Tbsp. all-purpose flour
- 3 cups organic chicken broth
  Giblets and neck from 1 turkey, finely chopped*
- 1 1/4 tsp. kosher salt
- 1/2 tsp. freshly ground black pepper
- 2 to 3 Tbsp. dry sherry
- 1 large hard-cooked egg, peeled and sliced

Melt butter in a small saucepan over medium heat. Add onion, and sauté 3 to 4 minutes or until tender. Add garlic; sauté 1 minute. Add flour, and cook, stirring constantly, 2 minutes. Stir in broth and next 3 ingredients, and bring to a boil. Reduce heat to low, and simmer, stirring occasionally, 10 to 15 minutes or until giblets are thoroughly cooked and gravy is thickened. Stir in sherry and egg just before serving.

* 1/4 cup each finely chopped chicken gizzards and livers may be substituted.

Ham Glazed With Spiced Plum Conserve

Ham Glazed With Spiced Plum Conserve

MAKES 8 TO 10 SERVINGS
HANDS-ON 15 MIN.
TOTAL 5 HOURS, 45 MIN., INCLUDING CONSERVE

Any brined, smoked supermarket ham will be welcomed on your holiday table in addition to (or in lieu of) the turkey. If you're using a spiral ham, there's no need to score it and stud with cloves.

- 1 (8-lb.) fully cooked, bone-in ham
- 1 Tbsp. whole cloves
- 3 cups Spiced Plum Conserve

Preheat oven to 325°. Place ham in an aluminum foil-lined 13- x 9-inch pan. Make shallow cuts in fat 1 inch apart in a diamond pattern. Insert cloves in centers of diamonds. Pour conserve over ham, add 1/2 cup water to pan, and cover with foil. Bake 4 hours or until a meat thermometer inserted into thickest portion registers 165°, basting with pan juices every hour. Remove from oven, and let stand 15 minutes before serving.

SPICED PLUM CONSERVE

MAKES ABOUT 6 CUPS
HANDS-ON 35 MIN.
TOTAL 1 HOUR, 15 MIN.

Experiment with your favorite seasonal fruit, including muscadines. This conserve also pairs well with roasted or smoked pork shoulder.

- 6 lb. red plums, quartered
- 1/2 cup apple cider vinegar
- 1/4 cup whole cloves
- 3 (3-inch) cinnamon sticks
- 3 cups sugar

1. Bring first 4 ingredients to a boil in a Dutch oven over medium-high heat, stirring occasionally; reduce heat to low, and simmer, stirring occasionally, 20 minutes or until mixture thickens. Pour through a fine wire-mesh strainer into a large bowl, discarding solids. Clean Dutch oven. Return plum mixture to Dutch oven.

2. Bring to a boil over medium heat; add sugar, and simmer, stirring often, 10 minutes or until slightly thickened. Let stand 15 minutes. Use immediately, or refrigerate in an airtight container up to 3 weeks.

Mimi's Cornbread Dressing

MAKES 8 TO 10 SERVINGS
HANDS-ON 30 MIN.
TOTAL 2 HOURS, 5 MIN.

Packaged mixes and store-bought cornbread vary in sweetness and moisture, so for this savory dressing, make yours from scratch. This simple buttermilk skillet version will give your dressing the best texture and flavor.

- 2 Tbsp. canola oil, divided
- 2 cups self-rising white cornmeal mix
- 1 1/3 cups buttermilk
- 1 cup self-rising flour
- 2 large eggs, lightly beaten
- 5 to 6 cups reduced-sodium chicken broth
- 3/4 cup butter, divided
- 3 cups chopped sweet onion (about 1 large)
- 2 cups chopped celery
- 4 large eggs, lightly beaten
- 2/3 cup chopped fresh flat-leaf parsley
- 1 Tbsp. chopped fresh sage
- 2 tsp. chopped fresh thyme
- 1 1/2 tsp. freshly ground black pepper
- 1/2 tsp. kosher salt

1. Preheat oven to 400°. Coat bottom and sides of a 10-inch cast-iron skillet with 1 Tbsp. oil; heat in oven 10 minutes.

2. Meanwhile, stir together cornmeal mix, next 3 ingredients, and remaining 1 Tbsp. oil. Pour batter into hot skillet.

3. Bake at 400° for 30 minutes or until golden. Remove from oven to a wire rack; cool 15 minutes. Crumble cornbread into a large bowl. Stir 5 cups broth into crumbled cornbread until moistened, adding more broth, 1 Tbsp. at a time, if necessary. (Mixture should resemble wet sand.)

4. Melt 1/4 cup butter in a large skillet over medium-high heat; add onion and celery, and sauté 8 to 10 minutes or until tender. Add onion mixture to cornbread mixture.

5. Microwave remaining 1/2 cup butter in a small microwave-safe bowl at HIGH 1 minute or until melted. Stir melted butter, eggs, and remaining ingredients into cornbread mixture; spoon into a lightly greased 13- x 9-inch baking dish.

6. Bake at 400° for 50 minutes to 1 hour or until golden brown. Serve immediately.

A Mess of Greens

MAKES 8 TO 10 SERVINGS
HANDS-ON 25 MIN.
TOTAL 2 HOURS, 30 MIN.

James' grandmother Mimi always added a knob of butter to her onions to boost the flavor as they browned in oil, and then simmered the greens slowly, adding water as needed to keep them submerged. For serving, James says, "I use my large, enameled cast-iron stew pot. It keeps the greens warm and offers a nice presentation."

- 2 Tbsp. butter
- 3 Tbsp. olive oil
- 1 small sweet onion, diced
- 3 garlic cloves, minced (about 1 Tbsp.)
- 1 smoked ham hock (about 12 oz.)
- 3 (1-lb.) packages fresh collard greens, washed, trimmed, and cut into thin strips
- 1/4 to 1/2 cup diced jarred jalapeño peppers, drained (optional)
  Pepper sauce

1. Melt butter with oil in a large Dutch oven over medium-high heat. Add onion, and sauté 5 minutes or until lightly browned. Add garlic; sauté 1 minute. Add ham hock, and gently stir.

2. Add half of collards and 2 cups water. Cover and cook over medium-high heat, stirring occasionally, 10 minutes. Add remaining collards and 8 cups water; bring to a boil. Cover, reduce heat to low, and simmer 2 hours. Stir in jalapeño peppers, if desired. Add table salt and black pepper to taste, and serve with pepper sauce.

Cranberry-Orange Relish

MAKES ABOUT 4 CUPS
HANDS-ON 10 MIN.
TOTAL 10 MIN.

The flesh and juice of oranges and a shot of orange liqueur help balance the tartness of cranberries in this coarsely chopped condiment.

- 1 (12-oz.) package fresh or frozen cranberries, thawed
- 1 orange, unpeeled, seeded, and cut into 6 wedges
- 3/4 cup chopped toasted pecans
- 1/2 cup sugar
- 1/2 cup fresh orange juice
- 1 Tbsp. orange liqueur (such as Grand Marnier)

Pulse cranberries in a blender or food processor 4 or 5 times or until coarsely chopped; transfer to a large bowl. Pulse orange wedges 4 or 5 times or until coarsely chopped. Stir pecans, next 3 ingredients, and oranges into cranberries. Serve relish immediately.

Note: To make ahead, prepare as directed, omitting pecans. Cover and chill up to 2 days. Add pecans just before serving.

Ambrosia With Apples

MAKES ABOUT 8 CUPS
HANDS-ON 45 MIN.
TOTAL 1 HOUR, 45 MIN.

Plan on sectioning the citrus and chopping the pineapple ahead of time. If you use canned or jarred fruit, save the juices and add them to the ambrosia.

- 4 oranges, peeled and sectioned
- 2 grapefruit, peeled and sectioned*
- 4 cups chopped fresh pineapple (about 1 small pineapple)
- 1 Fuji or Granny Smith apple, chopped
- 2 tsp. fresh lemon juice
- 1 cup frozen grated coconut, thawed
- 1/4 cup chopped fresh mint

1. Layer first 4 ingredients (in the order listed) in a large glass serving bowl or trifle dish. Sprinkle apple with lemon juice. Cover and chill 1 to 4 hours.

2. Sprinkle fruit mixture with coconut and mint. Gently toss just before serving.

*Blood oranges may be substituted.

Buttermilk-Glazed Mini Fig Cakes with Vanilla Hard Sauce

MAKES 20 MINI CAKES
HANDS-ON 15 MIN.
TOTAL 1 HOUR, 30 MIN., INCLUDING GLAZE AND SAUCE

Muffin pans make the perfect baking vessels for these little fig cakes. Gussy them up by spooning a dollop or piping a silver dollar of hard sauce on top, and then garnish them with halved fresh figs, fresh herbs, or even pecan halves.

- 2 cups all-purpose flour
- 1 cup sugar
- 1 tsp. baking soda
- 1 tsp. table salt
- 1 tsp. ground cinnamon
- 1 tsp. ground cloves
- 1 cup vegetable oil
- 3 large eggs
- 1 cup buttermilk
- 1 tsp. vanilla extract
- 1 cup fig preserves
- 1/2 cup chopped toasted pecans
  Buttermilk Glaze
  Vanilla Hard Sauce
  Garnishes: fresh rosemary sprigs, fresh fig quarters

1. Preheat oven to 350°. Stir together flour and next 5 ingredients in a large bowl. Gradually add oil, beating at medium speed with an electric mixer until blended. Add eggs, 1 at a time, beating until blended. Add buttermilk and vanilla, beating until blended. Fold in preserves and pecans.

2. Spoon batter into 2 lightly greased (12-cup) muffin pans, filling 20 muffin cups about three-fourths full.

3. Bake at 350° for 15 to 18 minutes or until a wooden pick inserted in center comes out clean. Cool in pans 5 minutes. Invert cakes onto wire racks. Cool 15 minutes.

4. Drizzle cakes with Buttermilk Glaze. Cool 10 minutes. Pipe Vanilla Hard Sauce onto warm cakes.

Buttermilk-Glazed Mini Fig Cakes with Vanilla Hard Sauce

BUTTERMILK GLAZE

MAKES ABOUT 3/4 CUP
HANDS-ON 10 MIN.
TOTAL 20 MIN.

- 1/2 cup sugar
- 1/4 cup buttermilk
- 4 Tbsp. butter
- 2 tsp. cornstarch
- 1/4 tsp. baking soda
- 1 1/2 tsp. vanilla extract

1. Bring sugar and next 4 ingredients to a boil in a small saucepan over medium heat, stirring often.

2. Immediately remove mixture from heat, and cool 10 minutes. Stir in vanilla.

VANILLA HARD SAUCE

MAKES ABOUT 1 1/2 CUPS
HANDS-ON 10 MIN.
TOTAL 10 MIN.

- 1 vanilla bean*
- 2 cups sifted powdered sugar
- 1 cup butter, softened

1. Split vanilla bean lengthwise, and scrape seeds into a large bowl. Stir in powdered sugar.

2. Beat butter into sugar mixture at medium speed with an electric mixer until blended.

*1 Tbsp. vanilla extract may be substituted. Omit Step 1. Stir extract into mixture after beating butter and sugar together in Step 2.

WARM & RUSTIC

TEXAS
THANKSGIVING

WITH THE CURRENS

2013

FOR TWO AUSTIN CHEFS,
TEXAS INGREDIENTS AND **BIG FLAVORS** ABOUND

It didn't take long for the two Texans to seek each other out in culinary school in New York back in 2003. Mary Catherine, a native Austinite, was 18 and Andrew (friends call him Drew) Curren, 7 years older, is from Houston. They bonded over a shared passion for honest home cooking. "We talked about what we'd name our restaurant on our first date," says Drew.

After graduation, they moved to New York City and landed jobs in high-end restaurants. But eventually the two began to long for things that don't come easy in New York: a backyard, a grill, and a dog. It was time to come home. They moved to Austin in 2008, just as the city was poised for a culinary renaissance.

Since then, Drew has amassed a mini-empire of thoughtful restaurants, including 24 Diner, Easy Tiger, and Arro. And each Thanksgiving, the Currens have a full table of enthusiastic eaters. "A perfect meal at our house begins with bubbles and ends with bourbon," Mary Catherine says. This year, the Champagne will partner with Chicken Liver Pâté and Cranberry-Pecan Chutney. When it comes to the bird, Drew breaks it down. "The number one question each November is, 'How do I roast a turkey so it's perfectly moist?' " The answer is cooking each piece separately to create the perfect level of doneness. Brining and smoking the breast creates a succulent texture; roasting the legs creates deep flavor.

By the time the Pumpkin Cheesecake Tart appears, single-barrel bourbon is poured and friends take turns playing DJ, selecting albums from Drew's sizable vinyl collection. Looking around, the Currens see a backyard with a grill that gets plenty of use; their dog, Lucy; and an easy, languid meal that starts early and goes late with good friends. They are indeed thankful. It's good to be home.

Lost in Texas

MAKES 1 SERVING
HANDS-ON 5 MIN.
TOTAL 5 MIN.

This refreshing beer cocktail balances a malty bock-style beer with fruit-tinged apricot brandy.

Combine 6 Tbsp. **bock beer**, 2 Tbsp. **vodka**, 2 Tbsp. **Italian bitter liqueur**, 1 to 2 Tbsp. **apricot brandy**, 1 Tbsp. **fresh lemon juice**, and 2 dashes of **Angostura bitters** in a cocktail shaker. Cover with lid, and shake vigorously until thoroughly chilled (about 30 seconds). Pour into a 12- to 16-oz. glass filled with **ice**. Garnish with an **orange peel strip**.

Note: We tested with Shiner Bock beer, Tito's Handmade Vodka, and Averna Amaro Italian bitter liqueur.

Chicken Liver Pâté

MAKES 1 1/2 CUPS
HANDS-ON 35 MIN.
TOTAL 6 HOURS, 45 MIN.

Serve this earthy, rustic spread with grilled bread and Cranberry-Pecan Chutney.

- 1 **lb. chicken livers**, trimmed
- 2 **cups milk**
- 4 **bacon slices**
- 2 **garlic cloves**, coarsely chopped
- 1 **jalapeño pepper**, seeded and chopped
- 1/2 **tsp. finely chopped fresh thyme**
- 1/2 **tsp. finely chopped fresh rosemary**
- 2 **Tbsp. butter**, melted
- 5 **Tbsp. bourbon**
- 1 **tsp. kosher salt**
- 1/2 **tsp. freshly ground black pepper**
- 2 **Tbsp. butter**, softened

1. Rinse livers, and pat dry with paper towels. Place livers in a large bowl, and add 1 cup milk; cover and chill 1 hour. Drain livers, and return to bowl. Add remaining 1 cup milk; cover and chill 1 hour. Drain livers, and pat dry with paper towels.

2. Cook bacon in a large skillet over medium heat 3 to 4 minutes on each side or until crisp. Drain on paper towels, reserving drippings in skillet. Finely chop bacon.

3. Cook livers, in batches, in hot drippings over medium heat 2 minutes on each side or until golden brown and done. Remove livers with a slotted spoon, and drain on paper towels. Discard drippings, and wipe skillet clean.

4. Sauté garlic, jalapeño, and next 2 ingredients in melted butter in skillet over medium-high heat 1 to 2 minutes or until fragrant. Stir in bourbon, salt, and pepper; simmer 1 minute. Remove from heat, and cool 10 minutes.

5. Process livers, bacon, and garlic mixture in a food processor 60 to 90 seconds or until smooth. Add softened butter, and process 10 seconds or until blended. Transfer to a bowl; cover and chill 4 hours.

Note: Chopped, cooked bacon may be omitted from the pâté and used as a topping instead, if desired.

Cranberry-Pecan Chutney

MAKES 3 ½ CUPS
HANDS-ON 25 MIN.
TOTAL 1 HOUR

Serve this versatile, zingy condiment with the pâté as a toast topper and with the turkey as a relish.

- 1 cup apple cider
- ¾ cup fresh orange juice
- ½ cup sugar
- 1 (3-inch) cinnamon stick
- 1 (1-inch) piece fresh ginger
- ½ tsp. kosher salt
- ½ tsp. whole cloves
- ⅛ tsp. dried crushed red pepper
- 1 (12-oz.) package fresh or frozen cranberries
- ¾ cup dried apricots, diced
- ½ tsp. loosely packed orange zest
- ½ cup chopped toasted pecans

1. Bring first 8 ingredients to a boil in a large saucepan over medium-high heat. Reduce heat to low, and simmer, stirring occasionally, 10 minutes. Remove cloves with a slotted spoon, and discard.

2. Add cranberries; increase heat to medium, and bring to a boil. Boil, stirring occasionally, 3 to 5 minutes or just until cranberries begin to pop. Discard cinnamon stick and ginger. Stir in apricots and orange zest; remove from heat. Cool completely. Serve immediately, or chill up to 2 days. Stir in pecans just before serving.

Herb-Roasted Turkey Legs

MAKES 6 SERVINGS
HANDS-ON 20 MIN.
TOTAL 3 HOURS, 30 MIN., PLUS 12 HOURS FOR CHILLING

While cooking a whole bird is traditional, most chefs smartly cook the white and dark meat separately to achieve the best flavor and perfect level of doneness. Brining and smoking the breast and curing and roasting the legs yields the most succulent results.

- ¼ cup kosher salt
- ¼ cup turbinado sugar
- ¼ cup fresh thyme leaves
- ¼ cup fresh rosemary leaves
- 3 bay leaves
- 2 garlic cloves
- 6 (1- to 1 ½-lb.) turkey legs
- ¾ cup reduced-sodium chicken broth

1. Process first 6 ingredients in a food processor 40 to 45 seconds or until finely chopped. Place turkey legs in a 13- x 9-inch baking dish, and rub with salt mixture. Cover and chill 12 to 15 hours.

2. Preheat oven to 400°. Transfer turkey to a roasting pan, discarding any accumulated liquid. Pour broth over turkey; let stand 30 minutes. Bake 1 hour.

3. Reduce temperature to 350°. Baste with pan juices, and bake 1 hour and 30 minutes to 1 hour and 45 minutes or until meat pulls away from bone, turning legs every 20 minutes. Let stand 10 minutes before serving.

Note: We tested with Sugar in the Raw turbinado sugar.

Smoked Turkey Breast

MAKES 8 TO 10 SERVINGS
HANDS-ON 20 MIN.
TOTAL 10 HOURS, 5 MIN.

- 1 (64-oz.) bottle apple cider
- 3/4 cup kosher salt (such as Diamond Crystal)
- 1/2 cup sugar
- 1/4 cup apple cider vinegar
- 3 (4-inch) fresh thyme sprigs
- 2 (4-inch) fresh rosemary sprigs
- 10 fresh sage leaves
- 1 garlic bulb, cut in half crosswise
- 4 cups ice cubes
- 1 (5 3/4- to 6-lb.) bone-in turkey breast
- 4 hickory wood chunks

1. Bring cider and next 7 ingredients to a boil in a large stockpot or 8-qt. Dutch oven over medium-high heat; reduce heat to medium, and simmer, stirring occasionally, 5 minutes. Remove from heat. Stir in ice. Cool completely (1 hour).

2. Place turkey in brine; cover and chill 5 to 12 hours.

3. Prepare smoker according to manufacturer's directions, bringing internal temperature to 225° to 250°; maintain temperature 15 to 20 minutes. Place wood chunks on coals.

4. Remove turkey from brine, and pat dry with paper towels. Smoke turkey, maintaining temperature inside smoker between 225° and 250°, for 3 1/2 to 4 hours or until a meat thermometer inserted into thickest portion registers 165°.

5. Remove turkey, cover loosely with aluminum foil, and let stand 10 to 15 minutes before slicing.

" A PERFECT MEAL AT OUR HOUSE BEGINS WITH BUBBLES AND ENDS WITH BOURBON. "

Green Beans with Citrus and Pecans

MAKES 6 TO 8 SERVINGS
HANDS-ON 20 MIN.
TOTAL 2 HOURS, 20 MIN.

A citrus vinaigrette adds fresh zing to crisp-tender green beans.

- 1 shallot, diced
- 3/4 cup olive oil
- 1 Tbsp. orange zest
- 1/3 cup fresh orange juice
- 1/3 cup fresh lemon juice
- 1/4 cup cane syrup
- 2 lb. haricots verts (thin green beans)
- 2 oranges, sectioned
- 1/2 cup chopped toasted pecans

1. **Whisk** together first 6 ingredients. Add salt and pepper to taste.

2. **Cook** green beans in boiling salted water to cover, stirring occasionally, 3 to 4 minutes or until crisp-tender; drain. Plunge into ice water to stop the cooking process; drain.

3. **Pat** beans dry with paper towels. Place beans and orange segments in a zip-top plastic freezer bag; add vinaigrette, and seal bag. Turn bag to coat beans and oranges. Chill 2 hours. Sprinkle with pecans before serving.

Smoked-Oyster-and-Andouille Dressing

MAKES 8 TO 10 SERVINGS
HANDS-ON 1 HOUR
TOTAL 2 HOURS, 10 MIN.

Give your dressing an extra-savory depth of flavor with the addition of humble canned, smoked oysters.

- 5 cups crumbled cornbread
- 8 oz. sourdough bread slices, cut into 1/2-inch cubes (5 cups)
- 1 cup butter
- 2 cups diced andouille sausage
- 2 cups chopped onion (about 1 large)
- 2 cups finely chopped celery (4 to 5 ribs)
- 1 cup chopped green bell pepper
- 1/4 cup chopped fresh sage
- 2 Tbsp. chopped fresh thyme
- 2 Tbsp. chopped fresh rosemary
- 1 Tbsp. Cajun blackened seasoning
- 1 Tbsp. poultry seasoning
- 1 tsp. black pepper
- 3 (3.75-oz.) cans smoked oysters, drained
- 4 cups chicken broth
- 4 large eggs, lightly beaten

1. **Preheat** oven to 400°. Stir together cornbread and bread cubes in a large bowl. Melt butter in a large saucepan over medium heat. Add sausage, and cook, covered and stirring occasionally, 5 to 7 minutes or until butter turns a light orange. Remove sausage with a slotted spoon; drain on paper towels.

2. **Add** onion and next 2 ingredients to butter; sauté 8 minutes or until tender. Add sage and next 2 ingredients, and sauté 1 minute. Stir in Cajun seasoning and next 2 ingredients; remove from heat.

3. **Stir** vegetables and sausage into cornbread mixture. Stir in oysters and next 2 ingredients. Spread in a lightly greased 13- x 9-inch pan; cover with aluminum foil.

4. **Bake,** covered, at 400° for 30 minutes. Uncover and bake 30 more minutes or until browned and thoroughly cooked. Let stand 10 minutes before serving.

Note: We tested with Weber New Orleans Cajun Seasoning and cornbread made with Martha White Cotton Country Cornbread Mix. (Do not use a sweet cornbread mix, such as Jiffy.)

Brussels Sprouts with Ham and Caramelized Onions

MAKES 8 SERVINGS
HANDS-ON 40 MIN.
TOTAL 40 MIN.

Easy seared Brussels sprouts get salty-sweet undertones from crispy ham and long-cooked onions.

- 4 oz. country ham, thinly sliced
- 5 Tbsp. olive oil, divided
- 2 lb. fresh Brussels sprouts, trimmed and halved
- 2 tsp. kosher salt, divided
- 2 lb. yellow onions, thinly sliced
- 1/4 cup honey
- 1/2 tsp. cracked black pepper
- 1/4 tsp. ground red pepper

1. **Sauté** ham in 3 Tbsp. hot oil in a large skillet over medium heat 3 to 5 minutes or until crisp; remove with a slotted spoon, and drain on paper towels.

2. **Add** Brussels sprouts to skillet, and cook, stirring occasionally, 7 to 8 minutes or until light brown and crisp-tender; toss with 1 tsp. salt. Transfer Brussels sprouts to a bowl. Wipe skillet clean.

3. **Heat** remaining 2 Tbsp. oil in skillet over medium-high heat; add onions, and cook, stirring occasionally, 15 to 20 minutes or until light brown and tender. Stir in honey, next 2 ingredients, and remaining 1 tsp. salt. Add Brussels sprouts, and cook, stirring constantly, 1 to 2 minutes or until thoroughly heated. Top with ham.

OVEN-ROASTED BRUSSELS SPROUTS
Preheat oven to 425°. Increase olive oil to 7 Tbsp. Heat a 15- x 10-inch jelly-roll pan in oven 10 minutes. Prepare recipe through Step 3, omitting Step 2. Toss sprouts with 2 Tbsp. olive oil, 1/2 tsp. freshly ground black pepper, and 1 tsp. kosher salt. Place sprouts, cut sides down, in hot jelly-roll pan, and bake 20 to 25 minutes. Toss with ham and caramelized onions.

Pumpkin Cheesecake Tart with Honey Swiss Meringue

MAKES 6 TO 8 SERVINGS
HANDS-ON 45 MIN.
TOTAL 13 HOURS, 10 MIN.

Begin with a toasted pecan crust, layer with cream cheese and a classic pumpkin filling, and then gild the lily with a creamy meringue.

TART CRUST

- ½ **cup chopped toasted pecans**
- 7 **Tbsp. butter, softened**
- 1 **cup powdered sugar**
- ¼ **tsp. table salt**
- 1 **large egg**
- ¼ **tsp. vanilla extract**
- 2 **cups all-purpose flour**

CREAM CHEESE LAYER

- 2 **(8-oz.) packages cream cheese, softened**
- ½ **cup granulated sugar**
- 1 **large egg**
- 1 **tsp. loosely packed orange zest**

PUMPKIN LAYER

- 1 **(15-oz.) can pumpkin**
- 3 **large eggs**
- ½ **cup heavy cream**
- ⅓ **cup firmly packed light brown sugar**
- 1½ **tsp. pumpkin pie spice**
- ½ **tsp. table salt**

TOPPING

Honey Swiss Meringue

1. Prepare Tart Crust: Process pecans in a food processor 10 to 12 seconds or until finely ground.

2. Beat butter at medium speed with an electric mixer 1 minute or until creamy. Gradually add powdered sugar and salt. Add egg, beating just until blended; stir in vanilla. Stir together flour and processed pecans; gradually add to butter mixture, beating at low speed until mixture is no longer crumbly and forms a ball, pulling away from sides of bowl. Press dough on bottom and up sides of a 9-inch deep-dish tart pan with a removable bottom. Chill 1 hour or until firm.

3. Preheat oven to 350°. Line crust with aluminum foil, and fill with pie weights or dried beans. Bake 20 minutes. Remove weights and foil; bake 12 to 14 more minutes or until crust is light brown. Cool completely on a wire rack (about 30 minutes). Increase temperature to 425°.

4. Prepare Cream Cheese Layer: Beat cream cheese, sugar, and egg at low speed with an electric mixer until smooth. Stir in orange zest. Spread over bottom of crust.

5. Prepare Pumpkin Layer: Whisk together pumpkin and next 5 ingredients until smooth; pour over cream cheese layer in crust. Cover tart edges with aluminum foil.

6. Bake at 425° for 15 minutes; reduce temperature to 350°, and bake 45 to 55 more minutes or until a knife inserted in center of pumpkin layer comes out clean. Transfer to a wire rack, and cool completely (about 1 hour). Cover and chill 8 to 12 hours.

7. Gently blot any moisture that collected on top of tart during chilling with a paper towel. Spread Honey Swiss Meringue over tart. Brown meringue using a kitchen torch, holding torch 1 to 2 inches from meringue and moving torch back and forth.

HONEY SWISS MERINGUE: Whisk together ⅔ cup **clover honey**, 4 large **egg whites**, and ¼ tsp. **table salt**. Pour **water** to depth of 1 inch into bottom of a double boiler over medium heat; bring to a boil. Reduce heat, and simmer; place honey mixture in top of double boiler over simmering water. Cook, whisking constantly, 10 to 12 minutes or until mixture reaches 160°. Quickly transfer mixture to bowl of a heavy-duty electric stand mixer, and beat, using whisk attachment, until stiff peaks form. **MAKES** about 4 cups

FRESH & ELEGANT
ALABAMA
THANKSGIVING
❧ WITH TASIA MALAKASIS ❧

JOIN ONE OF THE SOUTH'S PREMIER CHEESEMAKERS AND HER FAMILY FOR A **HARVEST FEAST** BRIMMING WITH NEW SEASONAL IDEAS

No matter where in the world we are living, we will always gather back at my house for Thanksgiving, my sisters and I promised each other years ago.

Now if only traveling to my home in Huntsville, Alabama, meant visiting from Athens, Georgia, instead of Athens, Greece, where our middle sister, Cynthia, lives. Carol, the youngest, lives in New York City.

I look forward to this day of the year like no other. My family has always centered our time around food, and my sisters and I spend Thanksgiving in the kitchen laughing, playing, cooking, and eating. As the head cook, I season the turkey skin with a homemade citrus salt and stuff the cavity with lemons and oranges as an homage to our Greek father, who always paired grilled and roasted meats with lemons. As Cynthia greets our guests, I keep Carol's prying hands out of the mixing bowl so she doesn't add extra spices to the lemony garlic mayonnaise, an aïoli inspired by the Greek yogurt sauce *tzatziki* that stands in for traditional Southern gravy. Like the cheese I make at my creamery, Belle Chèvre, the menu is fresh and full of modern, playful spins, such as my Stuffing-Stuffed Onions, in which I use hollowed-out roasted onions as mini serving vessels for a simple sage stuffing.

The menu may change from year to year, but one thing will not: My sisters will be home for Thanksgiving. That's because a promise made by sisters is a promise that is taken seriously.

Tasia Malakasis is the author of *Tasia's Table: Cooking with the Artisan Cheesemaker at Belle Chèvre.*

Citrus-Roasted Turkey with Lemon Aïoli

MAKES 10 SERVINGS
HANDS-ON 45 MIN.
TOTAL 5 HOURS

Seasoning with a citrus-salt rub and stuffing the cavity with lemons and oranges imparts fresh flavor and citrus fragrance and keeps the turkey extra juicy.

- 1 (14- to 16-lb.) whole fresh turkey
  Citrus-Salt Rub
- 2 lemons, quartered
- 2 small oranges, quartered
- 2 celery ribs, chopped
- 1 onion, coarsely chopped
- 2 Tbsp. chopped fresh oregano
- 2 tsp. chopped fresh thyme
- 2 tsp. black pepper
- 1/2 cup extra virgin olive oil, divided
- 6 Tbsp. fresh lemon juice, divided
- 1 1/2 tsp. kosher salt, divided
  Kitchen string
- 3 Tbsp. fresh orange juice
- 2 cups reduced-sodium chicken broth
  Lemon Aïoli

1. Remove giblets and neck from turkey, and rinse turkey with cold water. Drain cavity well; pat dry. Rub 4 Tbsp. Citrus-Salt Rub into cavity. Rub skin with remaining rub. Cover and chill 18 to 24 hours.

2. Preheat oven to 350°. Rinse turkey; drain cavity well, and pat dry. Toss together lemons, next 6 ingredients, 1/4 cup olive oil, 3 Tbsp. lemon juice, and 1 tsp. salt in a large bowl; spoon mixture into cavity of turkey.

3. Tie ends of legs together with kitchen string; tuck wing tips under. Place turkey, breast side up, on a lightly greased roasting rack in a large roasting pan.

4. Whisk together orange juice, remaining 3 Tbsp. lemon juice and 1/2 tsp. salt in a bowl; gradually whisk in remaining 1/4 cup oil until blended. Brush half of orange juice mixture over turkey.

5. Bake at 350° on lowest oven rack 1 hour. Brush remaining orange juice mixture over turkey, and bake 45 more minutes. Pour 1 cup broth into pan; bake 45 minutes. Pour remaining 1 cup broth into pan; bake 45 more minutes or until a meat thermometer inserted into thickest portion of thigh registers 165°. Remove from oven, reserving pan juices. Cover loosely with foil; let stand 30 minutes. Transfer to a platter; serve with pan juices and Lemon Aïoli.

CITRUS-SALT RUB Stir together 1/3 cup **kosher salt**; 2 Tbsp. each chopped fresh **oregano, lemon zest, orange zest,** and minced **garlic;** and 1 Tbsp. **freshly ground black pepper. MAKES** 3/4 cup

LEMON AÏOLI: Whisk together 1 cup **mayonnaise,** 2 tsp. **lemon zest,** 3 Tbsp. **fresh lemon juice,** 2 tsp. **Dijon mustard,** and 4 small minced **garlic cloves.** Add **salt** and **pepper** to taste. **MAKES** 1 1/4 cups

Kale-and-Collards Salad

MAKES 8 TO 10 SERVINGS
HANDS-ON 30 MIN.
TOTAL 1 HOUR, 35 MIN.

When making this bracing salad, dress the kale and collards in advance to tenderize them.

- 1 **bunch fresh collard greens** (about 8 oz.)
- 1 **bunch Tuscan kale** (about 8 oz.)
- 3/4 **cup sweetened dried cranberries** Lemon Dressing
- 3 **Bartlett pears, sliced**
- 2 **avocados, peeled and diced**
- 1 **Tbsp. fresh lemon juice**
- 1 **small head radicchio, shredded**
- 3/4 **cup chopped toasted pecans**
- 6 **cooked bacon slices, crumbled**

1. Trim and discard tough stalks from centers of collard and kale leaves; stack leaves, and roll up, starting at 1 long side. Cut into 1/4-inch-thick slices. Toss collards and kale with cranberries and Lemon Dressing in a large bowl. Cover and chill 1 hour.

2. Toss together pears and next 2 ingredients just before serving. Toss pear mixture, radicchio, pecans, and bacon with collard mixture. Serve immediately.

LEMON DRESSING Whisk together 1/4 cup **fresh lemon juice;** 2 **garlic cloves,** minced; 2 tsp. **Dijon mustard;** 1 tsp. **kosher salt;** and 1/2 tsp. **freshly ground black pepper** in a small bowl; add 1/2 cup **olive oil** in a slow, steady stream, whisking constantly until smooth. **MAKES** about 1 cup

Corn Pudding

MAKES 8 SERVINGS
HANDS-ON 25 MIN.
TOTAL 1 HOUR, 25 MIN.

This is the one dish that Tasia's son, Kelly, requests every Thanksgiving. Take one bite of the rich custard and you'll know why.

- 1/2 **cup unsalted butter**
- 5 **cups fresh yellow corn kernels**
- 1 **cup diced yellow onion**
- 4 **large eggs**
- 1 **cup milk**
- 1 **cup half-and-half**
- 1 **cup softened goat cheese**
- 3 **Tbsp. chopped fresh basil**
- 1 **Tbsp. sugar**
- 1 **Tbsp. kosher salt**
- 3/4 **tsp. freshly ground black pepper**
- 1 **cup (4 oz.) shredded extra-sharp Cheddar cheese**

1. Preheat oven to 350°. Melt butter in a large skillet over medium-high heat; add corn and onion, and sauté 4 minutes. Remove from heat, and cool 10 minutes.

2. Meanwhile, whisk together eggs and next 2 ingredients in a large bowl; gradually whisk in goat cheese until blended. Whisk in basil and next 3 ingredients; stir in corn mixture and 3/4 cup Cheddar cheese until blended. Spoon mixture into a lightly greased 2-qt. baking dish; sprinkle with remaining 1/4 cup Cheddar cheese.

3. Bake at 350° for 40 to 45 minutes or until golden brown and a knife inserted in center comes out clean. Remove from oven to a wire rack, and cool 15 minutes.

Roasted Root Vegetables

MAKES 6 SERVINGS
HANDS-ON 30 MIN.
TOTAL 1 HOUR, 45 MIN.

Use any 4-lb. combo of hardy root vegetables to make this simple side.

- 1 **lb. turnips**
- 1 **lb. rutabagas**
- 1 **lb. carrots**
- 1 **lb. parsnips**
- 3 **shallots, halved**
- 1/2 **cup olive oil**
- 2 **Tbsp. chopped fresh rosemary**
- 2 **tsp. kosher salt**
- 1 **tsp. black pepper**
- 8 **garlic cloves**

ENJOY!

Persimmon Salsa

Stir together 4 'Fuyu' **persimmons** (about 6 oz. each), peeled and chopped; 1/4 cup chopped **red onion;** 1/4 cup chopped **fresh cilantro;** 1 **jalapeño pepper,** seeded and minced; 2 Tbsp. **fresh lime juice;** 1 Tbsp. **olive oil;** and **salt** and **pepper** to taste. Serve with **tortilla chips. MAKES** about 3 1/2 cups. **HANDS-ON** 10 min., **TOTAL** 10 min.

Preheat oven to 400°. Peel first 4 ingredients; cut into 1-inch pieces. (If your carrots are small enough, leave them whole.) Toss with shallots and next 4 ingredients. Place in a single layer in a 17- x 11-inch jelly-roll pan. Bake 30 minutes, stirring halfway through. Add garlic; bake 45 minutes or until tender, stirring at 15-minute intervals.

Note: You can prepare 4 hours ahead: Cool in pan 30 minutes or to room temperature; bake at 450° for 10 to 15 minutes or until hot.

Stuffing-Stuffed Onions

MAKES 8 SERVINGS
HANDS-ON 45 MIN.
TOTAL 2 HOURS

Hollow out and fill roasted onions with a chunky stuffing for a twist on the hearty casserole version.

- 8 small yellow onions (about 2 1/4 lb.)
- 1 1/2 cups organic chicken broth, divided
- 1/2 cup butter, divided
- 2 celery ribs, thinly sliced
- 1/4 cup finely chopped fresh flat-leaf parsley
- 1 Tbsp. finely chopped fresh sage
- 2 1/2 cups fresh French-bread breadcrumbs, toasted
- 1 tsp. kosher salt
- 1/2 tsp. freshly ground black pepper

1. Preheat oven to 425°. Cut a thin slice from bottom (rounded end) of each onion, forming a base for onions to stand. Cut 1/2 inch from sprout end of each onion, and discard. Peel onions. Remove and reserve center of each onion, leaving 2 layers of onion as a thick shell. Finely chop 1 cup reserved onion centers. Reserve remaining onion centers for another use, if desired.

2. Place hollowed onions in a 2-qt. baking dish, and add 1 cup broth. Cut 2 Tbsp. butter into 8 pieces, and place 1 piece in each onion. Cover with aluminum foil, and bake at 425° for 25 to 30 minutes or until shells are tender. Remove from oven to a wire rack, and cool 20 minutes.

3. Pour liquid from onions into a measuring cup, and add broth (about 1/4 cup) to equal 1 cup. Reduce oven temperature to 350°.

4. Melt 4 Tbsp. butter in a large skillet over medium-high heat; add celery and 1 cup chopped onion, and sauté 5 minutes or until tender. Stir in parsley and sage, and cook, stirring constantly, 1 minute or until fragrant. Stir in breadcrumbs, salt, pepper, and 1 cup reserved broth mixture. Remove from heat.

5. Fill hollowed onions with stuffing, and place in a shallow 9-inch baking dish or pie plate. Add remaining 1/4 cup broth to pan. Bake at 350° for 30 to 35 minutes or until stuffing is golden brown and thoroughly heated. Transfer to a serving platter. Stir remaining 2 Tbsp. butter into cooking liquid, and spoon over onions.

Corn Pudding, Roasted Root Vegetables, and Stuffing-Stuffed Onions

Sweet Potato Gratin

MAKES 8 SERVINGS
HANDS-ON 30 MIN.
TOTAL 1 HOUR, 35 MIN.

You'll know when the potatoes are perfectly cooked when a table knife slides easily through the center.

Preheat oven to 400°. Cut 2 large **sweet potatoes** (about 2 lb.) and 2 large **russet potatoes** (about 1 3/4 lb.) into 1/8-inch-thick slices, using a mandoline or sharp knife. Toss together potatoes, 3/4 cup **heavy cream,** and 1 1/2 tsp. **table salt** in a large bowl. Transfer to a lightly greased 2-qt. gratin dish, and spread potatoes into layers. Top with 1 cup (4 oz.) shredded **Gruyère cheese.** Pour 3/4 cup more **heavy cream** over potatoes, and sprinkle with 1/2 cup (2 oz.) more shredded Gruyère. Cover loosely with aluminum foil. Bake at 400° for 40 minutes. Uncover and bake 20 to 25 minutes or until potatoes are tender and cheese is golden brown. Transfer to a wire rack; cool 5 minutes.

Carrot Cake with Chèvre Frosting

MAKES 8 SERVINGS
HANDS-ON 40 MIN.
TOTAL 2 HOURS, 35 MIN.

Substituting goat cheese for the standard cream cheese gives this frosting an extra-tangy kick.

CAKE

- Parchment paper
- 2 cups all-purpose flour
- 2 tsp. baking soda
- 1 tsp. table salt
- 1 tsp. ground cinnamon
- 2 cups sugar
- 1 1/4 cups canola oil
- 3 large eggs
- 3 cups grated carrots
- 1 (8-oz.) can crushed pineapple in juice, drained
- 1 1/4 cups coarsely chopped walnuts, toasted
- 2 Tbsp. minced fresh ginger

FROSTING

- 8 oz. goat cheese or cream cheese, softened
- 1/2 cup butter, softened
- 1 (16-oz.) package powdered sugar
- 1 vanilla bean
- Garnishes: walnuts, carrot curls

1. Prepare Cake: Preheat oven to 350°. Grease 2 (8-inch) round cake pans; line bottoms with parchment paper, and grease and flour paper.

2. Stir together flour and next 3 ingredients.

3. Whisk together sugar and oil in a large bowl until well blended. Add eggs, 1 at a time, whisking until blended after each addition. Add flour mixture, stirring just until blended. Fold in carrots and next 3 ingredients. Spoon batter into prepared cake pans.

4. Bake at 350° for 40 to 45 minutes or until a wooden pick inserted in center comes out clean. Cool in pans on wire racks 15 minutes. Remove from pans to wire racks; discard parchment paper. Cool completely (about 1 hour).

5. Prepare Frosting: Beat goat cheese and butter at medium speed with an electric mixer 2 to 3 minutes or until creamy. Add powdered sugar, 1 cup at a time, beating at low speed until blended after each addition.

6. Split vanilla bean; scrape seeds into goat cheese mixture. Beat 30 seconds to 1 minute or until frosting is light and fluffy. Spread 1/2 cup frosting between cake layers; spread remaining frosting on top and sides of cake.

Fresh Berry Topping

Use this sweet topper as the crown jewel on a purchased or homemade cheesecake. (Visit southernliving.com/cheesecake for recipes.) Also use the fruit over pancakes or ice cream.

Arrange 4 cups **assorted fresh berries, pitted cherries,** or sliced **strawberries** over **cheesecake.** Stir together 1/2 cup **seedless blackberry jam** and 1/4 cup **orange liqueur;** drizzle over fruit. Garnish with **fresh mint.**

NOT-SO-HUMBLE

★

PIES

FROM THE SOUTH'S MOST TRUSTED KITCHEN

20 ✕ 13

SHOW OFF WITH TWO SOUTHERN SPECIALTIES: **HOMEMADE PIE** AND **HEIRLOOM CHINA**

Coconut-Pumpkin Chiffon Pie

MAKES 8 TO 10 SERVINGS
HANDS-ON 35 MIN.
TOTAL 2 HOURS, 15 MIN.

Make and refrigerate without the topping a day ahead. Whip and add the topping before serving.

- ½ cup milk
- 2 envelopes unflavored gelatin
- 1 (15-oz.) can pumpkin
- 1 tsp. ground cinnamon
- ½ tsp. table salt
- ½ tsp. ground nutmeg
- ½ tsp. ground ginger
- 4 large pasteurized eggs, separated
- 1 cup plus 3 Tbsp. sugar, divided
- 1¼ cups sweetened shredded coconut, divided
- 1 cup graham cracker crumbs
- 5 Tbsp. butter, melted
- 2 cups heavy cream
- 2 tsp. vanilla extract

1. Preheat oven to 350°. Whisk together milk and gelatin in a 3-qt. saucepan; let stand 1 minute. Cook over medium heat, stirring constantly, 1 minute or until gelatin dissolves. Stir in pumpkin, next 4 ingredients, egg yolks, and ½ cup sugar. Cook, stirring constantly, 5 to 7 minutes or until slightly thickened. (Do not boil.) Transfer to a bowl; chill 40 minutes or to room temperature, stirring halfway through.

2. Meanwhile, place coconut in a single layer on a baking sheet, and bake at 350° for 8 to 10 minutes or until golden, stirring occasionally.

3. Stir together graham cracker crumbs, butter, 1 Tbsp. sugar, and 1 cup coconut. Press mixture into a 10-inch pie plate. Freeze 10 minutes or until ready to use.

4. Beat egg whites at high speed with a heavy-duty electric stand mixer, using whisk attachment, 8 minutes or until soft peaks form. Add ¼ cup sugar, and beat 2 to 3 minutes or until stiff peaks form.

5. Gradually fold egg whites into pumpkin mixture. Pour into crust. Chill 2 hours or until set.

6. Beat cream and vanilla at medium speed 1 to 2 minutes or until soft peaks form. Add remaining 6 Tbsp. sugar, and beat 1 to 2 minutes or until stiff peaks form. Top pie with cream mixture and remaining ¼ cup coconut. Serve immediately.

Recipe from Barbara Delaney, Columbia, MD

Mocha-Espresso Cream Pie

MAKES 6 TO 8 SERVINGS

HANDS-ON 20 MIN.

TOTAL 5 HOURS, 5 MIN.

CRUST

- 1 (9-oz.) package chocolate wafers
- 1/2 cup finely chopped toasted pecans
- 1/2 cup butter, melted

FILLING

- 2/3 cup sugar
- 1/4 cup cornstarch
- 2 Tbsp. instant espresso
- 2 cups half-and-half
- 4 large egg yolks
- 2 oz. bittersweet chocolate baking squares, chopped
- 2 Tbsp. butter

TOPPING

Coffee Whipped Cream

1. Prepare Crust: Preheat oven to 350°. Pulse chocolate wafers in a food processor 8 to 10 times or until finely crushed. Stir together wafer crumbs, pecans, and butter. Press on bottom, up sides, and onto lip of a lightly greased 9-inch pie plate. Bake 10 minutes. Cool completely (about 30 minutes).

2. Prepare Filling: Whisk together sugar and next 2 ingredients in a large saucepan. Whisk together half-and-half and yolks in a large bowl. Gradually whisk egg mixture into sugar mixture; bring to a boil over medium heat, whisking constantly. Boil 1 minute, whisking constantly; remove from heat.

3. Microwave chocolate in a small bowl at HIGH 1 1/2 minutes or until melted, stirring at 30-second intervals. Whisk 2 Tbsp. butter and melted chocolate into sugar mixture; spoon into prepared crust. Place plastic wrap directly onto filling (to prevent a film from forming). Chill 4 to 24 hours. Top with Coffee Whipped Cream just before serving.

COFFEE WHIPPED CREAM Beat 2 cups **heavy cream** and 1 Tbsp. **coffee liqueur** at medium-high speed with an electric mixer until foamy; gradually add 1/3 cup **sugar**, beating until soft peaks form. **MAKES** about 3 1/2 cups

Note: We tested with Kahlúa coffee liqueur.

Salted Caramel-Chocolate Pecan Pie

MAKES 8 SERVINGS

HANDS-ON 25 MIN.

TOTAL 1 HOUR, 20 MIN.

A cross between a fudge pie and pecan pie, this is all the more stunning if you arrange the pecans from the center in a spiral pattern. (Pictured on page 1)

CHOCOLATE FILLING

- 1 1/2 cups sugar
- 3/4 cup butter, melted
- 1/3 cup all-purpose flour
- 1/3 cup 100% cacao unsweetened cocoa
- 1 Tbsp. light corn syrup
- 1 tsp. vanilla extract
- 3 large eggs
- 1 cup toasted chopped pecans
- 1 (9-inch) unbaked deep-dish piecrust shell

SALTED CARAMEL TOPPING

- 3/4 cup sugar
- 1 Tbsp. fresh lemon juice
- 1/3 cup heavy cream
- 4 Tbsp. butter
- 1/4 tsp. table salt
- 2 cups toasted pecan halves
- 1/2 tsp. sea salt

1. Prepare Filling: Preheat oven to 350°. Stir together first 6 ingredients in a large bowl. Add eggs, stirring until well blended. Fold in chopped pecans. Pour mixture into pie shell.

2. Bake at 350° for 35 minutes. (Filling will be loose but will set as it cools.) Remove from oven to a wire rack.

3. Prepare Topping: Bring 3/4 cup sugar, 1 Tbsp. lemon juice, and 1/4 cup water to a boil in a medium saucepan over high heat. (Do not stir.) Boil, swirling occasionally after sugar begins to change color, 8 minutes or until dark amber. (Do not walk away from the pan, as the sugar could burn quickly once it begins to change color.) Remove from heat; add cream and 4 Tbsp. butter. Stir constantly until bubbling stops and butter is incorporated (about 1 minute). Stir in table salt.

4. Arrange pecan halves on pie. Top with warm caramel. Cool 15 minutes; sprinkle with sea salt.

Note: We tested with Hershey's 100% Cacao Special Dark Cocoa and Maldon Sea Salt Flakes.

Pear-Rosemary Pie with Cheddar Crust

MAKES 8 SERVINGS

HANDS-ON 30 MIN.

TOTAL 3 HOURS

Cheddar cheese gives this crust a unique, out-of-this-world flakiness.

- 2 1/2 cups all-purpose flour
- 1/8 tsp. table salt
- 3 Tbsp. granulated sugar, divided
- 1 cup finely grated sharp Cheddar cheese
- 1 cup cold butter, cut into 1/2-inch cubes
- 3 Tbsp. cold heavy cream
- 4 to 5 Tbsp. ice-cold water
- 3 1/4 lb. Bartlett pears, peeled and sliced
- 1/3 cup firmly packed light brown sugar
- 2 1/2 Tbsp. cornstarch
- 2 Tbsp. fresh lemon juice
- 1 1/2 tsp. vanilla extract
- 1 tsp. chopped fresh rosemary
- 1/4 tsp. table salt
- 1 large egg, lightly beaten

1. Pulse first 2 ingredients and 2 Tbsp. granulated sugar in a food processor 3 or 4 times or until combined. Add cheese and butter; pulse 10 to 12 times or until mixture resembles coarse meal. Drizzle cream and water over mixture; pulse 4 or 5 times or just until moist clumps form. Divide dough in half, and flatten into disks. Wrap disks in plastic wrap, and chill 30 minutes.

2. Meanwhile, stir together pears, next 6 ingredients, and remaining 1 Tbsp. granulated sugar in a large bowl.

3. Preheat oven to 400°. Roll 1 dough disk into a 12 1/2-inch circle on a lightly floured surface. Fit piecrust into a 10-inch pie plate; fold edges under, and crimp. Spoon pear mixture into crust.

4. Roll remaining dough disk to 1/8-inch thickness on a lightly floured surface, and cut into 6 (2 1/2-inch) strips. Arrange strips in a lattice design over filling; press ends of strips into crust, sealing to bottom crust, and crimp. (Reroll scraps if you do not have enough strips to cover pie.) Whisk together egg and 2 Tbsp. water. Brush lattice with egg mixture.

5. Bake at 400° for 55 minutes to 1 hour, shielding with aluminum foil after 30 minutes to prevent excessive browning. Let cool on a wire rack 1 hour.

PEAR-CHERRY PIE WITH CHEDDAR CRUST Prepare as directed, adding 1 cup dried cherries to pear mixture and increasing cornstarch to 1/4 cup.

Apple Slab Pie

MAKES 12 TO 14 SERVINGS
HANDS-ON 35 MIN.
TOTAL 3 HOURS, 5 MIN.

Baked in a jelly-roll pan, this rectangular pie feeds a crowd.

CRUST

5	cups all-purpose flour
2	Tbsp. granulated sugar
1	Tbsp. ground cinnamon
1	tsp. table salt
2	cups cold butter, cubed
1 1/2	cups ice-cold water

FILLING

2	Tbsp. butter
3	lb. tart apples, peeled and sliced (about 6 large)
1	cup dried cranberries
1/2	cup firmly packed dark brown sugar
1/2	cup amaretto liqueur (optional)
6	Tbsp. cornstarch
3	Tbsp. fresh lemon juice
1 1/2	tsp. table salt
1	tsp. ground ginger
1	tsp. ground cinnamon
1	tsp. ground allspice

REMAINING INGREDIENTS

2	Tbsp. heavy cream
1	large egg

1. Prepare Crust: Stir together first 4 ingredients in a large bowl. Cut butter into flour mixture with a pastry blender or fork until butter is pea-sized. Gently stir in 3/4 cup ice-cold water until blended. Add remaining 3/4 cup ice-cold water, and stir until a dough forms. Shape into a ball, using your hands. (If dough feels dry, add up to 4 Tbsp. cold water, 1 Tbsp. at a time, until dough comes together. Butter should not be fully incorporated into dough; you will be able to see small butter pieces.)

2. Turn dough out onto a floured surface, and knead lightly 10 times or until dough begins to look smooth. Divide in half, and shape into two 7- x 5-inch rectangles. Wrap rectangles in plastic wrap, and chill 1 hour.

3. Prepare Filling: Melt 2 Tbsp. butter in a Dutch oven or large saucepan over medium heat. Add apples; cook, stirring occasionally, 3 minutes. Increase heat to medium-high, and add cranberries and next 8 ingredients. Cook, stirring occasionally, 3 minutes. Remove from heat, and chill 20 minutes.

4. Assemble Pie: Preheat oven to 375°. Line a 15- x 10-inch jelly-roll pan with 2 layers of aluminum foil, allowing 2 to 3 inches to extend over short sides.

5. Roll 1 dough rectangle into a 20- x 15-inch rectangle (about 1/4 inch thick) on lightly floured surface. Transfer to prepared pan, allowing dough to hang over edges. Gently press dough into corners of pan. Top with apple mixture. Chill until ready to use.

6. Whisk together cream and egg. Roll remaining dough into a 20- x 15-inch rectangle (about 1/4 inch thick) on lightly floured surface. Place dough over apple mixture. Trim excess dough from top and the bottom crusts; crimp edges. Cut slits in top for steam to escape. Brush with egg mixture.

7. Bake at 375° for 1 hour to 1 hour and 10 minutes or until golden and bubbly. Cool on a wire rack 10 minutes. Lift pie from pan, using foil sides as handles, and transfer to wire rack. Serve warm or at room temperature.

Note: Dough may be chilled up to 3 days or frozen up to 1 month.

Apple Butter Pie

MAKES 8 SERVINGS
HANDS-ON 15 MIN.
TOTAL 2 HOURS, 50 MIN.

- 8 oz. gingersnaps
- 3 Tbsp. butter, melted
- 1 (14-oz.) can sweetened condensed milk
- 1 cup spiced apple butter
- 3 large egg yolks
- 1 1/2 tsp. apple cider vinegar
  Garnishes: whipped cream, crumbled gingersnaps

1. Preheat oven to 350°. Pulse gingersnaps in a food processor 20 times or until finely ground. With processor running, pour butter through food chute, processing until blended. Press mixture into a 9-inch pie plate.

2. Bake at 350° for 15 minutes. Cool on a wire rack 5 minutes.

3. Meanwhile, whisk together sweetened condensed milk and next 3 ingredients. Pour into prepared crust. Bake at 350° for 15 minutes. Chill 2 to 24 hours.

Note: We tested with Smucker's Spiced Apple Butter.

Recipe from Sheri Castle, Chapel Hill, NC

Sliced Sweet Potato Pie

MAKES 8 SERVINGS
HANDS-ON 20 MIN.
TOTAL 3 HOURS, 15 MIN.

We love the layered look of this ever-so-sweet streusel-topped treat.

- 1/2 (14.1-oz.) package refrigerated piecrusts
- 2 1/2 lb. small, slender sweet potatoes, peeled and cut into 1/8-inch to 1/4-inch rounds
- 1/2 cup granulated sugar
- 2 (4- x 1-inch) orange peel strips
- 1/2 cup firmly packed light brown sugar
- 2 Tbsp. all-purpose flour
- 2 tsp. pumpkin pie spice
- 1 tsp. loosely packed orange zest
- 1/2 tsp. table salt
  Streusel Topping

1. Preheat oven to 375°. Fit piecrust into a 9-inch deep-dish pie plate; fold edges under, and crimp. Bring potatoes, next 2 ingredients, and 1 cup water to a boil in a Dutch oven. Cover, reduce heat to medium, and simmer 6 minutes or until potatoes are just tender.

2. Transfer potatoes to a large colander, reserving cooking liquid. Rinse potatoes with cold water. Transfer cooking liquid and orange peel strips to a small saucepan, and bring to a boil over medium-high heat. Reduce heat to medium, and simmer, stirring occasionally, 10 to 12 minutes or until reduced to 1/4 cup. Reserve 2 Tbsp. potato-orange liquid; discard remaining liquid.

3. Transfer potatoes to a bowl; toss with brown sugar, next 4 ingredients, and reserved 2 Tbsp. potato-orange liquid. Spoon into crust; sprinkle with streusel.

4. Bake at 375° for 1 hour and 5 minutes to 1 hour and 15 minutes, shielding with aluminum foil after 30 minutes to prevent excessive browning. Cool completely.

STREUSEL TOPPING Stir together 3/4 cup **coarsely chopped pecans**, 1/4 cup plus 1 Tbsp. **all-purpose flour**, 1/4 cup firmly packed **light brown sugar**, 3 Tbsp. **melted butter**, 1 Tbsp. **granulated sugar**, 1/4 tsp. **pumpkin pie spice**, and 1/8 tsp. **table salt.** Let stand 30 minutes. Crumble into small pieces. **MAKES** 1 1/4 cups

Recipe from Sheri Castle, Chapel Hill, NC

TEST KITCHEN  INTERVENTION

HOW TO MAKE THE MOST OF YOUR GREATEST
KITCHEN ALLY: THE FREEZER

① CAKES AND PIE DOUGH Get a jump start on dessert. Wrap each baked layer of cake or disk of uncooked pie dough tightly in plastic wrap, and freeze in zip-top freezer bags.

② CASSEROLES Save time (and dirty dishes!) with lidded bakeware that goes from oven to freezer to fridge with ease ($14.95; *crateandbarrel.com*).

③ SMALL SERVINGS Portion individual servings and freeze in containers that are freezer- and microwave-safe. This allows you to reheat dinner for one, two, or the entire family. (Five 24-oz. containers start at $2.57. Visit *glad.com* for a list of online retailers.)

④ LIQUID ASSETS Small plastic freezer jars are perfect for stocks, gravies, cranberry sauces, or individual portions of soups and stews. Liquids expand when frozen, so leave 1/2 inch of headspace below the rim of the container. (Three 8-oz. plastic jars start at $3.99 at *kmart.com*.)

⑤ SINGLE ITEMS To freeze big items like cooked potatoes (recipe on page 285) and meatballs, arrange in a single layer on a jelly-roll pan, and freeze 1 to 2 hours; transfer to a zip-top bag. You'll avoid one frozen mass, plus single servings thaw faster.

⑥ FAMILY-SIZE PORTIONS Use empty cereal boxes to save space. Line an upright box with a zip-top bag (like lining a trash can). Fill, then seal the bag and freeze flat while still in the box. Once frozen, remove the bag from the box and stack.

The Fix & Freeze Recipes

▶ Fool your crowd into thinking you spent all day at the stove with these easy, freezer-friendly recipes. Find more smart freezer tips and techniques on previous page.

Jambalaya

MAKES 8 TO 10 SERVINGS
HANDS-ON 30 MIN.
TOTAL 1 HOUR

Build deep flavors by sautéing the aromatic trinity of onion, celery, and pepper in the andouille drippings with herbs, garlic, and spices.

- 1   lb. andouille sausage, sliced
- 2   Tbsp. canola oil
- 2   cups diced sweet onion
- 1   cup diced celery
- 1   large red bell pepper, diced
- 4   garlic cloves, minced
- 1   bay leaf
- 2   tsp. Creole seasoning
- 1   tsp. dried thyme
- 1   tsp. dried oregano
- 2   (10-oz.) cans diced tomatoes and green chiles, drained
- 3   cups chicken broth
- 2   cups uncooked long-grain rice
- 2   cups shredded cooked chicken
- 1   lb. peeled, medium-size raw shrimp, deveined
- ½   cup chopped fresh flat-leaf parsley
     Garnish: chopped green onions

1. Cook sausage in hot oil in a Dutch oven over medium-high heat, stirring constantly, 5 minutes or until browned. Remove sausage with a slotted spoon.

2. Add diced onion and next 7 ingredients to hot drippings; sauté 5 minutes or until vegetables are tender. Stir in tomatoes, next 3 ingredients, and sausage. Bring to a boil over high heat. Cover, reduce heat to medium, and simmer, stirring occasionally, 20 minutes or until rice is tender.

3. Stir in shrimp; cover and cook 5 minutes or just until shrimp turn pink. Stir in parsley. Serve immediately.

To Freeze: Prepare recipe as directed. Line bottom and sides of a 13- x 9-inch baking dish with heavy-duty aluminum foil, allowing 2 to 3 inches to extend over sides; fill with jambalaya. Cover and freeze. To

serve, remove foil, return casserole to original baking dish; cover and thaw in refrigerator 24 hours. Let stand at room temperature 30 minutes. Bake at 350° until thoroughly heated.

Sausage-and-Grits Quiche

MAKES 6 SERVINGS
HANDS-ON 35 MIN.
TOTAL 2 HOURS, 10 MIN.

Impress your brunch company with this clever, simple spin on a traditional quiche.

- 1   (10-oz.) package frozen chopped spinach
- 1   (16-oz.) package ground pork sausage
- 2   cups reduced-sodium chicken broth
- 1   cup whipping cream
- ½   tsp. table salt
- 1   cup uncooked regular grits
- 1   cup grated Asiago cheese
- ¼   tsp. ground black pepper
- 1   cup (4 oz.) freshly shredded white Cheddar cheese, divided
- 3   large eggs, lightly beaten
- 1½ Tbsp. plain white cornmeal

1. Thaw spinach; drain well, pressing between paper towels.

2. Cook sausage in a large skillet over medium-high heat, stirring often, 5 minutes or until sausage crumbles and is no longer pink; remove from skillet, and drain.

3. Preheat oven to 350°. Bring broth, cream, and salt to a boil in a large saucepan over medium-high heat. Gradually whisk in grits, and return to a boil. Cover, reduce heat to medium-low, and simmer, whisking occasionally, 12 to 15 minutes or until thickened. Remove from heat; stir in Asiago, pepper, and ¾ cup Cheddar until melted. (Mixture will be very thick.)

4. Gradually stir about one-fourth of hot grits into eggs; stir egg mixture into remaining hot grits. Stir in spinach and sausage until blended.

COOKED RICE
Make a double batch to spin this inexpensive staple into countless meals. Cool the rice, portion, and freeze in a zip-top freezer bag. To reheat: Transfer rice to a bowl, and sprinkle with water. Cover with a paper towel; microwave on HIGH 2 minutes.

5. Sprinkle bottom and sides of a lightly greased 10-inch deep-dish pie plate with cornmeal. Spoon grits mixture into pie plate; sprinkle with remaining Cheddar cheese.

6. Bake at 350° for 55 minutes or until set. Remove from oven to a wire rack, and cool 30 minutes.

To Freeze: Prepare recipe as directed through Step 5. Cover tightly with plastic wrap and heavy-duty aluminum foil. Place quiche in a 2-gal. zip-top plastic freezer bag. Freeze up to 1 month. Thaw in refrigerator 24 hours. Let stand at room temperature 30 minutes, and bake as directed.

Note: Recipe may be doubled and baked in a 13- x 9-inch baking dish for 1 hour.

Four-Ingredient Slow-Cooker Pot Roast

MAKES 6 TO 8 SERVINGS
HANDS-ON 20 MIN.
TOTAL 8 HOURS, 20 MIN.

For freezing instructions, see our tip below.

- 1 (3- to 4-lb.) chuck roast, trimmed
- 1 Tbsp. canola oil
- 1 (12-oz.) can beer
- 1 (0.7-oz.) envelope Italian dressing mix

Brown roast in hot oil in a skillet over medium-high heat 3 to 5 minutes on each side; transfer to a 6-qt. slow cooker. Whisk together beer and dressing mix; pour over roast. Cover; cook on LOW 8 to 10 hours or until tender. Remove roast from slow cooker. Skim fat from sauce; serve with roast.

SLOW-COOKED MEATS

Freeze pot roasts and braised pork shoulders in their cooking liquid—it preserves the juicy flavor and tender texture while guarding against freezer burn. Portion cooled meat into zip-top freezer bags, add cooking liquid, and freeze up to 1 month.

Curried Chicken Chowder

MAKES ABOUT 16 CUPS
HANDS-ON 40 MIN.
TOTAL 1 HOUR

- 2 cups diced sweet onion (about 1 large)
- 1 cup diced celery
- 1 cup diced carrots
- 2 Tbsp. canola oil
- 2 garlic cloves, minced
- 6 cups chicken broth
- 1 lb. Yukon gold potatoes, peeled and cubed
- 1 lb. sweet potatoes, peeled and cubed
- 4 cups shredded cooked chicken
- 3 cups fresh yellow corn kernels (about 6 ears)
- 2 cups uncooked, shelled frozen edamame (green soybeans)
- 1 (13.5-oz.) can unsweetened coconut milk
- 1 Tbsp. curry powder
- 2 tsp. table salt
- 1 tsp. ground black pepper
  Toppings: toasted coconut, green onions, peanuts, lime wedges

Sauté first 3 ingredients in hot oil in a large Dutch oven or stockpot over medium-high heat 5 minutes or until tender; add garlic, and sauté 1 minute. Add broth and next 9 ingredients; bring to a boil, stirring often. Reduce heat to medium, and simmer, stirring occasionally, 20 to 25 minutes or until vegetables are tender. Season with salt and pepper to taste. Serve with desired toppings.

To Freeze: Cool hot soup completely. Transfer to airtight containers or zip-top freezer bags. Freeze up to 1 month. Thaw in refrigerator 8 hours.

Twice-Baked Potatoes Four Ways

MAKES 8 POTATOES
HANDS-ON 15 MIN.
TOTAL 1 HOUR, 40 MIN.

- 4 (10- to 12-oz.) russet potatoes
- ½ (8-oz.) package ⅓-less-fat cream cheese, cubed and softened
- ½ cup milk
  Desired Potato Filling

1. Preheat oven to 400°. Pierce potatoes several times with a fork, and bake directly on oven rack 1 hour or until potatoes are tender. (Baking directly on the rack keeps skins crisp and firm to hold the filling.) Cool 10 minutes.

2. Cut potatoes in half lengthwise; carefully scoop pulp into a large bowl, leaving shells intact. Mash together potato pulp, cream cheese, and milk; stir in desired Potato Filling. Spoon mixture into potato shells, and place on a lightly greased baking sheet.

3. Bake at 400° for 15 to 20 minutes or until thoroughly heated.

To Freeze: Prepare through Step 2. Freeze potatoes on a baking sheet 1 hour or until firm. Wrap each potato in plastic wrap, place in a zip-top plastic freezer bag, and freeze up to 1 month. Thaw in refrigerator overnight. To serve, unwrap potatoes, and bake at 350° for 45 minutes or until hot. Or microwave at HIGH 5 minutes or until hot, checking at 1-minute intervals.

Potato Fillings

CHICKEN, BROCCOLI, CHEDDAR: Melt 2 Tbsp. **butter** in a large skillet over medium-high heat; add 1 **small onion,** diced, and 1 (10-oz.) package frozen **chopped broccoli,** thawed and drained; sauté 5 minutes or until tender. Stir together broccoli mixture, 2 cups chopped cooked **chicken,** 1½ cups (6 oz.) shredded **sharp Cheddar cheese,** ¾ tsp. **table salt,** and ½ tsp. **freshly ground black pepper. TOTAL TIME** 20 min.

BBQ PORK AND PEPPER JACK: Stir together 2 cups (about ½ lb.) chopped **barbecued pork** (without sauce), 1½ cups (6 oz.) shredded **pepper Jack cheese,** ⅓ cup minced **green onions,** and 4 tsp. **Ranch dressing mix.** Serve potatoes with barbecue sauce. **TOTAL TIME** 10 min.

CARAMELIZED ONION, BACON, AND GOAT CHEESE: Melt 2 Tbsp. **butter** in a large skillet over medium-high heat; add 2 cups chopped **red onion** and 2 tsp. **sugar,** and sauté 10 to 12 minutes or until caramelized. Stir in 2 Tbsp. **dry sherry,** and cook 1 minute or until liquid evaporates, stirring to loosen particles from bottom of skillet. Stir together onion mixture; 1 (4-oz.) **goat cheese log,** softened; 8 cooked and crumbled **bacon slices;** 2 Tbsp. chopped **fresh thyme;** ¾ tsp. **salt;** and ½ tsp. **ground black pepper. TOTAL TIME** 20 min.

Thanksgiving Appetizers

▶ A taste of who and what online got the most raves in the *Southern Living* Test Kitchen

RECIPES FROM
THE
SOUTH'S
Tastiest
BLOGS
★

From the Kitchen of
MARINA DELIO

YUMMYMUMMYKITCHEN.COM
SANTA BARBARA, CA

"These cranberries look like beautiful little jewels and can be prepared two days in advance." Serve them with baked Brie or as a pretty garnish for cakes or pies.

SPARKLING CRANBERRIES

Cook 1 cup **pure maple syrup** in a saucepan over medium-low heat 1 to 2 minutes. (Don't let syrup get too hot or cranberries will pop.) Remove from heat; stir in 2 cups **fresh cranberries.** Cover and chill 8 to 12 hours. Place 1 cup **sugar** in a large bowl or baking dish. Drain cranberries in a colander (about 15 minutes). Add 4 to 5 cranberries at a time to sugar; gently toss to coat. Repeat with remaining cranberries. Place cranberries in a single layer on a **parchment paper**-lined baking sheet; let stand until completely dry. **MAKES** 2 cups

From the Kitchen of
MEG VAN DER KRUIK

BEARDANDBONNET.COM
ATLANTA, GA

"This is my go-to fall snack when I'm craving guilty pleasures like pumpkin pie, because I could eat a whole pie by myself!"

PUMPKIN PIE-SPICED TRAIL MIX

Preheat oven to 350°. Spread 1 cup **raw pecan halves,** 1/2 cup raw **cashews,** and 1/2 cup **raw almonds** in a single layer on a **parchment paper**-lined baking sheet. Bake 10 minutes or until lightly toasted and fragrant, stirring once. Remove from oven, and transfer to a bowl. Reduce oven temperature to 300°. Bring 1/4 cup **maple syrup,** 1 tsp. **vanilla extract,** 1/4 tsp. **ground cinnamon,** 1/4 tsp. **ground ginger,** 1/8 tsp. **ground nutmeg,** and a pinch each of **ground cloves** and **table salt** to a rolling boil in a saucepan over medium-high heat. Drizzle hot syrup over nut mixture in bowl; toss to coat. Spread coated nut mixture in a single layer on same parchment-lined baking sheet. Bake at 300° for 25 to 30 minutes or until glaze begins to harden. Spread mixture onto lightly greased parchment paper, and cool completely. Transfer to a bowl, and stir in 1/4 cup each **dried cranberries** and 1/2-inch-thick **crystallized ginger slices. MAKES** about 3 cups

From the Kitchen of
NEALEY DOZIER

DIXIECAVIAR.COM
ATLANTA, GA

"This bruschetta is great for holiday gatherings. It's hearty enough to satisfy but not decadent enough to distract from the main event."

MUSHROOM-AND-ARUGULA BRUSCHETTA

Preheat oven to 350°. Bake 4 (1/2-inch-thick) **sourdough bread slices** on a wire rack on a baking sheet 12 to 14 minutes or until toasted. Meanwhile, melt 2 Tbsp. **butter** in a large nonstick skillet over medium heat. Add 1 large **shallot,** minced, and cook, stirring often, 4 to 5 minutes or until softened. Add 1 (8-oz.) package sliced fresh **mushrooms,** and cook 8 to 10 minutes or until golden brown and tender. Stir in 1 Tbsp. **all-purpose flour,** and cook, stirring constantly, 2 minutes or until blended. Add 3 Tbsp. **sherry,** and cook, stirring constantly, 1 to 2 minutes or until liquid evaporates. Add 1/2 cup **vegetable broth,** and simmer 3 to 4 minutes or until sauce thickens. Stir in 1 Tbsp. chopped fresh **flat-leaf parsley** and 2 tsp. fresh **lemon juice.** Add **table salt** and **black pepper** to taste. Remove from heat, and let stand 5 minutes. Toss 2 cups **baby arugula** with 2 tsp. **olive oil.** Spoon one-fourth of mushroom mixture onto each piece of toast. Top each with 1/2 cup arugula mixture and 1 (1-oz.) **goat cheese slice.** Add desired amount of table salt and black pepper; serve immediately. **MAKES** 4 servings

A Note from Nealey: "For an extra layer of flavor, rub toasted bread with a garlic clove and brush with olive oil, or stir a dollop of sour cream into the mushroom mixture after cooking."

December

THE 12 days OF CHRISTMAS

PRESENTED BY THE SOUTH'S MOST TRUSTED KITCHEN. WHEN IT COMES TO ENTERTAINING, A PARTRIDGE IN A PEAR TREE FEEDS ONLY A FAMILY OF THREE. SO HERE'S A 12-STEP SONG OF RECIPES FOR EVERY MAGICAL MOMENT OF THE SEASON, FROM ROASTS AND SIDES TO COOKIES AND, OF COURSE, ONE BIG WHITE CAKE. COOK (AND SING ALONG) WITH US NOW ....

1 Magical White Cake

Take a bow as you reveal the revelry inside this sophisticated cake

Red Velvet-White Chocolate Cheesecake

MAKES 10 TO 12 SERVINGS
HANDS-ON 45 MIN.
TOTAL 13 HOURS, 45 MIN.

CHEESECAKE LAYERS

- 2 (8-in.) round disposable aluminum foil cake pans
- 1 (12-oz.) package white chocolate morsels
- 5 (8-oz.) packages cream cheese, softened
- 1 cup granulated sugar
- 2 large eggs
- 1 Tbsp. vanilla extract

RED VELVET LAYERS

- 1 cup butter, softened
- 2 1/2 cups granulated sugar
- 6 large eggs
- 3 cups all-purpose flour
- 3 Tbsp. unsweetened cocoa
- 1/4 tsp. baking soda
- 1 (8-oz.) container sour cream
- 2 tsp. vanilla extract
- 2 (1-oz.) bottles red liquid food coloring
- 3 (8-in.) round disposable aluminum foil cake pans

WHITE CHOCOLATE FROSTING

- 2 (4-oz.) white chocolate baking bars, chopped
- 1/2 cup boiling water
- 1 cup butter, softened
- 1 (32-oz.) package powdered sugar, sifted
- 1/8 tsp. table salt

GARNISHES

Store-bought coconut candies
White Candy Leaves

1. Prepare Cheesecake Layers. Preheat oven to 300°. Line bottom and sides of 2 disposable cake pans with aluminum foil, allowing 2 to 3 inches to extend over sides; lightly grease foil.

2. Microwave white chocolate morsels in a microwave-safe bowl according to package directions; cool 10 minutes.

3. Beat cream cheese and melted chocolate at medium speed with an electric mixer until creamy; gradually add 1 cup sugar, beating well. Add 2 eggs, 1 at a time, beating just until yellow disappears after each addition. Stir in 1 Tbsp. vanilla. Pour into prepared pans.

4. Bake at 300° for 30 to 35 minutes or until almost set. Turn oven off. Let cheesecake stand in oven, with door closed, 30 minutes. Remove cheesecake from oven to wire racks; cool completely (about 1 1/2 hours). Cover and chill 8 hours, or cover and freeze 24 hours to 2 days.

5. Prepare Red Velvet Layers. Preheat oven to 350°. Beat 1 cup butter at medium speed with a heavy-duty electric stand mixer until creamy. Gradually add 2 1/2 cups sugar, beating until light and fluffy. Add 6 eggs, 1 at a time, beating just until blended after each addition.

6. Stir together flour and next 2 ingredients; add to butter mixture alternately with sour cream, beginning and ending with flour mixture. Beat at low speed just until blended after each addition. Stir in 2 tsp. vanilla; stir in red food coloring. Spoon batter into 3 greased and floured 8-inch disposable cake pans.

7. Bake at 350° for 20 to 24 minutes or until a wooden pick inserted in center comes out clean. Cool in pans on wire racks 10 minutes. Remove from pans to wire racks, and cool completely (about 1 hour).

8. Prepare White Chocolate Frosting. Whisk together white chocolate and 1/2 cup boiling water until chocolate melts. Cool 20 minutes; chill 30 minutes.

9. Beat 1 cup butter and chilled chocolate mixture at low speed until blended. Beat at medium speed 1 minute. Increase speed to high, and beat 2 to 3 minutes or until fluffy. Gradually add powdered sugar and salt, beating at low speed until blended. Increase speed to high; beat 1 to 2 minutes or until smooth and fluffy.

10. Assemble Cake. Place 1 Red Velvet Layer on a serving platter. Top with 1 Cheesecake Layer. Repeat with remaining Red Velvet Layers and Cheesecake Layers, ending with a Red Velvet Layer on top. Spread top and sides of cake with White Chocolate Frosting. Store in refrigerator.

TO MAKE THE WHITE CANDY LEAVES:

1. Select nontoxic leaves such as bay leaves. Thoroughly wash leaves, and pat dry. Melt approximately 2-oz. vanilla candy coating in a saucepan over low heat until melted (about 3 minutes). Cool slightly. Working on parchment paper, spoon a 1/8-inch-thick layer of candy coating over backs of leaves, spreading to edges.

2. Gently transfer leaves, by their stems, to a clean sheet of parchment paper, resting them candy coating sides up; let stand until candy coating is firm (about 10 minutes). Gently grasp each leaf at stem end, and carefully peel the leaf away from the candy coating. Store candy leaves in a cold, dry place, such as an airtight container in the freezer, up to 1 week.

3. When garnishing, handle the leaves gently or they'll break or melt. Arrange candy leaves around the base of the cake and store-bought coconut candies (such as Confetteria Raffaello Almond Coconut Treats) in the center of the cake. Accent the top of the cake with additional candy leaves. For candy pearls, simply roll any remaining candy coating into balls, and let stand until dry.

2 Dozen Cookies

Talk about redefining a baker's dozen because you can never make and take too many

Ambrosia Macaroons

MAKES ABOUT 6 DOZEN
HANDS-ON 20 MIN.
TOTAL 1 HOUR, 15 MIN.

Soft and chewy, these perfectly sweet macaroons get most of their sugar from the flaked coconut and dried pineapple. Give them a different look by garnishing with different candied or dried fruit like orange peel or green cherries.

1	large egg white
1/4	cup sugar
1/4	cup butter, melted and cooled
1/4	cup fresh lime juice
1/2	tsp. vanilla extract
1/2	tsp. kosher salt
1	tsp. loosely packed orange zest
1/2	cup all-purpose flour
1	(14-oz.) package sweetened flaked coconut
1/2	cup finely diced dried pineapple
	Parchment paper
36	red maraschino cherries, drained, halved, and patted dry

1. Preheat oven to 350°. Beat egg white at high speed with a heavy-duty electric stand mixer, using whisk attachment, until foamy; gradually add sugar, 1 Tbsp. at a time, beating until soft peaks form.

2. Gently stir in butter and next 4 ingredients until blended. Stir in flour. Stir in coconut and pineapple until blended.

3. Drop batter by teaspoonfuls, 1 inch apart, onto 2 parchment paper-lined baking sheets. Place 1 cherry half in center of each cookie.

4. Bake at 350° for 12 to 15 minutes or until edges are golden brown, switching baking sheets halfway through. Cool on baking sheets 10 minutes; transfer cookies on parchment paper to wire racks, and cool completely.

Gritscotti

MAKES ABOUT 4 DOZEN
HANDS-ON 30 MIN.
TOTAL 3 HOURS

Grits + biscotti=Griscotti. After baking the logs, gently cut them with a serrated knife for even slices. If you end up with a few broken slices, bake them anyway and save the bits to sprinkle over yogurt at breakfast.

3	cups all-purpose flour
1 1/2	cups instant grits
1	Tbsp. baking powder
1	tsp. kosher salt
1 1/2	cups sugar
3/4	cup butter, softened
1	Tbsp. loosely packed orange zest
4	large eggs
1 1/2	cups sweetened dried cranberries
	Parchment paper

1. Preheat oven to 325°. Stir together first 4 ingredients in a large bowl. Beat sugar, butter, and orange zest at medium speed with an electric mixer until creamy. Add eggs, 1 at a time, beating well after each addition. Add flour mixture and cranberries, beating just until blended.

2. Divide dough into 3 equal portions; shape each portion into a 12 1/2- x 9-inch slightly flattened log, using lightly floured hands. Place about 2 inches apart on a parchment paper-lined baking sheet. Bake at 325° for 30 to 35 minutes or until light brown. Transfer to wire racks; cool 15 minutes. Reduce oven temperature to 300°.

3. Cut each log into 1/4- to 1/2-inch-thick slices with a serrated knife, using a gentle sawing motion. Place on 3 parchment paper-lined baking sheets.

4. Bake at 300° for 30 to 35 minutes or until golden brown. Cool on baking sheets 10 minutes; transfer cookies on parchment paper to wire racks, and cool.

Hummingbird Oatmeal Cookies

MAKES ABOUT 4 DOZEN
HANDS-ON 30 MIN.
TOTAL 1 HOUR, 40 MIN., INCLUDING FROSTING

No time to make the frosting? No problem. These moist oatmeal cookies are delicious on their own.

2	cups all-purpose flour
2	tsp. ground cinnamon
1	tsp. baking soda
1/2	tsp. kosher salt
1	cup butter, softened
1	cup firmly packed light brown sugar
1	tsp. vanilla extract
2	large eggs
1/2	medium-size ripe banana, mashed
1 1/2	cups regular oats
1	cup finely chopped pecans
1/2	cup finely chopped dried pineapple
	Parchment paper
	Cream Cheese Frosting
1/2	cup chopped dried banana chips
1/2	cup toasted coconut
1/2	cup toasted chopped pecans

1. Preheat oven to 350°. Stir together first 4 ingredients in a medium bowl until blended. Beat butter, brown sugar, and vanilla at medium speed with an electric mixer 3 to 5 minutes or until creamy. Add eggs, 1 at a time, beating well after each addition. Add flour mixture and banana; beat just until blended. Add oats and next 2 ingredients, and stir until blended.

2. Drop by heaping tablespoonfuls, 2 inches apart, onto 2 parchment paper-lined baking sheets. Flatten each, using a lightly floured flat-bottom glass.

3. Bake at 350° for 12 minutes or until golden brown. Cool 10 minutes on baking sheets; transfer cookies on parchment paper to wire racks, and cool.

4. Spread Cream Cheese Frosting over half of each cookie (about 1 1/2 tsp. per cookie); sprinkle with chopped banana chips, toasted coconut and chopped toasted pecans, pressing to adhere.

CREAM CHEESE FROSTING

MAKES ABOUT 2 CUPS
HANDS-ON 10 MIN.
TOTAL 10 MIN.

- 2 cups powdered sugar, sifted
- 1/2 (8-oz.) package cream cheese, softened
- 1 tsp. vanilla extract
- 1/2 tsp. kosher salt
- 1/4 cup heavy cream

Beat first 4 ingredients in a medium bowl at medium speed with an electric mixer 3 to 5 minutes or until smooth. Add cream, and beat until smooth.

Peppermint Divinity Bars

MAKES 32 BARS
HANDS-ON 50 MIN.
TOTAL 2 HOURS, 10 MIN.

This recipe must be made all the way through, from start to finish. For the best result, spread the warm divinity onto a still-warm cookie base. If the divinity is too cool, it will tear the cookie base as you spread it.

- 3 cups all-purpose flour
- 1 Tbsp. baking powder
- 1 tsp. kosher salt
- 1 vanilla bean
- 1 1/4 cups butter, softened
- 2 cups sugar, divided
  Parchment paper
- 1/4 cup light corn syrup
- 2 large egg whites
- 1 tsp. vanilla extract
- 1/4 tsp. peppermint extract
- 3/4 cup finely crushed hard peppermint candies

1. Preheat oven to 375°. Stir together first 3 ingredients in a medium bowl.

2. Split vanilla bean; scrape seeds into bowl of a heavy-duty electric mixer. Add butter and 1 cup sugar; beat at medium speed with a heavy-duty electric stand mixer 2 minutes or until creamy. Add flour mixture; beat just until blended.

3. Line bottom and sides of a 13- x 9-inch pan with parchment paper, allowing 2 to 3 inches to extend over sides; lightly grease parchment paper. Press dough into bottom of prepared pan. Bake at 375° for 20 minutes or until edges are golden brown.

4. Meanwhile, stir together corn syrup, 1/4 cup water, and remaining 1 cup sugar in a small saucepan over high heat, stirring just until sugar dissolves. Cook, without stirring, until a candy thermometer registers 250° (7 to 8 minutes).

5. While syrup cooks, beat egg whites at medium speed with a heavy-duty electric stand mixer, using whisk attachment, until foamy.

6. When syrup reaches 250°, beat egg whites at medium-high speed until soft peaks form. While mixer is running, gradually add hot syrup to egg whites. Increase speed to high, and beat until stiff peaks form. (Mixture should still be warm.) Add vanilla and peppermint extracts, and beat at medium speed just until combined. Fold in 1/2 cup crushed peppermint candies.

7. Working quickly, spread mixture on warm cookie base, using a butter knife or small offset spatula. Sprinkle with remaining 1/4 cup crushed peppermint candies, and cool completely (about 1 hour).

8. Lift mixture from pan, using parchment paper sides as handles; cut into 32 bars.

Sugar Cookie Cutouts with Holiday Glazes

MAKES ABOUT 4 DOZEN
HANDS-ON 30 MIN.
TOTAL 2 HOURS, 30 MIN., NOT INCLUDING GLAZES

We think 1/8 inch thick is the perfect thickness for a crisp, buttery cookie, but this dough can be rolled to 1/4-inch-thick if you prefer a softer texture.

- 4 cups all-purpose flour
- 1 tsp. baking powder
- 1/2 tsp. kosher salt
- 2 cups granulated sugar
- 1 1/4 cups butter, softened
- 2 tsp. vanilla extract
- 2 large eggs
  Parchment paper

1. Stir together first 3 ingredients in a large bowl.

2. Beat sugar and next 2 ingredients at medium speed with an electric mixer 2 to 3 minutes or until creamy. Add eggs, 1 at a time, beating after each addition. Gradually add flour mixture, beating just until blended.

3. Divide dough into 4 equal portions; flatten each portion into a 1/2-inch-thick disk. Wrap each disk in plastic wrap, and chill 30 minutes.

4. Working with 1 disk at a time, place disks on a lightly floured surface, and roll to 1/4-inch thickness. Cut with a 3-inch round cutter. Place 1 inch apart on 2 parchment paper-lined baking sheets. Chill 30 minutes.

5. Preheat oven to 350°. Bake 10 minutes or until edges begin to brown, switching baking sheets halfway through. Cool on baking sheets 10 minutes; transfer cookies on parchment paper to wire racks, and cool completely. Glaze as desired.

HOLIDAY GLAZES

Each recipe makes about 1 1/4 cups, enough to glaze 48 cookies.

EGGNOG

HANDS-ON 5 MIN.
TOTAL 5 MIN.

- 2 cups powdered sugar
- 3 Tbsp. plus 2 tsp. whipping cream
- 1 Tbsp. bourbon
- 1/4 tsp. kosher salt
- 1/4 tsp. freshly grated nutmeg

Stir together all ingredients until smooth. Stir in 1 tsp. water at a time, up to 2 tsp., until desired consistency.

CHICORY COFFEE

HANDS-ON 5 MIN.
TOTAL 5 MIN.

- 2 cups powdered sugar
- 2 Tbsp. strong brewed chicory coffee (such as Café Du Monde)
- 2 Tbsp. whipping cream
- 1/4 tsp. kosher salt
  Garnish: crushed coffee beans

Stir together first 4 ingredients until smooth. Stir in 1 tsp. water at a time, up to 2 tsp., until desired consistency. Garnish, if desired.

KEY LIME

HANDS-ON 5 MIN.
TOTAL 5 MIN.

- 2 cups powdered sugar
- 2 Tbsp. Key lime juice
- 2 Tbsp. sweetened condensed milk
- 1/4 tsp. kosher salt
- 2 tsp. loosely packed lime zest
  Garnish: thinly sliced lime peel strips

Stir together first 5 ingredients until smooth. Stir in 1 tsp. water at a time, up to 2 tsp., until desired consistency.

MULLED WINE GLAZE

HANDS-ON 20 MIN.
TOTAL 20 MIN.

- 1 cup red wine
  (such as Merlot)
- 1 Tbsp. light brown sugar
- 1/8 tsp. ground allspice
- 1/8 tsp. ground cloves
- 1/8 tsp. ground nutmeg
- 1 (4- x 1/2-inch) orange peel strip
- 1/8 tsp. ground cinnamon
- 1/4 tsp. kosher salt
- 2 cups powdered sugar

Bring first 7 ingredients to a boil in a small saucepan over high heat; boil 7 to 10 minutes or until reduced to 1/4 cup. Remove from heat, and stir in salt until dissolved. Discard orange peel, and stir in sugar until smooth.

Bourbon-Pecan Gingerbread Cookies

MAKES ABOUT 2 DOZEN
HANDS-ON 20 MIN.
TOTAL 1 HOUR, 30 MIN., INCLUDING GLAZE
(PLUS 12 HOURS FOR CHILLING)

Important: Bake the dough while cold. Otherwise it will spread too much, and the cookies will lose their fluffy, cakey texture.

- 4 cups all-purpose flour
- 2 tsp. kosher salt
- 2 tsp. ground cinnamon
- 2 tsp. ground ginger
- 1 tsp. baking soda
- 1/2 tsp. ground cloves
- 1/2 tsp. ground allspice
- 1/2 tsp. ground nutmeg
- 4 cups finely ground toasted pecans
- 2 cups firmly packed dark brown sugar
- 1/2 cup bourbon
- 1/2 cup buttermilk
- 2 Tbsp. unsulphured molasses
- 6 large eggs, lightly beaten
- 1 Tbsp. loosely packed lemon zest
- 1 Tbsp. loosely packed orange zest
  Parchment paper
- 2 cups toasted pecan halves
  Bourbon Glaze

1. Stir together first 8 ingredients in a large bowl. Stir together ground pecans and next 7 ingredients in another bowl. Stir bourbon mixture into flour mixture until smooth. Cover and chill 12 hours.

2. Preheat oven to 350°. Drop level portions of dough 2 inches apart, onto 2 parchment paper-lined baking sheets, using a 2-oz. ice-cream scoop. Place 3 pecan halves in a star pattern on each cookie.

3. Bake at 350° for 15 to 18 minutes or until lightly browned at edges. Cool on baking sheets 5 minutes. Drizzle with Bourbon Glaze. Transfer cookies to wire racks, and cool completely.

BOURBON GLAZE

MAKES ABOUT 1 1/2 CUPS
HANDS-ON 5 MIN.
TOTAL 5 MIN.

Stir together 6 Tbsp. **bourbon** and 3 cups **powdered sugar**, sifted, in a small bowl. Stir in 1 tsp. **water** at a time, up to 1 Tbsp., until desired consistency.

Praline Rugelach

MAKES ABOUT 4 DOZEN
HANDS-ON 40 MIN.
TOTAL 4 HOURS, 20 MIN.

For the best results, thoroughly chill the rolled cookies before baking. It will keep the filling from melting out of the dough.

- 1 (8-oz.) package cream cheese, softened
- 1 cup butter, softened
- 3/4 cup firmly packed light brown sugar, divided
- 3 tsp. vanilla extract, divided
- 1 tsp. kosher salt, divided
- 2 cups all-purpose flour
- 1/4 cup butter, melted and cooled
- 2 Tbsp. cane syrup*
- 2 Tbsp. whipping cream
- 1/2 tsp. ground cinnamon
- 2 cups finely chopped toasted pecans
  Parchment paper
- 1 large egg, lightly beaten

1. Beat cream cheese, softened butter, 1/4 cup brown sugar, 1 tsp. vanilla, and 1/2 tsp. salt, at medium speed with a heavy-duty electric stand mixer 2 to 3 minutes or until creamy. Gradually add flour, beating until smooth. Divide dough into 4 equal portions; flatten each into a disk. Wrap each disk in plastic wrap, and chill 2 hours.

2. Stir together melted butter, next 3 ingredients, and remaining 1/2 cup brown sugar, 2 tsp. vanilla, and 1/2 tsp. kosher salt.

3. Unwrap 1 dough disk, and roll into a 10-inch-wide circle (about 1/4 inch thick) on a lightly floured surface. Spread about 3 1/2 Tbsp. butter mixture in a thin layer on dough circle, leaving a 1/2-inch border around edges. Sprinkle 1/2 cup pecans over butter mixture, pressing to adhere. Cut circle into 12 wedges, and roll up wedges, starting at wide end. Place, point sides down, on a parchment paper-lined baking sheet. Chill 20 minutes. Repeat procedure with remaining dough, butter mixture, and pecans.

4. Preheat oven to 350°. Whisk together egg and 1 Tbsp. water. Brush each roll with egg mixture, and bake 18 to 22 minutes or until golden brown, switching baking sheets halfway through. Cool on baking sheet 10 minutes; transfer cookies on parchment paper to wire rack, and cool.

*Maple syrup may be substituted.

Cane Syrup Slice-and-Bakes

MAKES ABOUT 5 DOZEN
HANDS-ON 35 MIN.
TOTAL 3 HOURS, 10 MIN.

Perfect for last-minute company, this dough can be made and stored in the refrigerator for up to 1 week, or frozen for up to 1 month.

- 2 cups butter, softened
- 3/4 cup granulated sugar
- 1/4 cup cane syrup*
- 1 1/2 tsp. kosher salt
- 2 tsp. vanilla extract
- 4 cups all-purpose flour
- 1 large egg, lightly beaten
- 1/2 cup turbinado sugar (such as Sugar in the Raw)
  Parchment paper

1. Beat first 5 ingredients at medium speed with an electric mixer 2 to 3 minutes or until creamy.

2. Add flour, and beat just until blended. Divide dough into 4 portions, and shape each portion into a 8- x 2-inch log. Wrap each log in plastic wrap, and chill 1 hour.

3. **Whisk** together egg and 1 Tbsp. water. Unwrap logs, and brush with egg mixture. Sprinkle turbinado sugar over logs, pressing to adhere, and rewrap logs. Chill 30 minutes.

4. **Preheat** oven to 350°. Cut logs into 1/4-inch-thick slices; place 1 inch apart on 2 parchment paper-lined baking sheets. Bake 10 to 14 minutes or until lightly browned at edges, switching baking sheets halfway through. Cool on baking sheets 5 minutes. Transfer parchment to wire racks, and cool.

*Sorghum syrup or light honey may be substituted.

BLACK-TIE BENNE SLICE-AND-BAKES
Prepare recipe as directed, reducing **butter** to 1 1/2 cups and adding 1/2 cup each **tahini** and **white sesame seeds** to first 5 ingredients. Substitute 3/4 cup **black sesame seeds** for turbinado sugar.

GINGERSNAP SLICE-AND-BAKES
Prepare recipe as directed, reducing **salt** to 1 1/4 tsp. and adding 2 tsp. **ground cinnamon,** 1 tsp. **ground cardamom,** and 1/4 tsp. each **ground allspice, ground cloves,** and **ground nutmeg** to first 5 ingredients. Stir in 1/2 cup finely chopped **crystallized ginger** after adding **flour.**

FRUITCAKE SLICE-AND-BAKES
Soak 1 cup **candied fruit,** 1 tsp. firmly packed **orange zest,** and 1 tsp. loosely packed **lemon zest** in 1/4 cup **spiced or dark rum** 30 minutes or until liquid is absorbed. Prepare recipe as directed, stirring in candied fruit mixture to dough after adding flour. Substitute 3/4 cup finely chopped **walnuts** for turbinado sugar.

LEMON-ROSEMARY SLICE-AND-BAKES
Prepare recipe as directed, omitting **egg** and **turbinado sugar** and adding 1 Tbsp. **lemon zest** and 2 tsp. minced **fresh rosemary** to first 5 ingredients. Reduce **flour** to 3 1/2 cups, and add 1/2 cup **cornmeal** with flour. Gently toss together warm cookies and 2 cups **powdered sugar** to coat.

Tex-Mex Brownies

MAKES 2 DOZEN
HANDS-ON 25 MIN.
TOTAL 2 HOURS, 20 MIN.

Not your mama's brownie. The subtle heat from the ground red pepper turns these delights into conversation starters.

1 1/2	**cups butter**
1	**(16-oz.) package bittersweet chocolate morsels**
2	**cups all-purpose flour**
2	**tsp. baking powder**
1	**tsp. ground cinnamon**
1/2	**tsp. kosher salt**
1/2	**to 1 tsp. ground red pepper**
1	**cup semisweet chocolate morsels**
1	**cup granulated sugar**
4	**large eggs**
3/4	**cup firmly packed dark brown sugar**
1 1/2	**Tbsp. vanilla extract**
	Parchment paper

1. **Preheat** oven to 350°. Cook first 2 ingredients in a large heavy-duty saucepan over low heat, stirring occasionally, 8 to 10 minutes or until smooth. Remove from heat; cool completely (about 20 minutes).

2. **Meanwhile,** whisk together flour and next 4 ingredients in a large bowl until blended; stir in semisweet chocolate morsels.

3. **Whisk** together granulated sugar and next 3 ingredients until smooth. Whisk in bittersweet chocolate mixture. Whisk chocolate mixture into flour mixture just until combined.

4. **Line** bottom and sides of a 13- x 9-inch pan with parchment paper, allowing 2 to 3 inches to extend over sides; lightly grease parchment paper. Pour batter into pan.

5. **Bake** at 350° for 35 to 40 minutes or until a wooden pick inserted in center comes out with a few moist crumbs. Cool in pan.

6. **Lift** mixture from pan using parchment paper sides as handles; cut into 24 squares.

TEXAS SHEET CAKE SANDWICHES Split each brownie horizontally, and sandwich 1 Tbsp. prepared chocolate frosting between top and bottom halves.

Apricot-Almond Thumbprints

MAKES ABOUT 6 DOZEN
HANDS-ON 30 MIN.
TOTAL 1 HOUR, 55 MIN.

2	**cups butter, softened**
2/3	**cup granulated sugar**
2/3	**cup firmly packed light brown sugar**
1	**tsp. almond extract**
1/4	**tsp. kosher salt**
4 2/3	**cups all-purpose flour**
1 1/2	**cups finely chopped sliced almonds**
3/4	**cup apricot preserves**

1. **Beat** first 5 ingredients at medium speed with an electric mixer 3 to 5 minutes or until creamy. Add flour; beat just until blended.

2. **Shape** dough into 1-inch balls (about 1 Tbsp. per ball), and roll in chopped almonds. Place 2 inches apart on 2 parchment paper lined-baking sheets. Press thumb or end of a wooden spoon into each ball, forming an indentation. Chill 20 minutes.

3. **Preheat** oven to 350°. Bake, in batches, 15 minutes or until bottoms are light golden brown. Cool on baking sheets 10 minutes; transfer cookies on parchment paper to wire racks, and cool 10 minutes. Spoon 1/2 tsp. apricot preserves into each indentation. Serve immediately, or cool completely.

Marble Snickerdoodles

MAKES 2 1/2 DOZEN
HANDS-ON 45 MIN.
TOTAL 1 HOUR, 50 MIN.

Use the bottom of a 1/2-cup measuring cup to flatten the cookies to the perfect size. Be sure to use salted butter.

- 3 2/3 cups all-purpose flour
- 2 1/2 tsp. cream of tartar
- 1 1/2 tsp. baking soda
- 1/2 tsp. kosher salt
- 1/3 cup unsweetened cocoa
- 1 3/4 cups salted butter, softened
- 2 1/2 tsp. vanilla extract
- 2 1/3 cups sugar, divided
- 4 tsp. ground cinnamon, divided
- 3 large eggs
- Parchment paper

1. Stir together 2 cups flour, 1 1/4 tsp. cream of tartar, 3/4 tsp. baking soda, and 1/4 tsp. salt in a medium bowl. Stir together cocoa and remaining 1 2/3 cups flour, 1 1/4 tsp. cream of tartar, 3/4 tsp. baking soda, and 1/4 tsp. salt in a separate medium bowl.

2. Beat butter, vanilla, 2 cups sugar, and 1 tsp. cinnamon at medium speed with an electric mixer until creamy. Add eggs, 1 at a time, beating well after each addition. Spoon half of butter mixture into cocoa mixture; spoon remaining butter mixture into flour mixture.

3. Beat plain batter until just blended; beat chocolate batter until just blended. Chill both dough mixtures 30 minutes.

4. Preheat oven to 350°. Stir together remaining 1/3 cup sugar and 3 tsp. cinnamon in a small bowl. Drop plain dough by tablespoonfuls onto aluminum foil. Top each with 1 Tbsp. of chocolate dough; roll together into a ball. Roll balls in cinnamon-sugar; place 3 inches apart on parchment paper-lined baking sheets. Flatten each ball using a flat-bottom glass.

5. Bake at 350° for 14 minutes or until edges are lightly browned, lightly tapping baking sheet halfway through to deflate cookies. Cool on baking sheets 5 minutes; transfer cookies to wire racks to cool.

MARBLE-CINNAMON SANDWICH COOKIES

Spread 2 cups **cinnamon-raisin swirl peanut butter** (such as Peanut Butter & Co.) on half of cookies (about 2 Tbsp. per cookie); top with remaining cookies.

Honey-Hazelnut Crisps

MAKES ABOUT 4 1/2 DOZEN
HANDS-ON 15 MIN.
TOTAL 1 HOUR, 30 MIN.

Lacy and delicate, these cookies store best in a cookie tin between sheets of wax paper.

- 3/4 cup powdered sugar
- 1/2 cup butter, softened
- 1 Tbsp. honey
- 1/4 tsp. vanilla extract
- 1/8 tsp. kosher salt
- 1/2 cup finely chopped hazelnuts
- 6 Tbsp. all-purpose flour
- 3 Tbsp. whole wheat flour
- Parchment paper

1. Preheat oven to 325°. Beat first 5 ingredients at medium speed with an electric mixer 4 to 5 minutes or until creamy. Add hazelnuts and next 2 ingredients; beat just until blended. Drop by level teaspoonfuls 3 inches apart onto 2 parchment paper-lined baking sheets.

2. Bake at 325° for 12 to 14 minutes or until edges are golden brown. Cool on baking sheets 5 minutes; transfer to wire racks, and cool.

HAZELNUT SANDWICHES

Spoon 1 1/2 cups **fig preserves** on half of cookies (about 1 tsp. per cookie); top with remaining cookies. Makes about 2 dozen.

Chocolate-Mint Cookies

MAKES ABOUT 4 DOZEN
HANDS-ON 35 MIN.
TOTAL 2 HOURS

Be sure to bake the cookies until they are crisp; the dark, chocolate colored dough makes it harder to tell when they're ready.

- 3 cups all-purpose flour
- 1 1/3 cups unsweetened cocoa
- 1/2 tsp. table salt
- 1 cup butter, softened
- 1 cup sugar
- 1/2 cup firmly packed light brown sugar
- 1 Tbsp. instant coffee granules
- 2 tsp. vanilla extract
- 1/2 tsp. peppermint extract
- 2 large eggs
- Parchment paper
- 1 cup crushed hard peppermint candies

1. Stir together flour and next 2 ingredients. Beat butter and next 5 ingredients at medium speed with an electric mixer 3 to 4 minutes or until creamy. Add eggs, and beat until smooth. Add flour mixture, and beat just until blended.

2. Divide dough into 2 equal portions. Flatten each into a disk between parchment paper. Roll each disk to 1/4-inch thickness; transfer to a baking sheet, and chill for 30 minutes.

3. Preheat oven to 350°. Place 1 dough disk on work surface, and remove top sheet of parchment paper. Cut with a lightly floured 2 1/2-inch round cutter; place 1 inch apart on 2 parchment paper-lined baking sheets.

4. Sprinkle 1 tsp. crushed peppermint candy onto each cookie. Repeat procedure with remaining dough and candy.

5. Bake at 350° for 12 minutes or until firm. Transfer cookies on parchment paper to a wire rack and cool.

WHITE CHOCOLATE LINZER COOKIES

Prepare recipe through Step 3. Cut centers out of half of cookies with a lightly floured 1 1/2-inch round cutter. Sprinkle 1 tsp. crushed **peppermint candy** over each hollow cookie. Proceed with Step 5. Spread 1 tsp. melted **vanilla candy coating** on each solid cookie; top with peppermint-covered cookie. Drizzle with melted vanilla candy coating, if desired. Makes 2 dozen. Hands-on 45 min.; Total 1 hour, 40 min.

3 Festive Menus

Celebrate the season with one of these elegant gatherings

'TIS THE SEASON FOR A

Cocktail Supper

[BY JULIA REED]

I LOVE GIVING PARTIES AT CHRISTMAS, mainly because the guests are already in the mood to make merry. They're primed to blow off their diets and imbibe more than usual; they want to dress up and show off and they're not embarrassed to stick holly in their hat. My favorite form of holiday entertainment is the cocktail supper, a big boozy bash featuring enough food to constitute supper.

Cheese Dreams

MAKES ABOUT 3 DOZEN
HANDS-ON 30 MIN.
TOTAL 45 MIN.

Make these the day before the party and refrigerate. Or freeze up to 3 weeks. If frozen, pop them in the oven directly from the freezer and allow for a longer baking time.

- 2 **cups finely grated sharp Cheddar cheese**
- 1 **cup butter, softened**
- 2 **Tbsp. heavy cream**
- 1 **large egg**
- 1 **tsp. Worcestershire sauce**
- 1/2 **tsp. table salt**
- 1/2 **tsp. dry mustard**
  Ground red pepper or hot sauce to taste
- 1 **(16-oz.) package firm white sandwich bread slices**

1. Preheat oven to 375°. Beat cheese and butter at medium speed with an electric mixer until blended. Beat in cream and next 5 ingredients.

2. Cut crusts from bread; cut each slice into 4 squares. Spread cheese mixture on half of bread squares (about 1 tsp. per square); top each with 1 remaining square. Spread remaining cheese mixture over top and sides of sandwiches. Place sandwiches, 1 inch apart, on a lightly greased baking sheet.

3. Bake at 375° for 15 minutes or until golden.

Montgomery Punch

MAKES 14 CUPS
HANDS-ON 15 MIN.
TOTAL 9 HOURS, 40 MIN., INCLUDING ICE RING

"Made the old-fashioned way, punch is, to quote one of my father's highest compliments, 'strong stuff.' When he uses the term, it's usually in reference to a good-looking woman or especially funny anecdote, but I'm sure its derivation comes straight from the punch bowl."

- 2 **cups fresh lemon juice**
- 1 1/2 **cups sugar**
- 1 **cup brandy**
  Ice Ring
- 2 **(750-milliliter) bottles chilled sparkling wine**
- 1 **(375-milliliter) bottle chilled dessert wine (such as Sauternes)**
  Garnishes: orange slices, lemon slices

1. Stir together first 2 ingredients until sugar dissolves.

2. Stir together brandy and lemon mixture. Pour over Ice Ring in a large punch bowl. Gently stir in wines. Serve immediately.

Note: To make ahead, stir together first 2 ingredients, and chill up to 24 hours. Proceed with recipe as directed.

ICE RING Freeze 3 cups water in a tube pan or Bundt pan (that will fit into a punch bowl) 4 hours or until set. Place sliced **fruit,** such as **lemons** and **oranges,** in a single layer over ice, and freeze 1 hour. Remove pan from freezer, and let stand 10 minutes. Add 5 cups ice-cold water, and freeze 4 hours or until set. Let stand at room temperature 10 minutes before unmolding. Makes 1 ice ring. Hands on 5 min., Total 9 hours, 25 min.

Salted Pecan Bourbon Balls

MAKES ABOUT 3 1/2 DOZEN
HANDS-ON 30 MIN.
TOTAL 30 MIN., NOT INCLUDING PECANS

- 1 **(12-oz.) package vanilla wafers, finely crushed**
- 1 **cup powdered sugar**
- 1 **cup finely chopped toasted pecans**
- 1/2 **cup bourbon**
- 2 **Tbsp. unsweetened cocoa**
- 2 **Tbsp. light corn syrup**
  Powdered sugar
  Toasted Pecans, coarsely chopped

Stir together first 6 ingredients in a large bowl. Shape into 1-inch balls, and roll in powdered sugar or Toasted Pecans. Refrigerate in an airtight container up to 2 weeks.

TOASTED PECANS

MAKES 4 CUPS
HANDS-ON 10 MIN.
TOTAL 1 HOUR, 5 MIN.

- 1/4 **cup butter, melted**
- 4 **cups pecan halves**
- 1 **Tbsp. kosher salt**
- 1/2 **tsp. ground red pepper**

1. Preheat oven to 325°. Toss together butter and pecans. Spread in a single layer in a jelly-roll pan; bake 25 minutes or until toasted and fragrant, stirring halfway through.

2. Remove from oven; sprinkle with salt and red pepper, tossing to coat. Cool completely in pan on a wire rack (about 30 minutes). Store in an airtight container up to 1 week.

Homemade Hot Mustard

MAKES 2 ¼ CUPS
HANDS-ON 20 MIN.
TOTAL 13 HOURS, 20 MIN.

- 1 cup dry mustard
- 1 cup apple cider vinegar
- 1 cup sugar
- 3 large pasteurized eggs, lightly beaten

1. Stir together first 2 ingredients in top of double boiler. Cover. Let stand 12 to 24 hours.

2. Pour water to depth of 1 inch into bottom of a double boiler over medium-high heat; bring to a boil. Reduce heat to low, and simmer; place top of double boiler over simmering water. Whisk sugar and eggs into mustard mixture, and cook, whisking constantly, 8 to 10 minutes or until thickened. Remove from heat, and cool completely (about 1 hour). (Mixture will continue to thicken as it cools.) Refrigerate in an airtight container up to 2 weeks.

Note: We tested with Colman's Mustard Powder.

Steamed Asparagus with Curry Dip

MAKES 2 ¼ CUPS
HANDS-ON 10 MIN.
TOTAL 10 MIN.

Stir together 2 cups **mayonnaise;** 1 Tbsp. **curry powder;** 2 Tbsp. **mustard-mayonnaise sauce;** 2 Tbsp. **ketchup;** 1 Tbsp. prepared **horseradish;** 1 Tbsp. **Worcestershire sauce;** 2 tsp. **grated onion;** 1 tsp. **celery seeds;** 1 tsp. **hot sauce;** 1 **garlic clove,** pressed; and **salt** to taste. Serve with 3 to 4 lb. steamed fresh **asparagus.**

Note: We tested with Hellmann's Mayonnaise and Durkee Famous Sauce.

Lump Crab Mornay

MAKES 10 TO 12 SERVINGS
HANDS-ON 20 MIN.
TOTAL 20 MIN.

- ½ cup butter, softened
- 1 bunch green onions, chopped
- 2 Tbsp. all-purpose flour
- 2 cups heavy cream
- 1 cup freshly grated Gruyère cheese*
- 2 Tbsp. dry sherry
- ¼ tsp. kosher salt
- ¼ tsp. ground red pepper
- 1 lb. fresh jumbo lump crabmeat
- ½ cup chopped fresh flat-leaf parsley
  toast points

Melt butter in a heavy saucepan over medium-high heat; add onions, and sauté 3 minutes or until tender. Whisk in flour, and cook, whisking constantly, 2 minutes. Add cream, and cook, whisking constantly, until smooth and sauce begins to bubble. Remove from heat, and stir in cheese until smooth. Stir in sherry, salt, and pepper. Fold in crabmeat and parsley. Keep warm in a chafing dish or slow cooker set on WARM or LOW. Serve with toast points.

*Swiss cheese may be substituted.

Cognac Cheese Spread

MAKES 1 ¼ CUPS
HANDS-ON 10 MIN.
TOTAL 2 HOURS, 10 MIN.

- ½ (8-oz.) package cream cheese, softened
- ¼ cup butter, softened
- 4 oz. Roquefort or other blue cheese, crumbled
- 1½ Tbsp. minced fresh chives
- 1 Tbsp. minced celery
- 1 Tbsp. cognac
- ⅛ tsp. ground red pepper
- ⅛ tsp. freshly ground black pepper
  Assorted crackers
  Assorted sliced fresh vegetables

Beat cream cheese and butter at medium speed with a heavy-duty electric stand mixer until smooth. Beat in blue cheese and next 5 ingredients on low speed until blended. Spoon into a serving bowl. Cover and chill 2 hours. Serve with crackers or sliced vegetables.

Perfect Beef Tenderloin

MAKES 8 TO 10 SERVINGS
HANDS-ON 10 MIN.
TOTAL 50 MIN.

As a rule of thumb, when seasoning roasts, 1 tsp. of salt per pound is sufficient.

- 1 (5- to 7-lb.) beef tenderloin, trimmed
- 3 Tbsp. butter, softened
- 5 to 7 tsp. kosher salt
- ¾ tsp. cracked black pepper

1. Preheat oven to 425°. Place tenderloin on a wire rack in a jelly-roll pan. Rub butter over tenderloin, and sprinkle with salt and pepper.

2. Bake at 425° for 25 to 35 minutes or until a meat thermometer inserted into thickest portion registers 135° (medium rare).

3. Cover tenderloin loosely with aluminum foil, and let stand 15 minutes before slicing.

Note: We tested with Diamond Crystal Kosher Salt.

Mini Corn Cakes with Smoked Salmon and Dill Crème Fraîche

MAKES ABOUT 2 DOZEN
HANDS-ON 20 MIN.
TOTAL 1 HOUR, 10 MIN.

Make these muffins in the morning, and garnish with salmon and crème fraîche just before your guests arrive.

- 1 (8.25-oz.) can cream-style corn
- 1 cup plain white cornmeal
- 1 cup sour cream
- 2 Tbsp. vegetable oil
- 1½ tsp. baking powder
- 1 tsp. table salt
- 2 large eggs
- 1 cup crème fraîche
- 2 Tbsp. finely chopped fresh dill weed
- 1 Tbsp. fresh lemon juice
- 2 (4-oz.) packages thinly sliced smoked salmon, flaked
  Garnish: fresh dill weed sprigs

1. Preheat oven to 350°. Whisk together first 7 ingredients until smooth. Spoon 1 heaping teaspoonful corn mixture into each cup of a well-greased 24-cup miniature muffin pan.

2. Bake at 350° for 20 minutes. Remove from oven, and cool 10 minutes.

3. Meanwhile, stir together crème fraîche, dill, and lemon juice. Top each muffin with crème fraîche mixture and smoked salmon.

Horseradish Sauce

MAKES ABOUT 2 CUPS
HANDS-ON 5 MIN.
TOTAL 5 MIN.

- 1⅓ cups sour cream
- ½ cup whipping cream, whipped to soft peaks
- 6 Tbsp. prepared horseradish
- 1½ tsp. Dijon mustard
- 2 to 3 tsp. fresh lemon juice
- ½ tsp. sugar

Fold together first 4 ingredients in a medium bowl. Stir in lemon juice and sugar. Add salt and pepper to taste. Serve immediately.

Cheddar Gougères

MAKES ABOUT 4 1/2 DOZEN
HANDS-ON 35 MIN.
TOTAL 1 HOUR, 10 MIN.

- ½ cup butter, cut into 8 slices
- ½ tsp. table salt
- 1 cup all-purpose flour
- 4 large eggs
- 1½ cups grated extra-sharp Cheddar cheese
  Parchment paper
- 3 Tbsp. grated Parmesan cheese
  Deviled Ham

1. Preheat oven to 425°. Bring first 2 ingredients and 1 cup water to a boil in a large saucepan over high heat. Reduce heat to medium. Add flour all at once, and beat vigorously with a wooden spoon 1 to 2 minutes or until mixture is smooth and pulls away from sides of pan, forming a ball of dough. Remove from heat, and let stand 2 minutes. Stir in eggs, 1 at a time, beating vigorously with a wooden spoon after each addition. (Mixture should be smooth and glossy.) Add Cheddar cheese, and stir until well blended.

2. Drop batter by level spoonfuls 1 inch apart onto a parchment paper-lined baking sheet, using a small cookie scoop (about 1 inch). Sprinkle with Parmesan cheese.

3. Bake at 425° for 10 minutes. Reduce oven temperature to 375°, and bake 17 to 20 more minutes or until golden brown.

4. Cut each gougère in half, and fill bottom half with desired amount of Deviled Ham. Top with remaining half.

Deviled Ham

MAKES ABOUT 8 SERVINGS
HANDS-ON 10 MIN.
TOTAL 10 MIN.

- 1 lb. cooked ham, cut into cubes
- ½ cup chopped sweet onion
- ¼ cup Dijon mustard
- 4 Tbsp. mayonnaise
- 3 Tbsp. chopped sweet pickles
- 1 tsp. prepared horseradish
- 1 tsp. Worcestershire sauce
- ⅛ tsp. ground red pepper

Pulse first 2 ingredients in a food processor 6 to 8 times or until finely chopped. Add remaining ingredients, and process 10 to 20 seconds or until smooth.

DEAR READER,

When I was growing up in Atlanta in the 60s and 70s, Christmas Eve in Atlanta was a quiet celebration, a relative calm before the storm of my mother's family's appearance for Christmas Lunch at 3 o'clock the next day. You see, I had these rambunctious cousins whose antics sometimes made my grandmother take an extra-long sip of the Christmas Champagne. And who could blame her? One year, after being excused from the table, her, uh, perfectly behaved grandchildren knocked over the 16-foot tree in her daughter's living room. Miraculously, all of us lived to tell about it.

This three-course holiday menu I've designed just for you ensures a perfect dinner. Everything can be made ahead, except the easy blender Hollandaise Sauce for the green beans, leaving extra time to batten down the hatches. Envision this: Champagne, cheese straws, and candied bacon kick off the meal. Sit down to a first course of brilliant Tomato Bisque. Out comes a whole side of salmon encrusted with pecans, and Potatoes Patio, named for my former restaurant because we served them with every dish in tarnation. For dessert, start a new tradition: Charlotte Russe, an unmolded sherry-flavored custard with ladyfingers. See there: You can do it!

Happy Christmas Eve!
Love, Alex

Potatoes Patio

MAKES 10 TO 12 SERVINGS
HANDS-ON 25 MIN.
TOTAL 1 HOUR, 40 MIN.

- 2 cups heavy cream
- 1¾ tsp. table salt
- 1 garlic clove, pressed
- ¾ tsp. freshly ground black pepper
- ¼ tsp. ground nutmeg
- 3 lb. russet potatoes, peeled and thinly sliced
- 2 cups freshly grated Gruyère cheese
- 2 Tbsp. freshly grated Parmesan cheese

1. Preheat oven to 350°. Stir together first 5 ingredients in a medium bowl. Let stand 5 minutes.

2. Arrange a single layer of potatoes in a buttered 13- x 9-inch baking dish. Pour ¼ cup cream mixture over potatoes, and sprinkle with ¼ cup Gruyère cheese. Repeat layers 7 more times. Top with Parmesan cheese.

3. Bake, covered with aluminum foil, at 350° for 45 minutes. Uncover and bake 15 to 20 more minutes or until golden brown and potatoes are tender. Cool on a wire rack 10 minutes before serving.

Green Beans with Hollandaise Sauce

MAKES 8 SERVINGS
HANDS-ON 15 MIN.
TOTAL 15 MIN.

For a festive presentation, dip 8 fresh chives into boiling water 5 to 10 seconds or until softened; remove and pat dry with paper towels. Divide green beans into 8 small bunches. Gently tie each bunch with 1 chive.

- ½ cup butter
- 4 large pasteurized egg yolks
- 2 Tbsp. fresh lemon juice
- ½ tsp. kosher salt
- ⅛ tsp. ground white pepper
  Dash of hot sauce (optional)
- 1 lb. haricots verts (French green beans), blanched or steamed

Melt butter in a small saucepan over medium heat; reduce heat to low, and keep warm. Process egg yolks, next 3 ingredients, 1 Tbsp. water, and, if desired, hot sauce in a blender or food processor 2 to 3 minutes or until pale and fluffy. With blender running, add melted butter in a slow, steady stream, processing until smooth. Serve immediately with green beans.

Pecan-Dill Crusted Salmon

MAKES 10 TO 12 SERVINGS
HANDS-ON 10 MIN.
TOTAL 30 MIN.

- 1 1/2 **cups pecan halves**
- 6 **Tbsp. butter, melted**
- 2 **garlic cloves, minced**
- 1 1/2 **tsp. dried dill weed**
- 1 **(3- to 3 1/2-lb.) boneless, skinless side of salmon**
- 1 1/4 **tsp. kosher salt**
- 1/2 **tsp. freshly ground black pepper**
  Parchment paper

1. Preheat oven to 400°. Pulse first 4 ingredients in a food processor 5 or 6 times or until mixture resembles coarse crumbs.

2. Sprinkle salmon with salt and pepper, and place on a parchment paper-lined baking sheet. Spread pecan mixture over salmon.

3. Bake at 400° for 18 to 20 minutes or just until fish flakes with a fork.

Tomato Bisque

MAKES ABOUT 2 QT.
HANDS-ON 15 MIN.
TOTAL 45 MIN.

This recipe is a signature of my partner at The Patio by the River, Mary Boyle Hataway. She developed it in the late 1960s, and it's a classic: full flavored, unique, rich, and delicious. The surprise addition of strong coffee is an inspiration from an old Italian cookbook, cited as the "secret ingredient" that Italians have understood for years.

- 3 **(14.5-oz.) cans diced tomatoes**
- 2 **cups diced onions**
- 2 **garlic cloves, minced**
- 2 **bay leaves**
- 4 **Tbsp. tomato paste**
- 3 **Tbsp. fresh brewed coffee**
- 1 **Tbsp. jarred beef soup base**
- 1 **tsp. jarred chicken soup base**
- 2 **fresh flat-leaf parsley sprigs**
- 1 1/2 **tsp. dried thyme**
- 1/2 **cup heavy cream**
- 2 **tsp. fresh lemon juice**
- 1 1/2 **tsp. kosher salt**
- 1/2 **tsp. black pepper**

1. Bring first 10 ingredients and 5 cups water to a boil in a large stockpot over high heat. Reduce heat to medium-high, and simmer, stirring occasionally, 20 minutes or until reduced by one-fourth. Cool 15 minutes.

2. Process with a handheld blender until smooth. Stir in cream and next 3 ingredients. Serve immediately.

Note: Refrigerate in an airtight container up to 4 days, or freeze up to 8 weeks. Reheat over medium heat until soup simmers. (Do not boil.) We tested with Superior Touch Better Than Bouillon beef and chicken soup bases.

Blue Cheese Silver Dollars

MAKES 3 DOZEN
HANDS-ON 20 MIN.
TOTAL 4 HOURS, 5 MIN.

The dough may be made up to a week ahead of time and refrigerated, or frozen up to a month in advance.

- 1/4 **cup butter, softened**
- 4 **oz. Stilton cheese, crumbled**
- 1/4 **tsp. cracked black pepper**
- 3/4 **cup all-purpose flour**
  Parchment paper

1. Beat first 3 ingredients at medium speed with an electric mixer until smooth. Add flour, and beat until just combined. (Do not overmix.)

2. Shape dough into a log (about 1 3/4 inches in diameter). Wrap in plastic wrap; chill 3 to 24 hours.

3. Preheat oven to 375°. Cut log into 1/4-inch-thick slices; place 2 inches apart on parchment paper-lined baking sheets. Bake, in batches, 10 minutes or until golden brown. Cool on pans 5 minutes. Transfer to a wire rack, and cool completely (about 20 minutes). Sprinkle with additional black pepper.

Millionaire's Bacon

MAKES 10 TO 12 SERVINGS
HANDS-ON 10 MIN.
TOTAL 1 HOUR, 25 MIN.

- 1 **(16-oz.) package thick bacon slices**
- 1 **cup firmly packed dark brown sugar**

1. Preheat oven to 350°. Arrange bacon in a single layer on 2 lightly greased wire racks in 2 aluminum foil-lined broiler pans. Let stand 10 minutes. Cover bacon with brown sugar, pressing lightly to adhere.

2. Bake at 350° for 45 to 50 minutes or until done. Cool completely (about 20 minutes). Cut into bite-size pieces.

Charlotte Russe

MAKES 8 TO 10 SERVINGS
HANDS-ON 45 MIN.
TOTAL 11 HOURS

- 1 **envelope unflavored gelatin**
- 1/2 **cup cold water**
- 5 **egg yolks**
- 1 1/2 **cups sugar**
- 2 **tsp. all-purpose flour**
- 1/2 **tsp. table salt**
- 2 **cups half-and-half**
- 1 **tsp. vanilla extract**
- 1/2 **cup dry sherry, divided**
- 2 **(3.5-oz.) packages hard ladyfingers**
- 2 **cups heavy cream**

GARNISHES
  Whipped cream
  Chocolate shavings
  Mandarin orange slices

1. Sprinkle gelatin over 1/2 cup cold water; stir and let stand 5 minutes. Whisk together egg yolks and next 3 ingredients in a medium bowl.

2. Bring half-and-half to simmer in a medium saucepan over medium heat. Whisk 1/4 cup hot half-and-half into egg mixture; add egg mixture to remaining hot half-and-half, whisking constantly. Reduce heat to medium-low, and cook, stirring constantly, 8 to 10 minutes or until mixture thickens and coats a spoon. Add vanilla, gelatin mixture, and 1/4 cup sherry, stirring until combined. Remove from heat, and let stand 15 minutes. Transfer to a large bowl. Cover and chill 2 hours or until pudding-like thickness, stirring every 30 minutes.

3. Arrange 23 ladyfingers in a single layer on a jelly-roll pan. Brush both sides of ladyfingers with remaining sherry.

4. Line a 9-cup charlotte mold or soufflé dish with plastic wrap, allowing 2 to 3 inches to extend over sides. Line sides of mold with ladyfingers.

5. Beat cream on medium speed with a heavy-duty electric stand mixer 2 to 3 minutes or until soft peaks form. Fold whipped cream into chilled half-and-half mixture. Gently pour mixture into prepared trifle dish. Cover and chill 8 to 24 hours or until fully set. To unmold, invert a flat plate over dessert. Holding containers together, invert. Lift off mold and gently remove plastic wrap. Cut dessert into wedges.

Note: We tested with Natural Nectar Biscotti Savoiardi Ladyfingers.

Brunch

[BY SARA FOSTER]

THIS TRADITION STARTED YEARS AGO when worked in a catering business that brought on a relentless holiday season starting around Halloween and continuing until we closed our doors on the last day of the year. This remains the nature of my business now, so for me, the first day of the year is not only my opportunity to exhale, and to celebrate another successful season with my friends and colleagues, it's also my one opportunity to have a holiday party (since Christmas would be out of the question). Whether you're in the food business or not, it's a casual and relaxed, come-when-you-want afternoon to bring the holiday season to a close—and to share a meal with family and friends.

Although I call it "brunch" and serve brunch-type foods, such as Bloody Marys and Cheesy Grits Soufflé, the party doesn't start until two in the afternoon. (I am realistic about what time my friends will wake up!) The menu changes from year to year, with a few constants: I always serve some type of biscuits—this year they're Sweet Potato Biscuits.

Rather than a typical buffet, I set up various stations around the house to get people mingling about and talking to each other, and also because that way I feel like there is an element of surprise when you walk into a room and discover a different dish there. My husband and I designed our house for easy entertaining, so it has an open format with the kitchen in the center, which is ideal for this kind of party. I make a dessert station on a counter that separates the kitchen from the den, and if I'm serving something hot, the stove becomes a warmer.

I'm the type of person who sets up her house two days in advance so I can enjoy how pretty everything looks for as long as possible. I also steal a few minutes here and there to do what can be done in advance. So on New Year's Day, I wake up, have a cup of coffee, pull cookie dough out of the refrigerator to bake, toss the salad with vinaigrette, and do other last minute touches while I wait for the house to fill up with friends. I can't think of a better way to start a new year.

Bloody Mary Bar

MAKES ABOUT 3 QT.
HANDS-ON 10 MIN.
TOTAL 10 MIN.

Fill small glasses with vegetable sticks, pickles, citrus, and let guests choose their own garnish.

Stir together 8 cups **tomato juice,** 2 cups **vodka,** 1/3 cup **prepared horseradish,** 1/3 cup **Worcestershire sauce,** 3/4 cup **fresh lime juice** (about 6 limes), 1 Tbsp. **hot sauce,** 2 tsp. **sea salt,** and 1 tsp. **freshly ground black pepper.** Serve over ice. Garnish as desired.

Chicks in a Blanket

MAKES 8 TO 10 SERVINGS
HANDS-ON 20 MIN.
TOTAL 1 HOUR, INCLUDING SAUCE

Move over pigs in a blanket. Dough-wrapped chicken-apple sausages are best fresh from the oven while still hot, so bake one batch at a time.

- 1 **(8-oz.) can refrigerated crescent rolls**
- 1 **(12-oz.) package mini smoked chicken-and-apple sausage (24 links)**
  Parchment paper
- 1 **large egg yolk, lightly beaten**
- 1 **Tbsp. sesame seeds (optional)**
- 1 **Tbsp. poppy seeds (optional)**
- 1 **Tbsp. fennel seeds (optional)**
  Spicy Dipping Sauce

1. Preheat oven to 375°. Unroll crescent rolls, and separate into triangles. Cut each triangle into 3 long triangles.

2. Place 1 sausage link on wide end of each triangle; roll up triangles around sausages, starting at wide end. Place, point sides down, on a parchment paper-lined baking sheet.

3. Brush each sausage roll with egg yolk. If desired, stir together sesame seeds and next 2 ingredients; sprinkle over rolls.

4. Bake at 375° for 14 to 15 minutes or until golden brown. Serve with Spicy Dipping Sauce.

Note: We tested with Aidell's Smoked Chicken & Apple Sausage Minis.

SPICY DIPPING SAUCE

MAKES ABOUT 1 CUP
HANDS-ON 5 MIN.
TOTAL 5 MIN.

Stir together 1/2 cup **honey mustard,** 2 Tbsp. **olive oil,** 1 Tbsp. **white wine vinegar,** 1 tsp. **dried crushed red pepper,** and 1 tsp. freshly ground **black pepper.** Serve immediately, or chill up to 12 hours.

Sweet Potato Biscuits

MAKES 3 DOZEN
HANDS-ON 30 MIN.
TOTAL 1 HOUR, 20 MIN.

Serve these mini scratch-made biscuits warm with butter, honey, and jam, along with two small platters—one with seared slices of country ham and a bowl of pepper jelly and another with slices of black forest ham and pimiento cheese—so guests can build their own breakfast sandwiches.

- 5 cups self-rising flour
- 1 Tbsp. sugar
- 1 tsp. kosher salt
- 1 cup cold butter, cut into small cubes
- ¼ cup cold vegetable shortening
- 2 cups buttermilk
- 1 cup cooked mashed sweet potato
  Parchment paper
- 2 Tbsp. butter, melted

1. Preheat oven to 425°. Stir together first 3 ingredients in a large bowl. Cut butter cubes and shortening into flour mixture with pastry blender or fork just until mixture resembles coarse meal. Cover and chill 10 minutes.

2. Whisk together buttermilk and sweet potato. Add buttermilk mixture to flour mixture, stirring just until dry ingredients are moistened.

3. Turn dough out onto a well-floured surface, and knead lightly 3 or 4 times. Pat or roll dough to ¾-inch thickness; cut with a 2-inch round cutter, reshaping scraps once. (Do not twist cutter.) Place rounds on a parchment paper-lined baking sheet.

4. Bake at 425° for 18 to 20 minutes or until golden brown. Remove from oven, and brush tops with melted butter. Serve immediately.

Beet-and-Citrus Salad

MAKES 8 TO 10 SERVINGS
HANDS-ON 30 MIN.
TOTAL 2 HOURS, 10 MIN.

Feel free to add or substitute different citrus fruits such as tangelos, blood oranges, Meyer lemons, or clementines.

- 3 medium-size fresh beets
- 3 Ruby Red grapefruit
- ¼ cup olive oil
- 2 Tbsp. maple syrup
- 2 Tbsp. white wine vinegar
- 1 tsp. kosher salt
- ¼ tsp. freshly ground black pepper
- 6 cups loosely packed arugula
- ¼ cup coarsely chopped pistachios

1. Preheat oven to 350°. Trim beet stems to 1 inch; gently wash beets, and place in an 8-inch square pan. Add ¼ cup water, and cover with aluminum foil. Bake 1 hour and 10 minutes or until tender. Uncover and cool completely (about 30 minutes).

2. Cut a ¼-inch-thick slice from each end of grapefruit using a sharp, thin-bladed knife. Place, flat ends down, on a cutting board, and remove peel in strips, cutting from top to bottom following the curvature of fruit. Remove any remaining bitter white pith. Holding peeled grapefruit over a bowl, slice between membranes, and gently remove whole segments. Reserve ¼ cup grapefruit juice.

3. Whisk together olive oil, next 4 ingredients, and reserved ¼ cup grapefruit juice in a small bowl.

4. Peel beets, and slice into wedges. Arrange arugula on a large platter; top with grapefruit segments and beets. Drizzle with vinaigrette; sprinkle with pistachios. Add salt and pepper to taste.

Cheesy Grits Soufflé

MAKES 8 TO 10 SERVINGS
HANDS-ON 25 MIN.
TOTAL 1 HOUR, 20 MIN.

- 4 tsp. kosher salt, divided
- 2 cups uncooked regular yellow grits
- 3 cups milk
- 1½ cups fresh corn kernels (about 3 ears)
- 6 large eggs, lightly beaten
- 2 cups (8 oz.) shredded sharp Cheddar cheese
- 6 Tbsp. butter
- 1 jalapeño pepper, seeded and diced
- 1 Tbsp. sugar
- 1 tsp. hot sauce
- ½ tsp. freshly ground black pepper

1. Preheat oven to 350°. Generously butter a 3-qt. baking dish; freeze 10 minutes.

2. Meanwhile, bring 3 cups water and 1 tsp. salt to a boil in a large saucepan over medium-high heat. Gradually whisk in grits; return to a boil. Reduce heat to medium-low, and cook, whisking often, 2 to 3 minutes or until thickened. Whisk in milk, and cook, stirring constantly, 3 to 4 minutes or until grits are creamy.

3. Remove from heat, and stir in corn, next 7 ingredients, and remaining 3 tsp. salt. Spread mixture in prepared dish. Place on an aluminum foil-lined jelly-roll pan.

4. Bake at 350° for 50 minutes or until puffed, firm around edges, and slightly soft in center. Remove from oven to a wire rack, and cool 5 minutes before serving.

Espresso Shortbread Cookies

MAKES ABOUT 4 DOZEN
HANDS-ON 45 MIN.
TOTAL 3 HOURS, 15 MIN.

Little bits of finely chopped chocolate-covered espresso beans are a perfect no-fail pick-me-up on New Year's Day. Make and chill the dough in advance and bake them in the morning.

- 1 cup butter, softened
- ½ cup granulated sugar
- 1 tsp. sea salt
- 1 tsp. vanilla extract
- 2 cups all-purpose flour
- ½ cup chocolate-covered espresso beans, chopped
- 1 Tbsp. finely ground espresso beans
- ½ cup Demerara sugar, divided*
  Wax paper

1. Beat first 3 ingredients at medium speed with a heavy-duty electric stand mixer 2 to 3 minutes or until light and fluffy. Stir in vanilla.

2. Stir together flour and next 2 ingredients in a medium bowl; gradually add to butter mixture, beating just until blended and stopping to scrape bowl as needed. (Do not overmix.)

3. Divide dough in half. Turn 1 dough portion out onto wax paper, and shape into a 10- x 2-inch log. Sprinkle log with 3 Tbsp. Demerara sugar, and roll log back and forth to adhere. Repeat with remaining dough portion and 3 Tbsp. Demerara sugar. Wrap logs in plastic wrap, and chill 2 to 3 hours.

4. Preheat oven to 350°. Cut chilled dough into ¼-inch-thick slices, and place 1 inch apart on 2 lightly greased baking sheets. Sprinkle 1½ tsp. Demerara sugar over cookies on each sheet.

5. Bake, in batches, at 350° for 12 to 15 minutes or until golden around edges, switching baking sheets halfway through.

6. Remove from oven to wire racks, and cool 5 minutes. Serve immediately, or cool completely. Store in an airtight container up to 4 days. Makes about 4 dozen.

*Turbinado sugar may be substituted.

4 Amazingly Tasty Roasts

Introducing four new bold statement pieces that will make you the holiday hero

Cracklin' Fresh Picnic Ham with Apple-Pomegranate-Cranberry Salsa

MAKES 8 TO 10 SERVINGS
HANDS-ON 30 MIN.
TOTAL 14 HOURS, 20 MIN., INCLUDING SALSA (PLUS 2 DAYS FOR CHILLING)

Ask your butcher: While a ham is traditionally a cured, brined, or smoked cut of pork using the hind leg, we're taking Christmas liberties with the word ham and choosing the best cut for the job, the shoulder. Look for a fresh picnic ham, a.k.a the picnic cut, whose marbling will give you the juiciest results. Bonus: a skin-on cut will give the prize on this roast: extra crackly skin.

Roast like a pro: Two keys: 1. Score the skin using an extra sharp paring knife or utility knife (see 6 Tools for Holiday Sanity on page 305) so the fat renders and exterior turns potato chip crunchy as the meat roasts. 2. Plan ahead. A bone-in roast this thick requires days of seasoning to allow the salt to penetrate to the bone. That's as many days as ingredients required to flavor this budget-minded wonder. A salty, crunchy cut like this begs for a fresh, easy, and crisp fruit condiment.

The right temp: Because we're talking shoulder, you want an internal temp of at least 175°, which will encourage the connective tissue and intramuscular fat to melt.

- 1 (11.6-lb.) bone-in, skin-on fresh pork picnic shoulder (picnic ham)
  Clean box cutter or one-sided razor blade
- ⅓ cup kosher salt
- 2 tsp. freshly ground black pepper
  Apple-Pomegranate-Cranberry Salsa

1. Wash ham, and pat dry. Make ¼-inch-deep cuts, ¼ inch apart, in skin with a clean box cutter. (The sharp blades cut through the skin with ease and make straight edges.) Stir together salt and pepper, and rub over ham, working into cuts in skin. Place ham in a large bowl, and cover with plastic wrap. Chill 2 days.

2. Remove ham from bowl. Remove salt from ham, and discard. Place ham, fat side up, on a wire rack in a jelly-roll pan, and chill, uncovered, 8 to 10 hours.

3. Let ham stand at room temperature 1 hour.

4. Preheat oven to 425°. Bake ham on lower oven rack 45 minutes. Reduce oven temperature to 325°, and bake 2 hours and 30 minutes. Increase oven temperature to 425°, and bake 30 to 35 minutes or until skin is crisp and a meat thermometer inserted into thickest portion registers 175°. Let stand 30 minutes before slicing. Serve with Apple-Pomegranate-Cranberry Salsa.

APPLE-POMEGRANATE-CRANBERRY SALSA

MAKES 2 CUPS
HANDS-ON 10 MIN.
TOTAL 35 MIN.

Bring ¼ cup **sugar**, ¼ cup **white wine,** and ¼ cup **water** to a boil in a small saucepan over medium heat. Remove from heat, and add ¼ cup **halved sweetened dried cranberries**; let stand 20 minutes. Drain cranberries; transfer to a medium bowl. Toss together 1 large **Granny Smith apple,** diced, and 2 Tbsp. **fresh lime juice.** Stir apple into cranberries. Stir in ¼ cup **pomegranate seeds,** ¼ cup **coarsely chopped toasted walnuts,** 1 Tbsp. **loosely packed orange zest,** and 1 Tbsp. **chopped fresh flat-leaf parsley.** Gradually stir in 2 Tbsp. **extra virgin olive oil.**

Turkey Breast Roulade with Figgy Port Wine Sauce

MAKES 6 TO 8 SERVINGS
HANDS-ON 1 HOUR, 10 MIN.
TOTAL 1 HOUR, 45 MIN.

- 8 thick bacon slices, chopped
- 2 shallots, minced
- 4 garlic cloves, minced
- ¼ tsp. dried crushed red pepper
- 2 (20-oz.) packages fresh baby spinach
- 1 (6- to 7-lb.) bone-in turkey breast
- 6 (6-inch) fresh rosemary sprigs
  Kitchen string
- ½ cup dried golden figs, finely chopped
- 1 cup port
- 3 Tbsp. olive oil
- ½ cup red wine vinegar
- 1 cup chicken broth
- 2 Tbsp. plum jam
- 1 Tbsp. cold butter

1. Cook bacon in a Dutch oven over medium heat 10 to 15 minutes or until crisp. Remove bacon, and drain on paper towels, reserving 3 Tbsp. drippings in Dutch oven. Sauté shallots and next 2 ingredients in hot drippings 1 to 2 minutes or until tender. Add spinach, in batches, and sauté 5 minutes or until wilted. Drain mixture, and coarsely chop. Stir together bacon and spinach mixture in a large bowl; add salt and pepper to taste. Cool 10 minutes.

2. Remove bone from turkey breast. Butterfly turkey breasts by making a lengthwise cut in 1 side, cutting to but not through the opposite side; unfold. Place breasts between 2 sheets of heavy-duty plastic wrap, and flatten to ¼-inch thickness, using a rolling pin or the flat side of a meat mallet. Sprinkle both sides with desired amount of salt and pepper, and place, skin sides down, on work surface.

3. Spoon half of spinach mixture on 1 breast, leaving a ½-inch border. Roll up, jelly-roll fashion, starting with long skinless side. Place 3 rosemary sprigs on breast, and tie breast with kitchen string, securing at 2-inch intervals. Repeat procedure with remaining breast, spinach mixture, and rosemary sprigs.

4. Preheat oven to 425°. Bring figs and port to a boil in a medium saucepan over high heat. Reduce heat to medium-low, and simmer, stirring occasionally, 5 minutes or until figs are tender. Remove from heat.

5. Cook turkey in hot olive oil in a 12- to 13-inch nonstick oven proof skillet over medium-high heat 2 minutes on each side or until browned. If necessary, turn turkey so that rosemary sides are up. Transfer skillet to oven, and bake at 425° for 25 to 30 minutes or until a meat thermometer inserted into thickest portion registers 165°.

6. Transfer turkey to a wire rack. Discard fat in skillet. Add fig mixture and vinegar to skillet, and cook over medium-high heat, stirring constantly, 4 to 5 minutes or until thickened. Stir in broth, and simmer, stirring occasionally, 5 to 8 minutes or until reduced by half. Stir in plum jam, and cook, stirring constantly, 1 minute. Whisk in butter and salt and pepper to taste.

7. Remove and discard string from turkey. Cut turkey into ½-inch-thick slices, and serve with fig mixture.

Standing Rib Roast with Red Wine Mushrooms

MAKES 8 TO 10 SERVINGS
HANDS-ON 30 MIN.
TOTAL 3 HOURS, 55 MIN.

Ask your butcher: Have the chine bone removed. A thin bone that runs perpendicular to the rib bones, it will get in the way of slicing once the meat is roasted.

Roast like a pro: Start roasting at 450° for 45 minutes to form the caramelized crust. Then reduce the temperature and finish cooking to keep the inside pink and juicy.

The right temp: 125° for prime rib lovers. The internal temp will continue to rise as the roast rests.

ROAST

- 1 (7-lb.) 4-bone prime rib roast, chine bone removed
- ⅓ cup Dijon mustard
- 3 garlic cloves, minced
- 1 Tbsp. chopped fresh rosemary
- 2 Tbsp. olive oil
- 7 tsp. kosher salt
- 2¼ tsp. freshly ground black pepper

RED WINE MUSHROOMS

- 2 Tbsp. butter
- 2 (8-oz.) packages fresh mushrooms
- 2 shallots, minced
- ½ cup dry red wine
- 1 cup beef broth

1. Prepare Roast: Let roast stand at room temperature 1 hour.

2. Preheat oven to 450°. Whisk together mustard and next 3 ingredients; reserve 1 Tbsp. Rub remaining mustard mixture over roast; sprinkle with salt and pepper. Place roast on a lightly greased rack in a roasting pan.

3. Bake at 450° on lower oven rack 45 minutes. Reduce oven temperature to 350°, and bake 1 hour and 10 minutes or until a meat thermometer inserted in thickest portion registers 120° to 130° (medium rare) or 130° to 135° (medium). Let stand 30 minutes; transfer roast to a serving platter, reserving drippings in pan.

4. Meanwhile, prepare Red Wine Mushrooms: Skim fat from reserved drippings; place pan on stove top over 2 burners. Melt butter in pan over medium-high heat, stirring occasionally and moving pan as necessary to prevent hot spots. Add mushrooms; sauté 3 minutes. Add shallots; cook, stirring constantly, 3 to 4 minutes or until tender. Stir in wine; cook, stirring constantly, 2 minutes. Stir in broth; reduce heat to medium, and simmer, stirring constantly, 5 minutes. Stir in reserved 1 Tbsp. mustard mixture. Add salt and pepper to taste Slice roast, and serve with mushroom mixture.

Sage-Crusted Double Pork Rack with Pear Chutney

MAKES 8 TO 10 SERVINGS
HANDS-ON 1 HOUR, 5 MIN.
TOTAL 13 HOURS, 50 MIN.

Ask your butcher: Leaving the meat on the bone will give bone-lovers more to gnaw on, but for a more elegant presentation, ask your butcher to french the racks, or trim the meat and fat clean from the bone.

Roast like a pro: The relatively neutral flavors of commercial pork call for a highly seasoned crust, in this case, a ground sage-chile-garlic and orange mixture. Pork loves fruit, so we pair it with an extra-chunky sweet-and-sour pear chutney.

The right temp: Thankfully, the USDA has relented on an across-the-board standard. Nowadays, we cook pork roasts like this until an instant-read thermometer reads 155°, which is medium to medium-well.

PORK

- 3 cups firmly packed fresh sage leaves (about 4 [1-oz.] packages)
- 3 garlic cloves
- 1¼ cups olive or canola oil
- 2 Tbsp. orange zest
- 1½ tsp. dried crushed red pepper
- 2 (3½- to 4- lb.) 6-rib bone-in pork loin roasts, chine bone removed
- 7 tsp. kosher salt

Pear Chutney

1. **Prepare** Pork. Process sage and garlic in a food processor 30 to 45 seconds or until finely chopped. Add 1 ¼ cups oil and next 2 ingredients, and process 10 to 15 seconds or until blended. Rub mixture over pork. Cover and chill 12 to 24 hours.

2. **Let** roasts stand at room temperature 30 minutes. Preheat oven to 500°. Place roasts on a lightly greased wire rack in a roasting pan. Sprinkle salt over roasts.

3. **Bake** at 500° for 30 minutes; reduce oven temperature to 325°, and bake 1 hour and 15 minutes or until a meat thermometer inserted into thickest portion registers 155°. Let stand 30 minutes.

PEAR CHUTNEY

Cook **5 ripe pears,** peeled and diced, in 2 Tbsp. hot **olive oil** in a Dutch oven over medium heat, stirring occasionally, 15 to 20 minutes or until tender. Transfer to a medium bowl; wipe Dutch oven clean. Heat 2 Tbsp. **olive oil** in Dutch oven over medium heat. Add 1 **large red onion,** cut into ½-inch slices, and sauté 8 to 10 minutes or until tender. Add ⅓ cup **golden raisins;** 3 **garlic cloves,** minced; and 1 tsp. **grated fresh ginger;** sauté 5 minutes. Add 1 Tbsp. **sugar,** 1 tsp. **ground cinnamon,** ½ tsp. **ground cloves,** and ¼ tsp. dried **crushed red pepper,** and cook, stirring constantly, 1 minute or until spices are fragrant. Stir in ⅓ cup each **red wine vinegar** and **maple syrup,** and cook 3 to 5 minutes or until reduced by half. Stir in pears; cook, stirring constantly, 5 minutes. Stir in ¼ cup **loosely packed fresh flat-leaf parsley.** Season with **salt** and **pepper** to taste. Makes 4 cups. Hands-on 45 min., Total 45 min.

5 Breakfast Breads

Greet the holidays with sticky sweet buns, rolls, and breads

Caramel-Glazed Monkey Bread

MAKES 10 TO 12 SERVINGS
HANDS-ON 30 MIN.
TOTAL 5 HOURS, 5 MIN., INCLUDING DOUGH AND GLAZE

We'd wager our presents under the tree that this is the best pull-apart bread on Earth. The dough is soft and cakey, and the loaf dons a scrumptious sugary crust.

> Wax paper
> ¾ cup granulated sugar
> ¾ cup firmly packed light brown sugar
> 1 Tbsp. ground cinnamon
> Breakfast Bread Dough
> ¾ cup butter, melted
> 1 cup chopped toasted pecans
> Caramel Glaze

1. **Generously** grease a 10-inch (12-cup) tube pan; line bottom with wax paper, and lightly grease wax paper.

2. **Stir** together granulated sugar and next 2 ingredients in a small bowl. Turn Breakfast Bread Dough out onto a lightly floured surface; knead 3 or 4 times. Shape dough into about 60 (1½-inch) balls. Dip each ball in melted butter, and roll in sugar mixture.

3. **Place** coated balls in a single layer in prepared pan, covering bottom completely. Sprinkle with ⅓ cup pecans. Repeat layers twice. Top with any remaining sugar mixture; drizzle wit any remaining melted butter. Cover and let stand 1 hour.

4. **Preheat** oven to 350°. Uncover and bake 40 to 45 minutes or until a wooden pick inserted in center comes out clean. Transfer to a wire rack, and cool 20 minutes. Remove from pan to wire rack, discarding wax paper. Invert onto a serving platter. Drizzle with Caramel Glaze. Serve warm.

Note: To make ahead, prepare recipe through Step 3. Cover and chill up to 24 hours. Let stand 1 hour and 30 minutes, and bake as directed.

CARAMEL GLAZE

MAKES ABOUT ¾ CUP
HANDS-ON 10 MIN.
TOTAL 10 MIN.

> ¾ cup firmly packed light brown sugar
> 6 Tbsp. butter
> 3 Tbsp. milk
> 1 tsp. vanilla extract

Bring first 3 ingredients to a boil in a small saucepan over medium heat, stirring constantly; boil, stirring constantly, 1 minute. Remove from heat, and stir in vanilla. Stir constantly 2 minutes; use immediately.

BREAKFAST BREAD DOUGH

MAKES 1 DOUGH PORTION
HANDS-ON 20 MIN.
TOTAL 2 HOURS, 25 MIN.

Incredibly versatile, this dough does double-duty and can be used in our Monkey Bread or Chocolate Rolls recipe. Similar to a refrigerator roll dough, it can be made and refrigerated for up to 3 days ahead of time.

> ½ cup warm water (100° to 110°)
> 1 (¼-oz.) envelope active dry yeast
> 1 tsp. sugar
> 5 cups all-purpose flour
> 3 Tbsp. sugar
> 5 tsp. baking powder
> 1½ tsp. table salt
> 1 tsp. baking soda
> ½ cup cold butter, cubed
> ½ cup shortening, cubed
> 2 cups buttermilk, at room temperature

1. **Stir** together first 3 ingredients in a 1-cup glass measuring cup; let stand 5 minutes.

2. **Stir** together flour and next 4 ingredients in a large bowl; cut butter and shortening into flour mixture with a pastry blender or 2 forks until crumbly. Add yeast mixture and buttermilk to flour mixture, stirring just until dry ingredients are moistened. Cover bowl with plastic wrap, and chill 2 to 72 hours.

Chocolate Rolls

MAKES 16 ROLLS
HANDS-ON 20 MIN.
TOTAL 4 HOURS, 25 MIN., INCLUDING DOUGH AND GLAZE

Be sure to use softened butter for spreading. It's the only way to keep the tender dough from tearing.

- Breakfast Bread Dough (see recipe on page 303)
- 1/2 cup butter, softened
- 1/3 cup granulated sugar
- 1/3 cup firmly packed light brown sugar
- 2 tsp. ground cinnamon
- 2 (4-oz.) bittersweet chocolate baking bars, chopped
- Vanilla-Orange Glaze

1. Turn Breakfast Bread Dough out onto a lightly floured surface, and knead 3 or 4 times. Roll dough into a 20- x 14-inch rectangle. Spread with softened butter, leaving a 1-inch border on all sides.

2. Stir together granulated sugar and next 2 ingredients. Sprinkle sugar mixture over butter. Sprinkle chopped chocolate over sugar.

3. Roll up dough tightly, starting at 1 long side; cut into 16 slices using a serrated knife. Place rolls, cut sides down, in a lightly greased 13- x 9-inch pan. Cover and let stand 1 hour.

4. Preheat oven to 350°. Uncover and bake 25 to 30 minutes or until golden brown. Cool in pan on a wire rack 10 minutes. Drizzle with Vanilla-Orange Glaze, and serve immediately.

Note: To make ahead, prepare recipe as directed through Step 3. Cover and chill 8 to 24 hours. Let stand 1 hour and 30 minutes, and bake as directed.

VANILLA-ORANGE GLAZE

MAKES ABOUT 1 CUP
HANDS-ON 5 MIN.
TOTAL 5 MIN.

Stir together 2 cups **powdered sugar**, 2 Tbsp. **milk**, 1 tsp. **vanilla extract,** and 1 tsp. **orange zest,** stirring in up to 1 Tbsp. **additional milk,** 1 tsp. at a time, until mixture reaches desired consistency and is smooth.

Kolaches

MAKES ABOUT 3 DOZEN
HANDS-ON 45 MIN.
TOTAL 10 HOURS, 10 MIN.

Just like biscuits, this dough will get tough if overworked. To portion it with ease, use a cookie scoop.

- 1 (1/4-oz.) envelope active dry yeast
- 1/2 cup warm water (100° to 110°)
- 1/2 cup butter, softened
- 1 1/3 cups sugar
- 2 1/2 tsp. table salt
- 2 large eggs
- 8 1/2 cups all-purpose flour
- 2 cups milk
- 3 (6-oz.) containers fresh blueberries (about 3 cups)
- 1/3 cup blueberry preserves
- 1/3 cup all-purpose flour
- 1/3 cup sugar
- 3 Tbsp. cold butter, cut up

1. Combine yeast and warm water in a 1-cup glass measuring cup; let stand 5 minutes.

2. Beat butter at medium speed with an electric mixer until creamy; gradually add 1 1/3 cups sugar and 2 1/2 tsp. salt, beating well. Add eggs, 1 at a time, beating just until blended after each addition. Stir in yeast mixture.

3. Add 8 1/2 cups flour to butter mixture alternately with milk, beginning and ending with flour mixture. Beat at low speed just until blended after each addition, stopping to scrape bowl as needed. Place in a well-greased bowl, turning to grease top. Cover with plastic wrap and chill 8 to 24 hours.

4. Shape dough into 35 (2-inch) balls (about 1/4 cup per ball), using floured hands, and place 1 1/2 inches apart on 2 lightly buttered baking sheets. Cover and let rise in a warm place 1 hour or until doubled in bulk.

5. Preheat oven to 375°. Stir together fresh blueberries and blueberry preserves. Combine 1/3 cup flour and next 2 ingredients in a bowl with a pastry blender until crumbly. Press thumb or end of a wooden spoon into each dough ball, forming an indentation; fill each with 1 Tbsp. blueberry mixture. Sprinkle flour mixture over balls. Bake 20 to 25 minutes or until golden brown.

Note: We tested with Smucker's Orchard's Finest Northwoods Blueberry Preserves.

MANGO KOLACHES Prepare recipe as directed, substituting 2 cups chopped fresh mango for blueberries and 1/3 cup peach preserves for blueberry preserves.

Ham-and-Swiss Sticky Buns

MAKES 16 BUNS
HANDS-ON 20 MIN.
TOTAL 1 HOUR, 10 MIN.

The trick to achieving a popover-like shape is to stuff the hefty rolls deep into the muffin tins. The tops will rise and form a cheesy dome while baking. If you want more kick, serve these with spicy mustard for dipping.

- 9 oz. deli ham, finely chopped
- 2 cups (8 oz.) shredded Swiss cheese
- 2 Tbsp. spicy brown mustard
- 1/2 cup firmly packed light brown sugar
- 2 (16.3-oz.) cans refrigerated jumbo biscuits
- Maple syrup (optional)

1. Preheat oven to 325°. Stir together first 3 ingredients.

2. Sprinkle brown sugar into a 12-inch square on a clean surface. Arrange biscuits in 4 rows on sugar, covering sugar completely. Pinch biscuits together to form a dough square. Roll dough into a 12- x 16-inch rectangle (about 1/4-inch thick), pinching dough together as needed. Spread ham and cheese mixture over dough. Roll up tightly, starting at 1 long side, pressing brown sugar into dough as you roll. Pinch ends and seam to seal. Cut into 16 slices using a serrated knife. Fit each roll into cups of a lightly greased 24-cup muffin pan. (Dough will extend over tops of cups).

3. Bake at 325° for 40 minutes or until golden brown and centers of dough are completely cooked. Cool in pan on a wire rack 10 minutes. If desired, drizzle with maple syrup.

Note: We used Pillsbury Grands! Flaky Layers Original refrigerated biscuits.

Gingerbread Muffins with Christmas Spice Streusel and Spiced Hard Sauce

MAKES 1 1/2 DOZEN
HANDS-ON 30 MIN.
TOTAL 1 HOUR, 45 MIN., INCLUDING STREUSEL AND SAUCE

We know, serving the streusel-topped muffins with hard sauce is really gilding the lily, but c'mon y'all, it's Christmas morning!

- 2 1/2 cups all-purpose flour
- 1/3 cup chopped crystallized ginger
- 1 tsp. baking soda
- 1/2 tsp. table salt
- 1/2 tsp. ground cinnamon
- 1/8 tsp. ground cloves
- 3/4 cup butter, softened
- 1/2 cup granulated sugar
- 1/2 cup firmly packed light brown sugar
- 2 large eggs
- 3/4 cup hot brewed coffee
- 2/3 cup unsulphured molasses
- 18 paper baking cups
  Christmas Spice Streusel
  Spiced Hard Sauce

1. Preheat oven to 350°. Process first 6 ingredients in a food processor 1 minute or until ginger is finely chopped.

2. Beat butter at medium speed with a heavy-duty electric stand mixer until creamy. Gradually add sugars, beating until light and fluffy. Add eggs, 1 at a time, beating just until blended after each addition.

3. Stir together hot coffee and molasses in a small bowl. Add flour mixture to butter mixture alternately with coffee mixture, beating at low speed just until blended after each addition.

4. Place baking cups in 2 (12-cup) muffin pans, and lightly grease; spoon batter into cups, filling two-thirds full. Sprinkle with Christmas Spice Streusel.

5. Bake at 350° for 18 to 20 minutes or until a wooden pick inserted in center comes out clean. Cool in pans on wire racks 5 minutes. Remove from pans to wire racks, and cool completely (about 30 minutes). Top with Spiced Hard Sauce.

Note: We tested with Grandma's Original Molasses.

CHRISTMAS SPICE STREUSEL

MAKES ABOUT 1 1/2 CUPS
HANDS-ON 10 MIN.
TOTAL 10 MIN.

- 1/2 cup firmly packed light brown sugar
- 2 Tbsp. all-purpose flour
- 1 1/2 tsp. ground cinnamon
- 1/4 tsp. ground cloves
- 1/4 tsp. ground nutmeg
- 1 cup coarsely chopped pecans
- 2 Tbsp. butter, melted

Stir together first 5 ingredients; stir in pecans and butter until crumbly.

SPICED HARD SAUCE

MAKES ABOUT 2 CUPS
HANDS-ON 10 MIN.
TOTAL 10 MIN.

- 1 cup butter, softened
- 2 Tbsp. milk
- 1/4 tsp. ground cinnamon
- 1/4 tsp. ground nutmeg
- 3 cups powdered sugar
- 2 tsp. vanilla extract

Beat first 4 ingredients at medium speed with an electric mixer until creamy. Gradually add powdered sugar and vanilla, beating until light and fluffy.

Note: To make ahead, refrigerate in an airtight container up to 1 week. Let stand 20 minutes before using.

ON THE SIXTH DAY OF CHRISTMAS *SOUTHERN LIVING* GAVE TO ME . . .

6 Tools for Holiday Sanity

These 6 gift-worthy tools were crucial to testing this year's holiday food section

1. UTILITY KNIFE It's not for opening boxes or presents, but for making "short cuts," literally. The sturdy handle and sharp blade make scoring skin and fat of large roasts simple, giving you the crispiest and most succulent cracklin' around.

2. BAKING MAT Get your roll on! This is the best baking prep surface we've ever tried. Just about any dough can be easily rolled and cut to exact measurements thanks to the printed rulers and guides. It's been our secret for perfect-sized biscuits, cookies, and pies; now it'll be yours.

3. JAPANESE MANDOLINE Want photo-worthy slices? Then grab this indispensable tool. It has a safety guard and is adjustable, allowing you to create everything from luxurious ribbons to slender coins.

4. COOKIE TINS Grandma was right: Holiday cookies are best kept in a tin. Find updated versions that sport bold colors and geometric patterns, which are great for sorting, storing, and gifting all your favorite varieties.

5. KITCHEN TOWELS A good towel is truly an all-purpose kitchen tool. Serving as oven mitt, trivet, napkin, and cleaning companion, these handy wipes are great gifts.

6. PROBE THERMOMETER You pay good money for a stunning holiday roast. Make sure it comes out perfectly by keeping track of its time and temperature. Complete with adjustable alarm tones, easy to read display, and probe thermometer, this canary will sing to help keep track of the prized main course.

7 Family Friendly Meals

Scoop into one of these delicious and hearty 1-dish and 1-pot meals that easily feed a full house.

One-Pot Shrimp and Grits

MAKES 8 SERVINGS
HANDS-ON 35 MIN.
TOTAL 1 HOUR, 5 MIN.

Spicy andouille, sautéed shrimp, and old-fashioned grits are the backbone of flavor for One-Pot Shrimp and Grits. Try not to overcrowd the pot when cooking the shrimp. Give them enough space so the shrimp brown and cook through quickly.

- 8 oz. andouille sausage, diced
- 3 Tbsp. olive oil
- 1 1/4 lb. peeled, large raw shrimp, deveined
- 1 medium-size sweet onion, chopped
- 2 celery ribs, chopped
- 3 garlic cloves, sliced
- 1 cup dry white wine
- 6 cups organic vegetable broth
- 1 (14 1/2-oz.) can fire-roasted diced tomatoes, drained
- 1/2 green bell pepper, diced
- 1/2 red bell pepper, diced
- 1/2 cup chopped green onions
- 1 1/2 tsp. Cajun seasoning
- 1 tsp. kosher salt
- 1/2 tsp. freshly ground black pepper
- 1 1/2 cups uncooked regular grits
- 2 Tbsp. chopped fresh oregano

1. Cook sausage in a large Dutch oven over medium heat, stirring often, 5 to 7 minutes or until browned. Remove sausage using a slotted spoon; reserve drippings in Dutch oven. Drain sausage on paper towels.

2. Stir oil into drippings. Cook shrimp, in batches, in hot drippings over medium-high heat 1 to 2 minutes on each side or until opaque; remove with a slotted spoon. Reduce heat to medium.

3. Sauté onion and celery in Dutch oven over medium heat 3 to 5 minutes or until tender. Add garlic, and sauté 1 minute. Stir in wine, and cook, stirring occasionally, 5 minutes or until reduced by half. Stir in broth and next 7 ingredients, and bring to

a boil over medium-high heat. Whisk in grits; return mixture to a boil, whisking constantly. Reduce heat to medium-low, and simmer, stirring occasionally, 20 to 25 minutes or until thickened. Stir in oregano, reserved sausage, and shrimp. Cook, stirring occasionally, 5 more minutes.

Chicken-and-Collard Green Pilau

MAKES 6 TO 8 SERVINGS
HANDS-ON 40 MIN.
TOTAL 1 HOUR, 5 MIN.

Chicken, rice, and greens fill the pot of our family friendly take on a Lowcountry staple. Quick-cooking basmati rice helps turn this dish into dinner in no time and stays fluffy throughout the cooking process.

- 6 oz. Cajun smoked sausage, diced
- 1 1/2 lb. skinned and boned chicken thighs, cubed
- 1 1/4 tsp. kosher salt
- 1/2 tsp. freshly ground black pepper
- 1 Tbsp. olive oil
- 1 cup chopped sweet onion
- 1 cup chopped celery
- 1 cup chopped carrot
- 2 garlic cloves, minced
- 3 cups organic vegetable broth
- 4 cups firmly packed chopped fresh collard greens
- 2 cups uncooked basmati rice
- 1/2 tsp. dried crushed red pepper

1. Preheat oven to 350°. Cook sausage in a Dutch oven over medium-high heat, stirring often, 5 to 7 minutes or until browned. Remove sausage using a slotted spoon; reserve drippings in Dutch oven. Drain sausage on paper towels.

2. Sprinkle chicken with salt and pepper. Add oil to hot drippings in Dutch oven, and cook chicken in hot drippings over medium-high heat, stirring occasionally, 8 to 10 minutes or until done. Add onion and next 3 ingredients. Cook, stirring often, 5 to 7 minutes or until onion is tender. Stir in broth, next 3 ingredients, and sausage.

3. Bring mixture to a boil over medium-high heat. Remove from heat; cover.

4. Bake at 350° for 20 to 25 minutes or until liquid is absorbed, stirring halfway through. Serve immediately.

Company Pot Roast with Creamy Mushroom Grits

MAKES 6 SERVINGS
HANDS-ON 40 MIN.
TOTAL 9 HOURS, INCLUDING GRITS

Seared flavorful chuck roast, slow cooked to perfection and served over creamy cheese grits with earthy mushrooms is easily made with the help of a slow cooker and quick-cooking grits.

- 6 medium leeks
- 4 thick bacon slices
- 1 (4- to 4 1/2-lb.) boneless chuck roast, trimmed
- 2 tsp. freshly ground black pepper
- 1 1/2 tsp. kosher salt
- 2 Tbsp. olive oil
- 3 garlic cloves, minced
- 1/3 cup firmly packed light brown sugar
- 1 cup dry red wine
- 1/3 cup balsamic vinegar
- 1 lb. carrots, cut into 4-inch sticks
- 1 lb. parsnips, cut into 4-inch sticks
- 1 cup chicken broth
- 1 Tbsp. cornstarch
  Creamy Mushroom Grits
  Garnish: fresh flat-leaf parsley sprigs

1. Remove and discard root ends and dark green tops of leeks. Cut a slit lengthwise, and rinse thoroughly under cold running water to remove grit and sand. Place leeks in a lightly greased 5- to 6-qt. slow cooker.

2. Cook bacon in a large skillet over medium heat 6 to 8 minutes or until crisp. Remove bacon, and drain on paper towels, reserving 3 Tbsp. bacon drippings in skillet. Crumble bacon.

3. **Sprinkle** roast with pepper and salt. Add olive oil to bacon drippings in skillet. Place roast in skillet, and cook over medium-high heat 2 to 3 minutes on each side or until browned. Transfer roast to slow cooker, reserving 1 Tbsp. drippings in skillet.

4. **Add** garlic to hot drippings, and sauté 30 seconds. Add brown sugar, stirring until sugar melts. Add wine and balsamic vinegar, and cook 2 minutes, stirring to loosen browned bits from bottom of skillet. Pour mixture over roast, top with carrots and parsnips.

5. **Cover** and cook on LOW 8 to 10 hours or until meat shreds easily with a fork.

6. **Transfer** roast to a cutting board; cut into large chunks, removing any large pieces of fat. Transfer roast and vegetables to a platter, and keep warm.

7. **Skim** fat from juices in slow cooker, and transfer juices to a 2-qt. saucepan. Add broth, and bring to a boil over medium-high heat. Stir together cornstarch and 2 Tbsp. water in a small bowl until smooth; add to pan, stirring until blended. Boil 1 minute. Add salt and pepper to taste. Serve gravy with roast and vegetables over Creamy Mushroom Grits. Top with crumbled bacon.

CREAMY MUSHROOM GRITS

MAKES 6 SERVINGS
HANDS-ON 20 MIN.
TOTAL 20 MIN.

Melt 1/4 cup **butter** in a medium skillet over medium-high heat; add 2 (3.5-oz.) packages **shiitake mushrooms,** stemmed and sliced, and sauté 3 to 4 minutes or until mushrooms begin to brown. Prepare 1 cup **quick-cooking yellow grits** according to package directions. Stir in 1/2 cup freshly grated **Parmesan cheese,** 1 tsp. **kosher salt,** and 1/2 tsp. **freshly ground black pepper.** Stir in mushrooms and 1/4 cup chopped fresh **flat-leaf parsley.**

Pizza Deluxe Casserole

MAKES 10 SERVINGS
HANDS-ON 40 MIN.
TOTAL 1 HOUR, 15 MIN.

Just about any large tube-shaped pasta will work in this Italian-style creation that kids and adults will crave.

- 1 (1-lb.) package ground mild Italian sausage
- 2 garlic cloves, minced
- 1 Tbsp. olive oil
- 1 (26-oz.) jar marinara sauce
- 1 tsp. kosher salt, divided
- 1/2 medium-size red onion, chopped
- 1/2 medium-size red bell pepper, chopped
- 1/2 medium-size green bell pepper, chopped
- 1/2 (8-oz.) package sliced baby portobello mushrooms
- 1 cup sliced black olives
- 1/2 cup pepperoni slices, chopped
- 1 (16-oz.) package rigatoni pasta
- 3 Tbsp. butter
- 3 Tbsp. all-purpose flour
- 3 cups half-and-half
- 2 cups (8 oz.) shredded fresh mozzarella
- 1/2 cup grated Parmesan cheese
- 1/2 tsp. freshly ground black pepper
- 1 (8-oz.) package shredded mozzarella cheese
- 8 to 10 pepperoni slices

1. **Preheat** oven to 350°. Cook sausage and garlic in hot oil in a large skillet over medium-high heat 5 to 7 minutes or until sausage crumbles and is no longer pink. Remove with a slotted spoon, reserving drippings in skillet. Drain sausage mixture on paper towels, and transfer to a medium bowl. Stir marinara sauce and 1/2 tsp. salt into sausage mixture.

2. **Sauté** onion and next 3 ingredients in hot drippings 5 minutes or until tender; stir in olives and chopped pepperoni. Reserve 1/4 cup onion mixture.

3. **Prepare** pasta according to package directions in a large Dutch oven.

4. **Melt** butter in a heavy saucepan over low heat; whisk in flour until smooth. Cook, whisking constantly, 1 minute. Gradually whisk in half-and-half; cook over medium heat, whisking constantly, 7 to 10 minutes or until mixture is thickened and bubbly. Stir in fresh mozzarella cheese, Parmesan cheese, pepper, and remaining 1/2 tsp. salt. Pour sauce over pasta in Dutch oven, stirring to coat. Stir in onion mixture.

5. **Transfer** pasta mixture to a lightly greased 13- x 9-inch baking dish, and top with sausage mixture, packaged mozzarella cheese, reserved 1/4 cup onion mixture, and pepperoni slices.

6. **Bake** at 350° for 30 minutes or until cheese is melted and lightly browned. Let stand 5 minutes before serving.

King Ranch Strata

MAKES 8 SERVINGS
HANDS-ON 40 MIN.
TOTAL 10 HOURS, 45 MIN.

To get the best baking results, don't forget to pour the remaining milk over top and knock off the chill by letting the strata stand 45 minutes before baking.

- 1/2 (16-oz.) French bread loaf, cubed (about 4 cups)
- 8 (6-inch) fajita-size corn tortillas, cut into strips
- 2 cups shredded cooked chicken
- 2 1/2 cups grated pepper Jack cheese, divided
- 3 Tbsp. butter
- 1 (14.5-oz.) can diced tomatoes, drained
- 3/4 cup chopped onion
- 1/2 cup chopped celery
- 1 (4-oz.) can diced green chiles, drained
- 2 garlic cloves, pressed
- 1 bell pepper, chopped
- 1 tsp. kosher salt
- 3/4 tsp. ground cumin
- 1/2 tsp. dried oregano
- 10 large eggs
- 1 (10 3/4-oz.) can cream of mushroom soup
- 2 1/2 cups milk, divided

1. **Toss** together first 2 ingredients, and place in a lightly greased 13- x 9-inch baking dish. Sprinkle with chicken and 2 cups cheese.

2. **Melt** butter in a medium saucepan over medium heat. Add tomatoes and next 8 ingredients, and cook, stirring often, 5 to 8 minutes or until tender. Remove from heat, and cool 10 minutes.

3. **Whisk** together eggs, soup, and 1 1/2 cups milk in a large bowl. Pour over bread mixture. Sprinkle with cooled onion mixture. Cover with plastic wrap, and chill 8 to 24 hours.

4. **Pour** remaining 1 cup milk over strata; top with remaining 1/2 cup cheese. Let stand 45 minutes.

5. **Preheat** oven to 325°. Bake 1 hour and 10 minutes. Serve immediately.

Pork Tacos with Pineapple Salsa

MAKES 8 TO 10 SERVINGS
HANDS-ON 20 MIN.
TOTAL 8 HOURS, 20 MIN.

Add fresh flavor to the tacos by getting creative with the toppings. Create a "taco bar" with plenty of options like shredded romaine, thinly sliced radish, fresh cilantro leaves, and crumbled queso fresco or goat cheese.

- 1 (4 1/2- to 5-lb.) boneless pork shoulder roast (Boston butt), trimmed
- 2 tsp. kosher salt
- 1 (12-oz.) bottle floral beer (such as Hoegaarden)
- 2 (8-oz.) cans pineapple tidbits in juice
- 1 (7-oz.) can chipotle peppers in adobo sauce
- 1 1/2 cups chopped fresh pineapple
- 1/3 cup chopped fresh cilantro
- 1/4 cup minced red onion
- 2 Tbsp. fresh lime juice
- 1 tsp. kosher salt
- 1/2 tsp. dried crushed red pepper
- 16 (6-inch) fajita-size corn tortillas, warmed
  Toppings: crumbled goat cheese, sliced radishes, fresh cilantro leaves, chopped avocado

1. Rub roast with salt, and place in a lightly greased 6-qt. slow cooker. Pour beer and 1 can of pineapple tidbits over roast. Process chipotle peppers and remaining can of pineapple in a blender or food processor until smooth. Pour over roast. Cover and cook on LOW 8 to 10 hours or until meat shreds easily with a fork.

2. Transfer pork to a cutting board; shred with two forks, removing any large pieces of fat. Skim fat from sauce, and stir in shredded pork.

3. Stir together fresh pineapple and next 5 ingredients. Serve pork in warm tortillas with pineapple mixture and desired toppings.

New Tuna Casserole

MAKES 8 SERVINGS
HANDS-ON 35 MIN.
TOTAL 1 HOUR, 30 MIN.

Our take on classic tuna casserole is creamy, cheesy, filled with fresh veggies, and has a salty crunch from a potato chip topping. Resist digging into the casserole right out of the oven. Give it a modest stand time of 10 minutes, allowing it to settle to the perfect consistency.

- 1 (16-oz.) package ziti pasta
- 1 (8-oz.) package haricots verts (French green beans), cut into 1-inch pieces
- 6 Tbsp. butter, divided
- 2 medium leeks, thinly sliced
- 2 (4-oz.) packages fresh gourmet mushroom blend
- 1/4 cup all-purpose flour
- 3 cups heavy cream
- 1 cup organic vegetable broth
- 2 cups (8 oz.) shredded sharp white Cheddar cheese
- 6 Tbsp. grated Parmesan cheese, divided
- 3/4 tsp. kosher salt
- 1/2 tsp. freshly ground black pepper
- 1 (12-oz.) can solid white tuna in spring water, drained
- 2 Tbsp. chopped fresh chives
- 1 Tbsp. chopped fresh tarragon
- 1/4 cup crushed potato chips
- 1/4 cup panko (Japanese breadcrumbs)
- 2 Tbsp. butter, melted

1. Preheat oven to 350°. Prepare pasta according to package directions.

2. Meanwhile, cook green beans in boiling salted water to cover 30 seconds to 1 minute or until crisp-tender; drain. Plunge into ice water to stop the cooking process; drain.

3. Melt 2 Tbsp. butter in a large skillet over medium-high heat. Add leeks, and sauté 2 minutes; add mushrooms, and sauté 5 minutes or until lightly browned. Transfer leek mixture to a small bowl. Wipe skillet clean.

4. Melt 4 Tbsp. butter in skillet over medium heat; whisk in flour, and cook, whisking constantly, 2 minutes. Gradually whisk in cream and broth. Bring mixture to a boil, stirring often. Reduce heat to medium-low; gradually whisk in Cheddar cheese and 4 Tbsp. Parmesan cheese until smooth. Stir in salt and pepper.

5. Stir cream mixture into pasta. Stir in tuna, next 2 ingredients, beans, and leek mixture; transfer to a lightly greased 13- x 9-inch baking dish.

6. Stir together potato chips, next 2 ingredients, and remaining 2 Tbsp. Parmesan cheese in a small bowl; sprinkle over pasta mixture.

7. Bake at 350° for 35 to 40 minutes or until bubbly. Let stand 5 minutes before serving.

8 Colorful Sides

Round out your holiday meal with these tasty side dishes

Glazed Turnips and Parsnips

MAKES 6 TO 8 SERVINGS
HANDS-ON 50 MIN.
TOTAL 55 MIN.

To make ahead, prepare recipe through Step 1, spread vegetables in a single layer in a jelly-roll pan, and cool to room temperature. Cover and let stand up to 4 hours or until ready to complete recipe.

- 2 lb. turnips, peeled and cut into 1/2-inch-thick wedges
- 1 lb. parsnips, peeled and cut into 1/2-inch slices
- 1 1/2 cups frozen pearl onions
- 2 tsp. kosher salt
- 3 Tbsp. cane vinegar, divided*
- 2 Tbsp. butter
- 2 Tbsp. olive oil
- 1 (3-inch) cinnamon stick
- 1 bay leaf
- 1/4 tsp. dried crushed red pepper
- 3/4 cup cane syrup
- 1/2 cup vegetable broth

1. Bring first 4 ingredients, 1 Tbsp. vinegar, and water to cover to a boil in a Dutch oven over medium-high heat. Cook, stirring occasionally, 12 to 15 minutes or until vegetables are just tender; drain.

2. Cook butter and next 4 ingredients in a large skillet over medium heat, stirring constantly, 1 minute or until butter melts and spices are fragrant. Add turnip mixture, and sauté 8 to 10 minutes or until lightly browned and thoroughly cooked. Discard cinnamon stick and bay leaf.

3. Stir in cane syrup, broth, and remaining 2 Tbsp. vinegar, and cook, stirring often, 8 to 10 minutes or until mixture is slightly thickened and vegetables are coated. Add salt to taste.

*Apple cider may be substituted.

Note: We tested with Steen's Pure Louisiana Cane Vinegar.

Collard Greens Gratin

MAKES 6 TO 8 SERVINGS
HANDS-ON 35 MIN.
TOTAL 2 HOURS, 30 MIN.

We found when using bagged chopped collards, the pieces can be a bit large and hard to eat. Our solution; give them a quick chop with a sharp knife to get them to bite-sized pieces.

- 5 cups heavy cream
- 3 garlic cloves, minced
- 2 cups freshly grated Parmigiano-Reggiano cheese, divided
- 1 tsp. cornstarch
- 2 (1-lb.) packages chopped collard greens
- 8 bacon slices, diced
- 2 cups chopped yellow onion
- 1/2 cup panko (Japanese breadcrumbs)
- 1 Tbsp. olive oil

1. Preheat oven to 350°. Bring first 2 ingredients to a light boil over medium-high heat. Reduce heat to low, and simmer 30 to 35 minutes or until reduced by half. Stir in 1 cup cheese. Stir together cornstarch and 1 Tbsp. water until smooth. Whisk into cream mixture until thickened.

2. Cook collards in boiling salted water to cover 5 to 7 minutes or until crisp-tender; drain and pat dry with paper towels. Cool 10 minutes; coarsely chop.

3. Cook bacon in a large skillet over medium-high heat, stirring often, 8 to 10 minutes or until crisp. Add onion, and cook 5 minutes or until tender. Stir in collard greens, and cook, stirring constantly, 3 minutes. Stir in cream mixture. Add salt and pepper to taste.

4. Pour mixture into a lightly greased 11- x 7-inch baking dish. Stir together panko, olive oil, and remaining 1 cup cheese; sprinkle over collard mixture.

5. Bake at 350° for 35 to 40 minutes or until breadcrumbs are golden brown. Let stand 5 minutes before serving.

Carrot-Cauliflower Salad

MAKES 8 SERVINGS
HANDS-ON 30 MIN.
TOTAL 1 HOUR, 10 MIN., INCLUDING VINAIGRETTE

We created this colorful, crunchy, and zesty side as a variation on the classic mayonnaise-based grated carrot salad. The sweet taste and light creaminess of the original are preserved through the addition of dried dates in the dressing and salad itself.

- 2 lb. carrots, thinly sliced
- 2 (6-oz.) packages baby rainbow carrots, diagonally sliced
- 1 Tbsp. kosher salt
- 2 Tbsp. apple cider vinegar
- 1 lb. fresh cauliflower, cut into small florets
  Orange Vinaigrette
- 1 cup loosely packed fresh flat-leaf parsley leaves
- 1/2 cup toasted walnuts, coarsely chopped
- 1/3 cup chopped dried dates
- 2 oz. feta cheese, crumbled

1. Toss together first 4 ingredients; drain in a colander 30 minutes.

2. Meanwhile, cook cauliflower in boiling salted water to cover, stirring occasionally, 1 to 2 minutes or until crisp-tender; drain. Rinse under cold running water until cool; drain.

3. Rinse carrots under cold running water; drain and pat dry. Toss carrots, cauliflower, Orange Vinaigrette, and remaining ingredients in a large bowl. Add salt to taste. Serve immediately.

ORANGE VINAIGRETTE

MAKES ABOUT 1 CUP
HANDS-ON 10 MIN.
TOTAL 10 MIN.

Process 1 tsp. loosely packed **orange zest,** 1/4 cup fresh **orange juice,** 2 Tbsp. chopped **dried dates,** 1 Tbsp. finely chopped **shallot,** 2 Tbsp. **apple cider vinegar,** 1 Tbsp. **honey,** 1 tsp. **Dijon mustard,** and 1/2 tsp. **kosher salt** in blender or food processor 30 to 60 seconds or until smooth. With processor running, pour 1/2 cup **canola oil** through food chute in a slow, steady stream, processing until smooth.

Savory Bacon-and-Leek Bread Pudding

MAKES 6 TO 8 SERVINGS
HANDS-ON 40 MIN.
TOTAL 1 HOUR, 20 MIN.

Spongy challah thoroughly soaks up the egg mixture, giving the dish a creamy and delicate texture when baked. The addition of hearty Parmigiano-Reggiano and smooth Gouda cheese add to the richness and depth of flavor.

- 8 large eggs, lightly beaten
- 1 cup half-and-half
- 1 cup heavy cream
- 2 tsp. kosher salt
- 1 tsp. dried thyme
- 1 tsp. dried marjoram
- 1 tsp. freshly ground black pepper
- 6 cups cubed challah bread (about 1-inch cubes)
- 1 1/4 cups grated Gouda cheese, divided
- 1 1/4 cups freshly grated Parmigiano-Reggiano cheese, divided
- 2 leeks, thinly sliced
- 2 Tbsp. butter
- 2 garlic cloves, minced
- 8 cooked bacon slices, crumbled

1. Preheat oven to 350°. Whisk together first 7 ingredients in a large bowl; stir in bread cubes and 1 cup each Gouda and Parmigiano-Reggiano cheeses.

2. Remove and discard root ends and dark green tops of leeks. Cut in half lengthwise, and rinse thoroughly under cold running water to remove grit and sand.

3. Melt butter in a medium skillet over medium heat. Add leeks, and cook, stirring occasionally, 7 to 8 minutes or until tender. Add garlic, and cook, stirring constantly, 1 minute. Fold leek mixture and bacon into egg mixture. Pour into a lightly greased 11- x 7-inch baking dish. Sprinkle with remaining 1/4 cup each Gouda and Parmigiano-Reggiano cheeses.

4. Bake at 350° for 35 to 40 minutes or until center is set. Let stand 5 minutes.

Citrus Salad with Pomegranate and Spiced Honey

MAKES 6 TO 8 SERVINGS
HANDS-ON 30 MIN.
TOTAL 1 HOUR, 5 MIN.

Cutting the citrus is the only real work you need for this palate-cleansing salad. Use any combination of citrus you have on hand; just peel and slice.

- 1/2 cup honey
- 1 (3-inch) cinnamon stick
- 1 bay leaf
- 1 tsp. black peppercorns*
- 1/4 tsp. dried crushed red pepper
- 4 whole cloves
- 3 medium-size oranges
- 3 mandarin oranges
- 2 Ruby Red grapefruit
- 2 limes
- 6 kumquats (optional)
- 1 (4.4-oz.) package fresh pomegranate seeds
  Toppings: fresh mint leaves, extra virgin olive oil, sea salt

1. Bring first 6 ingredients and 1/2 cup water to a boil over medium-high heat. Boil, stirring often, 1 minute. Remove from heat, and let stand 30 minutes.

2. Meanwhile, peel oranges, next 3 ingredients, and, if desired, kumquats. Cut away bitter white pith. Cut each fruit into thin rounds. Arrange rounds on a serving platter, and sprinkle with pomegranate seeds. Pour honey mixture through a fine wire-mesh strainer, discarding solids. Drizzle fruit with desired amount of spiced honey mixture; reserve remaining for another use (such as flavoring iced tea or cocktails). Top salad with a few drops of olive oil, a handful of fresh mint leaves, and sea salt.

*Pink or red peppercorns may be substituted.

Note: Salad may be made up to a day ahead. Prepare recipe as directed; cover and chill up to 24 hours.

Roasted Squash with Farro and Almonds

MAKES 6 TO 8 SERVINGS
HANDS-ON 25 MIN.
TOTAL 1 HOUR, 35 MIN.

With a texture similar to pearled barley, farro is quickly becoming a popular grain for many Southern cooks. This simple side dish highlights farro's hearty texture and nutty flavor and pairs it with sticky sweet roasted squash.

- 1 cup uncooked farro*
- 1/2 small butternut or kabocha squash, peeled and cut into 1/2-inch pieces (about 2 lb.)
- 1/4 tsp. kosher salt
- 1/4 tsp. ground cinnamon
- 1/8 tsp. ground nutmeg
- 1/8 tsp. freshly ground black pepper
- 6 Tbsp. olive oil, divided
- 1/4 cup roasted unsalted almonds, coarsely chopped
- 3 Tbsp. balsamic vinegar
- 2 Tbsp. honey
- 1/8 tsp. ground red pepper
- 1 shallot, minced
- 2 cups chopped radicchio or Belgian endive
- 1 cup loosely packed fresh flat-leaf parsley leaves
- 3 oz. crumbled blue cheese (optional)

1. Bring 6 cups salted water to a boil in a Dutch oven over high heat. Add farro, and boil, stirring occasionally, 25 to 30 minutes or until tender. Drain farro, and spread in a single layer in a lightly greased jelly-roll pan. Chill, uncovered, 30 minutes.

2. Meanwhile, preheat oven to 450°. Toss together squash, next 4 ingredients, and 2 Tbsp. olive oil in a large bowl. Spread squash in a single layer in a lightly greased jelly-roll pan, and bake 10 to 15 minutes or just until tender. Cool in pan on a wire rack 30 minutes.

3. Stir together almonds, next 4 ingredients, and remaining 1/4 cup olive oil in a small bowl. Add salt to taste. Let stand 10 minutes.

4. Stir together farro, radicchio, and parsley in a medium bowl; spoon desired amount of almond vinaigrette over farro mixture. Toss gently to coat; transfer mixture to a serving platter. Top with roasted squash and, if desired, blue cheese. Serve with remaining vinaigrette.

MAKE AHEAD: All elements can be made ahead individually and assembled before serving.

Glazed Sweet Potato Soldiers

MAKES 6 SERVINGS
HANDS-ON 40 MIN.
TOTAL 1 HOUR, 35 MIN.

This stripped down take on traditional glazed sweet potatoes is one of our favorites. We used the slender Garnet sweet potato, commonly grown in North Carolina, for this version, but if you can't find them in your area, a petite sweet potato will work in its place.

- 2 lb. small fingerling-style sweet potatoes (about 6 [7- x 1 1/2-inch] potatoes), unpeeled
- 1/2 cup fresh orange juice
- 1/4 cup butter
- 1/4 cup firmly packed light brown sugar
- 1/4 cup honey
- 2 Tbsp. dark rum or bourbon
- 1/2 tsp. ground ginger
- 1 Tbsp. butter
- Sea salt

1. Preheat oven to 425°. Pierce potatoes several times with a fork. Arrange in a single layer in a jelly-roll pan, and bake 25 to 35 minutes or until just tender. Transfer potatoes to a wire rack; cool completely (about 30 minutes).

2. Meanwhile, bring orange juice and next 5 ingredients to a simmer in a small saucepan over medium-low heat. Simmer, stirring often, 5 minutes or until thickened.

Remove from heat, and let stand at room temperature until ready to use.

3. Peel sweet potatoes, and cut crosswise into 1 1/2-inch pieces, discarding ends. Melt 1 Tbsp. butter in a 10-inch cast-iron skillet; cook over medium heat 1 minute or until butter begins to brown. Carefully add sweet potatoes, cut sides down, and cook 5 minutes. (Do not stir; move the skillet across the cooking eye to promote even browning.) Pour orange juice mixture over potatoes, and cook 10 minutes or until glaze is slightly thickened. Transfer sweet potatoes, seared sides up, to a platter; pour glaze over potatoes. Sprinkle with salt.

MAKE AHEAD Prepare recipe as directed through Step 2. Place cooked potatoes in a zip-top plastic freezer bag, and place glaze in an airtight container; refrigerate up to 3 days. Heat glaze in a small saucepan over medium heat 10 minutes, and proceed with Step 3.

Sweet Potato Spoonbread

MAKES 8 TO 10 SERVINGS
HANDS-ON 1 HOUR
TOTAL 2 HOURS

The addition of cornmeal to this soufflé-like side provides critical structure, helping it not to fall in the center. You may now scoop out a serving without fear of sunken spoonbread.

- 2 1/2 cups milk
- 1 Tbsp. fresh thyme leaves
- 2 tsp. sea salt
- 1/2 tsp. freshly ground black pepper
- Pinch of ground red pepper
- 1 cup plain yellow cornmeal
- 6 Tbsp. butter
- 3 medium-size sweet potatoes, baked, peeled, and mashed
- 5 large eggs, separated
- 2 tsp. baking powder

1. Preheat oven to 350°. Bring first 5 ingredients to a simmer in a 3-qt. saucepan over medium heat. Whisk cornmeal into milk mixture in a slow, steady stream.

Cook, whisking constantly, 2 to 3 minutes or until mixture thickens and pulls away from bottom of pan. Remove from heat, and stir in butter until melted. Cool 10 minutes.

2. Place potatoes in a large bowl; stir in cornmeal mixture. Stir in egg yolks and baking powder until well blended.

3. Beat egg whites at high speed with an electric mixer until soft peaks form; fold into potato mixture. Spoon batter into a well-buttered 3-qt. baking dish.

4. Bake at 350° for 40 to 45 minutes or until golden brown and puffy. (Edges will be firm and center will still be slightly soft.) Remove from oven to a wire rack, and cool 10 minutes before serving.

9 White Desserts

Bring out the sugar. Whip up the cream. Let the frosting billow.
Reveal a magical dessert for the grand finale to your feast.

Merry Cherry Cakes

MAKES 10 CAKES
HANDS-ON 45 MIN.
TOTAL 2 HOURS

- 2 (14.5-oz.) cans pitted tart cherries in water
- 1 (15.25-oz.) package white cake mix
  Vegetable cooking spray
- 3/4 cup sugar
- 3 Tbsp. cornstarch
- 1 (12-oz.) container frozen whipped topping, thawed
- 2 Tbsp. clear cherry brandy (optional)

1. Preheat oven to 350°. Drain cherries, reserving 3/4 cup liquid from cans. Coarsely chop 1/2 cup cherries, and drain well, pressing between paper towels to squeeze excess juice.

2. Prepare cake mix batter according to package directions; stir chopped cherries into batter.

3. Lightly grease 2 (6-cup) jumbo muffin pans with cooking spray. Spoon batter into 10 muffin cups, filling two-thirds full.

4. Bake at 350° for 17 to 19 minutes or until a wooden pick inserted in center comes out clean. Cool completely in pans (about 30 minutes).

5. Meanwhile, bring remaining cherries, sugar, and reserved cherry liquid to a boil in a medium saucepan over medium-high heat. Reduce heat to low, and simmer, stirring constantly, 1 minute. Stir together cornstarch and 2 Tbsp. water until combined. Quickly stir cornstarch mixture into cherry mixture, and cook, stirring often, 2 minutes or until mixture begins to thicken. Remove from heat, and cool 15 minutes.

6. Cut rounded top off each muffin to flatten; discard tops. Cut muffins in half crosswise. Dollop 1 rounded tablespoonful cherry mixture on each bottom half. Cover with top halves, and freeze 15 minutes.

7. Spoon whipped topping into a medium bowl. Stir in cherry brandy, if desired. Spread whipped topping over cakes, and top with remaining cherry filling. Serve immediately, or chill up to 24 hours.

Note: We tested with Oregon Fruit Products Pitted Red Tart Cherries In Water.

Milk Punch Frozen Custard

MAKES 8 SERVINGS
HANDS-ON 20 MIN.
TOTAL 6 HOURS, 35 MIN.

For a formal fête, freeze the custard in elegant wine glasses or brandy snifters. For a casual gathering, use milk shake glasses or punch cups.

- 3 large pasteurized eggs
- 2 large pasteurized egg yolks
- 3/4 cup sugar
- 1/2 cup brandy
- 1/4 tsp. ground cinnamon
- 1/4 tsp. ground nutmeg
- 1 1/2 cups heavy cream
  Garnishes: freshly grated nutmeg, whipped cream

1. Pour water to depth of 1 inch into bottom of a double boiler over medium heat; bring to a boil. Reduce heat to low, and simmer. Whisk together eggs, egg yolks, and next 4 ingredients in top of double boiler over simmering water, and cook, whisking constantly, 6 to 8 minutes or until thickened. Remove from heat, and cool completely (10 to 15 minutes), stirring often.

2. Meanwhile, beat cream at high speed with an electric mixer 3 to 5 minutes or until soft peaks form. Stir one-third of whipped cream into cooled egg mixture until well blended. Fold in remaining whipped cream. Spoon mixture into 8 (8-oz.) cups or glasses, filling half full; cover with plastic wrap. Freeze 6 hours to 2 days.

Red Berry Pavlova Tower

MAKES 10 TO 12 SERVINGS
HANDS-ON 40 MIN.
TOTAL 4 HOURS, 20 MIN., INCLUDING ICING

Easier to assemble than a layer cake, this tall pavlova will steal the show. The meringues and the frosting can be made a day ahead, and the tower should be stacked just before guests arrive.

- 2 cups sugar
- 2 Tbsp. cornstarch
- 8 large egg whites, at room temperature
- 1/2 tsp. cream of tartar
- 1/4 tsp. table salt
- 1/2 tsp. almond extract
  Parchment paper
  Cheesecake Frosting
  Whipped cream
- 2 lb. assorted fresh red berries (such as sliced strawberries, raspberries and fresh currants)

1. Preheat oven to 225°. Whisk together sugar and cornstarch. Beat egg whites at medium-high speed with a heavy-duty electric stand mixer, using whisk attachment, 1 minute; add cream of tartar and salt, beating until blended. Gradually add sugar mixture, 2 Tbsp. at a time, beating until mixture is glossy, stiff peaks form, and sugar dissolves. (Do not overbeat.) Beat in almond extract. Reserve 1 cup mixture.

2. Gently spread enough mixture onto a parchment paper-lined baking sheet to make a 10-inch round (about 1- to 1 1/2-inches high). Repeat process twice on another parchment-paper lined baking sheet, making an 8-inch round and a 6-inch round. Make an indentation in center of each meringue to hold filling.

3. Spoon reserved 1 cup meringue mixture into a large zip-top plastic freezer bag. (Do not seal.) Snip 1 corner of bag to make a small hole, and pipe meringue onto baking sheet next to 10-inch round to resemble a large chocolate kiss.

4. Bake at 225° for 1 hour and 30 minutes or until outside has formed a crust. Turn oven off; let meringues stand in oven, with door closed, 2 to 10 hours.

5. Place 10-inch meringue on a cake plate. Fill indentation with desired amount of Cheesecake Frosting, whipped cream, and berries. Top with remaining meringue layers, frosting, whipped cream, and berries. Top with kiss-shaped meringue. Serve within 1 hour.

CHEESECAKE FROSTING

MAKES ABOUT 3 CUPS
HANDS-ON 10 MIN.
TOTAL 10 MIN.

- 1/4 cup butter, softened
- 1 (8-oz.) package cream cheese, softened
- 1/2 cup sour cream
- 1/2 cup powdered sugar
- 1/4 tsp. table salt

Beat butter and cream cheese at medium speed with a heavy-duty electric stand mixer until smooth. Add sour cream, and beat until smooth. Gradually add powdered sugar and salt, beating at low speed until well combined. Use immediately, or cover and chill up to 48 hours.

Cranberry Dreamsicle Trifle

MAKES 10 TO 12 SERVINGS
HANDS-ON 30 MIN.
TOTAL 1 HOUR, 15 MIN.

- 3 1/2 cups frozen or fresh cranberries
- 3/4 cup sugar
- 1/2 cup orange juice
- 2 1/2 cups milk
- 2/3 cup sugar
- 1 Tbsp. orange zest
- 1 tsp. vanilla extract
- 3 large egg yolks
- 1/3 cup cornstarch
- 3 Tbsp. orange juice
- 1 (16-oz.) frozen pound cake, thawed
- 1 1/2 cups whipping cream, whipped to soft peaks

1. Bring first 3 ingredients to a simmer in a medium saucepan, and cook, stirring occasionally, 6 minutes or until sugar dissolves and orange juice is reduced by half.

2. Remove from heat, and cool 15 minutes. Cover and chill until ready to use, or refrigerate in an airtight container up to 4 days.

3. Whisk together milk and next 3 ingredients in a saucepan over medium-low heat, and cook, whisking occasionally, 2 to 3 minutes or until sugar dissolves. Remove from heat.

4. Whisk together egg yolks and next 2 ingredients in a medium bowl until smooth. Gradually whisk 1/2 cup milk mixture into egg yolk mixture, whisking constantly until smooth. Pour yolk mixture into remaining warm milk mixture in pan, whisking until blended. Cook over medium-high heat, whisking constantly, 3 to 5 minutes or until mixture thickens and begins to bubble.

5. Transfer to a bowl, and place plastic wrap directly on mixture (to prevent film from forming). Chill 30 minutes to 3 days.

6. Cut pound cake into 1-inch cubes. Layer one-third of cake cubes in a 2.5-qt. trifle dish. Top with one-third each orange pastry cream, cranberry mixture, and whipped cream. Repeat layers twice. Serve immediately, or cover and chill up to 24 hours.

Note: We tested with Sara Lee All Butter Pound Cake.

Ambrosia Coconut Cake

MAKES 12 SERVINGS
HANDS-ON 30 MIN.
TOTAL 11 HOURS, INCLUDING FILLING, FROSTING, AND CHERRIES

- 1 cup butter, softened
- 2 cups sugar
- 4 large eggs, separated
- 3 cups all-purpose flour
- 1 Tbsp. baking powder
- 1/2 cup milk
- 1/2 cup coconut milk
- 1 tsp. vanilla extract
- 1/4 tsp. coconut extract
- 1/8 tsp. table salt
  Vanilla Buttercream Frosting
  Ambrosia Filling
  Dipped Cherries
  Garnish: toasted shaved coconut

1. Preheat oven to 350°. Beat butter at medium speed with a heavy-duty electric stand mixer until fluffy; gradually add sugar, beating well. Add egg yolks, 1 at a time, beating until just blended after each addition.

2. Combine flour and baking powder; stir together milk and coconut milk. Add flour mixture to butter mixture alternately with milk mixture, beginning and ending with flour mixture. Beat at low speed until blended after each addition. Stir in extracts.

3. Beat egg whites and salt at high speed until stiff peaks form. Stir about one-third of egg whites into batter; fold in remaining egg whites. Spoon batter into 3 greased and floured 9-inch round cake pans.

4. Bake at 350° for 18 to 22 minutes or until a wooden pick inserted in center comes out clean. Cool in pans on wire racks 10 minutes; remove from pans to wire racks, and cool completely (about 30 minutes).

5. Place 1 cake layer on a serving platter. Spoon 1/3 cup Vanilla Buttercream Frosting into a zip-top plastic freezer bag. (Do not seal.) Snip 1 corner of bag to make a small hole. Pipe a ring of frosting around cake layer just inside the top edge. Top with half of Ambrosia Filling, and spread to edge of ring. Top with a second cake layer. Repeat procedure with frosting and remaining filling. Top with remaining cake layer, and spread frosting on top and sides of cake. Garnish with Dipped Cherries and coconut.

AMBROSIA FILLING

MAKES ABOUT 2 1/4 CUPS
HANDS-ON 25 MIN.
TOTAL 8 HOURS, 25 MIN.

- 1 medium-size navel orange
- 1 (8-oz.) can crushed pineapple in juice
- 3/4 cup sugar
- 1 Tbsp. cornstarch
- 1/4 tsp. table salt
- 3/4 cup heavy cream
- 3 large egg yolks
- 2 Tbsp. butter
- 1/4 tsp. coconut extract
- 1 cup toasted sweetened coconut

1. Grate zest from orange to equal 2 tsp. Peel and section orange; chop segments. Place oranges and pineapple in a fine wire-mesh strainer, and drain.

2. Whisk together sugar and next 2 ingredients in a 3-qt. heavy saucepan. Whisk in cream and egg yolks. Bring to a boil over medium heat, whisking constantly; boil, whisking constantly, 1 minute or until thickened. Remove from heat, and whisk in butter and coconut extract. Stir in orange-pineapple mixture, coconut, and orange zest.

3. Transfer to a small bowl, and place plastic directly on warm filling (to prevent a film from forming); chill 8 to 12 hours.

VANILLA BUTTERCREAM FROSTING

MAKES 4 1/2 CUPS
HANDS-ON 20 MIN.
TOTAL 20 MIN.

- 1 cup butter, softened
- 1 tsp. vanilla extract
- 1 (2-lb.) package powdered sugar, divided
- 3/4 to 1 cup heavy cream

1. Beat butter at medium speed with a heavy-duty electric stand mixer until creamy. Gradually add vanilla and 1 cup powdered sugar, beating at low speed until well blended.

2. Gradually add remaining powdered sugar alternately with cream, beating at low speed until blended after each addition. Beat at high speed until smooth and spreading consistency.

DIPPED CHERRIES

MAKES ABOUT 1 DOZEN
HANDS-ON 15 MIN.
TOTAL 45 MIN.

- 2 (2-oz.) almond bark candy coating squares
- 11 to 12 jarred maraschino cherries with stems, patted dry
  White sanding sugar (optional)
  Wax paper

Melt almond bark according to package directions. Holding onto stem, dip each cherry into melted bark, leaving a small amount of cherry visible. Sprinkle with sanding sugar, if desired, while almond bark is still soft. Place cherries on wax paper to dry completely (about 30 minutes). Remove stems, if desired.

Red Velvet Zebra Bundt Cake

MAKES 10 TO 12 SERVINGS
HANDS-ON 30 MIN.
TOTAL 2 HOURS, 45 MIN., INCLUDING GLAZE

- 1 cup butter, softened
- 1/2 cup shortening
- 2 1/2 cups sugar
- 6 large eggs
- 3 cups all-purpose flour
- 1 tsp. baking powder
- 1/2 tsp. table salt
- 3/4 cup milk
- 1 tsp. vanilla extract
- 1 Tbsp. unsweetened cocoa
- 1 Tbsp. red food coloring
  Snowy White Vanilla Glaze

1. Preheat oven to 325°. Beat butter and shortening at medium speed with a heavy-duty electric stand mixer until creamy. Gradually add sugar, beating until light and fluffy. Add eggs, 1 at a time, beating just until blended after each addition.

2. Stir together flour and next 2 ingredients. Add to butter mixture alternately with milk, beginning and ending with flour mixture. Beat at low speed just until blended after each addition. Stir in vanilla. Transfer 2 1/2 cups batter to a 2-qt. bowl; stir in cocoa and food coloring.

3. Drop 2 scoops of plain batter into a greased and floured 10-inch (16-cup) Bundt pan, using a small cookie scoop (about 1 1/2 inches); top with 1 scoop of red velvet batter. Repeat procedure around entire pan, covering bottom completely. Continue layering batters in pan as directed until all batter is used.

4. Bake at 325° for 1 hour to 1 hour and 5 minutes or until a long wooden pick inserted in center comes out clean. Cool in pan on wire rack 10 minutes; remove from pan to wire rack, and cool completely (about 1 hour). Drizzle with Snowy White Vanilla Glaze.

SNOWY WHITE VANILLA GLAZE

Whisk together 2 1/2 cups **powdered sugar**, 3 Tbsp. plus 1 tsp. **milk**, and 1 tsp. **vanilla extract** until smooth. Makes about 1 cup. Hands-on 5 min., Total 5 min.

Peppermint-Pretzel Bark

MAKES 12 SERVINGS
HANDS-ON 15 MIN.
TOTAL 20 MIN.

- 1 (16-oz.) package vanilla candy coating, chopped
- 1/2 tsp. peppermint extract
  Parchment paper
- 1 cup coarsely chopped pretzel sticks
- 2/3 cup coarsely chopped peppermint candy canes

1. Microwave candy coating in a 1-qt. microwave-safe glass bowl at MEDIUM (50% power) 1 minute; stir. Microwave until melted and smooth, stirring at 30-second intervals. Stir in peppermint extract.

2. Spread half of melted candy coating about 1/8 inch thick in a parchment paper-lined jelly-roll pan. Sprinkle 1/2 cup chopped pretzels and 1/3 cup chopped candy canes over melted candy coating, and press into coating. Repeat process with remaining ingredients on another parchment paper-lined jelly-roll pan. Chill 5 minutes or until cool and firm. Break into pieces.

Note: We tested with Log House Candiquik Vanilla Candy Coating and Nielsen-Massey Pure Peppermint Extract.

Raspberry Panna Cotta

MAKES 8 SERVINGS
HANDS-ON 20 MIN.
TOTAL 2 HOURS, 20 MIN.

- 1 (1-oz.) envelope unflavored gelatin
- 2 cups cold milk
- 2 pt. fresh raspberries, divided
- 3 Tbsp. sugar
- 2 Tbsp. fresh lemon juice
- 1 tsp. ground cardamom (optional)
- 1/3 cup sugar
- 1 Tbsp. vanilla extract

- 1/4 tsp. table salt
- 1 1/2 cups heavy cream

1. Sprinkle gelatin over milk in a medium saucepan; let stand 5 minutes.

2. Meanwhile, place 3 raspberries in each of 8 (6-oz.) parfait glasses or jars. Mash together 3 Tbsp. sugar, 2 Tbsp. lemon juice, remaining raspberries, and, if desired, cardamom in a medium bowl. Spoon 1 Tbsp. mashed raspberry mixture into each parfait glass. Reserve remaining berry mixture.

3. Stir 1/3 cup sugar, vanilla, and salt into milk mixture in saucepan, and cook over low heat, stirring constantly, 3 minutes or until sugar dissolves and milk begins to steam. Remove from heat; stir in cream. Pour milk mixture over raspberries in parfait glasses (about 1/2 cup per glass). Chill 2 hours or until firm.

4. Top each parfait with a heaping tablespoon of reserved mashed raspberry mixture just before serving.

Peppermint Ice-Cream Cake

MAKES 10 TO 12 SERVINGS
HANDS-ON 45 MIN.
TOTAL 25 HOURS, 40 MIN.

WHITE CAKE LAYERS

- 4 (8-inch) round disposable aluminum foil cake pans
  Wax paper
- 2 cups sifted cake flour
- 2 1/2 tsp. baking powder
- 1/2 tsp. table salt
- 1 1/4 cups granulated sugar, divided
- 1/2 cup canola oil
- 1/2 cup milk
- 1 tsp. vanilla extract
- 4 large egg yolks
- 8 large egg whites
- 1 tsp. cream of tartar

PEPPERMINT ICE-CREAM LAYERS

- 3 (8-inch) round disposable aluminum foil cake pans
- 1/2 gal. vanilla ice cream, softened
- 1 cup finely crushed hard peppermint candies (about 40 pieces)

Whipped Cream Frosting
- 3 cups heavy cream
- 1 tsp. vanilla extract
- 1/2 cup powdered sugar

Garnish
  Crushed hard peppermint candies

1. **Prepare** White Cake Layers: Preheat oven to 325°. Lightly grease bottoms of 4 disposable cake pans; line bottoms of pans with wax paper, and lightly grease wax paper.

2. **Whisk** together flour, next 2 ingredients, and 1 cup sugar in bowl of a heavy-duty electric stand mixer.

3. **Whisk** together oil and next 3 ingredients; add to flour mixture, and beat at medium speed 1 to 2 minutes or until smooth.

4. **Beat** egg whites in a large bowl at medium speed until foamy. Add cream of tartar; beat at high speed until soft peaks form. Gradually add remaining 1/4 cup sugar, 1 Tbsp. at a time, beating until stiff peaks form and sugar dissolves. Gently stir one-fourth of egg white mixture into flour mixture; gently fold in remaining egg white mixture .Divide cake batter among prepared pans, spreading with an offset spatula. Sharply tap pans once on counter to remove air bubbles.

5. **Bake** at 325° for 14 to 16 minutes or until a wooden pick inserted in center comes out clean. Cool in pans on wire racks 10 minutes. Remove from pans to wire racks; discard wax paper. Cool completely (about 30 minutes). Wrap layers in plastic wrap, and freeze 12 to 24 hours.

6. **Meanwhile,** prepare Peppermint Ice-Cream Layers: Line 3 disposable cake pans with plastic wrap, allowing 6 to 8 inches to extend over sides. Stir together vanilla ice cream and crushed peppermint candies in a large bowl. Divide ice-cream mixture among prepared pans (about 2 1/2 cups per pan), spreading to within 1/2 inch from sides of pans. (Cake layers shrink a little as they cool.) Cover with plastic wrap, and freeze 12 to 24 hours.

7. **Assemble** Cake: Remove plastic wrap from all layers. Place 1 cake layer on a serving plate; top with 1 ice-cream layer. Repeat with remaining white cake layers and ice-cream layers, ending with a cake layer on top. Wrap entire cake with plastic wrap, and freeze 12 to 24 hours.

8. **Prepare** Whipped Cream Frosting: Beat heavy cream and vanilla at medium speed until foamy. Increase speed to medium-high, and gradually add powdered sugar, beating until stiff peaks form. (Do not overbeat, or cream will be grainy.)

9. **Remove** frozen cake from freezer, and discard plastic wrap. Spread top and sides of cake with Whipped Cream Frosting. Garnish, if desired. Serve immediately, or freeze up to 2 hours. Store in freezer.

ON THE TENTH DAY OF CHRISTMAS
SOUTHERN LIVING GAVE TO ME . . .

10 Pouring Wines

Don't break the bank (or a sweat) pairing the perfect wine for the occasion. Let Inez Ribustello, queen of the $12 bottle and co-owner of Tarboro, NC's On the Square Restaurant, be your guide.

1. LA ARDILLA MOSCATO SPAIN $11
A sparkling liquid dessert from Spain that has a price tag lower than a Pecan Pie. For those who love something a little sweet, this spritzer is nectar in a bottle. Chill in an ice bucket to keep beside the Ambrosia Macaroons (page 290), and you'll be the most popular host on the block.

2. SAN GUILHEM CÔTES DE GASCOGNE FRANCE $10
Move over Sauvignon Blanc and Pinot Grigio, and go Gascony with light, crispy white that will be a fantastic pairing with just about any hors d'oeuvre. When you want to have a crowd-pleaser at your holiday party for 100, this Frenchie is a home run.

3. WILLIAMSBURG WINERY "JOHN ADLUM" CHARDONNAY VIRGINIA $12.50
Laden with ripe apples and creamy vanilla, this medium-to-full-bodied Chardonnay is not only totally proper, but it's big enough to pair with the Sage-Crusted Double Pork Rack with Pear Chutney (page 302) yet gentle enough to highlight Lump Crab Mornay with toast points (page 296).

4. HONORO VERA OLD VINES GARNACHA CALATAYUD, SPAIN $9
Did somebody say mistletoe? A bottle of this juicy, berry-laden red will make your lover's heart skip four beats. It's a fantastic match with that beef tenderloin in the oven, and because of the great price tag, you can buy more than one.

5. BENTON LANE PINOT NOIR OREGON $29
Splurge-worthy! Boasting a reputation as the healthiest wine in the world (thanks to all of the resveratrol found in the grapes), this light-bodied red with cranberries, cherry, and wild mushroom notes is as pretty as a present wrapped with red satin sashes.

6. SHELTON RIESLING YADKIN VALLEY, NORTH CAROLINA $11
One of the premier spots in the Yadkin Valley, Shelton Vineyards makes a killer Riesling that has loads of fruity personality and a dry finish. Want to add a little extra to the gift? Add a tag saying how great this wine is with chicken & waffles!

7. PADRILLOS MALBEC ARGENTINA $10
Secret Santa, I fear you not. This red from South America tastes like a blend of plums, dark chocolate, and roasted espresso beans. If you have a red wine lover in your midst, this gem says Happy Holidays in all languages.

8. VISION CELLARS BLANC GRIS CALIFORNIA $24
Worth the splurge! A blend of Sauvignon Blanc and Pinot Gris, Texas native Mac McDonald makes this wine in honor of his wife, Lil. Orange blossom, nectarines and plenty of pep, this fantastic white pairs with spicy poultry as much as Pimiento Cheese Gougéres (page 316). Buy it for your beautiful wife. Tell her that Lil recommended it; it's a wine that says the wife is in charge.

9. SUN GARDEN RIESLING NAHE, GERMANY $12
The only gift to give your friend who swears she doesn't like wine. Off-dry with loads of peach and ripe apple fruit, the turquoise bottle alone is a gift in itself. This one is the wine that turns the Grinch into a believer. Amazingly versatile, you can pair it with the Red Berry Pavlova Tower (page 312).

10. DIBON CAVA PENEDES $9
The perfect gift for your neighbor who is entertaining every garden club in the county this December. My husband, Stephen, and I drink our weight in this delicious sparkler from Spain. Perfectly priced, super fun and an awesome gift that will truly show friends just how wine savvy you are. Its tiny bubbles and crispy green apple flavor are so refreshing it will make a believer out of anyone who says they're not sure about sparklers.

11 Finger Friendly Appetizers

Serve these tasty pick-up foods at your next gathering

Pimiento Cheese Gougères

MAKES ABOUT 4 ¹/₂ DOZEN
HANDS-ON 35 MIN.
TOTAL 1 HOUR, 45 MIN.

We stamped a Southern accent on this classic French hors d'oeuvre. You can use a decorating bag with a ¹/₂-inch round tip or even a zip-top plastic freezer bag with a corner snipped off to pipe the gougères on the baking sheets.

¹/₂ **cup butter, cut up**
³/₄ **tsp. kosher salt**
1¹/₄ **cups all-purpose flour**
1 **(4-oz.) jar diced pimiento, drained**
4 **large eggs**
1¹/₂ **cups (6 oz.) finely shredded sharp Cheddar cheese**
1¹/₂ **tsp. Dijon mustard**
¹/₄ **tsp. ground red pepper**
Parchment paper

1. Preheat oven to 425°. Bring first 2 ingredients and 1 cup water to a rolling boil in a 3-qt. saucepan over medium heat; cook, stirring constantly, 1 minute. Add flour all at once, and beat vigorously with a wooden spoon 1 minute or until mixture is smooth and pulls away from sides of pan, forming a ball of dough. Reduce heat to low, and cook, stirring constantly, 2 minutes. (Dough will begin to dry out.) Remove from heat, and let stand 5 minutes.

2. Meanwhile, pat pimiento dry with paper towels, and finely chop.

3. Add eggs to dough, 1 at a time, stirring until blended after each addition. (If dough separates, don't worry. It will come back together.) Add pimiento, cheese, and next 2 ingredients; stir 2 minutes or until fully combined.

4. Drop half of dough by level tablespoonfuls 1 inch apart onto 2 parchment paper-lined baking sheets.

5. Bake at 425° for 10 minutes, placing 1 baking sheet on middle oven rack and other on lower oven rack. Reduce temperature to 325°, switch baking sheets, and bake 10 to 12 more minutes or until golden and crisp. Cool on baking sheets 5 minutes. Repeat with remaining dough. Serve warm.

Test Kitchen Tip: You can make the recipe ahead, and freeze completely cooled gougères in zip-top plastic freezer bags up to 1 month. To reheat, place frozen gougères on baking sheets, cover loosely with aluminum foil, and bake at 350° for 10 minutes or until warm.

Rosemary-Salt-and-Vinegar Chips

MAKES 6 APPETIZER SERVINGS
HANDS-ON 25 MIN.
TOTAL 25 MIN., PLUS 24 HOURS FOR BRINING

A tart, homemade brine gives these chips a more delicate vinegar tang than mouth-puckering bagged varieties.

2 **cups malt or white vinegar**
2 **Tbsp. sugar**
2 **Tbsp. kosher salt, divided**
2 **large russet potatoes (about 2 ¹/₄ lb.)**
1 **Tbsp. finely chopped fresh rosemary**
1 **tsp. freshly ground black pepper**
Peanut oil

1. Combine vinegar, sugar, 1 Tbsp. salt, and 1 cup water in a medium glass bowl, stirring until sugar dissolves. Cut potatoes into thin slices, using a mandoline or sharp knife. Stir potatoes into vinegar mixture, and chill 24 hours.

2. Stir together rosemary, pepper, and remaining 1 Tbsp. salt in a small jar.

3. Drain potatoes; gently pat dry with paper towels.

4. Pour oil to depth of 3 inches into a large Dutch oven; heat to 340°. Fry potatoes, in batches, stirring occasionally, 2 to 3 minutes or until golden brown. Drain on paper towels, and immediately sprinkle with rosemary mixture. Serve warm, or cool completely (about 10 minutes). Store in an airtight container up to 1 day.

Roasted Shallot Dip

MAKES ABOUT 4 CUPS
HANDS-ON 20 MIN.
TOTAL 5 HOURS, 35 MIN.

Caramelized sweet shallots and silky mascarpone cheese update the old-school onion soup dip. No need to waste time peeling all the shallots; after roasting, the papery skins easily slip away. This can be made 1 day ahead.

1¹/₂ **lb. shallots, unpeeled and root ends trimmed**
3 **garlic cloves, unpeeled**
2 **Tbsp. vegetable oil**
1 **(8-oz.) container sour cream**
1 **(8-oz.) container mascarpone cheese**
¹/₃ **cup thinly sliced fresh chives**
1 **Tbsp. fresh lemon juice**
2 **tsp. whole grain Dijon mustard**
³/₄ **tsp. kosher salt**
¹/₂ **tsp. freshly ground black pepper**
Dash of hot sauce
Garnishes: crumbled bacon, lemon zest, sliced fresh chives

1. Preheat oven to 425°. Cut shallots in half. Toss together shallots and next 2 ingredients in a jelly-roll pan; sprinkle with desired amount of salt and pepper. Bake 45 to 50 minutes or until shallots are light brown and skins are charred, stirring twice. Cool completely in pan on a wire rack (about 30 minutes). Remove and discard papery skins from shallots and garlic; coarsely chop shallots and garlic.

2. Stir together sour cream and next 7 ingredients; fold in shallot mixture. Add salt and pepper to taste. Cover and chill 4 to 24 hours. Stir before serving. Add salt and pepper to taste just before serving, if desired.

Warm Kale-and-Asiago Dip

MAKES ABOUT 3 1/2 CUPS
HANDS-ON 35 MIN.
TOTAL 1 HOUR, 5 MIN.

Trendy kale, a healthy dose of bacon, and Italian cheese replace traditional spinach in this baked crowd-pleasing dip.

- 5 bacon slices, chopped
- 1 bunch fresh Lacinato kale, stemmed and finely chopped (about 16 oz.)
- 1/2 medium-size sweet onion, chopped
- 2 garlic cloves, chopped
- 1/4 cup dry white wine
- 1 (8-oz.) package 1/3-less-fat cream cheese, softened
- 1/2 cup mayonnaise
- 1 cup plus 2 Tbsp. (4 1/2 oz.) shredded Asiago cheese
- 1 cup plus 2 Tbsp. (4 1/2 oz.) shredded fontina cheese
- 1 Tbsp. red wine vinegar
- 1/4 to 1/2 tsp. dried crushed red pepper
- 1/4 tsp. freshly ground black pepper
  Assorted crackers and crudités

1. Preheat oven to 350°. Cook bacon in a Dutch oven over medium-high heat, stirring often, 6 to 7 minutes or until crisp; remove bacon, and drain on paper towels, reserving 1 Tbsp. drippings in Dutch oven. Sauté kale, onion, and garlic in hot drippings 7 to 8 minutes or until onion is tender. Add wine, and cook, stirring constantly, 1 to 2 minutes or until particles loosen from bottom of Dutch oven.

2. Stir together cream cheese and mayonnaise in a large bowl until smooth. Stir in cheeses, next 3 ingredients, and kale mixture. Spoon into a lightly greased 1- to 1 1/2-qt. baking dish.

3. Bake at 350° for 25 to 30 minutes or until center is hot and cheese is melted. Let stand 5 minutes; top with chopped bacon. Serve with assorted crackers and crudités.

Test Kitchen Tip: To make ahead, prepare recipe as directed through Step 2. Cover and chill up to 24 hours. Let stand 30 minutes, and bake as directed.

Black-eyed Pea Pâté

MAKES 4 CUPS
HANDS-ON 25 MIN.
TOTAL 45 MIN., PLUS 8 HOURS FOR CHILLING (NOT INCLUDING ONIONS AND CUKES)

A touch of salty country ham and shiitake mushrooms adds a smoky touch to this Southern twist on pâté. This can be made a day ahead.

- 1 1/2 cups frozen black-eyed peas
- 1/2 jalapeño pepper, seeded
- 3/4 cup chopped country ham
- 1 (3.5-oz.) package fresh shiitake mushrooms, sliced*
- 3 garlic cloves, chopped
- 1/2 cup olive oil, divided
- 1/4 cup dry white wine
- 1/2 cup finely chopped toasted walnuts
- 1/2 cup finely chopped fresh flat-leaf parsley
- 2 tsp. chopped fresh thyme
  Pickled Red Onions and Cukes, drained
  Crostini

1. Cook black-eyed peas according to package directions, adding jalapeño pepper to water. Drain.

2. Sauté ham and next 2 ingredients in 2 Tbsp. hot olive oil over medium-high heat 4 to 5 minutes or until lightly browned. Stir in wine, and cook, stirring occasionally, 1 minute.

3. Process peas, jalapeño, ham mixture, and remaining 6 Tbsp. olive oil in a food processor just until smooth. Stir in walnuts and next 2 ingredients; add salt and pepper to taste. Cover and chill 8 to 24 hours.

4. Stir pâté, and add salt and pepper to taste, if desired. Transfer to a shallow bowl, or spoon into small jars. Top with desired amount of Pickled Red Onions and Cukes. Serve with crostini.

*1/2 (8-oz.) package sliced fresh button mushrooms may be substituted.

PICKLED RED ONIONS AND CUKES

MAKES ABOUT 1 1/2 CUPS
HANDS-ON 10 MIN.
TOTAL 2 HOURS, 10 MIN.

Stir together 1/2 medium-size **red onion,** thinly sliced; 1/2 **English cucumber,** seeded and sliced; 1 cup **seasoned rice wine vinegar;** 1 **garlic clove,** minced; 1/4 cup **water;** 1 Tbsp. **sugar;** and 1 1/2 tsp. table **salt** in a large bowl. Cover and chill 2 hours to 2 days. Serve with a slotted spoon.

Sesame Salmon Croquettes

MAKES ABOUT 3 1/2 DOZEN
HANDS-ON 45 MIN.
TOTAL 1 HOUR, 45 MIN., NOT INCLUDING RÉMOULADE

Fragrant fresh ginger gives these croquettes a bright punch of flavor. If you can't find fresh ginger, substitute with half the amount of dried ground ginger.

- 1 lemon
- 2 Tbsp. kosher salt
- 1 (1-lb.) salmon fillet
- 2 1/2 cups panko (Japanese breadcrumbs), divided
- 2 large eggs
- 2 green onions, thinly sliced
- 1/4 cup chopped fresh cilantro
- 1/4 cup mayonnaise
- 2 tsp. loosely packed lime zest
- 2 Tbsp. fresh lime juice
- 1 Tbsp. finely grated fresh ginger
- 1 (1.62-oz.) jar toasted sesame seeds
- 2 garlic cloves, minced
- 1/2 tsp. kosher salt
- 1/4 tsp. freshly ground black pepper
- 1/3 cup butter, melted
  Ginger Rémoulade (see page 318)

1. Cut lemon in half. Squeeze juice from lemon into a 3-qt. saucepan. Add lemon halves, 2 Tbsp. salt, and 6 cups water, and bring to a boil over medium-high heat. Add salmon fillet (cut into 2 pieces, if necessary); cover and reduce heat to low. Simmer 4 minutes. (Center of salmon will be raw.) Carefully transfer salmon to a large bowl, and cool completely (about 10 minutes). Remove and discard skin, and flake salmon.

2. Preheat oven to 425°. Stir 1/2 cup panko and next 11 ingredients into flaked salmon.

3. Stir together melted butter and remaining 2 cups panko. Spoon 1 tsp. panko mixture into each cup of a lightly greased 24-cup miniature muffin pan. Add 1 Tbsp. salmon mixture to each muffin cup. Top each with 1 tsp. panko mixture.

4. Bake, in batches, at 425° for 10 minutes or until topping is golden brown. Serve warm with Ginger Rémoulade.

Note: We tested with McCormick Gourmet Collection Toasted Sesame Seed.

Contemporary Shrimp Cocktail

MAKES 12 SERVINGS
HANDS-ON 10 MIN.
TOTAL 35 MIN., INCLUDING RÉMOULADE, CREAM, AND SAUCE

A rule of thumb: Plan on 1 pound of large shrimp for every 4 to 5 guests.

- 3 lb. peeled, large cooked shrimp with tails
  Ginger Rémoulade
  Avocado Cream
  Tequila-Lime Cocktail Sauce

GINGER RÉMOULADE

MAKES 1 1/3 CUPS
HANDS-ON 5 MIN.
TOTAL 5 MIN.

Stir together 1 cup **mayonnaise,** 2 minced **green onions,** 2 Tbsp. **Asian chili-garlic sauce,** 1 Tbsp. whole grain **Dijon mustard,** 1 Tbsp. fresh **lime juice,** and 4 tsp. grated **fresh ginger.** Add **salt** and **pepper** to taste. Serve immediately, or cover and chill up to 3 days. Stir well before serving.

AVOCADO CREAM

MAKES 1 3/4 CUPS
HANDS-ON 10 MIN.
TOTAL 10 MIN.

Scoop pulp from 1 large **avocado** into a medium bowl, and mash until very smooth. Stir in 1 (8-oz.) container **sour cream,** 2 Tbsp. chopped **fresh dill,** 2 Tbsp. chopped **fresh flat-leaf parsley,** 1 tsp. loosely pack **lemon zest,** 2 Tbsp. fresh **lemon juice,** and 1 **green onion,** minced. Add **salt** and **pepper** to taste. Serve immediately, or cover and chill up to 1 day. Stir well before serving.

TEQUILA-LIME COCKTAIL SAUCE

MAKES 1 1/2 CUPS
HANDS-ON 10 MIN.
TOTAL 10 MIN.

Stir together 1 (12-oz.) bottle **chili sauce,** 2 Tbsp. chopped **fresh cilantro,** 3 Tbsp. **tequila,** 2 Tbsp. prepared **horseradish,** 1 tsp. loosely packed **lime zest,** 1 Tbsp. fresh **lime juice,** and if desired, 1/2 **jalapeño pepper,** minced. Add **salt** and **pepper** to taste. Serve immediately, or cover and chill until up to 3 days. Stir well before serving.

Cranberry-Goat Cheese Canapés

MAKES 36 PIECES
HANDS-ON 25 MIN.
TOTAL 55 MIN., INCLUDING TOAST SQUARES

Make the cranberry mixture up to 3 days ahead of time and assemble the canapés the day of your party.

- 1 1/2 cups fresh cranberries, chopped
- 3 Tbsp. chopped fresh cilantro
- 3 Tbsp. sugar
- 1 1/2 Tbsp. minced fresh jalapeño pepper
- 3/4 tsp. grated fresh ginger
  Canapé Toast Squares
- 1 (5.3-oz.) container spreadable goat cheese
  Garnish: roasted, salted, and shelled pepitas (pumpkin seeds)

1. Stir together first 5 ingredients in a medium bowl. Let stand 10 minutes, stirring occasionally. Add salt and pepper to taste.

2. Spread each toast square evenly with cheese, and top with a small spoonful of cranberry mixture.

Note: We tested with Chavrie Original Mild Goat Cheese.

CANAPÉ TOAST SQUARES

MAKES 36 PIECES
HANDS-ON 10 MIN.
TOTAL 20 MIN.

Preheat oven to 350°. Cut 9 sandwich **bread** slices into quarters using a 2-inch square cutter. Place in a single layer on a baking sheet. Coat 1 side of bread slices with **vegetable cooking spray.** Bake 7 to 9 minutes or until lightly toasted.

Note: We tested with Pepperidge Farm Original White and 100% Whole Wheat Stone Ground Sliced Bread.

Asparagus-Gorgonzola Canapés

MAKES 36 PIECES
HANDS-ON 30 MIN.
TOTAL 50 MIN., INCLUDING TOAST SQUARES

If you're not a blue cheese fan, use any kind of soft, crumbly cheese you like.

- 3 oz. Gorgonzola cheese, softened
- 3 oz. cream cheese, softened
- 1/3 cup finely chopped toasted walnuts
- 2 Tbsp. half-and-half
- 2 Tbsp. butter
- 1 large shallot, finely chopped
- 2 cups thinly sliced fresh asparagus
  Canapé Toast Squares

1. Stir together first 4 ingredients in a small bowl. Melt butter in a medium skillet over medium-high heat; add shallot, and sauté 2 minutes. Add asparagus, and sauté 2 minutes or just until crisp-tender. Add salt and pepper to taste.

2. Spread each toast square with cheese mixture, and top with asparagus mixture.

Pumpkin-Carrot Soup with Coconut Cream

MAKES 6 CUPS
HANDS-ON 35 MIN.
TOTAL 1 HOUR, 25 MIN., INCLUDING COCONUT CREAM

Inexpensive glass votives or demitasse cups are perfect for serving this soup. Fry 4 long strips of prosciutto or center cut bacon in 1 tsp. hot oil to make a crisp, salty garnish to pair with the silky soup. Smoked paprika can easily be substituted for pimentón. If you prefer a thinner soup, add vegetable broth, 1 Tbsp., at a time until desired consistency.

- 3 Tbsp. butter
- 2 large shallots, sliced
- 1 small red bell pepper, chopped
- 3 garlic cloves, chopped
- 1/2 jalapeño pepper, seeded and diced (optional)
- 1 (1-lb.) package baby carrots, coarsely chopped
- 1 Tbsp. finely grated fresh ginger
- 1/4 tsp. pimentón (sweet smoked Spanish paprika)
- 6 cups vegetable broth
- 1 (15-oz.) can pumpkin
- 3/4 tsp. kosher salt
- 1/4 tsp. freshly ground black pepper
- 1/2 cup heavy cream
  Coconut Cream

1. Melt butter in a Dutch oven over medium-high heat; add shallots, next 2 ingredients, and, if desired, jalapeño, and sauté 5 minutes or until golden. Add carrots, and sauté 5 minutes. Stir in ginger and pimentón, and cook, stirring constantly, 1 minute. Stir in broth and next 3 ingredients. Bring to a boil, reduce heat to low, and simmer, stirring occasionally, 25 minutes or until tender. Remove from heat; cover and let stand 5 minutes.

2. Process with a handheld blender until smooth. Stir in cream and salt and pepper to taste. Cook over medium heat, stirring occasionally, 5 minutes or until thoroughly heated. Pour into small glasses or demitasse cups; dollop with Coconut Cream.

COCONUT CREAM

MAKES ABOUT 1 ½ CUPS
HANDS-ON 5 MIN.
TOTAL 5 MIN.

Place ½ cup cold **heavy cream** and a pinch of table **salt** in a chilled bowl, and beat at medium-high speed with an electric mixer until foamy. Add ⅓ cup **coconut milk**, and beat until soft peaks form.

Pepper Jelly Palmiers

MAKES ABOUT 4 DOZEN
HANDS-ON 20 MIN.
TOTAL 2 HOURS, 10 MIN.

Party-staple pepper jelly goes uptown in this flaky, sweet-and-savory cookie.

- 1 (17.3-oz.) package frozen puff pastry sheets, thawed
  Parchment paper
- 1 cup plus 2 Tbsp. finely shredded Parmesan cheese
- 6 Tbsp. chopped fresh chives
- ½ tsp. kosher salt
- ½ tsp. freshly ground black pepper
- ½ cup hot pepper jelly

1. Roll 1 pastry sheet into a 12- x 10-inch rectangle on lightly floured parchment paper. Sprinkle with half of cheese, 3 Tbsp. chives, and ¼ tsp. each salt and pepper. Roll up pastry, jelly-roll fashion, starting with each short side and ending at middle of pastry sheet. Wrap pastry tightly with parchment paper. Repeat procedure with remaining pastry sheet, cheese, chives, salt, and pepper. Freeze pastries 1 to 24 hours.

2. Preheat oven to 375°. Remove pastries from freezer, and let stand at room temperature 10 minutes. Cut each roll into ¼-inch-thick slices, and place on parchment paper-lined baking sheets. Bake, in batches, 20 minutes or until golden.

3. Microwave pepper jelly in a microwave-safe bowl at HIGH 1 minute. Spread ½ tsp. pepper jelly onto each palmier. Serve immediately.

Test Kitchen Tip: To make ahead, prepare as directed through Step 1. Wrap uncut pastry rolls in heavy-duty plastic wrap, and freeze up to 1 month. To serve, proceed as directed in Steps 2 and 3.

12 Gifts for Sharing

Show them you love them (and save money) with 12 handmade & from-the-heart stocking stuffers for everyone on your list

FOR THE
CHEESE LOVER

Amp up the holiday cheese platter with a new cheese ball, briny cubes of marinated feta, and a spicy honey for drizzling.

MAKE IT:
Smoky Bacon-Cheddar Cheese Ball

Cook 6 **hickory-smoked bacon** slices in a skillet over medium heat 5 to 8 minutes or until crisp; remove bacon, and drain on paper towels, reserving 2 Tbsp. drippings in skillet. Crumble bacon. Sauté ½ cup chopped **pecans** in hot drippings 2 minutes. Remove skillet from heat, and cool 10 minutes. Stir together 2 cups (8 oz.) freshly shredded **sharp Cheddar cheese,** ⅓ cup **mayonnaise,** ¼ cup sliced **green onions,** ½ tsp. **kosher salt,** ¼ tsp. **ground red pepper,** 3 oz. softened **cream cheese,** crumbled bacon, and pecans. Shape into a ball, or use as a spread. Total 15 min.

To package: Wrap neatly in plastic wrap, and refrigerate up to 1 week.

Marinated Feta

Cook 1 cup **olive oil** and 3 smashed **garlic cloves** in a small saucepan over medium-low heat 2 to 3 minutes or until garlic starts to bubble. (Do not brown.) Remove pan from heat; cool completely (about 15 minutes). Layer 2 oz. **feta cheese,** cubed; 2 **lemon slices;** 4 small fresh **thyme sprigs;** and ¼ cup **Castelvetrano olives** in 1 (1-pt.) jar. Repeat layers once. Pour oil-and-garlic mixture over feta mixture. Add additional oil to fill jar. Cover and chill 24 hours to 3 days. Total 15 min.

Chile-Infused Honey

Stir together 1 cup **honey;** ½ tsp. dried crushed **red pepper;** ¼ tsp. **kosher salt;** and 2 fresh **peppers** (such as serrano or jalapeño), sliced; and 1 (4-inch) fresh **rosemary sprig** in a small saucepan over medium heat 2 to 3 minutes or until bubbles begin to appear around edges of pan. Remove from heat, and cool completely (about 15 minutes).

To package: Spoon into 1 (8-oz.) jar. Use immediately, or cover and chill up to 2 weeks.
To serve: Let mixture stand at room temperature 30 minutes. Serve with cheese.

2

FOR THE
BRUNCH BUNCH

Which came first: The chicken or the waffle? Decide over a brunch of pecan-crusted chicken tenders with a bacon-studded waffles.

MAKE IT:
Pecan-Cornmeal Dredge

Stir together 2 cups coarsely chopped **pecans,** 2 cups **all-purpose flour,** 1 cup plain **yellow cornmeal,** 1/2 cup chopped **shallots,** 1 Tbsp. **kosher salt,** 1 Tbsp. chopped fresh **rosemary,** and 1 tsp. freshly ground black **pepper.** Refrigerate in an airtight container up to 1 week. Makes 5 1/2 cups. Hands-on 15 min. Total 15 min.
To package: Spoon into a bag, and refrigerate.
To make chicken tenders: Place dredge in a shallow bowl. Whisk together 1 large **egg** and 1/2 cup **milk** in another shallow bowl. Dip 16 **chicken breast tenders,** 1 at a time, in egg mixture; dredge in Pecan-Cornmeal Dredge. Pour vegetable oil to depth of 2 inches into a Dutch oven; heat to 325°. Fry chicken, in batches, 5 to 6 minutes or until done. Drain on a wire rack over paper towels. Makes 4 servings. Hands-on 35 min. Total 35 min.

Bacon Waffle Mix

Whisk together 2 cups **all-purpose flour,** 2 Tbsp. **sugar,** 1 Tbsp. **baking powder,** 1/2 tsp. **kosher salt,** and 5 cooked and crumbled **bacon** slices.
To package: Spoon into a bag and refrigerate.
To make Bacon Waffles: Place Bacon Waffle Mix in a medium bowl; stir in 1 1/4 cups **milk,** 1/4 cup melted **butter,** and 2 large **eggs.** Cook in a preheated oiled waffle iron until done. Makes 8 (4-inch) waffles (about 1/2 cup batter per waffle). Hands-on 35 min. Total 35 min.

3

FOR THE
SLOW COOKER SET

MAKE IT:
Green Chile Chili Starter

Sauté 4 **poblano peppers,** seeded and chopped; 10 **garlic cloves,** smashed; 2 large **carrots,** chopped; and 1 medium-size **white onion,** chopped, in 2 Tbsp. **olive oil** in a large skillet over medium heat 4 to 5 minutes or until tender. Remove from heat, and stir in 2 (15.5-oz.) cans **white hominy,** drained; and 1 (16-oz.) jar **salsa verde.** Stir in 2 tsp. **kosher salt,** 2 Tbsp. **ground cumin,** 2 tsp. **dried oregano,** and 1/2 tsp. **ground red pepper.**
To package: Spoon into 2 (1-qt.) canning jars, leaving 1/2 inch room at the top. Cover with metal lids, and screw on bands. Chill up to 1 week. Total 25 min.
To make Green Chile Chili: Place 12 boned and skinned **chicken thighs** in a 5-qt. slow cooker. Pour both jars Chili Starter over chicken; cook on LOW for 6 to 7 hours or until chicken is done. Skim the fat. Serve with Mexican crema and cilantro.

Hoppin' John Stew Starter

To make Ham Base: Cook 6 **bacon** slices in a skillet over medium heat 8 to 10 minutes or until crisp. Remove bacon, and drain on paper towels, reserving drippings in skillet. Crumble. Cook 8 oz. chopped smoked **pork** in hot drippings 3 to 4 minutes or just until beginning to brown. Combine crumbled bacon, pork, and 1/3 cup jarred ham soup base.
To package: Spoon Ham Base into 1 (8-oz.) jar. Chill up to 2 weeks.
To make pea mixture: Combine 1 1/4 cups dried **black-eyed peas,** 1 cup uncooked converted **white rice,** 1/4 cup **dried onion flakes,** 2 tsp. freshly ground **black pepper,** 1 tsp. **smoked paprika,** 1/2 tsp. **garlic powder,** 1/4 tsp. **baking soda,** and 2 **bay leaves.**
To package: Spoon in a decorative bag; tie with a ribbon. Store at room temperature up to 3 weeks. Total 20 min.
To make Hoppin' John Stew: Stir together pea mixture and bacon mixture in a slow cooker; stir in 8 cups water. Cover and cook on LOW 7 to 8 hours or until peas are tender. Serve with pepper vinegar. Makes 8 to 10 servings. Hands-on 5 min. Total 7 hours, 5 min., not including starter

4

FOR THE
CARAMEL CONNOISSEUR

MAKE IT:
Orange Caramel Taffy

Line bottom and sides of an 8-inch square pan with aluminum foil, allowing 2 to 3 inches to extend over sides. Generously grease foil. Melt 1 cup **butter** in a 3-qt. saucepan over low heat. Stir in 1 (16-oz.) package **dark brown sugar,** 1 (14-oz.) can **sweetened condensed milk,** and 1 cup **light corn syrup** until smooth. Bring mixture to a boil. Cook over medium heat, stirring constantly, until a candy thermometer registers 235° (about 20 minutes). Remove from heat; add 1 Tbsp. orange zest, and stir 1 minute or until mixture is smooth and no longer bubbling. Quickly pour mixture into prepared pan. Let stand 2 hours. Lift caramels from pan, using foil sides as handles. Makes 32 pieces. Total 2 hours, 20 min.
To package: Cut caramels into 2- x 1-inch pieces with a buttered knife. Wrap each piece in a taffy wrapper.

Boozy Caramel Fudge

Bring 3/4 cup **sugar,** 1/4 cup **water,** and 1 Tbsp. fresh **lemon juice** to a boil in a small saucepan over medium-high heat. Boil 8 to 10 minutes or until sugar begins to brown. (Do not stir.) Stir in 1/3 cup **heavy cream** and 2 Tbsp. **butter;** remove from heat. Let stand, stirring constantly, until mixture is no longer bubbling. Microwave 2 (14-oz.) cans **sweetened condensed milk** and 2 (12-oz.) packages **semisweet chocolate morsels** in a large microwave-safe bowl at HIGH 3 minutes, stirring at 1-minute intervals. Stir in 1/4 cup **dark rum,** 2 1/2 Tbsp. **butter,** and 1/4 tsp. **table salt.** Immediately pour into a greased and parchment paper-lined 9-inch square pan. Immediately pour caramel mixture over chocolate mixture, and gently swirl with a knife. Chill 2 to 4 hours. Hands-on 20 min. Total 2 hours, 20 min.
To package: Cut into squares, and wrap in wax paper. Store in refrigerator. Let stand at room temperature 15 minutes before serving.

5

FOR THE
ITALIOPHILE

Use these versatile spiced nuts and roasted sweet peppers as condiments for bruschetta and stir-ins for pasta.

MAKE IT:
Roasted Sweet Peppers

Preheat oven to 450°. Toss together 1 ½ lb. **sweet mini bell peppers, 3 garlic cloves,** unpeeled, and 2 Tbsp. **olive oil.** Bake in a single layer in a jelly-roll pan 25 to 30 minutes or until peppers look blistered, stirring every 10 minutes. Peel, seed, and coarsely chop peppers. Peel and slice garlic; stir into peppers. Stir in ¼ cup torn **fresh basil,** 2 Tbsp. chopped **fresh chives,** 1 tsp. loosely packed **lemon zest,** ¾ tsp. **kosher salt,** and ½ tsp. **dried crushed red pepper.** Total: 40 min.
To package: Spoon into 1 (1-pt.) jar. Chill up to 1 week.
To make sweet pepper bruschetta: Spoon pepper mixture over toasted French bread slices.

Garlicky Mixed Nuts

Cook ½ cup chopped **pecans** and ¼ cup each **pine nuts,** sliced **almonds** and blanched **hazelnuts** in 1/3 cup hot **olive oil** in a medium skillet over medium heat, stirring constantly, 2 minutes or until toasted. Remove from heat. Stir in ½ cup **golden raisins;** ½ cup chopped fresh **flat-leaf parsley;** 2 tsp. chopped fresh **thyme;** 1 tsp. loosely packed **orange zest;** ½ tsp. **dried crushed red pepper;** 1/4 tsp. **table salt,** and 1 large **garlic clove,** sliced.
To package: Pour mixture into 1 (8-oz.) jar. Chill up to 2 weeks.
To use the nuts: Cook **Garlicky Mixed Nuts** in 2 Tbsp. hot **olive oil** in a medium skillet over medium heat 1 to 2 minutes or until fragrant. Toss with 16 oz. **hot cooked pasta.** Serve immediately with **grated Parmesan.** Makes 6 to 8 servings. Total 10 min.

6

FOR THE
SOUTHERN BAKER

Easy homemade self-rising flour with cornmeal gives biscuits added texture. A decadent pie filling shortcuts pie baking.

MAKE IT:
Hot Fudge Pie Filling

Microwave 1 cup **half-and-half,** ¼ cup **butter,** and 8 oz. chopped **bittersweet chocolate** in a microwave-safe bowl at HIGH 2 minutes or until chocolate melts. Stir until smooth. Stir together 1 ½ cups **sugar,** ¾ cup **unsweetened cocoa,** ¼ cup **all-purpose flour,** and ¼ tsp. **table salt** in a medium bowl. Stir in 2 large **eggs,** 3 large **egg yolks,** and melted chocolate mixture.
To package: Pour Hot Fudge Pie Filling into a 1-qt. jar; cover and chill 1 hour to 7 days. (Mixture thickens as it chills.)

To make your pie: Preheat oven to 350°. Fit 1 refrigerated **piecrust** into a lightly greased 9-inch deep-dish pie plate according to package directions; fold edges under, and crimp. Pour **Hot Fudge Pie Filling** into prepared crust; bake 45 minutes or until filling puffs, center is set, and top begins to crack around the edges. Cool 10 minutes. Makes 1 (9-inch) pie. Hands-on 5 min. Total 1 hour.

Homemade Self-Rising Cornmeal Flour

Stir together 3 cups **all-purpose flour,** ½ cup **plain yellow cornmeal,** 4 tsp. **baking powder,** and 1 tsp. **table salt.** Place in a zip-top plastic freezer bag, and seal. Freeze up to 4 weeks. Makes 3 ½ cups Total 5 min.
To package: Transfer flour mixture to paper bags.
To use: Replace self-rising flour in any recipe (such as biscuits) with this cornmeal-enriched homemade version.

7

FOR THE
BACKYARD GRILLMASTER

Fire up their imagination with an all-purpose BBQ rub and sweet and sticky sauce.

MAKE IT:
Smoky Grill Rub

Stir together 3 Tbsp. **sweet paprika,** 3 Tbsp. **ground cumin,** 2 Tbsp. **kosher salt,** 2 Tbsp. **dark brown sugar,** 1 Tbsp. **smoked paprika,** 2 ½ tsp. **ground red pepper,** 1 ½ tsp. **garlic powder,** and 1 tsp. **celery seeds.** Total 5 min.
To package: Spoon into an 8-oz. jar or container, and store at room temperature.
To serve: Rub on chicken, pork, or full-flavored fish, such as salmon.

Sweet Tomato BBQ Sauce

Melt ¼ cup **butter** in a small saucepan over medium-high heat. Add 1 ½ cups coarsely chopped **yellow onion;** sauté 3 minutes. Add 4 smashed **garlic cloves;** sauté 1 minute. Drain 1 (28-oz.) **can whole peeled plum tomatoes;** crush tomatoes. Stir ½ cup **sugar,** ½ cup **cider vinegar,** ¼ cup **white vinegar,** 2 Tbsp. **tomato paste,** 2 tsp. **kosher salt,** 2 tsp. **Worcestershire sauce,** 1 tsp. freshly ground **black pepper,** and crushed tomatoes into onion mixture; bring to a boil. Reduce heat to low; simmer, stirring occasionally, 2 hours or until color is deep red and most of liquid evaporates. Remove from heat; let stand 15 minutes. Process in a blender or food processor until smooth.
To package: Spoon into 3 (8-oz.) glass containers. Refrigerate up to 3 weeks. Hands-on 10 min. Total 2 hours, 30 min.

FOR THE
LOWCOUNTRY LOVER

Show them love with a sachet of spiced boil mix and pair it with a mustardy dipping sauce for peel 'n' eat shrimp.

MAKE IT:
Shrimp and Crab Boil Sachets

Place 2 (8- x 8-inch) triple layers of cheesecloth on a flat work surface. Heat 3 Tbsp. **black peppercorns,** 3 Tbsp. **coriander seeds,** 2 Tbsp. **dried crushed red pepper,** 2 Tbsp. **mustard seeds,** 1 Tbsp. **dill seeds,** 1 Tbsp. **celery seeds,** and 3 crushed **bay leaves** in a hot skillet over medium-high heat, stirring constantly 1 to 2 minutes or until fragrant. Cool 10 minutes. Stir in 1/4 cup **kosher salt.**
To package: Divide mixture between 2 cheesecloth stacks. Gather edges of cheesecloth; tie with kitchen string. Makes 2 sachets Total 15 min. Store at room temperature 2 weeks. Before giving, package sachets with 3 **lemons,** 2 **yellow onions,** and 2 **garlic bulbs.**
To prepare shrimp: Bring 6 **cups water;** 3 **lemons,** sliced; 2 **yellow onions,** sliced; 2 **garlic bulbs,** and 1 **Shrimp and Crab Boil Sachet** to a boil in a large Dutch oven over medium-high heat; boil 30 minutes. Add 3 lb. unpeeled, large raw **shrimp;** cover and remove from heat. Let stand 10 minutes or just until shrimp turn pink. Discard sachet, and serve shrimp with sauce. Makes 6 servings. Hands-on 15 min. Total 1 hour, 5 min.

Carolina Mustard Sauce

Stir together 1/2 cup **Dijon mustard,** 1/2 cup **mayonnaise,** 2 tsp. **Worcestershire sauce,** and 1 Tbsp. **Asian hot chili sauce** (such as Sriracha) in a small bowl. Chill until ready to serve. Note: We tested with Maille Dijon Originale Mustard.

FOR THE
BEAU FROM THE BIG EASY

Celebrate New Orleans with a bag of chicory coffee, a savory sandwich condiment and a sweet praline syrup.

MAKE IT:
Pickled Muffuleta Salad

Pulse 1 (32-oz.) jar mixed **pickled vegetables,** drained, in a food processor 5 or 6 times or until coarsely chopped. Transfer mixture to a large bowl. Pulse 2 cups pitted **Spanish olives** and 1 cup **black olives** 5 or 6 times or until coarsely chopped; stir into vegetable mixture. Add 2 large **garlic cloves,** minced; 1/2 cup **olive oil;** 2 tsp. **dried Italian seasoning;** 1/4 tsp. **dried crushed red pepper;** and 1 Tbsp. **Champagne vinegar.** Stir in 3/4 cup thinly sliced **pickled okra.** Spoon into airtight containers, and chill until ready to use. Makes about 6 cups. Hands-on 15 min. Total 15 min.
To package: Spoon into 3 (16-oz.) jars; cover and refrigerate up to 2 weeks.

Praline Drizzle

Bring 1/4 cup **butter,** 1/4 cup firmly packed **light brown sugar,** and 1/4 cup **water** to a boil in a medium saucepan over medium heat. Boil 1 minute, stirring constantly. Remove from heat, and stir in 1 1/4 cups **maple syrup,** 1/2 cup chopped toasted **walnuts,** 1/2 cup chopped toasted **pecans,** 1/2 cup toasted sliced **almonds,** 1/2 tsp. **ground cinnamon,** 1/4 tsp. **ground nutmeg,** and 2 tsp. loosely packed **orange zest.** Let stand 30 minutes.
To package: Spoon mixture into 3 (8-oz.) jars, leaving 3/4 inch of room at the top; wipe jar rims. Cover with metal lids, and screw on bands. Chill 10 minutes to 7 days. Spoon over pancakes, French toast, or serve with soft cheeses. Makes 3 jars. Total 10 min.

FOR THE
NICEST NEIGHBOR

MAKE IT:
Homemade Hot Cocoa Mix

Stir together 1 cup **instant nonfat dry milk,** 1 1/2 cups **53% cacao dark chocolate morsels,** 1 1/4 cups **sugar,** and 2/3 cup **dark unsweetened cocoa.**
To package: Spoon into 1 (2-qt.) jar. Total 5 min. Store at room temperature up to 1 month.
To make your hot cocoa: Heat 1 cup milk to 180°; stir in 1/4 cup Homemade Hot Cocoa Mix. Makes 1 serving Total 5 min.

Honey-Vanilla Marshmallows

Sprinkle 3 envelopes **unflavored gelatin** over 1/2 cup **cold water** in bowl of a heavy-duty electric stand mixer. Split 1 **vanilla bean,** and scrape seeds into a 4 1/2 -qt. saucepan. Stir in 1 1/2 cups **granulated sugar,** 1 (16-oz.) bottle **orange blossom honey,** and 1/2 cup **water.** Cover and cook over medium-high heat 3 minutes, bringing to a boil. Uncover and boil, stirring often, until syrup thickens and a candy thermometer registers 240° (about 8 to 12 minutes; lower heat as necessary to prevent mixture from boiling over). Gradually add hot sugar mixture to gelatin mixture, beating at low speed, using whisk attachment, 30 seconds or until blended. Increase speed to high (cover bowl with a towel to prevent splattering); beat 10 to 12 minutes or until mixture cools to room temperature and is thick but pourable. Whisk together 1/4 cup **cornstarch** and 1/4 cup **powdered sugar.** Dust a buttered 13- x 9-inch baking dish with 1 Tbsp. **cornstarch mixture.** Pour gelatin mixture into prepared dish; smooth with a lightly greased spatula. Dust with 1 1/2 Tbsp. **cornstarch mixture.** Cover remaining cornstarch mixture tightly; reserve. Let mixture stand, uncovered, in a cool, dry place 8 to 14 hours or until dry enough to release from baking dish and no longer sticky. Invert marshmallow slab onto cutting board; cut into squares (about 1 inch each). Toss squares in reserved cornstarch mixture to coat. Store in an airtight container at room temperature up to 2 weeks.
To package: Put 10 to 12 marshmallows in a cellophane bag; tie closed with ribbon. Makes about 9½ dozen. Hands-on 40 min. Total 8 hours, 50 min.

FOR THE
JETSETTER

MAKE IT:
Chai Tea Truffles

Bring ³/₄ cup **whipping cream**, 1 tsp. **ground cardamom**, 1 tsp. **ground ginger**, ¹/₂ tsp. **ground cinnamon**, and ¹/₄ tsp. freshly **ground black pepper** to a boil; remove from heat. Add 2 (12-ounce) packages **semisweet chocolate morsels**, and stir until melted. Pour into a lightly greased 11 x 7-inch baking dish. Chill 2 hours. Remove from refrigerator, and let stand at room temperature for 20 minutes. Shape into 1-inch balls (about 2 tsp. per ball). Whisk together ²/₃ cup **Dutch-process unsweetened cocoa**, ¹/₂ cup **powdered sugar**, 2 tsp. freshly **ground black pepper**, 1 ¹/₂ tsp. **ground cinnamon**, ¹/₂ tsp. **ground cardamom**, and ¹/₄ tsp. **kosher salt** in a shallow dish, stirring with a whisk. Roll balls in cocoa mixture. Makes about 4 dozen. Hands-on 15 min. Total 2 hours, 35 min.

Coconut Irish Cream Truffles

Bring ¹/₂ cup **whipping cream** to a boil in a 1-qt. saucepan over high heat. Place 2 (10-oz.) packages **60% cacao bittersweet chocolate morsels** in a heatproof bowl. Pour cream over chocolate, and gently stir until melted and smooth. (If chocolate does not melt completely, place bowl over a pan of simmering water, and stir until melted and smooth.) Stir in 2 Tbsp. **softened butter** and ¹/₄ cup **Irish cream liqueur**. Spread chocolate in a lightly greased 11- x 7-inch baking dish. Chill 1 hour. Remove from refrigerator, and let stand 20 minutes. Shape mixture into 1-inch balls (about 2 tsp. per ball). Roll balls in 1 cup unsweetened shredded coconut. Makes about 4 dozen. Hands-on 30 min. Total 1 hour, 50 min.
To package: Place 1 dozen truffles in a cellophane bag, and tie with ribbon. Refrigerate up to 2 weeks.

FOR THE
COCKTAIL COGNOSCENTI

Shaken or stirred? Naughty or nice? Herewith, two options, one sweet and one briny, for however you take your cocktail.

MAKE IT:
Naughty Olives

Cook 2 tsp. **fennel seed**, ¹/₂ tsp. **black peppercorns**, and ¹/₄ tsp. **dried crushed red pepper** in a small saucepan over medium heat, stirring constantly, 1 to 2 minutes or until fragrant and lightly toasted. Add ¹/₂ cup **liquid from jarred Spanish olives**, 4 **bay leaves**, 4 (3-inch) **orange rind strips**, and 1 (6-inch) fresh **rosemary**, and bring to a boil. Remove from heat, and add 1 cup **extra-dry vermouth** mixture in each jar. Combine 3 cups drained **Spanish olives** and 1 cup drained **cocktail onions** in a medium bowl; spoon into 4 (8-oz.) canning jars. Place 1 **bay leaf** and 1 **orange rind strip** from vermouth mixture in each jar, and fill with vermouth mixture. Cover with metal lids, and screw on bands. Chill up to 4 hours to 3 weeks. Serve as a cocktail garnish or bar snack. Makes 4 jars. Total 35 min.

Naughty Martini

Combine 3 Tbsp. **gin** and 1 to 1 ¹/₂ Tbsp. **Naughty Olive liquid** in a cocktail shaker filled with ice cubes. Stir until thoroughly chilled (about 30 seconds). Strain into a 10-oz. stemmed cocktail glass. Garnish with a **Naughty Olive**. Makes 1 serving . Total 5 min.

Nice Vanilla-Lemon Syrup

Split 1 **vanilla bean;** scrape seeds into a large saucepan; place pod in pan. Add 3 cups **sugar;** 2 cups **water;** and 6 **lemons,** sliced. Bring to a boil over medium heat. Reduce heat to low, and simmer, stirring occasionally, 10 minutes. Remove from heat, and let stand 5 minutes. Pour through a fine wire-mesh strainer into a large bowl; discard solids, and cool completely (about 30 minutes). Pour into 4 (8-oz.) canning jars; cover with metal lids, and screw on bands. Use immediately, or chill up to 3 weeks. Makes 4 jars Hands-on 15 min. Total 55 min.
To serve: Add to cocktails, iced tea, or lemonade.

The Nice Guy Cocktail

Combine ¹/₄ cup **gin** and 2 Tbsp. **Nice Vanilla-Lemon Syrup** in a cocktail shaker filled with ice cubes. Cover with lid, and shake until thoroughly chilled (about 30 seconds). Strain into a 10-oz. cocktail glass filled with ice cubes. Top with desired amount of club soda. Garnish with 1 **lemon** peel strip. Makes 1 serving. Hands-on 5 min. Total 5 min.

Festive Holiday Drinks

▶ A taste of who and what online got the most raves in the *Southern Living* Test Kitchen

---

From the Kitchen of
GEORGIA JOHNSON

AUSTIN, TEXAS
THECOMFORTOFCOOKING.COM

....

"Simmered with a cinnamon stick, vanilla extract, and a touch of chili powder, this hot chocolate is amazingly fragrant and delicious with a dollop of whipped cream"

....

MEXICAN HOT CHOCOLATE

Bring 3 cups **milk**, 3 Tbsp. **unsweetened cocoa**, ½ tsp. **vanilla extract,** and 1 (3-inch) **cinnamon stick** to a boil in a medium saucepan over medium-high heat, stirring occasionally. Reduce heat to low, and stir in 1 (3.5-oz.) **chili chocolate bar,** chopped, until melted. Remove from heat, and if desired, add ¼ tsp. **chili powder.** Remove cinnamon stick, and serve immediately. **MAKES** 4 servings.

Note: We tested with Lindt Excellence Chili Dark Chocolate.

From the Kitchen of
SHWANDA HORN

HOUSTON, TEXAS
JASONANDSHWANDA.COM

....

"We love the cranberry margarita because it's beautiful, festive and a reminder that margaritas aren't just for summer."

....

CRANBERRY MARGARITAS

Dip rims of 6 (8-oz.) glasses in 1 Tbsp. **cranberry juice;** dip rims in **sugar** to coat. Fill glasses with **ice.** Process 1½ cups fresh **cranberries***, ¾ cup **tequila,** ¾ cup **cranberry juice,** ¾ cup fresh **lime juice,** ½ cup **orange liqueur** (such as Triple Sec or Grand Marnier), and ⅓ cup **sugar** in a blender 30 seconds or until smooth. Pour mixture through a fine wire-mesh strainer into a large pitcher. Stir in 1¼ cups chilled **club soda** and ¼ cup fresh **orange juice.** Pour into prepared glasses. Garnish with whole **cranberries,** if desired. **MAKES** 6 servings.

*Frozen cranberries, thawed may be substituted.

From the Kitchen of
AMY MIKKELSEN

ATLANTA, GEORGIA
WWW.YOURSOUTHERNPEACH.COM

....

"This cocktail was inspired by the Southern side dish that's popular during the holidays. Mini marshmallows and cherries make a festive garnish."

....

AMBROSIA COCKTAIL

Fill an 8-oz. glass with **ice.** Stir in ¼ cup **coconut rum,** 2 Tbsp. fresh **orange juice,** 2 Tbsp. **pineapple juice,** and a splash of **grenadine.** Garnish with **miniature marshmallows** and whole **maraschino cherries,** if desired. **MAKES** 1 serving.

From the Kitchen of
NATALIE BROULETTE

NEW YORK, NEW YORK
THE SoHo

....

"It's unusual to find a cold drink that gives you that sense of holiday coziness, but this one does the trick. Grate your own nutmeg. It makes all the difference."

....

HOLIDAY MILK PUNCH

Whisk together 2 cups **milk**, 2 cups **half-and-half,** 1 cup **brandy** or **bourbon,** ½ cup sifted **powdered sugar,** and 1½ tsp. **vanilla extract** in a large pitcher. Serve over crushed **ice.** Top each serving with freshly grated **nutmeg. MAKES** about 4 servings.

Dreamy Cake

Raspberry Curd Cake with Lemon Buttercream Frosting

MAKES 12 SERVINGS
HANDS-ON 32 MIN.
TOTAL 4 HOURS, 7 MIN.

(Pictured on cover)

- 1 ⅓ cups butter, softened
- 2 ⅔ cups sugar
- 5 large eggs
- 4 cups all-purpose flour
- 1 ⅓ Tbsp. baking powder
- 1 ⅓ cups milk
- 1 ⅓ Tbsp. lemon juice
- 2 ⅔ tsp. lemon zest
- 1 ⅓ tsp. vanilla extract
  Raspberry Curd
  Lemon Buttercream Frosting
  Garnish: Fondant Trees

1. Preheat oven to 350°. Beat butter at medium speed with a heavy-duty stand mixer until fluffy; gradually add sugar, beating well. Add eggs, one at a time, beating until just blended after each addition.

2. Combine flour and baking powder; add to butter mixture alternately with milk, beginning and ending with flour mixture. Beat at low speed until blended after each addition. Stir in lemon juice, zest, and vanilla.

3. Spoon batter into 4 greased and floured 8-inch round cake pans.

4. Bake at 350° for 18 to 22 minutes or until a wooden pick inserted in center comes out clean. Cool in pans on wire racks 10 minutes; remove from pans, and cool completely on wire racks.

5. Spread Raspberry Curd between layers, leaving a one-half inch border. Spread Lemon Buttercream Frosting on top and sides of cake. Garnish with Fondant Trees.

RASPBERRY CURD

MAKES 1 CUP
HANDS-ON 10 MIN.
TOTAL 2 HOURS, 15 MIN.

- 2 (6-oz.) packages fresh raspberries
- ½ cup sugar
- 3 Tbsp. cornstarch

1. Process raspberries in a blender or food processor until smooth, stopping to scrape down sides as needed. Press raspberries through a wire-mesh strainer into a medium bowl, using back of a spoon to squeeze out juice; discard pulp and seeds.

2. Combine sugar and purée in a 3-qt. saucepan; gradually whisk in cornstarch and 3 Tbsp. water. Bring mixture to a boil over medium heat, whisking constantly, and cook, whisking constantly, 1 minute. Remove from heat.

3. Place plastic wrap directly on warm curd (to prevent a film from forming); chill 2 hours or until cold.

LEMON BUTTERCREAM FROSTING

MAKES 5 CUPS
HANDS-ON 10 MIN.
TOTAL 10 MIN.

- 1 cup butter, softened
- 1 Tbsp. plus 2 tsp. loosely packed lemon zest
- 1 (32-oz.) package powdered sugar
- 4 Tbsp. fresh lemon juice
- 5 to 6 Tbsp. heavy cream

Beat butter and lemon zest at medium speed with an electric mixer 1 to 2 minutes or until creamy; gradually add powdered sugar alternately with lemon juice and 5 Tbsp. heavy cream, beating at low speed until blended after each addition. Add additional 1 Tbsp. heavy cream, 1 tsp. at a time, until desired consistency is reached. Beat on high speed until light and fluffy, about 1 minute.

FONDANT TREES: Roll out white fondant to ¼-inch thickness. Using a Christmas tree cookie cutter, cut out shapes. Using a #61 Wilton pastry tip, lightly press the curved end of tip into the shapes to impress the shape of the tip. If desired, press tip all the way through tree to create cut outs of tip shape. Set aside trees to dry for about 2 hours. Lightly brush trees with water and sprinkle with desired decorating sugars. Allow to dry at least 30 minutes.

Drink of the Month

▶ Some of our cocktails can be influenced by the flavors of the seasons. Here are a few that we think you'll want to try.

JANUARY

ORANGE SPICED TEA

Heat 2 (3 1/2-inch) **cinnamon sticks** and 1/2 tsp. **whole cloves** in a large saucepan over medium heat, stirring occasionally, 3 minutes or until fragrant. Stir in 6 cups **boiling water.** Add 6 regular-size **wild sweet orange tea bags** (such as Tazo) and 1 (10-inch) **orange peel strip;** cover and steep 5 minutes. Discard solids. Stir in **1/2 cup sugar** until dissolved; if desired, add 1/3 cup **orange liqueur.** Pour into 6 mugs. Garnish with orange slices. **MAKES** 6 servings

FEBRUARY

THE CORDUROY JACKET

Muddle 1 fresh **orange slice,** 1 **brown sugar cube,** and 2 dashes **Angostura bitters** in a cocktail shaker to release flavors. Fill shaker with ice cubes, and add 1/4 cup **cognac;** cover with lid, and shake vigorously until thoroughly chilled (about 30 seconds). Strain into a stemmed 10-oz. glass. Top with 6 Tbsp. **chilled sparkling apple cider.** Garnish with 1 (3 1/2-inch) **orange peel strip** and **fresh thyme sprig. MAKES** 1 serving

MARCH

THE DOGWOOD

Combine 1/4 cup **white grapefruit juice,** 3 Tbsp. **vodka,** and 1 Tbsp. **elderflower liqueur** in a cocktail shaker filled with ice cubes. Cover with lid, and shake vigorously until thoroughly chilled (about 30 seconds). Strain into an 8-oz. glass filled with ice cubes. Garnish with a **lemon wheel** and **fresh rosemary sprig. MAKES** 1 serving

APRIL

THE PALAFOX FIZZ

Muddle 8 to 10 **fresh basil leaves** and 3 to 5 **cucumber slices** in a cocktail shaker to release flavors. Fill shaker with **ice cubes,** 3 Tbsp. **gin,** 1 Tbsp. **fresh lime juice,** and 1 Tbsp. **simple syrup.** Cover with lid, and shake vigorously until thoroughly chilled (about 30 seconds). Strain into a 12-oz. glass filled with ice cubes; top with **club soda. MAKES** 1 serving

MAY

PIMM BOB

What happens when an Old Fashioned meets a Pimm's Cup with a touch of Sazerac flair? A Pimm Bob!

Muddle 2 **fresh tarragon sprigs**; 1 **lemon slice**; 1 **orange slice**; 1 **strawberry**, quartered; 1 to 1 1/2 Tbsp. **simple syrup**; and 2 dashes of **Peychaud's bitters** in a 12-oz. glass to release flavors. Fill glass with ice cubes. Add 1/4 cup each **rye whiskey** and chilled **club soda**; stir gently. **MAKES** 1 serving

---

JUNE

WATERMELON LEMONADE

Squeeze juice from 10 **large lemons** to equal 2 cups; reserve 4 squeezed lemons. Bring 6 cups **water**, 1 1/2 cups **sugar**, and 1/4 tsp. **kosher salt** to a boil, stirring occasionally. Remove from heat; add reserved lemons. Cool; strain into a large pitcher. Process 4 cups chopped **watermelon** and 1 cup **water** in a blender until smooth; strain into pitcher. Stir in juice. Serve with ice. **MAKES** 12 cups

---

JULY

BLACKBERRY-LIME AGUA FRESCA

Process 1 (12-oz.) package **fresh blackberries**, 1 cup **powdered sugar**, and 1/2 cup **fresh lime juice** in a blender until smooth (about 30 seconds). Press mixture through a fine wire-mesh strainer into a large pitcher, using back of a spoon to squeeze out juice. Discard pulp and seeds. Stir in 4 cups **chilled water** or **club soda**. Garnish with **lime wedges** and **fresh blackberries**. **MAKES** 6 cups

---

AUGUST

JALAPEÑO-TEQUILA SMASH

Muddle 2 **lime slices**, 2 **orange slices**, 1 **fresh jalapeño pepper slice**, and 2 to 3 tsp. **simple syrup** in a 12-oz. glass to release flavors. Fill glass with **ice cubes**, and add 3 Tbsp. **tequila**; stir until thoroughly chilled (about 30 seconds). Top with 1/2 cup **lemon-lime soft drink**, **club soda**, or **seltzer water**. **MAKES** 1 serving

SEPTEMBER

THE SCREENED PORCH

Muddle 2 tsp. **fig preserves**, 1 tsp. **honey**, and 1 **lemon wedge** in a cocktail shaker to release flavors. Fill shaker with **ice cubes,** and add ¼ cup **rye whiskey.** Cover with lid, and shake vigorously until thoroughly chilled (about 30 seconds). Strain into a stemmed 10-oz. glass. Garnish with a thin lemon slice. **MAKES** 1 serving

OCTOBER

LAST-WORD FIZZ

This frothy cocktail was adapted from the new book Pickles, Pigs & Whiskey *by chef John Currence.*

Combine 4 ½ tsp. **gin**, 4 ½ tsp. **green Chartreuse**, 4 ½ tsp. **maraschino liqueur** (such as Luxardo Originale 32°), 4 ½ tsp. **fresh lime juice,** 1 Tbsp. **powdered sugar,** and 1 **pasteurized egg white** in a cocktail shaker. Cover with lid, and shake vigorously until frothy (about 20 seconds). Remove lid, and fill shaker with **crushed ice.** Cover with lid, and shake vigorously until chilled (about 15 seconds). Strain into 2 (10-oz.) stemmed glasses, and top each with a splash of chilled **club soda.** Twist a **lime peel strip** over each drink, and rub around rim of each glass; garnish with lime peel strip. **MAKES** 2 servings

NOVEMBER

FIRST SNOW

Muddle 2 Tbsp. **powdered sugar,** 2 (2½ inch) **orange peel rind strips,** and 2 tsp. **coarsely chopped fresh ginger** in a cocktail shaker to release flavors. Fill shaker with ice cubes, 6 Tbsp. **half-and-half,** and 3 Tbsp. **brandy.** Cover with lid and shake vigorously until throughoughly chilled (about 30 seconds). Strain into a 10-oz. stemmed cocktail glass. Garnish if desired with an orange twist. **MAKES** 1 serving

Holiday Favorites

Daybreak in Dixie

▶ Family arrives from all directions both near and far to gather together to celebrate the season

Morning Menu
serves 8

MERRY MIMOSAS
FOR A CROWD

CINNAMON COFFEE
WITH BOURBON CREAM

SPINACH-ARTICHOKE
STRATA

APPLE-MAPLE
BREAKFAST SAUSAGE

WINTER FRUIT
COMPOTE

CINNAMON-APPLE
COFFEE CAKE WITH
CREAM CHEESE GLAZE

Game Plan

2 DAYS BEFORE:
- ❑ Chill juices and Champagne.
- ❑ Prepare compote; cover and chill.

1 DAY BEFORE:
- ❑ Assemble strata; cover and chill unbaked.
- ❑ Set up coffeemaker.
- ❑ Make sausage patties; cover and chill.
- ❑ Prepare coffee cake; store at room temperature.

1½ HOURS BEFORE:
- ❑ Bake strata; let stand.

45 MINUTES BEFORE:
- ❑ Prepare bourbon cream; cover and chill.

30 MINUTES BEFORE:
- ❑ Bring compote to room temperature.
- ❑ Brew coffee.

20 MINUTES BEFORE:
- ❑ Fry sausage patties.

15 MINUTES BEFORE:
- ❑ Stir together mimosa, and garnish.

Merry Mimosas for a Crowd

MAKES 7 CUPS
HANDS-ON 5 MIN.
TOTAL 5 MIN.

We put a festive twist on the traditional mimosa by adding a splash of cranberry juice.

- 3 cups fresh orange juice, chilled
- 1 cup cranberry juice cocktail, chilled
- 1 (750-milliliter) bottle Champagne or sparkling wine, chilled
- Garnish: frozen cranberries

Combine orange juice and cranberry juice in a large pitcher. Add Champagne just before serving. Serve immediately.

Note: Mimosas can be made 1 at a time by stirring together orange juice and cranberry juice, and then pouring equal parts orange juice mixture and Champagne into Champagne flutes.

Cinnamon Coffee with Bourbon Cream

MAKES 8 CUPS
HANDS-ON 11 MIN.
TOTAL 21 MIN.

The fragrance of aromatic cinnamon will fill the air as this coffee brews.

- 1 cup medium-roast ground coffee
- 1 tsp. ground cinnamon
- 1 cup heavy cream
- 2 Tbsp. light brown sugar
- 2 Tbsp. bourbon
- Additional ground cinnamon
- 8 cinnamon sticks (optional)

1. Combine ground coffee and 1 tsp. cinnamon in a coffee filter. Brew coffee in a 12-cup coffeemaker according to manufacturer's instructions using 8 cups water.

2. Beat heavy cream at high speed with an electric mixer until foamy; add brown sugar, 1 Tbsp. at a time, beating until soft peaks form. Stir in bourbon. Chill until ready to serve.

3. Top each serving with bourbon cream, additional ground cinnamon, and, if desired, a cinnamon stick.

Note: 8 cups of water poured into a coffeemaker show as 12 cups in the coffeepot.

Merry Mimosas for a Crowd

Spinach-Artichoke Strata

MAKES 8 SERVINGS
HANDS-ON 16 MIN.
TOTAL 9 HOURS, 36 MIN.

This crusty brunch dish delivers everything we love in the classic spinach-artichoke dip.

- 1 1/2 (8-oz.) packages sliced fresh mushrooms
- 1 small onion, chopped (about 1 1/4 cups)
- 1 Tbsp. olive oil
- 1 (12-oz.) French or Italian bread loaf, torn into 1-inch pieces and divided
- 2 (6-oz.) packages fresh baby spinach
- 8 large eggs
- 3 cups milk
- 1 (8-oz.) container sour cream
- 1 tsp. dried Italian seasoning
- 1/4 tsp. freshly ground black pepper
- 2 (5-oz.) packages shredded Parmesan cheese, divided
- 1 cup (4 oz.) shredded mozzarella cheese
- 1 (14-oz.) can artichoke hearts, drained and chopped
- 1 (12-oz.) jar roasted red bell peppers, drained and chopped

1. Cook mushrooms and onion in oil in a large skillet over medium-high heat 8 to 10 minutes or until onion is tender.

2. Meanwhile, measure 1 1/2 cups torn bread pieces, and place in a small food processor. Pulse bread 3 or 4 times to make coarse breadcrumbs; set aside.

3. Gradually add spinach to cooked mushroom mixture. Cook over medium-high heat, stirring constantly, just until spinach wilts. Remove from heat, and let cool slightly.

4. Whisk together eggs and next 4 ingredients in a large bowl. Stir in remaining bread pieces, 1 1/2 packages Parmesan cheese, mozzarella cheese, artichokes, and bell peppers. Stir in mushroom mixture. Spoon into a greased 13- x 9-inch baking dish. Top with remaining Parmesan cheese and reserved breadcrumbs. Cover and chill 8 hours.

5. Preheat oven to 350°. Uncover strata, and bake for 1 hour and 20 minutes or until browned and set.

Apple-Maple Breakfast Sausage

MAKES 8 SERVINGS
HANDS-ON 41 MIN.
TOTAL 1 HOUR, 41 MIN.

- 2 lb. ground pork
- 2 Tbsp. maple syrup
- 2 tsp. finely chopped fresh sage
- 1 1/2 tsp. table salt
- 1 1/2 tsp. freshly ground black pepper
- 1 Gala apple, peeled, cored, and finely chopped
- 1 Tbsp. canola oil

1. Combine first 6 ingredients in a large bowl. Shape mixture into 16 patties. Cover and chill at least 1 hour.

2. Heat oil in a large skillet over medium-high heat. Cook patties, in 2 batches, 3 to 4 minutes on each side or until no longer pink.

Winter Fruit Compote

MAKES 8 SERVINGS
HANDS-ON 7 MIN.
TOTAL 37 MIN.

Dried fruit plumped with wine provides a great way to enjoy a colorful midwinter fruit dish.

- 1 cup sweet white wine
- 1/2 cup sugar
- 1 cup dried cherries
- 1 cup dried apricots
- 1/2 cup dried cranberries
- 1 cinnamon stick
- 2 Bosc pears, peeled and cut into 1-inch pieces
- 1/4 tsp. almond extract
- 2 (8-oz.) containers plain yogurt
- 1/2 cup sliced almonds

Combine first 6 ingredients in a large saucepan; bring to a boil over medium-high heat. Reduce heat to medium-low; cover and simmer 15 minutes. Add pears, and simmer 15 more minutes or until pear is almost tender. Remove from heat; stir in extract. Discard cinnamon stick. Serve warm or at room temperature. Top each serving with a dollop of yogurt and 1 Tbsp. sliced almonds. (Compote can be prepared 2 days in advance and stored in refrigerator. Let stand 30 minutes before serving.)

Note: We tested with Riesling sweet white wine.

Cinnamon-Apple Coffee Cake with Cream Cheese Glaze

MAKES 8 TO 10 SERVINGS

HANDS-ON 50 MIN.

TOTAL 4 HOURS, 40 MIN., INCLUDING STREUSEL AND GLAZE

This tall coffee cake is gooey good, packed with sour cream richness and cinnamon sugar.

- 1 cup peeled, finely chopped Golden Delicious apple
- 3/4 cup finely chopped toasted walnuts
- 1/4 cup firmly packed light brown sugar
- 1 1/2 tsp. ground cinnamon
- 1 cup butter, softened
- 2 cups granulated sugar
- 2 large eggs
- 1 (8-oz.) container sour cream
- 2 tsp. vanilla extract
- 2 cups all-purpose flour
- 1 tsp. baking powder
- 1 tsp. ground cinnamon
- 1/2 tsp. table salt
- Streusel Topping
- Cream Cheese Glaze

1. Preheat oven to 350°. Combine first 4 ingredients, stirring well; set aside.

2. Beat butter at medium speed with an electric mixer until creamy; gradually add granulated sugar, beating 3 to 5 minutes or until light and fluffy. Add eggs, 1 at a time, beating just until blended after each addition. Stir in sour cream and vanilla.

3. Combine flour, baking powder, 1 tsp. cinnamon, and salt; gradually add to butter mixture, beating at low speed just until blended. Spread half of batter into a greased and floured 9-inch springform pan. Spoon reserved apple mixture over batter to within 1/2 inch of edge. Spread remaining batter over apple mixture. Sprinkle with Streusel Topping.

4. Bake at 350° for 1 hour and 25 to 30 minutes or until a wooden pick inserted in center comes out clean. Let cool in pan on a wire rack 10 minutes. Remove sides of pan; let cool completely (about 1 1/2 hours). Drizzle with Cream Cheese Glaze.

Cinnamon-Apple Coffee Cake with Cream Cheese Glaze

STREUSEL TOPPING

MAKES 1 1/2 CUPS

HANDS-ON 8 MIN.

TOTAL 8 MIN.

- 1/2 cup all-purpose flour
- 1/3 cup firmly packed light brown sugar
- 1 tsp. ground cinnamon
- 1/3 cup cold butter, cut into pieces
- 3/4 cup chopped walnuts

Combine first 3 ingredients in a medium bowl; cut in butter with a pastry blender or fork until crumbly. Stir in walnuts.

CREAM CHEESE GLAZE

MAKES 1 CUP

HANDS-ON 5 MIN.

TOTAL 5 MIN.

- 1 (3-oz.) package cream cheese, softened
- 1 tsp. vanilla extract
- 1 1/2 cups powdered sugar
- 3 to 4 Tbsp. milk

Beat cream cheese at medium speed until creamy; add vanilla, beating well. Gradually add powdered sugar, beating at low speed just until blended. Gradually add enough milk to reach desired consistency.

Road Trip to Grandma's

▶ Make the trip home for the holidays as memorable as the main event. Enjoy a picnic in the pines with great make-ahead, portable dishes that trump anything you could get from a drive-through

Pack a Picnic
serves 6

ROSEMARY-SCENTED COLD CIDER

COLD SKILLET-FRIED CHICKEN

APPLE-CABBAGE SLAW

SWEET POTATO SALAD

CHAMELEON ICEBOX COOKIES

CARAMEL DROP-BANANA BREAD TRIFLE DESSERT

Game Plan

2 DAYS BEFORE:

❑ Prepare cider, omitting ginger ale; cover and chill.

1 DAY BEFORE:

❑ Prepare chicken; cool, cover, and chill.

❑ Prepare sweet potato salad; cover and chill.

❑ Prepare slaw; cover and chill.

❑ Prepare trifle; cover and chill.

❑ Prepare cookies; store in an airtight container.

30 MINUTES BEFORE THE TRIP:

❑ Pack up, placing chilled items in a cooler.

JUST BEFORE:

❑ Stir ginger ale into cider.

Rosemary-Scented Cold Cider

MAKES 9 ½ CUPS
HANDS-ON 5 MIN.
TOTAL 8 HOURS, 5 MIN.

Pick up a jug of fresh-pressed cider for optimum results with this refreshing drink.

- 5 cups apple cider
- 4 (4- to 5-inch) fresh rosemary sprigs
- 2 cups cranberry-apple juice drink, chilled
- 2 (12-oz.) cans ginger ale, chilled

1. Bring cider and rosemary sprigs to a boil in a saucepan over medium-high heat. Reduce heat to medium-low; simmer 3 minutes. Remove from heat; let cool to room temperature. Cover and chill 8 to 24 hours. Remove and discard rosemary sprigs.

2. Combine cider and cranberry-apple drink in a pitcher or thermos. Add ginger ale just before serving.

Cold Skillet-Fried Chicken

MAKES 4 TO 6 SERVINGS
HANDS-ON 11 MIN.
TOTAL 2 HOURS, 37 MIN.

Enjoy this crispy, well-seasoned chicken hot from the skillet at home, or cool and chill it, and nibble on the road to Grandma's.

- 2 cups buttermilk
- ¼ cup dill pickle juice
- 1 Tbsp. chopped fresh rosemary
- ½ tsp. paprika
- ¼ tsp. ground red pepper
- 2 garlic cloves, pressed
- 1 (4-lb.) cut-up whole chicken
- 1 cup self-rising flour
- 1 Tbsp. plus 1 tsp. seasoned salt
- 2 tsp. freshly ground black pepper
  Peanut oil

1. Place 1 large zip-top plastic freezer bag inside another zip-top plastic freezer bag. Combine first 6 ingredients in the inside bag. Add chicken pieces, tossing to coat. Seal both bags, and chill at least 2 hours or overnight.

2. Remove chicken from marinade, discarding marinade. Combine flour, salt, and black pepper. Dredge chicken in flour mixture, shaking off excess.

3. Pour oil to depth of 1 1/2 inches in a deep skillet or Dutch oven; heat to 350°. Add chicken, a few pieces at a time; cover and cook 6 minutes. Uncover, and cook 9 minutes. Turn chicken; cover and cook 6 minutes. Uncover and cook 5 to 9 minutes, turning chicken the last 3 minutes for even browning, if necessary. Drain on paper towels. Serve immediately, or let cool; cover and chill.

Apple-Cabbage Slaw

MAKES 8 TO 10 SERVINGS
HANDS-ON 5 MIN.
TOTAL 5 MIN.

Adding dried fruit and nut mix to this slaw is an easy way to add color, flavor, and crunch with a single ingredient.

- 1/2 cup canola oil
- 3 Tbsp. apple cider vinegar
- 2 Tbsp. honey
- 1/2 tsp. table salt
- 1/8 tsp. black pepper
- 1 (10-oz.) package finely shredded cabbage
- 1 cup dried fruit and nut mix
- 2 Fuji apples, cored and finely chopped
- 2 green onions, minced

Whisk together first 5 ingredients in a large bowl; add cabbage and remaining ingredients. Toss well. Cover and chill until ready to serve.

Sweet Potato Salad

MAKES 6 TO 8 SERVINGS
HANDS-ON 11 MIN.
TOTAL 56 MIN.

This salad is great warm or chilled. With honey-mustard undertones, it pairs well with fried chicken, turkey, or ham.

- 4 large sweet potatoes, peeled and cubed
- 1 Tbsp. olive oil
- 1/2 tsp. table salt
- 1/2 tsp. black pepper
- 2 Tbsp. mustard seeds
- 1/4 cup rice vinegar
- 3 Tbsp. honey
- 1/4 tsp. ground cinnamon
- 1/4 tsp. curry powder
- 1/4 tsp. dry mustard

1. Preheat oven to 450°. Toss together sweet potatoes, oil, salt, and pepper on a lightly greased large rimmed baking sheet or roasting pan. Roast at 450° for 45

minutes or until potatoes are tender and lightly browned. (Do not stir.)

2. Meanwhile, toast mustard seeds in a small skillet over medium heat until fragrant, stirring or shaking skillet to prevent burning. Add vinegar, honey, and spices; bring to a boil. Remove from heat. Pour over sweet potatoes in a serving bowl; toss. Serve warm, or cover and chill.

Chameleon Icebox Cookies

MAKES ABOUT 4 DOZEN
HANDS-ON 18 MIN.
TOTAL 1 HOUR, 49 MIN.

Old-fashioned icebox cookies become a creative and tasty blank canvas for Christmas stir-ins. Our staff had a hard time choosing a favorite variation.

- 1 cup butter, softened
- 1 cup superfine sugar
- 1 large egg
- 2 tsp. vanilla extract
- 2 1/4 cups all-purpose flour
- 1/2 tsp. table salt
- Wax paper

1. Beat butter at medium speed with an electric mixer until creamy; gradually add sugar, beating well. Add egg and vanilla; beat well.

2. Combine flour and salt; add to butter mixture, beating at medium-low speed just until blended. Cover and chill dough at least 1 hour.

3. Shape dough into 2 (6-inch) logs. Wrap logs in wax paper or parchment paper; chill or freeze until firm.

4. Preheat oven to 350°. Slice dough into 1/4-inch-thick slices. Place on ungreased baking sheets. Bake at 350° for 12 minutes or until barely golden. Remove to wire racks, and let cool completely (about 10 minutes).

BITTERSWEET CHOCOLATE & ORANGE ESSENCE ICEBOX COOKIES: Stir 1/2 cup (4 oz.) finely chopped **bittersweet chocolate** and 1 Tbsp. **orange zest** into dough. Proceed with recipe as directed. Bake 12 to 13 minutes or until golden.

STRAWBERRY-PECAN ICEBOX COOKIES: Stir 3/4 cup finely chopped **dried strawberries** into dough. Roll logs in 1 cup finely chopped **pecans.** Proceed with recipe as directed.

KIDS' ICEBOX COOKIES: Roll 1 log of dough in 1/3 cup **green decorator sugar crystals**. Roll remaining log in 1/3 cup **red decorator sugar crystals**. Proceed with recipe as directed.

LAVENDER ICEBOX COOKIES: Stir 1 1/2 Tbsp. **dried lavender,** lightly crushed, into dough. Proceed with recipe as directed.

Note: We used a mini food chopper to crush the lavender.

Caramel Drop-Banana Bread Trifle Dessert

MAKES 8 TO 10 SERVINGS
HANDS-ON 30 MIN.
TOTAL 2 HOURS

Instead of using vanilla wafers in this yummy banana pudding dessert, we chopped a loaf of banana bread. Pick up a loaf at a local bakery or grocer's bakery section. Assemble this dessert in a large, shallow plastic container with a lid; chill and take it to a holiday gathering.

CUSTARD

- 1 cup sugar
- 2/3 cup all-purpose flour
- 1/2 tsp. table salt
- 5 cups milk
- 5 large egg yolks
- 1 Tbsp. vanilla extract
- 1 Tbsp. butter

TRIFLE DESSERT

- 1 (1-lb.) banana bread loaf without nuts (about 8 x 4 inches)
- 2 large ripe bananas, sliced
- 1 (13.4-oz.) can dulce de leche
- 1 (8-oz.) container frozen whipped topping, thawed
- 1 cup chopped pecans, toasted

1. Prepare Custard: Combine first 3 ingredients in a heavy saucepan; whisk in milk. Cook over medium heat, stirring constantly, until thickened and bubbly (about 12 minutes).

2. Whisk egg yolks until thick and pale. Gradually stir about one-fourth of hot mixture into yolks; add yolk mixture to remaining hot mixture, stirring constantly. Cook over medium heat, stirring gently, 3 minutes. Remove from heat; add vanilla and butter, stirring until butter melts. Cool to room temperature. Cover and chill up to a day ahead. (Custard will be thick.)

3. Prepare Trifle Dessert: Chop banana bread loaf into 3/4-inch pieces to yield about 5 cups. Place banana bread pieces in a 13- x 9-inch baking dish or similar size heavy-duty plastic container. Spoon and spread Custard over banana bread; top with banana slices. Top dessert with small dollops of dulce de leche. Top with whipped topping, spreading to edges; sprinkle with pecans. Cover and chill 1 to 24 hours.

Vintage Southern Holiday

▶ Set the table with your most prized family heirlooms and celebrate the holidays with this elegant meal of Southern classics

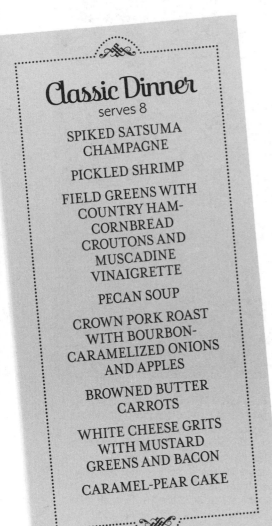

Classic Dinner

serves 8

SPIKED SATSUMA CHAMPAGNE

PICKLED SHRIMP

FIELD GREENS WITH COUNTRY HAM-CORNBREAD CROUTONS AND MUSCADINE VINAIGRETTE

PECAN SOUP

CROWN PORK ROAST WITH BOURBON-CARAMELIZED ONIONS AND APPLES

BROWNED BUTTER CARROTS

WHITE CHEESE GRITS WITH MUSTARD GREENS AND BACON

CARAMEL-PEAR CAKE

Game Plan

1 DAY BEFORE:
❑ Make simple syrup for Champagne; cover and chill. Freeze orange slices.
❑ Prepare PickledShrimp; cover and chill.
❑ Prepare croutons for salad; cover.
❑ Prepare vinaigrette for salad; cover and chill.
❑ Bake cake layers, and drizzle with syrup; cover and chill overnight.

MORNING OF:
❑ Fill and frost cake.

3 ½ HOURS BEFORE:
❑ Assemble and bake pork roast.

1 ½ HOURS BEFORE:
❑ Prepare soup; keep warm.

1 HOUR BEFORE:
❑ Prepare carrots.

45 MINUTES BEFORE:
❑ Prepare grits dish; keep warm.

20 MINUTES BEFORE:
❑ Prepare and plate salads.

JUST BEFORE:
❑ Assemble beverage.
❑ Stir parsley into shrimp.

Spiked Satsuma Champagne

MAKES 9 ½ CUPS
HANDS-ON 13 MIN.
TOTAL 43 MIN.

Frozen orange slices serve double duty as ice cubes and garnish in this bubbly elixir.

- 2 **satsumas, thinly sliced**
  Wax paper
- 1/2 **cup sugar**
- 2 **cups fresh satsuma orange juice*** **(about 9 satsumas)**
- 1/2 **cup orange liqueur**
- 2 **(750-milliliter) bottles chilled dry Champagne**

1. Arrange orange slices on a baking sheet lined with wax paper; freeze 30 minutes.

2. Combine 1/2 cup water and sugar in a 2-cup glass measuring cup. Microwave at HIGH 1 minute or until very hot. Stir until sugar dissolves.

3. Combine sugar syrup, juice, and liqueur in a pitcher; chill until ready to serve.

4. Place 1 frozen orange slice in each Champagne glass. Pour 1/4 cup juice mixture into each glass. Top with Champagne, and serve immediately.

*Bottled tangerine juice may be substituted. Look for it in the produce section.

Pickled Shrimp

MAKES 12 SERVINGS
HANDS-ON 20 MIN.
TOTAL 8 HOURS, 20 MIN.

Use decorative picks to serve these well-seasoned, piquant shrimp.

- 2 lb. unpeeled, large raw shrimp
- 3 large garlic cloves, sliced
- 3 bay leaves
- 2 large lemons, thinly sliced
- 1 small red onion, thinly sliced
- 1/2 cup olive oil
- 1/4 cup white wine vinegar
- 2 Tbsp. Old Bay seasoning
- 2 Tbsp. drained capers
- 1 Tbsp. whole black peppercorns
- 1 Tbsp. Worcestershire sauce
- 1 Tbsp. hot sauce
- 2 tsp. kosher salt
- 1 tsp. sugar
- 1/2 tsp. dried crushed red pepper
- 1/4 cup chopped fresh parsley

1. Peel shrimp; devein, if desired. Cook shrimp in boiling water to cover 3 to 5 minutes or just until shrimp turn pink; drain. Rinse with cold water.

2. Combine shrimp and next 4 ingredients in a large bowl. Whisk together oil and next 9 ingredients; pour over shrimp mixture. Cover and chill 8 hours, stirring occasionally. Remove and discard bay leaves. Stir in parsley just before serving.

Field Greens with Country Ham-Cornbread Croutons and Muscadine Vinaigrette

MAKES 12 SERVINGS
HANDS-ON 7 MIN.
TOTAL 2 HOURS, INCLUDING CROUTONS AND VINAIGRETTE

A homemade sweet vinaigrette brings this salad together with great flavor.

- 2 (5-oz.) packages sweet baby greens
- 2 Fuji or Honey Crisp apples, halved, cored, and thinly sliced
  Country Ham-Cornbread Croutons
  Muscadine Vinaigrette

1. Divide greens evenly between 12 salad plates. Top evenly with apple slices and Country Ham-Cornbread Croutons. Drizzle with Muscadine Vinaigrette.

COUNTRY HAM-CORNBREAD CROUTONS

MAKES ABOUT 6 DOZEN
HANDS-ON 12 MIN.
TOTAL 1 HOUR, 35 MIN.

- 2 Tbsp. butter
- 1 cup chopped onion
- 1/2 cup finely chopped country ham
- 2 cups buttermilk
- 1 large egg, lightly beaten
- 1 3/4 cups plain yellow cornmeal
- 1 tsp. baking powder
- 1 tsp. baking soda
- 1 tsp. table salt

1. Preheat oven to 450°. Melt butter in a large skillet over medium-high heat. Add onion and ham. Sauté 6 minutes or until ham is browned and onion is tender. Remove from heat; cool slightly.

2. Combine buttermilk, egg, and sautéed ham mixture in a medium bowl. Combine cornmeal and remaining ingredients in a separate bowl. Gradually add buttermilk mixture to cornmeal mixture, whisking until blended. Pour batter into a lightly greased 13- x 9-inch pan.

3. Bake at 450° for 15 minutes or until golden brown. Cool in pan on a wire rack 10 minutes. Run a knife around edges to loosen cornbread from sides of pan. Remove cornbread from pan; cool completely on a wire rack (about 20 minutes). Reduce oven temperature to 400°.

4. Cut cornbread into 1-inch cubes. Place cornbread cubes in a single layer on a large rimmed baking sheet. Bake at 400° for 18 minutes, stirring occasionally, or until toasted. Cool completely in pan on a wire rack (about 20 minutes).

MUSCADINE VINAIGRETTE

MAKES 1 1/4 CUPS
HANDS-ON 5 MIN.
TOTAL 40 MIN.

- 1 1/4 cups sweet muscadine wine
- 1 Tbsp. country Dijon mustard
- 1 large shallot, minced
- 1/2 cup olive oil
- 1/2 tsp. table salt
- 1/2 tsp. freshly ground black pepper

1. Bring wine to a boil over medium-high heat in a small saucepan. Cook 15 minutes or until wine is reduced to 1/2 cup. Let cool completely (about 20 minutes).

2. Combine wine reduction, mustard, and shallot in a 2-cup glass measuring cup. Gradually add oil in a slow, steady stream, whisking constantly. Whisk in salt and pepper.

Pecan Soup

MAKES 13 CUPS
HANDS-ON 36 MIN.
TOTAL 1 HOUR, 6 MIN.

This velvety, rich appetizer is like chestnut soup with Southern flair. If serving as an appetizer, ladle it into small cups.

- ½ cup butter
- 3 celery ribs, coarsely chopped
- 2 sweet onions, chopped
- 1 large baking potato, peeled and coarsely chopped
- 4 cups chicken broth
- 3 cups heavy cream
- 1 tsp. table salt
- ½ tsp. ground white pepper
- 1 lb. pecan halves, toasted
   Garnishes: crème fraîche, chopped chives, additional pecan halves

1. Melt butter in a Dutch oven over medium heat; add celery and onion. Sauté 20 minutes or until translucent.

2. Add potato and next 5 ingredients. Bring to a boil; reduce heat to medium-low, and simmer, uncovered, 30 minutes or until slightly thickened and potato is very tender. Remove from heat; cool slightly.

3. Process soup mixture, in batches, in a blender until smooth, stopping to scrape down sides as needed. Ladle into serving bowls. Serve hot.

Crown Pork Roast with Bourbon-Caramelized Onions and Apples

MAKES 12 SERVINGS
HANDS-ON 20 MIN.
TOTAL 3 HOURS

Call ahead to your local butcher to reserve this company-worthy roast. Ask the butcher to french the rib bones and tie the roast into a circle with kitchen string for easy roasting.

- 1 (16-rib) crown pork roast, trimmed and tied (10 to 11 lb.)
- 1 Tbsp. dried thyme
- 2 tsp. table salt
- 2 tsp. freshly ground black pepper
- 3 large sweet onions, cut into wedges
- 1 tsp. table salt
- 1 tsp. freshly ground black pepper
- 2 Braeburn apples, coarsely chopped
- 2 Tbsp. butter
- ¼ cup bourbon
   Garnishes: fresh thyme sprigs, small Lady apples

1. Preheat oven to 450°. Rub meaty portion of ribs with dried thyme, and 2 tsp. each salt and pepper. Place roast in a greased broiler pan. Cap the end of each bone with aluminum foil to prevent tips from burning. Bake at 450° for 20 minutes. Reduce oven temperature to 350°. Bake 2 hours or until a meat thermometer inserted between ribs 2 inches into meat registers 145°. Meanwhile, toss onions with 1 tsp. each salt and pepper. Scatter seasoned onions around pork roast after 1 hour of baking.

2. Carefully transfer roast to a serving platter. Let pork roast stand 15 minutes before slicing. Meanwhile, place broiler pan with onions across 2 burners. Add chopped apple and butter. Cook over medium-high heat 8 minutes or until apples are tender. Remove from heat; stir in bourbon.

3. Spoon onion-apple mixture into middle of roast, if desired. To serve, carve roast between bones using a sharp knife.

Note: To keep roast upright, if butcher does not tie crown roast securely into a circle with heavy string, we recommend placing roast, rib ends down, in a 1-qt. round soufflé dish. Place soufflé dish on a baking sheet, and proceed with recipe as directed, except add raw onions to cook with apples in broiler pan, cooking 18 minutes or until onions and apples are tender.

Browned Butter Carrots

MAKES 12 SERVINGS
HANDS-ON 23 MIN.
TOTAL 46 MIN.

- 3 lb. carrots
- ⅓ cup butter
- 1 tsp. table salt
- 1 tsp. freshly ground black pepper
- ⅓ cup firmly packed dark brown sugar
- ⅓ cup apple cider vinegar
- 2 tsp. vanilla extract
   Garnish: fresh herbs such as flat-leaf parsley or thyme

1. Cut carrots in half lengthwise; cut into 2-inch pieces. Cut thick pieces in half lengthwise. Melt butter in an extra-large skillet or sauté pan over medium heat; cook, stirring constantly, 3 minutes or until butter begins to turn golden brown. Add carrots, salt, and pepper; cook 8 to 10 minutes, stirring occasionally, or until carrots are barely tender.

2. Add 1/2 cup water; cover and cook 10 minutes. Uncover and add brown sugar and vinegar; cook 8 to 10 minutes or until carrots are glazed and most of liquid evaporates. Remove from heat; stir in vanilla.

White Cheese Grits with Mustard Greens and Bacon

MAKES 12 SERVINGS
HANDS-ON 32 MIN.
TOTAL 32 MIN.

- 6 thick bacon slices
- 5 cups packaged, fresh chopped mustard greens, sliced
- 1 (32-oz.) container chicken broth
- 2 cups uncooked quick-cooking grits
- 4 oz. goat cheese, crumbled
- 2/3 cup whipping cream or half-and-half
- 2 Tbsp. butter
- 1/2 tsp. freshly ground black pepper

1. Cook bacon in a skillet over medium heat 8 minutes or until crisp; remove bacon, and drain on paper towels, reserving drippings in skillet. Crumble bacon.

2. Sauté mustard greens in hot drippings 6 to 8 minutes or just until tender. Season with salt and pepper to taste. Set aside.

3. Meanwhile, bring broth and 3 cups water to a boil in a large saucepan over medium-high heat. Gradually whisk in grits; bring to a boil. Reduce heat to medium-low; cover and simmer, stirring occasionally, 5 to 7 minutes or until thickened. Add cheese and remaining 3 ingredients, stirring until cheese and butter are melted. Transfer grits to a serving bowl; spoon sautéed greens down center of grits, and sprinkle with bacon.

Caramel-Pear Cake

MAKES 12 SERVINGS
HANDS-ON 1 HOUR
TOTAL 3 HOURS, 30 MIN., PLUS 1 DAY FOR CHILLING

The pièce de résistance to any holiday menu should indeed be the dessert. This cake will leave your guests wanting more—because of its cornmeal crumb and yum-factor caramel frosting.

HAZELNUT SYRUP
- 1/2 cup sugar
- 3 Tbsp. hazelnut liqueur

CAKE LAYERS
- 3 cups all-purpose flour
- 1 cup plain yellow cornmeal
- 3/4 tsp. table salt
- 2 cups butter, softened
- 1 1/2 cups granulated sugar
- 1 cup firmly packed light brown sugar
- 8 large eggs
- 1/2 cup sour cream
- 1 Tbsp. vanilla extract

CARAMELIZED PEAR FILLING
- 1/4 cup butter
- 6 large, firm ripe red Anjou or Bartlett pears (2 1/2 lb.), peeled, cored, and chopped
- 2 Tbsp. sugar
- 1 Tbsp. lemon juice
- 1 Tbsp. hazelnut liqueur
- Pinch of table salt

CARAMEL FROSTING
- 1 1/2 cups firmly packed light brown sugar
- 3/4 cup butter
- 6 Tbsp. evaporated milk or whipping cream
- 2 1/4 cups powdered sugar
- 1 Tbsp. vanilla extract

1. Prepare Hazelnut Syrup: Combine 3/4 cup water and sugar in a small saucepan. Bring to a boil over medium-high heat, stirring frequently. Boil 1 minute or until sugar dissolves. Remove from heat; stir in liqueur. Cool completely; cover and chill thoroughly.

2. Prepare Cake Layers: Preheat oven to 350°. Grease and flour 3 (9-inch) round cake pans; set aside.

3. Combine flour, cornmeal, and salt; set aside. Beat butter at medium speed with a heavy-duty electric stand mixer until creamy (about 2 minutes). Gradually add sugars, beating well (5 minutes). Add eggs, 1 at a time, beating just until yellow disappears after each addition. Gradually add dry ingredients to butter mixture, beating just until blended after each addition. Stir in sour cream and vanilla. Pour batter into prepared pans.

4. Bake at 350° for 24 to 25 minutes or until a wooden pick inserted in center comes out clean. Cool in pans on a wire rack 10 minutes. Remove from pans to wire rack, and cool completely (about 1 hour).

5. Place each cake layer on a large piece of plastic wrap. Pierce each layer multiple times using a wooden skewer; slowly drizzle or brush Hazelnut Syrup over layers, allowing syrup to soak in. Wrap layers, and refrigerate overnight.

6. Prepare Caramelized Pear Filling: Melt butter in a large skillet or sauté pan over medium-high heat (we had best results with a 12-inch sauté pan). Add pears; sauté 6 minutes or until just tender. Sprinkle pears with sugar and next 3 ingredients. Cook over high heat 6 to 8 minutes or until pears are very tender and beginning to caramelize, stirring twice. Remove from heat; cool to room temperature.

7. Place 1 cake layer on a serving plate; top with half of Caramelized Pear Filling. Top with another cake layer and remaining pear filling. Top with remaining cake layer. Set cake aside while preparing Caramel Frosting.

8. Prepare Caramel Frosting: Bring first 3 ingredients to a boil in a 3-qt. saucepan over medium heat, whisking constantly; boil, whisking constantly, 1 minute. Remove from heat; gradually whisk in powdered sugar and vanilla until smooth. Beat vigorously with a wooden spoon 3 to 5 minutes or until mixture begins to cool and thickens slightly. Use immediately.

9. Frost top and sides of cake with Caramel Frosting. Let cake stand at least 1 hour before serving.

METRIC EQUIVALENTS

The recipes that appear in this cookbook use the standard United States
method for measuring liquid and dry or solid ingredients (teaspoons, tablespoons,
and cups). The information on this chart is provided to help cooks outside
the U.S. successfully use these recipes. All equivalents are approximate.

METRIC EQUIVALENTS FOR DIFFERENT TYPES OF INGREDIENTS

A standard cup measure of a dry or solid ingredient will
vary in weight depending on the type of ingredient.
A standard cup of liquid is the same volume for any type of
liquid. Use the following chart when converting standard cup
measures to grams (weight) or milliliters (volume).

Standard Cup	Fine Powder (ex. flour)	Grain (ex. rice)	Granular (ex. sugar)	Liquid Solids (ex. butter)	Liquid (ex. milk)
1	140 g	150 g	190 g	200 g	240 ml
¾	105 g	113 g	143 g	150 g	180 ml
⅔	93 g	100 g	125 g	133 g	160 ml
½	70 g	75 g	95 g	100 g	120 ml
⅓	47 g	50 g	63 g	67 g	80 ml
¼	35 g	38 g	48 g	50 g	60 ml
⅛	18 g	19 g	24 g	25 g	30 ml

USEFUL EQUIVALENTS FOR DRY INGREDIENTS BY WEIGHT

(To convert ounces to grams, multiply
the number of ounces by 30.)

1 oz	=	¹⁄₁₆ lb	=		30 g
4 oz	=	¼ lb	=		120 g
8 oz	=	½ lb	=		240 g
12 oz	=	¾ lb	=		360 g
16 oz	=	1 lb	=		480 g

USEFUL EQUIVALENTS FOR LENGTH

(To convert inches to centimeters,
multiply the number of inches by 2.5.)

1 in				=	2.5 cm		
6 in	=	½ ft		=	15 cm		
12 in	=	1 ft		=	30 cm		
36 in	=	3 ft	=	1 yd	=	90 cm	
40 in				=	100 cm	=	1 m

USEFUL EQUIVALENTS FOR LIQUID INGREDIENTS BY VOLUME

¼ tsp						=	1 ml		
½ tsp						=	2 ml		
1 tsp						=	5 ml		
3 tsp	=	1 Tbsp			= ½ fl oz	=	15 ml		
		2 Tbsp	=	⅛ cup	= 1 fl oz	=	30 ml		
		4 Tbsp	=	¼ cup	= 2 fl oz	=	60 ml		
		5⅓ Tbsp	=	⅓ cup	= 3 fl oz	=	80 ml		
		8 Tbsp	=	½ cup	= 4 fl oz	=	120 ml		
		10⅔ Tbsp	=	⅔ cup	= 5 fl oz	=	160 ml		
		12 Tbsp	=	¾ cup	= 6 fl oz	=	180 ml		
		16 Tbsp	=	1 cup	= 8 fl oz	=	240 ml		
		1 pt	=	2 cups	= 16 fl oz	=	480 ml		
		1 qt	=	4 cups	= 32 fl oz	=	960 ml		
					33 fl oz	=	1000 ml	=	1 l

USEFUL EQUIVALENTS FOR COOKING/OVEN TEMPERATURES

	Fahrenheit	Celsius	Gas Mark
Freeze Water	32° F	0° C	
Room Temperature	68° F	20° C	
Boil Water	212° F	100° C	
Bake	325° F	160° C	3
	350° F	180° C	4
	375° F	190° C	5
	400° F	200° C	6
	425° F	220° C	7
	450° F	230° C	8
Broil			Grill

Menu Index

This index lists every menu by suggested occasion. Recipes in bold type are provided with the menu and accompaniments are in regular type.

Oscar-Worthy Party Menu

SERVES 6
(page 44)

Gougéres
Fried Chicken Wings
Broccoli Slaw
Best-Ever Brownies

Easter Brunch

SERVES 8 TO 10
(page 62)

Watercress-Buttermilk Soup
Asparagus, Orange, and Lentil Salad
Scalloped Potato and Herb Tart
Cornmeal-Chive Biscuits
Pepper Jelly and Ginger Glazed Ham
Jasmine-Buttermilk Panna Cotta with Berry Sauce

Lee Bros. Party

SERVES 10 TO 12
(page 70)

The Hugo
Savory Benne Wafers
Romaine With Toasted Pecans and Pickled Strawberries
Rice and Ham Croquettes with Tomato Sauce
Smoked Egg Salad Toasts
Pickled Shrimp With Fennel
Grapefruit Chess Tart

Texas-Style Crawfish Boil

SERVES 10 TO 12
(page 94)

The Crawfish Boil
Woodshed Margarita
Blue Cheese Coleslaw
Bean-Jicama Salad
Tequila-Key Lime Meringue Pie

The Winning Spread

SERVES 12
(page 112)

Beef Tenderloin Crostini
Corn-Avocado Salad
Next-Day Pickled Shrimp
Moonshine-Cherry Blush
Berry Pies

Backyard Bash

SERVES 6
(page 126)

Frozen Peach Old Fashioneds
Buttermilk-Ricotta Cheese Dip
Grilled Summer Vegetable Platter with Veggie Vinaigrette
Smoked Beef Tenderloin with Chimichurri Sauce
Charred Corn with Garlic-Herb Butter
Whiskey Pie with Tipsy Berries and Vanilla Ice Cream

Sunday Supper

SERVES 6 TO 8
(page 142)

Sweet Tea-Brined Fried Chicken
Tomato-and-Fruit Salad
Zucchini, Squash, and Corn Casserole
Shout Hallelujah Potato Salad
Skillet Green Beans
Two-Step Fresh Peach Pound Cake
Butterscotch Banana Pudding Pie
Patchwork Cobbler

No-Cook Party Menu

SERVES 8
(page 159)

Cucumber Gin & Tonic
Tomato-Tequila Fizz
Easy Summer Appetizer Board
White Cheddar-Chive Pimiento Cheese
Riesling Peaches
Whipped-Cream Corn Salad
Sweet-Hot Cukes and Peppers
Carrot-Avocado Tabbouleh
BLT Salad with Olive Vinaigrette
Snappy Beans and Peas with Pecorino

New Year's Brunch

SᴇʀᴠᴇS 8

(page 299)

Bloody Mary Bar
Chicks in a Blanket
Sweet Potato Biscuits
Beet-and-Citrus Salad
Cheesy Grits Soufflé
Espresso Shortbread Cookies

Daybreak in Dixie

SᴇʀᴠᴇS 8

(page 330)

Merry Mimosas for a Crowd
Cinnamon Coffee with Bourbon
    Cream
Spinach-Artichoke Strata
Apple-Maple Breakfast Sausage
Winter Fruit Compote
Cinnamon-Apple Coffee Cake with
    Cream Cheese Glaze

Road Trip to Grandmas

SᴇʀᴠᴇS 6

(page 333)

Rosemary-Scented Cold Cider
Cold Skillet-Fried Chicken
Apple-Cabbage Slaw
Sweet Potato Salad
Chameleon Icebox Cookies
Caramel Drop-Banana Bread Trifle
    Dessert

Vintage Southern Holiday

SᴇʀᴠᴇS 8

(page 336)

Spiked Satsuma Champagne
Pickled Shrimp
Field Greens with Country Ham-
    Cornbread Croutons and
    Muscadine Vinaigrette
Pecan Soup
Crown Pork Roast with Bourbon-
    Caramelized Onions and Apples
Browned Butter Carrots
White Cheese Grits with Mustard
    Greens and Bacon
Caramel-Pear Cake

Weeknight Winter Supper

SᴇʀᴠᴇS 6 ᴛᴏ 8

Rosemary-Garlic Chicken Quarters
    (page 38)
Caramelized Spicy Green Beans
    (double recipe) *(page 52)*
Mashed potatoes
Lemon-Yogurt Crumb Cake *(page 50)*

Casual Spring Get-Together

SᴇʀᴠᴇS 10

Green Pea Hummus *(page 76)*
Spinach-Artichoke Cups *(page 76)*
Hot Chicken Dip *(page 76)*
Pound Cake Cupcakes *(page 89)*

Backyard Cookout

SᴇʀᴠᴇS 6

Steak and Fingerling Potato Kabobs
    (page 120)
Tomato-Goat Cheese Tart with
    Lemon-Basil Vinaigrette *(page 116)*
Blackberry-Peach Cobbler Bars
    (page 131)
Tea and lemonade

Ladies Lunch

SᴇʀᴠᴇS 4 ᴛᴏ 6

Blue & White Chicken Salad
    (page 148)
Cheese Straw Tomato Tartlets
    (page 118)
Summer Sangria Salad *(page 148)*
Nancy Reagan's Vienna Chocolate
    Bars *(page 149)*

Vegetable Plate

SᴇʀᴠᴇS 6

Fried Zucchini Straws *(page 152)*
Pimiento-Cheese Stuffed Okra
    (page 153)
Watermelon "Steak" Salad *(page 155)*
Cornbread

Recipe Title Index

This index alphabetically lists every recipe by exact title.

Month-by-Month Index

This index alphabetically lists every food article and accompanying recipes by month.

Drink of the Month

Holiday Favorites

General Recipe Index

This index alphabetically lists every recipe by exact title.

353

ISBN-13: 978-0-8487-3968-3
ISBN-10: 0-8487-3968-X
ISSN: 0272-2003

Printed in the United States of America
First printing 2013

Oxmoor House

Editorial Director: Leah McLaughlin
Creative Director: Felicity Keane
Senior Brand Manager: Daniel Fagan
Senior Editor: Rebecca Brennan
Managing Editor: Elizabeth Tyler Austin

Southern Living® 2013 Annual Recipes

Editor: Susan Hernandez Ray
Project Editor: Emily Chappell Connolly
Assistant Designer: Allison Sperando Potter
Photography Director: Jim Bathie
Recipe Editor: Alyson Moreland Haynes
Food Stylist: Catherine Crowell Steele
Senior Production Manager: Greg A. Amason

Contributors

Copy Editor: Donna Baldone
Proofreaders: Rebecca Benton, Polly Linthicum, Barry Wise Smith
Indexer: Mary Ann Laurens
Editorial Interns: Elizabeth Laseter, April Smitherman, Megan Thompson
Photographer: Iain Bagwell
Photo Stylist: Lydia DeGaris Pursell
Food Stylist: Maggie Ruggiero

Cover: Raspberry-Lemon Curd Cake with Lemon Buttercream Frosting, page 325
Page 1: Salted Caramel-Chocolate Pecan Pie, page 280

Time Home Entertainment Inc.

Publisher: Jim Childs
Vice President, Brand & Digital Strategy: Steven Sandonato
Executive Director, Marketing Services: Carol Pittard
Executive Director, Retail & Special Sales: Tom Mifsud
Director, Bookazine Development & Marketing: Laura Adam
Executive Publishing Director: Joy Butts
Publishing Director: Megan Pearlman
Finance Director: Glenn Buonocore
Associate General Counsel: Helen Wan

Southern Living®

Editor: M. Lindsay Bierman
Creative Director: Robert Perino
Managing Editor: Candace Higginbotham
Executive Editors: Rachel Hardage Barrett, Hunter Lewis, Jessica S. Thuston
Food Director: Shannon Sliter Satterwhite
Senior Food Editor: Mary Allen Perry
Deputy Food Director: Whitney Wright
Test Kitchen Director: Robert Melvin
Associate Food Editor: Norman King
Recipe Editor: JoAnn Weatherly
Assistant Recipe Editor: Ashley Arthur
Test Kitchen Specialist/Food Styling: Vanessa McNeil Rocchio
Test Kitchen Professionals: Pam Lolley, Angela Sellers
Editorial Assistant: Pat York
Style Director: Heather Chadduck Hillegas
Director of Photography: Jeanne Dozier Clayton
Photographers: Robbie Caponetto, Laurey W. Glenn, Melina Hammer, Hector Sanchez
Senior Photo Stylist: Buffy Hargett Miller
Assistant Photo Stylist: Caroline Murphy Cunningham
Copy Chief: Susan Emack Alison
Assistant Copy Chief: Katie Bowlby
Copy Editor: Ashley Leath
Production Manager: Mary Elizabeth McGinn Davis
Assistant Production Manager: Christy Coleman
Production Coordinator: Paula Dennis
Office Manager: Nellah Bailey McGough

To order additional publications,
call 1-800-765-6400.

For more books to enrich your life,
visit oxmoorhouse.com

To search, savor, and share thousands of recipes,
visit myrecipes.com

Favorite Recipes Journal

Jot down your family's and your favorite recipes for quick and handy reference. And don't forget to include the dishes that drew rave reviews when company came for dinner.

Recipe	Source/Page	Remarks